Prepare your students with the power of classroom practice

adopt and assign
MyEducationLab today
www.myeducationlab.com

What is MyEducationLab?

MyEducationLab is a powerful online tool that provides students with assignments and activities set in the context of real classrooms. MyEducationLab is fully integrated in your course and provides practice for your students in an easy to assign format.

Children: "Oo"
Teacher: Good job.

ASSIGNMENTS AND IN-CLASS ACTIVITIES:
Each chapter in MyEducationLab includes assignable Activities and Applications exercises that use authentic classroom video, teacher and student artifacts, or case studies to help students understand course content more deeply and to practice applying that content.

PRACTICE TEACHING: Building Teaching Skills and Dispositions exercises use video, artifacts, and/or case studies to help your students truly see and understand how specific teaching techniques and behaviors impact learners and learning environments. These exercises give your students practice in developing the skills and dispositions that are essential to quality teaching.

Does it work?

A survey of student users from across the country tells us that it does!

93% MyEducationLab was easy to use.

70% MyEducationLab's video clips helped me to get a better sense of real classrooms.

79% I would recommend my instructor continue using MyEducationLab.

*Percentage of respondents who agree or strongly agree.

Where is it?

- Online at www.myeducationlab .com
- Integrated right into this text! Look for margin annotations and end-of-chapter activities throughout the book.

What do I have to do to use MyEducationLab in my course?

Just contact your Pearson sales representative and tell him/her that you'd like to use MyEducationLab with this text next semester. Your representative will work with your bookstore to ensure that your students receive access with their books.

What if I need help?

We've got you covered 24/7. Your Pearson sales representative offers training in using MyEducationLab for you and your students. There is also a wealth of helpful information on the site, under "Tours and Training" and "Support." And technical support is available 24 hours a day, seven days a week, at http://247pearsoned.custhelp.com.

Creative Thinking and Arts-Based Learning

Preschool Through Fourth Grade

FIFTH EDITION

Joan Packer Isenberg
George Mason University

Mary Renck Jalongo
Indiana University of Pennsylvania

Merrill
Upper Saddle River, New Jersey
Columbus, Ohio

Library of Congress Cataloging-in-Publication Data

Isenberg, Joan P.

   Creative thinking and arts-based learning : preschool through fourth grade / Joan Packer Isenberg, Mary Renck Jalongo. — 5th ed.

       p. cm.

   Includes bibliographical references and index.

   ISBN-13: 978-0-13-603978-5

   ISBN-10: 0-13-603978-2

   1. Early childhood education—Activity programs.   2. Creative activities and seat work.

I. Jalongo, Mary Renck.   II. Title.

   LB1139.35.A37I86 2010

   372.13—dc22

                                                                            2008036908

Vice President and Editor in Chief: Jeffery W. Johnston
Acquisitions Editor: Julie Peters
Development Editor: Bryce Bell
Editorial Assistant: Tiffany Bitzel
Senior Managing Editor: Pamela D. Bennett
Senior Project Manager: Linda Hillis Bayma
Production Coordination: Christian Holdener, S4Carlisle Publishing Services
Senior Art Director: Diane C. Lorenzo
Cover image: Jupiterimages
Cover Design: Janna Thompson-Chordas
Photo Coordinator: Valerie Schultz
Media Producer: Autumn Benson
Media Project Manager: Rebecca Norsic
Senior Operations Supervisor: Matthew Ottenweller
Operations Specialist: Susan Hannahs
Vice President, Director of Sales & Marketing: Quinn Perkson
Marketing Manager: Erica DeLuca
Marketing Coordinator: Brian Mounts

This book was set in Palatino by S4Carlisle Publishing Services. It was printed and bound by Hamilton Printing Company. The cover was printed by Lehigh Phoenix.

Chapter Opener Photo Credits: p. 2, David Mager/Pearson Learning Photo Studio; p. 32, T. Lindfors/Lindfors Photography; p. 70, Scott Cunningham/Merrill; p. 101, Silver Burdett Ginn; p. 150, Ryan McVay/Getty Images, Inc. – Photodisc; p. 194, Krista Greco/Merrill; p. 232 Patrick White/Merrill; p. 274 BananaStock/SuperStock Royalty Free; p. 314, Anthony Magnacca/Merrill; p. 350 Michael Newman/PhotoEdit Inc.

Pearson Education Ltd., London
Pearson Education Singapore, Pte. Ltd.
Pearson Education Canada, Inc.
Pearson Education—Japan
Pearson Education Australia PTY, Limited

Pearson Education North Asia, Ltd., Hong Kong
Pearson Educación de Mexico, S.A. de C.V.
Pearson Education Malaysia, Pte. Ltd.
Pearson Education Upper Saddle River, New Jersey

Merrill
is an imprint of

www.pearsonhighered.com

10 9 8 7 6 5 4 3 2 1
ISBN-13:   978-0-13-603978-5
ISBN-10:   0-13-603978-2

For Jacob and Sara Pearlstein who fill my life with love, joy, and creative endeavors. May your childlike qualities flourish inside each and every one of us.

Joan Packer Isenberg
George Mason University

For educators worldwide who nurture every child's creativity and artistic expression.

Mary Renck Jalongo
Indiana University of Pennsylvania

Preface

Creative thought and artistic expression: What is the value of these processes and the resulting products for children and families, communities, and society at large? Why should educators be concerned about such things at a time when tough talk about academic standards, teacher accountability, and international ranking on tests dominates the educational scene? As this book will argue, the ability to think in innovative and productive ways is a survival skill in a world where we are inundated daily with information. In the past, the educated person took pride in knowing something about many things and knowing a few things reasonably well. Today, knowing no longer suffices. Instant access to information has made it relatively easy for us to know, or at least to quickly find out, about virtually any topic. In fact, if the information explosion continues and artificial-intelligence technology advances, the children we work with today will have even less need for the rote memorization of basic content that has characterized traditional early and elementary education.

The audience for this book needs only to look around to see that expectations for children, teachers, and teacher educators have changed dramatically. Contemporary children are immersed in a world of fleeting images and multiple symbol systems; their challenge is to negotiate the complexities of that increasingly chaotic context. Contemporary teachers are expected to teach for understanding to an increasing number of local, state, and national benchmarks and to improve their respective country's reputation for academic excellence. Today's college and university faculty are being challenged to demonstrate that their teacher candidates have attained not only knowledge of pedagogy but also the practical/professional abilities of an effective early childhood or elementary teacher. Across all of these groups, the message is consistent: aim higher, achieve more, and contribute further to society. When the pressure is on, there is a tendency to discredit, disregard, or completely overlook the very thing that is most necessary in the preparation of students and their teachers. We contend that creative thinking is necessary to survive and thrive in an uncertain future.

Why have so many others failed to arrive at a similar conclusion? Individuals and groups define, recognize, and support creativity in distinctive ways. Creativity and the arts are aspects of human functioning that are sometimes perplexing, often controversial, and challenging to assess.

Even within the same person, ideas about creative thought can be contradictory. The age of the person who creates a product can affect recognition of its value. An adult who is awestruck by the inventiveness reflected in the latest piece of technology, for example, may disregard the imaginative life of a child as the wellspring for that ingenuity. In other cases, the domain in which creative thought is expressed can influence perceptions of its relative merits. As a result, a teacher who delights in young children's drawings and writings may fail to recognize opportunities for creative thought in mathematics or science, treating them as "one right answer" subjects. In still other cases, the social organization in which creative thinking operates can unduly influence point of view. As a result, a political leader who extols the virtues of innovative thought and entrepreneurship in business also may be a shrill voice for "back to basics" in the public schools.

Few people possess an understanding of creative thought and artistic expression that is not woefully outdated. They are uninformed or misinformed about decades of research in cognitive psychology, on the human brain, and on the contributions of the arts to cognitive functioning. Their ideas about creativity and the arts emphasize natural talent, inspiration, and art as a curricular "frill," when the research supports instead the importance of training and practice, materials and opportunities, and the arts as a genuine basic (Jalongo, 2003). It is imperative that those of us who work with young children do an effective job in supporting creative thinking and arts-based learning, because, as Shavinina and Ferrari (2004) contend, "All human cultural development builds on the amazing technological, scientific, educational, and moral achievements of the human mind" (p. 3).

Our Vision for This Book

Our vision for this book is that it will equip practitioners in the fields of early childhood and elementary education to counteract stereotypes that run rampant about the contributions of children's creative thinking; to educate professional colleagues and the general public about creativity and the arts; and to influence schools and communities to regard the creative processes and artistic products of children's minds with new appreciation and respect. As Karen Gallas (2003) points out, children:

> are open to joy, curiosity, wonder, intuition, experimentation, and exploration . . . But somehow, for most of us and for our children, those things fade into the background as the years pass. School and life become hard, filled with drudgery, repetition, and 'have-to's.' Joy, curiosity, wonder, intuition, experimentation, and exploration are shunted aside as the educational process moves forward. We are told that that is the way the process is meant to work: Our children must leave behind childish things like play, performance, invention, and wonder and redirect their attention toward organization, detail, and conformity to archaic concepts of work and the workplace. This is a pronouncement that comes from deep in our culture's past, from a historically distant moment that did not appreciate the boundless potential that all our children represent. (p. 169)

Challenges to Misconceptions About Children's Creativity

Although many college-level textbooks use the word *creativity* or *art* in their titles, many of these "creative activities" books make minimal contributions to teachers' creative growth, much less children's. Any book that claims to center on children's creative thinking must begin with respect for the child's intellect. Effective teachers acknowledge children's ability to construct their own understandings about their world and to express their ideas in original, inventive ways. We resent the condescending message of materials that presume to give young children patterns to copy, lines to color inside, and activities that are completely initiated and directed by adults. We decided to write a book that would do a better job of enabling teachers and caregivers to articulate a more enlightened view of children's creative and artistic growth to families, colleagues, and administrative personnel.

Purpose

Above all, in this fifth edition we want to orient both preservice and inservice teachers to the profound and lifelong contributions of an emphasis on children's creative thinking and arts-based learning. There is little question that most educators' backgrounds in nurturing children's creativity and promoting learning through the arts are inadequate. For many teachers, preparation for educating students to become creative, critical thinkers and communicate through the arts consists of a single college course. In this text, we have attempted to distill the essential research-based perspectives that can guide classroom teachers in promoting creativity, play, art, music, dance, and drama for all children. *Creative Thinking and Arts-Based Learning: Preschool Through Fourth Grade* also delineates the teacher's role from a philosophical, pedagogical, and curricular stance by addressing key components, including the classroom environment, materials and resources, behavior management, assessment, and culturally responsive teaching.

Audience

This book is an outgrowth of our combined more than 60 years of teaching college courses on children's creativity and the arts. Because the book is firmly grounded in theory and research, it is well suited for students seeking initial licensure or certification, whether they are enrolled in a community college, a four-year teacher-preparation program, or a fifth-year program for practicing professionals who are pursuing certification or a master's degree in early childhood or elementary education. *Creative Thinking and Arts-Based Learning: Preschool Through Fourth Grade* is equally appropriate to early childhood and elementary students at various stages in their careers. The book's universal message of fostering creative and artistic expression is important to professionals who work with children throughout the world.

Description of the Book's Contents

The book begins with three chapters that form the foundation for the remaining chapters. Chapter 1 discusses creative thought: how it is defined, how it develops, and what adults can do to foster its growth. Chapter 2 examines children's play, games, and inventions and how these modes of inquiry support children's learning across the disciplines, and Chapter 3 explores ways to foster children's creative thought and expression.

After establishing this base, Chapters 4 through 6 cover the topics that are traditionally associated with the creative arts (art, music, dance, dramatic arts), and Chapters 7 through 9 discuss topics that are foundational to creative teaching and assessment (designing the environment, using materials and resources effectively, and assessing creative processes and products). Chapter 10 examines the influence of cultural contexts on creative thought and artistic expression and the important role that families play in supporting children's creativity.

Features of This Book

The first edition of this book was published in 1993. It was the first co-authored textbook for both of us, and, as is the case with many textbooks, we wrote it because we could not find a suitable book for the classes we were teaching in creative expression and play. It began as an early childhood book and continued as one through the second and third editions. As we have talked with college faculty at various institutions, however, we discovered that the book often is used in college-level courses that include both early childhood and elementary teachers. In 2006 we broadened the book's scope up to and including fourth grade and incorporated more material on the influence of culture on creative thinking and products. In order to accomplish all of this, both the book's content and its title changed to reflect this new focus. Each chapter includes

Classroom Perspectives, scenarios from preschool through kindergarten, first through second grade, and third through fourth grade—presented at the beginning of each chapter to serve as the basis for class discussion.

Teachers' Reflections . . . the voices of our students as they learn about the contributions of creative thinking and arts-based learning to their teaching effectiveness.

Frequently Asked Questions to dispel misconceptions about creativity and the arts. Common questions and research-based and experience-based responses are provided.

Meeting Standards, a compilation of guidelines from various organizations and states to demonstrate how learning experiences in each of the creative arts and play align with standards.

New to the Fifth Edition

High-quality contemporary early childhood and elementary classrooms are inclusive. Teachers make adaptations that enable all students to express themselves in creative ways. To provide additional support, we have included a new feature in the chapters on creativity, play, music, art, drama, and materials and resources that we call *Curriculum Accommodations for Diverse Learners.* It begins with general suggestions and then offers practical ideas for including children with emotional and intellectual, visual, hearing, and orthopedic impairments in creative thinking and arts-based learning.

MyEducationLab

Go to MyEducationLab and select the topic "Child Development." Under Activities and Applications, view the artifact Guitar Drawing. *As you look at the artifact, think about how it meets the criteria for art.*

Effective teachers also know how to integrate the arts across the curriculum. To illustrate how this is achieved, we have included a table in five chapters called *Integrating the Curriculum.* This feature identifies a teaching theme that is suitable for each group—toddlers, preschool, primary, intermediate—and shows how it can be taught across the curriculum. The areas of the curriculum included are Communication (Literacy, Language Arts, and Technology), the Sciences (Mathematics/Science) and Social Studies (Social Studies, Health and Safety).

MyEducationLab *Integration*

Margin notes within each chapter enable students and instructors to access **MyEducationLab,** a carefully selected collection of video clips, artifacts, assignable questions in "Activities and Applications," and more elaborate exercises in "Building Teaching Skills and Dispositions." To start using MyEducationLab, activate the access code packaged with your book. If your instructor did not make MyEducationLab a required part of your course or if you are purchasing a used book without an access code, go to *www.myeducationlab.com* to purchase access to this wonderful resource!

Expanded Ancillary Package

The fifth edition includes an **expanded ancillary package.** Please note that material from the fourth edition Companion Website has been moved to the *Instructor's Manual* and *Test Bank*. The *Test Bank* includes test questions with responses, and the *Instructor's Manual* lists outstanding children's literature to accompany the content-area chapters, as well as a suggested Interview and a Write-to-Learn activity. Another technology-based support for the instructor is a complete set of color PowerPoint slides that highlight key concepts from the chapters. PowerPoint slides can be used as provided in an onscreen show using a computer and projector. Or, instructors can make them into overhead transparencies. Additionally, instructors can duplicate the notes page version of the slides in PowerPoint and distribute them to students for use as a study aid. All instructor ancillary products are available online and can be downloaded from the Educators section at *www.pearsonhighered.com* by educators who adopt the text. Finally, WebCT and Blackboard versions of the *Test Bank* are also available for downloading.

Using This Book

Instructors will find that this exceptionally versatile book includes an array of text features that can be emphasized for different audiences. Those working with more advanced students may want to stress the theoretical framework and the Frequently Asked Questions in each chapter. Those working with early childhood and elementary educators who are at the beginning of their careers may want to place greater emphasis on the classroom scenarios and the Interviews and Write-to-Learn activities (available in the *Instructor's Manual*). All teachers will find the new "Integrating the Curriculum" and the "Meeting Standards" sections helpful in designing an integrated curriculum. Of particular value in contemporary inclusive classrooms is the "Curriculum Accommodations for Diverse Learners" that appears in Chapters 1, 2, and 4–8. By offering instructors various features that they can use as assignments and as in-class activities, *Creative Thinking and Arts-Based Learning: Preschool Through Fourth Grade* lends extensive support to instructors who are themselves at different levels of experience in working with future and current early childhood and elementary teachers.

Acknowledgments

We are deeply indebted to the many people who contributed to the development of this book. First and foremost, we would like to thank the colleagues and doctoral advisees who helped us expand the book's scope to include the elementary years. Their names are listed in the table of contents, but we also wish to acknowledge their contributions here. Laurie Nicholson Stamp, faculty member and Dean's Associate at Indiana University of Pennsylvania, co-authored Chapter 5 on music, movement, and dance. Marilyn J. Narey, faculty member at Edinboro University and former art teacher, collaborated on the art and assessment chapters. Shana Barr and Karen Curtis, former graduate assistants, assisted with the dramatic arts and environment chapters. We wish to acknowledge the graduate and undergraduate students at George Mason University and Indiana University of Pennsylvania for their cooperation in field-testing this book and for providing us with many of the rich classroom examples that appear throughout these chapters. Natalie K. Conrad, now a faculty member at University of Pittsburgh Johnstown and Norah Hooper, now a faculty member at Mary Washington University, our former graduate assistants, merit special recognition for their work on the *Instructor's Manual* and *Test Bank* that accompany the fifth edition of the text. Elizabeth Silvia and Jennifer Durham worked on the text features Curriculum Accommodations for Diverse Learners and Integrating the Curriculum as well as the MyEducation-Lab navigation. We are also grateful to the many teachers, parents, and children whose photographs, art material, and stories are an integral part of this text. Thanks, too, to our many colleagues who helped us further clarify our thinking about children's creative thought and artistic expression.

We want to thank our editor for this edition, Julie Peters, who offered unflagging guidance and support. We are also grateful to the rest of the staff at Pearson/Merrill who made the publication of this book possible, particularly our former editor, Ann Davis. They are a fine group of professionals and have been a pleasure to work with throughout the book's production. In addition, we appreciate the valuable input from those who reviewed the book: Linda Aiken, Southwestern Community College; Michelle Brown, University of Oklahoma; Colleen Finegan, Wright State University; Wendy McCarty, Illinois College; and G. Patricia Wilson, University of South Florida.

Finally, we wish to acknowledge the continuous and unwavering support of our families and close friends. We are especially grateful for their encouragement, understanding, and willingness to listen through each phase of the development of the book from the first to the fifth edition.

A Final Word

In education, there are three common misconceptions about teaching and learning—that it is all content, that it is all process, and that there is one best curriculum for all children (Eisner, 1990, 1998). Fortunately, any instructor who would choose our book for a course would also be likely to avoid these three errors. When it is approached with an open mind, the study of children's creative thought and artistic expression is a powerful reminder that neither coverage nor aimlessness is the answer and that, clearly, there are no panaceas. Rather, the teacher must create a classroom learning community that emphasizes quality over quantity of materials, balances freedom with control, and respects children as individuals while socializing them into an increasingly diverse society and global village. By bringing these perspectives to teaching, teachers and teacher educators not only avoid the pervasive pitfalls of which Eisner speaks, but also become more effective and reflective practitioners.

It has been gratifying to see the book that began as hopeful dreaming evolve into print. It has been humbling to realize, with each edition of the work, the amount of information we need to master in order to remain current in a rapidly changing field. It also has been encouraging to watch our collaborative efforts endure in the fiercely competitive college textbook market for more than fifteen years. As authors, we have been privileged to revisit our work and refashion it—each time, we trust, into a college-level text that better meets the needs of contemporary children, educators, and teacher educators.

Joan Packer Isenberg
Fairfax, Virginia

Mary Renck Jalongo
Indiana, Pennsylvania

Brief Contents

Contents

NOTE: Every effort has been made to provide accurate and current Internet information in this book. However, the Internet and information posted on it are constantly changing, so it is inevitable that some of the Internet addresses in this textbook will change.

Creative Thinking and Arts-Based Learning

Preschool Through Fourth Grade

PART 1
FOUNDATIONS OF CREATIVE THOUGHT

Chapter 1

Understanding Children's Creative Thought and Expression

Students displaying creative behaviors tend to be unappealing to teachers. This claim is very important for the future of human advancement. When teachers do not know what creativity is, how it manifests and how it is important, they may ignore teaching for creativity; thereafter, loss of creative talent is reflected in scientific and artistic advancements in particular, and in human civilization in general.

Ugur Sak, 2004, p. 216

 CLASSROOM PERSPECTIVES ON CREATIVITY

Preschool–Kindergarten

Two 4-year-old boys balance empty margarine tubs on their heads, hum loudly, and play imaginary instruments, as if they were in a marching band. The teacher tells them that the plastic tubs are for holding puzzle pieces and directs them to put everything away. The boys comply with her request but a few moments later they disrupt play in the family living center and are reprimanded for misbehavior.

First Grade–Second Grade

A group of kindergarten and first-grade children are playing house. Their teacher is surprised by some of the gender roles and themes reflected in their dialogue:

Girl 1: *(speaking to a boy while running a toy sweeper)* Get out, you're making a mess!

Boy: I didn't do anything wrong. I'm playing by myself.

Girl 2: Don't, honey. I already swept the floor, now I'll have to do it again. *(sweeps the floor, picks up a doll, and speaks to the boy)* You're her daddy. Our little girl needs to see you. You're her daddy.

Boy: No, I'm not. I have ten brothers and we are going to see a movie that's rated PG.

Girl 1: Daddy, dad, come here.

Boy: This is stupid. I didn't do anything bad. Let's play. *(moves a wooden ramp across the entrance to the housekeeping area)* Honey, pretend this is a jail and I can't get out. See, I got on handcuffs. *(puts wrists together)*

Girl 1: I can get you out. See, I just did.

Girl 2: Daddy, daddy. I want to be the baby.

Girl 1: No, you will not be the baby.

Girl 2: I am the baby—goo, goo, ga, ga. *(grabs baby bottle and crawls on the floor with it in her mouth)*

Girl 1: Then who's going to be the father?

Boy: Not me, I'm going to work.

Third Grade–Fourth Grade

Children who are at least one year below grade level in reading are enrolled in summer school and their district's program emphasizes using literacy to accomplish important community goals. Today, the students are presented with a challenge: The local animal shelter is full to capacity with homeless dogs and cats and the director asks them to help. The children form small groups to plan their strategy. One group does research on the Internet to find innovative ideas that promote pet adoption. Another group helps to implement the idea of posting videos of the animals on the shelter's Web site. A third group uses digital photos to design posters advertising an "adoptathon" at the local pet store chain. As they work on these projects, the students use their research skills, creative thinking, interpersonal skills, and literacy skills to save animals and make a contribution to their community.

These vignettes raise many questions about creativity, including what creative thought is, how children's creative thinking is distinct from that of adults, and what adults do to help or hinder children's creative growth. In this chapter, we explore the role of creative thought and expression in children's lives and its rightful place in the curriculum.

DEFINING CREATIVE THOUGHT

The word *create* comes from the Latin word *creare*, which means "to make a thing which has not been made before; to bring into being" (Barnhart & Barnhart, 1983). Based on these origins, the word *create* is used in contemporary society to mean to invent, or produce; to approach the realm of art (imaginative, artistic, literary); and to produce something useful or worthwhile (constructive, purposeful). In addition, because creative thought can be put to negative or destructive ends, positive intentions must underlie **creativity** (Craft, 2006). To summarize, the creative process consists of "the interaction among aptitude, process, and environment by which an individual or group produces a perceptible product that is both novel and useful as defined within a social context" (Plucker & Beghetto, 2004, p. 90).

Over the years, originality has been a constant factor in discussions of creative processes and products but being different is not enough (Runco, 2004). It would surely be different for a college student to decide to dress in a gorilla costume and sit on the roof of the tallest building on campus to eat lunch; however, this is merely bizarre behavior. The creative response or product must also be effective, defined as relevant to the issue at stake and capable of offering some type of genuine solution (Cropley, 2001).

A first step in clearing up the confusion about creativity is to treat creativity as a form of intelligence (Webster, 1990). Creativity is a key component in Sternberg's (2008) triarchic theory of intelligence, which combines three interrelated ways of thinking:

1. *Creative thought*, which includes creating, designing, imagining, and supposing
2. *Analytical thought*, which includes analyzing, comparing/contrasting, evaluating, and explaining
3. *Practical thought*, which includes using, applying, and implementing

As Sternberg (2008) explains, "We need creative abilities to generate ideas, analytical abilities to determine whether they are good ideas, and practical abilities to implement the ideas and to convince others of the value of our ideas. Most people who are successfully intelligent are not equal in these three areas, but they find ways of making the three abilities work harmoniously together" (p. 153).

Four Cognitive Dimensions
Creativity as a Thinking Process

1. Fluency

- Generating a large quantity of relevant responses
- Following a train of thought
- Building up collections of related ideas

2. Flexibility

- Approaching things in alternative ways
- Changing categories as appropriate
- Viewing the problem from a different perspective

3. Originality

- Producing unusual, novel, unique, or clever ideas
- Combining known ideas into some new form and connecting the seemingly unconnected

4. Elaboration

- Filling out ideas and adding interesting details
- Stretching or expanding on an idea

Four Affective Dimensions
Creativity as a Feeling Process

1. Curiosity

- Wondering, puzzling about something
- Playing with ideas
- Following intuition to see what happens

2. Complexity

- Feeling challenged to do things in detailed ways
- Seeking many different alternatives
- Bringing order out of chaos
- Seeing missing parts between what is and what could be

3. Risk-Taking

- A willingness to express ideas to others
- The courage to expose self to criticism or failure
- The confidence to follow a hunch and "invest" in a humble idea

4. Imagination and Fantasy

- The ability to form rich and varied mental images ("what if"/"as if")
- The ability to put oneself in another place, time, or person's shoes
- An intuitive sense of what might be or what something might become

Figure 1.1   Dimensions of Creativity
Note: Data from Guilford (1984) and Sternberg (2006).

Creativity is both a cognitive (thinking) and affective (feeling) process (Feldhusen, 1995). Figure 1.1 is an overview of the cognitive and affective dimensions of creative thought. To observe a teacher addressing stereotypes, watch the video "Explode Stereotypes" online at MyEducationLab.

The children described in the vignettes that introduced this chapter demonstrated this cognitive/affective connection as they referred to their previous experiences (an absent father), responded to objects (making margarine tubs into band hats), used symbols (hands joined to represent handcuffs), discussed ideas (a PG-rated movie), collaborated with other people (animal shelter personnel), and responded to situations (homeless animals).

MyEducationLab

Go to MyEducationLab and select the topic "Diversity." Under Activities and Applications, watch the video Explode Stereotypes *and complete the activity.*

 EVIDENCE OF CREATIVE THOUGHT IN CHILDREN

Consider these activities of children at different ages and stages:

- Jessica, a 30-month-old, has wrapped a block in a blanket that she now refers to as "baby"; she is using an object to symbolize something else.

Children need social support to develop their potential for creative thought.

- Sydney, age 3, paints a mandala (a shape that looks like the sun); it is new to her even though adults have seen this in children's drawings many times.
- Arwen, age 5, is painting at the easel in response to a dream he had the night before in which he could fly; he is using his imagination.
- Miguel, a gifted third grader, is designing his own home page on the computer; he is using his knowledge of other home pages he has seen previously and applying his skills in technology to accomplish a goal.

As the behavior of these children suggests, creativity is novel behavior with a purpose (Peterson, 2001/2002).

Nevertheless, understandings of creativity are full of contradictions. People may, for example,

- Say that creativity is an asset, but have difficulty explaining it or identifying it (McDaniel & Thorn, 1997).
- Claim that everyone is creative yet think that only "cultured" people have the right to participate in the arts (Kerka, 2002).
- Recognize the importance of creativity both for the individual and society, yet continue to think of creative pursuits as frivolous activities that take away time from more serious, academic study (Horibe, 2001; Robinson, 2001).
- View creativity as inspired where inventions and technological advances are concerned, yet say that creative individuals are impractical or socially maladjusted (Peterson, 2001/2002).

Figure 1.2 is an overview of the theoretical perspectives and theorists that have contributed to an understanding of creative thought.

It is a common misconception that creative thought exists only inside the individual when, actually, it is understood and built by society. "All human achievements are influenced by and produced in a cultural context that defines high ability and excellence and determines its relative value in society"(Dorn, Madeja, & Sabol, 2003, p. 81). Just think about how the definition of "creative" differs from one academic department to another at your college. If you interviewed education, drama,

---

Classical Theories

Theory: Humanistic

- **Carl Rogers: The creative person is fully functioning.**

Implications: If the young child's natural curiosity, passion for learning, and active imagination are deadened by adults, the child becomes less rather than more capable from a creative standpoint.

- **Abraham Maslow: The creative person is self-actualized.**

Implications: When schedules are rigid and tasks are predetermined, children do not have an opportunity to make choices or solve interesting problems. Over time, they learn to depend on others for ideas rather than trusting their own ideas.

- **Rollo May: Being creative is courageous.**

Implications: Young children's ideas often seem outrageous or silly to adults who seek large amounts of predictability and control. Yet children need permission to pursue their unorthodox ideas so that they can "dare to be different" throughout life.

Theory: Psychoanalytic

- **Alfred Adler: Creativity is a way of compensating for perceived physical or psychological inferiority.**

Implications: Rather than having a "talent scout" mentality, in which only those children with potential to become great artists or inventors are afforded opportunities for creative expression, teachers need to cultivate creativity in all children.

- **Carl Jung: Creative ideas emanate from a deeper source, from the "collective unconscious."**

Implications: It is essential that children become familiar with the creative processes and products of other times, cultures, ethnic groups, and races so that they can make personal connections with the sum of human creativity.

Theory: Constructivist

- **Jean Piaget: Creativity is a type of problem solving that depends on the child's thinking processes.**

Implications: Developing the young child's problem-solving processes gives children the time and opportunity to explore materials and use hands-on approaches in pursuing interesting challenges.

Contemporary Theories

Multiple Intelligences Theory

- **Howard Gardner: Creativity consists of a constellation of nine different intelligences.**

Implications: Every young child possesses at least nine distinctive ways of knowing that must be considered and valued when planning any curriculum that claims to meet individual needs.

(Continued)

Figure 1.2   Theories of Creativity

Triarchic Theory of Creativity

- **Robert J. Sternberg: Creativity is a cluster of three types of abilities: synthesizing, analyzing, and practicing.**

Implications: Children need to have role models of creativity, raise questions, have time to use trial-and-error, take sensible risks, define and pursue their own problems, puzzle over ideas, overcome obstacles, earn support for their ideas, and be evaluated in ways that respect creativity.

Optimal Experience or "Flow" Theory

- **Mihalyi Csikzentmihalyi: Creative individuals acquire competence in a domain of interest and pursue that interest with passion and enjoyment.**

Implications: Throughout the world, young children will play spontaneously and persist at their play even though no one is directing it or reinforcing them. In studies of eminently creative adults, one consistent finding is that the lines between play and work are blurred and they tend to approach their work playfully.

Figure 1.2   *(Continued)*

science, business, or music majors their definitions of creativity would differ somewhat, depending upon their field of study—and this is all at the same institution in the same location. Ideas of creativity differ even more dramatically when the cultural background differs. This is why contemporary experts view creativity as a socially constructed trait. The experience of 6-year-old Theran shows what this means. Theran's grandfather sings in the church choir and often takes his grandson along to practice. The boy is enthralled by the music and, now that he is learning to read, he tries to follow along by identifying some of the words that he knows. Theran also sings along with his grandpa as he practices in the car. This first grader's behavior illustrates four key points about the way that creativity develops (Faulkner, Coates, Craft, & Duffy, 2006; Sawyer, 2003).

1. *There are important relationships between creativity and the child's culture during the early years.* If Theran did not have this experience with church music, his life would be different. As he enjoys the singing of the choir and gains insight into the practice required, Theran begins to regard it as a significant part of his family's and community's life.

2. *Creativity emerges through interactions with other people and with the environment.* Theran is not just hearing about his grandfather's participation in the choir or even enjoying it on Sunday; rather, he is immersed in it and begins to think about joining the choir someday.

3. *Creative development is mediated by physical and symbolic artifacts within specific domains.* Every type of creative endeavor has particular physical contexts and artifacts—in the case of the choir, the church is the setting and sheet music is an artifact that captures Theran's imagination.

4. *The culture of children differs from that of adults.* Although the child barely notices it, his grandfather is concentrating on the director, his individual performance, and the overall sound of the group. Theran, on the other hand, is applying new things he has learned at each practice. For example, he was very excited when he could use a letter and number to "look up" the selections that the group would sing all by himself. He also came to the realization that the musical notation on each page is a different kind of symbol system used to direct the group's efforts.

One way that teachers promote creativity is by teaching children to use tools for thinking. Graphic organizers are a widely recognized strategy for integrating thinking across subject areas as described in Table 1.1.

TABLE 1.1 Integrating the Curriculum: Using Graphic Organizers

What is a graphic organizer?

A graphic organizer is a way to make thinking more visible. Also referred to as concept maps or webs, graphic organizers structure information and arrange important aspects of a concept or topic into a visual pattern that is labeled with words (Mosco, 2005). The most common graphic organizers are concept maps (with a main vocabulary word/idea and details radiating out from the center), sequence charts (that show a process in step-by-step fashion), compare/contrast diagrams (such as the Venn diagram), and cause-and-effect diagrams.

Why use graphic organizers?

There is a large body of research to suggest that graphic organizers support learning across subject areas (Baxendell, 2003; Gallenstein, 2005; Kim, Vaughn, Wanzek, & Wei, 2004). When children work with concepts in a more organized fashion, it helps them to construct mental models of ideas and their interrelationships.

Why are graphic organizers particularly suitable for children with special needs?

Visually displaying information can assist children's ability to organize and remember information; therefore, graphic organizers appear to be a particularly strong form of support for diverse learners. It is not enough, however, to use graphic organizers in a haphazard, occasional way. They are most effective when they are consistent (teachers select a few models and use them often), when they are coherent (deal with a limited number of concepts and clearly label the interrelationships among them), and creative (teachers use them at the beginning, middle, and end of lessons; use them for homework/review; pair pictures with words; use them across subject areas; and incorporate them into partner or cooperative group work) (Baxendell, 2003). An example of a graphic organizer is creating a web for a work of art. At the center of the web might be a print or photograph of the work. Radiating out from the center might be categories such as works of similar type (such as other sculptures), works with a similar subject or theme (such as animals), works by the same artist (such as Winslow Homer), works of similar style (such as picture books that use collage), and so forth. In this way, children are using literacy and art together.

	COMMUNICATION Literacy, Language Arts, and Technology	THE SCIENCES Mathematics/Science	SOCIAL STUDIES Social Studies/ Health and Safety
Toddler Theme *Caring for the Young*	Share books about parents caring for their offspring such as *Over in the Meadow* (Keats, 1971). Use computer clip art to make a song chart that depicts animal mothers caring for their offspring.	Teach one-to-one correspondence. Use a collection of large and small stuffed animal toys and ask children to match mothers with babies; watch a nature film about animal parents caring for babies; create a photo collage of animal parents and babies.	Set up a baby bath time outdoors. Provide tub, water, plastic dolls, no-tears soap and shampoo, towels, diaper, clothing, and baby blanket so that children can enact familiar caregiving rituals.

(Continued)

TABLE 1.1   Integrating the Curriculum: Using Graphic Organizers—continued

	COMMUNICATION Literacy, Language Arts, and Technology	THE SCIENCES Mathematics/Science	SOCIAL STUDIES Social Studies/ Health and Safety
Preschooler Theme *Using Symbols to Represent Ideas*	Choose a story with a simple, one-line plot, such as *Rosie's Walk* (Hutchins, 1987) and have children create a story map on the floor.	Lay two hula hoops or circles of yarn on the floor as in a Venn diagram. Use attribute blocks and pose questions ("If the blocks on this side are red, and the blocks on this side are big, what could we put in the middle that is *both* big and red?").	Share the classic book, *The Listening Walk* (Showers, 1993), then take a walk outdoors and make a list of the sounds that the children heard. Use a concept web or map to categorize the sounds by their source (e.g., made by people, animals, machines, etc.).
Primary Theme *Favorite Songs*	Have children compare three versions of the same basic song, such as *Six Little Ducks* and make an Alike/Different chart.	Use a big book to sing a counting song such as *Five Little Monkeys Jumping on the Bed* (Christelow, 2006). Use clip art to represent each verse of the song and make cue cards.	Invite family members with different cultural backgrounds to share the folk songs that they learned in childhood.
Intermediate Theme *Intellectual Property*	Point out the credits and copyright information in several books. Have children work as writer/illustrator teams to produce an original picture story book. Include a brief bio for each child and a copyright page.	Visit the United States copyright information center online and determine the basic rules for copyright of ideas. Look at several pieces of software for copyright information and discuss the steps that are taken to keep intellectual property secure.	Invite a local inventor to the class to discuss the process of obtaining copyright. Have children create a sequence diagram for the copyright process based on their interview.

THEORETICAL AND RESEARCH BASE: SOCIAL CAPITAL THEORY

Think about some of the popular talent shows that give people an opportunity to share their accomplishments and further develop their potential, such as *American Idol, Dancing with the Stars*, or *America's Got Talent*. Now think about what happens during childhood that makes it possible for two children who begin life with comparable levels of innate ability to perform at dramatically different levels in the arts. One theory that attempts to explain such differences is social capital theory. In every person's life, there is a range of resources that is intellectual, economic, cultural, and institutional in nature (Li, 2004; McLaughlin, 2001). These resources are referred to as capital, because, like personal wealth, they are not equally distributed and allocated. Use of the resources depends on an individual's circumstances in society, access to resources, and ability to elicit appropriate support. According to social capital theory, bringing creativity to fruition requires more than personal ability or even individual determination; it requires social support (Gruber & Wallace, 1999; Zimmerman & Zimmerman, 2000). As Ferrari (2004) explains, "impressive artistic and creative achievements result when students' ideals correspond with what is valued in a culture and when they have the means (e.g., social upbringing, practice, and innate ability) that enable them to excel" (p. 226). Cultural capital "is a product of individual social history but is often misrecognized as inborn talent . . . we should not underestimate the extent to which dedicated training and masterful teaching contribute to producing 'stars' in a particular cultural field" (Ferrari, 2004, p. 233). Thus, whether the work in question is a technological breakthrough, a paradigm-shifting scientific theory, an aspiring singer's first CD, or an elementary school child's drawing, successful innovation requires some access to social capital. According to social capital theory, all individuals and groups are capable of making contributions to society and human potential merits the same development as a country's natural resources or financial resources.

Lev Vygotsky (1933), a Russian theorist, contended that learning is fundamentally cultural and interactive in nature. Through social interaction, children internalize the cultural tools that the world of others presents to them and draw upon their imaginative thought processes (Davis & Gardner, 1992; Eckhoff & Urbach, 2008, in press; Gajdamaschko, 2005). For example, if we examine the drawings by a Japanese child or a Navajo child, we will see that their early representational drawings resemble the art from the culture they know; their style has been influenced by the art that they have experienced in their societies.

A basic concept in Vygotsky's theory is the *zone of proximal development*, or ZPD, the level at which the child feels reasonably confident in pursuing an activity, yet not bored by it; the level at which the child feels challenged intellectually, yet not frustrated. The ZPD is one reason why giving children printed pictures to color and/or cut out while sitting quietly at their seats—a common activity in American schools—is not recommended. True, this activity keeps children occupied, but it does nothing to challenge them intellectually, undermines creative thought, and offers no social support. Such an activity creates no feeling of functioning in a community of learners; it is simply busywork performed in quiet isolation.

TEACHERS' REFLECTIONS ON CREATIVITY

Consider these preservice and inservice teachers' reflections as they completed a course on creativity:

Preservice Teachers

"My knowledge of creativity was really limited. I knew that it was beneficial, but I didn't really have any facts to back it up—just a vague feeling that it's basically good. Now I have reasons why creative thinking benefits the whole child in all areas of development."

Inservice Teachers

"I have always believed that creative expression was important to children's development, but I think I only considered the content—art, music, dance, etc. I think I viewed these subjects as something to be appreciated rather than in terms of ways they can support children's learning."

Your Reflections

*   How do these teachers think about creativity in their students?

*   What are your assumptions and understandings about creative thought?

*   What role might creative thought play in learning and teaching?

 ## FAMILIES' ROLES IN PROMOTING CREATIVITY

Try to picture a creative child in your mind's eye. If you are like most people, you will envision a "little professor" child with thick glasses, a child with encyclopedic knowledge of a particular topic (e.g., dinosaurs), a child who is precocious (i.e., can perform academic tasks well in advance of peers), or perhaps a child who seems to be an eccentric and a loner (Kerr & Cohn, 2001; Piirto, 1998). Such views, however, tend to link creativity to superior academic skills or to social maladjustment and result in harmful stereotypes about creativity. Creative behavior often is misinterpreted in a negative way by uninformed or insensitive adults. The child who is playful, energetic, excitable (Tieso, 2007), and intrinsically motivated could be labeled as "hyperactive," the child who is independent, perceptive, and confident as a "smart aleck," and the child who is original, nonconforming, and adventuresome as "strange" or "stubborn." Most adults prefer children who are subdued, compliant, quiet, neat, and polite and who fit in easily with peers. This is one reason why it is so important for teachers to be well informed about children's creativity. Errors in teachers' judgment can damage children's self-esteem and thwart creative growth.

Does this mean that everyone is creative to some extent? Yes. While there are different dimensions and levels of creativity, every child is creative if given the chance to be; "everyone has creative potential but developing it requires a balance between skill and control and the freedom to experiment and take risks" (Robinson, 2001, p. 445). This does not mean that everyone will produce a remarkable invention, perform on stage, or see his or her art displayed in a gallery. A teacher who designs an engaging learning activity for the students is being creative. A mother who provides nutritious, tasty meals on a very limited food budget is being creative. A child who fashions an imaginary dinosaur out of clay is being creative. When we meet life's challenges and resolve problems, we are being creative (Ripple, 1989; Runco, 1996).

Creative thinking in children is both like and different from that of adults. It is alike in that children "have experiences that are similar in complexity, challenge, and creativity to those of creative experts" (Caine & Caine, 1999, p. 117). It is different in terms of experience and style. Mature individuals' creative processes and products emphasize expertise, which involves the technical skill, artistic ability, talent, or knowledge of useful information that they bring to whatever they produce, and work habits, which include work style, concentration and persistence, the ability to generate new possibilities, and openness to new ideas (Amabile, 1983; Epstein, in press). In comparison to most adults, young children have fewer expe-

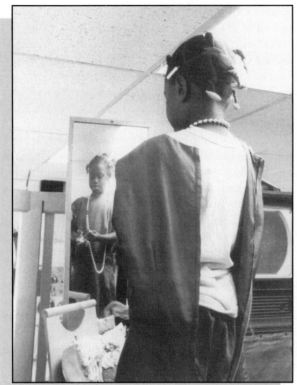

Anne Chamberlain

*All children display creative behaviors at various times
or in particular situations.*

riences, less expertise, and less well-developed work habits and styles. But whatever children may lack in these areas they more than compensate for in their
unique ways of thinking and approaching a task.

One way of glimpsing creativity in action is to listen and watch while children talk and draw (Coates & Coates, 2006). Here is what Caitlin, a 3 and ½-year-
old, says out loud as she draws a picture. Notice Caitlin's vivid imagination as well
as her lack of inhibition about revealing her thoughts:

> I'm makin' a butterfly. This is grass, this green stuff is grass. I'm making a bridge
> this time. The butterfly's gonna go over the bridge—under the bridge, I mean . . .
> Now I'll make myself. I need some pink. Hmm, no pink. *(she chooses a red crayon)*
> I'll just have to color light if I want to make some pink. There, that's my honker
> *(nose)*. This is my hair. I'm going to make some hair. There I am! *(she smiles)* I
> want black. Purple will do. I have some blush on—there! Ha-ha! I'll have to make
> a sidewalk here. Those are drainers *(drains)*, like little logs. *(in a singsong voice)* I
> need a blue log log, blue log, blue log log. Can you make a flower, Caitlin? Blue
> will do it! Blue water. See, this is a log. I forgot to make the sunshine. I'll pretend
> this is Rudolph *(the Red-Nosed Reindeer)*. Sunshine. There! Now I'm going to make
> an elephant . . .

As Caitlin's talk and drawing suggest, children excel at three characteristics
thought to be related to creative genius: responsiveness to internal and external
stimuli, lack of inhibition, and the ability to become completely absorbed in an

activity (Holden, 1987). Both for children and for adults, creativity is a paradox because it is serious and playful at the same time (Rea, 2001).

Marina, a 3-year-old, is a good example of a child with *responsiveness to stimuli*. The bishop of her Greek Orthodox church was visiting and all of the adults were quiet and reserved. Marina walked right up to the bishop and asked, "Do you know how to color? Would you like to draw pictures with me?" Marina seemed to sense that others felt ill-at-ease so she applied her strategy for making a friend in a way that the entire congregation still remembers fondly.

Five-year-old Lauren exemplifies the child's *spontaneity and lack of inhibition*. She has created an imaginary friend named "Mousie," and before her family travels anywhere, she lifts the gas tank door and puts her hand, palm up, next to the opening so that Mousie can crawl inside. Lauren talks aloud to her imaginary pet and gives him instructions on how to behave, completely unconcerned that anyone might overhear her.

As fourth grader Kevin settles in for a cross-country airplane ride, his play with an electronic game demonstrates *complete absorption in an activity*. He is determined to move to the next level and has been working with a friend to invent an idea for a similar game that peers would like to play. As the behavior of Marina, Lauren, and Kevin illustrates, children can become totally absorbed in pretending. They surprise us by their perceptivity, spontaneity, and playfulness. Because they are newer to the world, their sensory impressions are particularly keen. These characteristics lead us to seek careers working with young children and endear them to us as adults. Out of all the creative thinking that children do, perhaps none is more charming than their world of pretend and sense of limitless possibilities, a topic that we will explore next.

Possibility Thinking, Imagination, and Fantasy

Possibility thinking occurs when children engage with everyday problems at a deep level and pose "what if?" questions (Craft, 2001a, 2001b, 2002). When children gain more experience with possibility thinking and are encouraged to seek novel and unusual solutions they become more adept with it, more confident in their ability to problem-solve, and eventually acquire the habit of thinking creatively (Sternberg, 2006). Conversely, in the absence of possibility thinking opportunities, creative potential can be squelched. To see possibility thinking in action, watch the "Interactive Writing" video online at MyEducationLab.

MyEducationLab

Go to MyEducationLab and select the topic "Early Literacy." Under Activities and Applications, watch the video Interactive Writing. *How does it illustrate possibility thinking?*

It is common to say that children have "active imaginations," meaning that the boundaries between reality and fantasy are not as clearly demarcated for children as they are for adults. **Imagination** is defined as the ability to form rich and varied mental images or concepts of people, places, things, and situations that are not present. Fantasy occurs when a person uses the imagination to create particularly vivid mental images or concepts that are make-believe, impossible, or at least not yet possible (Weininger, 1988). Experts on creativity have long believed that, for most human beings, imagination and fantasy are very active during early childhood. Howard Gardner (1993a) observed that "The child is not bothered by inconsistencies, departures from convention, nonliteralness . . . which often results in unusual and appealing juxtapositions and associations" (p. 228).

Kindergartner Mallory's drawings in Figure 1.3 offer a good example of possibility thinking at work. She is intrigued by flowers—not just ordinary flowers, but flowers that exist only in her mind's eye. As she imagines what she calls "an acrobatic flower" and "a flower with pineapple teeth," Mallory has combined ap-

Figure 1.3
Mallory's Flowers

parently unrelated elements in her drawings to produce surprising new forms and we can glimpse fantasy in her work.

Stages in the Creative Process

According to the classic theory of creativity, the creative process consists of four stages (Wallas, 1926). The stages are recursive, meaning that a person may move back and forth between and among them, rather than following them in an invariant sequence from first to last. These stages in the creative process are summarized in Figure 1.4.

✳ **Preparation/Brainstorming** (accessing information)

The thinker applies knowledge, skill, and understanding to materials, objects, problems, or combinations of these things. Creative individuals "engage" with the materials, objects, or problems with a playful or experimental attitude. Engagement with the ideas may be deliberate or accidental.

↓

▢ **Incubation** (processing information internally)

The mind begins to formulate and work on a problem, often through images and associations.

↓

▯ **Illumination/Inspiration** (arriving at a solution)

The thinker selects some ideas and rejects others; this is an evaluative phase.

↓

✓ **Verification/Communication** (evaluating the solution, communicating it to others, and validating its contributions)

The thinker tests the product of creative thought in terms of usefulness, completeness, and correctness. This testing may occur at three different levels (Glover, 1980): the individual level (a personal consideration of the work's originality and purpose), the peer level (soliciting the evaluation of peers), or the social level (assessing the contributions of the work to society at large).

Figure 1.4   Stages in the Creative Process

Note: Data from Cropley (1997), Glover (1980), Runco (1997), and Wallas (1926).

Joan Isenberg

Imagination and fantasy are the great creative assets of early childhood.

 ## PROMOTING CREATIVE THINKING

Adults share responsibility for developing the rich resources of imagination, creativity, curiosity, and playfulness that characterize childhood (Cobb, 1977; Martindale, 2001). In order to fulfill that responsibility, they first have to recognize the creative behavior. In a study of more than 1,000 teachers' ideas about children's creative behavior, only about half of the teachers realized that divergent thinking—thinking "outside the box"—is a key element of creative thought (Fryer, 2003). Figure 1.5 describes how to recognize children's creative thinking in action.

Here is what Scott's mother had to say about her son's imaginary companion:

> My son, who just turned 4, became fascinated by deer. This happened, I think, because while we were visiting friends out in the country, a doe and her fawn came into the yard. Now Scott has created a pretend friend named "Fawnbelly." His bedroom window faces the front porch, and that, according to my son, is where she sleeps. He feeds her by putting a plastic apple on the windowsill and, in return, she protects him at night. When he talks about Fawnbelly, I can picture this gentle, expectant doe with huge brown eyes keeping watch over our house.

This mother obviously values her son's vivid imagination and rich fantasy life, and rightly so. Innovation and resourcefulness are essential to sur-

- Playful, persistent, and intrinsically motivated
- Become intensely absorbed in activities, persist at work or play, and concentrate on a single task for a relatively long period of time
- Explore, experiment, manipulate, play, ask questions, make guesses, and discuss findings
- Use imaginative role play, language play, storytelling, and artwork to solve problems and make sense out of their world
- Curious, intuitive, and resourceful
- Ask many questions
- Are capable of tolerating ambiguity as they explore alternatives
- Are strongly intuitive and perceptive
- Enjoy thinking and working independently
- Resourceful, nonconforming, and adventuresome
- Tend to challenge assumptions or authorities based on well-reasoned differences of opinion
- Formulate hypotheses and conduct trials to test their ideas
- Try to bring order out of chaos by organizing their environment
- Do something new with the old and familiar and display interest in new ideas
- Use repetition as an opportunity to learn more from an experience rather than becoming bored with it

Figure 1.5
Observable Characteristics of Children's Creative Thought Processes
Note: Data from Davis and Rimm (1994), McAlpine (1996), Healy (1996), and Maxim (1989).

vival (Craft, 2003a, 2003b, 2006). Most of the problems we encounter throughout life are complex, "unscripted" ones. Resolving them depends on two sets of internal psychological conditions: psychological safety and psychological freedom (Rogers, 1991). Psychological safety is external; it depends on a low-risk environment in which people treat one another with respect. Psychological freedom is internal; it is what enables us to play with ideas, be open to experience, and acquire ego strength—the ability to rely more on self-evaluation than the evaluations of others (Runco, 2004). To see an artifact that illustrates a child's ability to play with ideas, look at "Scribble Writing" online at MyEducationLab. A mother described her son's play as follows:

> Lance [age 5] loves farming and he has lots of toy farm equipment that once belonged to his Dad. One day he was playing farmer and took his toy manure spreader into the kitchen, filled it up with coffee grounds, and began spreading "manure" on his land, which just happens to be the kitchen floor!

Lance's mother knew that he was completely wrapped up in his farm fantasy and that his intentions were good, even if the outcomes were messy. She did insist that Lance help her clean up the coffee grounds, yet she did not punish him or make him feel ashamed of his desire to really "test out" his farm equipment. By taking this approach, she supported both psychological safety and psychological freedom.

As we have seen, psychological safety, psychological freedom, and social support are essential to promote optimal creative growth in children. How well are the schools meeting these requirements?

MyEducationLab

Go to MyEducationLab and select the topic "Early Literacy." Under Activities and Applications, view the artifact Scribble Writing (Preschool). *As you look at the artifact, think about psychological safety and psychological freedom.*

THE DECLINE OF CREATIVITY

Although it is sad to think that education would be responsible in any way for thwarting the child's creative potential, it evidently does (Imagine Nation 2008; Sternberg, 2006). As children mature, their creative thinking tends to decline (Dacey, 1989; Olson, 2006) and often is "stalled" by age 5 (Tysome, 2003). For example, in case studies of children 3 to 7 years of age, young children's art often went unappreciated by teachers and they tended to create their own "studios" at home to pursue drawing; however, these activities tended to fall away as they grew older (Anning, 2003; Anning & Ring, 2004).

By age 9 to 10, there is a tendency throughout the world for children to become very conventional and conforming (Craft, 2005). Then, as children approach adolescence, they think of themselves as "ordinary" and therefore inferior in creative thinking. By the time most people reach adulthood, they start to see innovation and artistic expression as avenues open only to those who are officially recognized as having exceptional talent (Kerka, 2002). Are school personnel deliberately suppressing children's creativity? Actually, it is more often the case that adults, including teachers, have misconceptions about creativity and act on those erroneous beliefs (Sharp, 2004; Williams, Brigockas, & Sternberg, 1997).

In general, educators seem to lack two types of knowledge. The first is how to recognize creative behavior in children and the second, how to promote creativity in the classroom. Following are four common mistakes that teachers make with respect to creative thinking:

1. *Confusing measures of intelligence with measures of creativity.* When asked to identify creative students, teachers tend to mention those with high test scores or grades (Nicholson & Moran, 1986). Although creative thinking is a form of intelligence, it is not the type usually emphasized in elementary schools, where the

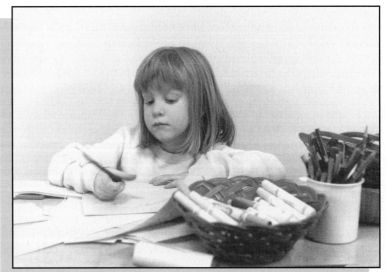

Schools that nurture creativity support children's experimentation and problem-solving efforts.

emphasis is on basic skills in reading and mathematics. Furthermore, a person might be a creative genius in one domain, such as composing music, but not be particularly creative in another domain.

2. *Being overly influenced by socially desirable behavior.* Academic environments are not always accepting of children who "dare to be different" (Fleith, 2000). History is full of examples of people who were called "daydreamers," "underachievers," or "troublemakers" during childhood only to become highly creative or even creative geniuses in later life, such as the politician Winston Churchill, the actress Sara Bernhardt, the scientist Albert Einstein, the inventor Alexander Graham Bell, and the dancer Isadora Duncan.

3. *Being overly influenced by the child's rate of development.* Adults react more readily and more favorably to children's uncommon (advanced) behavior than to children's unconventional (creative) behavior (Nicholson & Moran, 1986). To illustrate, think about two 3-year-old boys, Aaron and Matt. Aaron's parents have taught him to identify several reading words printed on flashcards. Matt's parents encourage independence and creative problem solving. In fact, one of Matt's favorite expressions is "I have an idea. We could. . . ." Matt is learning to problem-solve while Aaron is being conditioned to imitate adult behavior as rapidly as possible. Aaron may be precocious (i.e., capable of doing something in advance of most peers) but his responses are not creative. To see creative problem solving in action, watch the "Building Blocks: Small Group Activity" online at MyEducationLab.

4. *Associating creativity with socioeconomic privilege.* Studies have shown that teachers—even teachers in gifted/talented programs—tend to overlook the influence of cultural background, social circumstances, and the individual circumstances that affect creativity (Lee & Seo, 2006). Some teachers associate creativity with economic privilege and fail to notice it in students who are not engaged in the fine arts (Torrance, 2003). The disturbing outcome of such attitudes is that when children from low income homes demonstrate creative behavior, their abilities often are overlooked or even actively discouraged by teachers. A review of 62 studies concluded that arts education has particular advantages for students from economically disadvantaged backgrounds, yet this population is least likely to have extensive opportunities and a wide variety of materials (Manzo, 2002). Many traits commonly displayed by African American children—a low tolerance for boredom; excitement and involvement with new designs, music, or ideas; language rich in imagery, humor, symbolism, and persuasion; and high divergent thinking ability—are associated with creative thinking but research suggests that some teachers treat it as misbehavior or disrespect (Baldwin, 2001).

MyEducationLab

Go to MyEducationLab and select the topic "Play." Under Activities and Applications, watch the video Building Blocks: Small Group Activity *and consider how play with blocks supports creative thinking.*

TEACHERS' ROLES AND RESPONSIBILITIES IN PROMOTING CREATIVITY

Creativity is a complex developmental system that is shaped by at least seven influences: (1) cognitive processes; (2) social and emotional processes; (3) family aspects, both while growing up and current; (4) education and preparation, both informal and formal; (5) characteristics of the domain and field; (6) sociocultural contextual aspects; and (7) historical forces, events, and trends (Feldman, 1999, pp. 171–172). We know that "the professional skill of the teacher is important in sustaining . . . creative effort, because creativity is easily extinguished" (Peterson, 2001/2002, p. 8).

Teachers succeed in promoting children's creativity when they:

1. *Understand what it means to be a creative teacher.* Teachers assume that "creative activities" are all about them when, in reality, the worth of creative activities is evaluated by the quality of the children's responses. Genuinely creative activities are not something that teachers *do for* children, such as designing "cute" games for them to play. To develop possibility thinking and problem finding, children need "playful teachers who constantly invent teaching strategies to surprise their students" (Pitri, 2001, p. 48). Teaching creatively activates children's potential rather than requiring teachers to perform in the arts (Egan, Stout, & Takaya, 2007). This should be good news for teachers who worry about their singing voices, their inability to draw, their clumsiness at dance, their inexperience with drama, or the fact that they never learned to play a musical instrument.

2. *Offer support for possibility thinking.* Possibility thinking happens when children engage with everyday problems at a deeper level and pose "what if" questions (Craft, 2001b, 2002). Researchers in the field of creativity have argued that the creative individual engages, to a considerable extent, not merely in problem solving but in problem *finding* (Dorn, Madeja, & Sabol, 2003). Problem-finding patterns of thinking forge connections between creative thought (such as "outside the box" thinking), values (such as decisions about what is effective, elegant, ethical), and intrinsic motivation (that is, self-directed to pursue a goal). Teachers might begin with a concrete object to stimulate creative thought, such as carpet squares used as "magic" carpets. Unusual situations are another avenue for developing possibility thinking. Pitri (2001) introduced a princess puppet and began with a story about her waking up in a forest when it suddenly started to rain. The children were given the task of creating something that would protect the princess from the rain. Note that this activity engages children in predicting events, reasoning about cause and effect, and arriving at conclusions. Picture books such as *Alice the Fairy* (Shannon, 2004); *Can You See What I See? Dream Machine* (Wick, 2003*); If I Were a Lion* (Weeks, 2004); *Ernst* (Kleven, 2002); *There Is a Flower at the Tip of My Nose Smelling Me* (Walker, 2006); and *Once Upon a Cloud* (Walker, 2005) are another way to stimulate possibility thinking.

3. *Value the process as well as the product.* Studies of creativity reveal that quantity affects the quality of work (Simonton, 2003). In other words, highly creative individuals need to amass considerable practice and often generate numerous unsatisfactory attempts before they arrive at a satisfying outcome. Therefore, children should be encouraged to play with ideas and explore solutions rather than being pushed into premature conclusions. When children are pressured to dash something off to meet someone else's schedule, they are not afforded the "luxury" of seeking many alternatives and refining the most promising ones and the essential creative skill of self-evaluation is undermined (Amabile, 1989).

4. *Provide the right amount of structure.* Research suggests that either too much or too little *structure* can interfere with the development of creative expression (McLeod, 1997). If a classroom is regimented, there is too much structure. On the other hand, if a classroom is "anything goes," there is too little structure to provide proper guidance. One way to create more flexibility is to relax the schedule for activities in which children are deeply absorbed. That way, children begin to appreciate intrinsic motivation and the "labor of love" satisfactions of creative pursuits (Amabile, 1986; Webster, Campbell, & Jane, 2006). Figure 1.6 summarizes strategies that teachers use to promote creativity.

Classroom Environment, Materials, and Climate

- Create organizational and structural conditions that allow open and flexible distribution of roles, themes, problems, and activities
- Provide challenging and stimulating learning materials
- Offer opportunities to work with varied materials under different conditions
- Establish a classroom climate that permits alternative solutions

Professional Attitudes and Values

- Provide support and positive feedback for problem finding, not just problem solving
- Serve as a model of creative thought
- Tolerate ambiguity, accept alternative solutions
- Allow for humor and playfulness

Social Support for Creativity

- Have a cooperative, socially integrative style of teaching
- Enable children to participate in joint projects with self-selected partners
- Surprise students with recognition for creative processes and products
- Extend mastery of factual knowledge through collaboration

Recognition of and Respect for Children's Creativity

- Enable self-directed work that allows for a high degree of initiative, spontaneity, and experimentation
- Encourage and accept constructive nonconformist behavior
- Take children's questions seriously and tolerate "sensible" or bold errors
- Help students learn to cope with frustration and failure
- Reward courage as much as being right
- Actively teach creative strategies
- Foster intense concentration and task commitment through high motivation and interest in self-selected topics
- Increase autonomy of learning by recognition and self-evaluation of progress

Figure 1.6   What Teachers Do to Promote Creativity in Students

Note: Data from Clark (1996), Cropley (2001), and Urban (1996).

MyEducationLab

Go to MyEducationLab and select the topic "Early Literacy." Under Activities and Applications, view the artifact Dialog Journal. *As you look at the artifact, think about the connection between cognition and creativity.*

5. *Establish mechanisms for peer support.* Children are encouraged to share ideas, not only with the teacher but also with one another. One of the ways that children begin to regard themselves as creative is in their reflected selves—in others' responses to them and their ideas. Therefore, it is important for children to give and receive supportive feedback, not only from adults but also from peers. Strategies for making curriculum accommodations for diverse learners so that all children are included in creative thinking are discussed in the next section. To view an artifact that illustrates how an activity can be adopted, look at "Dialog Journal" online at MyEducationLab.

6. *Minimize competition and external rewards.* Creativity is promoted when teachers enjoy experiences along with children rather than singling out particular products for praise or rewards. When children are informed that there will be a contest, that some will win a tangible reward and others will lose, three things happen. First, they become more cautious and tend to "play it safe"; second, they feel pressured to please someone else and lose their intrinsic motivation; and third, they tend to rush to get the reward. All of these things result in less spontaneous, less complex, and less varied products; in other words, less creative responses.

7. *Encourage rather than praise.* In praise, the teacher passes judgment on the quality of the child's work ("You did a very good job on your story"); encouragement acknowledges the child's efforts ("I noticed that you worked very hard to revise your story until it was ready to be published online"). Effusive praise can actually suppress children's creativity. Suppose that a child paints an orange pumpkin with black triangle eyes and nose and a toothy grin. If adults shower the child with praise, saying, "Oh, that's so wonderful! It's just the cutest little pumpkin!" the child may get "stalled" at this stage because he or she is trying to please the adult. It is better to show genuine, personal interest and comment specifically on the child's work ("Carla, that pumpkin looks really happy") or ask questions about it ("How did you figure out how to make the stem?"). Sheets (2006) describes, for example, how an African American child who had the freedom to invent a jack-o-lantern decided to make it more like herself with elaborate braids and eyelashes; the teacher followed up with the book *Meet Danitra Brown* (Grimes, 1994) as a way to encourage the child's creative choices. Figure 1.7 suggests appropriate comments about children's creative work.

A first-grade teacher helps illustrate how these principles are put into practice. Ms. Kastenbaum uses a four-phase strategy that begins with awareness, then moves to exploration, next to inquiry, and finally to utilization (Copple & Bredekamp, 1997). She builds the children's awareness by asking, "What is a robot? How are robots made? What is special about robots? What robots have you seen?" Krish says that robots are "sort of like people, only they're machines." Taro mentions R2-D2 from *Star Wars,* and Joelle expresses a wish for a toy robot. Exploration begins as the children share and discuss a collection of robot pictures and the teacher summarizes by asking, "What have you learned about robots? What questions do you still have about robots?" Now Ms. Kastenbaum moves the group into inquiry as she invites them to examine a wide array of recycled materials and invent a robot puppet. One child begins with an old sock, another with a cardboard box; one child uses Styro-

Figure 1.7
Responses to
Children's Work

Note: Data from Cecil and Lauritzen (1994).

How did you get the idea for this work?

This makes me feel . . .

I like the way you used _____ because . . .

This reminds me of . . .

What were you trying to do?

Maybe you could combine . . .

This interests me because . . .

How does this work compare with other work you have created?

I wonder what would happen if . . .

I like the part where . . .

I'd like to know more about . . .

You used some powerful ideas such as . . .

The part where you explained . . .

This is like your . . .

You are really good at . . .

foam egg carton cups for "buggy eyes," while another chooses aluminum foil and cardboard tubes for arms. All of the children experiment with different fixatives such as glue, staples, tape, and sewing. The activity turns to utilization as the children's finished robot puppets move to electronic music.

🦋 CURRICULUM ACCOMMODATIONS FOR DIVERSE LEARNERS IN CREATIVE ACTIVITIES

When young children have a disability it is common for people to approach it as a "problem" and to become preoccupied with the things the child cannot do (Whitehurst & Howells, 2006). Effective teachers take a positive approach. They unlock the creative potential in children with disabilities through a persistent focus on children's strengths and capabilities (Carpenter & Shevlin, 2004). The teacher's goal is to include rather than exclude: "Inclusion is about much more than the type of school that children attend: it is about the quality of their experience; how they are helped to learn, achieve and participate fully in the life of the school" (Department for Education and Skills [DFES], 2006, p. 25).

Tips to Support Creativity in an Inclusive Classroom

- Support possibility thinking that relies on "What if?" questions, open-ended activities, and experiences in solving unstructured problems
- Provide models for children, not to copy but to stimulate thinking
- Use cooperative groups that include children with different talents and strengths
- Provide a variety of tools for creative expression and demonstrate how to use them

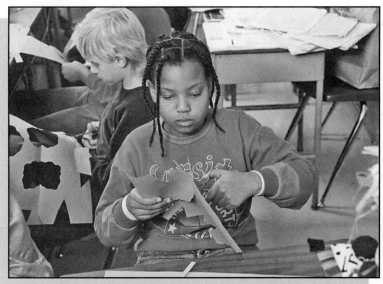

Scott Cunningham/Merrill

Children's behavior is creative when it is original, appropriate, fluent, and flexible.

- Anticipate conditions that contribute to boredom—e.g., stop an activity before children become tired of it
- Encourage students to take initiative and make use of unscheduled time— e.g., provide independent activities at centers in the classroom so that children have creative outlets
- Seek professional development in creativity (Strom & Strom, 2002)
- Pursue partnerships with outside agencies (e.g., museums) and individuals (e.g., artists) that support young children's growth in creativity

Practical Suggestions

Students with Emotional and Intellectual Challenges

- Remember that "The arts are often the one area in which students who are challenged by academic content can first succeed" (Bafumo, 2005, p. 1). Children with a variety of intellectual and emotional challenges, such as mental retardation, ADHD (Healey & Rucklidge, 2005), or bipolar disorder (Simeonova, Chang, Strong, & Ketter, 2005) can express themselves creatively.
- Pair a child with attentional or intellectual challenges with a typically developing child and use the talking drawings strategy. In this approach, children draw their understanding of a nonfiction concept (e.g., the Statue of Liberty), then listen to an information book read aloud, and finally redraw and label the parts of their drawing now that they have obtained additional information from listening or reading (Fello, Paquette, & Jalongo, 2006/2007).
- Use a big book with a definite rhyme pattern, such as *Down by the Cool of the Pool* (Mitton, 2002) and practice until the children can recite (or read) the story aloud with expression. Engage children in creating sound effects or soft musical backgrounds for their performance of the book.

Students with Visual Impairments

- A child with a visual disability may not be able to use crayons to produce a drawing that is pleasing to the eye, but that child can use fabrics to create a texture collage that is pleasing to the touch.
- To support children with visual impairments in enjoying picture books, record the text of the story and "narrate" the pictures as well, describing each illustration (Isbell, Sobel, Lindauer, & Lowrance, 2004).
- Give children with visual impairments opportunities to explore various story listening and story producing media—cassette tapes, DVDs, CDs, text-to-speech and speech-to-text software (Cassell, 2004).

Students with Hearing Impairments

- Drawing and writing are important tools for self-expression, particularly for children with hearing impairments (Heath & Wolf, 2005).
- Children with hearing impairments often are very capable at expressing ideas through gesture and pantomime (Roush, 2005). Use picture books that invite physical participation to involve children with hearing impairments (Nespeca, 2005).
- Experience books, in which the child dictates or writes an account of a personal experience and then illustrates it with digital photos or drawings, are a means for creative self-expression (Pakulsky & Kadavarek, 2004).

- Teach all children in the class some simple sign language to facilitate the ability to communicate for the child with hearing impairments (see Murray, 2007).
- Opportunities for pretend play are an important way of supporting vocabulary growth in children with (and without) hearing impairments. Make collections of puppets and other props that focus on a particular theme (e.g., The Little Red Hen), label the storage containers with pictures, and store them so that children can access them easily.
- Make word walls of vocabulary that enable children to express themselves creatively—lists of the names of imaginary creatures (e.g., unicorn, fairy), lists of verbs (galloped, fly), and lists of descriptive words (flowing mane, glittery wings).
- Use video technology, such as captioned stories, to support understanding for the child with hearing impairments.

Students with Orthopedic Impairments
- Adapt the physical environment so that wheelchairs, walkers, and other orthopedic equipment can be accommodated and children can participate in pretend play (Doctoroff, 2001).
- The child whose physical condition affects fine motor skills for sculpting or painting at an easel may be able to mold large objects with clay or use hand and arm movements to finger-paint. Think of ways to make art materials accessible to the child with orthopedic impairments.
- Investigate group games that have been adapted to include children with various disabilities (Torbert, 2005).

MEETING STANDARDS THROUGH CREATIVE ACTIVITIES

For a behavior to be creative, it must meet four basic criteria (Guilford, 1984; Jackson & Messick, 1965). These criteria are described next using examples of young children's behavior.

1. *Criterion 1: Creative behavior is original; it has a low probability of occurrence.* Two-year-old Adam attended a college hockey game with his father, and the toddler now wants to be a hockey player. When Adam asked for hockey equipment, his parents told him he was too little and that it was too expensive, so Adam invented his own. He used a wooden spoon for a hockey stick, his sister's empty lip gloss container for a puck, socks for hockey gloves, and the open door to a closet as the goal net. Now "playing goalie" while his dad or older brother do the sports commentary is Adam's favorite game. Adam's behavior is unusual and surprising rather than typical and predictable. Thus it has a low probability of occurrence, and it is original.

2. *Criterion 2: Creative behavior is appropriate and relevant.* Six-year-old twins Becky and Belinda both love Hans Christian Andersen's story "The Little Mermaid." They want to look like mermaids and need to create long, flowing hair, so Becky suggests using scarves attached with bobby pins. To create a tail, Belinda has the idea of using a sock. Their mother helps out and gives them an old pair of socks to use. Belinda cuts off the foot portion and stretches the ankle part over both of her ankles, turning her feet outward to represent "fins." The twins' behavior is a good illustration of appropriateness. In order for behavior to be creative, it needs to be relevant to the goals of the person who produced it.

3. *Criterion 3: Creative behavior is fluent; it results in many new, meaningful forms.* Six-year-old Louie likes to invent things and does so frequently. One day he "invented a wind tunnel" with his dad's help. Louie attached a small sheet to the sides of a large box fan with duct tape. Then his dad plugged in and turned on the fan and the fabric billowed out. Louie could sit inside and read. Fluency in creativity is comparable to fluency in language; it means that the child can generate one idea after another with apparent ease.

4. *Criterion 4: Creative behavior is flexible; it explores and uses nontraditional approaches to problem solving.* Lucia is seated next to Tomas, a fellow first grader who is disassembling a grease pencil. He pulls the string and unwraps the paper coiled around the lead. Lucia watches as Tomas throws the curls of paper in the trash can, and then she retrieves them. She cuts two pieces of curled paper, glues them on her drawing, and attaches a piece of string to each one. "There," she says aloud. "The windows of my house have shades just like this." The teacher comments on Lucia's picture, saying, "And the shades on the windows you drew really roll up and down, too! This looks like a very special picture—will you choose it for your portfolio?" Lucia's behavior is a good example of flexibility. She wanted to make her drawing three-dimensional, and she used a different method that involved materials that others considered useless. As the behaviors of these children suggest, children's thinking is creative when it is original, appropriate, fluent, and flexible.

Three basic intellectual functions support creative expression and arts-based learning: finding out how existing things work, finding out what has happened, and producing new or unique things (Dorn, Madeja, & Sabol, 2003; Hope, 1991). As you review the following examples, refer to Figure 1.8.

Preschool: Finding Out How Existing Things Work

In a classroom for 3- to 5-year-olds, the food preparation gadgets in the cooking center have captured the children's imaginations. Among the children's favorites are the hard-boiled egg slicer, the melon baller, a manual orange juicer, an ice cream scoop, and an apple corer.

Primary: Finding Out What Has Happened

A second-grade teacher's observations of her second graders on the playground reveal that many of the students from low-income homes are much more adept at inventing games and playing cooperatively than the children who come from economically advantaged homes. Rather than allowing this important strength to go unnoticed, the teacher asks the children to show the class some of their games, which involve syncopated hand clapping and original jump rope chants. When the other children try to participate in the games these students have created, they gain a new appreciation for their classmates' skills. The teacher further supports and extends the children's activity by sharing several books of jump rope jingles, by inviting each child to discuss favorite childhood games with various family members, by giving children the opportunity to share what they learned from their interviews, by inviting parents to come in to demonstrate favorite childhood games, and by teaching the children new games from other eras and lands. Some picture

Activities stimulate creative thought and problem solving when they:

- Are relevant to the learner, meaning that they are developmentally appropriate, understandable to the learner, and have "real world" applications
- Meet the needs of children at different levels of development because the challenges have multiple answers (rather than one right answer)
- Enable students to engage in long-term, open-ended projects and pursue a narrower range of ideas and materials in greater depth
- Capitalize on children's interests, curiosities, and passions and allow the child to set the pace and take the lead
- Support children as they use the processes of exploring, selecting, combining, and refining a form
- Are framed by teachers and students, with teachers structuring or limiting as necessary
- Give the students something practical and worthwhile to do that engages thoughts and feelings, mind and body
- Encourage children to look for models and make connections, emphasizing the influence and the works of others
- Use a variety of perspectives (such as critic, philosopher, inventor)
- Help students develop a set of standards for evaluating their performance and peers' performance that goes beyond "good" or "bad" and carefully analyzes the dimensions of a work
- Expand opportunities for learning and lead to new, interesting challenges

Figure 1.8   Features of Creative Experiences and Activities

Note: Data from Felton and Stoessiger (1987), Jalongo and Stamp (1997), and Lindstrom (1997).

books that are particularly intriguing to the children are *Hopscotch Around the World* and *Jumprope Around the World*. As a result of this second-grade teacher's interest and encouragement, all of the students now recognize what has happened: Some children's outdoor play is remarkable for its resourcefulness, reliance on cooperation, and reflection of the children's culture and community.

Intermediate: Producing New or Unique Things

A wide array of strategies to promote creative thinking have been designed and implemented over the years (see Cropley [2001] for a review). What follows are some of the most well-known strategies that are used to facilitate creative thinking in older children and a description of how teachers might put them to use in a classroom. Brainstorming is a technique that is used to capitalize on the creative-thought and problem-solving capacities of a group. Feldhusen (2001) offers the following guidelines for brainstorming:

1. Make sure that students understand the task dimensions.
2. Indicate that generating many ideas or responses is the goal.
3. State that there will be no evaluation or judgment of responses while ideas are being produced.
4. Assure students that they should feel free to proffer unusual and original ideas.
5. Urge students to strive to connect, relate, or alter their own and others' ideas.
6. Suggest that students be brief in responding; lengthy statements should be avoided. (p. 12)

A creative-thinking technique that is used to stimulate "out of the box" type thinking uses the acronym SCAMPER. Barnes (2002) elaborates on the SCAMPER strategy originally developed by Osborn (1972) by using a series of questions to coax thinking out of routine and taken-for-granted ways:

S SUBSTITUTE   To have a person or thing act or serve in the place of another.
   Question: Can you think of a new way of using this?

C COMBINE   To bring together or unite.
   Question: What do you think might happen if you try to put these together?

A ADAPT   To adjust for the purpose of suiting a condition or purpose.
   Question: What else is like this?

M MODIFY   To alter, change the form or quality.
   MAGNIFY   To enlarge, make greater in form or quality.
   MINIFY   To make smaller, lighter, slower, less frequent.
   Question: Can you imagine this bigger? Smaller?

P PUT TO OTHER USES To use for purposes other than originally intended.
   Question: Do you think we might use this for . . . ?

E ELIMINATE   To remove, omit, or get rid of a quality, part, or whole.
   Question: What might this be like if you got rid of . . . ?

R REVERSE   To place opposite or contrary, to turn around.
   REARRANGE   To change the order, plan, layout, or scheme.
   Question: What happens if you turn it backward . . . or upside down? (Barnes, 2002, pp. 53–54)

 ## CONCLUSION

Effective teachers capitalize on the creative propensities of childhood in three basic ways: (1) by teaching the skills and attitudes of creative thinking to students, (2) by orienting students to the creative methods of various disciplines, and (3) by creating a "problem friendly" classroom in which lines of inquiry with relevance for learners can be pursued through multidisciplinary methods (Starko, 2001). In order to function at full creative capacity, children need the freedom to pursue questions that captivate them and work in learning environments that offer a blend of high support and high expectations (Rea, 2001).

 ## CHAPTER SUMMARY

1. Creativity is a behavior characterized by originality, relevance, fluency, and flexibility.
2. Children's thinking is different from adults' thinking because, generally speaking, children are highly sensitive to stimuli, are less inhibited, and can become completely absorbed in imagination ("as if") and pretend ("what if").
3. If teachers regard the dimensions of children's creative behavior— originality, appropriateness, relevance, fluency, and flexibility—they can further develop children's creative potential.

Frequently Asked Questions About Creativity

Is it true that children have active imaginations?

Even when wide awake, children experience more frequent theta wave activity, a daydream-like state that mature adults experience primarily as their minds hover between being awake and falling asleep (Diamond & Hopson, 1999). Theta wave brain activity is more relaxed, freewheeling, and receptive to fleeting mental images. Eminent creative individuals in various fields report a host of techniques to capture theta wave activity (Goleman & Kaufman, 1992; Runco & Pritzker, 1999). Evidently, children are adept at forming varied and unusual images while adults tend to have the advantage when it comes to storing and retrieving information, drawing upon experience, and making judgments about what is appropriate and effective. So children may not be "more" imaginative, but they certainly do have active imaginations.

Are children more or less creative than adults?

Children are differently creative than adults. Children have unique ideas but may not yet have the ability to execute them well or communicate them clearly to others. Originality in children "reflects their lack of inhibitions rather than their intentional and metacognitive efforts . . ." (Runco, 2004, p. 22). Evidently the creative assets of childhood include a tolerance for ambiguity, a propensity for nonlinear thinking, and receptivity to ideas that might be quickly discarded by an adult as too fanciful to merit further

consideration. The line of demarcation between fantasy and reality is not as firmly drawn for children as it is for adults, so ideas from one realm slip through easily into another. This may enable children to respond in ways that are nonstereotypic, a trait that many adults, particularly those in the arts, find enviable (Kinkade, 2002).

Is being creative valued mainly because it provides an emotional release?

Creativity is more than "letting off steam." There is a difference between making noise and making music and between jumping around and dancing, for example. The artist's behaviors are planned, controlled, and practiced. This tendency to treat the arts as emotional outlets distances creative work not only from the cognitive and physical processes used to attain excellence, but also from the cultural contexts in which creative works are produced. Creativity is much more than an emotional outlet; it is an expression of values, a source of national pride, and, for those outside the culture, a way of promoting intercultural understanding.

How can teachers support the creative expression of all children?

It is no mistake that Amabile's (1986) "creativity killers" include such things as inflexible schedules, intense competition, reliance on extrinsic rewards, and lack of free time. Educators bear major responsibility as advocates for children's creative thought and expression. Fulfilling this important role often involves unlearning common assumptions and replacing them with more enlightened perspectives.

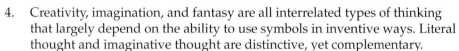

4. Creativity, imagination, and fantasy are all interrelated types of thinking that largely depend on the ability to use symbols in inventive ways. Literal thought and imaginative thought are distinctive, yet complementary.
5. Theories that attempt to explain the desire to create may be categorized as humanistic, psychoanalytic, and constructivist.
6. The creative process can be described in four stages: preparation, incubation, illumination, and verification/communication.
7. Some ways that classroom environments support creativity include providing psychological safety by reducing stress and anxiety, valuing process over product, removing time limits, valuing self-expression, encouraging peer interaction, and minimizing competition and external rewards.
8. Active, child-initiated experiences give the child authentic opportunities for creative expression and build the child's inner sense of psychological freedom or ego strength. When teachers provide a classroom environment in which children feel safe to experiment, to take the risks associated with

learning something new, and to learn from their mistakes as an accepted part of the learning process, the condition of psychological safety has been met.

9. Teachers and parents play a crucial role in fostering the creative process in children. One recommended teaching strategy is to begin by building children's awareness, then move next to exploration, then to inquiry, and finally to utilization.

10. All children are creative. If all children are to develop their creative potential to the fullest extent, every classroom must provide a wide range of opportunities for creative expression. This means that teachers will need to respect children's ethnic and cultural diversity, acknowledge the role of multiple intelligences, adapt materials to each child's needs, and encourage authentic self-expression.

 Discuss: Perspectives on Creative Expression

1. Do you agree that teachers sometimes discourage creativity? Why or why not? What might teachers do (or fail to do) that would undermine young children's creative expression?

2. Sometimes children's creativity is mistaken for misbehavior. Were you ever punished as a child for creative thinking?

3. Cite several current examples of imagination and creativity at work in various fields (medical research, business, new inventions, film, music). How would an education that fosters creativity and artistic expression prepare children for the workplace of the future?

Chapter 2

Supporting Children's Play, Games, and Inventions

Ample evidence points to the enormous health and professional benefits of laughter, lightheartedness, games, and humor. In the Conceptual Age, in work and life, we all need to play.

Daniel Pink, 2006, p. 66

CLASSROOM PERSPECTIVES ON PLAY, GAMES, AND INVENTIONS

Preschool–Kindergarten

Preschoolers Jonah, Dylan, and Sarena recently heard the book *Today Is Monday* by Eric Carle (1993), and they are re-creating their own version of it in the dramatic play center. The children are pretending to be different restaurant workers, talking about their roles as cook, server, and cashier, and spontaneously developing and role-playing a familiar restaurant theme. At one point, Jonah announces, "I think we should make this a restaurant," and initiates the restaurant play episode with Sarena and Dylan. Dylan becomes the cook, who makes alphabet soup. They check their own imaginative play against the reality of restaurants when they decide to "make alphabet soup . . . lock up the store . . . clean up the kitchen . . . and put the dishes away." Their words, actions, and gestures show their understanding of what a restaurant needs based on their experiences, the media, and the play context.

First Grade–Second Grade

Ms. Lee's first graders have been reading the Dr. Seuss book *Bartholomew and the Oobleck* (1949). Some of the children ask Ms. Lee if they can make oobleck, so she provides some cornstarch, water, and red food coloring. The children explore the cornstarch—feeling, smelling, and tasting the white powder—and then mix it with water and red food coloring to produce red goo. Then they explore the mixture, squeeze it, talk about it, shape it into balls, describe it as soft and gushy, and call it such names as "mushy mess." They laugh when they hold it in their hands to make it drip. Some add more water to see what happens; others add more cornstarch to see what happens.

Third Grade–Fourth Grade

Fourth graders Eli and Maya are playing chess in the game area of their classroom. During the game, you hear them using such terms as *jeopardy, capture, check,* and *checkmate* as well as reminding each other of the appropriate directions in which the different pieces can move. Their faces, body language, and conversation reveal their use of different thinking processes needed to protect their king piece. Eli and Maya's choice of a game that interests them shows their high level of cognitive activity, social interaction, and autonomy.

Each of these perspectives reveals information on the importance of children's play, games, and inventions. They provide information about these children's knowledge and ways of thinking as they play, create, imagine, invent, figure things out, and make things work. This chapter explores the essential role of play, games, and inventions as critical childhood activities that help all children learn, develop, and create.

✄ THEORETICAL AND RESEARCH BASE: WHAT IS PLAY?

Over the years, theorists, researchers, and educators have documented that play is the optimal vehicle for learning and development. They also suggest that the *absence of play* is often an obstacle to developing happy, healthy, and creative individuals. Although experts who study play disagree on some of its aspects, there is genuine agreement on the characteristics that distinguish play from other types of human behavior (Fromberg, 2002; Fromberg & Bergen, 2006; Frost, Wortham, & Reifel, 2008).

Characteristics of Play

At least five essential elements characterize play. Each element was illustrated in at least one of the opening scenarios.

1. *Play is voluntary and intrinsically motivated.* In play, children are free to choose the content and direction of their activity. The play is self-satisfying because it does not respond to external demands or expectations. In their self-chosen roles as cook and restaurant workers, Jonah, Dylan, and Sarena controlled how to play them out.

2. *Play is symbolic, meaningful, and transformational.* Play helps children to connect their past experiences to their current world. It empowers them to transform themselves into others' roles as they switch back and forth and in and out of different situations. By pretending to be others, they assume a *"what if"* or *"as if"* attitude. When Dylan imagined himself as a cook making alphabet soup, he assumed a *"what if"* attitude by imagining what a cook might say or do. When he pretended to be a cook, he transformed himself into a cook by imagining cooking, stirring, and serving soup, like a cook. This *"as if"* attitude (the play) is what facilitates the further generation of ideas.

3. *Play is active.* In play, children explore, experiment, investigate, and inquire with people, objects, or events. Notice how the first graders making "oobleck" explored what different proportions and combinations of cornstarch, water, and food coloring would do to it—making it drier, wetter, or mushier, depending on the amounts used. They also used language such as "mushy mess," to describe their experiences. Active play experiences increase children's awareness of what materials can do and what children can do with materials while at the same time increasing their skills of observation and description.

4. *Play is rule-bound.* Children are governed by either explicit or implicit rules during play. Younger children both create and change rules in play that apply to appropriate role behavior and object use. Older children accept predetermined rules that guide the play. In the *restaurant scenario*, the preschoolers created their own rules about paying, cooking, and cleaning up; in the *chess scenario*, the children focused on the appropriate language and moves for the individual pieces.

5. *Play is pleasurable.* Children play for the intrinsic pleasure it brings—not for an extrinsic reward. In each of the opening classroom perspectives, the children you read about were playing because they chose to play as they wished and played with total concentration on what they were doing. Clearly, these children were pursuing their play because it made sense to them.

Play helps children to construct understandings of their world from their own experiences and strongly influences their optimal growth, development, and learning. In play, children become empowered to do things for themselves, to feel in control, to test out and practice their skills, and to affirm self-confidence. The play context is an important one for children's developing sense of competence (Wassermann, 2000).

These five characteristics describe what play is. While it is important to understand what play is, it is equally important to consider what play *is not*. Table 2.1 (p. 36) lists a continuum of behavior from play to work that differentiates between play and nonplay behaviors and also relates them to the type of learning that each generates.

Controversies Surrounding Play

With agreed-upon characteristics of play, why would there be any controversy about its definition and purposes? First, theorists and researchers differ in their assumptions about play and its primary purpose, yet all attest to its significance in children's physical, social/emotional, language, and intellectual growth and development. Freud (1958) and Erikson (1963) emphasized the emotional significance of play, the way children use play to express and release powerful emotions; Piaget (1962), on the other hand, emphasized play's cognitive significance, the way individual children use play to practice known information and construct understanding. Vygotsky (1967, 1978) emphasized the way children use play as a vehicle for social and cultural learning and the development of the social tool called language.

Second, our own culture makes a clear distinction between play and work (Fromberg & Bergen, 2006; Frost et al., 2008; Zigler & Bishop-Josef, 2006). Children are pressured more and more to participate in high-stakes, fast-paced, teacher-directed, formal lessons leaving little, if any, time to learn through play. Many teachers believe that play experiences should be the centerpiece of their curricula. Yet they feel obligated to justify the use of play with the phrase "Play is children's work," which implies that work is serious and play is trivial. This misconception equates "real" school with a narrow view of learning that focuses on isolated facts and skills rather than making information one's own. Yet if we look at the best practices in each area of the curriculum, such as hands-on science, math manipulatives, music laboratories, and writers' workshops, it is easy to see that all of these approaches are play-based and support children's curiosity, motivation, attention, and insightful thinking.

An illustration of how your own orientation to play will affect your classroom comes from the following two very different second-grade classrooms. In Ms. Liu's room, children plan their daily schedules with Ms. Liu during their morning meeting. Then, during a 90-minute uninterrupted block of planned learning experiences, the second graders complete some teacher-selected stations related to the current unit of study and then choose from a wide variety of accessible and well-organized learning materials; they play games, paint, design and construct with manipulatives, write in their math or writing journals, or investigate science ideas. There is a quiet buzz from the children's interactions with these carefully planned but diverse activities. They also have daily opportunities for outdoor play or recess.

Mr. White's second graders, on the other hand, sit in desks in neat rows and work in whole groups to complete teacher-prepared activities, such as completing worksheets and making an art project by copying Mr. White's sample. Because he expects his second graders to do their own work, there is little time for the children to talk with one another about what they are doing, thinking, or making. Outdoors,

TABLE 2.1 Continuum of Behavior from Play to Nonplay and Types of Learning

	Child-Initiated Play	Facilitative Play	Directed Play	Work Disguised as Play	Work (Nonplay)
Focus of play	Child has greatest degree of control over situation, event, or other players. Can freely interact and choose.	Child plays within a flexible environment of social rules, requiring players to attend to externally imposed control. Adults monitor play and often redirect, challenge, and add materials.	Adults impose play elements and often lead the play. Child does not usually choose whether, what, how, or when to play.	Task oriented activities that are not inherently playful but can be transformed into directed or guided play activities if the potential for internal control, motivation, and reality can be tapped.	Activities designed to reach an externally defined goal and for which motivation is external. No opportunity to bend reality. Adult's expectations are central and often evaluated.
Example	Child freely chooses when, how, what, and with whom to play. High levels of social and pretend play occur.	Child may have a limited number of choices or be expected to engage in a specified number of play activities within a particular time period.	Group games, finger plays, directed story reenactment.	Rote memory activities such as singing ABC songs, spelling games, addition facts races.	Adults decide when, how, where, or on what to work. Goal-oriented tasks, such as worksheets, dittos, and other drill-and-practice activities.
Type of learning	Discovery learning	Guided, discovery learning	Receptive learning	Rote learning	Repetitive learning

Note: Data from Bergen (1987), Christie (2001), and Frost, Wortham, & Reifel (2008).

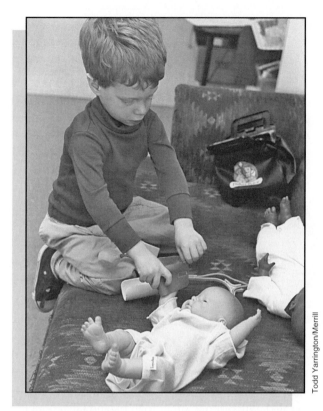

Play with objects empowers children to do things for themselves, to feel in control, to test and practice skills, and to develop a sense of competence.

children play organized ball games or practice motor skills on the climbing equipment. How do these classrooms reflect each teacher's assumptions about play?

In a classroom like Mr. White's, little attention is given to the powerful relationship of play to learning and development. His classroom experiences deny children the opportunity to engage in challenging tasks in a playful context. Historically, early childhood educators have valued and supported the centrality of play in the early childhood classroom (Isenberg & Quisenberry, 2002; Johnson, Christie, & Yawkey, 1999; Singer, Golinkoff, & Hirsh-Pasek, 2006). However, recent educational developments have emphasized a more academic, structured orientation and have undermined the role of play in the curriculum. Classroom practices such as the use of inquiry-based learning, problem-solving activities, and cooperative learning groups offer one way of including play-based experiences in today's curriculum.

The Educational Value of Play

If we could travel back in time and interview three educational leaders about the value of play, what would they say? John Dewey, Patty Smith Hill, and Susan Isaacs all strongly promoted play in the classroom. Dewey (1916, 1938) advocated that play was a major way all children learn about themselves and their world. While children build on what they know in their play, their play continually changes by their experiences. For Dewey, play becomes a recurring cycle of learning that is essential to

John Dewey believed that children learn about themselves and their world through their play.

Patty Smith Hill recognized the importance of play for children's learning.

what children know and can do. Through meaningful, active experiences with concrete materials coupled with opportunities to think and talk about these experiences, children build understanding. The peer interactions and the negotiations that inevitably occur during play enhance children's social competence. Dewey's ideas about **active learning** continue to permeate today's curriculum.

Patty Smith Hill (1923), strongly influenced by Dewey's ideas, recognized the importance of play for children's learning. She designed child-centered activities and curriculum based on children's development, special needs, and social development and used large classroom spaces to enhance children's learning through play. In her work-play period, kindergarten children freely explored the objects and materials in their environment, initiated and carried out their own ideas, and engaged in cooperative learning groups with their peers.

Susan Isaacs (1933), another historical figure, believed that play contributes to all aspects of children's development. Her work was especially useful to teachers as they helped children develop mastery of their emotions. Isaacs ardently defended children's right to play and challenged parents to support play, which she regarded as children's natural resource for learning.

Prior to the large-scale societal and educational reforms beginning in the 1960s, most early childhood practitioners recognized the importance of play. They believed that play reflects children's experiences, is meaningful and relevant, and is a rich resource for learning. The translation of Piaget's (1962) work in the 1960s began to find support for the idea that children of all ages are active learners.

At the same time, other researchers documented the importance of the early years for influencing intellectual development (Bloom, 1964; Bruner, 1966; Hunt, 1961). Educators soon began putting these research ideas into practice to improve the academic performance and social skills of "disadvantaged" children (Bronson, 2006, p. 47), but did so in inappropriate ways. As curriculum designers became driven by the belief that earlier is better, academic skills and a "back to basics" philosophy replaced play as central to the early childhood curriculum, to the grave concern of many educators.

Since the 1990s, new research on brain development, the rediscovery of inquiry learning as taught in the schools of Reggio Emilia, and the reemergence of looking at the whole child influenced the way educators viewed early learning and play in particular. This research supports children's need for many opportunities to learn spontaneously, to engage in constructive social relationships, and to think about the consequences of their actions (Jensen, 2000; Santrock, 2007). Opportunities for children to learn through play were slowly reintegrated into the early childhood curriculum.

But the educational climate is once again changing. Recent policies and legislation, such as the *No Child Left Behind* (NCLB) Act passed in 2001, has placed an increasing emphasis on higher expectations for children and more accountability that has led teachers to teach more scripted, rote lessons. The emphasis on annual testing has increased the pressure on teachers "to teach to the test" while denying children the opportunities to learn through play and other developmentally appropriate ways.

Yet, in today's world, educational leaders and the business community are calling for schools to teach the necessary skills and develop the abilities that will be required of future workers and are raising questions about rote learning (National Center on Education and the Economy, 2007). Schools and curricula at all levels must be refashioned to develop children's initiative, inventiveness, and planning and focus on fostering their problem-solving ability, divergent thinking, and social skills.

Play provides the vehicle for children to develop such competencies. Thus, all teachers must understand its value for all children. As the next section details, play is what childhood is all about. First, read what teachers have to say about play and then think about your own reflections.

TEACHERS' REFLECTIONS ON PLAY, GAMES, AND INVENTIONS

Preservice Teachers

"I never realized that there was so much to learn about play and games. I was surprised that a whole course could be designed on this topic. I've learned some reasons why so many people do not believe that play is important."

"I never really thought of play and games as learning tools. Rather, I thought of them as things to take up time with the children. Now I realize that play and games are excellent tools for learning, not just something children do to keep busy."

Inservice Teachers

"I realized I needed play in my classroom when the children began complaining of headaches and I was having no fun. I haven't changed any of my curriculum objectives; I've just looked for better ways to make learning meaningful for children."

"I never thought that the absence of play could be detrimental to children's development. As an experienced elementary school teacher, I struggle with my own philosophy of teaching that keeps swinging back and forth between play-centered learning experiences and teacher-directed ones."

Your Reflections

- What role do you think play, games, and inventions should have in the curriculum?

- Can you envision different types of play in the curriculum?

- How might your beliefs about play, games, and inventions enhance or inhibit children's learning and development?

 ## WHY IS PLAY IMPORTANT?

Guidelines from the Association for Childhood Education International (ACEI) and the National Association for the Education of Young Children (NAEYC), two respected professional associations, affirm that play is essential for all children's healthy development and learning across all ages, domains, and cultures. Play does the following:

- Enables children to make sense of their world
- Develops social and cultural understandings
- Allows children to express their thoughts and feelings
- Fosters flexible and divergent thinking
- Provides opportunities to meet and solve real problems
- Develops language and literacy skills and concepts (Bredekamp & Copple, 1997; Gronlund, 2006; Isenberg & Quisenberry, 2002)

In the following vignettes, consider how play contributes to children's cognitive, language, literacy, social/emotional, and creative development.

Cognitive Development

Ellen, Taralyn, and Jasmine are first graders. On this day early in the school year, they come into their classroom, hang up their backpacks, and then choose to play school at the chalkboard. Ellen decides that Jasmine and Taralyn should get a chair and bring it up to the board. They each also find a yardstick.

Ellen: We better have two chairs.

Taralyn: (*writing on the chalkboard*) Today is . . .

Jasmine: I need to check the size. (*using the yardstick, begins to measure herself while sitting down*) I am the big teacher. My size is up to here. (*pointing to where she measured herself*)

Ellen: (*gets up from the chair acting like a teacher*) I will write it. You sit down.

Jasmine: Today is what? (*gets up*) I want to be the teacher.

Ellen: It's my turn first. You can be the teacher next.

(*As Ellen looks at the calendar to find the words she wants to use, Taralyn measures herself with the yardstick.*)

Taralyn: Today is October 8, 2007.

Jasmine: Ellen, can I write, too?

Ellen: After I am finished. (*Taralyn and Jasmine begin giving Ellen weather words to write.*)

Taralyn: Read the calendar sentence. Hey, you forgot the 7.
Ellen: Yeah. (*She goes back and inserts the number 7. Then she writes* Tody *and* wet.)
Taralyn: What is the weather? It's my turn.
Ellen: Raise your hand for the weather.
Taralyn: Today the weather is sunny.
Ellen: (*Writing on the board, she asks Taralyn for help.*) What comes after *s-u-n?*
Taralyn: *n-y.*

These first graders are using play as a tool for cognitive development or how children make sense of their world. They do this by building on what they already know to interpret new experiences. In their play, Ellen, Taralyn, and Jasmine demonstrate the following four essential elements of cognitive development (Perkins, 1984):

1. *Problem solving.* When Jasmine uses the yardstick to measure herself sitting down and standing up, she figures out the concept of size.
2. *Mental planning.* As Ellen comes to the chalkboard area, tells Taralyn and Jasmine to get two chairs, sits down in front, and stands at the chalkboard to write, she clearly plans to play school. Mental planning also occurs when Ellen states she will be the teacher first.
3. *Self-monitoring.* We see Ellen checking her own spelling skills when she asks Taralyn for help spelling the rest of the word *sunny.*
4. *Evaluation.* When Taralyn is reading the calendar sentence and notices that Ellen forgot the 7, she demonstrates her understanding of writing the date.

Much of the research on play shows its relationship to the development of children's thinking and more sophisticated classification skills (Frost, Wortham, & Reifel, 2008; Perkins, 1984; Santrock, 2007) and the ability to use what they already know to construct new knowledge. In this case, these first graders are building on what they already know (the routines of school, specific teacher behaviors, and basic literacy concepts and skills) and extending it through playful interactions. They play with words and letters as they test the spelling of weather words and the way to record the day and date.

The cognitive skills children use in pretend play are essential for school success (Smilansky, 1968; Smilansky & Shefatya, 1990). All subjects and problems include cognitive skills children use to pretend, yet many subjects (such as social studies) are those with which children have limited experience. To illustrate, after a teacher shares books about the Chinese New Year, such as *Lion Dancer* (Waters & Slovenz-Low, 1990) or *China's Bravest Girl* (Chin, 1997), children's imaginations are stimulated. During play we might notice the children imagining a Chinese New Year celebration with its special dances to ward off evil spirits, colorful dragons and decorations, and special Chinese festival foods, because they are using their make-believe ability to play. In this way, real and pretend become complementary as children use make-believe to enhance their cognitive understanding (Berk, 2005; Johnson, Christie, and Yawkey, 1999; Smilansky & Shefatya, 1990).

Language Development

Evan and Anna are preparing a birthday celebration for their mother in the housekeeping area of their Head Start classroom. When they realize they need a present, Anna says, "Let's ask Mr. Bear." This is a reference to the book *Ask Mr. Bear* by

Marjorie Flack (1932), in which Danny tries to find the perfect birthday present for his mother by asking several different animals for suggestions. After locating the book in the library area, Evan and Anna become the goose, the goat, the cow, the hen, and the bear as they search for the perfect present. The book becomes the content for their play as they assume the roles of the animals, experiment with the intonations and inflections of the different animals, and use language to guide their own behavior and direct the behavior of others. Evan and Anna's play is contributing to their language growth and vice versa.

Proficiency in oral language is essential for all children's success in school (Han, Benavides, & Christie, 2001; Morrow, 2009). In the previous scenario, we see at least four ways that Anna and Evan's play of a birthday celebration helps them to practice important language skills:

1. *Communication.* In pretend play, children use role-appropriate statements and metacommunication, or language used to maintain the play episode; plan a story line; and assign roles. Pretending to be someone else allows children to use voice inflections and language in situations they may or may not have encountered. Play helps children internalize the many rule systems associated with the language they are speaking. It also helps them express their thinking in different ways (Santrock, 2007).

2. *Forms and functions.* During play, children learn to use language for different purposes in different settings and with different people. Michael Halliday (1975) calls this "learning how to mean," as children discover that what they say translates to what can be done. Talking in play settings provides opportunities for children to practice the necessary forms and functions of language (Halliday, 1975) and think about ways to communicate. Moreover, for English language learners, play offers opportunities to talk in safe, social settings in school (Han et al., 2001; Morrow, 2009).

3. *Purposeful conversation.* In play with others, children often use language to ask for materials, ask a question, seek out information and provide information to others, express ideas, explore language, and establish and maintain the play. For *younger children*, verbal give-and-take during sociodramatic play is important because children plan, manage, problem-solve, and maintain the play by verbal explanations, discussions, or commands (Smilansky & Shefatya, 1990). For *older children*, the ability to use reflective and analytical language is related to their level of linguistic awareness and achievements, which are essential to all forms of play.

4. *Play with language.* Children of all ages enjoy playing with language because, in doing so, they feel in control of it. Play is their arena for experimenting with and coming to understand words, syllables, sounds, and grammatical structure. Language play for *elementary school children* manifests itself in the jokes, riddles, jump rope rhymes, and games they use. Elementary school children are intrigued by the sound and meaning ambiguity of "knock-knock" jokes as well as by the humor of enacting scripts that include dialogue with multiple meanings and rhymes. These forms of language play require the transformational ability to explore the phonological, syntactic, and semantic rules of language (Bergen, 2002; Clawson, 2002; Isenberg & Quisenberry, 2002).

Literacy Development

A growing body of evidence shows how children's play contributes to their literacy development—the ability to read and write. By the time children come to school, they already possess a well-developed spoken language in their native language (Christie, Enz, & Vukelich, 2007). We know, too, that children learn to read and write in meaningful social settings that involve both social and cognitive abilities (Morrow, 2009). Elementary children become proficient readers if reading is an enjoyable way of learning and an important means of communication to them. Proficient readers demonstrate some of the same characteristics of good players; they are strategic, engaged, fluent, and independent.

Children at play can reveal the following literacy understandings:

1. *Knowledge of story elements and story comprehension.* Evan and Anna displayed knowledge of story elements (character, plot, setting, goal, and conflict) and exhibited story comprehension in their pretend dramatization of preparing for a birthday based on the story, *Ask Mr. Bear*. Children's first attempts at reading and writing often occur during dramatic play as they read environmental print, make shopping lists, or play school. Most beginning readers rely on their oral language to gain meaning from books as they internalize the structure and meaning of language. More proficient readers have a more complex and developed concept of the interrelatedness of story elements. Dramatic play develops improved story comprehension and an increased understanding of story elements (Christie et al., 2007).

2. *Understanding fantasy in books.* In dramatic play, children enter the play world "as if" they were another character or thing. The ability to transform oneself in play enables children to enter the world often created in books featuring talking animals (such as *Ask Mr. Bear* or *Charlotte's Web* [White, 1952]) or to write stories in which they create hypothetical characters. Elementary children's ability to play with reality is necessary to understand science fiction as well as other types of fantasy books (Christie et al., 2007; Fields, Groth, & Spangler, 2007).

3. *Use symbols to represent their world.* As children invent their own versions of stories, they make their world their own by representing their understandings symbolically. This symbolic behavior is the basis of the abstract thinking children

Children become proficient readers if reading is an enjoyable way of learning.

need to become literate. You can see evidence of *younger children's* use of symbols to represent what they know in their language, role enactment, or use of props (Fields et al., 2007; Owocki, 1999). Similarly, you can see evidence of *older children's* abstract understanding in literacy through their story retellings, writing, word-play, and the Internet to represent the literacy behaviors they know. Classroom teachers need to understand the many ways children's play, games, and inventions contribute to their language and literacy development. Figure 2.1 is a checklist for documenting children's literacy learning through play.

Social and Emotional Development

During play, children also increase their social competence, confidence, relation-ship building with both peers and adults, and emotional maturity. These life skills greatly influence children's school success, and later on, workplace success (Singer et al., 2006; Singer & Singer, 2005; Smilansky & Shefatya, 1990). Play supports chil-dren's social development through:

MyEducationLab

Go to MyEducationLab and select the topic "Guiding Children." Under Activities and Applications, watch the video Facilitating Peer Interaction *and answer the questions provided.*

- Practicing both verbal and nonverbal communication skills as they negotiate roles and responsibilities, try to gain access to ongoing play, and appreciate the feelings of others.
- Responding to their peers' feelings while waiting for their turn and sharing materials and experiences.
- Experimenting with roles of the people in their home, school, and community as they come into contact with the needs and wishes of others through cooperative learning and play.
- Experiencing others' points of view by working through conflicts about space, materials, rules, or responsibilities positively. You can observe a teacher helping a young child welcome another child into her play activity in the video "Facilitating Peer Interaction" online at MyEducationLab.

Play supports emotional development by providing a way for both preschool-ers and elementary children to *express and manage* both positive and negative feel-ings. Play helps children *express* feelings in the following ways (Piaget, 1962):

- *Simplifying events* by creating an imaginary character, plot, or setting to match their emotional state. A child afraid of the dark, for example, might eliminate darkness or night from the play episode.
- *Compensating for situations* by adding forbidden acts to pretend play. A child may, for example, eat cookies and ice cream for breakfast in play, whereas in reality this would not be permitted.
- *Controlling emotional expression* by repeatedly reenacting unpleasant or frightening experiences. Children who have experienced trauma from a natural disaster, such as a hurricane, bombing, or shooting may "play out" those experiences through games, invented stories, jokes, or pretend play.

In addition to expressing feelings, play helps children learn to *manage* their feelings as they act out being angry, sad, or worried in a situation they control (Erikson, 1963; Singer et al., 2006). A good example for a preschooler is Alexander, a 4-year-old whose dog was recently hit by a car. In his dramatic play in the pet hospital, his teacher heard him say to another child, "I'm sad because the car hurt my dog." Here he was trying to cope with unpleasant feelings from a frightening situation. Play enabled Alexander to express his feelings so that he could cope with

Child's Name: _____

Demonstrates "readinglike," literate behaviors

- ✓ Looks at books and print materials that reflect their interests
- ✓ Does pretend writing
- ✓ Shares reading/writing ideas with friends
- ✓ Uses sound spelling to write notes
- ✓ Practices reading familiar stories

Shows understanding of stories and narrative language

- ✓ Acts out pretend stories
- ✓ Tells a story through drawing, puppets, or other media
- ✓ Engages in dramatic retellings that include _____ characters, _____ setting, _____ conflict, _____ plot, and _____ solution
- ✓ Dramatic retellings use story structure (e.g., beginning, middle, and end)

Explores conventions of print

- ✓ Writes messages in dramatic play center
- ✓ Copies letters and words from other print materials
- ✓ Reads messages to others during dramatic play or story retellings

Investigates book knowledge and the language of books

- ✓ Turns pages left to right
- ✓ Distinguishes between pictures and print
- ✓ Makes up words and stories to match pictures
- ✓ Reads books with familiar patterns or repetitive language
- ✓ Names some print while reading

Experiments with a variety of forms of written language

✓ Announcements	✓ Library cards
✓ Calendars/ Invitations	✓ Notes/Recipes
✓ Money/cash registers	✓ Signs
✓ Coupons/Labels	✓ Tickets
	Other: _____

Statement of literacy behaviors demonstrated:

Ideas for furthering literacy development:

Suggestions for parents:

Figure 2.1   Documenting Children's Literacy Learning Through Play
Note: Data from Owocki (1999).

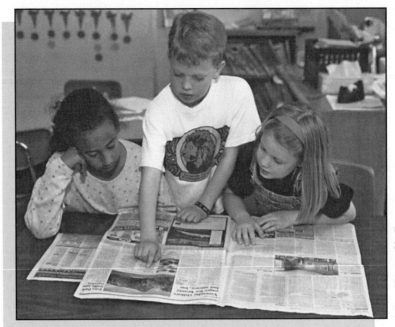

Anthony Magnacca/Merrill

During play, children increase their social competence, confidence, relationship building, and emotional maturity.

his worry about his dog (Landreth & Homeyer, 1998). Through games and inventions, elementary children learn valuable emotional skills, such as increasingly realistic self-perceptions, the ability to manage their emotions, and self-control that improves over time. As *elementary children* engage in spontaneous and structured play activities, they come to see themselves as good in some areas and less good in others. These opportunities to monitor and discriminate among feelings and emotions contribute to children's beliefs about their own capacity and are foundational to children's ability to meet the academic and social requirements in school.

Physical Development

Play contributes to children's fine and gross motor development and body awareness as they actively use their bodies. Learning to use a writing tool, such as a marker, is an example of fine motor development through play. Playing with writing tools helps children craft their fine motor skills as they move developmentally from scribbles to shapes and forms to representational pictures. Gross motor development, such as hopping and skipping, develops in a similar way. When children first learn to hop, they practice hopping on different feet or just for the pure joy of hopping. As *elementary* children, they integrate their hopping skill into many games, such as hopscotch and jump rope. Using their bodies during play also helps them to feel physically confident, secure, and self-assured (Isenberg & Quisenberry, 2002).

While all children need active play for healthy physical development, the physical benefits are particularly valuable for children with joint or muscular illnesses, such as juvenile rheumatoid arthritis and multiple sclerosis. These children cannot engage in repeated strenuous exercise; they can, however, engage in active play. Active play helps them build or maintain energy, joint flexibility, and muscular strength (Majure, 1995). It also helps their development of social skills and an increasing ability to endure stressful situations.

Creative Development

In Chapter 1, "Understanding Children's Creative Thought and Expression," we talked about the important role of creative thought and expression in children's development and learning. Nearly 50 years ago, Sigmund Freud (1958) suggested that every child at play "behaves like a creative writer, in that he creates a world of his own, or, rather, rearranges the things of his world in a new way which pleases him. . . . The creative writer does the same as the child at play. He creates a world of phantasy which he takes very seriously—that is, which he invests with large amounts of emotion" (pp. 143–144).

Play is an ideal context for supporting children's creative development because it offers a risk-free environment. Research shows that play and creative thought are related behaviors as they both rely on children's ability to use symbols (Johnson, Christie, et al., 1999; Singer et al., 2006; Singer & Singer, 1998; Spodek & Saracho, 1998). The ability to make-believe, invent activities and materials, and play games is evidence of children's developing ability to create internal imagery, be curious, and experiment with alternative responses to different situations. This capacity, practiced in various types of play, enhances children's ability to be successful in new situations.

Creative thought can also be viewed as an aspect of problem solving, which has its roots in play. When children use their imaginations in play, they are more creative, perform better at school tasks, and develop a problem-solving approach to learning (Dansky, 1980; Dansky & Silverman, 1973; Fromberg & Bergen, 2006; Frost et al., 2008; Pepler & Ross, 1981; Singer, 1973; Sutton-Smith, 1986).

The importance of play in children's lives is well documented. As children grow and change, play develops with them in a developmental sequence.

 ## HOW DOES PLAY DEVELOP?

Meet Jessie, a fourth grader. If you could go back in time and catch glimpses of her play behavior, this is what you would see:

> As a 10-month-old, Jessie plays pat-a-cake with Grandma Marji. At age 2, Jessie pours sand back and forth into different-sized plastic containers. When Jessie is 4, she pretends to make pizzas and take delivery orders over the telephone with her friends, Lara and Michelle. At age 6, Jessie and two friends pretend to eat space food in a spaceship they have constructed. At age 8, Jessie plays a card game, I Doubt It, and is becoming quite adept at rummy. And now, at age 10, Jessie invents a memory game that matches ten inventors' names with their inventions.

As Jessie's experiences illustrate, play matures over time, becomes more complex and organized, and parallels and strengthens children's development (Scarlett, Nadeau, Salonius-Pasternak, & Ponte, 2005). Play at all ages has been studied from two major perspectives, cognitive and social. Think about the following questions as you read the next section: What types of play do children demonstrate at different ages? Do these types of play reappear at later ages? How does play reflect children's cognitive and social development?

Development of Cognitive Play

Cognitive play reflects children's age, conceptual understandings, and experiential background. The ideas of Piaget (1962), Smilansky (1968), and Smilansky and Shefatya (1990) describe the following cognitive types of play: functional play, symbolic play, constructive play, and games with rules. While each type of play peaks at a particular age, they all continue in some form throughout life, have unique characteristics, and contribute to children's understanding of themselves, others, and their world. Table 2.2 provides an overview of the four types of cognitive play, their characteristics, and age-appropriate examples.

Functional Play

Functional play (birth to age 2) is characterized by simple, pleasurable, repeated movements with objects, people, and language to learn new skills or to gain mastery of a physical or mental skill. It is also referred to as sensorimotor, practice, or exercise play (Piaget, 1962; Smilansky & Shefatya, 1990). Functional play dominates the first 2 years of development, about one-third of the play of preschoolers, and less than one-sixth of the play of elementary school children (Rubin, Fein, & Vandenberg, 1983), and continues in some form through adulthood. To observe pre-schoolers engaged in functional play as they are painting, view the video "Parallel Play: Children Painting Outdoors" online at MyEducationLab.

<u>**MyEducationLab**</u>

Go to MyEducationLab and select the topic "Play." Under Activities and Applications, watch the video Parallel Play: Children Painting Outdoors *and answer the questions provided.*

TABLE 2.2   Types, Characteristics, and Examples of Cognitive Play

Types	Characteristics	Examples
Functional play	Repetition of movements when new skills are being learned, with or without objects.	*Infants and toddlers:* grasping and pulling a mobile *Preschoolers and kindergartners:* repeating a pattern on a pegboard *School-aged children:* practicing throwing, catching, or doing acrobatics
Symbolic play	Imagination and role play used to transform the self and objects and to satisfy needs.	*Infants and toddlers:* pretending to drink from a baby bottle
	Early symbolic play: mental representation that transforms one object for another.	*Preschoolers and kindergartners:* transforming a block into a broken car and pretending to fix it
	Later symbolic play: mental representation that transforms self and objects.	*School-aged children:* using secret codes or made-up languages to communicate
Constructive play	Manipulation of objects or materials that children regulate to make something. Combines functional play repetitive activity with symbolic representation of ideas.	*Preschoolers and kindergartners:* constructing a hospital room for a sick animal *School-aged children:* creating an exhibit for a project or designing virtual games and figures with electronic icons
Games with rules	Activities with predetermined rules that are goal-oriented and often competitive with one or more individual.	*Infants and toddlers:* playing pat-a-cake with an adult *Preschoolers and kindergartners:* playing simple singing and circle games *School-aged children:* playing tag, marbles, hopscotch, or relay races

Note: Data from Piaget (1962) and Smilansky & Shefatya (1990).

Brian Smith, Photographer

Using their bodies during play helps children feel competent and confident.

Through functional or practice play, children develop coordinated motor skills and begin to feel confident and competent with their bodies, as in the following examples:

The 1-year-old who stacks and unstacks rings on a pole

The 4-year-old who incessantly repeats "I'm the king of the castle"

The 5-year-old who intentionally places pegs in a pattern on a pegboard

The 7-year-old who practices bicycling skills on a two-wheeler at every available minute

The 9-year-old who does variations on jump rope movements

Symbolic Play

Symbolic play (ages 2 to 7), also called pretend, dramatic, sociodramatic, fantasy, or make-believe play, emerges in the second year and continues in different forms throughout adulthood. It arises when children can transform their world into symbols and usually contains three elements: props, plot, and roles. Symbolic play reflects children's growing mental ability to make objects, actions, gestures, or words stand for something or someone else (Piaget, 1962; Van Hoorn, Monighan-Nourot, Scales, & Alward, 2007). Symbolic play focuses on social roles and interactions (Smilansky & Shefatya, 1990) and reveals children's ability to play with ideas or symbols. In symbolic play, children make mental and verbal plans of action, assume roles, and transform objects or actions to express their feelings and ideas (Van Hoorn et al., 2007). Let's look at children's symbolic play at different ages.

Infants and toddlers imitate actions associated with a particular prop in symbolic play, learn to substitute one thing for another, and act as if they were someone else who is familiar to them. For example, as a young toddler, Naomi picks up her toy cup and pretends to drink from it. As an older toddler, she may offer her doll a drink from the cup. Her symbolic play shifts from pretense about herself to pretense about others.

Preschool and kindergarten children's symbolic play is more complex. They pretend alone or with others, use nonrealistic objects, assume roles, and use objects as symbols in addition to what they stand for (Van Hoorn et al., 2007). Three-year-old Miriam uses her hand as a pretend hairbrush for the baby's hair. Five-year-olds Jimbo and Celeste become firefighters as they collaborate to rescue people from a burning building. These transformations are essential for symbolic play. Symbolic play peaks during the preschool years, the golden age of make-believe, but reappears later as daydreaming, hypothetical thinking, or private fantasies from the middle grades through adulthood.

School-age children's symbolic play differs from the play of children at other ages because now their thinking is less public. They can integrate their symbols into age-appropriate, socially acceptable mental games and language play such as riddles, number games, secret codes, and daydreaming (Elias & Berk, 2002; Johnson et al., 1999). It is not uncommon to find 7-year-olds delighting in the use of secret code, a form of symbolic and language play, or to find 9-year-olds daydreaming. For school-age students, engaging in simulations and games provides an opportunity to participate in situations that they cannot actually experience, thus increasing their interest and intrinsic motivation. The elements of fantasy and pretense make what otherwise would be a boring activity more meaningful (Pintrich & Schunk, 2002). Research shows that symbolic play increases children's memory (Newman, 1990), enriches language and expands vocabulary (Christie, 2001; Holmes & Geiger, 2002), enhances children's ability to reason with contradictory facts (Fromberg & Bergen, 2006), and fosters flexible and inventive thinking (Pepler & Ross, 1981).

Sociodramatic Play

When symbolic play involves two or more children who communicate verbally about the play episode, it is called **sociodramatic play**. Because it is person-

These girls are transforming their world into symbols by using props, creating a story, and assuming new roles as they reenact a "beauty shop."

oriented rather than object-oriented, sociodramatic play is considered a higher level of symbolic play. Here children exchange information and ideas during a jointly elaborated play sequence or theme; they can also simultaneously be actors, interactors, and observers (Smilansky & Shefatya, 1990). Repeated opportunities to engage in this type of play offer children a rich arena for refining concepts, solving problems, feeling in control by making things happen, enhancing peer relationships, and learning self-regulation (Berk, Mann, & Ogan, 2006; Elias & Berk, 2002). Sociodramatic play correlates highly with children's intellectual and social abilities (Smilansky & Shefatya, 1990). Table 2.3 (p. 52) describes Smilansky's six criteria for determining dramatic and sociodramatic play. Note that the last two characteristics (interaction and verbal communication) define symbolic play as sociodramatic. A discussion of the Smilansky scale for assessing sociodramatic play elements can be found in Chapter 9, "Assessing the Creative Process and Products of Children".

Constructive Play

In **constructive play**, children create something or engage in problem-solving behavior according to their own preconceived plan. Constructive play often combines functional and symbolic play and predominates during the preschool years (Forman, 1998). The following example from a kindergarten and first-grade classroom illustrates constructive play.

Emily, Porsche, and Elizabeth chose to play in the block center. They had just visited the Washington, D.C., memorials and decided to build the Jefferson Memorial. To do this, they had to decide which blocks would be appropriate for the entrances, where to place them, how to make the river, and who would be the statue. After they built their structure, which resembled the real Jefferson Memorial, they engaged in symbolic play. In this play episode, the girls combined constructive play (building a memorial) with symbolic play (visiting the memorial) by representing their ideas with the materials (blocks) and elaborating on them in symbolic play (playing house inside the memorial). In constructive play, the child focuses on a lasting end product (Forman, 1998).

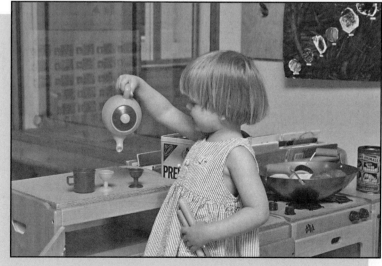

In sociodramatic play, children imitate familiar roles and develop social skills.

TABLE 2.3   Smilansky's Characteristics of Dramatic and Sociodramatic Play

Play Behavior	Characteristics	Examples	Levels
Imitative role play	Child assumes a make-believe role of a person or object and expresses it in imitation and/or verbalization	"Let's pretend that I am the baby."	Beginning: Role relates to the familiar world, (e.g., mommy, daddy, baby) Advanced: Role relates to world outside the family (e.g., doctor, teacher, police)
Make-believe with regard to objects	Child uses movements, verbal statements, or materials or toys that are *not* replicas of the object itself or real objects	Uses Lincoln Logs to make a house for the baby and uses chimneys from Lincoln Logs to make beds for the dogs.	Beginning: Real objects or replicas used (e.g., real toy car) Advanced: Uses prop as part of play scenario (e.g., stirs soup with a block)
Verbal make-believe with regard to actions and situations	Child substitutes verbal descriptions or declarations for actions and situations	Uses Lincoln Logs to outline a square for the house and says "This is a house for the baby."	Beginning: Imitates simple actions of adult (e.g., holds vacuum and moves back and forth) Advanced: Child's actions are integral to the play episode (e.g., "I'm vacuuming this floor so the baby can crawl around and not hurt herself")
Persistence in role play	Child stays within a role or play theme for at least 10 minutes	Plays role of baby, mother, and daughter within a family play theme for 10 minutes.	Beginning: Short, sporadic involvement (e.g., child enters area, picks up the baby, and leaves) Advanced: Child stays involved in area and the theme for more than 10 minutes
Interaction	At least two players interact within the context of a play episode		Beginning: Plays alone with no obvious awareness of others nearby Advanced: Cooperative effort to work together around a common theme
Verbal communication	There is some verbal interaction related to the play episode		Beginning: Simple dialogue around the use of toys (e.g., "Give me the bottle") Advanced: Dialogue about the roles, props, plot of the play scenario

Note: Data from Smilansky (1968) and Dodge, Colker, & Heroman (2002).

School-age children engage in some constructive play in the classroom because it is easily accommodated in work-oriented settings (Bergen, 2002; Christie, 2001; Forman, 1998). Typical constructive play might include creating a play around a social studies topic (such as occupations), writing a story, creating an interactive exhibit, using invented spelling, building virtual systems on a computer screen, or making a mobile out of recycled materials. In order for the play to qualify as constructive, however, children must maintain a playful attitude (for instance, keeping the focus on "What if I do this?" rather than "Why won't it do that?"), must become absorbed in the process, and must find it pleasurable. In that way, the child keeps the goal in mind, but it does not dominate the play.

Games with Rules

Games with rules rely on prearranged rules that guide acceptable play behavior of *reciprocity and turn-taking*. Board games (such as Clue), card games (such as rummy), and outdoor games (such as kickball) are the most prominent form of games with rules among elementary school children. Their more logical ways of thinking and advanced social skills make it possible for older elementary school children to follow a set of rules and negotiate with peers. Games with rules (see Chapter 8, "Using Creative Materials and Resources Effectively," for detailed discussion) enhance children's physical coordination, refine their social and language skills, build conceptual understandings, and increase children's understanding of cooperation and competition (DeVries, 1998; Johnson et al., 1999; Torbert, 2005).

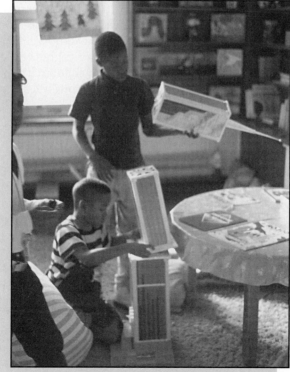

Scott Cunningham/Merrill

In constructive play, children become absorbed in the process of creating a lasting end product.

In the following example of the card game *Addition War*, think about the rules fourth graders Tom and Chang use and how they reason their way through problems. The boys are sitting side by side so they can see each other's addition facts and lay their cards down like a vertical math problem.

Tom: I have 18. How many do you have?
Chang: I have 17.

(Tom picks up all four cards and places them face down at the bottom of his stack. They each put down two more cards.)

Tom: I win.
Chang: I have 9 and 8. You know what that is? That equals 17 so I win this time.
Tom: We haven't had a war yet.
Chang: I have 18; what do you have?
Tom: I have 11 and 8.
Chang: 11 and 8 is 19.
Tom: How much is an ace worth?
Chang: 11. Oooh, you win! *(They lay down more cards.)* A jack and king equal 20. I have 20. Let me see. You have 16 and I have 20. I win. *(When the game ends, Chang quickly counts his cards)*. I have 39 cards and that means I win because it's more than half the deck.

In this card game, Tom and Chang use their knowledge of addition facts to play a rule-based game. They demonstrate understanding of prearranged rules (acknowledging the winner of each round and assigning a numerical value to the ace), conceptual understanding (the winner holding 39 cards has more than half the deck), and turn-taking (knowing who goes next after each pair is placed on the table).

In sum, children use all types of cognitive play at different ages and for a variety of purposes. The unique nature of each type of cognitive play reflects what children know and are able to do. Because much of children's play occurs with or around others, the next section describes how play contributes to children's social competence.

Development of Social Play

Social play, the ability of children to interact with their peers, matures over time in a similar way as cognitive play. This kind of play often develops rapidly during the preschool years and continues to be refined over the years. The now-classic ideas of Mildred Parten (1932) have focused attention on the social aspects of play during early childhood. Parten identified six types of play, beginning with the least socially mature (solitary play) and moving toward the most socially mature (cooperative play). Today, most researchers consider Parten's "levels" as descriptive of styles of play rather than social maturity because as children grow older, they cycle back and forth between the types of social play (Van Hoorn et al., 2007). Table 2.4 describes the characteristics of Parten's six levels of social play.

Knowing how play develops will help you to provide appropriate learning opportunities for children. It also offers a way for you to enjoy and encourage age-appropriate play. Play is children's natural resource for developing social and cognitive skills that affect their present and future social competence. To appreci-

TABLE 2.4   Levels of Social Play

Type of Play	Characteristics of the Child
Unoccupied behavior	Is not engaged in play and does not seem to have a goal. Plays with body, gets on and off chairs, walks about aimlessly.
Onlooker behavior	Observes, asks questions, and talks to other children but does not enter play itself. Stands within speaking distance to see and hear. More active interest and involvement than unoccupied behavior.
Solitary play	Plays independently and is not involved with other children. Playing with own toys is the primary goal. Most typical of 2- and 3-year-old children. Older children use solitary play for needed privacy and for elaborate individual dramatic play.
Parallel play	Plays alongside or nearby, but not with, others. Uses shared toys but plays independently. Does not share toys. Typical of young preschool children. Often considered the beginnings of group play.
Associative play	Plays with others in a similar, loosely organized activity. Conversation involves asking questions, using one another's toys. Some attempts made to control who may join the group. Is often the transition from parallel to cooperative play.
Cooperative play	Uses common goals involving negotiation, division of labor, and differential role taking, such as taking turns and organization of play themes. Organizes group for the purpose of making a product, dramatizing a situation, or playing a game with a strong sense of belonging to the group.

Note: Data from Parten (1932).

ate the essential role of play in children's lives, it is important to understand the different theories of why children play and how these theories influence teachers' views of play.

 ## WHY DO CHILDREN PLAY?

For more than 150 years, none of the theories of play that have been proposed adequately explain why children play. Some suggest that children play because they feel physically safe during play (the house is not really burning, so they can escape); others suggest that children play because they feel emotionally safe (playing out events after a natural disaster provides a way for children to confront the realities of their environment). Still others suggest that play helps children take in new information and make it their own, such as creating a new flying machine as part of a unit on space or using invented spelling to write a message. Collectively, however, these theories represent a belief in the power of play in children's development, which has greatly influenced teachers' thinking about its importance. These theories can be categorized as **classical theories** (those that were prominent in the nineteenth century through World War I) and **modern theories** (those that were prominent after World War I) (Frost et al., 2008; Johnson et al., 1999; Scarlett & New, 2007).

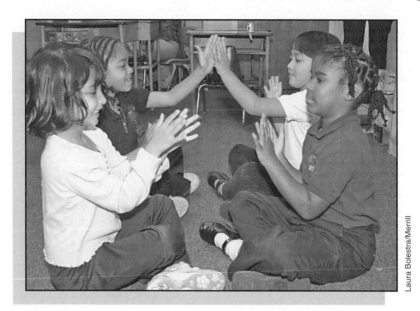

Play is children's natural resource for developing social and cognitive skills.

Classical Theories

Classical theorists sought to explain the causes and purposes of play through theories of surplus energy, recreation/relaxation, practice, and recapitulation (Ellis, 1973). We can see evidence of these theories in how today's teachers view children's behaviors in the classroom.

Surplus-energy theory suggests that human beings have a certain amount of energy to be used for survival. Energy not used for survival is spent on play and becomes surplus energy. When children have limited opportunities to move around, they seem to have bursts of energy that relieve stress and tension so they can settle down again. Teachers' views about "getting rid of excess energy on the playground" support this theoretical perspective.

Recreation/relaxation theory, in contrast to surplus-energy theory, suggests that play replenishes energy used in work. The influence of this theory is evident in early childhood classrooms where children alternate between quiet and active activities and in elementary classrooms where children have daily opportunities for recess to provide balance in their daily lives.

Practice theory, also known as instinct theory, proposes that play prepares children for the future roles and responsibilities needed to survive in their culture. When *young children* pretend to be a mother, father, or teacher and invent ways to use available materials to represent adult tools and then create play episodes, they are practicing the behaviors and characteristics of significant adults in their lives. When *elementary children* play board games, they practice such essential life skills as strategic thinking, reasoning, and self-regulation.

Recapitulation theory also focuses on instincts. In contrast to practice theory, it posits that play allows children to revisit developmental stages observed in their ancestors and shed any negative behaviors. Play is seen as developing in stages and is a vehicle for learning to live in today's world. Popular games of chase and pursuit can be categorized within recapitulation theory for all ages.

Modern Theories

Modern theories of play emphasize the consequences of play for the child (Frost et al., 2008; Scarlett & New, 2007). Three major modern theoretical orientations are psychoanalytic, supporting emotional development; cognitive-developmental, supporting mental development; and sociocultural, focusing on social development.

Psychoanalytic theory views play as an important vehicle for emotional release (Freud, 1958) and for developing self-esteem as children gain mastery of their thoughts, bodies, objects, and social behaviors (Erikson, 1963). Play helps children enact feelings, without pressure, by actively reliving experiences and mastering them in reality. Moreover, it provides adults with clues to children's individual needs. After the birth of a new baby, it is not uncommon to hear a preschool brother or sister at play saying to a doll, "I'm taking you back to the hospital." Expressing resentment through play enables children to gain control of it in real situations.

Cognitive-developmental theory examines play as a mirror of children's developing mental abilities (Bruner, 1966; Piaget, 1962; Sutton-Smith, 1986). Piaget proposes that children individually create their own knowledge about the world through their interactions with people and materials. They practice using known information while consolidating new information and skills, test new ideas against their experiences, and construct new knowledge about people, objects, and situations.

Bruner (1966) and Sutton-Smith (1986) interpret play as flexible thinking and creative problem solving in action. Because children focus on the process of play, they engage in multiple combinations of ideas and solutions that they use to solve relevant life problems. For Bruner, play allows children to discover ideas for themselves and to view children as "knowers" even before we explicitly teach them.

Sociocultural theory emphasizes the centrality of the social and cultural contexts in development (Vygotsky, 1967, 1978). Vygotsky (1978) believes that play is a "leading factor in development" (p. 101) and that "in play a child behaves beyond his average, above his daily behavior; in play it is as though he were a head taller than himself" (p. 102). Because children first encounter knowledge in their social world that later becomes the origin of their conceptual understandings, play acts as a mental support so that children can think through and solve problems in new ways. This "zone of proximal development" (Vygotsky, 1978) gives children the freedom to bend reality and do things in play that they are often unable to do on their own outside the play setting. For example, Ms. Rodriques's fourth graders have a weekly time for playing games they have constructed. In pairs or small groups, the children create variations of common board games such as bingo or Clue that often contain the content they are studying, such as questions about the properties of liquids, constants and variables, and vocabulary words such as *volume, weight,* and *graduated cylinder.* Notice that Ms. Rodriques provides the context for her fourth graders to understand these properties first in a social setting (pairs or small groups) and then as individuals in constructing their knowledge.

Each of these theorists supports the essential role of play for children's optimal development. They illustrate the many ways play can support children's learning in meaningful and authentic ways. Table 2.5 (p. 58) lists the major theories, theorists, and purposes of play. Collectively, these theories provide teachers with a framework for promoting the development of play and play skills of all children in

TABLE 2.5   Theoretical Perspectives of Children's Play

Theories	Theorists	Purpose of Play
Classical		
Surplus-energy	Schiller and Spencer	Expend excess energy to survive
Recreation/relaxation	Lazarus	Restore energy used in work
Practice/instinct	Groos	Practice future survival skills
Recapitulation	Hall	Reenact ancient activities
Modern		
Psychoanalytic	Freud	Master unpleasant experiences
	Erikson	Master physical and social skills to build self-esteem; express wishes and needs
Cognitive	Piaget	Practice and consolidate known information and skills through different types of play:

		Functional play (repeated motions)
		   Symbolic play (make-believe)
		   Games with rules (predetermined rules)

	Bruner and Sutton-Smith	Promote flexibility and creative problem-solving through symbolic transformations
Sociocultural	Vygotsky	Foster abstract thinking and self-regulation through symbolic play. Contribute to potential development (performance with a more capable peer or an adult or the zone of proximal development).
		Enable child to grapple with unrealizable desires.
Other	Bateson	Operate on two levels at the same time. On one level, children are engrossed in pretending; on another level, they are aware of their true identities.

the classroom. A crucial role for teachers is making curriculum adaptations for diverse learners so that all children can participate.

 # CURRICULUM ACCOMMODATIONS FOR DIVERSE LEARNERS IN PLAY

As classrooms become more inclusive, teachers need to know how to adapt their curriculum to include all children in meaningful play-based experiences. Research shows that play supports the developmental needs of children with language, motor, cognitive, or social disabilities (Deiner, 2005; Johnson, Christie, & Wardle, 2005; Mindes, 1998). Because there are no "right" or "wrong" ways to play, children's needs can easily be accommodated through play (Casey, 2005).

Tips for Play in an Inclusive Classroom

- Provide opportunities for children to invent their own games both indoors and outdoors.

- Observe children at play to identify their strengths and needs. Then provide play experiences that support those strengths.
- Model and teach children specific skills needed to play with peers who have disabilities, such as touching a child with vision loss, or pairing children so that one models the activity or game for the other.
- Suggest "easy-out" options, such as scorekeeper, banker, or batboy, so that children can leave a game and reenter easily.
- Provide simple props to make roles clear, such as having the child who is "it" in tag wear a hat or give teams colored vests to wear.
- Modify materials to facilitate play such as using pictures to show game rules and sequence, creating a bingo card with fewer spaces, and giving a young child fewer rings to stack on a tube.

Specific Suggestions for Diverse Learners
Children with Developmental or Language Delays
Children with mild disabilities often follow the same stages of play as their nondisabled peers, but their social interaction skills are often delayed. This often leads to more solitary, less cooperative play (Guralnick & Hammond, 1984, 1999; Hestenes & Carroll, 2000). Consider the following accommodations for these children:

- Use "scripted play" through a prepared script that guides play in particular situations. For example, you may create and practice a script to help children understand and use the language needed to enter a play situation (Neeley, Neeley, Justen, & Tipton-Sumner, 2001).
- Break down directions and uses for games and toys into language that the child can understand.

Children with Visual Impairments
Children with total vision loss or limited sight often do not pick up unfamiliar toys causing them to engage in repetitious and predictable play with familiar objects (Johnson et al., 2005). You might try the following:

- Encourage children to feel play objects to familiarize themselves with the functions of materials and toys. If you make changes to play areas, be sure to have children explore these changes through touch and by walking the new areas.
- Teach other children how to physically guide their friend into play situations. Use verbal or physical cues to direct children to the location of equipment, friends, and toys during outdoor play.

Children with Autism Spectrum Disorder (ASD)
Children with ASD have difficulty with social skills and often lack the mental representations and language needed for pretend and spontaneous play (Guralnik & Hammond, 1999; National Institute of Mental Health, 2008). Consider these strategies:

- Teach children the skills needed to play through modeling and intervention, such as turn-taking, asking for an object, or sharing.
- Respect children's preference for a particular area of the room, need for personal space, and ability to tolerate others in an activity (Peter, 2003).

- Explain what is happening in the play setting, such as adding a new toy to the play area, introducing another child, or engaging in fantasy play.
- Keep experiences familiar to the child; gradually extend their comfort level with others, objects, and types of play.
- Create clear physical boundaries when outdoors and specify how to use each toy and piece of equipment.

Play is a natural part of all children's daily lives. You can include all children in play by assuming a variety of roles that support the play of all children.

TEACHERS' ROLES AND RESPONSIBILITIES

Teachers have an essential role in supporting children's play so that it becomes more elaborate and complex (Reifel, 2001; Singer, 2006; Smilansky & Shefatya, 1990; Vygotsky, 1978). You will need a good blend of strategies that facilitate, not control, the way children play and think about their play. Teachers often ask why, how, if, or when they should intervene in children's play. How you think about these questions determines whether you use play to enrich or disrupt learning.

Why Should Teachers Support Children's Play?

Guidance in answering this question comes naturally from the theories of Lev Vygotsky (1978), who suggested that play scaffolds children's advancement to higher ability levels in all domains. Scaffolding is particularly important as we examine the range of teachers' roles in play settings. Often a child cannot accomplish a particular task independently but can accomplish the same task with the assistance of an adult or a more capable peer. This "zone of proximal development" is the optimum time for teachers to assist children in their learning.

When Should Teachers Support Children's Play?

There will be times when you will want to scaffold children's play. Yet under no conditions should you dominate the direction of children's play, nor should you participate in play when children clearly do not want you there. Usually, teachers support play in the following situations:

1. When play is absent from children's behavior, such as aimless wandering and inability to engage with another child, material, or activity.
2. When a child finds a task far too difficult, like being unable to make a bridge out of blocks or construct a math game.
3. When a child needs assistance to get something done, such as playing a board game or creating an invention.
4. When a child knows very little about a role, object, or situation, like reenacting a scene from a literature selection.
5. When children ask you to participate; for example, you may assume the role of ticket taker at an imaginary airport or ask questions (Singer, 2006).

As you read each of the different roles teachers assume, think about when and how to use each role to support children's play.

What Are Teachers' Roles in Children's Play?

The following six roles describe the kinds of support teachers can provide.

Teachers as Observers

Teachers must be good observers of play so that they can determine whether children need help with a problem; whether toys or materials are adequately stimulating; and whether play is contributing to children's developing social, motor, and cognitive skills. Skilled observers note which child plays what role, which child chooses particular themes, how children enter and exit a play setting, which children seem to "get stuck" in a play theme and can't move forward with it, who needs one-to-one interaction, and which children are developing the ability to participate in group activity. Skilled observers also note when not to intervene, such as when children are already playing cooperatively or when they do not seem interested in adult participation. Careful observation and interpretation are the bedrock of all the other roles teachers assume in facilitating children's play (Jones & Cooper, 2006; Singer, 2006). For an extended discussion of informal observation measures to study play, see Chapter 9.

Teachers as Collaborators

Sometimes children continuously repeat actions and cannot move forward with a role, theme, or idea. Teachers can extend their play by adding a new toy or prop or by asking a question that elaborates on but does not change the theme. One *kindergarten teacher* had a fast-food restaurant in her theme corner. After a week of play, she added a "Drive Thru" sign and a cardboard window that the children used to add a new dimension to their play. She also suggested adding the role of "cashier." In doing so, she extended the children's thinking and imagination without undermining their original intentions (Fromberg & Bergen, 2006). A *fourth grade teacher* provided opportunities for children to collaborate with others to compose stories out of a set of random words that had been a part of their social studies unit and then watch as other children in the class added to the story. Occasionally, children enacted the final story. This teacher understood the importance of her role as a collaborator in children's exploratory play with words.

Teachers as Planners

Teachers must plan for play. Selma Wassermann (2000) describes a K–2 multi-age classroom that shows a teacher's careful attention to planning for play. She writes about "breathing out," the first 45 minutes of the day when children transition from home to a school environment that absorbs their interest and prepares them for a day of learning. This environment includes plenty of space and materials for learning stations including construction materials, dramatic play, and art; investigative centers that operate later in the day where children explore explicit content; and a choosing board where children select how they will spend their time at centers. As children become absorbed in their play activities, teachers work individually with children on particular skills. Orchestrating this kind of play activity requires considerable planning.

Teachers as Responders

When teachers describe children's actions and words or ask questions about the role or theme, they provide feedback on what the children are doing and saying.

For *younger children*, making statements such as "I see you have bought a large bag of groceries" or "I noticed the tower is as tall as you are" gives children an opportunity to elaborate on that behavior if they choose. Asking questions, making suggestions, and helping children connect with others are all ways in which teachers respond to children's play (Jones & Cooper, 2006; Smilansky & Shefatya, 1990). These strategies, however, address the role of the child and not the child. In this way, you validate that playing is a valued activity. For *elementary children*, providing feedback to their playful learning requires that you have in mind the major concepts and skills that children can demonstrate. Your questions and responses support children's examination of a particular idea. Further, your responses, through either paraphrasing, further questioning, or making statements about what you see, contribute to children's ability to further explore an idea (Wassermann, 2000).

Teachers as Models

Sometimes teachers actively *model* a particular behavior or role relevant to the on-going play theme. In this way, you teach individuals or groups of children a needed play skill or behavior. Consider the following example. In Ms. Blum's inclusive preschool class, two 4-year-old girls are playing in the home-living areas. Ms. Blum notices that one child rocks with a doll while the other repeatedly opens and closes the oven door. She enters the play, sits at the table, and announces: "It is time for lunch." She asks, "What smells so good in the oven?" and later asks, "Could I help set the table?" Ms. Blum's modeling of family roles and behaviors encourages children to practice some of those skills, which children will then be able to transfer to other settings on their own.

Teachers as Mediators

MyEducationLab

Go to MyEducationLab and select the topic "Guiding Children." Under Activities and Applications, watch the video Managing Challenging Behavior: Dealing with Conflict and answer the questions provided.

As a **mediator**, you help children construct meaning from play by serving as a bridge between children's initial understanding of a concept or event and their deeper understanding as a result of experiencing that concept or event. For example, teachers of *young children* frequently encounter children's conflicts and disputes about toys, space, roles to play, or rules. As a mediator, you will want to use strategies that help children develop peaceful resolutions. These can include being aware of children's intentions; helping children use words to express their needs and feelings; making play spaces accessible and providing enough materials to share; and giving children enough time to negotiate their own solutions to problems (Wheeler, 2004). Teachers of *elementary children* often encounter conflicts over rules of the game, participation, and friends. In the role of mediator, you will want to help children develop strategies for solving conflicts so that they can participate in group activities. Finding the right balance as a bridge between ideas is a powerful role for the teacher as mediator. You can see how one preschool teacher mediates a dispute over materials between two children with special needs in the video "Managing Challenging Behavior: Dealing with Conflict" online at MyEducationLab.

You will be using each of these six roles throughout your school day. These roles are especially important, however, as you integrate play, games, and inventions across the curriculum. Table 2.6 provides a variety of ways to integrate the curriculum by using games.

TABLE 2.6   *Integrating the Curriculum: Using Games*

What is a game?

A game is a form of play in which children follow an agreed-upon set of rules, predetermine an outcome, assign players specific roles, and assign sanctions for violations (DeVries, 1998; Hughes, 1999; Kamii & DeVries, 1980). While very young children often change rules in the middle of a game, rules do exist. Most children's games involve physical skill, chance, strategy, or some combination of these elements to determine the outcome. Games of strategy, such as checkers or Boggle, require decision-making skills and compel players to take turns, follow complex directions, and employ complicated strategies.

Why use games?

Games provide children with opportunities to learn and practice many skills across different learning domains. They support children's cognitive skills, such as decision-making, turn-taking, and problem-solving abilities; language skills, social skills, and self-regulation skills, such as exercising control over their emotions, thinking, and actions and physical skills (Click & Parker, 2009; DeVries, 1998; Hirsh-Pasek & Golonkoff, 2003; Rule, 2007).

Games suitable for *preschool and kindergarten children* have one or two simple rules, include all children who want to participate, encourage children to figure things out for themselves, and do not stress being first, winning, or losing. Young children like noncompetitive guessing games such as "I'm thinking of something in the room that is . . . ," simple sorting and matching games, simple board games (if they can change the rules), and basic running and chasing games.

Children in *first through fourth grades* enjoy strategy games that develop problem-solving and decision-making abilities. Board games and active outdoor group games are typical of this age for both boys and girls. With an emphasis on involvement, mutual enjoyment, and respect, group games can promote basic intellectual and social skills in children through fourth grade (Bergen & Coscia, 2000; Jensen, 2000; Santrock, 2007). Children need many opportunities to practice regulating themselves (Bodrova & Leong, 2007; Diamond, Barnett, Thomas, & Munro, 2007) and practice and refine critical cognitive and life skills (Frost, Wortham, & Reifel, 2008; Isenberg & Quisenberry, 2002; Rule, 2007; Tolbert, 2005; Wassermann, 2000).

Why games are suitable for children with special needs

Researchers (Bodrova & Leong, 2007 and Diamond et al., 2007) suggest that games have potential benefits for children with special needs. They argue that games help them practice self-regulation—the ability to control emotions and behavior and practice self-discipline. Children with reduced self-regulation skills may be showing up in the increased numbers of children diagnosed with ADHD.

Children with special needs can be encouraged to engage in all kinds of appropriate games in the classroom. Many games simply require that adults determine what kinds of adaptations need to be made so individual children can participate (Frost et al., 2008).

	COMMUNICATION Literacy, Language Arts, and Technology	THE SCIENCES Mathematics/Science	SOCIAL STUDIES Social Studies/ Health and Safety
Preschool/Kindergarten *Circle Time Games*	"Nursery Rhyme Changes" Have children change words in familiar nursery rhymes and other chants that rhyme with the correct word, such as Jack and Jill went up the (child supplies rhyming word for "hill").	"I'm Thinking of . . ." Have a child think of an object and give a clue to that object. Provide one clue at a time until someone guesses the object another was thinking of.	"Cooperation Games" that have no winners or losers such as "Call Ball" during which a child in the center tosses a ball to a child and calls his or her name and the game continues or "Basket Ball" in which children stand before a plastic basket and toss the ball with a focus on hitting the basket and not keeping score.

(Continued)

TABLE 2.6 Integrating the Curriculum: Using Games—continued

	COMMUNICATION Literacy, Language Arts, and Technology	THE SCIENCES Mathematics/Science	SOCIAL STUDIES Social Studies/ Health and Safety
First/Second Grade *Guessing Games*	"Character Riddles" Have individual or small groups of children write and share riddles of a book character using three clues.	"Feely Bags or Closed Boxes" Fill bags or boxes with natural science or other objects, such as stones, sticks, bones, shells. Pass the box around for children to feel, shake, and listen to what is inside.	Create "word searches" that contain different kinds of social studies vocabulary to test children's creativity and knowledge.
Third/Fourth Grade *Games with Rules*	"Playing with Words" Have children construct their own crossword puzzles for others to complete.	"Invent a Board Game" that uses the content and concept of a current social studies unit, such as the environment, economics, or geography. Play the game with other small groups in the class.	Adapt familiar games such as "Twenty Questions" or "Jeopardy" for social studies, famous people, places, and things. Goal for "Twenty Questions" is to guess the person, place, or thing in 20 or less questions; goal for "Jeopardy" is to ask the question to the answer that is given.

MEETING STANDARDS THROUGH PLAY

Incorporating Play in Inquiry-Based Units on "Change"

Standards are statements that guide what children should know and be able to do in a given content area at a given time. They are used to *assess student learning* and *promote accountability.* While there are no specific standards in the area of play, play-based learning provides an important way for you to teach to standards in each curriculum area, use an inquiry approach to learning, and gain important knowledge about children's thinking. Play experiences also meet national teacher education standards.

The four forms of cognitive play discussed in this chapter—functional play, symbolic play, constructive play, and games with rules—provide a framework for an inquiry-based approach to learning. They give children many opportunities to explore and clarify ideas, describe, internalize, and synthesize information as they come to understand their world. For example:

In *functional play*, children explore objects with all of their senses, which involve experimenting and tinkering with materials.

In *symbolic play*, children transform their world into symbols, which involves brainstorming, role-playing, and teamwork.

In *constructive play,* children create something or engage in problem-solving behavior according to a preconceived plan, which involves problem solving and "thinking out of the box."

In *games with rules,* children rely on prearranged rules that guide acceptable play behavior of reciprocity and turn-taking, which involves strategic thinking and teamwork.

Youngquist and Pataray-Ching (2004) suggest that play-based experiences be viewed as acts of inquiry, a term that requires creative, reflective, and investigative thinking. When viewed as a form of inquiry, play-based learning experiences become a powerful vehicle for children to express what they know. The thinking abilities humans develop through play are mental characteristics critical to successful school-based learning—curiosity, persistence, imagination, and inventiveness. Many teachers find that the concepts students have to learn in the content areas lend themselves naturally to play-based learning.

What follows are examples of how teachers incorporate play-based experiences across grade levels and content areas in different inquiry-based units on the broad concept of change. First is a list of key content-area standards for students. Next is a brief description of an appropriate unit followed by examples of play-based, age-appropriate experiences. Each example identifies the types of play used and the content-area standard it addresses. Following the content-area student standards are the teacher education standards that can be met.

Content-Area Standards Related to the Concept of Change

Social Studies Standard: Time, Continuity, and Change: Students should study the ways human beings view themselves in and over time.

Mathematics: Patterns, Functions, and Algebra: Students should be able to analyze change in various contexts.

Science Standard: Science as Inquiry: Students develop abilities necessary to do scientific inquiry and understandings about scientific inquiry.

Language Arts Standard: Students should use language appropriately in daily use as well as use new vocabulary to describe feelings, thoughts, experiences, and observations.

Teacher Education Standards

National Association for the Education of Young Children (NAEYC): Standard 4b Teaching and Learning: Teachers use effective approaches to positively influence child development and learning.

INTASC Standard 2: Student Development: Teachers understand how children learn and develop and can provide learning opportunities that support children's intellectual, social, and personal development.

Examples for Preschool/Kindergarten

As part of a unit on change, preschool and kindergartners are studying about themselves and their personal pasts. Their earliest understandings of history begin with learning about themselves and their own changing characteristics. They are learning about the changes in the way they look, what they eat, what they play with, what they wear, what they can do, and what they know.

Appropriate Play-Based Learning Experiences

Functional Play

- Explore with senses different tastes of baby food compared with real food. Graph with pictures favorite tastes of baby food and food they like now. (Math)

Symbolic Play

- Role-play familiar roles such as baby, toddler, and adult. Include diapers, baby clothes, dolls, infant and toddler toys, sippy cups, booster seats, and a variety of adult clothing. Children can enact what they use today, compare with what they used when they were babies, and what they might use when they are grown up. (Language Arts/Social Studies)

Constructive Play

- Construct a picture-rebus timeline of children's lives. Use photos and drawings to chronicle children's lives and changing abilities from birth to present, such as changes in height, number of teeth, amount of hair, how many letters they know, or how much they weigh. Be sure to use drawings for every child to be sensitive to children who do not have access to photos of their childhood. (Math/Social Studies)

Games with Rules

- Play "Guess Who I Am?" or a Name Chant. (Language Arts/Social Studies)

Now, add to these examples using one or more of the content-area standards.

Examples for First Grade–Second Grade

As part of their unit on change, first and second graders often study the water cycle, which involves learning about evaporation, condensation, precipitation, and collection. They learn that water moves in a continuous cycle between the air, the ground, and plants and animals. Children are naturally motivated to use the following kinds of play-based inquiry experiences to find out how the water cycle works.

Appropriate Play-Based Learning Experiences

Functional Play

- Explore the changes that water causes in the soil. Using soil, pebbles, and containers, children can explore soil changes when adding different amounts of water and what happens to water when they make a channel. Explore also samples of muddy water to observe the sediment when it settles. Describe patterns. (Math/Science)

Constructive Play

- Collaborate with others to build a model of the water cycle using clear plastic containers, sand, pebbles, a small amount of water, and leaves. (Science/Math/Language Arts)

Games with Rules
- Create a game that includes "water facts." (Science/Language Arts)
- Create a word search using different water cycle terms, such as *water, fresh, gallons, safe, clean.*
- Make a puppet and some rain sticks and tell the story of *It Rained on the Desert Today* (Buchanan, 1994) or *Peter Spier's Rain* (Spier, 1997). What happens to the dry desert or your backyard when it rains? (Science/Language Arts)

Symbolic Play
- Role-play different parts of the water cycle. (Science)

Now, add to these examples using one or more of the content-area standards.

Examples for Third Grade–Fourth Grade

As part of their historical study of the colonial period, third and fourth graders study about the founding and expansion of the 13 original colonies. Through research and interpretation of daily life in the colonial period, the children learn about such things as the types of homes, transportation, activities, games, recipes, clothing, and tools that were used in colonial days. They also learn about people and places.

Appropriate Play-Based Learning Experiences
Constructive Play
- Construct a three-dimensional or salt dough map that illustrates different features of colonial times and colonial communities. (Social Studies/Math/Language Arts)
- Visualize a timeline starting with colonial games and toys and compare them to the kinds of toys and games we use today. Select, organize, and sequence information about the toy's functional role in the historical era. Brainstorm reasons why and how some of these toys were used. (Math)
- Construct scale models of a colonial ship of choice. (Math)

Games with Rules
- Construct a game on the chronology of toys using various sources of information such as pictures, charts, inventors, and photographs to show an understanding of the past. (Social Studies/Language Arts)
- Create colonial word problems using metrics. (Math/Language Arts)

Symbolic Play
- Write a skit to communicate to younger children the different toys, clothing, and foods used long ago and why they were appropriate. Enact that skit for children of different ages. (Language Arts/Social Studies)
- Role-play the different occupations such as blacksmith, cooper, miller, cobbler, silversmith, tinsmith, and town crier that were common in colonial days. (Language Arts/Social Studies)

Frequently Asked Questions About Play, Games, and Inventions

Why is recess so important for elementary school children?

Recess is the time for children to "take a break" from the focused academic activities of the classroom and engage in active, unstructured activity. Whether it occurs indoors or outdoors, recess is an educational activity that has many benefits. First, recess provides children with opportunities to interact with peers on their own terms without the structure of the rest of the school day. Second, it allows children to maximize their ability to pay attention to academic tasks after a recess break; and third, it provides another opportunity for children to refine their social competencies of sharing, cooperation, and problem solving through the play and games traditionally seen at recess (Frost et al., 2008; O'Brien, 2003; Pellegrini & Holmes, 2006).

Today, recess in schools is in jeopardy. As a result, the National Association of Early Childhood Specialists in State Departments of Education (NAECSSDE) and the National Association for Sport and Physical Education (NASPE) have recommended that elementary children get at least 1 hour of exercise each day, preferably in 15-minute blocks without the structure of a physical education class. Recess should be a time when children choose their activity and playmates with supervision from teachers.

I want to teach older children. Why do I need to know about play when most principals and parents oppose the use of play in elementary schools?

While some consider play trivial and simple, and even a waste of time, play is not wasted time but rather time spent building new knowledge from previous experience (Fromberg, 2002; McCune & Zanes, 2001; Piaget, 1962). Information about typical age-related play behaviors provides a useful framework for understanding the different forms and functions of children's play. Play is a major way children take ownership of new information by playing with it. Learning requires an interactive balance of gaining skills and knowledge and making them one's own. Active play fosters personal meaning. When children perceive learning as relevant, it becomes part of their long-term memory; when children perceive learning as irrelevant, such as a continuous series of memorizing isolated facts and meaningless concepts, it typically will not become part of long-term memory.

How does play support children from diverse backgrounds?

With greater frequency, today's classrooms include children whose native language is not English and children who have different cultural and ethnic backgrounds. Children's play provides information about who they are and enables them to better understand others. Teachers can help realize play's potential for children from different cultures, races, and ethnic backgrounds in a variety of ways (Banks, 2001; Jalongo, 1991; Tiedt & Tiedt, 2000). First, teachers must recognize and respect ethnic and cultural differences by asking themselves some difficult questions to discover their basic attitude toward others, such as the following: *Am I aware of my own biases toward different populations? Do I recognize that different child-rearing practices affect a child's play?* Second, teachers can help children explore their cultural backgrounds through appropriate play-based experiences. A curriculum sensitive to diversity helps children appreciate their personal histories. As a teacher, you need to know enough about children and their families to make informed curriculum decisions, such as learning the background and culture of the children, finding out how long families have been in this country, what toys and materials children use at home, and what experiences have the children had outside the home (such as eating in a certain kind of restaurant or observing cars being repaired at a gas station). This information is critical to providing relevant and familiar play experiences. Third, teachers need to be particularly sensitive to gender and racial issues as children enact familiar roles. Play is a powerful vehicle for understanding gender and racial issues. How teachers communicate messages about what girls, boys, and people of color can do affects how children view themselves and their competencies. In preparing children for today's and tomorrow's world, be sure to use culturally diverse materials and experiences, such as puppets, dolls, puzzles, music, art, and books in the room; that they provide enough novelty and challenge for all; and that all children are free to enact different roles.

CHAPTER SUMMARY

1. Play has been studied from different perspectives, yet experts still have no consensus about its definition or primary purpose. Yet, there are accepted identifiable characteristics.
2. Both classical and modern theories have influenced how play is viewed in the early childhood curriculum. These theories are essential to understanding why children play and must be used as a basis of curriculum planning.
3. Play contributes to all areas of children's development. It is the primary vehicle through which their cognitive, language, literacy, social/emotional, and creative development occurs.
4. Teachers have at least six roles in supporting children's play—observer, collaborator, planner, responder, role model, and mediator. Each of these roles must be fulfilled to support children's learning and development through play.
5. Teachers must make curriculum accommodations so that all children can benefit from the power of play, games, and inventions. Each can be utilized to enhance the diversity of their classrooms, to challenge children's imagination, and to integrate children with special needs.

 ## *Discuss: Perspectives on Play, Games, and Inventions*

1. This chapter has described the difficulty surrounding the study of play and games. Explain to your colleagues how assumptions about play and the play/work distinction have contributed to this confusion. Describe how you used to think about play and games before reading this chapter and the questions you now have after reading this chapter. How can you begin to find answers to these questions?
2. Your role as a classroom teacher is crucial in supporting play. Review the six roles of the teacher discussed in this chapter. Of what significance is it to assume these different roles? Cite some examples from your personal or field experience that illustrate these roles. Were these the most useful roles to assume? Why or why not?
3. Reread the "Teachers' Reflections on Play, Games, and Inventions" early in this chapter. In what ways are these teachers' reflections similar in their thinking about play? What differences did you notice? Talk about which of these teachers' reflections made an impression on how you think about play after reading this chapter. Of what importance are teacher reflections?
4. With the increasing emphasis on test scores and high standards, can you envision the play context as fundamental to learning? How do you think play can help children develop the knowledge and skills they need to be successful in school and in the workplace of the future? What do you believe about the importance of play? Tell why.

Chapter 3

Fostering Creative Thought and Expression

The mind of the five-year-old represents, in one sense, the height of creative powers. Accordingly, the challenge to the educator is to keep alive the mind and the sensibility of the young child.

Howard Gardner, 2007, p. 84

CLASSROOM PERSPECTIVES ON FOSTERING CREATIVE THOUGHT AND EXPRESSION

Preschool–Kindergarten

It is center time in Ms. Manning's kindergarten classroom. David and Ahmad are making puppets so that they can dramatize their original stories about farm animals. When their puppets are finished, they begin tugging on each other and wrestling with their puppets. The boys become increasingly boisterous, so Ms. Manning comes over.

Ms. Manning: Pardon me, David and Ahmad. Please talk with me over here. *(she goes to a quiet corner, kneels down, and talks to them at their eye level)* What was in your story that made you wrestle with each other so roughly? *(she listens intently to their responses)*

Ahmad: Playing pigs and robbers. The robbers were getting my pigs and we needed to catch them to get our pigs back. *(David nods in agreement)*

Ms. Manning: David, tell me in your own words about what you were doing.

David: Playing pigs and robbers. But I was done with the game and didn't want to be the robber anymore, and Ahmad kept wrestling with me and my puppet.

Ms. Manning: You were done playing with your puppets for your story. When you are play wrestling you need to tell each other when you stop playing. *(David nods)* David, did you tell Ahmad when you wanted to stop? *(shakes head no)* Look at my eyes, David. How will Ahmad know that you want to stop the game if you don't tell him? Next time you could say in your own words, "Ahmad, I don't want to play this game anymore." *(David looks down and shakes his head)* When you leave the game, tell the person you're playing with so they know. Let's go back to finishing your puppet stories about the farm animals. *(all three get up and leave)*

First Grade–Second Grade

In Mr. Connor's second grade, the children are studying underwater mammals. During their language arts and music block, the children read the book *I'm a Manatee* (Lithgow, 2003) in which a little boy dreams of becoming a manatee, sing the accompanying music, and write about their dreams of becoming a real or fictional underwater mammal. Knowing that children who have just read about a manatee might want to write about one, Mr. Connor primes the children's thinking by leading them in a guided-imagery trip under the sea, encouraging divergent thinking to inspire their writing. He sets the mood using recorded sounds of the ocean and invites the children to close their eyes and picture the world around them. He asks, "What does your mammal look like? What do you see? Hear? Smell? Touch? Taste?" Through guided imagery, the children visualize and imagine almost simultaneously how they would live as an underwater mammal (Annarella, 1999).

Third Grade–Fourth Grade

As part of Mrs. Barr's social studies unit, she uses the book *Shiloh* (Naylor, 1991), in which 11-year-old Marty cares for a mistreated beagle pup as his own. When Marty discovers that the pup belongs to a neighbor, he faces many difficult questions. Should he return the dog to its owner? Should he tell his parents? Should he steal food to help the abused pup? Through small-group and whole-class discussions, Mrs. Barr invites children to respond to Marty's dilemmas and relate them to their own everyday experiences at home and school. In a culminating activity, the children reenact scenes from the book that show how Marty's behavior affects the relationships of the people he cares for the most.

In each of these scenarios, the teachers use different strategies to foster children's creative thought and expression. Ms. Manning uses *modeling and discussion* to seek solutions to problems ("You know, next time you could say in your own words, 'Ahmad, I don't want to play this game anymore.'") Mr. Connor uses *guided imagery* to spark creative thinking, and Mrs. Barr uses *story reenactment* to illustrate moral and ethical dilemmas. The teachers' underlying beliefs that children can guide their own behavior and become fully functioning individuals (Rogers, 1961) are an important part of fostering children's creative growth.

Fostering children's creative thought and expression can be accomplished by the strategies teachers choose to use. How you create environments and use materials directly and indirectly affects how children think and act. As teachers, we are responsible for offering children many opportunities to engage in creative endeavors that serve as an important bridge to learning (Eisner, 2003; Gordon & Browne, 2007; Hearron & Hildebrand, 2005; Marion, 2007). This chapter explores ways teachers can promote children's creative thought and expression.

THEORETICAL AND RESEARCH BASE: FOSTERING CREATIVE THOUGHT

Teachers use three major developmental theories to foster children's creative thought: constructivism, humanism, and behaviorism/social-learning theory. Each theory provides a way to understand how and why children think, act, and learn as they do as well as ways to guide their own and children's creative thinking and behavior.

Constructivism

Constructivists, like Piaget (1952) and Vygotsky (1978), view children as active agents in their own development. They study the mental process of creativity (how children think about their world, other people, and how to behave) and focus on how children come to understand their world and solve problems they face (Papalia, Olds, & Feldman, 2007). Constructivists assume that

- Creative growth refers to concept building and problem solving, which depend on a child's level of cognitive development.
- Children are doers—they actively construct or build understandings of their world.
- Children think differently from adults and gradually come to understand the viewpoints of others.

For constructivists, fostering creative thought and behavior would include the following adult-child interactions:

- Adapting to children's different ways of working together and solving problems.
- Providing many opportunities to communicate thoughts and feelings.
- Supporting children's investigations and experimentation with tasks and materials.
- Providing a respectful, comfortable, and accepting environment that has clear, consistent, and fair limits for all children.
- Understanding that children's emotions provide motivation for learning.
- Facilitating development of self-control and self-directed behavior (Bredekamp & Copple, 1997; Edwards, 2006; Hyson, 2008; Santrock, 2007).

Using constructivist theory to guide children's creative thinking is most effective when the adults working with children understand their social and intellectual development, encourage children's interaction with others to increase their perspective-taking and social interaction skills, and probe children's thinking about ideas.

Humanism

Humanists such as Carl Rogers and Abraham Maslow believe that people are capable of controlling their lives if their basic needs are met. They do this positively through choice, creativity, and self-realization (Papalia et al., 2007). Thus, how children feel about themselves strongly influences their ability to be cooperative, curious, and creative learners. From a humanistic perspective, human beings strive to become fully functioning individuals. Such an individual possesses four characteristics:

- Positive self-regard.
- Awareness of personal feelings and those of others.
- Acceptance of responsibility for decisions.
- Ability to solve problems (Rogers, 1961).

Children who interact with supportive, accepting adults learn to view themselves as competent and worthwhile. In contrast, children who are deprived of supportive, accepting adults do not develop such feelings and often seek approval in inappropriate ways. Teachers who draw on humanistic traditions foster children's creative growth by helping them to think about and investigate problems, by encouraging them to express a range of feelings, and by accepting a range of solutions to problems. They also value qualities such as spontaneity, freshness of appreciation, and a sense of humor.

Supportive, accepting, resourceful teachers facilitate children's investigative capacity. They help children talk about feelings, especially during conflicts, and guide them toward self-regulation (Charney, 2002; Edwards, 2006).

Behaviorism and Social-Learning Theory

Behaviorists view the environment as the single most important variable in shaping behavior and focus on observable, measurable behaviors. From this perspective, children react to the forces in their environment. Consequently, behaviorist theory does not address feelings or emotional states. Behaviorists assume that

- All behavior is learned. Learned behavior is shaped by external influences and causes development by rewarding observable behaviors.
- All children gradually learn how to respond to environmental influences.
- Adults in the environment are the major catalysts in changing or shaping children's behavior (Papalia et al., 2007).

The behavioral perspective has provided the foundation for the extensive use of behavior modification programs currently used in educational settings. The danger, of course, is that overreliance on these intrusive methods may make children more dependent on adults to resolve problems and less independent in defining problems and seeking solutions to them. For example, using time-out repeatedly to allow children to regain control often does not achieve the desired behavior. Rather, children perceive it as an opportunity to gain additional attention.

Social-learning theorists view social interaction as the major influence on learning and development. Rather than relying on reinforcement to influence children's behavior, social-learning theorists hold that children learn socially appropriate behavior by observing and imitating *models* in their world (Papalia et al., 2007). In this way, children learn by example—a powerful teaching and parenting tool because children typically imitate role models in their world.

An Eclectic Approach

MyEducationLab

Go to MyEducationLab and select the topic "Curriculum." Under Activities and Applications, watch the video Conducting an Investigation: Small Group "Taste Test" Activity.

Most teachers use several theoretical perspectives for techniques that foster creative thought and expression, including Howard Gardner's view of multiple intelligences (see Chapter 10, "Children's Creative Work in Diverse Families and Communities"). In other words, our philosophy of creative growth tends to be *eclectic*. An eclectic approach applies a variety of theories that fit our beliefs and help us make the best educational decisions for children's creative thought and behavior. We need an eclectic approach because no one theory is ever comprehensive enough to foster children's creativity (Marion, 2007).

To understand how an eclectic philosophy operates, recall the three opening scenarios. Ms. Manning adopts a constructivist and behavioral/social-learning approach to guide David's understanding of appropriate behavior; Mr. Connor helps the children construct their own understanding of their underwater world through the use of guided imagery; and Mrs. Barr adopts a constructivist and humanistic approach by facilitating children's investigations in solving dilemmas. You can observe a teacher helping children to construct knowledge of different types of apples using their senses in the video "Conducting an Investigation: Small Group 'Taste Test' Activity" online at MyEducationLab.

A growing research base supports the importance of nurturing children's creative expression. Teachers often underestimate the influence of their own upbringing and value system on guiding the creative expression of others. To a considerable extent, our orientations derive from our experiences. We need to be aware of how and why we are selecting particular strategies that promote creative expression.

As teachers, we must understand that each child brings a rich history of experiences, cultural backgrounds, and personality traits to the classroom. Consequently, we need to be as flexible as possible in guiding their creative thought and expression. Like an artist who selects particular paints, colors, and paper to convey an idea or image, teachers must select the most appropriate strategies to foster each child's creativity. The more you understand the different perspectives and your own beliefs and values about creativity, the more able you will be to respond appropriately to children's creative ideas and behaviors. Table 3.1 presents three theoretical perspectives that affect creative thought and expression and provides examples of each. Consider which ones reflect your current views.

TABLE 3.1   Theoretical Perspectives on Creative Thought

Theory	Outcome	Teacher Role	Strategies
Behaviorism and social learning	Increase desired behavior.	Direct the process.	• **Provide a cue:** Remind child before expected behavior (e.g., "Johnny, see if you can find your mailbox for your painting.") • **Ignore the behavior:** Do not acknowledge minor behavioral infractions (e.g., ignore child in circle who dominates others' conversations). • **Model appropriate behavior:** Demonstrate how to ask for a toy or to gain entry into an ongoing play situation.
Humanism	Develop a strong self-concept, which is the child's image of himself or herself.	Guide children's ability to control and direct their own behavior.	• **Own the problem:** If the problem is an adult's, say, "I have a problem, and I need your help." If the problem is the child's, say, "It seems as though there is a problem here; do you need my help?" • **Listen actively:** Listen to the message the child is conveying. Do not interrupt the child or make a judgment. • **Use I-messages:** Name the behavior causing the problem and your feelings, such as "I feel angry when I see you grab the block from Johnny."

(Continued)

TABLE 3.1   Theoretical Perspectives on Creative Thought (*Continued*)

Constructivism	Gain understanding and control of their world through development of problem-solving abilities and conceptual understanding.	Facilitate and guide children's investigations with materials and with one another.	• **Provide opportunities to learn:** Use circle or meeting times for children to tell their versions of the problem to solve, talk about appropriate behaviors, and suggest alternative solutions.
			• **Set clear and appropriate limits:** Focus the child's attention and set predictable limits.
			• **Redirect behavior:** Provide new options, introduce a new material or idea, or limit choices, if necessary.
			• **Take social conflicts seriously:** Be at eye level while listening to children; empathize with all children involved in the conflict.

Note: Data from Marion (2007), and Papalia, Olds, & Feldman (2007).

TEACHERS' REFLECTIONS ON FOSTERING CREATIVE THOUGHT

Preservice Teachers

"I am beginning to understand that I need to help children develop their creative thinking, which is something that never occurred to me. I now own a poster of Albert Einstein with his quote, 'Creativity is more important than knowledge,' which I plan to hang in my own classroom as one way to remind me."

"In my student teaching, I used different strategies to encourage the children's creative thinking. In my culminating unit activity, the first graders in my classroom worked in cooperative groups to produce creative works of art, music, and drama to show what they learned about different shelters."

Inservice Teachers

"As a preschool teacher, I look for ways to help families foster their children's creative thought and expression. I have started to use home-school journals with my preschool parents as a place to share examples of divergent thinking, problem solving, and imagination. Parents are responding with such positive statements as 'I am looking at my child in a whole new way.'"

"After our school completed a museum-in-progress project, one teacher told our principal that she wasn't sure she'd ever be able to go back to 'textbook only' teaching. Her comment not only indicates that the children showed her that they really learn by doing research for projects but also shows that the teacher is becoming more comfortable with children learning through projects."

Your Reflections

- What are some ways to support children's creative thought and problem-solving ability?

- How do you think a creative teacher would manage his or her classroom?

- What new awareness about creative thought and expression comes to mind for you after reading these teachers' reflections?

 ## YOUR ROLE IN FOSTERING CREATIVE THOUGHT

Consider the different responses of these second graders to their teachers' challenge of using a blank piece of corrugated cardboard to make something. Each teacher gave the children an 8½-by-11-inch piece of corrugated cardboard and asked them to think of a way to use it, create what was in their mind, and then share how they made it. Becky quickly saw the possibility of folding the cardboard, making it into a bird feeder, and decorating it with birds, flowers, and seeds. Sam stared at the blank cardboard with tears welling up in his eyes. When his teacher asked him what the problem was, he said, "I can't do this. I don't know what you want me to make." He could not think of any way to use the cardboard. Andrea hastily folded her piece of cardboard into a "crayon box," but after a few unsuccessful attempts to figure out how to get it to stay closed, she left the project unfinished on the table.

Clearly, children respond to creative tasks in different ways. A teacher who tells Sam, "You're just not trying hard enough; put on your thinking cap," may be providing choices and freedom, but without support. A sensitive teacher realizes that Andrea needs encouragement and recognition of her efforts to persist at a task. She might encourage Andrea with a statement such as, "I like your idea of a crayon box. I wonder if this stapler would help you close those edges." On the other hand, teachers who are not accepting make it difficult for children to develop a creative, problem-solving approach to ideas and tasks. You can see an example of how one creative teacher helps children investigate the properties of painting using a hands-on approach in the "Creative Arts" video online at MyEducationLab.

Your role as a teacher is one of support, acceptance, and promotion of desirable behavior through prevention, redirection, and collaboration. Creative teachers promote children's expression through their active engagement in real, firsthand learning experiences, such as enactments, projects and thematic units, field trips, and use of community resources. They also use developmentally appropriate strategies to foster children's creative expression. Figure 3.1 lists suggestions for your different roles in teaching children to think creatively.

In the next section, we look at adults' interactions with children. Those interactions exert a major influence on the way they express their creative thinking.

Go to MyEducationLab and select the topic "Visual Arts." Under Activities and Applications, watch the video Creative Arts.

 ## STYLES OF ADULT-CHILD INTERACTIONS

There are three basic styles of adult-child interactions—autocratic, permissive, and democratic (Baumrind, 1967, 1993; Papalia et al., 2007). Each refers to how demanding or responsive teachers are with children; each also cultivates typical behaviors and mind-sets to creative thought and expression.

Figure 3.1
Guidelines for
Fostering Creative
Thought and
Expression

*Note: Based on
Bredekamp & Copple
(1997), Hearron &
Hildebrand (2009), and
Marion (2007).*

All children need adults' respect and acceptance to nurture their creative thought and expression. Teachers can use these guidelines to promote children's creative thought when and where appropriate:

1. *Provide children with opportunities for choices and decisions.*

    Example: As a group, young children have less experience in making choices, so they need to begin with two or three alternatives so that they are not overwhelmed by the possibilities. The range of choices can be increased as children gain in self-confidence and experience with decision making.

2. *Model care and respect for all people in your setting.*

    Example: In constructions, children often share ideas in deciding what structure to build and support one another in finding the appropriate places and materials to build it.

3. *Prepare interesting and challenging activities that promote prosocial behavior and independent thought.*

    Example: Children can find out information for a science project, take responsibility for care of part of the room, or choose a topic of study that helps children consciously manage their unpredictable world with new solutions and reflects the conscious beliefs of the teachers and caregivers.

4. *Use positive guidance techniques,* such as setting clear limits for younger children and helping older children set their own limits, modeling appropriate behavior, and redirecting inappropriate behavior.

    Example: Enlist children in creating and monitoring classroom rules. Introduce and model the "You can't say you can't play" rule (Paley, 1992) so that children know how to ask to join an ongoing play situation and to help children learn positive ways of communicating with one another.

5. *Help children verbalize their feelings and emotions.*

    Example: When a very shy child tries to enter ongoing doctor play and is "not allowed in," she sits alone in a corner looking sad and dejected. Teachers can help shy children by saying "I know you feel sad about not playing with the others. Let's see if they could use a pharmacist to get the sick baby's medicine."

6. *Be a creative teacher.*

    Example: To guide children's creative growth, you first need to determine what beliefs and values you bring to your classroom. It is the positive, confident teacher who understands and accepts himself or herself who can bring out the best in children.

Autocratic Interactions

Autocratic adults demand that children respond to an inflexible set of rules and standards. The autocratic teacher does the following:

*   Maintains stern and formal interactions with children.
*   Devalues adult-child verbal interactions in which there are disagreements.
*   Emphasizes a "no-nonsense" classroom environment.
*   Discourages individuality or autonomy in children.

When teachers are autocratic, children do not learn self-control or risk-taking; rather, they become dependent on the adults in their lives to control their behavior. Autocratic methods tend to develop children who have difficulty with peer relations, lack initiative, and tend to be anxious, withdrawn, and apprehensive.

Creative teachers promote children's expression through their active engagement in real, firsthand learning experiences.

Permissive Interactions

Permissive adults have an "anything goes" orientation. They place few demands and controls on children's decision making and problem solving in a poorly organized environment with unclear and inconsistent standards for behavior. The permissive teacher does the following:

- Projects a laissez-faire, uninterested attitude.
- Presents an inconsistent, unpredictable environment.
- Fails to set clear, firm limits on behavior.

The methods of permissive teachers tend to develop children with little self-control, self-reliance, or exploratory or investigative behavior. Because the standards for behavior are so inconsistent and the environment is so unpredictable, children cannot anticipate that their rights will be protected, or even clearly determine what their rights are.

Democratic Interactions

Democratic adults believe that children need firm but reasonable limits for behavior as well as opportunities for choice, verbal negotiation, and decision making. The democratic teacher does the following:

- Exhibits confidence in his or her ability to guide children's thinking and expression.
- Understands child development, limits, and potentials.
- Listens to children and respects their ideas and opinions.

- Has high expectations for all children.
- Responds to children's initiatives and suggestions.
- Prepares the environment with choices.
- Expects students to be responsible for the consequences of their decisions.

You can see an example of how a democratic preschool teacher responds to children's input and interest by watching the video "Emergency Curriculum Built on Children's Interests: A Hospital Project in Preschool" online at MyEducationLab.

Children who live and work with democratic teachers appear to feel secure, know what is expected of them, and be self-sufficient, self-controlled, and self-assertive. They also tend to be "self-starters" who can initiate and complete projects independent of adults. Democratic teachers do more than cover material—they develop children's thinking and problem-solving skills by engaging them actively in learning and empowering children to accept responsibility for their own learning and actions. Democratic teachers embody the principles held by teachers in Reggio Emilia—that teachers facilitate children's creative interpretations of their worlds and that children are competent decision makers about what they want to learn. The Reggio Emila principles are discussed in depth in Chapter 4 "Promoting Children's Art," and Chapter 7 "Designing Environments That Support Creativity and the Arts".

Teachers can look to guidelines from Reggio Emilia schools (Edwards, Gandini, & Forman, 1998), the National Association for the Education of Young Children (Bredekamp & Copple, 1997), and the Northeast Foundation for Children (Charney, 2002) to foster children's creative growth. These guidelines provide a framework for encouraging children to unlock their creative potential, to investigate their worlds in many ways, and to promote their ability to communicate in multiple forms (revisit Figure 3.1 for these guidelines).

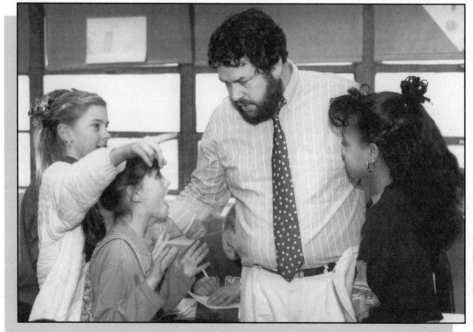

Democratic teachers really listen to and respect children.

🦋 ENCOURAGING CREATIVE THOUGHT IN THE CLASSROOM

To be successful adults in the work world of tomorrow, today's children need to develop a different kind of mind—a mind that has qualities of "inventiveness, empathy, joyfulness, and meaning" (Pink, 2006, p. 3). These qualities are equally important to each child's psychological, physical, and social success as well. Think about how you can encourage creative thought in your own classroom as you read the following descriptions of children's interactions in the classroom.

Three-year-old Hans uses a wheelchair, but he wants to participate in a movement activity. Justine suggests that he can be the engine when the group sings "Little Red Caboose." Five-year-old Sandy is trying to make her picture "look snowy" after the first snowfall. Ralph remembers that they used a mixture of soap flakes, water, and silver glitter in his Sunday school class. He asks the teacher if he and Sandy can try the recipe at after-school care. Eight-year-old Monica helps Jeffrey rig a pulley system to send messages across the room. Later, Jeffrey sends a note to Monica: It reads: "Thank you to Monica. Your friend, Jeff."

These children are demonstrating prosocial behavior—spontaneously sharing with or helping another. Prosocial behavior develops in children who live and work in supportive environments where adults model cooperative, helping behaviors. It is characteristic of children who have a high level of self-esteem, self-control, and emotional understanding. Teachers can foster prosocial behavior in the classroom community.

Fostering Prosocial Behavior

When children see adult models of prosocial behavior and feel accepted in a group, they not only develop cooperative, helping, and responsible behaviors themselves but also learn to respect themselves through their accomplishments (Charney, 2002; Marion, 2007; Papalia et al., 2007). In creative learning environments there is mutual respect among teachers and children.

Picture the following scenario in Ms. Payne's 4-year-old class. After a few days of playing in the camping center, Ms. Payne introduced the idea of fishing. She added a pup tent, a blue paper lake, and a small grill filled with crumpled black and orange paper inside to represent a glowing charcoal fire. She developed the fishing theme by including fishing licenses, some magnetic fishing poles, a bucket, and some paper fish shapes with paper clips attached to the ends. She stimulated the children's interest in the idea by relating that she noticed people fishing nearby, so that the pond was probably well stocked with fish. In the following play text, try to identify examples of *prosocial behavior* in the 4-year-olds (such as cooperative, helping, sharing, and respectful behaviors). What role did the teacher have in fostering such behavior? Look at the photos on page 82 to better understand the children's interactions.

(Katie, Steven, Melanie, and Harold fish excitedly at the pond)

Katie: *(at the pond)* Got the fish. One, two, three . . .
Steven: I need a fish. That one. *(points to the big one)* I caught a fish for myself. Look how big!
Harold: Here's a fish.
Katie: Pick it up. *(says to Harold)* Put it over here. *(points to the bowl)* I caught it for you.

Joan Isenberg

Steven: *(cutting the fish and eating)* That was good. I need more.
Katie: Hey, all the fish are gone. *(everyone has caught all of the fish)*
Steven: We have to put some back.
Harold: We have to catch them all over again. *(they put some of the fish back; Katie catches one and starts to put it back in the water)*
Steven: Don't throw him back!
Harold: We have to put them back after we catch them.

(Ms. Payne passes by the center and adds ideas about baiting the hook to catch the fish, cleaning the fish before cooking and eating them, and throwing back those that are too small)

Katie: I am the mother and I am going to cook everything.
Melanie: No, I am the mother. I want to cook.
Katie: No, you can be the grandma and help me cook, but we can have only one mother.
Melanie: Okay. *(they both go over to the grill and start to cook fish)*
Katie: *(to the fish)* Hey, you! Don't burn! Are you done? I need a fork and a cup.
Melanie: I'll get one. *(returns with a long stick)* We have to turn the fish with a fork. I think I burned my finger. Ouch! Ouch! *(blows on finger)*
Katie: Come over here, Grandma. I can put a bandage on it, and it will make it feel real good. *(pretends to take out some bandages and fix the finger)*

Steven:	I want pink fish. They taste better.
Harold:	I have a pink one and I have a big fish.
Steven:	Can I have the pink one?
Harold:	I'll give you another one. You can have two and I'll have two.
Steven:	Okay. Hey, Grandma, where are the fishies? Are they done yet?
Melanie:	No, I burned them. So now I have to clean the grill because the fish are burnt on it. *(she takes the sponge and pretends to wipe it up)* All clean.
Katie:	Dinner today will be fish, macaroni, and juice.
Steven:	*(starts setting up for dinner and then goes back to fish with Melanie; they fish and put the fish in bowls for dinner)*

While this play scene may seem unimportant to the novice, it is actually rich with examples of creative thought and prosocial behavior. These children are not only drawing upon their experiences, but are also solving problems as they arise, practicing social skills, using their imaginations to engage in friendly interactions, and working as members of a cooperative group. From an experiential perspective, the children have shared a common episode—helping to prepare, cook, and eat food together with family and friends. They used their *imaginations* as they solved problems—how to cook fish on the grill and what to do when the fish were gone from the lake. They practiced *social skills* as they negotiated who was to play the mother when both Katie and Melanie wanted the role. And they engaged in *friendly fantasy interactions* as they caught fish and threw them back in the lake. In this 45-minute play episode, the children were responsible for the contents, roles, and sequence of events. After the play began, Ms. Payne intervened only once with a comment about catching, cleaning, and cooking the fish.

Using the preceding play text and the guidelines for creative growth in Figure 3.1, identify which specific episodes supported children's prosocial behavior. What was Ms. Payne's role in this scenario?

Although it is important to encourage positive behaviors in children, teachers must also prepare children to cope with and think about conflicts that inevitably arise. How teachers interact with children in conflict situations largely determines how children will approach problem solving and thinking of imaginative solutions, both of which are essential attributes of creative thought (Edwards, 2006; Marion, 2007; Wheeler, 2004; Woolfolk, 2007).

UNDERSTANDING CHILDREN'S CONFLICTS

In Ms. Balboa's Head Start classroom, Juanita joins Erik at the play-dough table. Within a few minutes, she rolls out a large, thick pancake shape, and the following dialogue occurs:

Juanita:	Look at my big thing! *(Points to a long, snakelike shape)*
Erik:	Oh man! That's big!
Juanita:	I'm gonna get it even bigger. *(She picks it up and shows Erik the thumbprint on the bottom)* See, on the back, Erik?
Erik:	Whoa! *(Erik leans on his rolled-out play dough, making a "tummy print"; Juanita cuts biscuit shapes with a plastic cup)*
Erik:	Hey! I need that cup!

Juanita: NO!
Erik: *(in increasingly loud, angry tones)* I need that cup! I need it. I need it. I'm gonna make balls and put the balls in it. So, gimme it. Gimme that. Teacher! Juanita won't let me have the cup.

A dispute over a toy is the number one cause of conflict among preschool children, whereas disputes over resources (such as school supplies and equipment) and preferences (such as what game to play or what activity to choose first) predominate for elementary children. Without a doubt, conflicts hold significance for the teacher and the children. What causes conflict? What are the consequences of various types of conflict resolution for their development of creative thought and expression? And what are some guidelines for conflict resolution?

Causes of Conflict

Children's conflicts are a natural part of their lives. Conflict occurs when one person does something to which a second person objects. Underlying reasons for the conflict may be either intentional or unintentional. Whatever the cause, conflict is a powerful tool for creative growth because children must negotiate ideas and actions that lead to some outcome (Kohn, 1996; Wheeler, 2004; Woolfolk, 2007).

Conflicts tend to follow a developmental sequence. Toddlers often have conflicts over possessions or toys because sharing toys and materials is an essential part of group functioning in classrooms. Preschool children's conflicts continue to focus on play materials but also include struggles over playing roles; gaining access to an ongoing group, space, or number of players allowed in a space; and fitting into the ongoing play needs by gender, size, or dress (Isenberg & Raines, 1992). Children in first through fourth grades often disagree with their peers over rules for games, initiating interactions, and maintaining relationships as well as about resources and preferences. They tend to be inflexible in thinking about rules and, as a result, often find themselves involved in disputes over them.

Most teachers want to stop conflicts at all costs as soon as they arise or try to prevent them from occurring. Yet conflict has a positive side. It offers children the opportunity to deal with their thoughts and feelings in social situations. Successful conflict resolution helps children develop the skills and attitudes needed for group living and perceive others' ways of thinking as they reflect on ways to find workable solutions. As a teacher, you can guide conflict to enhance children's creative thought and expression.

Types of Conflicts

Today, educators are spending as much time helping children learn nonviolent ways of solving problems as they spend on creating other ways of learning. Whether children are bickering over a plaything or calling one another names, conflicts are a fact of life. Your own comfort level with conflict, such as how quickly you look for solutions, how sensitive you are to hurt feelings, how much you choose to ignore a problem hoping it will go away, and how willing you are to find mutually agreeable solutions, influences greatly how you approach conflict and model conflict resolution in the classroom. Table 3.2 lists some typical conflicts children experience, describes those conflicts, and suggests appropriate strategies for prevention and intervention.

TABLE 3.2 What Teachers Can Do for Specific Children's Conflicts

Conflict	Description	Appropriate Strategies
Possession disputes	Occur when children argue over ownership of a toy or material.	• Discourage the practice of bringing items to school from home that children will not or should not share. • Ask children to share the material or toy. • Redirect the behavior by suggesting an alternative material or way to use that material. • Ignore the dispute.
Power struggle disputes	Occur when children want to be first or force other children to do something "their way."	• Suggest different ways of playing the same role or using the same materials for different purposes. • Reassure children they will get a turn. • Keep track of turn-taking to ensure that every child really does get a turn.
Group-entry disputes	Occur when children try to join the ongoing activity of another group.	• Use the "You can't say you can't play" rule to deal with problems of insiders and outsiders. • Be clear that all children are expected to get along with one another. • Model ways to approach an ongoing group of children already engaged in activity.
Aggressive play	Occurs when violent, boisterous play escalates in intensity and tempers flare and frustration rises.	• Set reasonable limits on play. • Temporarily disband the group and redirect the children to a different activity. • Establish a caring classroom where adults and children demonstrate cooperation, kindness, and respect for others. • Have conversations about what kindness, cooperation, and respect mean and how children can show those behaviors in the classroom.
Peer and adult disputes	Occur when children have differences over rules, preferences for games or activities, or initiating or maintaining interactions.	• Provide opportunities for peer acceptance. • Provide opportunities to participate in rule-governed games. • Model constructive ways of dealing with conflict and problems.

Note: Data from Jalongo & Isenberg (2008), Marion (2007), and Wheeler (2004).

Tips for Teaching Children How to Resolve Conflicts

The following techniques will help you teach children how to resolve conflicts peaceably and in ways that enrich their ability to solve problems, take another person's perspective, and enhance social skills (Charney, 2002; Marion, 2007; Wheeler, 2004). When families are also invited to use these techniques, then children receive the same messages in both home and school.

1. *Encourage children to find solutions to conflicts on their own, where possible, before intervening.* Teachers who nurture children to be responsive to the needs of others must provide opportunities that guide children toward caring about and helping others. You might remind *elementary children* to "look at the class suggestions about what to do when something is bothering you" or suggest that *younger children* "think about the problem and come back to it in a few minutes." In conflict situations, focus on what can be done rather than unraveling the complex causes of the dispute. Ask children questions, such as, "What do you think we can do about this problem?" or "What are your ideas of how we can make this work?" Taking action will help children resume their activity, and this in itself is reinforcing. Eventually, children learn that making a few concessions can keep their activity going instead of bringing it to an abrupt halt. Teachers who teach children the skills of cooperative conflict resolution promote children's prosocial understandings.

2. *Teach specific social skills to children who are aggressive, unpopular, and rejected by their peers.* Children often suffer peer rejection because they lack the skills for gaining entry into existing play groups, rely overly on adults to solve problems for them, or dominate the activity. Consider, for example, a kindergarten classroom where children have been assigned to small groups to reenact "The Three Little Pigs." Dana takes total control. She shoves the other children and berates them if they deviate from her planned script. Just as the group is about to perform, a shy child named Rolando, who was completely excluded by Dana, says quietly to his teacher, "But I was supposed to be the narrator." Dana is desperately in need of guidance. She needs to see that she can experience success in the group without being overbearing. Rolando needs to have his rights protected as well. If the adults in this kindergarten classroom ignore this peer conflict, neither child's social skills will be enhanced.

3. *Use group meetings to discuss how to handle conflicts.* Group meetings are a powerful way to teach children the skills needed to manage conflicts positively, because the atmosphere is calm and children are not caught up in the immediacy of the dispute. Role playing, puppets, children's illustrations of their own conflicts, and children's literature dealing with conflict resolution provide rich opportunities for talking about conflicts, discussing ways to resolve them, and generating alternative solutions to the conflict. *Younger children* can generally describe the problem and give information, give their own opinions, and accept more than one possible solution to a problem. *Older children* can develop more than one solution, explore different points of view, and anticipate the pros and cons of different outcomes (Charney, 2002).

Children's conflicts hold important opportunities for encouraging creative thought and expression with both peers and adults. In all classrooms, the following three strategies are particularly well suited to fostering children's creative thinking.

Teachers can help children resolve conflicts in ways that enrich their creative expression.

TEACHING STRATEGIES FOR FOSTERING CREATIVE THOUGHT AND EXPRESSION

A major goal of any curriculum is to enable all children to become divergent thinkers. Three teaching strategies designed to meet this goal include inquiry- and problem-based learning groups (Johnson, Johnson, & Holubek, 1998; Tegano, Sawyers, & Moran, 1989; Woolfolk, 2007); investigative play (Wassermann, 2000); and project work (Katz & Chard, 2000).

Inquiry- and Problem-Based Learning Groups

Inquiry- and problem-based learning groups involve a major concept or big idea, a shared goal or interest, a difference of opinion, and an active exchange of ideas. In these groups the children and adult work together to solve essential questions in ways that emphasize positive interaction and individual responsibility to the group. This kind of group cooperation exposes children to different points of view, enhances their perspective-taking ability, and increases social interaction skills.

All children can inquire and solve problems. A child's incessant "why" questions show that motivation to inquire and wonder is fully alive. Teachers can help children become more skillful inquirers by using "big ideas" both as part of the daily classroom life and as a way of learning subject matter. Children who have developed their inquiry abilities can draw conclusions based on evidence and judge whether that evidence supports the conclusions drawn by others (Parker, 2009; Woolfolk, 2007).

Children solve problems regularly through their cooperative play and daily interactions as they decide how to bridge two blocks, fit two children on a swing, or paint a mural together. However, not all problems lead to inquiry or cooperative problem solving, which depends on good communication and positive relations in working through issues. Inquiry- and problem-based learning are enhanced when there are good problems to solve. Figure 3.2 describes the characteristics of good problems.

Fostering Inquiry- and Problem-Based Learning

Use the following guidelines for fostering inquiry- and problem-based learning that contributes to children's creative thought and behavior.

1. *Plan activities with a common goal.* A group of kindergartners were building a school bus to enact the song "The Wheels on the Bus." Before they began, their teacher encouraged them to discuss their ideas, to agree on how to build the bus, and to decide what to include on it (such as steering wheel, seats, horn, driver, steps, and a door). Many children find these kinds of groups a less intimidating setting to test ideas. Helping children work together on a common goal encourages cooperative problem-based learning.

2. *Probe children's thinking.* As part of a unit on environmental responsibility, a third-grade teacher invited children to collect clean, recyclable materials and encouraged the children to use them as they wished. Nothing much came from her suggestion. Later, she decided to try the same activity with small groups, asked guiding, open-ended questions that focused children's thinking on particular attributes, and then had them imagine different uses for the recycled materials. This teacher realized how to capitalize on children's sense of wonder and curiosity. Most children responded more favorably to this activity because they were able to build on one another's ideas as well as suggest their own.

3. *Provide children with specific roles and responsibilities.* To promote the necessary social, decision-making, and conflict management skills, children need to participate regularly in cooperative-learning groups. By designating and rotating group members' roles as leader, recorder, questioner, or reporter, children experience different group roles. Participation in cooperative-learning groups motivates second-language learners by giving them more face-to-face interactions, enriching their group relations and self-esteem, and improving their communication in both languages.

All children can engage in inquiry- and problem-based learning activities during spontaneous play, planned open-ended activities, or planned content-specific

Figure 3.2
Characteristics of
Good Problems

*Note: Based on
Bredekamp & Copple
(1997), Tudge & Caruso
(1988), Wassermann
(2000), and Woolfolk
(2007).*

- Are relevant and interesting to children.
- Involve real or simulated materials and/or people.
- Require the child to modify, move, or transform the materials.
- Elicit many possible solutions.
- Can be solved by the child, yet provide interesting challenges.
- Help the child believe in his or her own problem-solving abilities.
- Encourage children to share differing points of view.
- Occur spontaneously in children's play.
- Occur in open-ended, content-specific, planned activities.

activities, such as science investigations. Through shared exchanges of ideas, children explore new possibilities together and enhance their creative thinking.

Investigative Play

Mr. Yoon's first graders are exploring the effect of different formulas on soap bubbles. Two groups of children are experimenting with different solutions of food colorings, liquid detergents, corn syrup, and glycerin. They are also using other materials—straws, lids, a plastic tennis racket, plastic tubing attached to a funnel, and the plastic rings from a six-pack of soda cans—to produce bubbles of various sizes. Mr. Yoon has given them an activity card with the following guidelines:

- Find out everything you can about bubbles.
- What did you observe about the different formulas? Colors?
- What solution made the biggest, strongest bubbles?
- What materials can be used to make many small bubbles? To make one huge bubble?
- Talk about what you noticed.

One group of children added glycerin to see if they could get stronger bubbles. They started with one teaspoon, and then increased to two, three, four, and five. Another group tried different ways of making different-sized bubbles. In both groups, all the children were involved in the tasks, either as investigators or as observers. Mr. Yoon served as a facilitator, encouraging and supporting children's investigations with such comments as, "I see you are now going to try a new color of bubbles."

This activity illustrates another strategy for fostering creative thought—a three-step model for organizing instruction that challenges children's divergent thinking, called **play-debrief-replay** (Wassermann, 2000). Each step is explained next.

Play

During *play,* children investigate and explore materials to make predictions, observe and classify information, and make both individual and collaborative decisions. Investigative play builds children's concepts about materials and ideas and enables them to examine key curriculum concepts such as, "Plants are living things" and "The work different people do requires special abilities and talents." In play, teachers set the stage and challenge children's learning, while children control their own learning. Wassermann reports that teachers using this model "feel exhilarated, energized and empowered" (2000, p. 28). Mr. Yoon's first graders were testing hypotheses about the "perfect" soap bubble formula. They were learning about viscosity, pressure, velocity, colors, and light—all basic concepts of physics.

Debrief

In the second step, *debriefing* becomes the common base for children's reflections. In either small or large discussion groups following exploratory play, Mr. Yoon asks the children questions that encourage them to reflect on their experiences, such as, "What did you notice about the bubbles?" and "How did you figure that out?" Good questions cause children to think carefully and to add their understandings to others. In the hands of a skillful, knowledgeable teacher, debriefing play experiences empower children as thinkers, invite new ideas, build self-esteem, and provide a foundation for future play with new insights about the same concept (Wassermann, 2000).

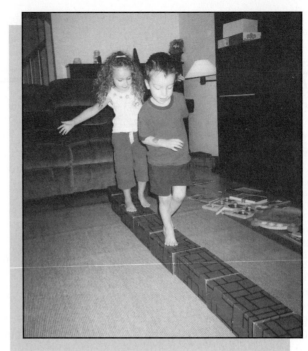

All children want to be competent learners.

Replay

Replay occurs after debriefing. Some replay may involve the same materials; other replay may involve some new materials to move the inquiry along. A teacher might invite children to figure out the best way to transfer a bubble from one person to another without breaking it or ask children to introduce some new ways of blowing into the bubble makers. Replay provides additional practice with the concept or skill and an opportunity to replicate and verify findings. As a result, replay gradually builds children's conceptual understandings. Children's creative thought is enhanced when they can investigate objects, ideas, and events. Investigations encourage children to ask questions, explore ideas, and reflect on their thinking to make learning meaningful and powerful. They enable children to participate with their own learning styles and to begin to assess their own ways of thinking through reflection and debriefing. Play-debrief-replay is an important strategy in long-term classroom projects.

Project Work

A third strategy for strengthening creative thought is project work. According to Katz and Chard (2000) and Allison (2004), a **project** is a focused study of something worth learning about undertaken by one or more children for as long as they remain interested. Projects offer children opportunities to apply skills, choose what topic to study, investigate questions that are personally meaningful, and revisit theories. These four characteristics support children's ability to think creatively.

Projects are an important teaching strategy because they foster meaningful learning, demand collaboration, require a range of skills, and can be as long or as short as children wish. In the following description of project activities related to construction, think about the possibilities for children's engagement in learning (Hartman & Eckerty, 1995; Hyson, 2008).

All of the children were at the window watching the construction workers and equipment. They had many questions: "Why do they dig a hole first?" "What happens next?" "How do they know what to do?" In response to their questions and interest and her belief that her children were capable of pursuing extended project activities, Ms. Hartman developed a project on construction that led to the following scenario.

Ms. Hartman located several picture books that illustrated basic building principles, including Byron Barton's *Building a House* (1981) and Gail Gibbons's *Tool Book* (1982). The class looked at a real blueprint, took a walking tour of the community to look for different building styles, and interviewed an architect. Ms. Hartman also brought in picture postcards of famous buildings and lavishly illustrated books from the library. It turned out that one of the teachers had built a house the previous year and had a set of photographs that documented each building stage.

In this scenario, Ms. Hartman initiated the construction project in response to children's interest and questions. She began with a class discussion about what the children already knew about construction and what they were interested in finding out. Through their investigation of books, their examination of postcards and real materials such as the blueprint, and a walking tour of the community the children developed their own construction site to build a "class house" from blocks and boxes. Through their project, the children used their math and science skills (measuring space for the rooms in the house), literacy skills (making lists of materials needed to build the house), and social studies skills (exploring the interdependent roles of the architect, builder, and construction worker). They also developed clearer concepts of the complexities of building a house.

Project work can heighten creative thought and expression by doing the following:

* Fostering children's independent, creative thinking and involvement at different levels.
* Providing diverse cognitive challenges so that all children can experience success.
* Utilizing academic skills in relevant, highly motivating contexts.
* Encouraging cooperation to ensure successful completion of the project.
* Providing opportunities to increase knowledge and understandings and interpretations (Allison, 2004; Katz & Chard, 2000).

To see an example of a project that incorporates multiple intelligences for learning through poetry, art, science, mathematics, and expression, view the video "Addressing Multiple Intelligences in a Project" online at MyEducationLab.

Or, you can see how one child's detailed drawing illustrates knowledge and understanding of undersea life based on a long-term study online at MyEducationLab.

Strategies such as *project work, investigative play,* and *inquiry- and problem-based learning* are appropriate for all children. They take a holistic approach to teaching and learning and make learning meaningful by enabling children to actually carry out long-term projects, investigate real-world problems, and relate what they need to learn to what they already know. Keeping children engaged in learning makes further learning possible. In the next section, we present some ways to meet standards while promoting creative thought and expression.

MyEducationLab

Go to MyEducationLab and select the topic "Curriculum." Under Activities and Applications, watch the video Addressing Multiple Intelligences in a Project *and answer the questions provided.*

MyEducationLab

Go to MyEducationLab and select the topic "Math, Science, and Technology." Under Activities and Applications, view the artifact Deep Sea Picture, Science (K-12) *and answer the questions provided.*

MEETING STANDARDS THROUGH CREATIVE EXPERIENCES

Activities That Foster Creative Thought and Expression

Fostering children's creative thought and expression are essential aspects of the curriculum. Perhaps more than anything else, all children want to be competent learners. We therefore must find ways to provide all children with opportunities for discovering unique solutions to problems, thinking flexibly, experiencing investigative activities, capitalizing on their sense of wonder, learning self-control, and demonstrating prosocial behavior.

What follows are snapshots of units of study at the preschool/kindergarten, first/second-grade, and third/fourth-grade levels followed by a chart containing selected examples of possible activities that foster creative thought and expression in that thematic unit. Each activity is aligned with the appropriate content, arts, and teacher education standards.

Preschool–Kindergarten

A group of kindergartners is learning about plants and other living things through some of their activities. In the dramatic-play center, the teachers have added farmer and chef clothes and props (such as fruits and vegetables, a cash register, materials for making signs) and related books such as *The Giant Carrot* (Peck, 1998) and the children are creating their own market and acting out stories. In the block center, some children are using pots, empty seed packets, and rulers to design their own gardens. In the kitchen center, the children use pretend fruits and vegetables, seeds, and recipe cards to make applesauce, roasted pumpkin seeds, vegetable stew, and fruit salad. In the art center, children paint signs of fruits and vegetables for the fruit and vegetable market and make pictures of their own gardens using seeds and glue. In the music center, children invent a dance to make their plants grow and pop out of the ground (just as Little Isabelle does in *The Giant Carrot*) and sing and move to various recorded songs about planting and growing seeds. In the math center, children estimate how many seeds are in apples and peapods and weigh and classify seeds. In the science center, children follow instructions (for example, use 1 cup of soil for every two seeds) on how to plant their own seeds in clear plastic cups so that they can observe and record the seeds' growth throughout the unit.

At all centers, an ample supply of paper and pencils encourages children to record measurements, map out their own gardens, create recipes, take orders, and write receipts. The culminating activity for the unit invites children to replant their plants at home with their family. The children will also work together to make a class fruit salad to enjoy during snack time. The following tables show the content, arts, and teacher education standards that are met within the array of activities. Standards are abbreviated as follows:

Student Content-Area Standards

Mathematics: National Council of Teachers of Mathematics (NCTM)

Social Studies: National Council for the Social Studies (NCSS)

Science: National Science Teachers Association (NSTA)

Literacy: National Council of Teachers of English (NCTE)

Student Arts Education Standards

National Standards for Arts Education

Teacher Education Standards

> National Association for the Education of Young Children (NAEYC)
> Interstate New Teacher Assessment and Support Consortium (INTASC)
> National Board for Professional Teaching Standards (NBPTS)

Preschool/Kindergarten: Unit on "Plants Are Living Things"			
Activity	**Student Content Standards**	**Student Arts Education Standards**	**Teacher Education Standards**
Science: *Planting seeds*	NSTA A: Ability to do scientific inquiry; Understanding about scientific inquiry	M1: K–4 Singing, alone and with others; a varied repertoire of music	NAEYC 4b: Using developmentally effective approaches
Music and movement: *Singing and dancing*	NSTA C: Characteristics of organisms; Life cycles of organisms; Organisms and environments	M8: K–4 Understanding relationships between music, the other arts, and disciplines outside the arts	NAEYC 4c: Understanding content knowledge in early childhood education INTASC Prin. 1: Content pedagogy; Prin. 4: Multiple instructional strategies; Prin. 5: Motivation and management
Math: *Estimating, weighing, and classifying seeds*	NCTM 5: Estimation NCTM 6: Number Sense and Numeration NCTM 10: Measurement	D2: K–4 Understanding choreographic principles, processes, and structures D7: K–4 Making connections between dance and other disciplines	NBPTS Prop. 2: Making learning accessible; Prop 4: Managing and monitoring student learning
Dramatic play: *Designing a fruit and vegetable market*	NCTM 4: Mathematical Connections NCTM 6: Number Sense and Numeration	VA1: K–4 Understanding and applying media, techniques and processes	See above
Acting out: The Giant Carrot	NSTA B: Properties of objects and materials NCSS 7: Production, distribution, and consumption	VA3: K–4 Choosing and evaluating a range of subject matter, symbols, and ideas	
Kitchen: *Making and creating recipes with pretend food*	NCTE 2: Read a range of literature from many periods in many genres to build understanding of the many dimensions of human experience	VA6: K–4 Making connections between visual arts and other disciplines T1: K–4 Acting by assuming roles and interacting in improvisations	

(Continued)

Preschool/Kindergarten: Unit on "Plants Are Living Things" (*Continued*)

Activity	Student Content Standards	Student Arts Education Standards	Teacher Education Standards
Art: *Making seed pictures and signs for the play center*	NCTE 4: Use spoken, written, and visual language to communicate effectively with a variety of audiences and for different purposes	T3: K–4 Designing by visualizing and arranging environments for classroom dramatizations	
Blocks: *Designing and building block gardens*	NCTE 12: Use spoken, written, and visual language to accomplish their own purposes		

Note: In the third column, the letters M, D, VA and T identify Music, Dance, Visual Arts, and Theater Standards.

First Grade–Second Grade

As part of their social studies unit, second-grade children become pioneers and plan their own expedition out west. They assign roles for all participants (such as husbands, wives, and children) and occupations (such as pioneers). The teacher provides each "pioneer" a budget and facilitates discussion on the items needed for their journey (such as an axle, wheels, and axe), travel to their destination, and factors that might affect their trip. Through a variety of explorations, investigations, and conversations, the pioneers work together to design and create a map of the West, decide how to spend their money, overcome each obstacle, and safely arrive at their new western home. During the unit, the children also sing pioneer mu-

First Grade–Second Grade: Unit on "Pioneers"

Activity	Student Content Standards	Student Arts Education Standards	Teacher Education Standards
What do we need for our trip? Budget activity and simple machine review	NCTM 1: Mathematics as Problem Solving NCTM 4: Mathematical Connections NCTM 7: Computation and Estimation NSTA B: Physical Science—Properties of objects and materials; Position and motion of objects NSTA E: Science and Technology—Abilities to distinguish between natural objects and objects made by humans NCSS 7: Production, distribution, and consumption	T5: K–4 Researching by finding information to support classroom dramatizations	NAEYC 4b: Using developmentally effective approaches NAEYC 4c: Understanding content knowledge in early childhood education INTASC Prin. 1: Content pedagogy; Prin. 4: Multiple instructional strategies; Prin. 5: Motivation and management NBPTS Prop. 2: Making learning accessible; Prop. 4: Managing and monitoring student learning

(Continued)

First Grade–Second Grade: Unit on "Pioneers" (*Continued*)

Activity	Student Content Standards	Student Arts Education Standards	Teacher Education Standards
What factors did early pioneers face that may affect the journey? Oregon Trail reenactment; pioneer diary	NCSS 2: Time, continuity, and change NCSS 3: People, places, and environments NCSS 5: Individuals, groups, and institutions AAHE 1: Comprehend concepts related to health promotion and disease prevention AAHE 6: Demonstrate the ability to use goal-setting and decision-making skills to enhance health NSTA F: Science in Personal and Social Perspectives—Personal health NCTE 5: Employ a wide range of writing strategies and use different writing process elements to communicate with different audiences for a variety of purposes	T1: K–4 Script writing by planning and recording improvisations T2: K–4 Acting by assuming roles and interacting in improvisations T3: K–4 Designing by visualizing and arranging environments for classroom dramatizations	See above
How do we get to our destination? (pioneer maps)	NCSS 3: People, places, and environments	VA1: K–4 Understanding and applying media, techniques, and processes VA3: K–4 Choosing and evaluating subject matter, symbols, and ideas VA6: K–4 Making connections between visual arts and other disciplines	See above

sic (such as "Home Sweet Home," "Oh Susanna," "Skip to my Lou," and "Buffalo Gals") and use the songs to inspire their pioneer letters home to family and friends. During each daily reenactment, the "pioneers" enact factors similar to those faced by early pioneers (such as cholera, weather, poor sanitation, accidental gunshots, and broken wagon axles) and each pioneer makes reflective entries in his or her diary that eventually will be part of a culminating assessment.

The following table shows the content, arts, and teacher education standards for each activity.

Third Grade–Fourth Grade

Mr. Gore's fourth-grade class is involved in a literature unit based on the Newbery Medal–winning book *Holes* (Sachar, 1998). In math, children are creating word problems for the character Zero, based on situations he faced in the story (for example, if a round hole is 5 feet in diameter and 5 feet deep, then what is the volume of the hole?). In science, children are exploring the different layers of Earth (crust, mantle, inner core, and outer core) by cutting a peach in half. The children use the peaches and other spices authentically to practice fractions while making their own recipes for the character Kate Barlow's spiced peaches. For their recipe, children design their food label including nutritional information for their cans of spiced peaches and investigate how canned peaches can be preserved. In the book *Holes*, Stanley's father is an inventor seeking the solution for foot odor. The children use the Internet to find out about the writing portion of the unit, create their own inventions using everyday found objects, and dramatize a commercial for their invention or write a jingle about it. An ongoing theme in the book and throughout the unit is power. The children also explore the topic by acting out scenes in the book and in daily life that show appropriate and/or unjust use of power.

The following table shows the content, arts, and teacher education standards for several unit activities.

Third Grade–Fourth Grade: Literature Unit on "Holes"

Activity	Student Content Standards	Student Arts Education Standards	Teacher Education Standards
Find out about the layers of Earth Recipes for spiced peaches Inventions	NCTM 1: Mathematics as Problem Solving NCTM 4: Mathematical Connections NCTM 7: Computation and Estimation NCTM 13: Measurement NSTA D: Earth and Space Science—Structure of the earth system NSTA F: Science in Personal and Social Perspectives—Personal health	VA1: K–4 Understanding and applying media, techniques, and processes VA6: K–4 Making connections between visual arts and other disciplines	NAEYC 4b: Using developmentally effective approaches NAEYC 4c: Understanding content knowledge in early childhood education INTASC Prin. 1: Content pedagogy; Prin. 4: Multiple instructional strategies; Prin. 5: Motivation and management NBPTS Prop. 2: Making learning accessible; Prop. 4: Managing and monitoring student learning

(Continued)

Third Grade–Fourth Grade: Literature Unit on "Holes" *(Continued)*

Activity	Student Content Standards	Student Arts Education Standards	Teacher Education Standards
Inventions	NCSS 3: People, places, and environments NCSS 4: Individual development and identity NCSS 8: Science, technology, and environment NCTE 2: Read a range of literature from many periods in many genres to build understanding of the many dimensions of human experience NCTE 4: Use spoken, written, and visual language to communicate effectively with a variety of audiences and for different purposes NCTE 5: Employ a wide range of writing strategies to communicate with different audiences for varied purposes NCTE 12: Use spoken, written, and visual language to accomplish their own purposes	T1: K–4 Script writing by planning and recording improvisations T2: K–4 Acting by assuming roles and interacting in improvisations M1: K–4 Singing alone and with others VA1: K–4 Understanding and applying media, techniques, and processes VA3: K–4 Choosing and evaluating a range of subject matter, symbols, and ideas VA6: K–4 Making connections between visual arts and other disciplines	See above
What do I know about power? Compare/contrast situations in the book and in daily life that show appropriate and/or unjust use of power. Subjects addressed: Social Studies Drama	NCSS 1: Culture NCSS 2: Time, Continuity, and Change NCSS 4: Individual Development and Identity NCSS 6: Power, Authority and Governance NCSS 10: Civic Ideals and Practices	T1: K–4 Script writing by planning and recording improvisations based on personal experience and heritage, imagination, literature, and history T2: K–4 Acting by assuming roles and interacting in improvisations	

Frequently Asked Questions About Fostering Creative Thought and Expression

How do I foster creative thinking with children from diverse backgrounds?

The arts and play provide children opportunities to express their cultural uniqueness, share cultural traditions, and discover their own personal identities before they can extend that learning to other cultures. A recent report (Stevenson, 2004) reveals that teachers who bring the arts into their classroom describe positive changes in their instruction for children from diverse backgrounds. Curricular modifications that strengthen self-expression in culturally sensitive ways include opportunities for children to build new understandings about accepting others, responsibility, and their own personal identities. Appropriate literature includes *Family Pictures* (Garza, 1990), which describes growing up in a Mexican-American community in Texas, and bilingual picture books that honor cultural and language differences for children with various heritages, such as the Kenyan tale *Bringing the Rain to Kapiti Plain* (Aardema, 1981) or *Abuela's Weave* (Castañeda, 1996), the story of how a Guatemalan girl learns of her family traditions from her grandmother (Diamond & Moore, 1995).

Other curricular modifications include the following:

- *Role-play* different problematic behaviors illustrated through a collection of pictures depicting problem situations (two children arguing over a toy, a child locked out of the house, a group of children teasing an Islamic girl wearing a headscarf or a Jewish boy wearing a kipa). Have children generate solutions to the problems, role-play some of them, and discuss why some solutions would be more appropriate than others.
- *Adapt existing games* such as lotto, bingo, and Memory to use words, numbers, or significant pictures representing the cultural backgrounds of the children in your class. Invite children and their families to supply materials to adapt classroom games.
- *Engage in dramatic play* with props and clothing from different cultures represented in your room, such as overnight bags for children to take pretend trips to a variety of places or travel folders and posters (Deiner, 2005).
- *Use music* to express cultural and ethnic differences and share family traditions, which can increase children's first- and second-language usage (Ray, 1997).
- *Encourage a creative climate.* Children of all ages can write poems, stories, illustrate ideas, and display their work in the halls and in the classroom. Each piece of work should exemplify a joyful place to create and a place where ideas and thinking are valued. Figure 3.3 suggests additional resources for obtaining information about culturally diverse groups.

How do I foster creative thought and expression with children with exceptionalities?

Inclusive classrooms benefit all children. However, children with disabilities in these settings require appropriate support to be able to participate meaningfully with their peers who do not have disabilities. According to *The Arts and Special Student Populations* (Arts Education Partnership, 2004b), "Students marginalized though self-imposed or induced withdrawal to the periphery of the classroom may increase their involvement, perhaps because they enjoy or feel competent enough to participate in arts activities. If, as a result, special populations gain self-concept through the arts, their classmates and teachers may perceive them in a new and more positive light, and a more reciprocal, inclusive social atmosphere in the classroom could enhance instructional effectiveness for all students" (p. 25). The goal of curricular and environmental adaptation is to ensure the participation and success of children at all levels. Students with exceptionalities need opportunities for decision making on projects, for being members of a classroom community that focuses on social acceptance, for using a variety of art materials, and for participating in experiences that address multiple intelligences, and teachers who accept their divergent responses (Bredekamp & Copple, 1997; Deiner, 2005; Erwin & Schreiber, 1999).

Everyone tells me that I have to meet the needs of individual students. How do I do that and still foster their creative growth?

In classrooms designed for children to succeed, all children participate in experiences that address the same curricular areas but at different levels of difficulty. When children and teachers are clear about the concepts to be learned, then teaching and learning with a focus on creative thought can occur for all children. According to *The Arts and Group Learning* (Arts Education Partnership, 2004a), "The arts are . . . a venue for exploring specific elements of collaborative learning environments such as scheduling, the nature of group work assignments, enlisting and managing subgroups or teams for various purposes, and the potential roles of the expert (whether teacher or mentor) in the group learning process" (p. 23). In one example, third- and fourth-graders studying ancient Greece work collaboratively in planning, researching, designing, and participating in their own class Olympics. Children

The following resources provide *free* information for classroom teachers. Be sure to mention why you need these materials and how you will use them in your classroom.

African-American Institute
School Services Division
www.aaionline.org

Asian-American Studies Center
www.aasc.ucla.edu

Canadian International
Development Agency (CIDA)
www.acdi-cida.gc.ca

(provides free poster kits of children in both urban and rural settings)

Multiculturalism National Office
www.pch.gc.ca

(provides resources for educators on multiculturalism in play)

National Information Center for
Children and Youth with Disabilities
(NICHCY)
www.nichcy.org

Office for Civil Rights
U.S. Department of Education
www.hhs.gov/ocr

(provides free pamphlets on multiculturalism)

Figure 3.3   Additional Teaching Resources for Diverse Groups
Note: Artwork and artifacts of children, families, and colleagues provide a free and ready source of relevant resources. Moreover, many embassies and consulates provide pamphlets, maps, and posters from their countries without charge.

have the opportunity to choose from activities that represent various cognitive and artistic ability levels and multiple-intelligence strength(s). Another example refers to a construction project in the community in which children with exceptionalities and children who are high achievers become city planners who evaluate community needs, such as a recycling center or a traveling library, and create possible ways to meet those needs. Children who are lower achieving might select and build the necessary buildings, make signs for the community areas, illustrate the types of buildings and equipment needed, or plan a playground. Each of these examples meets the needs of individual learners in a group setting that has the potential to unlock children's creative thought and expression.

CHAPTER SUMMARY

1. Teachers use three fundamental theoretical perspectives to foster children's creative thought: constructivism, humanism, and behavioral/social learning. *Constructivists* view children as active agents in their own development. *Humanists* assume that people are capable of controlling their own lives. *Behavioral/social-learning* theorists view individuals as products of their environment.

2. The three basic styles of adult-child interactions—autocratic, permissive, and democratic all refer to how demanding or responsive teachers are with children. However, each cultivates typical behaviors and approaches to problem solving differently.

3.   Fostering children's creative thought includes facilitating the development of prosocial, cooperative, and helping behaviors. Teachers encourage children to become more caring, respectful, and self-responsible.

4.   Children's conflicts are a natural part of their lives. Most conflicts among toddlers involve possessions; most preschoolers' disputes are over role playing and play materials; and many elementary-grade children's disagreements with peers are over rules, social interactions, resources, and preferences.

5.   Helping children learn to resolve their own conflicts peaceably encourages their ability to solve problems, take another person's perspective, and enhance social skills.

6.   Three culturally relevant strategies to help children become better thinkers are inquiry- and problem-based learning groups, investigative play, and project work.

Discuss: Perspectives on Fostering Creative Thought and Expression

1.   Refer to the opening scenario in which Ms. Manning intervenes in David and Ahmad's play. Think about the consequences of her actions. Suppose she had said, "Boys, stop that fighting right now!" What difference would that have made in their future ability to negotiate or to express feelings?

2.   Imagine that you are responsible for making a presentation on parents' night that explains the importance of fostering creative thought. How would you show parents how this meets standards?

3.   Brainstorm some curriculum projects that would be appropriate for inquiry- and problem-based learning. Select one project and identify the common goal, find the problem, test hypotheses, and provide feedback.

4.   Refer to the chapter opening quote by Howard Gardner. After reading and discussing the material in this chapter, present your views on why "we need to keep alive the mind and the sensibility of the young child." Give some examples from your own experience.

PART 2
THE CREATIVE ARTS

Chapter 4

Promoting Children's Art

Mary Renck Jalongo and
Marilyn J. Narey

Art is an integral part of an early childhood classroom. For children, it is a tool that encourages them to express themselves graphically, emotionally, and verbally. For family members, it provides concrete evidence of their child's work, in addition to increasing their understanding of their child's development. For teachers, it is an observation tool, an assessment support, and a means of sharing with children as well as their families.

Kimberly B. Moore, 2003, p. 1

 CLASSROOM PERSPECTIVES ON ART

Preschool–Kindergarten

When the 4- and 5-year-olds in Ms. Lin's preschool class draw themselves, their artwork is typical for their age and usually consists of a circular shape with a face and lines radiating out to represent legs and/or arms. Their teacher's goal is to focus children's attention to various body parts so that they elaborate in their drawings. The teacher shares the book *Whose Shoes?* (Hines, 2001) and asks "What kinds of shoes do people wear? Look at your own shoes; what do you see? Do your shoes have ties, buckles, or Velcro?" Then the preschoolers draw a picture of themselves wearing their favorite shoes and some children now scribble or draw shapes to represent shoes. For the children who do not, Ms. Lin accepts it as normal and does not point out the omission. Throughout the year she poses many new artistic challenges, such as "I am smelling a flower" (nose), "I am holding a flag" (hands and arms), "I am combing my hair" (hands and hair), and "I am pushing a cart in the store" (arms and legs). By the end of the school year, the children's drawings are considerably more detailed (see Golomb, 2004).

First Grade–Second Grade

Mr. Pena knows that young children often will respond to the sensory qualities of artwork (e.g., bright, intense colors), relate their experiences to the subject matter in art, invent stories about the shapes, colors, and images found in works of art, and respond more to what is pictured (subject or theme) than to the artist's style (Kerlavage, 1995). Mr. Pena's preparation for the first graders' museum visit begins with *Squeaking of Art* (Wellington, 2002), a picture book about an imaginary art museum tour by ten mice. The teacher also displays fine art reproductions throughout the room (e.g., a print by Bruegel that depicts children at play), uses a projector to discuss selected works of art posted at (http://www.indiana.edu/~ssdc/artlinks.htm), and encourages children to connect these works of art with their experiences. Mr. Pena leads children to discover themes in works of visual art (fantasy, realism, multiculturalism, caricature, still life, land/city/seascapes, and so forth). Mr. Pena then invites each child to choose an artwork from prints and postcards to "show" the class and "tell" the meaning ("This picture is about _____," "I like it because _____," "It looks like the artist. . . "). Prior to the trip to the art museum, all of the students responded both through drawing and writing to the book *To Be an Artist* (Aimera & Ivanko, 2004) and the question, "What is art?" After the trip, the students revise their definitions as they

103

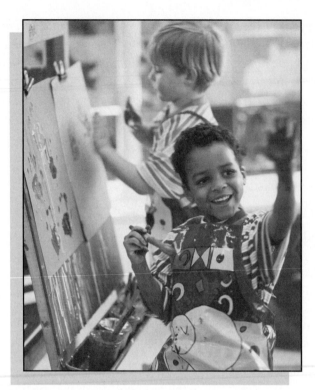

Making art relies on thought as well as emotions.

discuss two additional thought-provoking books about art (Renshaw, 2007; Renshaw & Ruggi, 2005).

Third Grade–Fourth Grade

The classroom teachers and school counselor collaborate with the art, music, and physical education teachers to develop a unit on mental health. Today's lesson is about coping with difficult emotions and the art teacher begins with a slide show of paintings and photographs of people's faces. Next, small groups of students use many different types of magazines and examples of collage in picture books (Prudhoe, 2003) to create poster-sized collages with the unifying theme of a particular emotion (joy, sorrow, surprise, confusion, anger, etc.). The groups then compose a short essay about the kinds of experiences that prompt the various emotions. Finally, all students identify a personal situation that caused them to have mixed emotions and they accompany their story with a drawing, painting, or sculpture.

DEFINING CHILDREN'S ART AND AESTHETIC EXPERIENCES

To evaluate your assumptions about children's art and aesthetic experiences, read each statement in Figure 4.1 and indicate whether it is true or false.

1. Artistic ability unfolds naturally so it is best to leave children to follow their own inclinations.

2. Producing art is an emotional process rather than a cognitive one.

3. Any sensory experience, such as playing with shaving cream, is an art experience.

4. Children need to produce artwork in a solitary fashion; otherwise, they might "copy" the work of their peers.

5. The primary purpose of art projects in school is, and should be, to celebrate holidays or make gifts.

You may be surprised to learn that all five of these statements are false. Here's why:

Question 1. False. It is not enough to throw children together with some art materials and hope for the best. Children need to learn techniques, such as preschoolers learning how to use just a bit of white glue so that wooden items will hold together and dry quickly.

Question 2. False. Art is every bit as much a cognitive (thinking) process as it is an affective (emotional) one. When a group of children plans a display of their work, they are engaging in problem solving (Where will we place our display? How will we organize it?) as well as responding to affective responses (How does this look?). Realize too that art can be a source of frustration, such as when a weaving unravels or a clay sculpture breaks after it is fired in a kiln. The arts can teach children how to respond to complex challenges with tenacity and grace.

Question 3. False. There is a useful distinction between "messing about" with materials and art experiences. A baby who plays with his food is not having an art experience because the behavior serves no purpose related to the arts.

Question 4. False. Art is a social activity, not merely a means of talent testing or promoting individual accomplishment. Children often are inspired by their peers to try new things in art, just as real artists are influenced by the works of artists they admire. Children should be allowed to interact with their peers during art activities.

Question 5. False. Art is not a commodity. When children paste cotton ball beards on a printed picture of a snowman, it is not art, it is an assembly task. Assembly tasks are not art because they offer no opportunities for creative expression and problem solving.

Figure 4.1   Test Your Assumptions About Children and Art

If all of the assumptions in Figure 4.1 are false, then what is true? Actually, it is easy to avoid some of the worst activities masquerading as art by asking a few simple questions (Jalongo & Stamp, 1997):

- *Are the children's responses predetermined?* If so, it is not art. A teacher who distributes patterns to color, trace, copy, or cut out in some designated way is not providing an art activity, no matter how clever it might be. It is an exercise in following directions and should be recognized as such.

- *Will one child's work look nearly identical to another's?* If so, it is not art. When you can view a display of children's work and see nothing original or surprising, it is not truly children's work and therefore, it is not art.

- *Who is the activity for?* If it is simply to convince parents that their child is keeping busy at school, it is not art. For example, the teacher who "fixes" children's cut-and-paste pictures by rearranging them to look more presentable for display not only has selected an inappropriate activity but also is undermining children's confidence in their ability to be makers of art.

- *Will the child's efforts lead to the creation of a new form that is satisfying to the child at his or her level of development?* If a child is being pushed, it is not art. An adult who grasps a 3- or 4-year-old's hand and forces the child to produce a stick figure is not "teaching" the child to draw! Most young children will strongly resist such impositions, and understandably so. When a child is at the scribbling stage, scribbles are new, interesting, and therefore appropriate. If adults have to do an activity for the child, it is not art. You can see an example of a child's original artwork at MyEducationLab.

Consider this example from Mr. Ortiz's first-grade class. His students have been collecting what he calls "beautiful junk" for several weeks. Included in these materials are items such as bits of fabric, yarn, buttons, lace, felt, boxes, and plastic bottles of various sizes and shapes. He begins by talking about Shrek and then sharing stories about other not-so-scary monsters, including *My Friend the Monster* (Taylor, 2008), *Where the Wild Things Are* (Sendak, 1963), *Leonardo, the Terrible Monster* (Willems, 2005), *The Very Worst Monster* (Hutchins, 1985), *There's a Nightmare in My Closet* (Mayer, 1968), *My Monster Mama Loves Me So* (Leuck & Buehner, 2002), *Harry and the Terrible Whatzit* (Gackenbach, 1977), and *Monster Mess* (Cuyler, 2008). Mr. Ortiz's challenge to his students is simply this: "Using any of the materials we have collected here or others you may have at home, create your own monster. Think about questions like these: What is a monster? What is special about your monster? What does it eat? Are people afraid of it? Why? Where does it live now? What makes it happy? What makes it sad? What does it like to do? After you have created your monster, you will tell the class all about it. Then you will make up a story about your monster." Is this art? Use the four preceding questions and the information in Table 4.1 to arrive at your answer.

MyEducationLab

Go to MyEducationLab and select the topic "Child Development," under Activities and Applications view the artifact Guitar Drawing. *As you look at the artifact, think about how it meets the criteria for art.*

TABLE 4.1 Is It Art? How to Decide	
Not Art	
Category	**Examples**
Assembly Tasks	Using craft store items to construct something (e.g., gluing a magnet on a clothespin); coloring, cutting out, and pasting pictured items onto a paper bag to make a puppet
	Why isn't this art? There is no creativity involved. Each child's work will appear very similar. The emphasis is on following directions.
Using Food as Art	Making macaroni necklaces; "painting" with pudding; making a "house" out of graham crackers and icing; "painting" on bread with food coloring; gluing beans, rice, and other food items onto paper
	Why isn't this art? Real artists generally do not use these materials. These projects waste good food and may be perplexing or offensive, particularly to people from communities where food is in short supply.
Copy Work	Coloring pictures from coloring books; follow-the-dots drawing; using clip art; tracing patterns or using templates; painting by the numbers
	Why isn't this art? These activities emphasize conformity and fine motor control rather than resourcefulness and originality.

TABLE 4.1 Is It Art? How to Decide (*Continued*)	
Art	
Category	**Examples**
Creative Problem Solving	Designing an original picture book; constructing a well-balanced mobile; mixing paints to arrive at the perfect color; figuring out how to achieve a goal, such as making doors and windows that open on a cardboard box house
	Why is this art? Each child's work will be a one-of-a-kind original. Children are choosing their own artistic challenges, making decisions about the medium, determining ways to share and display their work, and evaluating the finished product.
Aesthetic Responses	Pairs of children examining art postcards and discussing them; describing/comparing/contrasting the artistic style of picture books, responding to beauty outdoors or in nature photographs; participating in a weekly "Artist's Circle" in which small groups of children share their work and peers comment on one thing that they like about each piece
	Why is this art? Children are developing emergent skills in art criticism and insights about style.
Art Centers	Teachers design several different learning centers so that children can move from one area to the next to conduct experiments (e.g., working with watercolors), complete various components of projects (e.g., creating materials for a puppet play), or achieve a goal (e.g., creating a painting that covers the entire page)
	Why is this art? Children are making choices, following their interests, acquiring skills, and gaining insight into both process and product.

Note: Data from Bae (2004), Bresler (1993), and Epstein (2001).

If you decided that the monster-inventing activity was art, you were correct.

✥ THEORETICAL AND RESEARCH BASE: ART AS A LANGUAGE AND THE SCHOOLS OF REGGIO EMILIA

Art is a set of processes that uses symbols and tools to communicate meaning. Art is also a language through which the child can communicate understanding (Narey, 2009). Participation in art activities enables children to elaborate on their ideas, interests, and experiences (Korn-Bursztyn, 2002). For children who are just learning to express their thoughts and feelings through words, art takes on even greater importance as a language (Danko-McGhee & Slutsky, 2003). Year after year, the majority of children report that art is one of their favorite subjects in school. It is not difficult to understand why, when we consider how art typically is taught in elementary school. In art, children have a greater opportunity to spontaneously seek new challenges, make meaningful choices, work at their own pace, attend to details, take pride in craft, and enjoy the satisfactions of a job well done.

Of all the early childhood programs in the world today, those in a municipality of Italy called Reggio Emilia are recognized as some of the very finest, particularly

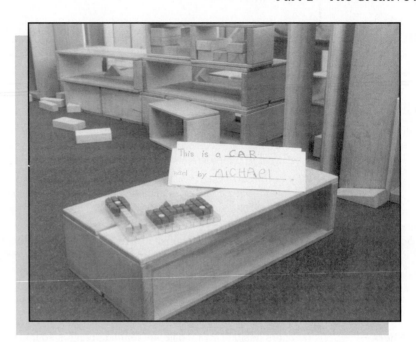

*Authentic art experiences emphasize the process, value originality, and
allow children to retain ownership of their artwork.*

where the art curriculum is concerned (Gandini, Hill, Cadwell, & Schwall, 2005). Providing opportunities for children's creative expression is a cornerstone of the early childhood programs in Reggio Emilia, and educators from around the globe have visited there or have viewed their traveling exhibitions of children's artwork. The first question that this raises is, Why? What occurs in these programs that supports children's creative expression? Surely no one would argue that Italian children are innately more creative than other children! So what is the teaching philosophy, what is the curriculum, and what are the conditions that lead to such amazing work from young children? Review Figure 4.2, then read the description of the Reggio schools written by Frankie DeGeorge that follows.

Prior experience with art materials: Do children have access to materials and art tools? Is the range, supply, or quality of materials limited?

Cultural opportunities: Do children have the opportunity to see various types of art in their environment? For instance, do they visit studios or museums, examine different types of architecture, or appreciate the folk art traditions of their culture and other cultures?

Family discipline: How do parents react to the child's artistic efforts? Is a child severely punished for drawing on the wall, for instance? Are boys actively discouraged from artistic pursuits?

Visual skills, mental capacity, and motor coordination: What strengths and abilities does the child bring to the art activity? Can the activity be adapted to challenges or special strengths of the child?

Figure 4.2   Variables Affecting Children's Artistic Expression
Note: Based on Henkes (1989).

Observations on Reggio Schools
Frankie DeGeorge

The Reggio Emilia approach to early childhood involves a system of interrelationships among children, parents, teachers, and the environment. Central to the approach is the view of the child as an active seeker and builder of knowledge (Gandini, Hill, & Cadwell, 2005).

Children's interests determine what will be investigated, experienced, and interpreted. This display of interest can be initiated in various ways: by a book, a local happening, or a problem that presents itself within the group. Children's interest in these projects may last only a few days, be sustained over several weeks, or appear intermittently over a number of months.

The teachers play an important role in these projects—as inquirers to encourage thinking, as co-learners who construct knowledge along with the children, as projectors of the possible directions of a project, and as resources for equipment or experiences to support the children's initiatives. It is important to mention here the role of the atelierista, *or arts educator, who assists the children and the teachers in providing the appropriate art medium for the children's use in expressing and creating, thereby documenting their own work as the project unfolds.*

This idea of documentation is another essential element in the Reggio Emilia approach. It begins in the asili nido *(infant center) for children approximately 1 to 3 years of age. Each child has an album filled with photographs, teacher descriptions of events, developmental milestones, and children's scribbles. Seeing these albums gives visitors, and surely parents, an overwhelming sense of the respect and value that teachers have for children. Quotations from parents were seen over each crib in one center. They had been gathered from interviews and conversations with parents. These words, held to be so special by the teachers, conveyed this same feeling for the parents.*

Documentation for ages 3 to 5 involves the display of children's artwork, which remains at school. It comprises photographs, questions, and comments of the children as they investigate, experience, and create, all beautifully displayed on classroom walls. Seeing this documentation contributes to the children's understanding that their words and work are valued by the adults around them. This knowledge engenders a continued interest in creating and participating by the children. Indeed, this documentation has a positive effect on parents, who can see the whole scope of a project and their child's development through it. This knowledge fuels interest in their child's work and furthers parental participation in the school.

Displays of children's artwork and photograph panels also play an important part in the interior decor of Reggio Emilia schools. The children's artwork is displayed with all the attention and care given to the work of professional artists. Mobiles hang from the ceiling, translucent works are attached to glass, some works are framed on a wall-mounted light box, and many sculptures are neatly arranged on shelves. The effect is delightful.

The environments draw the children, as well as the adults, into a world of light, reflection, and involvement. Mirrors are seen everywhere—at entrances, along stairwells, under blocks, and particularly in the totally mirrored, small triangular houses where a child can see multiple reflections. All the schools visited included a large, tiled central square or piazza, where gatherings take place and special play centers are available. These areas were lovely with plants, artifacts, and equipment neatly and artistically arranged.

Each of the schools also provided a puppet stage frequently used by the municipal puppeteer, who entertains and intrigues the children with issues of reality versus fantasy— "It is and it isn't." This recurring theme is also played out in the dress-up centers where, to quote a teacher, "A child goes in one person and comes out another." A large shadow screen where children can create settings and dramatize is also provided.

Other materials found in the schools include blocks with many props, table games, comfortable book corners, housekeeping areas, water play activities, music rooms for listening and creating, and indoor climbing equipment.

The dining rooms were especially inviting with decorative items that added a home-like touch. Small tables were covered with cloths. Each table was graced with a centerpiece; at one school, it was an African violet, at others, children's creations.

In the art rooms varieties of paper, art supplies, and other materials were neatly stored on open shelves for everyone's use. The tops of the storage units held divided trays of bits and pieces, beads, seeds, buttons, sequins, and marvelous collections of items to be used creatively. Wire and other metal fencing materials were available for shaping and weaving. Also in supply were translucent papers for painting and transparent material for encasing three-dimensional works of art. One display of clay sculptures created by children showed adults, each holding a child in a different way. One adult held a child's hand, one carried a child on his back, one held a child in her arms, and one bounced a child on his extended leg. The pieces were individually designed, detailed, well proportioned, and expressed sensitivity to feelings.

The atelierista *(art teacher) explained that the children are encouraged to be attentive to the details of the object they are representing. The teachers may point out the shape, curve, or other specifics to the children. In addition, the children are given the opportunity to "revisit" their previous works in the same area and improve on them, since the work remains at school. This practice allows children to see mistakes or missed details as their knowledge of the subject matter improves and their project continues. Learning and creativity are purposely intertwined in the program. As this description suggests, creative expression and play are at the heart of practice in the exemplary schools of Reggio Emilia.*

Clearly, the early childhood program in Reggio places a high value on children's creativity. Their curriculum also suggests many ideas that will make the program in which you teach more successful, such as:

- Listening to children's ideas and respecting their thoughts by taking them seriously
- Observing children's work with various media and supporting them with gentle questions and positive comments
- Allowing children to think about projects over a long period and work on them for as long as they are interested
- Providing unhurried and unstructured time for children to work with art materials
- Enlarging the art area to include more materials and providing places for "works in progress" to be stored overnight or between work sessions
- Adding new and different media and recycled materials to your room often
- Sharing the talents of a staff person who is creative and loves art with the students (Moore, 2003, p.1).

Figure 4.3 highlights key principles of developmental theory and their implications for the child's growth in art. For additional information on children's development in art, visit the Arts Education Partnership Web site at www.aep-arts.org.

Principle 1: Children think about art in ways that are different from that of most adults.

Children have their own ways of thinking and representing their worlds (Gardner, 2000). When a typical adult judges a drawing, it is based on how much it "looks like" the original. Not so for the young child who uses drawing more like a language, as a way to organize thoughts and construct meaning (Goodenough, 1954; Kellogg, 1979). Young children draw patterns rather than events or objects; they do not approach art as many adults do—as mere decoration (Vygotsky, 1925).

Principle 2: Growth in art is indicated by sequential stages of development that cannot be forced.

It is foolish for adults to push children to draw in a particular way long before they are sufficiently mature to accomplish such tasks (Vygotsky, 1986). Illustrating this point, Lowenfeld and Brittain (1982) describe a study in which researchers attempted to teach nursery school children the task of copying a square. Despite "saturating" the children with square-making instruction, square-making ability did not improve. Furthermore, when the children who had been pressured to copy squares reached age 4, their skill level did not differ from that of peers without direct instruction. The ability to draw people and animals in a variety of poses develops slowly in the child (Vygotsky, 1925). For example, kindergartners often draw the body first, then draw the clothes, making the clothes appear "transparent." Elementary school-aged children draw people primarily from frontal view and find it challenging to depict a body in motion—jumping to play basketball, eating food, or walking the dog. Development in art centers on the representation of space and understanding of spatial-geometrical constructs (Kindler, 1997). For instance, children who have not yet reached Piaget's stage of concrete operations (age 7 to 11) find it difficult to consider the way objects look when viewed from different angles (Cox & Ralph, 1996; Li, 1996). This understanding of space can be observed in children's drawings of trees growing on a hillside, a chimney on a roof, or a path leading up to the front door of a building: in each case, a child who has not yet reached a level of spatial understanding will draw these objects perpendicular to the surface.

Principle 3: Children learn to express themselves through art by interacting with their environments.

Learning takes place in the context of what is known (Lowenfeld & Brittain, 1982). The brain assimilates new information only by understanding it in relation to information that it has already processed. The drawings of young children, for example, seldom have a baseline; rather, figures appear to float on the page. As children gain experience with representational drawing, however, their works begin to show the ground, often with grass or flowers or asphalt—whatever the child has experienced or can imagine. Most first-grade students are not cognitively or conceptually ready to deal with space in terms of linear perspective or to learn body proportion. It is more important that they spend time developing their own schema for the world that surrounds them, investigating and interpreting their environment. As the students begin to realize that their technical skills do not allow them to communicate their environment in the representational way that older children tend to prefer, it is then appropriate to provide instruction in linear perspective and human proportion.

(Continued)

Figure 4.3   Developmental Principles and Children's Art

Principle 4: With competent assistance, a child can reach a higher level in art development than what could be reached alone.

There is a middle ground between, at one extreme, leaving children entirely to their own devices and, at the other extreme, giving children a predetermined model to imitate. In art, that middle ground is Vygotsky's (1986) ZPD or zone of proximal development. It is the place where a teacher or more competent peer can provide assistance so that a child can move beyond the level that could be reached on her or his own (Gilbert, 1996). Vygotsky calls this support a "scaffold" and, like a house painter's scaffold, it provides the support needed to accomplish a task.

Figure 4.3   *(Continued)*

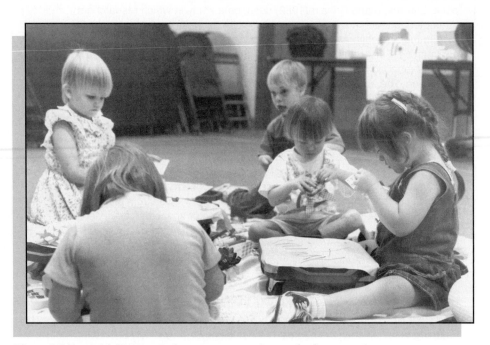

These children with Down syndrome are preparing crafts for a parade.

TEACHERS' REFLECTIONS ON ART

Preservice Teachers

"After we talked about children's art in class, I decided to use what I am learning to plan the activities for my volunteer work at the Community Center program. It was a theme that I had used with success before, during my student teaching. I started with Rowena Bennett's poem about the gingerbread man from the collection *Sing a Song of Popcorn* (White, Moore, DeRegniers, & Carr, 1988) prior to making gingerbread cookies. That part still seemed good, so I kept it. I used to make a pattern of a gingerbread person that I found in a book with decorations for them to color, cut out, and paste. But after taking this class, I decided to let the children create their own drawings and decorations. I was so impressed by what they produced on their own!"

Inservice Teachers

"Because I have been substitute teaching, I have done many of the things that were criticized in this chapter. Usually, I have to follow plans left by the teacher. Most of these activities result in exactly the same thing from each student, such as a Valentine's Day heart to trace. Now that I have my own class, I feel encouraged to break away from this."

"Teaching the fourth grade, I always felt that we have to focus on the core subjects. I never realized that art is really a core subject, too! I have begun to integrate the arts into my entire curriculum and I notice that, when the arts are included, children think more broadly and deeply. They are not just taking in information, they must synthesize it, evaluate it, and restructure it."

Your Reflections

*   What criteria can be used to differentiate between art activities and other types of classroom activities?

*   What contributions does art make to every child's overall development?

*   What concerns do you have about integrating art into your curriculum?

To observe ways to share children's artwork with families, watch the video "Families and Communities" online at MyEducationLab.

MyEducationLab

Go to MyEducationLab and select the topic "Family/Parent Involvement." Under Activities and Applications, watch the video Portfolio Exhibitions and complete the activity.

HOW CHILDREN LEARN THROUGH ART

Generally speaking, four types of learning are promoted through the arts. Figure 4.4 (p. 114) provides an overview of the four major types of learning (Katz, 1988) promoted through the arts.

Through art, children learn to do the following:

*   Observe carefully and record their observations
*   Organize ideas and express their feelings
*   Work with purpose and maintain a focus
*   Solve unstructured problems through trial and error
*   Respect themselves and their achievements
*   Communicate feelings and ideas with others
*   Express their own points of view while respecting others' points of view
*   Appreciate the contributions of different cultural groups
*   Create changes in their environments using a wide range of media
*   Make aesthetic discoveries and render evaluative judgments (Cohen & Gainer, 1995; Jalongo & Stamp, 1997).

Understanding children's artistic development, the role of art in promoting meaningful self-expression, and the basic principles of a high-quality art education is essential to a well-balanced curriculum. Skillful teachers have learned to use the arts not as an afterthought or add-on, but as a key to the elementary curriculum (Rasmussen, 1998).

1. **Knowledge about the arts** *is developed by:*
   - Sensory experiences and the exploration of materials.
   - Meeting real, live artists and watching them at work.
   - Thoughtful examination and discussion of works of art.

   What practitioners can do:

   Select high-quality art materials that children will want to return to again and again.

   Teach children to respect and care for art materials (e.g., cleaning up, proper storage).

   Use community resources to provide role models of craftspersonship.

   Use the library, the media center, the Internet, and museum-quality reprints and reproductions to stimulate children's thinking about art.

   Extend children's vocabulary by using descriptive words when talking about art.

2. **Skills in the arts** *are developed by:*
   - Experimenting with arts materials, tools, and processes in a low-risk environment.
   - Gentle guidance from others who have already acquired the skills.
   - Trial and error; making mistakes and learning from them.

   What practitioners can do:

   Provide a wide variety of high-quality art materials.

   Make time for art experiences every day.

   Experiment yourself with the materials that you provide for children.

   Emphasize the process that children use to create art products.

3. **Dispositions toward the arts** *are developed by:*
   - Interaction with role models—more competent peers, teachers, and professional artists.
   - Experiencing the arts alongside enthusiastic arts advocates.
   - Participating successfully in the arts.

   What practitioners can do:

   Encourage children to use their own imaginations and ideas in their work and to find their own ways of responding to lesson objectives.

   Teach children to be observant and aware of the visual arts in their surroundings.

   Invite children to select their best work and display artwork created by every child.

4. **Feelings about the arts** *are developed by:*
   - A sense of belonging to a community and feeling support from the group.
   - Opportunities to respond to works of art created by others.
   - The sense of efficacy that results when a child's artistic efforts evoke a positive response from others.

Figure 4.4   Four Types of Learning Promoted Through the Arts

Note: Based on Cohen & Gainer (1995), Jalongo & Stamp (1997), and State of Florida Department of State (1990).

> *What practitioners can do:*
>
> Teach children to respect the work created by peers.
>
> Model for children ways to respond thoughtfully to the works of professional artists.
>
> Invite children to consider why their work evoked particular responses from others.

Figure 4.4   *(Continued)*

✿ DEVELOPMENTAL SEQUENCE FOR CHILDREN'S ART

When we speak about art, we are talking about something that is perceptual, cognitive, developmental, graphic, and affected by the context and culture. Consider Figure 4.5, an original picture book by Vickie, a first grader whose mother is expecting a baby. Vickie's original picture book reminds us that:

> *Art is perceptual.* Artists of any age must be keenly aware of sensory input. It is clear from Vickie's story that she is aware of the changes in her mother's body.

Figure 4.5   Vickie's Book

Art is cognitive. When Vickie forms symbols, she must know the material (in this case, the media of paper and crayons), know the referent (in this case, the mother and baby), and use that material/medium to express something about that referent (in this case, original drawing and writing).

Art is developmental, meaning that as Vickie matures, her art will continually change along with her.

Art is graphic, meaning that she is learning the art techniques necessary to give form to her feelings, ideas, and experiences by her use of color, line, arrangement, proportion, and placement.

Art is affected by the context. Because the birth of a new child is celebrated as an important life event in her family, Vickie has chosen it as a worthy subject for her art. Figure 4.6 illustrates the stages in children's drawings from age 2 through 9.

Art-Making Activities

Art-making activities in the visual arts typically include such things as:

Painting, drawing, printmaking, collage

Sculpture, including mobiles, assemblages, and light

Photography, films, television, theater design, videography, and digital imagery

Crafts—ceramics, fiber arts, jewelry, metalwork, enameling; works in wood, paper, plastic, and other materials

Environmental arts—architecture, urban design, landscaping, interior design, product design, clothing design, and graphic communication in both personal and public environments

Technology—computer-generated graphics, multimedia design, and use of the Internet as a resource (National Art Education Association, 1999)

Infants and Toddlers

Developmental Profile: The child communicates directly through body movements, such as enjoying the medium of finger paint and observing the effects of different hand movements on the patterns on the paper. For the very young, visual artworks are more of a happening, more of an experience and an event than a means of communicating with others. An infant's attempt at drawing tends to be random. If the drawing implement makes contact with the paper, that is what is produced.

Typical Art Activities: Infants tend to engage in sensory experiences—touching, tasting, smelling, and mouthing objects. During early infancy, they begin to focus their gaze and then track objects with their eyes. Young infants have a definite preference for high-contrast pictures (such as black-and-white patterns) and the human face. During later infancy, they study objects intently and manipulate toys and objects that interest them. They frequently are fascinated by variation in what they see (a mobile over the crib, a blinking light). Toddlers begin to explore simple art materials in ways that do not demand high levels of manual dexterity, such as finger paints, play dough, scribbling with a fat crayon on paper, and so forth.

Figure 4.6　Developmental Sequence for the Making of Art
Note: Data from Feeney, Christensen, & Moravcik (1991).

NONREPRESENTATIONAL/SCRIBBLING STAGE

Approximate Age: 2 years
Art Skills: Explores media through all the senses
Makes random marks on paper
Begins scribbling

(Continued)

NONREPRESENTATIONAL/SCRIBBLING STAGE

Approximate Age: 3 years

Art Skills: Explores and manipulates materials   Scribbles are more controlled
Makes scribbles one on top of the other   May cover paper with layers of color
Process, not product, is important to child

Preschool and Kindergarten

Developmental Profile: The child begins to learn how to communicate through symbols and to use one thing to represent another. The drawings typically produced by 3-year-olds are **controlled scribbles**, because the child is better able to deliberately make marks on paper. Although a young preschooler's scribble in response to a cat may not look anything like a cat, that scribble might represent all of the child's sensory impressions of an experience with a cat—sandpapery tongue, beautiful fur, the sound of its purr, and its playfulness. The child may announce, "That's kitty," hence this stage is referred to as naming of scribbles. As control of drawing increases, typically developing 3- and 4-year-olds often begin to produce repeated small shapes, almost like geometric designs. By the time most children are in kindergarten, they recognize that art has the power to communicate. They often use artwork as a "narrative prop"—as a way of telling a story. Their drawings and play-dough creations begin to resemble the objects that they have in mind. This is referred to as **representational art**.

Typical Art Activities: Basic art materials and techniques are used, such as crayons and paper; finger paints and wet paper; large paintbrushes, tempera paints and easels; modeling dough or clay; white glue and wood; torn-paper constructions; simple collages; crayon rubbings of objects (leaves, shoe sole); painting with objects (for example, marbles dipped in paint and rolled around in a box on paper); learning to use scissors; and simple printmaking with Styrofoam shapes dipped in paint. At this stage, children learn to use crayons, scissors, paste, and paint to design, cut, arrange, and paste various items, such as child-made books, murals, simple masks, and replicas of objects (for example, a large cardboard box transformed into a house), and consider ways of displaying art.

Figure 4.6   *(Continued)*

NONREPRESENTATIONAL/SCRIBBLING STAGE

Approximate Age: 3–4 years
Art Skills: Scribbling stage continues
Perceives shapes in work
Attempts to make shapes
Often names scribbles

(Continued)

EMERGING REPRESENTATIONAL

Approximate Age: 4–5 years

Art Skills: Combines two shapes, often a circle and a cross, to make m andalas"
(sun shapes)

Represents humans as a circle with arms and legs, a "tadpole" person

Figures appear to float on the page

Art is used to represent feelings and ideas

Represents what has made an impression, rather than everything that is
seen or known

Figure 4.6 *(Continued)*

REPRESENTATIONAL

Approximate Age: 6–8 years

Art Skills: Child's art clearly resembles whatever it represents
Baseline begins to appear in drawings
More planning and inclusion of details
Child strives to master various art skills and begins to evaluate own work
Work tends to be more realistic in terms of proportion and arrangement

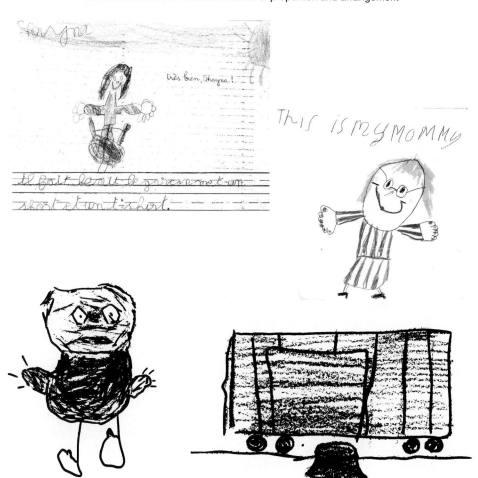

First Grade

Developmental Profile: The child becomes more confident as a symbol maker. With greater mastery of language, the child frequently chooses to weave symbols together (as when making a picture book).

Typical Art Activities: New and more involved techniques such as papier-mâché, paper weaving, and collage construction are introduced. Materials and techniques involving yarns, fabrics, and stencils are experienced. More sophisticated clay construction techniques (such as using coils of clay to construct items, or planning constructions that will stand and stay together) are used. Children create simple stitchery (for example, yarn and plastic needle on burlap) and puppets (such as rod and sock puppets).

(Continued)

Second and Third Grade
Developmental Profile: This stage corresponds to the industry-versus-inferiority stage of Erikson's psychosocial theory. The child seeks to build competence by undertaking a wide variety of art activities. Crafts such as toymaking, painting with acrylics, fashioning items from fabric, and making ceramic items or holiday decorative items are all common during this stage that Davis and Gardner (1992) refer to as "youth as craftsperson."
Typical Art Activities: Students learn more complex uses of art tools (for example, the clay sculpting tools used by artists). They develop more manual control and ability (as when exploring watercolors and fine brushes). Children begin to explore stitchery (by making a class quilt or a simple stuffed toy), create more elaborate props (such as by painting on fabric to create a scenery backdrop), investigate design problems (as in creating posters for an event), and explore multistep group projects that are fashioned to scale (such as using chicken wire and papier-mâché to construct a dinosaur).

Figure 4.6 *(Continued)*

 ## INTEGRATING THE ARTS

Arts integration is an intentional effort to build a set of relationships between learning in the arts and learning in the other subjects (Deasy, 2002; Stevenson & Deasy, 2005). When teachers integrate two or more subject areas, it is not only more efficient (that is, it avoids duplication) but also a better way for children to develop and demonstrate a depth of understanding (Burnaford, Brown, Doherty, & McLaughlin, 2007). Integrating the arts also offers children multiple ways to represent what they have learned; therefore, it enables teachers to do a better job of meeting the needs of diverse groups of learners (Kendrick & McKay, 2004; Merriman & Marazita, 2004). For example, students who are frustrated by typical school assignments often are motivated by tasks that enable them to use their strong visual and spatial intelligences. Claudia Cornett (2006) describes four different approaches to integrating the arts:

1. *Teaching with the arts*—combining the arts with other subjects in the curriculum (Althouse, Johnson, & Mitchell, 2003), such as literacy (Egan, 2006; Mantione & Smead, 2003; Narey, 2009).
2. *Teaching about the arts*—helping students to acquire knowledge about the arts, such as searching for shapes (Browne, 2003), going on a color-hunt using a spinner, or asking them to tell a painting's story (Eckhoff, 2008; Epstein & Trimis, 2002; Savva & Trimis, 2005).
3. *Teaching in the arts*—guiding children to develop the skills and strategies used by real artists, such as working with an artist in residence to learn technical terms, the proper use of artist's tools, and ways to plan/execute/evaluate a project (Heath & Wolf, 2005).
4. *Teaching through the arts*—using creative and artistic approaches to teach all curricula (Bamford, 2006), such as maintaining a journal in science (Brenneman & Louro, 2008).

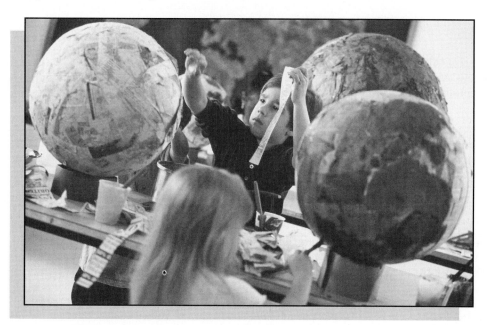

Effective teachers integrate the arts into other subject areas.

Table 4.2 gives an example of how the arts can be integrated into the various subject areas through the study of artifacts.

As you think about creating new interdisciplinary units or evaluating the ones planned by others, refer to the guidelines in Figure 4.7.

TABLE 4.2   Integrating the Curriculum: Studying Artifacts

What is an artifact?

An artifact is an object or symbol that was created by a human being to have meaning and value for a particular culture. A painting, a picture book, a piece of software, a DVD, a kitchen gadget—all of these items are artifacts. The artifacts that a particular society treasures are preserved and shared with successive generations as a way to "foster creative and innovative new ways for students to think about, understand, and represent their knowledge" (Zwirn & Graham, 2005, p. 53).

Why use artifacts?

When children study the artifacts created by others, they begin to see how they might contribute to society through their artistic efforts. Young children gradually learn that artifacts possess certain features that make them suitable for particular activities (Casler & Keleman, 2007). Take, for example, a picture book; a toddler may chew, walk on, or pound with a book until he or she recognizes the book's purpose (Zeece, 2008).

Why is the study of art and artifact particularly appropriate for children with special needs?

Artifacts are concrete objects so children can approach them at different levels. For instance, if a teacher is discussing the art produced by a well-known illustrator of picture books, some children can identify the topic of the work, others the action in the picture, still others the theme, or they can analyze how the style compares with other works by the same artist or different artists.

(Continued)

TABLE 4.2 Integrating the Curriculum: Studying Artifacts—*continued*

	COMMUNICATION Literacy, Language Arts, and Technology	THE SCIENCES Mathematics/Science	SOCIAL STUDIES Social Studies/ Health and Safety
Toddler Theme *Using Art Postcards*	Familiarize young children with works of art by creating a matching game of art postcards. Teach concepts such as under, over, beside, above, and below as children talk about pictures and real pets.	Children can identify and count pets in artwork, then visit a pet store to see the animals that were represented.	Familiarize children with a variety of images from various historical periods and cultures.
Preschooler Theme *Virtual Field Trips*	Utilize visually-rich literacy Web sites such as *Starfall.com* that provide auditory and visual avenues for children to experience language arts. Raise children's awareness of visual culture which includes the fine arts, folk traditions of art making, photography, commercial illustration, cinema and television, and computers (Duncum, 2002; Efland, 2004). For example, what are some of the different ways in which lions are portrayed in paintings, on DVDs, in African crafts, and in the media?	Children can go on a scavenger hunt for different categories of artwork (e.g., sculpture, painting, mask, architecture) and work in groups to produce posters with the images they've printed out from the computer. For an integrated unit on weather and light, see Fisher & McDonald, 2004. Address children's misconceptions in science through art and literacy via the "talking drawings strategy" (Fello, Paquette, & Jalongo, 2006/2007).	Take advantage of Web sites such as *national-geographic.com* that allow children to listen to stories, play games, etc., based on a variety of social studies topics. Jones (2005): "Study games around the world, such as cricket, soccer, rugby, red rover, double Dutch, and foursquare" (pp. 11–12). Link drawing, story, and social studies (Bloom & Hanny, 2006; Coufal & Coufal, 2002).
Primary Theme *Traveling Museums and Borrowed Artifacts*	Use picture books about art and online art collections to connect literacy with the visual arts (Hollander & Richwine, 2004; Justice, Pence, & Beckham, 2005; Kasten, Kristo, McClure, & Garthwait, 2004).	Children can observe specimens of organisms found in the natural environment, and record these observations through drawings: Then have children categorize drawings based on similar characteristics. Have the children use flashlights to individualize and heighten children's skills of observation (Cobb, Mallett, Pridmore, & Benford, 2007).	Invite a guest speaker, such as a person who collects antique kitchen gadgets, to share with the children. Use a children's museum's lending program to bring art into the classroom. Use books from the Adventures in Art and Architecture Series (http://www.prestel.com) to stimulate thinking about art.

TABLE 4.2 *Integrating the Curriculum: Studying Artifacts—continued*

	COMMUNICATION Literacy, Language Arts, and Technology	THE SCIENCES Mathematics/Science	SOCIAL STUDIES Social Studies/ Health and Safety
Intermediate Theme *Creating a Classroom Museum*	Create a classroom poetry museum. Create a picture of family heirloom museum. Have children write the story of each and interview family members. Go on a virtual field trip of a museum at de Grummond Children's Literature Collection, the Eric Carle Museum or the Mazza Museum.	Have students bring in a fossil, bird's nest, etc. from the outdoors to contribute to a classroom natural history museum. Discuss how the fossil was made, how the nest was made, etc. Visit classroom museums online (Hileman, 2008).	Have teachers borrow historical artifacts from lending museums. Host a "museum night," where children dress appropriately for that era and explain to parents what their artifact is, what time period it is from, etc. (Hileman, 2008).

Evaluation Questions for Curriculum

In this interdisciplinary unit of study,

_____ Are meaningful connections made between or among the disciplines?

_____ Is in-depth learning promoted?

_____ Are high quality examples from the arts and the other discipline(s) used?

_____ Is appropriate technology used?

_____ Are the artistic processes of creating, performing, and responding incorporated?

_____ Is the assessment ongoing throughout the project?

_____ Is there a final evaluation of student learning?

Evaluation Questions for School Personnel

In this educational setting,

_____ Is there planning time and ongoing professional development for teachers?

_____ Are sufficient resources available?

_____ Is the schedule sufficiently flexible?

_____ Is there administrative support and involvement?

Figure 4.7 Criteria for Evaluating Interdisciplinary Curriculum

Note: Data from Ulbricht (1998) and Consortium of National Arts Education Associations (2002).

✿ TEACHERS' ROLES AND RESPONSIBILITIES IN ART

Phyllis is a 5-year-old who has just started kindergarten. One day she comes home from school looking distraught. She bursts into tears, reaches into her pocket, and takes out a tissue with a broken crayon wrapped inside. It seems that the teacher had been especially harsh in cautioning children about taking care of school supplies and not breaking the crayons. Phyllis knew she had committed the unpardonable sin—"pressing too hard." To avoid punishment, she had resorted to concealing her "crime." Phyllis's experience illustrates how important it is for classroom teachers to understand their role in promoting the arts.

Emphasize Process As Well As Product. When children are required to color pictures neatly in designated areas, cut out predetermined shapes on the lines, paste them onto paper in some preordained way, and take the result home to decorate a refrigerator door, this is skipping over the process and rushing to a product. Activities such as these communicate the message that children's original artwork is inferior to that of adults.

Value Originality Rather Than Conformity. The very essence of art is to break, rather than perpetuate, stereotypes. Art is not coloring pages, following the dots, or painting by numbers; art is not a hand-traced turkey for Thanksgiving, a tree that looks like a lollipop, or a square-plus-triangle house. If it isn't original, it isn't art. After the classroom pet of a group of second graders in a church-affiliated school died, their teacher read Cynthia Rylant's *Dog Heaven* and each child created a drawing of what paradise might be like for the gentle spirit of the long-haired guinea pig named Fuzzy. Every drawing was different and the children combined their ideas to make a poster-sized image of "guinea pig heaven."

Allow Children to Retain Ownership. Children retain ownership of their artwork when they (1) choose their own ideas or subject matter, (2) have the freedom to express their ideas in their own way, and (3) have the right to organize their art in their own way (Jefferson, 1963). Children need the latitude to use many different art media. The goal is not to compete and make comparisons between and among children by using the teacher's model as the standard for all to follow. To see a child's orginal drawing look at the "Flying Baseball" online at MyEducationLab.

Develop the Child's Appreciation for Mixtures and Balances. Think about how different your life would be without the visual art of film. Now think about a favorite film that you have watched many times. What was it about the style of the film that captured your imagination? Are there other films by this same director that you also like? Answers to questions such as these illustrate the importance of a concept in aesthetics called mixtures and balances. Clearly, many films can be made, but it is the particular combination of ingredients and the interplay of those elements that creates a satisfying whole. Skillful mixtures and balances transform the ordinary and the mundane into a work of art. Working with mixtures and balances is something that children need to experience for themselves in order to respect it in others.

Provide a Safe and Healthy Environment. Teachers are often unaware of the potential hazards of art materials and activities. Figure 4.8 provides a checklist that you can use to assess your knowledge about safety issues in working with art materials.

MyEducationLab

Go to MyEducationLab and select the topic, "Early Literacy." Under Activities and Applications, view the artifact Flying Baseball. *As you look at the artifact, think about how it meets the criteria for art.*

The Environment	Yes	No
Is the area free of dirt, debris, and dust?	☐	☐
Is the floor clean and dry to avoid slipping and falling?	☐	☐
Is equipment arranged to avoid tripping, falling, and pulling items down (e.g., electrical cord taped to baseboard)?	☐	☐
Is ventilation (e.g., fresh air, open window, fan) adequate?	☐	☐
Is the lighting adequate?	☐	☐
Is protective gear (e.g., dust masks, plastic gloves, eye protection) in use?	☐	☐
Are safety rules posted (e.g., no running, no using art tools as weapons)?	☐	☐
Are emergency procedures posted and is the Poison Control Center number displayed?	☐	☐
Supplies and Storage		
Are the items to which children need independent access stored so that children can obtain them readily?	☐	☐
Are materials that require teacher supervision stored in a locked cabinet?	☐	☐
Health and Safety Practices		
Are health and safety considerations part of the planning of activities?	☐	☐
Are health and safety issues part of the explanation of activities to children?	☐	☐
Is there evidence that children have been taught safe and healthy practices (e.g., pictorial warning signs, a poster about washing hands)?	☐	☐
Are the art materials and equipment that children use maintained and inspected regularly?	☐	☐
Instructional Practices		
Does the teacher use good sense in selecting activities that are both age-appropriate and individually appropriate (e.g., "painting" with shaving cream is *not* appropriate for toddlers, who may attempt to taste it or accidentally rub their eyes)?	☐	☐
Are children taught the way to use tools properly?	☐	☐
Is the teacher aware of environmental toxins and their effects?	☐	☐
Does the teacher know about the ratings of art supplies (e.g., nontoxic, AP/Approved Product or CP/Certified Product of the Art and Craft Materials Institute) and avoid using inexpensive imported products that may be hazardous?	☐	☐
Are policies and procedures clear (e.g., handling scissors, distributing or collecting tools, no horseplay with art materials)?	☐	☐
Is the teacher aware of potential hazards due to ingestion, inhalation, or absorption through the skin?	☐	☐

(Continued)

Figure 4.8   Health and Safety Issues in Art: A Checklist

Note: Based on Qualley (1986) and National Safety Council, www.nsc.org/resources/Factsheets/ environment/indoor_air_quality.aspx.

	Yes	No
Special Needs		
Does the teacher have detailed information about which children have allergies, chemical sensitivities, respiratory problems, fine or large motor impairments, etc.?	☐	☐
Has the teacher carefully considered the characteristics of students, such as their manual dexterity or familiarity with the tools, when planning art activities?	☐	☐
Is there evidence of low-tech and high-tech adaptations that will enable young children with special needs to participate in art activities?	☐	☐
Teacher Knowledge		
Did you know that . . .		
Clay is 60% silica, and if clay dust becomes airborne, it can aggravate respiratory problems or even cause lung disease with prolonged exposure?	☐	☐
Powders and mixtures that are often used to make art materials (e.g., flour, cornstarch, plaster of paris) can be inhaled and precipitate an asthma attack in children with this disease?	☐	☐
Even if children do not deliberately eat art supplies, they can accidentally ingest them by touching their mouths, biting their fingernails, or putting an art tool in their mouths?	☐	☐
Food dyes once believed to be completely harmless are now considered carcinogenic (cancer-causing)?	☐	☐
Real clay, dug from the earth, can contain molds and bacteria that may trigger allergies or cause infections?	☐	☐
Children may rub their eyes and accidentally get dyes, paints, ink from markers, and other substances in their eyes, causing swelling and irritation?	☐	☐
The main ingredient in play dough and paste is wheat flour, and the main ingredient in white glue is milk. Therefore, if children with an allergy to wheat (celiac condition) or milk products (lactose intolerance) ingest these substances, they can become very ill?	☐	☐

Figure 4.8   *(Continued)*

Establish Rules and Limits.   Effective teachers should establish rules and limits that enable children to get the most from their art experiences. Figure 4.9 (p. 130) is a suggested list of classroom management considerations in art (Schirrmacher & Fox, 2008).

Select Appropriate Materials and Demonstrate Skills Effectively.   When children first begin using paints, a teacher might present the basic concepts of using protective clothing, putting the brush back in the same color, and cleaning up after painting. As they gain some experience, the teacher could present the strategy of wiping each side of the brush on the rim of the paint container to avoid drips and grasping the brush with the fingers (rather than the fist) above the metal rim, which increases the child's control over the brush. Next, the teacher could show children how to avoid smearing by letting one color dry before putting wet paint over or very close

---

1. Decide on a few important general rules rather than many insignificant specific rules.

2. Limit the number of children at a center at any one time. This avoids disputes over materials and accidental damage to a child's work caused by overcrowding.

3. Impress on children the need to wear protective clothing. Provide smocks, aprons, or simply a man's old shirt worn backward with sleeves rolled up.

4. Teach children how to use and care for art tools, such as rinsing paintbrushes, putting the lid on paste, and returning materials to their original location when finished.

5. Model for children the importance of conserving materials and using only what is needed. You could give them a dab of white glue on an old margarine tub lid, for example, rather than the whole bottle.

6. Teach children to share supplies and respect others. Model for children, asking rather than grabbing ("May I use the stapler next?" "Are you finished with the pink Play-Doh?"). Discuss with children the importance of accepting the art activities of other children.

7. Rather than simply announcing, "Time to clean up," demonstrate how children are supposed to clean up after each art activity.

Figure 4.9   Establishing Rules and Limits in Early Childhood Art Programs
Note: Data from Schirrmacher & Fox (2008).

to it, how to use different-sized brushes for different purposes (narrow/pointed for details, wide/flat for large areas), and how to rinse brushes in cool water and store them with bristles up. As children gain experience with paints in the primary grades, they can learn different brush strokes, learn how to sketch before they paint, or experiment with paints that are more difficult to control, such as watercolors.

Evaluate Materials and Experiences.   Walk down the hall of an elementary school, look at children's artwork, and you will notice a definite trend. In kindergarten and first grade, there is a freshness and spontaneity to children's work. Most kindergartners and first graders will tackle nearly any illustration challenge—a suspension bridge, a giraffe, or a trailer court. By second or third grade, however, many children have begun to trace and copy rather than create their own drawings.

You will know that your efforts to promote creativity through the arts are successful when:

- Children use and request specific art materials.
- Children confidently accept new challenges in art.
- Children pursue art activities during free time at home and at school.
- Children express positive attitudes toward art and artistic abilities during class discussions.

Responding Appropriately to Children's Art

Two-year-old Katie likes to curl up with Kirstie, a border collie, while she is looking at books, and the toddler produces a scribble that she names Kirstie. Young children do not separate their sensory impressions from one another. Katie's scribble might represent the softness of the animal's fur or the pleasurable feeling of being surrounded by warmth and closeness rather than the dog's appearance. The adult who remarks, "Very good, but what happened to the dog's tail?" or demands, "What is it?" fails to appreciate young children's early forms of artistic expression. Sometimes, children are not representing at all and are responding to the sensory pleasure of materials, such as the squish of modeling dough between their fingers or the glide of finger paint on wet paper. Even when they are attempting to represent an idea, children may interpret the task quite differently, such as the preschooler who drew "a scary house" by drawing a regular-looking house, but growling all the while (Davis & Gardner, 1992).

For all of these reasons, it is better to talk about artistic elements when discussing art with very young children. You could comment on color ("Look at all that yellow, Ishaka!"), on arrangement ("Lester, you covered the whole page with paint"), texture ("This clay feels smooth now that you rolled it out"), line ("I see the interesting patterns you made with the toothpick and paint on your paper, Claudia"), or shape and arrangement ("I noticed that you used circles and triangles!"). For older children who are creating representational art, it is best to follow the children's lead. You might begin by saying, "Tell me about your picture," and then follow the child's lead in the discussion. It is best to really notice what children are working to accomplish through art and remark on it rather than pass judgment on the quality of the work.

As you respond to children's artwork, keep the following guiding principles in mind:

- *Treat child artists and their work with respect.* Let children know that their work is valued by displaying it proudly, helping them transport it home safely, and finding something positive to say about their work (Rankin, 1995).
- *Emphasize feelings and responses.* Rather than treating art as an assembly task or an exercise in following directions, encourage children to explore emotions via the arts.
- *Suggest alternatives when children seem stalled or frustrated.* Ask questions that will help children to take a different approach or perspective rather than falling into a rut or quitting in frustration. Encourage children to persist when tasks are challenging rather than giving up when the way to proceed is not clear or obvious.
- *Help children sort out what is essential from what is unnecessary.* Teach them the skill of emphasizing what is most important in their creative products and help them understand that many times "less is more" and aesthetic experiences are improved by the elimination of extraneous details.
- *Guide children in doing their best.* Do not encourage or accept slapdash work. When it is clear that children did not produce their best work, try to find out why and give them an opportunity to revise and excel.
- *Recognize children's efforts.* Encourage self-evaluation and avoid a contest mentality. It is better to encourage all children than to single out a few for prizes (Cohen & Gainer, 1995).

Locating Resources and Storing Materials

Few teachers have the luxury of purchasing whatever art materials they please. More often, it is a matter of making choices among many possible alternatives. Materials such as paints, paper, crayons, clay, and wood are usually referred to as consumable because they need to be replenished constantly. When budgets are tight, the focus is often on nonconsumables, materials that need replacement less often.

Many times, adults are not particularly unhappy to see messy materials go. But these art materials are a basic means of self-expression and something that children should have access to every day. Rather than eliminating them altogether, teachers need to be creative problem solvers and seek out resources for art materials.

Use art materials that:

1. *Extend children's experience.* Figure 4.10 highlights ways that children's picture books can be used to extend the children's art experience. See also *Talking*

A story guide is a set of activities designed to accompany and extend a particular children's book. A good story guide integrates content areas and invites children to respond to the book in meaningful ways. Below are two story guides that emphasize the arts, play, creativity, and imagination.

Story Guide for *Tar Beach*

Book *Tar Beach,* by Faith Ringgold (1996)

Summary City apartment dwellers pretend that their apartment building roof is a beautiful beach. On their "tar beach," they have a picnic and enjoy one another's company. Then the narrator, a young African American girl, and her younger brother go on a flight of fancy through the neighborhood before returning safely home. Illustrations for the book come from a quilt created by the author.

Introduction Today we are going to hear a story about pretending. What are some make-believe games that you play? Look at the cover of this book by Faith Ringgold. It is about a girl and her brother who like to pretend. The pictures in this book are very special. Instead of drawing the pictures, Faith Ringgold sewed them. Then she put them all together into a quilt.

Questions

1. What are some things that you like to pretend?
2. Why did the people in the story pretend to have a beach?
3. If you could fly, what would you choose to fly over? Why?
4. Who would you choose to go with you?

Props A real quilt or a book of quilts with picture patterns.

Follow-Up

- Look at other books with unusual illustrations—the plasticine illustrations in *Have You Seen Birds?* by Joanne Oppenheim and Barbara Reid (1988); the collage in *The Snowy Day,* by Ezra Jack Keats (1962); or the moving parts in *The Wheels on the Bus,* by Paul O. Zelinsky (1990).
- Try sewing some pictures of your own with burlap, large plastic needles, and yarn.
- Look at a book or calendar or magazine pictures of prize-winning quilts. Take a survey on which quilt each member of the class likes best and why.
- Ask someone who makes quilts to visit the class and bring several quilts in different stages of completion.

(Continued)

Figure 4.10   Using Children's Picture Books to Develop Arts Awareness

- Read some other books about quilts that tell a story, such as Patricia Polacco's *The Keeping Quilt* (1988), Tony Johnston's *The Quilt Story* (1984), and Lauren Mills's *The Rag Coat* (1991).
- Read another book about another flight of fancy, such as *Abuela,* by Arthur Dorros (1991), or watch a video of Raymond Briggs's *The Snowman* (1978).
- Watch the movie *Peter Pan.* Then read *Amazing Grace,* a story by Mary Hoffman (1991) about an African American girl who wants to play Peter Pan in the school play.

Story Guide for *Seven Blind Mice*

Book *Seven Blind Mice,* by Ed Young (1992)

Summary In this variant of the Indian tale "The Blind Men and the Elephant," each mouse examines one small portion of the elephant's anatomy (ear, tusk, tail, etc.) and draws an incorrect conclusion about the total object. It is only after the seventh mouse examines the entire elephant and puts all of their observations together that they realize what the object really is!

Introduction Make a pair of old sunglasses into a blindfold by gluing black paper over the lenses. Let children wear the "blindfold" while attempting to guess what various objects are by touch alone.

Questions

1. Why were six of the mice wrong in their guesses about what the object was?
2. What did the last mouse do that was different from the other six mice? How did that help him make a good guess?
3. Did your eyes ever play a trick on you? Did you ever see one thing and think it was something else?

Props Create a large silhouette of an elephant and seven felt finger puppets or paper stick puppets of mice.

Follow-Up After you read the story, have children retell the story using the elephant silhouette and mouse puppets they have created.

- Create a "Guess What?" class book using children's drawings or photographs cut out from magazines. Cover each picture with a piece of cardstock and create small, numbered flaps to lift. Children should try to guess what is pictured by seeing only a small portion of the total picture. After guessing what the picture is, they can lift the entire sheet to see the total picture. Bind each child's page into a large class book.
- Try using bright acrylic paints on a black background to create some of the same effects that the artist used in the book.
- Read other stories with surprises, including *Boo! Who?* by Colin and Jacqui Hawkins (1984) or the *I Spy* picture riddle books series by Jean Marzollo.
- Look at several optical illusions. (Psychology books or reference books about vision are good sources.) Also look at some books that show how animals hide using various types of camouflage.

Figure 4.10 *(Continued)*

Exploring Art Media Through Picture Books

(Amann, 1993; Kiefer, 1995)

Watercolor Transparent paint mixed with water. It is usually painted on a white background, giving it a luminous quality.

Examples of watercolor illustrations from children's books

Sue Williams/Julie Vivas, *I Went Walking* (1992)

Uri Shulevitz, *Dawn* (1988)

Allen Say, *Grandfather's Journey* (1993)

Experiencing watercolor with children Teach children how to control the color intensity by the amount of water that they use to mix with the paints; teach them to rinse the brush out thoroughly when switching from one color to another.

Pastel chalk A stick of color made from powdered pigment in soft hues.

Examples of pastel chalk illustrations from picture books

Judith Hendershot/Thomas Allen, *In Coal Country* (1987)

Experiencing chalk with children Use sidewalk chalk to create a life-size board game, to draw a hopscotch board, to advertise an upcoming event in the classroom, to guide a walk around the playground, to draw oversized pictures, or to make giant scribbles.

Pen and ink Pigment (usually black) applied with a pen to paper (usually white).

Examples of pen-and-ink illustrations from picture books

Chris Van Allsburg, *Two Bad Ants* (1988)

Mercer Mayer, *Frog Goes to Dinner* (1977)

Experiencing pen and ink with children Give children white shelf paper or shirt or hosiery cardboard and an assortment of black ballpoint pens and black felt-tip pens so that they can create pictures in black and white; look at sketches done by artists in black and white.

Acrylic paints Pigments bound with vinyl that resemble oil paint but are faster drying.

Examples of acrylics from picture books

Donald Hall and Barbara Cooney, *Ox-cart Man* (1984)

Experiencing acrylics with children Visit an artist's studio or a display of art at a local bank, museum, or university. If you have access to some acrylics, allow the children to experiment with them on a small scale (these paints are rather expensive), but be sure to protect the children's clothing (these paints will not wash out).

Airbrush A mechanical tool used by commercial artists that looks like a pen. An airbrush takes a small amount of paint and sprays it very evenly on a surface using a small compressor.

Examples of airbrush techniques from picture books

Donald Crews, *Freight Train* (1978)

Leo and Diane Dillon, *Why Mosquitoes Buzz in People's Ears* (1983)

Experiencing an airbrush with children To see an airbrush in use, watch *A Video Visit with Donald Crews,* published by Trumpet Book Club. Invite a commercial artist to demonstrate the use of the airbrush and let children use it.

(Continued)

Try mixing thin tempera and using a pump spray (like the ones used for hairspray) to create outlines of shapes created by the children.

Collage The use of an assemblage or collection of materials and textures to create a picture.

Examples of collage illustrations from picture books

Eric Carle, *The Very Hungry Caterpillar* (1969)

Ezra Jack Keats, *The Snowy Day* (1962)

Experiencing collage with children Invite children to create books using collage illustrations; to create a collage that represents a feeling or characterizes a person; or to make a nature collage of leaves, seed pods, branches, dried flowers, etc.

Resist The technique of masking a surface so that it repels paint, dye, or ink. Batik uses this process with fabric.

Examples of batik illustrations from picture books

Roni Schotter and Marcia Sewall, *Captain Snap and the Children of Vinegar Lane* (1988)

Margaret Mahy and Patricia MacCarthy, *Seventeen Kings and Forty-Three Elephants* (1993)

Experiencing resist with children Use crayon resist and paste batik.

Linoleum or block prints A pattern or picture is cut into metal, wood, or linoleum so that raised lines and shapes are created. Then paint or ink is applied to the surface of the block and the pattern is printed on paper.

Examples of prints from picture books

Gail Haley, *A Story, A Story* (1988)

Ashley Wolff, *A Year of Birds* (1984)

Experiencing prints with children Use a cut-out piece of Styrofoam glued onto a block of Styrofoam to create a stamp, use a small screwdriver to create a shape on the Styrofoam, and make a print.

Photography The technique of using film to record a picture of something.

Examples of photography in picture books

Tana Hoban, *A Children's Zoo* (1985)

Dav Pilkey, *Dogzilla* (1993)

Experiencing photography with children Get children involved in using inexpensive, durable cameras to take pictures during a special event; ask children to bring in family snapshots.

Oil paint Paint that uses oil as a base for the pigment.

Examples of oil paintings in picture books

Hans Christian Andersen and Thomas Locker, *The Ugly Duckling* (1985)

Paul O. Zelinsky, *Rumpelstiltskin* (1986)

Experiencing oil paints with children Collect scraps of canvas board so that children can paint on the same surface that real artists use. Use a plastic lid from a small jar as a palette and place a small daub of various colored oil paints inside. Invite children to comment on the texture and rich colors oil paints produce.

Figure 4.10 *(Continued)*

Plasticine A modeling material similar to clay that does not harden when exposed to air.

Examples of plasticine in picture books

Joanne Oppenheim and Barbara Reid, *Have You Seen Birds?* (1988)

Barbara Reid, *Two by Two* (1993)

Experiencing plasticine with children Use various types of modeling material, including plastic clay. Invite children to study the illustrations and invent some pictures with bits of brightly colored clay.

Children's picture books about art experiences

Carle, E. (1992). *Draw me a star.* New York: Philomel.

Cohen, M. (1980). *No good in art.* New York: Greenwillow.

de Paola, T. (1988). *The art lesson.* New York: Putnam.

Lionni, L. (1991). *Matthew's dream.* New York: Knopf.

Rylant, C. (1988). *All I see.* New York: Orchard.

Velthuijs, M. (1992). *Crocodile's masterpiece.* New York: Farrar, Straus & Giroux.

Wolkstein, D. (1992). *Little mouse's painting.* New York: Morrow.

---

with Artists I and *Talking with Artists II* (Cummings, 1992, 1993) and, for older students, *Side by Side: Five Favorite Picture-Book Teams Go to Work* (Marcus, 2001).

2. *Are plentiful.* Recycling is a way to acquire an ample supply of free paper. Newspaper printers sometimes give away the ends of paper rolls, and wrapping paper from gifts can be saved by everyone in the class. For special papers, make contact with a printer that prints stationery and invitations or get in touch with a frame shop. Another way to achieve greater variety in classroom resources is to send home a list at the beginning of the year asking for such things as sewing and craft materials (buttons, trim, pieces of fabric, yarn, and ribbon) and throwaway materials that can be put to another use (plastic bottle caps, detergent bottles, food containers, six-pack holder rings, and foil canisters of various sizes).

3. *Are accessible.* It is important for children to use materials when they wish, rather than being completely dependent on adults for access to materials. Be alert to inexpensive alternatives. An old microwave cart, divided trays, or a lazy Susan can all help provide children access to many different materials, keep the materials organized, and make the collection more mobile.

4. *Are age-appropriate.* When a mother volunteered to work in her preschool son's Head Start classroom, both she and the teacher were surprised to see him take the paper off the easel and put it on newspaper on the floor to paint. Apparently, the child's only experience with painting was on a horizontal rather than a vertical surface. Gradually, the teacher was able to extend his experience to painting at an easel.

5. *Are of high quality.* Adults sometimes insist that children use crayons rather than markers, because markers are expensive and can easily be ruined by leaving the caps off or pressing too hard. But rather than avoiding markers, teachers need to demonstrate how to use and care for them.

Displaying Children's Art

Some general guidelines for displaying children's art include placing the work at children's eye level where they can enjoy it, rotating art regularly, and utilizing a variety of spaces—not just walls or bulletin boards, but also cardboard box panels, doors, windows, shelves, and display cases. Consider also how you will deal with works in progress as opposed to finished projects. Usually, the works in progress need to be placed where children can return to them again easily. A part of displaying children's art that is often neglected is the finishing touch, such as a frame for a picture. Frames for children's art can be colored paper, Styrofoam meat trays, plastic microwave food trays, plastic coffee can lids, or boxes and lids of every description. With older children, you may want to develop an art gallery of their framed art, tape-record children's descriptions of their art, or even make a walking-tour tape similar to that used in a museum.

Remember, displaying art is for everybody, not just the small percentage of children who might become professional artists someday. Rather than singling out only a few pieces of artwork to be displayed, teachers should recognize every child's efforts at self-expression. Rather than every child's work displayed on the same project, consider more of an art gallery approach in which children choose their best work. Children should be permitted to take their work home within a reasonable time period if they wish or to leave it on display at school. Teachers who care about children's art make sure that the paint is dry before rolling up the picture or, if the art is three-dimensional, plan a way for the child to transport the item home safely. Clean, recycled milk cartons with the tops cut off are good carriers for clay creations, for example.

Talking About Art

Children need a wide range of opportunities to look at art and talk about it (Burton, 2001; Isbell & Raines, 2006). Discussions about works of art with young children are effective when teachers consider the physical environment (e.g., position the work so that everyone can see it), select appropriate artworks (e.g., choose something that intrigues children, such as an antique toy), encourage a multiplicity of voices (e.g., invite everyone to comment), and provide closure to the discussion (e.g., "wrap up" with a comment such as, "We found all of the shapes we have learned in these paintings.") (Barrett, 2004). Figure 4.11 provides an overview of discussion strategies to be used in discussing works of art and art reproductions.

Developing a child's vocabulary of art involves three things:

1. *Encouraging children to discuss the artwork first in ordinary language.* If children discuss art in their own words first, it permits an equal sharing of adult and child perceptions. Five-year-old children who examined a large, colorful book of American artist Mary Cassatt's paintings made interesting observations such as "She must like little kids" and "The pictures look soft." By allowing children to make these observations first, the teacher can follow their lead, explaining briefly about the artist's life ("Deidra was right, Mary Cassatt did love little children. Sometimes she used her own family as models for her paintings"). Teachers might pose interesting challenges such as, "What could an artist do to lines to make the picture 'look soft,' like Harrold said? Let's try to make some pictures that way, pictures without dark lines, pictures that look softer."

2. *Introducing the vocabulary in context.* If children use new words in conjunction with direct experience, they are more likely to incorporate new words such as *texture, etching,* or *symmetry* into their vocabularies.

Types of Questions

Questions on aesthetics—Look at the lines on your paper. On the ceiling. Can you find other lines? Thin lines? Thick lines?

Questions on art criticism—Here are pictures of some famous buildings in the world. If you could choose one to be built in our town, which one would it be? Why?

Questions about art history—Which of these sculptures was made a long time ago? Why do you think so?

Questions on art production—What are some ways artists can make their pictures look smooth? Rough?

1. *Who made it?*

Situation: Looking at a UNICEF calendar of children's artwork.

Question: "Do you think these drawings were made by adults or children? What are you seeing right now that can give you a clue?"

2. *How was it made?*

Situation: Looking at a large metal sculpture

Question: "Does anyone know how pieces of metal are joined together?"

3. *When was it made?*

Situation: Looking at an ancient piece of sculpture

Question: "If you look at this carefully, you will notice that some of the pieces are broken off. Do you think this sculpture is new or old? Why?"

4. *For whom was it made?*

Situation: Looking at a wooden toy

Question: "One of my neighbors makes toys out of wood like the ones I brought today for you to play with. Who do you think he makes the toys for?"

5. *What is the message or meaning, if any?*

Situation: Looking at a heritage quilt

Question: "Do you know anyone who makes their clothes by sewing them instead of buying them already made at the store? The owner of this quilt said that her great-grandmother made it from scraps of fabric that were left over from the sewing she did for her family. Why would their grandmother do all of this work to make a quilt?"

6. *What is its style?*

Situation: Looking at the art in picture book illustrations

Question: "On this table, we have several books written and illustrated by the same person. These three are by Rosemary Wells, these by Keith Baker, these by Jerry Pinkney, and these by Diane Goode. What can you say that explains what each artist's work is like? How are these drawings by Rosemary Wells alike? How are they different from all the others?"

7. *What is the quality of experience it affords?*

Situation: After viewing a film

Question: "You all know the book *Frog Goes to Dinner* by Mercer Mayer (1975). Which did you like better, the movie or the book?"

(Continued)

Figure 4.11 Questions About a Work of Art

Note: Data from Althouse, Johnson, & Mitchell (2003); Amann (1993); Barrett (2004); Heberholz (1974); Jalongo & Stamp (1997); and Rowe (1987).

8. *What was its place in the culture in which it was made?*

Situation: Watching a Navajo sand painter at work from the video on sight by Diane Ackerman from the PBS series *Mystery of the Senses*

Question: "Were you surprised to see that someone could paint with sand? Why are these sand paintings made?"

9. *What is its place in the culture or society of today?*

Situation: Visit to an art museum

Question: "How do you decide which of your art projects or paintings to keep and which ones to throw away? One of the people we will be meeting has a special job in taking care of these paintings. The paintings need to be cleaned, and sometimes they need to be fixed. Can you think of some reasons why people think these paintings are important enough to keep?"

10. *What peculiar problems does it present to understanding and appreciation?*

Situation: Looking at an art print that uses pointillism

Question: "Some of you were wondering why this picture looks so different close up than it does from a distance. If you look very closely, you will see that the picture is made up of hundreds of dots. Did any of you ever experiment with dots as a way to make pictures? When you work at the computer to make a picture, the computer actually makes the dots for you. Use this magnifying glass to look at one of the pictures you made last week. Now look at this piece of a newspaper. You can see that the print is made of dots too."

Additional Questions about a Work of Art

What is this work of art?

What is it made from?

What is the most interesting thing about this work of art?

Is there a story here? What is it?

What is the artist trying to tell us?

Does the artist suggest new ways of seeing things?

How does the work make you feel? Why?

What does it make you think of?

What did the artist use (medium, techniques, tools, ways of organization, effects, composition)?

How is this the same (or different) from other pieces you have seen by this artist? By other artists?

What makes a work of art great?

What makes an artist great?

Do you like this work of art? Why or why not?

Sources for Art and Art Reproductions

Children's picture books, prints of famous works of art borrowed from the library, picture postcards of art, walls of a local gallery, an artist's studio, a display of

Figure 4.11 *(Continued)*

children's work at a public building, a museum exhibit, a university, slides, art history books, encyclopedias, film. Specific sources include:

Full-size (approximately 22" × 28")

Metropolitan Museum of Art
New York, NY 10028

Modern Learning Press
P.O. Box 9067
Cambridge, MA 02139-9067
(800) 627-5867

Miniature (such as postcard size)

Art Visuals
P.O. Box 925
Orem, UT 84059

Parent Child Press
P.O. Box 675
Hollidaysburg, PA 16648

University Prints
21 East Street
Winchester, MA 02138

3. *Using accurate, appropriate vocabulary.* Teachers need to provide new vocabulary words readily and unobtrusively so that they underscore the child's experience. Building a vocabulary of art is important because it enables children to participate in the world of art both in and out of school throughout their lives.

To view an artifact that a child produced, look at "Joy Fund" online at MyEducationLab.

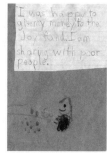

MyEducationLab

Go to MyEducationLab and select the topic "Family/Parent Involvement." Under Activities and Applications, view the artifact Joy Fund.
As you look at the artifact, think about conferencing with a student.

CURRICULUM ACCOMMODATIONS FOR DIVERSE LEARNERS IN ART

In order to make art accessible to all children, teachers need to make appropriate adaptations for students with special needs. The visual arts are another language for communication. For young children in particular, drawing and other means of visual expression are equally, if not more, important than written communication. Through interactive experiences with the arts, children engage in the learning processes of exploring ideas, creating meaning, constructing knowledge, and communicating concepts, thoughts, and feelings (Varnon, 1997, p. 325). The arts are a major way of meeting needs of diverse learners (Jones, 2005).

Tips for Art in an Inclusive Classroom

- Teachers need to have a clear idea of what constitutes good standards in art, and to have high expectations for all children; these should be communicated through instruction, discussion, and the display of art in school. See www.ket.org/arttoheart for many excellent art activities.
- Think the 4Es: enable, empower, engage, extend (Hermon & Prentice, 2003). *Enable* refers to the child's entitlement and access to the curriculum and achievement; *empower* refers to the child's autonomy and self-esteem; *engage* means involvement in the learning contexts and activities; and *extend* means to "stretch" and go beyond current levels of knowledge, understanding, and skill.
- Realize that art is an especially important means of communication for the young English language learner (Meier, 2004). The realism of

photographs can be particularly useful in teaching concepts (see Geyer & Geyer, 2005).

- Build children's ability to make informed judgments about art through discussion of various artifacts—not only paintings but also architecture, sculpture, textiles, and so forth.
- Demonstrate your appreciation of children's artwork by creating displays with simple, one-color backgrounds (to allow children's artwork to stand out), and arrange the materials in a way that is attractive and draws children's attention to them throughout the school and community. Consider displays in hallways, near offices, on bulletin boards, at the mall, in a doctor's office, or at local stores.
- When making art displays, keep them neat and contained in their own designated spaces. Allow children to make choices of which work they would like to display and ask them to include a simple label, title, or headline to explain the focus of the display. Display work by every child, but not every child's work in every display. Encourage children to help create and change displays (Moore, 2003).
- Send artwork home regularly or place it in portfolios periodically to decrease clutter.
- A social worker reported that, every year, many of the children in the shelter for homeless and abused women requested art kits as Christmas presents. Support families with limited access to or financial resources for art materials by identifying durable, inexpensive containers (e.g., a small plastic suitcase or box with a secure lid) and equipping them with art materials. Include suggestions on projects that children can complete independently and ask the children to bring their work to school to share (see Hutinger, 1997).

Specific Suggestions
Students with Emotional and Intellectual Challenges
- Assign children to work together on various projects—construct something using bits of wood, mat board, cardboard; create a mural, working with an artist-in-residence. Group projects encourage children with attentional difficulties to focus and persist at tasks.
- Consider assigning roles matching the children's strengths that "nudge" them to take on a new challenge. For example, if students are making a diorama or display, a child with autism might be assigned to conduct the research, a child with mental retardation might work on cutting out the pieces for the display, and a child with attentional difficulties might be given the challenge of managing the group.
- Realize that children with autism tend to experience things in the present and in a concrete rather than imagined way. The child with autism may reject attempts to communicate on a verbal level or be disturbed by the physical presence of others (Osborne, 2003); therefore, it is important to provide quiet areas, established routines, and concrete instructions. Coach the child on dealing with frustration productively and build on small successes.
- Teach children with emotional and intellectual challenges to discuss the art of picture books using a five-step sequence that develops their language and reading skills. The steps are to identify: (1) the person, (2) the objects, (3) the person with the objects, (4) the action, and (5) the sequence of the action (Alberto & Frederick, 2000).

- Work with an art specialist to have teams of older students (or teams that include a gifted student) write, illustrate, and share picture books for and with younger students (Jones & Ross, 2005). "Fractured" fairy tales can be an interesting picture book project for teams or groups of older students (Holder & Pearle, 2005).

Students with Visual Impairments

- Get in the habit of identifying yourself, letting the child know you are talking to him or her, and announcing when you are walking away (Pappalardo, 1990). Make available lots of modeling materials with different textures and smells such as clay or homemade dough.
- Use art materials that work to children's strengths, such as scented markers for drawing, "big paper" for large movements of the hands and arms, finger paint (bought or homemade). For instance, children with visual impairments can be part of a group that is creating a giant tree for the fall or spring. It begins with a large trunk and branches constructed of brown craft paper. Some of the children can cut out or tear leaf shapes, others can overlap them on the branches.
- Teach children simple weaving with paper strips, yarn, or raffia. Consider equipment such as the Easy Weaver that enables children to complete more sophisticated weaving projects.
- Include sculpture so that children can feel the contours and participate in the discussion. Try using favorite stuffed toys for a contour drawing experience (Crumpecker, 2004) or have children make their own stuffed toys using silhouette shapes and working with a volunteer who can stitch the fabric for them using a portable sewing machine.
- Try crafts that rely more on touch than on vision—such as supersize stringing beads (Young, 2006) or using the different types of paper punches used in scrapbooking to create interesting arrangements.
- Share a picture book such as Liao's (2006) *The Sound of Colors: A Journey of the Imagination* to help other children understand blindness.

Students with Hearing Impairments

- Realize that art is a major means of expression for children with hearing impairments (Coufal & Coufal, 2002). Keep background noise low because hearing aids amplify everything, including background noise (Doctoroff, 2001). Provide ample lighting in settings, as visual cues are important for children who are hard of hearing (Doctoroff, 2001).
- In the Japanese tradition, create a classroom space called a "beauty area" where interesting and lovely items from nature are displayed (e.g., in the spring, display pussy willows, a forsythia spray, daffodils, tulips, milkweed, a small branch from a fruit tree).
- Have children with hearing loss caption their drawings with written words or, if the child has an aide, have them sign their captions with the aide translating.
- Explore story making software, such as Dream Weaver, as a way for children with hearing impairments to produce and share original storybooks.
- Give them an opportunity to respond to works of visual art through gesture and drawing.
- Partner them with a hearing child to work with printed lists or a word wall of rhyming words and then draw pictures of pairs of things that rhyme or construct a mobile out of pictures of words that rhyme.

- Help children to analyze how packaging is used to make food items more appealing. Bring in empty junk food packages to analyze how they invite people to purchase them and then have children work in groups to invent a package for a fruit or vegetable that would encourage people to purchase it.

Students with Orthopedic Impairments

- Keep access to work areas clear of obstacles; allow ample space for wheelchairs, walkers, etc. (Doctoroff, 2001). Get tables with a semicircular cutout to accommodate orthopedic equipment and tray tables for wheelchairs with rims that prevent dropping of art materials.
- Think of ways to control the movement of materials. Secure, or remove materials that can be knocked over (i.e., paint) in the workspace of a child who cannot control movements (e.g., cerebral palsy) (Doctoroff, 2001). Place art paper inside a box, to limit the extent of the artwork (Gould & Sullivan, 2004). Place art paper in a box, on a wall, to limit or control the movement necessary for a child to draw/paint (Gould & Sullivan, 2004).
- Explore adapted art materials, for example: extra large crayons that are triangular shaped or flat on one side to minimize rolling; oversized colored pencils and chalk that are easier to grip, or adaptive grip paintbrushes (e.g., with egg-shaped handles that are flat on one side, with rubber grips to reduce slippage, with shaving brush-type handles). For large posters and murals, look into equipment such as paint poles and paint rollers (see http://www.zotartz.com/).
- Try projects that require less fine motor skill, such as a cut/ripped paper collage. Use adapted scissors with oversized handles, with springs to keep them in the open position when not cutting, with long looped handles that can be operated by thumb and the remaining fingers, or with double loops (Johnson, 2008).
- If a child has muscular atrophy, has limited mobility, is confined to a wheelchair, and the needs help swallowing and breathing, the child might be able to comment on art using a voice output communication aid (VOCA) (Hennebery, Soto, & Yu, 2007).
- If a child lacks the motor coordination to draw with hands, the child might be able to use assistive technology, such as Eyedraw. This software program, when run on a computer with an eye tracking device, enables children with severe motor disabilities to draw pictures by just moving their eyes.

For more ideas on adaptations, see: Art Express, 2002; Art Ideas for Special Artists, 2008; National Institute of Arts and Disabilities; Start with the Arts; Teaching Special Kids: On-Line Resources for Teachers, 2008; Gould & Sullivan, 2004; Vize, 2005.

MEETING STANDARDS

Interdisciplinary Curriculum and Key Experiences in the Arts

The National Art Education Association (1999) has identified nine key opportunities that teachers should provide to students through art.

1. **Examining extensively both natural and human-made objects from many sources.**

A group of second graders has been examining both real items and representations of things. During their unit on animals, the teacher shared books about elephants and invited a collector to share her assortment of elephants. Included in the collection were ceramic, wood, metal, plastic, and fabric elephants. The children saw a hand-carved wooden elephant from India, a stuffed toy, and a green elephant sculpted from malachite. The children were able to examine these objects closely and compare/contrast them with photographs and drawings. Afterward, the elephant items were on display so that children could vote for their favorites and give a reason for each choice that was written on a sentence strip and placed next to each one. During math class, the children learned how to make a simple bar graph that summarized their choices by using self-stick notes labeled with their names arranged next to a digital photo of each item.

2. **Expressing individual perceptions, ideas, and feelings through a variety of art media suited to the manipulative abilities and expressive needs of the student.**

The drawings of young children frequently focus on "I" and "my" experiences. ("I am eating a Popsicle." "I am jumping in a puddle." "My toy is broken.") As children move into the primary grades, it is helpful to provide new challenges such as "jumping rope with my friends," "lying on the grass and looking at the clouds," or "the day we got caught in a thunderstorm." Asking directed questions such as, "How does the grass feel? Soft? Tickly? Prickly? How can we show that in your picture (or sculpture)? What happens when it storms? Is it windy? Can you see the wind? How can you show that the wind is blowing hard in your artwork?" will help children learn to select the most effective media to communicate their ideas.

3. **Experimenting with art materials and processes to understand their potentials for personal expression.**

Demonstrations of how to use art materials—paint, finger paint, clay, and so forth—can be followed by student experimentation with the material. Students can also work with different implements (thin and thick markers, chalk and crayons, bingo markers, colored pencils) on paper of different sizes (3-by-3-inch squares, long narrow strips, large rolls of paper) or paper with different surfaces (construction paper, corrugated paper, sandpaper). At first, children may seem as if they are reverting to an earlier stage of development as they just "try out" the medium. A child who is drawing representationally, for instance, might make scribbles with the new medium as a way of exploring it. The teacher's main role is to relate the new materials and processes to the child's expressive needs. If, for instance, a child is fortunate to have 166 different colors of crayons at home and just 16 colors at school and is disappointed to see that the color he uses for his hair is not available, the teacher might suggest some color-mixing experiments.

4. **Working with tools appropriate to the students' abilities to develop manipulative skills needed for satisfying aesthetic expression.**

Beginning teachers are sometimes surprised to encounter preschoolers who do not know how to cut with scissors. Figure 4.12 is a developmental sequence for learning to use scissors.

Question: At what age do children typically know how to use scissors? When you teach a skill, begin with a task analysis and break the task down into simple steps (Schirrmacher & Fox, 2008). Arrange the list below in a developmental sequence and designate the approximate age at which you might expect this behavior. Across all of the ages, accommodations can be made through the use of adapted scissors with oversized handles, with springs to keep them in the open position when not cutting, with long looped handles that can be operated by thumb and all of the remaining fingers, or with double loops so that teachers can assist the child with a physical disability (Johnson, 2008).

- Use projects that do not require scissors at all, such as a cut/ripped paper collage.

- Teach the child how to hold the scissors. Then teach the child how to move fingers to make the cutting motion. Try rolling play dough thin and have the child take "bites" of it with scissors.

- Demonstrate how to cut through half-inch-wide strips of stiff construction paper (cheaper paper often bends in the blades and does not result in a successful cut, which can frustrate the child). Show them how to rest the scissors on the desk to steady them.

- Practice making multiple cuts ("fringe") along the sides of a small sheet of paper (approximately 3 by 6 inches).

- Have children cut along a straight line from one edge of a small rectangle of paper to the other. The child can be shown how to make a cut and then open the scissors without removing them from the cut to take another "bite."

- Teach the child to cut around contours or other, more intricate shapes.

- Teach children how to cut out small interior spaces such as the eyeholes for a mask or to control their scissor cutting to make lift-the-flap books or "windows" with hinged shutters on each side that open and close.

- Have the children experiment with special equipment and materials, such as using pinking shears on fabric. This is more difficult because the scissors must be kept at a right angle to the fabric in order to function properly.

Figure 4.12   A Developmental Sequence for Learning to Use Scissors
Note: Data from Schirrmacher & Fox (2008).

5. **Organizing, evaluating, and reorganizing works in progress to gain an understanding of the formal structuring and expressive potential of line, form, color, and texture in space.**

One teacher invited women from the senior center to talk with the children. Before they arrived, he shared the picture book *The Seasons Sewn: A Year in Patchwork* (Paul, 2000) and drew the children's attention to classic quilt patterns and their names through a matching game made from the pictures of a calendar. On the first visit, the ladies developed the concept that a quilt can tell a story. They also brought several completed quilts and shared examples in quilt pattern books. Next, the ladies shared their plans and pattern for the quilt and gave each child a small scrap of fabric to keep. The students read several picture books about quilts—*The Quilt* (Jonas, 1989b), *Quilt Story* (Johnston, 1984), and *The Patchwork Quilt* (Flournoy, 1985)—and watched excerpts from a movie about quilting borrowed from the library. On the second visit, the ladies demonstrated how a quilt is put together. The children learned about stitching, appliqués, polyester fiberfill, and a quilting frame. On the third visit, a portion of the quilt was finished and a piece was added while the children observed, and on the last visit, the quilt was finished.

6. **Reading about, looking at, and discussing works of art and design from contemporary and past cultures using a variety of educational media and community resources.**

7. **Seeing artists and designers at work in their studios and in the classroom through the use of technology.**

A kindergarten teacher included fine art in a unit on shapes and colors. The children searched for circles in Vincent van Gogh's painting *Starry Night,* and afterward, one mother reported that her daughter commented that the bubbles in her bath water looked like the circles in van Gogh's painting. Meanwhile, a group of first graders searched for triangles in Winslow Homer's *Croquet Scene.* Their work with shapes is more challenging because they have to identify some "hidden" triangles—in background space, in negative space, or in the "dot to dot" arrangement of the players' heads. At this same school, the fourth graders are studying the style of Japanese artist Hokusai (Ray, 2001; http://www.prestel.com) and making a list of characteristics that define his style. Their teacher uses Mike Venezia's series *Getting to Know the World's Greatest Artists* and the *Smart about Art* series to expand students' understanding of style and to familiarize them with artists such as Edgar Degas (Cocca-Leffler, 2001), Claude Monet (Kelley, 2001), Jackson Pollock (Greenberg & Jordan, 2002), Leonardo da Vinci (Stanley, 1996), Benjamin West (Brenner, 2003), and Andy Warhol (Warhola, 2003).

8. **Evaluating art of both students and mature artists, industrial products, and home and community design.**

As part of a unit on consumer education, a group of fourth graders decided to compare/contrast the features of three comparable pieces of computer software. The students established a rating sheet for the product, tried each program, compiled their data and then, using published software reviews as a guide, wrote a critique for each. In this way, children gained firsthand experience in the evaluation of industrial/technical products.

9. **Engaging in activities that provide opportunities to apply art knowledge and aesthetic judgment to personal life, the home, and the workplace.**

Aesthetic judgment is a process that develops over time. Therefore, it is important to teach children to observe closely and consider what makes an object beautiful and worthy of appreciation. One third-grade teacher involved her students in re-organizing their classroom space. She used the room arrangement grid and shapes in a school furniture catalog; the children experimented with many different room arrangements by shifting the items around at the overhead projector until they decided on the best classroom layout.

 ## CONCLUSION

The personal inclinations developed by the arts include such things as learning to play with images, ideas, and feelings, recognizing and constructing the multiple meanings of events, and perceiving things from various perspectives (Eisner,

Frequently Asked Questions About Art in the Curriculum

How will I know if an activity truly is art?

The three most common errors in teaching art are as follows: (1) advocating formulas and requiring conformity, (2) mistaking lack of guidance for freedom, and (3) unduly emphasizing copying and neatness (Gaitskell, Hurwitz, & Day, 1982). Surprisingly many, if not most, of the "art" activities that adults do with young children are not art at all (Szyba, 1999). More often than not, they are exercises in following directions.

Shouldn't art be left to unfold naturally?

Like any other ability, creativity needs active encouragement, gentle guidance, and appropriate instruction in techniques. Too often, a belief in natural unfolding leads teachers to see themselves as distributors of art materials. Children need to be apprenticed into understanding the repertoire of skills necessary to attain excellence and be given the opportunity to practice those skills alongside helpful, observant professionals and peers.

How can teachers recognize children's gifts in the arts?

Research on young gifted children suggests that they may (a) strive for realistic portrayals, many details, and complete accuracy in what they represent, (b) become intensely interested in particular topics not routinely of interest to peers (such as meteors or sea creatures), (c) go beyond what is immediately observable and explore the subject in greater depth (for example, making a cross-section drawing of the *Titanic*), (d) display exceptional sensitivity to emotion and ways of expressing it (for example, choosing to explore the subtleties and complexities of humor), or (e) produce works of visual art that display types of perception not commonly found in young children's work (such as light and shade or near/far perspective) and that require advanced development in the physical domain (Harrison, 1999).

How can work in the visual arts support the goals of multicultural education?

In order for all children to flourish as artists, they must communicate about a wide range of artistic styles and forms, see those styles and forms accepted by others, freely experiment with art media, and learn to accept one another's art. Art offers a way of communicating and accepting other cultures. Mexican piñatas, Navajo pottery, and Ukrainian decorated eggs each give children insight into the history, values, and aesthetic sensibilities of others. The newly immigrated child who is an English-language learner can express ideas, thoughts, and feelings nonverbally through paper, sculpture, pottery, and fabric.

How important are the materials in art?

All children need the challenge and excitement of working with new art media. It is thrilling to draw with brand-new, sharply pointed, soft-leaded colored pencils or to draw and color a picture with watercolor markers that include unusual colors such as silver or gold. Unusual papers are appealing too. Paper that is heavy, embossed, glossy, or foil, such as that used in greeting cards and wrapping paper, often can be recycled for a lasting supply of high-quality material. Many children do not have access to art materials (other than crayons and paper) at home. Materials such as oil pastels, colored chalk, washable acrylic paints, and clay are generally unavailable because parents cannot afford them, do not recognize their value, or are concerned about the mess. Even fewer children have access at home to artist's tools such as an easel, woodworking tools, or crafts materials. Consider supplying some of the real tools used by artists, demonstrating how they are used, and making them available to children.

How do children connect the symbol system of art with the symbols of language?

Children ages 5 to 9 tend to use drawings as objects to label, as catalysts for generating ideas, as ways of making the abstract concrete, and as aids to their thinking (DuCharme, 1991). Many young children who draw representationally use narrative art, pictures that tell a story. Sometimes their storytelling depends entirely on the pictures; sometimes the pictures are combined with captions. Five-year-old Isabell explained the advantage of drawing over writing this way: "I'll draw you what I would write, but drawing is funner." Even before children are writing alphabetically, teachers can develop the concept of pictures accompanied by print—squiggles, letterlike forms, or letters and numbers that the child happens to know.

2003). Yet studies show that, while teachers believe that task persistence and creative problem solving are important lessons in the arts, they seldom make children aware of these purposes. When this occurs, children assume that their art is "just for fun" and that the only "real" purpose for art in the lives of adults is fame and fortune. Both assumptions are damaging to promoting the arts in society because they teach children that their art does not count and that appreciating art is for the wealthy while creating art is for eccentrics or tortured souls. It is essential to help children to see *themselves* as artists. This demands that teachers continually address three fundamental questions: Who do we teach? (the needs of the learner), Why do we teach? (the goals of society), and What do we teach? (identifying appropriate subject matter, skills, and processes) (Hicks, 2001; Katz, 1988; Stankiewicz, 2000; Walling, 2001). It will not be enough to follow the path of many of our predecessors in the field of early childhood because, all too often, art has been treated as a second-class subject. "A picture may be worth a thousand words, but these words can remain unsaid or misunderstood when adults do not attend to their development. Beyond fostering the artistic development of the young children we work with through media and processes, we must also guide children's aesthetic development—verbal and visual literacy—in the aesthetic domain. Otherwise, their art may be misinterpreted or neglected and the young artists' meanings never communicated" (Althouse, Johnson, & Mitchell, 2003, p. 79).

 ## CHAPTER SUMMARY

1. In order for a classroom activity to qualify as art, it must value process as well as product, emphasize originality rather than conformity, allow children to retain ownership of their work, and develop an appreciation of mixtures and balances.
2. Understanding children's art depends on an appreciation of the child as artist, knowledge of the developmental sequence in children's art, an understanding of the principles of art education, and a recognition of the many contributions art makes to children's overall development.
3. In a quality art program, children learn not only to become artists but also to appreciate the artwork of others.
4. To support the goals of art education, teachers should locate quality art and art reproductions from many sources and discuss these works skillfully with children. Critical issues in art programs for young children include health and safety considerations as well as the selection, presentation, evaluation, storage, and display of art and art materials.
5. Effective teachers provide quality art experiences with a variety of materials as a way of building every child's artistic sensibilities and skills and integrating art into the curriculum.
6. Art is a true curricular basic, a way of knowing that is just as valuable in the real world as other types of know-how.
7. Art must be integrated into different subject areas so that it receives the attention that it merits.

Discuss: Promoting Children's Art

1. Use Allen Say's (2003) book *Emma's Rug* to spark a discussion about how artists get ideas for their work. Work in groups to plan how you would introduce and discuss this book with preschoolers, children in the primary grades, and older students.
2. A friend asks you how to tell if her child is artistic. How would you respond, based on what you have learned from this chapter?
3. McKean (2000) found that the two most powerful influences on teachers' attitudes toward art were: (1) their experiences during childhood and (2) their formal training. How will you overcome past experiences with art that were inappropriate?
4. Suppose that a parent volunteers to work in your classroom and you observe the parent with his or her hand on top of a child's hand and paintbrush, forcibly showing the child how to paint a flower. After the children leave, the parent tells you that the child was rude and unappreciative. How would you respond?
5. Collect some of these picture books about art and artists and discuss how you could build a lesson around each book: *Visiting the Art Museum* (Brown & Brown, 1990), *The Fantastic Journey of Pieter Bruegel* (Shafer, 2003), *Leonardo da Vinci* (Stanley, 1996), *You Can't Take a Balloon into the Museum of Fine Arts* (Weitzman & Glasser, 2002), *Cherries and Cherry Pits* (Williams, 1986), *Emily's Art* (Catalanotto, 2001), *Drawing Lessons from a Bear* (McPhail, 2000), *The Boy Who Loved to Draw: Benjamin West* (Brenner, 2003).

Chapter 5

Engaging Children in Music, Movement, and Dance

*Mary Renck Jalongo and
Laurie Nicholson*

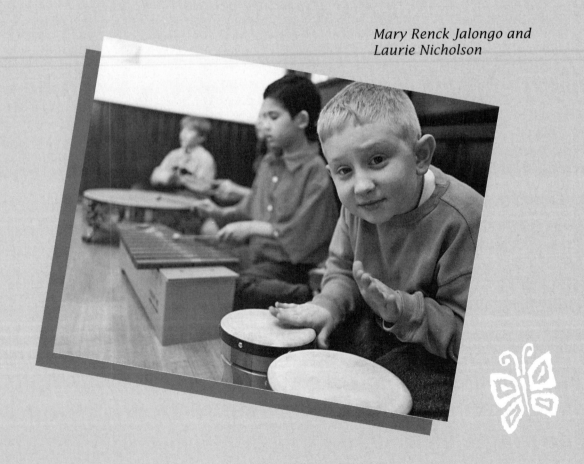

Music is an intensely social experience. To sing or play instruments in a group, children must listen to themselves, their leader (often the teacher), and each other. To be successful, everyone has to conform to the spirit and structure of the music, starting and stopping together and coordinating their musical activity from moment to moment. Singing, playing instruments, and joining in games are intensely integrative learning activities. They build on children's natural drive to join in and exercise their auditory discrimination or hearing ability as well as fine and gross motor coordination.

Elizabeth M. Armistead, 2007, pp. 89–90

CLASSROOM PERSPECTIVES ON MUSIC, MOVEMENT, AND DANCE

Preschool–Kindergarten

It is a warm summer afternoon and the local concert band is giving a free performance at the community park. Children from the toddler class at the university child-care center have arrived in their multiseat wagons and strain to see where the music is coming from. As they are lifted up from their seats, 2-year-old Marcus puts his chubby fists to his mouth and blows, imitating the trumpet players featured in the patriotic tune being played. Jasmine claps her hands almost in time to the music, and Shenay takes the hands of her teacher and sways from side to side. Then a group of 4-year-olds arrives, walking hand-in-hand with their partners. The preschoolers excitedly begin to point out and identify the instruments that their teacher displayed in the classroom as preparation for their walking field trip. Curtis and Lexie imitate the snare drummer and cymbal player, Maurice sits down to watch, and Jennica finds a stick on the ground that she uses to mimic the conductor's animated gestures. All of these young children have responded to a live musical performance by spontaneously connecting music with movement.

First Grade–Second Grade

Since the first week of school Mr. Torrez's second graders have found music playing each morning when they arrive. "First Circle," a jazz tune by Pat Metheny, is today's selection. Davis taps his eraser lightly in time as he visits his mailbox and reads a message from his teacher about yesterday's math assignment. Kayla reads the liner notes from the CD that her teacher has displayed, and Matthias, a recently immigrated child from Kenya, tries out the percussion instruments Mr. Torrez has on display. Mr. Torrez has been collaborating with the music teacher to reinforce concepts and integrate ideas from her weekly class.

Third Grade–Fourth Grade

As part of Mrs. Arnett's fourth-grade social studies unit on World War II, children work in small groups with replicas of posters, books, and note cards from the era. Renee and Enrique plan to demonstrate popular dances and they have just downloaded a clip of dancers from the 1940s performing to a song by the Andrews

Sisters. A second group is investigating swing orchestras, while a third is delving into patriotic music of the time. Around the room, reproductions of work by photographers and painters of the 1940s are displayed. Mrs. Arnett has invited veterans from the community to their culminating activity, and in doing so, found that elderly twin sisters from her church worked as USO hostesses in San Diego during the war. Emma and Francine, both widows now, will enrich the children's understanding of the period by sharing scrapbooks, recordings, and song sheets from their volunteer days.

These vignettes point out the variety of roles that music, movement, and dance can and should play in the classroom life of the developing child.

❧ UNDERSTANDING MUSIC, MOVEMENT, AND DANCE

Music, movement, and dance are rich and natural teaching resources for educators. Music is not merely a content area; it is also a unique way of communicating and a domain of intelligence. Musical/rhythmic intelligence refers to sensitivity to sounds and patterns of sound that results in the ability to appreciate, participate in, and perform music. Music supports the goals of inclusion because "It offers varying levels of engagement—from simply listening to participating or even performing" (Humpal & Wolf, 2003). Throughout the world, musical experiences begin in the earliest days of life. Adults from many different cultural backgrounds have taken note of children's positive responses—the fussy baby being lulled to sleep, the toddler or preschooler laughing delightedly first watching and later joining in an action song, or the elementary school child proudly playing a musical instrument during a concert at school (see Custodero & Johnson-Green, 2007; Zur & Johnson-Green, 2008).

Parents and caregivers instinctively communicate with infants in a musical fashion because, although infants don't understand the lyrics, melodic stimulation always gets their attention (Weinberger, 1998). Similarly, action songs are used to entertain toddlers or preschoolers, and older students are taught to sing, move to music, and play musical instruments, both simple and sophisticated.

Three-year-old Mira, a recent immigrant from Russia, exemplifies the powerful attraction that music has for the young child. Mira speaks only Russian, and she has been quiet and withdrawn during her first two weeks in the preschool class. The children are learning the hand and body motions that accompany *Ten in the Bed* (Cabrera, 2006) and Mira is captivated by the teacher's visual aid—a quilted pillow sham with small stuffed toys tucked inside, labeled from 1 to 10. As the teacher sings the song, she invites the children to join in on whatever parts they know and to clap as they count down after each one falls out. Mira creeps closer to the circle and bobs her head animatedly in time to the music, and her teacher wonders if Mira knows the song. Later that day, the teacher overhears singing and is delighted to turn the corner and find Mira standing on a stepstool at the sink and singing in a mixture of English, Russian, and tuneful syllables while looking in the mirror and clapping as she counts.

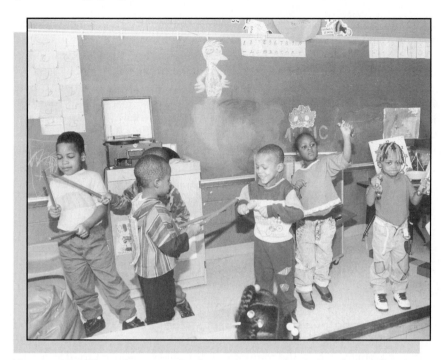

For young children, the connection between movement and understanding is very strong.

As Mira's behavior suggests, movement is quite often part of a child's initial response to music. The terms *creative movement, movement,* and *creative dance* are used interchangeably to refer to the child's natural physical response to music. Teachers of young children often speak of creative movement rather than dance to differentiate movement from formal lessons and on-stage performances (see Werner, Timms, & Almond, 1996). For young children, the connection between movement and understanding is particularly strong. One team of researchers found, for example, that it was not until after children were asked to physically rotate their bodies that they were then able to understand the mental concept of rotation (Wohlschlaeger & Wohlschlaeger, 1998). From the earliest days of life, infants respond differently to slow, quiet music and lively tunes and toddlers respond to the rhythmic flow, beat, and expressiveness of music through movement (Merrill, 2004). Both movement and dance rely on kinesthetic intelligence, which is the ability to coordinate the body and orchestrate one's physical movements in space and time. Physical/spatial/temporal or kinesthetic intelligence is possessed and cultivated to a high degree by dancers and athletes.

Dance is distinctive from movement in that it is a more formal and structured type of movement; it is a physical language that integrates the mind and the body (Ross, 1994). Unlike creative movement, dance tends to denote an organized and discrete set of steps or body movements that have a right and wrong manner of performance. Dance depends on cultural and symbolic resources to make meaning and express creativity using the human body (Johnson, 2003). Children's kinesthetic intelligence grows when adults provide (1) a supportive physical and emotional environment, (2) opportunities for social interaction, and (3) role models to emulate.

Obviously, music, movement, and dance are interconnected. Everyone has seen young children spontaneously "walk, run, rock, or twist as they sing or speak in rhythm" (Tarnowski, 1999, p. 28). Ideally, musical and kinesthetic intelligence also are integrated with other areas of the curriculum. One Massachusetts school district's experience with integrating music, literature, and movement illustrates how this can occur. Creative and innovative classroom teachers and music specialists decided to explore the fairy tale and ballet called *Firebird* with kindergarten children. Repeated readings of the story, opportunities to listen to the music, and a virtual treasure trove of props allowed these kindergartners to retell the enchanting story of the Firebird through their own words. They also made observations such as: "The music helped our ears hear the story. There is another way to tell a story—with feet. Dancers can dance a story. A dancing story is called a ballet" (Roebuck, 1999, p. 34).

✿ HISTORICAL INFLUENCES ON MUSIC, MOVEMENT, AND DANCE FOR CHILDREN

The history of music, movement, and dance education is distinguished and exceptionally international in scope because "Dancing is every child's cultural birthright . . . Music, too, is the memory of our people brought to life . . . [In music and dance] our children can awaken to a knowledge of themselves—their community and their country—in ways that cannot be duplicated" (D'Amboise, 1991, p. 5). Table 5.1 highlights educators who have had a major influence on music education for children.

Contemporary educators often take an eclectic approach to music that draws on the best features of each tradition. We recognize the importance of early experience as Rousseau did, we help children understand movement through time and space as Dalcroze did, we prepare a musical environment as Montessori did, we

TABLE 5.1	Leaders in Music Education	
Educator and Country of Origin	**Background and Philosophy**	**Major Contributions to Music Education**
Jean Jacques Rousseau (1712–1778) *France*	Rousseau's mother died when he was born, his father abandoned him, and the boy endured a variety of difficult foster-care situations. Rousseau's contention that people are born free and equal was revolutionary for its time. He advocated respect for the natural ways of children, which was at odds with most of his contemporaries who favored harsh punishment.	In his book about an imaginary "everychild" named *Émile*, Rousseau argued that music and movement go hand in hand. He emphasized the importance of singing to children and recommended that mothers should sing simple, interesting songs suitable for children. Rousseau believed that singing to and with children would make the child's voice accurate, uniform, flexible, and sonorous as well as make the child's ear sensitive to meter and harmony.

TABLE 5.1   *(Continued)*

Émile Jacques-Dalcroze (1865–1950) *Switzerland*	An accomplished composer appointed to the Conservatory of Music at age 27, Jacques-Dalcroze challenged the prevailing views of musical training that relied on imitation, repetition, and harsh criticism. He argued for an approach that considered time, space, and energy.	The Dalcroze method emphasizes coordination of the eye, ear, mind, and body. Components of the method are (1) eurhythmics (expression of physical and mental rhythms and the laws affecting their performance), (2) solfege (training the ear, eye, and voice in pitch, melody, and harmony), and (3) improvisation (use of musical, physical, and verbal rhythms for spontaneous personal expression). The Dalcroze method continues to be popular today.
Maria Montessori (1870–1952) *Italy*	Montessori was the first woman in Italy to qualify as a physician. She was assigned to working with children living in poverty who were considered "ineducable." The general educational principle of her method was *first the education of the senses, then the education of the intellect.*	Montessori argued for sound exploration activities for young children. She invented a set of mushroom-shaped bells that helped children discover musical concepts. Montessori-method schools were established throughout the world and continue to exist today.
Zoltan Kodaly (1882–1967) *Hungary*	An active composer, Kodaly wrote a great deal of choral, vocal, and orchestral music. He advocated using traditional music to teach children about their cultural heritage.	Kodaly proposed that musical literacy be developed through a carefully sequenced program of folk music that began with 3-year-olds. It combined vocal and movement activities. Kodaly's method was responsible for major changes in approaches to training in listening and appreciating music. It also inspired music educators worldwide to regard music as a way to preserve the cultural heritage of their respective countries.
Carl Orff (1895–1982) *Germany*	Orff was a composer of music, primarily stage pageants. As a teacher, Orff founded a school for gymnastics, music, and dance that influenced his thinking about early musical training. He developed creative musicianship in children by engaging them in spontaneously producing and creating their own music, rhythmic responses, and imaginative actions.	Orff's approach was child-centered and focused on activities that children do naturally and with pleasure. He provided children with ways to make music using their voices and simple percussion instruments. Carl Orff schools were established throughout the world to educate children using his methods.
Shinichi Suzuki (1898–1998) *Japan*	Suzuki was one of 12 children and his father owned a violin factory. Although he initially regarded these instruments as toys, Suzuki taught himself to play the violin, inspired by a stunning performer. He later took lessons and began to teach young children. Suzuki believed that all children have talent if they are taught well by loving parents and teachers. When the young children Suzuki had trained performed, people worldwide were amazed by the level of proficiency these children had attained at such an early age. Thousands of parents enrolled their children in Suzuki training.	Suzuki originated a program that taught very young children to play the violin and cello using a series of child-sized instruments. The success of the program, which took a musical literacy approach, relied on extensive parent involvement. Suzuki's mission was unique in that it did not have the production of more concert violinists or cellists as its major mission; rather, his goal was to introduce children to a world of beauty and appreciation through music. Suzuki contended that hearing and playing beautiful music helped children mature into people with good hearts.

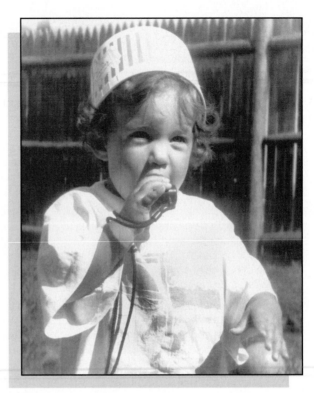

This child's exploration of musical sounds illustrates her emerging understandings about music.

attend to the developmental levels of children as Kodaly did, we emphasize spontaneity and originality as Orff did, and we appreciate the importance of parental involvement as Suzuki did. Even though there are various published music (Anderson & Lawrence, 2006) and dance curriculum guides (Dunkin, 2006), effective teachers incorporate music and movement throughout the day. Look in on any high-quality program for children from toddlerhood through the elementary grades and you will see children chanting, singing, clapping, swinging, tapping, marching, skipping, doing simple dances, and fully engaging in all kinds of music and movement activities.

THEORETICAL AND RESEARCH BASE: NEUROSCIENCE, COGNITIVE PSYCHOLOGY, AND MUSIC/MOVEMENT

Research on the human brain from the fields of neuroscience and cognitive science indicates that music, movement, and dance are ways to enrich the brain (Jensen, 2006). The connections that are formed between the cells of the brain, called synapses, are strengthened through use, and music and dance provide a unique form of cognitive stimulation (Ratey, 2001; Wilcox, 2000). The brain appears to be more malleable during the first 10 years of life than in adulthood (Flohr, Miller, & Debeus, 2000). Thus, the absence of the particular forms of cognitive stimulation provided via music and dance can have long-term adverse consequences for cognitive development. It is generally accepted, for example, that the singing voice of the "average" adult does not develop much beyond that acquired by age 7 or 8 when no training or additional opportunities are provided. Nevertheless, increasing pressure on teachers to meet academic standards and raise children's test scores often leads to the neglect of music during early childhood and elementary years, which diminishes not only children's musical potential but also their cognitive development throughout life. While many school districts employ music specialists, few districts have the luxury of enough musical instruction time, and educational settings that include children younger than kindergarten age may have no specialist at all.

Cognitive psychology suggests that children's abilities in the musical and kinesthetic domains tend to progress through three stages: (1) enactive, (2) iconic, and (3) symbolic (Bruner, 1968). At the *enactive stage*, physical activity and music are intertwined (Mang, 2005). Just think about all of the rhythmic games that adults play with infants and toddlers, and how they combine physical activity with music. We rock babies to sleep with a lullaby such as "Rock-a-Bye Baby," sing a lively song and bounce them on our knees, tickle a baby's toes to the chant of "This Little Piggy," or share simple action songs such as "Eensy Weensy Spider" with toddlers. Bruner's enactive stage relates to Piaget's (1952) sensorimotor stage and Erikson's (1950) trust-building stage. When we think about the enactive music stage of babies and toddlers, it is clear that the activities adults select not only stimulate the child's senses and foster cognitive development, but also build social relationships by communicating warmth and acceptance.

During the *iconic stage*, which is typical of preschoolers, children use tangible items (real objects and pictorial representations of objects, such as photographs and drawings) to represent their experiences. At this stage, children are highly imaginative (Piaget, 1962) and assert their autonomy, yet want to be accepted by the group (Erikson, 1950). Musical experiences that are appropriate for this stage recognize all of these characteristics of preschoolers. Consider, for example, a teacher who extends the musical game "The Farmer in the Dell" by providing a prop to represent each character in the game (e.g., a straw hat for the farmer, a cow bell for the cow, and so forth). Such an activity gives children a chance to connect music and dance with words, actions, and objects. It also paves the way for understanding symbols.

At the *symbolic stage*, children begin to use abstract symbols, primarily language, to represent ideas. By the time most children are in elementary school, they rely less on icons (pictures) and learn to use multiple-symbol systems that are more abstract, including words, musical notation, and the movement and gesture of dance. School-age children think more logically and realistically (Piaget, 1952). They also have a sense of industry, which is manifested in their drive to master many different skills (Erikson, 1950). Intellectual development from birth through the school years runs the course of the enactive, iconic, and symbolic systems "until the human being is able to command all three" (Bruner, 1968, p. 12). Throughout the early childhood and elementary years, music, movement, and dance are important ways for children to demonstrate their intelligence. Figure 5.1 presents an overview of musical development and activities suitable for each stage.

INFANTS

Music

Sensitive to dynamics, the loudness or softness of a sound; startle at loud sounds and are comforted by soft, rhythmic, melodious sounds (e.g., musical toys, lullabies). Respond to the human voice, especially the primary caregiver's voice; respond in more lively ways to action songs and more subdued ways to lullabies.

Movement

Tend to respond to music with the entire body. "Lap babies" will bounce to lively music; babies who are standing may rock from side to side, sway back and forth, or bounce up and down by flexing their knees.

TODDLERS

Music

Discriminate among sounds and may attempt to imitate sound or to approximate pitches; listen to music and respond more enthusiastically to certain songs. Explore sound making with household objects (e.g., hitting a pan with a wooden spoon), musical toys, (e.g., a toy xylophone), or musical instruments; express greater interest in recordings. Can demonstrate knowledge of sounds and music by identifying familiar sounds or instruments played on a tape or outside their view. Experiment with songs and voice and gain some control of the singing voice; occasionally match melody and may join in on certain phrases of familiar songs; sing or hum improvisationally during play.

Movement

Use primarily arms and legs and can move in response to the tempo (fast/slow) of a rhythm instrument (e.g., run, walk, "freeze"). Will often "dance" on request while music is playing and show more control over physical responses. Respond well to large and small motor musical activities that emphasize repetition and rhyme— simple finger plays and action songs.

Recommended Picture Books for Infants and Toddlers

The Baby Dances (Henderson, 1999); *Old MacDonald Had a Farm* (Carter, 2001); *If You're Happy and You Know It, Clap Your Hands* (Carter, 2001); *Hanukkah, Oh Hanukkah* (Roth, 2003); *Baby Danced the Polka* (Beaumont, 2004); *Knick-Knack Paddy Whack!* (Zelinsky, 1992); *God Bless the Child* (Pinkney, 2003).

THREE-YEAR-OLDS

Music

Have better voice control, rhythmic responses, and mastery of song; most have names for their favorite tunes, can recognize familiar tunes, and can sing portions of them with a fair degree of accuracy (Day, 1988). With experience, most can play a simple rhythm instrument in ways that reveal an emerging awareness of beat, tempo, and pitch in response to songs with simple, definite rhythm patterns.

Movement

Move in a more coordinated way to music (usually running) and may experiment with different types of body movements, such as walking on tiptoe; movements tend to be more graceful than previously. Usually try to participate in action songs and finger plays by performing the gestures; often combine creative drama with song.

Figure 5.1 Developmental Sequence for Music, Movement, and Dance

FOUR-YEAR-OLDS

Music

Capable of learning some basic musical concepts such as pitch (high/low), duration (long/short), tempo (fast/slow), and loudness (soft/loud) and can use language to express these ideas; can classify musical instruments by sound, shape, size, pitch, and quality. Sing complete songs from memory with greater pitch control and rhythmic accuracy; sing both original songs and structured songs spontaneously. Vocal range, rhythmic ability, and vocabulary expand rapidly; can sing an average of five notes. Usually enjoy group singing games and more complex songs. Longer attention span in guided listening to records.

Movement

Movements suggesting rhythm (e.g., swinging on a swing) are likely to be accompanied by spontaneous song. Master new movements and can switch rapidly from one type of movement to another when the word is substituted (e.g., "Hop, hop, hop to my Lou").

FIVE-YEAR-OLDS

Music

Sense of pitch, rhythm, and melody emerge; usually understand some melodic contours and intervals (skips and steps in a melody); can demonstrate some musical concepts (e.g., fast/slow, high/low, short/long duration) on a small keyboard. Enjoy longer songs with predictable structures (e.g., colors, numbers, repetition, rhyme). Can reproduce the melody in an echo song and have a vocal range of five to six notes.

Movement

Movements have a more rhythmic quality than previously. Can march around in a circle while playing in a rhythm band and participate in a variety of group singing games with simple dance movements to songs such as "Looby Lou."

Recommended Picture Books for Preschoolers

Dancin' in the Kitchen (Gelsanliter & Christian, 1993); *Song and Dance Man* (Ackerman, 1988); *I Know an Old Lady Who Swallowed a Fly* (Gulbis, 2001); *Ah, Music!* (Aliki, 2002); *The Ants Go Marching* (Manning, 2003); *Mole Music* (McPhail, 1999); *The Philharmonic Gets Dressed* (Kuskin, 1982); *Giraffes Can't Dance* (Andreae, 2001); *Violet's Music* (Johnson & Huliska-Beith, 2004); *Ty's One-Man Band* (Walter, 1987); *Max Found Two Sticks* (Pinkney, 1994); *Dance!* (Cooper, 2002); *Presenting Tanya, the Ugly Duckling* (Gauch, 1999); *Zin! Zin! Zin! A Violin* (Moss & Priceman, 1995); *My Mama Had a Dancing Heart* (Gray, 1996); *The Moon Jumpers* (Udry, 2002); *From Miss Ida's Porch* (Belton, 1993); *There Was an Old Lady Who Swallowed a Fly* (Taback, 2002); *That Dancin' Dolly* (Merz, 2004); *What Charlie Heard* (Gerstein, 2002); *The Jazz Fly* (Gollub, 2000); *Hip Cat* (London, 1996); *Music Is* (Moss & Petit-Roulet, 2003); *Our Marching Band* (Moss, 2001); *The Musical Life of Gustav Mole* (Meyrick, 1990).

SIX-, SEVEN-, AND EIGHT-YEAR-OLDS

Music

Singing voice is at nearly mature level. Sing "in tune," with a vocal range of approximately eight to ten notes; are aware of a song being pitched at a comfortable singing level. Sense of harmony is emerging. By second or third grade, can sing a

(Continued)

round and may master a simple two-part harmony if given adult direction. Enjoy silliness and begin to understand wordplay in song lyrics; learn to read song lyrics; able to master songs that place greater demands on memory and sequencing skills. Greater awareness of printed music and its relationship to the way that music is sung or played; usually able to conceptualize musical notes as "stairsteps." Musical preferences are fairly well established; may express an interest in learning to play a musical instrument.

Movement and Dance

Able to improvise movements and match movements to the beat of the music (i.e., clapping "in time," playing a rhythm instrument "to the beat"). Capable of following more complex instructions and can learn simple folk dances with adult direction.

Recommended Picture Books for Children in the Primary Grades

Lion Dancer: Ernie Wan's Chinese New Year (Waters & Slovenz-Low, 1990); *Meet the Orchestra* (Hayes & Thompson, 1995); *Here's Bojangles: Think of That!* (Dillon & Dillon, 2002); *Handel, Who Knew What He Liked* (Anderson, 2002); *Strange Mr. Satie* (Anderson, 2003); *My Country 'Tis of Thee* (Smith, 2004); *Horace and Morris Join the Chorus (But What about Dolores?)* (Jave, 2002); *The Story of the Incredible Orchestra: An Introduction to Musical Instruments and the Symphony Orchestra* (Koscielniak, 2000); *Lives of the Musicians: Good Times, Bad Times (and What the Neighbors Thought)* (Krull, 1993); *Raggin': A Story about Scott Joplin* (Mitchell, 1992); *If Only I Had a Horn: Young Louis Armstrong* (Orgill, 1997); *Duke Ellington: The Piano Prince and His Orchestra* (Pinkney, 1998); *Ella Fitzgerald: The Tale of a Vocal Virtuosa* (Pinkney, 2002); *John Coltrane's Giant Steps* (Raschka, 2002); *Ragtime Tumpie* (Schroeder, 1989); *Charlie Parker Played Be Bop* (Raschka, 1997); *Music for Alice* (Say, 2004); *Snow Music* (Say, 2003); *When Marian Sang* (Ryan, 2002); *Aaron Copland* (Venezia, 1995); *John Philip Sousa* (Venezia, 1999).

Figure 5.1   *(Continued)*

As children participate in music, movement, and dance at the enactive, iconic, and symbolic stages, they acquire the following attitudes (data from Hall, 1989):

• *I can listen to music and watch dance.* Children recognize different ways of using their senses to experience, appreciate, and differentiate among various types of music and dance. To achieve this, they need adults who model appreciation and respect for music, movement, and dance. Many studies, of both exceptionally talented musicians and adults in general, suggest that early experiences that were relaxed, informal, and enjoyed in the company of supportive adults contributed to the child's early attachment to music (Wilson & Roehmann, 1990). In fact, parents' own singing might be the single most important influence on an infant's musical activity (Kelley & Sutton-Smith, 1987). On the other hand, when significant others express disdain for music and dance, these negative pronouncements tend to narrow children's range of interests. If, for example, a child hears others ridicule males who are interested in dance or music, the child often learns to devalue these activities too. Contrary to popular opinion, music and dance education is not limited to the few individuals who are sufficiently talented to make their living at it. Practically everyone is capable of enjoying music and dance performed by others.

• *I can join in music and movement.* Think about the continuum of participation in music and dance reflected in 9-year-old Colleen's history. When she was a toddler, her version of the traditional singing game "Ring Around the Rosy" was simply "rindaround . . . pocketful . . . boom," and she delighted in holding her mother's hands, moving in a circle, and dropping to the floor at the song's end. As a 3-year-old in nursery school, Colleen mastered all of the words (substituting "Ashes, ashes, we all fall down" for "boom") and learned how to move together with the other children around the circle. Now that she is in elementary school, Colleen takes dance lessons and has learned to coordinate her movements with those of her dance group. She also sings in her church choir and is inspired by the religious music and camaraderie. Colleen has learned that she can participate in music and dance composed and choreographed by others.

• *I can create music, movement, and dance.* Children need to feel free to explore sound and motion in response to music and dance. Consider the response of Owen, a 3-year-old who is waiting for his mother at the hairstylist's shop. After he hears a lively Sheryl Crow song on the radio, he begins to move his head back and forth. Owen's mother smiles and the stylist turns to see the small boy responding to the music. When the stylist asks him if he feels like getting up and dancing, Owen replies, "Well, my feet don't want to, but my head sure does." Education should help a child like Owen acquire the confidence to translate his feelings into dance and music compositions.

• *I can understand the language of music and dance.* A basic goal for children is for them to learn to use the vocabulary of music and dance. One preschool teacher encouraged her students to pick up and put away work and play materials while listening to music. She would sometimes ask, "Does anyone know a work song?" and was delighted to hear their ideas, which often consisted of bits of familiar songs (e.g., "Just Whistle While You Work") as well as their invented song ideas. She worked alongside them, stooping, reaching, and stretching, all the while modeling how cleanup could be done "in time" to the distinctive rhythms of a Sousa march, a portion of Benjamin Britten's *Young Person's Guide to the Orchestra,* and an excerpt from Edward Elgar's *Enigma Variations.* The teacher did not stop there, however. She also used vocabulary that would prepare her students to talk about

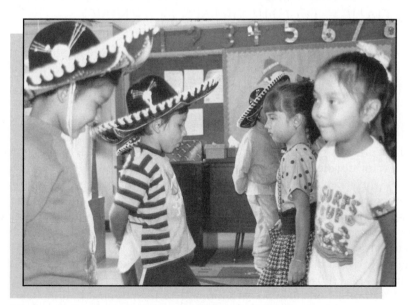

Music and dance are part of every child's cultural heritage.

music in more precise and satisfying ways, with terminology words such as *tempo, style,* and *rhythm.*

MyEducationLab

Go to MyEducationLab and select the topic "Music and Movement." Under Activities and Application, watch the video A Web-Based Music Project *and complete the activity.*

• *I can compose music and choreograph movements.* Naturally, the selection of both music and movement activities depends on the developmental levels of the children. Toddlers can rock a teddy bear to a lullaby, preschoolers can make "dancing dolls" (empty detergent bottles and fabric skirts) and swirl them about in response to a Strauss waltz, and primary-grade children can lope along to a cowboy song as they hold the reins of their horse (a length of ribbon or yarn encircling the waist of a partner). Children spontaneously create and sing original songs, invent dances to accompany musical selections, or think of ways to use streamers, scarves, paper fans, or feathers to accompany a musical selection. With older children, a task such as composing a simple melody using the pentatonic scale (C-D-E-G-A) to accompany various three-line haiku poems might pose an interesting musical challenge (Burns, 2002). When children record their compositions in some way and lead others in performing them (e.g., using bells or a xylophone) they are learning the rudiments of composing. To view an example of a child's web-based music project, go to MyEducationLab online.

• *I can perform music and dance.* "Musical activities should give pleasure to all who are participating, and if they don't, they are probably worse than useless" (Boyd, 1989, p. 8). It is not enough to simply "bathe" children in music or let children race around aimlessly to expend surplus energy because, to the young child, music is both active (something that you do) and interactive (something that you share with others). Even young children can perform music and movement at some basic level, such as using simple instruments from various cultures to accompany Raffi's (2008) *Songs of Our World.* As school-age children begin to acquire performance skills, they also learn another lesson—that performances in music and dance often demand a level of excellence that exceeds those in other fields. Professional musicians and dancers continue to practice until even a single wrong note or missed step is avoided.

CONTRIBUTIONS OF MUSIC, MOVEMENT, AND DANCE TO CHILDREN'S LEARNING

Music contributes to the child's total development: psychomotor, perceptual, affective, cognitive, social, cultural, and aesthetic. Figure 5.2 highlights ways that teachers can use music and dance more effectively in the classroom.

Psychomotor Development

As children participate in music, movement, and dance, it contributes to their psychomotor development. Babies who have not yet learned to crawl usually will raise their arms and legs up off the floor and make rapid swimming motions in response to lively music. Preschoolers learn to coordinate the small muscles of their hands and arms, or fine motor skills, when they tap lightly on a tambourine; they use the large muscles of their bodies when they invent actions to go along with a song or interpret the mood of a musical selection through creative dance. Elementary students coordinate their voices and body movements with those of their classmates in order to perform at a musical event at their school. In all of these situations, music, movement, and dance offer physical benefits to children. Failure to develop competence in fundamental

- To begin the day and greet one another
- To create a warm, positive atmosphere
- To establish a particular mood
- To ease transitions from one activity to another
- To link the arts with other subject areas
- To focus children's attention
- To make special events even more special
- To celebrate diversity
- To establish social solidarity
- To refresh and relax
- To sharpen thinking skills
- To promote creative expression
- To bring the day or an event to a satisfying conclusion

Figure 5.2   How Teachers Use Music and Dance in the Curriculum
Note: Data from Hildebrandt (1992).

skills of movement may result in a poor body image (Green, 2001), and may deter children from participating in any organized sport or physical endeavor (Garcia, Garcia, Floyd, & Lawson, 2002).

Thus, the need for children to develop competence and confidence in their own abilities to move and use their bodies is critical. Figure 5.3 provides recommendations on ways to incorporate music and dance in your classroom.

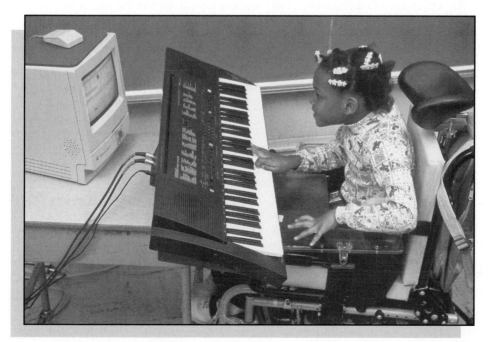

Music contributes to this child's physical development as she learns to play a song on a keyboard.

General Principles

- Base the program on four elements: listening (e.g., playing the music of different cultures in the background), moving (e.g., inviting children to experiment with dance steps that accompany musical selections with distinctive beats), playing (e.g., teaching children a story song and inviting them to dramatize it), singing (e.g., encouraging joyful, spontaneous singing in response to activities such as swinging on a swing).

- Provide a balance of large-group, small-group, partner, and individual music and movement activities. Adapt the environment and materials to give children with special needs opportunities to participate. Also provide a balance of teacher-facilitated and child-initiated activities.

- Expect children's responses to vary and invite children to respond in their own ways to music and dance rather than requiring everyone to do the same thing. For instance, balance the use of songs that have the motions predetermined (like "Eensy Weensy Spider") with opportunities for children to invent their own actions to accompany songs.

- Build the children's self-confidence as people who can enjoy, participate in, and respond to music and dance. Invite children to share their ideas, but do not force them to perform or ask the group to critique their performance.

- Avoid generic praise ("That's great, everyone!") and use personalized encouragement instead ("I notice that you are using your whole body, Jason," and "I see that Chelsea decided to use mostly her arms.").

- Actively seek to build the children's vocabularies related to music and movement. While toddlers may focus on simpler concepts (e.g., fast/slow, turning around), older children can learn the terminology used by artists (e.g., dynamics, pirouette).

- Encourage and support the children's spontaneous songs and dances by observing and documenting what they have created on audio or videotape. Invite the child to teach his or her song or dance to you.

- Join in as appropriate, by offering to sing with a child or accompany the child's song or dance on whatever instrument you can play (e.g., a drum, a kazoo, a guitar, a keyboard).

- For children who seem reluctant to express themselves through music and movement, model joyful responses and invite the child to sing or move with you in response to music.

- Avoid a talent-scout mentality, in which you focus on a few children who appear to be precocious in music or dance. Give all children opportunities to engage in music and movement to the best of their abilities.

Preparation

- For safety's sake, when children are engaged in movement activities, make sure that they are wearing shoes with nonslip soles. Make certain also that children are not being asked to sing during snack or meal times, as food may get caught in their throats and cause them to choke.

- Select a space that will accommodate the activity. During creative movement activities, use a large, open, uncluttered area and tell children to behave like

Figure 5.3 How to Incorporate Music and Dance in Your Classroom

Note: Based on Bennett, Wood, & Rogers (1997), Gold & Cuming (1999), Greenberg (1979), Persellin (1998), and Turner (1999).

peanut butter and s-p-r-e-a-d out! Even if space is more limited, ask children to extend their arms and turn slowly about to be sure that they will not bump into anyone else. You will need a large group area for playing circle games (e.g., "Ring Around the Rosy"), and a listening center equipped with high-quality sound equipment and musical selections from throughout the world. Remember to include outdoor musical experiences, such as galloping to music with stick horses.

- When you set up learning centers, provide music and movement opportunities every day (e.g., a listening center, a music center) as well as centers that change periodically (e.g., a musical prop-making center, materials for making sandpaper blocks at the woodworking center). Have a center that includes scarves, ropes, balls, streamers, and other materials that encourage movement and dance. Consider a special dramatic play area for conducting music that includes a music stand, baton, and podium. Plan a music laboratory where children can invent their own music, equipping it with a set of bells, a keyboard, xylophone, drums, and rhythm band set. Add music to the home-life center by including a cassette or CD player, musical stuffed toys, a music box, or some musical instruments.

- At various times, combine music and movement with all other subject areas and centers in the classroom (e.g, a work song playing in the woodworking area for preschoolers, or a group of second graders who invent a song parody about energy in science, or a third-grade class that composes and performs a musical puppet play on sets and subsets for the first grade).

Materials and Resources

- Don't choose a book, recording, or piece of software simply because it is "popular"—much of the "children's music" in wide use is of inferior quality and simply well marketed. Strive to provide the very best. Choose high-quality materials and sound equipment. You might be able to use the CD player on a computer to provide better sound quality than that provided by old records or cassette tapes, for example.

- Song lyrics should be matched to the interests and developmental levels of *children* (e.g., romantic songs are not appropriate). Songs need to be pitched at the child's singing range.

- When young children sing or move to music, they should be responding sincerely and genuinely rather than mimicking adults. Strive for a neat, clean appearance and avoid makeup, suggestive song lyrics, or risqué costumes.

- Teach children to respect and care for props, instruments, equipment, and software. Organize your classroom so that it is easy for children to see where things belong and how they are to be put away.

- Give children independent access to musical experiences by providing a listening center, a place to record music, a center or cart with homemade and real musical instruments, and computer software about music and dance. Teach children how to operate the equipment and provide posters with illustrated instructions.

- Expand children's appreciation for different types and styles of music and dance by introducing the music and dance of many eras, ethnic groups, and cultures throughout the entire year.

- Use community resources to provide a wide array of recorded and live performances in music and dance. Collaborate with families, colleagues, and

(Continued)

professionals in other fields. Send out a request to those who have skill in music, asking them to share their talent and level of accomplishment with children.

- Begin a file of online and print resources for parents/families about young children's music and dance. When parents turn to you for advice about lessons in music or dance, have authoritative answers ready.

Presentation

- Don't reserve music and movement activities for one specific time block. Rather, use music and creative movement throughout the day, particularly during transition times such as arrival/departure at the school or center; as children move in and out of free play; before, during or after a story session; or as children move inside and outside for outdoor play.

- Remember that young children enjoy repeating familiar songs and dance movements. Feel free to revisit the familiar as well as introduce something that is new.

- When young children are moving to music, the emphasis should be on developing techniques rather than on displays of athleticism or stunts. Incorrect technique can cause physical damage to the young child's body.

- Pay attention to variety and pacing. Even a brief music or creative dance time period will require several different activities. Stop an activity before the children grow tired of it and save some of that enthusiasm for next time.

Evaluation

- Quality music and movement programs help all children develop positive attitudes and emotional responses. Early musical experiences should inaugurate a lifelong love of music and dance.

- Closely observe how children respond to particular music and movement activities. Make some brief notes about what was particularly well received and what was not.

- Realize that a lukewarm response to a song or a movement experience may mean that it was not developmentally suited to the children at that time. Perhaps if it is introduced later on, children will respond more favorably.

- Don't allow yourself to get caught up in high-pressure, on-stage performances for large audiences. Even people who have extensive musical training may not understand the needs of young children very well and you will need to advocate for the children's needs. Remember, you aren't selling tickets, you are teaching children.

- Exercise good judgment about how formal a music or dance experience should be for children. Help parents and community members to understand that when children are acting tense and anxious, rather than enjoying the activity, it is time to reconsider.

- Remain current with the recommendations of leading organizations in music and movement, such as Music Educators National Conference, and use their guidelines as a basis for ongoing self-evaluation.

- You will know that your music and movement program is achieving its goals when children learn to listen and observe appreciatively, sing tunefully, move expressively and rhythmically, play classroom instruments, develop age-appropriate musical concepts, create self-satisfying responses, and value music and dance as part of everyday life.

Figure 5.3 (Continued)

Participating in a rhythm band teaches both musical skills and cooperation.

Perceptual Skills

Children are accustomed to hearing music—at shopping malls, on television programs, on Web sites, or from windup musical toys—but these experiences do not really teach children to listen thoughtfully to music. Children may hear others attempt to sing along with a CD, mimicking a particular vocal style, but this does not make them aware of the voice and breath control that go into singing. Likewise, children often see others jumping around as if they were dancing or may attempt to imitate real dancers they see—such as walking on tiptoe after watching ballet—but these experiences do not make children aware of the control and precision necessary in order to dance. Appreciation of and participation in the arts demands heightened perceptual skills.

From the earliest days of life, children show that they are capable of perceiving music and movement. A baby who recognizes her mother's voice is differentiating between it and all the other voices in her environment. Toddlers' perceptions of music may be so intense that they may think sounds have a physical substance. After hearing a note played on the piano, a toddler might run around to search for that note, expecting to see and touch as well as hear it. Perceptual skills are evident when a kindergartner remarks that "The Flight of the Bumblebee" sounds "buzzy" and makes a connection between music and his prior experience. As children mature, their ability to perceive the mood of music and articulate that mood in words increases. After some third graders heard the mournful tune "Ashokan Farewell," the theme song for Ken Burns's *The Civil War* series on PBS, one child remarked, "It's kind of slow and sad and makes you feel the way you feel if your friend moves away." Music, movement, and dance are an effective way of heightening the perceptual development of children.

Emotional and Social Development

Darren, a kindergarten teacher, shared this story from his classroom: "The other day, I wanted to introduce the children to the song 'Old Brass Wagon.' We've been working on right and left and I thought that would be a great reinforcement for the concept. So I invited the children to the carpeted area of the classroom to join me for a game. Many came over at once, but Keisha and a few of her friends stayed in their places. 'Come on'. . . I invited, 'we need you, too.' Then Keisha asked, 'Mr. Martin . . . is this a fun game or a WINNING game?'" Keisha's question points out another contribution of musical games and movement activities: They can be adapted to allow everyone to feel competent, successful, and accomplished, thereby support socioemotional development.

Many music and movement activities encourage participation, sharing, and cooperation and, in most cultures throughout the world, music and dance are part of the bonding process across the generations. "Musical ability is developed in a relationship, in a succession of relationships—musical self in relation to musical selves" (Bernstein, 1990, p. 401). A classroom activity such as the group singing game "London Bridge," for example, teaches children to learn to subordinate their individual wishes to the goals of the group—the essence of cooperation.

Cognitive Skills

Musical intelligence involves children's ability to process mentally the tonal aspects of rhythm and melody. The child who learns to sing "This Old Man," for instance, has learned to focus on a task, sequence material, and link words with actions. Musical experiences, such as creating a tune at a keyboard, can develop all the higher-level thinking skills of application, analysis, synthesis, and evaluation. There are cognitive connections between learning music and learning to do mathematics or learning to read, since all of these tasks depend on mastering a language.

Multicultural Development

Music familiarizes children with the musical heritage of various geographic regions, cultures, and ethnic groups. A group of second graders who heard the Grammy award–winning African music group Ladysmith Black Mambazo were captivated by their majestic Zulu harmonies. The children with African roots felt renewed pride in their ethnic heritage, while children with a different cultural heritage felt admiration for the music of a culture different from their own. Likewise, when a Lakota Sioux group performed their breathtaking ceremonial dances at a university and a beautifully synchronized troupe of Greek folk dancers demonstrated the power of their art at an ethnic festival, their audiences were not only enthralled, but also filled with admiration. Many compilations feature the music and songs of various groups, such as *Fiestas: A Year of Latin American Songs of Celebration* (Orozco, 2004) and *Dance, Sing, Remember: A Celebration of Jewish Holidays* (Kimmelman, 2000). Another good resource for recordings of multicultural music is Putumayo Kids available from Music for Little People.

Aesthetic Awareness

Effective teachers heighten children's awareness of the beauty of music and dance with questions that invite reflection. Some general questions are:

- What do we hear in the music and notice in the dance?
- Why do we respond the way that we do to what we hear and see?
- What is beautiful in music and dance?

- How might we show appreciation for music and dance?
- What are some ways that each of us might participate in music and dance?
- Can you teach us the song that you were singing?

   More specific examples of good questions are:

- Can you show me with your body that the music is getting louder? Softer? Higher? Lower? Can you show me with just your hands? Can you show me with your whole body that it is getting faster? With just your head? With just your feet?
- Can you show me giant steps as you move around the circle? Baby steps? Can you imagine how an elephant might dance to this music? How about a mouse?
- Show me *happy*. How would your face look if you just opened the best present ever? Now add your arms. Next, show your whole body being happy. Show me how *happy* moves around the room. Now choose a prop that makes you look even happier, joyful.
- Show me how a leaf flutters down from the tree using your whole body. Can you show me with a paper streamer? With just your arms?

MyEducationLab

Go to MyEducationLab and select the topic "Early Literacy." Under Activities and Applications, view the video Contextual Analysis and Story Dramatization *and complete the activity.*

Note that the teacher is not performing music, movement, or dance *for* the children; rather, the teacher is urging children to think and respond aesthetically.

   To observe children combining music and drama, watch the video "Contextual Analysis and Story Dramatization online at MyEducationLab.

TEACHERS' REFLECTIONS ON MUSIC, MOVEMENT, AND DANCE

Preservice Teachers

"After reading this chapter and contrasting it with what happened in the name of music at the child-care center where I worked last summer, I can see that we were really missing the whole point. We basically used music as a 'cheap filler' or tried to drill children on some skill through music, like 'The Alphabet Song.' Now I see how much more we could have been doing in terms of selecting, presenting, and simply enjoying music together."

"You haven't really enjoyed 'The Hokey Pokey' until you've heard Sharon, Lois, and Bram's rock version and compared it to Michael Doucet's zydeco version! And you have forgotten how 'Skip to My Lou' is supposed to be sung until you've listened to John McCutcheon's lively version!"

Inservice Teachers

"After programs such as *Riverdance* and *So You Think You Can Dance* appeared on television, several of my fourth graders became interested in dance. I think that watching these programs helped the children to appreciate the energy, strength, control, and hours of practice that go into these performances."

"Our school never has enough instruments so we sponsored an instrument donation drive. It was amazing how many people were willing to sponsor a child by providing an instrument that was useable but no longer in use. The donators were our special guests at the elementary school concert."

Your Reflections

- How would you characterize your current thoughts about how music, movement, and dance activities contribute to children's lives and their overall development?

- What types of musical experiences, artists, and resource materials, both traditional and contemporary, would you choose for young children? Why?

- What concerns do you have about your own abilities to foster young children's creative expression through music, movement, and dance?

Table 5.2 offers recommendations on using song picture books across the curriculum.

TABLE 5.2   Integrating the Curriculum: Using Song Picture Books

What is a song picture book?

A song picture book is an illustrated version of a song's lyrics (Jalongo, 2007; Jalongo & Ribblett, 1997). It is common for folk songs, counting rhymes, and action songs that are suitable for young children to be produced in song picture book format. These books bring a familiar song to life and usually provide the music, are accompanied by a recording, such as *Over in the Meadow* (Keats, 1971), or may tell the history of the song, such as *Follow the Drinking Gourd* (Winter, 1988). It is easy to locate these books at the library by conducting a search that uses the categories of "picture book" and "song." For more ideas on combining music with the visual arts, see Cosenza (2006).

Why use song picture books?

These books are particularly useful for meeting the needs of diverse groups of learners because they demonstrate the link between the kinesthetic (singing or doing the motions to a song), pictorial representations of the concepts in the song (viewing the illustrations), and print (reading the lyrics/words to the song).

Why are song picture books particularly appropriate for children with special needs?

For children with difficulty focusing, song picture books provide a concrete prompt; for ELLs, song picture books support language learning; for children with visual impairments, song picture books can be sung; and for children with hearing impairments, song picture books can be viewed.

	COMMUNICATION Literacy, Language Arts, and Technology	THE SCIENCES Mathematics/Science	SOCIAL STUDIES Social Studies/ Health and Safety
Toddler Theme *Fingerplays*	Children's responses to musical play and singing games are very positive (Gluschankof, 2002; Temmerman, 2000; Young, 2003a). Participate in a phonemic awareness fingerplay to the tune of "Fi fie fo fum." For more fingerplays, see (IbcTech, 2007). Combine music and story (DeVries, 2008, in press) such as the board book *Miss Mary Mack* (Hoberman, 2001).	Combine the study of insects with music "Butterfly" (IbcTech, 2007). On a rainy day, tape construction paper "raindrops" and "puddles" on the floor so that children can stomp, jump in, and splash through puddles. Supply small umbrellas so children can stretch to make large steps between raindrops or balance between small steps (Armistead, 2007).	Teach the fingerplay "Five Police Officers," and explain their importance in society (IbcTech, 2007).

TABLE 5.2 Integrating the Curriculum: Using Song Picture Books—continued

	COMMUNICATION Literacy, Language Arts, and Technology	THE SCIENCES Mathematics/Science	SOCIAL STUDIES Social Studies/ Health and Safety
Preschooler Theme *American Folk Songs*	Have children listen to or read lyrics to traditional folk songs (Gershon & Gershon, 2008); have them explain what each song is about, guess why it was written, etc. Link literacy with music and movement through questions such as: Who can show me how the little billy goat would cross our balance beam bridge to this music?	Learn simple counting songs that feature animals. Use real objects to practice math. For more math integration ideas, see Charlesworth & Lind, 2006; for science and music ideas, see Schiller & Willis, 2006.	Have children listen to or read the lyrics to folk songs of other cultures, and compare them with American folk songs. Teach simple dances (Morin, 2001; McIntyre, 2005) and perform multicultural dances for parents/families.
Primary Theme *Conducting an Author Study*	Dedicate some of reading time each day to songs or chants such as Eric Carle's *Today Is Monday* (Rouleau & Buchberg, 2008). Supply a collection of picture books that show why people are passionate about music or dance, such as *Jazzy Miz Mozetta* (Roberts, 2004). Invite a music or dance performer to class for children to interview.	Use *The Grouchy Ladybug* by Eric Carle to study how the sun rises and sets (Rouleau & Buchberg, 2008). Send home math-based story sacks that include song picture books and math activities such as board games, activities using calculators, and so forth (Mitchell, 2004).	Send home picture books from various lands and accompanying materials such as a recording of the song, Web resources, and simple puppets. Have children identify the different cultural origins of the characters, and locate these countries on the globe (Griffiths, 2001; Rouleau & Buchberg, 2008).
Intermediate Theme *How Books Are Published*	Have children work in groups to produce an illustrated song chart of a familiar song. Begin with simple substitutions such as "If you're happy and you know it, _____," then move to song parodies such as *On Top of Spaghetti* (Glazer, 1982), a parody of "On Top of Old Smokey," or *Old MacDonald Had a Woodshop* (Shulman, 2004), a parody of "Old MacDonald Had a Farm." Or *Sing a Song of Piglets* (Bunting, 2002), which is sung to the tune of "Sing a Song of Sixpence." Edit each other's work. Publish their own song picture book, using *Read Write Think Printing Press* (Verizon Foundation, 2004). For more music/language arts ideas, see Andrews & Sink, 2002; Schiller & Willis, 2006.	Produce a song picture book parody with an ecology theme (e.g., "We Have the Good Earth in Our Hands" to the tune of "He's Got the Whole World in His Hands") and illustrate it with photographs. Create song lyrics that include facts and figures about going green.	Have students compile a "printing inventory," or a list of all published sources that they use on a daily basis. Then research on the Internet William Caxton, the first English printer (Read, Write, Think, 2007).

TEACHERS' ROLES AND RESPONSIBILITIES

At one time in the history of the United States, teachers were required to complete as many as 15 credits in the arts prior to teaching, and kindergarten teachers often had a piano in their classrooms, which they were expected to play and use throughout the day when teaching. Now it is commonplace for teachers to have just one or two classes and hope that a music and art specialist will be available. Yet even when these services are available, each group of children typically gets just 20–30 minutes per week of the specialist teacher's time. Therefore, no matter what your training or setting, you will have responsibility for providing quality music and movement experiences for young children.

Teachers often think that unless they can sing beautifully, play an instrument, or have professional training in dance they won't be able to do much to promote children's development in music, movement, and dance. But leading children to and through these activities does not require polished performance skills from you. Some practical alternatives are described in Figure 5.4.

Even teachers who are relatively untrained in music and movement and feel they have very little ability in music or dance can, with the right attitude and resources, provide a high-quality musical program for children.

1. **Identify the source of your inhibitions.** Did someone tell you that you couldn't carry a tune? Are you concerned that the children will judge you? First, keep in mind that you are teaching children, not a contestant on *American Idol!* Judge your voice by the ability to sing children's songs, not by your ability to imitate famous vocalists. The great majority of songs for preschoolers have a range of about five notes. An ordinary singing voice coupled with extraordinary enthusiasm is perfectly adequate to sing most songs for young children. You probably know many of the songs already or can quickly learn them by singing along with a tape or record.

2. **Use recorded materials and live performances.** Teachers can obtain many excellent CDs, tapes, and children's concert videotapes through their public library. To avoid fumbling around to find a particular selection on a tape or CD, make copies on tape with just the songs you will be using that day, or use the counter on the videotape machine and write down the exact location of each song. This will enable you to move smoothly from one selection to another. What if you find the sheet music to a song in a book but cannot find a recorded version? Find a person who plays an instrument well to make a tape for you. You might ask the person to sing the song the first time so that you can learn it, then play just the background music the second time. Videotapes of skilled children's musicians in action are not only for children's viewing, but are also useful self-teaching tools for early childhood educators. Tapes such as *A Young Children's Concert with Raffi* (Raffi, 1984) model the enthusiasm and ways of presenting material that achieve maximum audience participation. Children often are inspired to try music and dance after watching performances. Show videos or CDs of great performances and work within your community to bring dancers and professional musicians to the school or center.

Figure 5.4   What If I Can't Sing? What If I Can't Dance?

3. **Start out right.** Singing requires breath control. Before you start singing, be certain that you stand or sit up straight. Determine your range, the low and high of what you can sing comfortably. Consult with someone who knows music about your range. To get off to a good start, consider playing a note and matching your voice to it; with older children, you might ask a child to start the song and then join in. What about dance? Are you fearful that you will be clumsy or undignified during creative movement or dance? Remember the African adage, "If you can talk, you can sing. If you can walk, you can dance." Actually, it isn't necessary to be a dancer yourself, only to guide children's expression through creative movement or dance. Children might understand the concept of rhythm better if it is related to a concrete experience many of them already have, such as the ticking of a clock. A teacher might pass around a clock, tell children to listen, and then ask, "How can we make our rhythm sticks sound like a clock?" Alternatively, the children might listen to the song "My Grandfather's Clock" or the music of the "Syncopated Clock" and move their heads, hands, or feet to the sounds of the clock. If a group of school-age children want to present a story such as "Coppelia" by Leo Delibes (1986) with musical sound effects, the teacher can relate it to their picture-symbol knowledge with questions such as, "How could you help the players remember when to play?" Children may decide to provide the director with pictorial cue cards of each instrument, to make a large story chart coded with the symbols, or to provide each player with the text of the story coded with the instrument symbols. It is appropriate to teach them dances that they will have the opportunity to enjoy throughout life as they attend celebrations—a waltz, a polka, a folk dance. Above all, avoid perpetuating the inhibitions you feel in your students. (See Moore, 2002, and Neely, 2002, for further suggestions).

4. **Accomplish curriculum goals through music, movement, and dance.** Is your goal to teach rhythm? If so, you could use a simple chant such as the Big Book version of *Peanut Butter and Jelly* (Wescott, 1987) to emphasize the rhythmic patterns of language. To pose a rhythmic challenge to third graders, you could select a complicated rap such as "The Little Shekere" on Sweet Honey in the Rock's *All for Freedom* album (1989). If your goal is to improve children's memory, you might select a song with several verses, such as Peter Spier's *The Fox Went Out on a Chilly Night* (1961) for first or second graders, or something simpler such as "If You're Happy and You Know It" for preschoolers.

5. **Use the simplest accompaniments.** You may have decided that, unless you can play the piano or guitar, you cannot lead children in song. But what about the simplest instruments, such as a tom-tom, a tambourine, or maracas? One simple instrument that children (and teachers) can learn to play is the chorded zither called an autoharp. Instead of having to learn the chords by positioning the fingers (as with a guitar), you simply press a button corresponding to that chord and strum down with your thumb and up with your finger in time to the music. The major drawback to the autoharp is that it must be tuned. The best way for nonmusicians to tune it is to ask a musician to do it for you or, better yet, learn to do it for yourself by matching each string's sound to those on a CD or tape (Peterson, 1979). Another alternative is the Omnichord, an electronic version of the autoharp that requires no tuning—you need only to push a button and stroke a pressure-sensitive keyboard. There are many different models of the Omnichord, and the smaller ones are reasonably priced.

6. **Seek opportunities for professional development.** When teachers are not specialists in music and dance, they need to rely on high-quality resources. Use

(Continued)

the library. Many of the most popular children's musicians have concert tapes that you can borrow. Weston Woods has several song picture books on video, including Pete Seeger's "The Foolish Frog", Aliki's "Hush Little Baby"; visit booths where you can review materials. One shortcut to high-quality materials is to find materials that have earned positive reviews from professional organizations and have earned awards (e.g., Parent's Choice Award and the American Library Association's Notable Recording). Consult professional journal and magazine articles about music, movement, and dance activities. Finally, talk with teachers, both music specialists and regular classroom teachers, about the materials and experiences in music and dance that that they have found particularly effective with children.

For general music resources, see Anderson & Lawrence, 2006; Dunkin, 2006; for free and inexpensive music downloads: http://www.musicforlittlepeople.com/Audio_Recordings/Downloads/Free_Downloads/

Figure 5.4 *(Continued)*

Teachers fulfill their musical roles and responsibilities effectively when they function as motivators, planners, observers, and facilitators.

Teachers as Motivators

It is not sufficient for teachers to set up a music center and a listening station and sing a few songs. Children need to be introduced to music and dance experiences in an engaging way, just as with a story or lesson. The motivation for a music activity should include a concrete object, thought-provoking questions, and active participation. Mrs. O'Malley introduced a new song to her kindergarten class by placing a four-sided wooden object with one pointed end and a stem in the center of the circle. The children were not really sure what it was or why it had unusual markings on it. When she gave the object a twirl and it began to spin around, they called out delightedly, "A top!" Mrs. O'Malley then explained that it was a very special type of top, a dreidel; that it was a traditional toy of Jewish children; and that the markings on the top were Hebrew letters. Then the children learned to sing "My Dreidel" while each child took a turn spinning the top. Additional motivational ideas include introducing "The Teddybears' Picnic" with a picnic basket and arranging chairs in bus seat formation to sing the action song *The Wheels on the Bus* (Zelinsky, 1990). Older students are often captivated by popular music and, with careful screening for appropriateness, some of this music can be used for listening enjoyment, for curriculum tie-ins, and to motivate students to complete academic tasks.

Teachers as Planners

Planning a musical experience involves preparation, pacing, and variety. Preparation includes identifying your purpose, deciding what to include, and assembling all of your materials. If you are using recording equipment, ensure that it is in working order. Careful preparation will enable you to keep your attention on the children rather than on the book, musical instrument, or recording equipment. Another aspect of preparation is getting the children assembled and ready. Teach the children some basic signals that are useful when transitioning into music or dance, such as shaking a tambourine to announce singing together or using the "freeze" command to calm them down if movement and dance get too rambunctious. Strive to reduce background noise and other distractions before beginning. Don't forget to make music part of planning processes for special events. For example, if a walking field trip to the post office is planned, you might teach the humorous Woodie Guthrie song, "I'm Gonna Mail Myself to You."

Pacing is important too. Do not drag out an activity or race through it. It is generally best to alternate "mostly listening" activities with "mostly movement," to limit the amount of unfamiliar material at any one session, and to conclude with a quiet song or a song that leads into the next activity planned. If children ask to sing a song again honor their request but stop before interest wanes.

Variety is another consideration. Give children a variety of opportunities to participate by listening, singing, moving, dancing, and playing simple instruments. Think of adaptations that will allow all children to participate in some way. Remember that the goal is to extend and balance children's musical experiences, so include varied musical selections (see Figure 5.5), not only during music time, but also throughout the day.

Lullabies—Traditional and Original, American and Multicultural
Examples: *Baby's Morning Time* (Judy Collins), *Lullaby Berceuse* (Connie Kaldor & Carmen Campagne), *Star Dreamer* (Priscilla Herdman), *Earthmother Lullabies I and Earthmother Lullabies II* (Pamala Ballingham), *Lullabies for Little Dreamers* (Kevin Roth), *Nitey-Night* (Patti Ballas & Laura Baron), *Nightsongs and Lullabies* (Jim Chappell)

American Folk Songs—Children's Chants, Play Songs, and Singing Games
Examples: *Let's Sing Fingerplays* and *Activity and Game Songs* (Tom Glazer), *Circle Time* (Lisa Monet), *Family Tree* (Tom Chapin), *Doc Watson Sings Songs for Little Pickers* (Doc Watson), *Stories and Songs for Little Children* and *American Folk Songs for Children* (Pete Seeger), *The Best of Burl's for Boys and Girls* (Burl Ives), *Come On In* and *Fiddle Up a Tune* (Eric Nagler), *This a Way, That a Way* (Ella Jenkins), *Stay Tuned* (Sharon, Lois, & Bram), *American Children* (various artists), *Peter, Paul, & Mommy* (Peter, Paul, & Mary)

Nursery Tunes and Songs for the Very Young
Examples: *Mainly Mother Goose* (Sharon, Lois, & Bram), *Singable Songs for the Very Young* and *More Singable Songs for the Very Young* (Raffi), *Baby Songs and More Baby Songs* (Hap Palmer), *The Baby Record* (Bob McGrath & Katherine Smithrim), *Lullabies and Laughter* (Pat Carfra), *Shake It to the One You Love the Best: Play Songs and Lullabies from Black Musical Traditions* (Cheryl Warren Mattox)

Multicultural Music from Around the World and Music of the Child's Ethnic Heritage
Examples: *Children's Songs of Latin America* and *Cloud Journey* (Marcia Berman), *All for Freedom* (African-American) (Sweet Honey in the Rock), *Family Folk Festival: A Multicultural Sing-Along* (various artists), *Mi Casa Es Su Casa* (Michele Valeri), *Beyond Boundaries: The Earthbeat! Sampler* (various artists), *Miss Luba and Kenyan Folk Melodies* (Muungano National Choir of Kenya), *Shake Shugaree* (various cultures) (Taj Mahal), *Le Hoogie Boogie: Louisiana French Music for Children* (Michael Doucet)

(Continued)

Figure 5.5   Types of Music

Holiday, Religious, and Seasonal Music
Examples: *Leprechauns and Unicorns* and *Oscar Brand and His Singing Friends Celebrate Holidays* (Oscar Brand), *Holiday Songs and Rhythms* (Hap Palmer), *Songs for the Holiday Season* (Nancy Rover), *Just in Time for Chanukah* (Rosenthal & Safyan), Mormon Tabernacle Choir, Vienna Boys Choir, Gregorian Chant (Benedictine Monks), Reverend James Cleveland, Mighty Clouds of Joy

Contemporary Children's Music
Examples: *Evergreen, Everblue* (Raffi), *Rosenshontz* (Gary Rosen & Bill Shontz), *Sillytime Magic* (Joanie Bartels), *All of Us Will Shine, Hug the Earth,* and *Circle Around* (Tickle Tune Typhoon), *1-2-3 for Kids* (The Chenille Sisters), *Little Friends for Little Folks* (Janice Buckner), *Singin' and Swingin'* (Sharon, Lois, & Bram), *Collections* (Fred Penner), *Take Me with You* (Peter Alsop)

Popular Music—Rock, Jazz, New Age, Pop, Electronic, Movie Music, Show Music
Examples: *Sebastian the Crab* (from *The Little Mermaid*) (various artists), *Peter and the Wolf Play Jazz* (Dave Van Ronk), *Star Wars Trilogy Soundtrack* (London Philharmonic), *Electronic Music II* (Jacob Druckman), *Really Rosie* (children's musical) (Carole King/Maurice Sendak), *Baby Road* (Floyd Domino), *Fresh Aire I and Fresh Aire II* (Manheim Steamroller), *The Lion King* (Elton John)

Chants, Rhymes, and Rap
Examples: "The Little Shekere" from *All for Freedom* (Sweet Honey in the Rock), "Fiesta Musical" from *Music for Little People Sampler* (Maria Medina Serafin), various playground chants and African chants from *Where I Come From!* (Cockburn & Steinbergh)

Classical Music
Examples: *Peter and the Wolf* (Sergei Prokofiev), *Sorcerer's Apprentice* (Dukas), *Carnival of the Animals* (Camille Saint-Saens), *Sleeping Beauty* (Peter Ilyich Tchaikovsky), *The Firebird* (Igor Stravinsky), *Fiedler's Favorites for Children* and *More Fiedler Favorites* (Arthur Fiedler and the Boston Pops Orchestra), *G'morning, Johann: Classical Piano Solos* (Ric Louchard), *Nutcracker Suite* (Peter Ilyich Tchaikovsky), *Symphonie Fantastique* (Hector Berlioz), *La Mer* (Claude Debussy), *Mr. Bach Comes to Call* (Toronto Boys Choir and Studio Arts Orchestra)

Music for Dancing, Patriotic Songs, and Marching Songs
Examples: *Play Your Instruments* (Ella Jenkins), Sousa marches, Strauss waltzes, *Swan Lake* (Peter Ilyich Tchaikovsky)

Music from Various Historical Periods
Examples: *Dance of the Renaissance* (Richard Searles & Gilbert Yslas), *Shake It to the One You Love the Best: Play Songs and Lullabies from Black Musical Traditions* (various artists), *Harpsichord Music* (Jean-Philippe Rameau)

Music by Contemporary Artists
Examples: *Who's Afraid of Opera* video (Joan Sutherland), Beverly Sills, Stevie Wonder, Luciano Pavarotti, *Songbird* (Kenny G)

Story Songs for Quiet Listening
Examples: "The Ugly Duckling" from *A Child's Celebration of Song* (Danny Kaye), "Puff the Magic Dragon" from *Peter, Paul, & Mommy* (Peter, Paul, & Mary), "My

Figure 5.5 *(Continued)*

Grandfather's Clock" from *Family Folk Festival: A Multicultural Sing-Along* (Doc Watson), "Mail Myself to You" from *Special Delivery* (John McCutcheon), "The Circus Song" from *Family Folk Festival: A Multicultural Sing-Along* (Maria Muldaur)

Sources for Children's Recordings

Children's Circle
Weston, CT 06883
(800) KIDS-VID

Music for Little People
Post Office Box 1460
1144 Redway Drive
Redway, CA 95560
(800) 346-4445

Educational Record Center
Building 400, Suite 400
1575 Northside Drive
Atlanta, GA 30318-4298
(800) 438-1637

Redleaf Press
450 North Syndicate Suite 5
St. Paul, MN 55104-4125
(800) 423-8309

It is also important to develop a variety of strategies for achieving learning goals. If you want to teach children a new song, for example, you could:

- Play the song in the background for several days so children will be familiar with it when it is introduced.
- Teach children the chorus while you sing the verses (at first).
- Sing along with a recording and tell children to join in singing with whatever portions of the song they feel comfortable with.
- Use lined poster paper to create a song chart that older students can read.
- Create a rebus (words and pictures) song sheet for children to use so that picture cues remind them of the content of each verse.
- Teach children the song one phrase or sentence at a time, then combine the phrases.
- Teach children the actions to an action song first, then teach them to sing the words (or vice versa).
- Have pairs of children make small take-home song books using computer software and clip art.

In the role of planner you will no doubt want to develop thematic units. Figure 5.6 is a thematic unit on African rhythms and harmonies.

What Is a Teaching Theme?

A teaching theme begins with the concepts that children are expected to acquire as a result of the theme. Using those concepts as a foundation, the teacher identifies a variety of activities that will further develop those concepts. Other concepts suggested by the experiences can also be identified and elaborated on as they emerge from the experiences and the children's interests.

(Continued)

Figure 5.6   Sample Teaching Theme on African Rhythms and Harmonies

Concepts to Be Developed

Concept #1: Rhythm is the pattern that we hear in music; rhythm is what some people call the beat.

Introduction to Concept #1: Use a drum to demonstrate a clear, steady rhythm and a random bunch of sounds. Then play a song with a strong, steady beat that children can easily pick out and replicate on their drums. Ask children to invent rhythms on coffee can or oatmeal box drums. Share the picture book *To Be a Drum* (Coleman, 2000).

Concept #2: Harmony is what makes music blend together well; harmony makes music pleasing to the ear.

Introduction to Concept #2: Use a simple musical instrument, such as a toy xylophone, to illustrate two notes played simultaneously. After each combination of notes, ask children whether the two sounded good together or not so good. Explain that when the notes complement one another and sound good together, it is called harmony.

Activities

Pulling Together Tie a rope around a relatively heavy object, such as a small desk, and ask several of the children to pull it across the floor. Listen to "Harambe," an African chant that means "Let's all pull together," from the album *The Evolution of Gospel* by The Sounds of Blackness (1991). Point out to the children that this is a work song, one that will enable them to work more effectively because they can tug in rhythm to the song. Play the song again and tap the rhythm on a drum or sticks. Tell the children to coordinate their pulling and to tug only when they hear the beat. Compare the progress that they made in moving the object in an uncoordinated way with the progress they made when they synchronized their pulling and worked together. Measure the distance that the object moved each time and contrast the two.

Talking Drums Tell the children that you are going to answer their questions yes or no by playing a drum. Invite them to guess whether your answer is yes or no by listening alone. Demonstrate with a simple question (e.g., "Can a dog fly?"). Hit the drum sharply once for no. Then demonstrate with another question (e.g., "Can a cow moo?") and play a light roll of the drum with your fingertips to mimic the sound of the word *yes.* Use the *All for Freedom* recording by Sweet Honey in the Rock (1989) to explain why drums are so important to the African culture. For older children, invite them to generate a list of other nonverbal methods of communication (e.g., smoke signals, the flash of a mirror, a telegraph, or signal flags). Then ask them to make a list of devices we use to amplify, transmit, and enhance verbal communication (e.g., a cellular phone, microphones, walkie-talkies, letters, or a paper-cup-and-string telephone). Look at a chart of the universal symbol codes for *school crossing, danger, stop,* etc. and/or look at books that combine pictures with words to communicate, such as Marc Brown's *Hand Rhymes* (1985), *If You're Happy and You Know It* (Weiss, 1987), or *"I Can't," Said the Ant* (Cameron, 1961). Ask children if they are aware of any other cultures that used pictures to communicate (e.g., Egyptian hieroglyphics, Native Americans).

Sets and Subsets Make a list of activities and ask the children to classify them into two groups: things they can do all by themselves (e.g., roller skating, riding a bike, reading a book, or putting together a puzzle) and things that they cannot do without others (e.g., playing a lotto game, playing in a rhythm band, or using a seesaw). For

Figure 5.6 *(Continued)*

older children, introduce the concept of the intersection of sets using hula hoops or circles of yarn as Venn diagrams. Include a list of things that lend themselves to individual and group participation, such as jumping rope.

Chants and Rap Listen to a recorded chant on an album by the Grammy award–winning Zulu a capella choral group Ladysmith Black Mambazo, or watch their performance on Paul Simon's *Graceland* video. Then teach the children to sing the African nonsense chant "Che Che Koolay" and compare/contrast it with American children's playground chants on the album *Where I Come From! Poems and Songs from Many Cultures* (Cockburn & Steinbergh, 1991). Use the work chant/song "There Come Our Mothers" by Ladysmith Black Mambazo and a children's chorus (1994) to sing a song in two languages. Use "Fiesta Musical" (Medina-Serafin, 1994), a Latino rap song, as an introduction to rap.

Life in Africa Develop children's understanding of African culture by reading books such as *A is for Africa* by Ifeoma Oneyefulu (1997), *A Country Far Away* by Nigel Gray (1998), *The Village of Round and Square Houses* and *Darkness and the Butterfly* by Ann Grifalconi (1986, 1987), and *Galimoto* and *When Africa Was Home* by Karen Williams (1990, 1994).

Teachers as Observers

In the role of observer, teachers notice how children are making music, movement, and dance a part of their daily lives. Three-year-old Tracy is playing in the house-keeping area. She has the baby doll propped on her hip as she stirs the soup at the stove. Clearly, Tracy has observed the multitasking of homemaking and child care. When she is satisfied that the soup is "enough peppery," she moves to the rocking chair, where she wraps the doll in a blanket, begins to rock, and softly sings an invented lullaby. Observing Tracy's play provides her teacher with important information concerning this young child's increasing knowledge of music; she notices that Tracy understands the use of soft dynamics, a slow melodic line, and a less lively rhythmic pattern for a soothing song.

When sharing music with young children, watch for these behaviors (Jalongo & Collins, 1985):

1. *What parts of the activity generate the most response?* Children generally prefer music and songs that have dominant rhythm patterns, repetition, and nonsense syllables; evoke a mood (such as calm or lively); emphasize enjoyment; suggest enactment and movement; and tell a story (Bayless & Ramsey, 1990). Watch for the behaviors that children perform without prompting such as clapping, swaying, nodding, bouncing, or joining in the singing.

2. *When do children follow along best?* Experiment with different methods of presenting concepts to children and note which are most effective. Try to relate explanations to something that the children have experienced previously, such as "Can you show me how baby bear might walk to this music? How about papa bear?" or "Listen and watch as I make this sound that is like the clip-clop of a horse's feet. Now you take a turn and make the halves of your coconut shells sound that way too."

3. *How do children use music spontaneously?* Note when and where children burst into song, dance around, or use musical instruments. If talk with a parent reveals that a child who never sings at circle time is singing away as she rides home in the car, an audiotape of the class singing might be sent home to build the child's confidence. If children seek a quiet corner in the classroom to play their instruments, a new music center and better room arrangement might be the answer. A well-balanced program contains many different types of simple musical instruments. Figure 5.7 provides a listing of some typical classroom instruments.

Figure 5.7 Simple Musical Instruments

Sources for classroom instruments: Suzuki, Rhythm Band, Inc., and Music for Little People.

RHYTHM

Wood Blocks   Bells   Sand Blocks

Maracas   Bongo Drums   Notched Rhythm Sticks

Clicking (tone blocks, wood blocks, coconut shells)
Ringing (bells, gong, jingle taps, wrist bells)
Rattling or swishing (sand blocks, rattles, gourds, maracas, cabasa)
Booming or thudding (drums—tom-tom, bongos, African drums)
Scratching or scraping (notched rhythm sticks, gourd rasp, washboard)

MELODY

Round Bell   Tone Bar   Xylophone

Hand bells, resonator bells, tone bars, step bells, xylophone

HARMONY

Ukulele   Autoharp   Electronic Keyboard

Accordion, guitar, ukulele, banjo, autoharp, keyboards

Teachers as Facilitators

When teachers act as facilitators of music, movement, and dance, they provide children with the resources and coaching they need to accomplish important musical/kinesthetic goals. Kai, Andre, and Tyler are working together in the block area. "Let's make a music video," Tyler says, taking two of the oblong blocks and placing them together in front of one of her eyes. "You guys be the band." Kai picks up a long block, placing his left hand near the top of it and propping the other end on the waistband of his jeans. He draws his hand in a strumming motion across the block, makes sounds to imitate guitar riffs, and begins to move as he has seen MTV and VH1 performers do. Meanwhile, Andre picks up a cylindrical block and holds it in front of his mouth. "This is my microphone thing," he announces. Their teacher, observing from nearby, asks if the children would like some music to use. She brings over a small CD player and lets them select from songs they know. They choose James Taylor and Carly Simon's recording of "Mockingbird" and Tyler "videotapes" with her block cameras from every angle as Andre and Kai perform their folk song variation. Their teacher offers to set up the video camera the next day so that the children's goal of making a music video is realized.

A crucial role for teachers seeking to facilitate musical/kinesthetic growth in students is making curriculum accommodations for diverse learners so that all children can participate.

CURRICULUM ACCOMMODATIONS FOR DIVERSE LEARNERS IN MUSIC AND MOVEMENT

Young children engaged in music activities—whether it is in the "regular" classroom or a music class taught by a specialist—might have physical, emotional, and intellectual disabilities that range from mild to severe. The single most important strategy for including all young children in musical activities is to consider the child's abilities, not just disabilities, when planning a lesson (Jellison, 2002). "The arts are often the one area in which students who are challenged by academic content can first succeed" (Bafumo, 2005, p. 1).

Music and Movement Tips for an Inclusive Classroom

- Use a variety of musical selections, high-quality recorded music, and related movement (fine motor/gross motor) activities that offer rich opportunities for expression of feelings (various styles and cultures with interesting elements of melody, rhythm, harmony, dynamics, tempo, texture) (Montgomery & Martinson, 2006; Sims & Cecconi-Roberts, 2003). Incorporate music into lessons across the curriculum.
- Strive to include everyone. The best way to achieve this is to design plans using a variety of sensory modes (visual, aural, kinesthetic)—maybe even taste and smell. Before you begin, evaluate the importance and developmental appropriateness of the concept or skill students are expected to learn, the levels students are expected to eventually reach, and the developmentally appropriate approaches.
- Develop a step-by-step plan. For example, a recommended sequence for an action song is to first learn movement, then icon (connect with objects or pictures), and last, symbol (such as a song chart).

- Consider how to make music and movement objectives part of each student's IEP and determine what measure or evidence can be used to document growth. Assess students by having them model or show their understanding of the music, rather than tell about it (Mazur, 2004).
- Be aware of children's musical instrument preferences; studies show that they seek out drums, step bells, keyboards, xylophones, ukuleles, guiros, and recorders when given free time to play instruments (Basinger & Killian, 2004).
- Encourage music and movement activities outside the classroom (e.g., during recess) and at home (e.g., share songs, recorded music, and recorded musical performances with families) (O'Neill, 2002).
- Identify human resources (special education teachers, music specialists, music performances, musicians in residence, and music therapists) and material resources. Use music to promote body awareness and movement, to foster communication and social interaction, and to enhance children's self-esteem (Malloch, & Trevarthen, 2002). Singing games, for example, can be an excellent way to include all children (Young, 2002).

Specific Suggestions
Students with Emotional and Intellectual Challenges

- Realize that "... music forms an important—some would say indispensable—element in the lives and learning of children and young people who have severe learning difficulties (SLD) or profound and multiple learning difficulties (PMLD)" (Ockelford, Welch, & Zimmerman, 2002, p. 178).
- For the child with attention disorders, creative dance is a way to concentrate because "dancing involves making movement significant in and of itself. The first step in making movement dance is to pay attention to it" (Stinson, 1990, p. 35).
- Keep the pace fast enough for typical students but still appropriate for children with emotional and intellectual challenges. Independent practice for children with special needs, such as listening on headphones and playing "in time" with recorded music is recommended. After a child is coached on how to identify the beat of the music, he or she could play the autoharp, xylophone, hand drum, jingle stick, or puili stick (a split-bamboo rhythm instrument of Hawaiian origin) while listening to a song with a clear and simple rhythm pattern.
- Minimize distractions and use physical participation and visual aids to focus attention. Concrete materials support children with emotional and intellectual challenges; they also assist ELLs in building vocabulary in L2. A picture book that connects visual images, printed words (in English and Spanish), and music with dance is *Spicy Hot Color: Colores Picantes* (Shahan, 2008).
- Avoid too much time in between activities, plan for smooth transitions, and try to anticipate problems when planning lessons. For example, when introducing a particular instrument, figure out, in advance, how each student will receive a turn with the instrument. Planning for these activities helps avoid potential problems.
- Use meaningful repetition, for example, singing "Skip to My Lou" with different physical actions depicted on cue cards (clap, tap, hop, march, sway).

- Children with Down syndrome frequently respond especially well to music, as do youngsters with autism. They can move freely and expressively to "Morning" from Peer Gynt Suite no. 1 by Edvard Grieg; pretend they are one of the animals in "Carnival of the Animals" by Camille Saint-Saens; fly or swim slowly and gracefully to "The Swan"; use a heavy, swinging motion to "The Elephant" (Merrill, 2004).
- Involve children in constructing simple musical instruments—dowel rods sanded smooth for rhythm sticks, coffee can drums with pieces of inner tubes for the drum head, sandpaper on wood blocks.
- Realize that the musical behavior of children with intellectual challenges might be more similar to that of younger children. At about 18 months, children without disabilities may begin to sing spontaneously, to "rework" known songs, or to incorporate familiar bits of songs into their own improvisations during play; although it is rare for them to master all of the lyrics of a song they still might know the overall musical structure (Young, 2002). Children usually understand the word meaning of simple songs better if they combine them with body movement and imaginative play.

Students with Visual Impairments
- Emphasize the auditory, kinesthetic, and tactile modes for students with visual impairments (Montgomery, 2003). Rhythm patterns can be traced with puff paint, a raised paint that the student can feel and visually impaired students can read and write music using Braille.
- Give clear and concise explanations, and repeat them if necessary. Support verbal instructions with nonverbal means of communication. For example, if you begin to pat a steady beat on your lap, looking at your students invites them to join in. You might invite the child with visual impairments to begin by gently touching the child's forearm, with permission.
- Another delightful way for children to represent the tempo of music is to pretend to give an imaginary friend a ride on different parts of their body so that they can become one with this music (Merrill, 2004).

Students with Hearing Impairments
- Adapt lessons so they are visual and kinesthetic. The visuals can explain the sequence, the technique, or the goal. Label the concepts with words. For example, if students are learning about high and low sounds, and the visual has a picture at the top and the bottom of the page, label these pictures as "high" and "low"; otherwise students may think they are learning about up and down.
- Students who are hearing impaired can also participate very effectively in musical activities through movement. Dancing, dramatizing, and moving can help all students to learn music concepts.
- Students with hearing impairments can feel vibrations of music. Expose these children to musical instruments that enable them to use touch to experience the music, such as the air that blows from a woodwind and the vibrations of a guitar string or drum head, or the vibrations from a sound system's speaker.
- Explore specialized equipment. Many children with hearing impairments can hear certain sounds or particular instruments. There are microphones,

headphones, earphones, and combinations of them that can enhance their hearing.

Students with Orthopedic Impairments

- Assess the physical environment and adapt it to accommodate to children's orthopedic challenges and equipment (Doctoroff, 2001).
- Children with cystic fibrosis often have limited breath control and this can affect singing. Try adaptations such as letting the child rest for a moment or sing just one part of the song.
- Cerebral palsy affects a child's motor skills but the child may have more motor control on one side of the body than on the other. Try having the child clap using one hand to tap on the table or slap his or her knee, for example.
- Adapt lessons to the sensory modes available to the students; this often means emphasizing the visual and auditory. For example, when teaching a rhythm pattern, a student who cannot use his hands might tap feet or verbalize the pattern.
- There are many instruments available that have been specially constructed for students with orthopedic impairments. These range from triangles to tubas. A useful reference for finding appropriate instruments is Clinically Adapted Musical Instruments.

 # MEETING STANDARDS

Music Educators National Conference and National Dance Standards

In general, appropriate music activities for children include singing songs together, playing and listening to records and tapes, learning the names and uses of musical instruments, discovering ways of making sounds, experiencing the different ways that music makes us feel, learning to participate with music through physical action and song, discovering rhythms in everyday life, observing different instruments being played, and playing simple musical instruments (Taylor, 1999). What principles should guide teachers as they strive to incorporate music, movement, and dance into the curriculum? Music Educators National Conference (MENC) and the National Dance Association (NDA) are the major organizations that have set the standards for pre-K through high school in music, movement, and dance. They offer detailed recommendations concerning opportunities to learn as well as criteria for appropriate facilities, curriculum and scheduling, staffing, materials, and equipment. Figure 5.8 offers a general framework of beliefs governing music, movement, and dance that is based on the recommendations of MENC and NDA.

The following section identifies key standards from Music Educators National Conference (Consortium of the National Arts Education Associations, 1994) that guide music education and offers examples of classroom activities that support each standard.

Singing, Alone and with Others, a Varied Repertoire of Music

Music Educators National Conference guidelines suggest that 12 percent of every day be spent in musical activities. During early childhood there often is an empha-

- All children have potential in music and movement.
- All children bring their own unique interests and abilities to the music and movement learning environment.
- Very young children are capable of developing critical thinking skills through musical ideas and movement activities.
- Children come to early childhood music and movement experiences with diverse backgrounds.
- Children should experience exemplary musical sounds, activities, and materials.
- Young children should not be pressured to perform on stage with an audience.
- Children's music and movement activities should be enjoyable and inaugurate a lifelong appreciation for music and movement.
- Children learn best in safe, pleasant physical and social environments.
- Diverse learning environments and varied opportunities are essential in order to serve the developmental needs of many children.
- Children need effective, enthusiastic adult models.

The National Dance Association believes that all children should acquire the following abilities in dance:

1. *Movement mechanics.* Students can do the movement they choreographed with attention to transitions, flow through phrases, and correct techniques.
2. *Spatial awareness.* Students demonstrate appropriate diagonal, circular, level, or zigzag motion in relation to other persons and space.
3. *Timing and rhythm.* Students dance with correct phrasing and counts per measure of music.
4. *Dynamics.* Students demonstrate contrasts between fast and slow, sharp and flowing motions.
5. *Performance.* Students demonstrate appropriate stage presence and facial expressions and don't let mistakes keep them from completing the dance.

Figure 5.8 A Framework of Beliefs About Young Children, Music, Movement, and Dance

Note: Data from Blizzard (1999), Palmer & Sims (1993).

sis on singing. How does singing ability develop? Barrett (2006) and Mang (2005) observed the following early singing behaviors:

- For many infants/toddlers, a combination of talking and singing in which the talk is rhythmic, has the inflection of a child's native language, and often is accompanied by movement.
- For many 2- and 3-year-olds, invented singing of nonsense words and syllables or stories that may or may not incorporate simplifications of learned songs or bits of songs and/or melodies that were recalled. Music is integrated with movement and imaginative play, interestingly, a child who sang "Mary Had a Little Lamb" stopped to search for an imaginary sheep!
- For preschoolers, a marked increase in the number of learned songs (e.g., *Bingo; Teddy Bear; Twinkle, Twinkle, Little Star; Old McDonald; I Love You; Jingle Bells; Happy Birthday; Baby Beluga; The Green Grass Grew All Around*).

Learning to sing a varied repertoire of songs is a national standard in music.

Children often rework known songs, may mix them together, or combine them with improvised singing. ELLs frequently combined melodic material from their first and second language. Children who had not learned songs or portions of songs rarely produced original songs. Most children seemed to rely on the words of the song to remember the musical elements and seemed to be more attracted to a song's words when accompanied with body movements.

"Children must be immersed in a playful musical environment in which their musical utterances are nurtured and treasured" (Taggart, 2000, p. 24). Choose songs that encourage active involvement; relate to children's interests; engage the whole child; have repetitive, easy-to-learn phrases; and emphasize rhyme, rhythm, and alliteration. Older students can learn to sing the parts of songs individually and then blend their voices together. One teacher involved the second-, third-, and fourth-grade classes in learning different parts of a song and recording them. That way, when each class came in to rehearse, they could practice blending their voices together even if schedules did not permit a total group rehearsal. The result was a stirring performance at the school's spring concert.

Performing on Instruments, Alone and with Others, a Varied Repertoire of Music

Having high-quality recorded music in the classroom is much easier today than ever before. Children can shake bell bracelets along to Leroy Anderson's "Sleigh Ride" or use guiros, hand drums, and tambourines to accompany Carlos Santana. Providing simple rhythm band instruments for children to play is naturally motivating. Even if resources are limited, rhythm sticks can be made from dowel rods, sandpaper blocks from scraps of wood and sandpaper, and drums from oatmeal boxes and coffee cans. For many ideas on making simple instruments, see *Listen!* (Wilt & Watson, 1977). Other inexpensive instruments such as kazoos, tuned bells, or toy electric keyboards are another resource for making music. Elementary school children often begin their music education by learning to play plastic flutes called recorders with the music specialist. Selecting a song that the whole class can play will allow for "half the group singing while the other half plays" types of performances. Another way to provide varied opportunities for performing music is to designate a child who is learning to play an instrument in band or orchestra to play along on his or her instrument to the morning's patriotic or opening song.

Improvising Melodies, Variations, and Accompaniments

Improvisation is often neglected because it requires materials and time as well as thoughtful planning and guidance. The Suzuki String Method, for example, introduces children to improvisation in a gradual way. Young Suzuki violinists learn a very simple version of "Twinkle, Twinkle Little Star" that begins with a simple back-and-forth bow stroke. After that is mastered, new challenges are posed, such as the "Mississippi hot dog" bow stroke, which can be identified by the rhythm of its four short strokes followed by two longer strokes.

Another opportunity for improvisation is in inventing musical accompaniment for stories read aloud. "Jack and the Beanstalk" can be accompanied by a slide whistle to represent characters' ascent and descent on the stalk and "The Three Billy Goats Gruff" with drums of different sizes to represent their footsteps across the bridge. Likewise, many high-quality recordings for young children contain at least one story with sound effects and music, such as "Bear Hunt" (Bayes, 1983), that can be used to illustrate the idea. Older students might use a story about a journey, such as *Frog Odyssey* (Snape & Snape, 1991) or *How Many Days to America: A Thanksgiving Story* (Bunting, 1990), to develop a corresponding musical journey (Mantione & Smead, 2003). For more on musical improvisation activities, see Scott (2007).

Composing and Arranging Music Within Specified Guidelines for Reading and Notating Music

One of the best ways of leading children to music is to provide an environment where they have the materials, time, and opportunity to discover and build their own knowledge about music (Fox, 1989; Upitis, 1990). A music laboratory is one way of achieving this. It functions much like a scientist's laboratory—it emphasizes active involvement and gives students a chance to explore and experiment with music. Work in the music laboratory is supported by teachers who observe, model, facilitate, encourage, comment on, and ask questions about the child's activities. In the music laboratory, children can compose, arrange, read, and notate music, depending on their interests and developmental levels.

Listening to, Analyzing, and Describing Music

One first-grade teacher broadened her students' listening opportunities by playing music every morning when the children arrived and creating a listening center with a variety of high-quality recordings. The teacher obtained, free of charge, recordings produced by different U.S. military bands and colleges' and universities' CDs of wind ensembles, concert bands, marching bands, orchestras, vocal groups, and jazz bands. Additionally, she borrowed CDs from the public library on a regular basis. As a result of her efforts to encourage children to listen to, analyze, and describe music, her first graders not only identified the mood that a particular piece evoked but also became adept at describing the emotion in music to others. Figure 5.9 suggests strategies for building concepts in music and dance.

Musical Element: Dynamics (Soft/Loud)
Reception Even before birth, during the last months of pregnancy, infants have a hearing ability comparable to that of an adult, although the sounds they can hear while immersed in amniotic fluid are muffled. They startle to loud, sudden noises and are comforted by soft sounds, such as quiet music or a lullaby. Newborns and young infants benefit from listening to music of different types, including classical music, traditional lullabies, and music of many different styles and cultures.
Imitation Toddlers and young preschoolers can be helped to understand the distinction between loud and soft if these concepts are made sufficiently concrete. Allow children to directly experience what happens when the volume is turned down low and then turned up high on a piece of listening equipment. Try tapping a drum very softly, then loudly. Invite them to slap their thighs very softly, then louder, or tap their feet softly, then stomp their feet loudly. Get them to use the words *loud* and *soft* to refer to their experiences (e.g., the thunderstorm was loud, the sound of rain falling was soft).
Production Most preschoolers are capable of demonstrating their understandings of dynamics by producing sounds. You might construct a large, cardboard dial that the children can see and ask them to begin singing, then allow children to operate the dial and "turn up" or "turn down" their voices.
Musical Element: Tempo (Fast/Slow)
Reception While still in the hospital nursery, infants respond differentially to slow music, such as lullabies, and lively music, such as action songs. Babies become more active when lively music is played (Wilcox, 1994).
Imitation Make the fast/slow aspect concrete by looking at things in nature. Look at animals that move quickly, others that move slowly. Ask children to show how they move slowly and quickly by walking/running or by making the wheels of their wheelchair move faster. Get children moving around the circle and ask them to change how they move in response to the music. Then play slow songs followed by fast songs.
Production Invite children to work at the music center to create fast and slow songs using the props provided there. Children may, for example, create a lively chant or cheer to go along with pom-poms and create a slow song to accompany scarves or paper fans.

Figure 5.9   Strategies for Building Concepts in Music and Dance

Musical Element: Pitch (High/Low)

Reception

Even young infants are apparently able to distinguish between high and low pitches. If the same pitch is played repeatedly, the infant grows accustomed to it. But when a new pitch is introduced, babies will often begin to suck on a pacifier vigorously, indicating that they detect the difference and are interested again.

Imitation

Differences in pitch are often introduced to preschoolers as stair steps because this gives them a concrete way of relating to high and low pitches. Try using a wooden rocking boat set upside down and a set of tonal bells or a toy xylophone as a prop. Begin with very dramatic differences between pitches. After several demonstrations of moving up on top of the boat when the music goes higher, give children a chance to play this high/low game. The game can be made more challenging by choosing notes on the scale that are closer in pitch or by adding steps.

Production

Using a pitch pipe, keyboard, bells, or xylophone, play each note on the scale and ask children to "match" it with their voices. Teach children the song "Do Re Mi."

Musical Element: Rhythm (The Patterns of Sounds)

Reception

Even before birth, infants grow accustomed to rhythmic sounds of the mother's heartbeat and respiration. Hospital nurseries sometimes have toys or sound equipment that plays similar sounds to comfort newborns. Babies frequently relax and drift off to sleep from the rhythmic motion of a caregiver's gentle rocking, a car, a stroller, or a swing.

Imitation

Rocking and gently bouncing babies and toddlers as a part of playful games and nursery tunes teaches them the rudiments of rhythm. A child who learns to play "Pat a Cake" is imitating the rhythm.

Production

Even preschoolers can begin to move their bodies "in time" to the rhythm of the music if it is modeled for them. A good rhythm song for kindergarten and primary is "Horsey, Horsey" by Sharon, Lois, and Bram. The entire song follows the clip-clop of the horse's hooves, which can be produced by using rhythm sticks or tapping together the shells of an empty coconut.

Musical Element: Harmony (The Blending of Complementary Sounds)

Reception

From the earliest days of life, children are immersed in the harmonies of their cultures. There is ample evidence to suggest that an understanding of harmony is accelerated by early exposure and atrophies with disuse.

(Continued)

Imitation
An understanding of harmony is generally considered the last to develop. Make the complementarity of sounds concrete by playing two musical notes together on a keyboard. Ask children whether the notes sound better together or not. Consider watching a video of an African choir or inviting musicians whose work relies on close harmony, such as a barbershop quartet or folksingers, to perform for the class.

Production
It is not until elementary school that most children are taught to sing a song in two or three parts and harmonize their voices. A good recording is the Chenille Sisters.

Figure 5.9 *(Continued)*

Evaluating Music and Music Performances

Just as we compare and contrast versions of favorite pieces of children's literature, we can offer students the opportunity to hear several versions of musical works performed by different singers or instrumentalists. In doing so, we build skills of listening, discernment, and musical preference. Exposing children to the very best quality in music and musical experiences is essential. Provide high-quality recorded music, but also invite young performers from the upper grades in the district to be a part of the musical culture of the classroom. Sarah, the 9-year-old cellist from the fourth grade, cannot be expected to play like the celebrated artist Yo-Yo Ma, but kindergarten children will meet a child to whom they can relate doing something that is interesting and engaging musically.

Understanding Relationships Between Music, the Other Arts, and Disciplines Outside the Arts

Musical intelligence and bodily/kinesthetic intelligence are two distinctive "kinds of smart." As a result, children who perform well in academic subjects may or may not be gifted musically or kinesthetically. In a special project involving elementary school students that was designed to identify talent in the performing arts, 62 percent to 82 percent of those identified as gifted in dance had reading levels in the bottom half of the class, and 34 percent were below grade level in mathematics (Kay & Subotnik, 1994). Just imagine what might happen to these students if no educational opportunities in music and dance—a chance for them to shine—were available. They probably would exit the educational system early, disillusioned and defeated. If all children are at least given the opportunity to try various kinds of music and movement activities, they can begin to appreciate more fully the rich diversity among their classmates and to recognize that each person has unique strengths and talents.

Understanding Music in Relation to History and Culture

Music and movement provide a common vehicle for children to know about, understand, appreciate, and preserve cultural traditions. Children can respond to dances from other cultures through recordings. Simple dances from the Far East, India, Africa, the Americas, and continental Europe can be taught using the Nonesuch Explorer series (Numbers 7–11) as a guide. Songs in picture book format such as *Tortillitas para Mama* (Griego, 1980), a Spanish work song, or *Moonsong Lullaby*

(Highwater, 1981), a Native American lullaby, expose children to the language and music of other cultures. Music is also ideal for fostering multicultural appreciation as children listen to a collection of songs, chants, and poems from a wide array of ethnic and cultural groups through a musical collection such as *Where I Come From! Poems and Songs from Many Cultures* (Cockburn & Steinbergh, 1991). Music for Little People has a series of recordings that are collections of various types of music such as opera, show tunes, soul, lullabies, and dance music.

CONCLUSION

In a democratic society, the overarching goal in music/movement/and dance is not to single out those who are gifted or talented in music. Rather, the goal is to maximize the musical abilities of every child. All children need opportunities to develop their musical/rhythmic and bodily/kinesthetic intelligences; such opportunities should not be restricted to the privileged children whose parents and families can afford private lessons in settings outside of school. All adults who care about children need to ask themselves, "Do we value children's music, movement, and dance only for its imitation of adults' music and dance, or do we appreciate it in its own right?" Attention to young children as musicians or dancers should not be based on a talent scout model that seeks only to identify those who will become concert pianists, successful rock singers, or ballet prima donnas someday. Rather, the focus should be on music and dance for today and every day, music and dance for everyone.

There are music and movement activities suitable for every child, regardless of age, talent, or disability. When teachers make music, movement, and dance an integral part of the school day, children's development in all areas—cognitive, physical, emotional, social, and aesthetic—is supported and enriched.

Frequently Asked Questions About Music and Dance

Do parents and families really support music and dance in schools?

Participation in the arts is clouded by stereotypes, gender bias, and prejudice. In a qualitative study of parental attitudes toward arts education for children, most parents considered the arts feminine, frivolous, and nonessential to getting ahead in the "real world," other than as a way to teach self-discipline (for example, practicing a musical instrument). They were conflicted about ways in which the arts affected social status, and even families that strongly supported arts education sometimes wanted it to be an extracurricular activity to preserve the exclusivity of their child's training (Gainer, 1997). Educators need to encourage parents, families, and communities to challenge the prevailing assumptions about creativity and talent (Kemple & Nissenberg, 2000; Kindler, 1997).

Isn't the purpose of a school music program to identify the children who have the talent to benefit from instruction?

Creative expression depends not on talent alone, but also on motivation, interest, effort, and opportunity. Contemporary psychologists are downplaying the role of innate talent and emphasizing instead deliberate practice (Ericsson & Charness, 1994). If it is talent we seek, then we must actively develop it rather than merely take notice of it after it has emerged. The appropriate role of education is to provide all children with a host of thoughtfully designed experiences in creative representation, beginning in early childhood (Brickman, 1999; Chenfeld, 2002) and continuing throughout school (Torff, 2000).

CHAPTER SUMMARY

1. Each child develops musical/rhythmic and bodily/kinesthetic intelligences through interaction with others, and enjoyment of a wide variety of music and movement suited to his or her developmental level.
2. The goal of music, movement, and dance activities is to support every child's growth in these domains and develop skills in each area beginning in the earliest days of life.
3. Research on the human brain suggests that experiences with music, movement, and dance exert an enduring influence on the way that the brain responds, functions, and ultimately is organized.
4. From a cognitive perspective, children proceed through the enactive, iconic, and symbolic modes in their understandings about music.
5. A supportive physical and emotional environment, positive adult and peer interaction, and varied opportunities to enjoy and create music, movement, and dance contribute to the child's overall development.
6. Teachers fulfill their roles and responsibilities in music education when they select, present, and evaluate musical experiences effectively; when they function as motivators, planners, facilitators, and observers; and when they integrate music, movement, and dance throughout the school day and across various subject areas.

 Discuss: Your Ideas About Music

1. Compare and contrast the beliefs, values, and attitudes that underlie a program to maximize every child's musical talent with those that seek to identify precocity in music. Use your readings to support the philosophy of building every child's abilities.
2. A parent tells you, "I don't sing to my child because I never learned to play an instrument, but I play his song tape for him at night." How would you respond? Why?
3. An administrator observes the children briefly during your lesson, then asks, "Why are they having music during social studies?" How would you support your decision without becoming defensive?
4. If money were available through the budget, a donation, or a small grant, what music, movement, and dance materials would you purchase for students at various ages and stages? Why?

Chapter 6

Inviting Children's Participation in the Dramatic Arts

Of all of the arts, drama involves the participant most fully: intellectually, emotionally, physically, verbally, and socially. As players, children assume the roles of others, where they learn and become sensitive to the problems and values of persons different from themselves. As spectators, children become involved vicariously in the adventures of the characters on stage.

Nellie McCaslin, 2006, p. 4

CLASSROOM PERSPECTIVES ON CHILDREN'S PARTICIPATION IN THE DRAMATIC ARTS

Preschool–Kindergarten

In Mrs. Paitsel's preschool class, the children have been reading *Brown Bear, Brown Bear, What Do You See?* (Martin, 1995) and are now ready to enact it. The children choose a headband that resembles one of the animals in the book. Now when Mrs. Paitsel rereads the book aloud, she asks the children to show her how a duck, a horse, or a bird moves. Then children are ready to pantomime moves when they hear their animal's name read. Mrs. Paitsel rereads the story so that all the children, including Andrew, a young boy who uses a wheelchair, have more than one opportunity to move like their chosen animal character. Through this drama experience, the children warm up their bodies and use their imagination in a low-risk environment that allows each of them to participate successfully.

First Grade–Second Grade

Five children in Ms. Clark's first-grade class have asked to enact "The Little Red Hen." Florence, a nonreader, asked to be the narrator. Jesse, a shy, obese boy, has asked to play the role of the hen. Ms. Clark knows how important it is for children to reenact a favorite, familiar story. So she encouraged them to choose roles, and to practice using their body, voice, and imagination. Jesse usually speaks softly and does not enunciate clearly, but because he wants to be the Little Red Hen, he practices using his voice like a hen. Florence is not yet reading, but her role as narrator has prompted her to listen to a tape recording over and over again until she can rely on familiarity with the story to read the book aloud. This simple enactment activity helps children learn about themselves and others, develop a sense of belonging in a community of learners, gain self-confidence, and master skills and concepts in meaningful situations.

Third Grade–Fourth Grade

Mr. Carson's fourth graders are reviewing for a social studies test on the Boston Tea Party. An essential part of their review is the preparation and videotaping of a news broadcast of the actual events prior to and on December 17, 1773. The children, representing different characters, assemble in corners of the classroom depicting the settings of England, Boston, and Washington, DC. Newscasters Dana, Brandon, and Emma are "Live on the Scene" at their different locations ready to interview people about their role in the historic event. Their researching, writing, rehearsing, and teamwork in a meaningful, integrated social studies, language-arts, and drama experience clearly reflected their knowledge and understanding of this historic event.

In each of these scenarios, the teachers intentionally engaged the children in drama activities that supported their learning in other subject areas. Why should teachers devote so much time to drama? This chapter explores the dramatic arts as a subject area in its own right and also as an important instructional strategy that makes learning meaningful to children.

THEORETICAL AND RESEARCH BASE: WHAT DO WE MEAN BY DRAMATIC ARTS?

Drama, often called *enactment,* uses the art of theater to enhance the participants' awareness of self, others, and their world. In drama, children act "as if" their imagined world were an actual world and represent familiar feelings, thoughts, and actions for themselves rather than memorizing a script for an audience (Gelineau, 2004; McCaslin, 2006). Drama not only gives children a meaningful way to communicate and an opportunity to imagine possibilities, but also is a useful tool for developing higher-order thinking, problem solving, concentration, and reflection as children show what they know through their mind, voice, and body.

Drama provides a strong foundation for all of the subject areas. In *literacy,* for example, drama supports each of the language arts—listening, speaking, reading, and writing (Furman, 2000b; Jalongo, 2007). It supports *social studies* by deepening children's appreciation for other people's ways and points of view with connections to past and present events. In *science,* drama helps children understand how the physical world works, how systems and processes work, and how to use science vocabulary. And in *mathematics,* drama helps children safely explore abstract terminology and concepts.

Drama experiences tap into four kinds of intelligences that capitalize on children's learning: (1) bodily/kinesthetic, (2) verbal/linguistic, (3) interpersonal, and (4) intrapersonal intelligence (Gardner, 1993a, 1993b). Gardner's work suggests that people develop and learn in many ways and that neither children nor adults possess intelligence that is "fixed" in one area. Children, like adults, depend on different areas of their brain in different situations, at different times, and for different reasons. As children act out stories, situations, and ideas, they use their bodily/kinesthetic and/or verbal/linguistic intelligence to express themselves through gesture, voice, or movement. They use their interpersonal intelligence to work cooperatively to determine how to dramatize a favorite story or interact with an audience, and they use their intrapersonal intelligence to express feelings and develop concentration. These ways of expression offer a window into children's understandings. Table 6.1 lists and defines these four types of intelligences, relates them to enactment, and provides age-appropriate examples.

Experiences with enactment provide a natural link to children's personal experiences and knowledge. This connection contributes to all children's success in school by uncovering their hidden strengths or by challenging undeveloped areas of learning. Consequently, opportunities for drama belong everywhere in the curriculum (Hennings, 2003; McCaslin, 2006).

TABLE 6.1   Multiple Intelligences Most Related to Enactment

Type	Definition	Relation to Enactment	Examples
Bodily/Kinesthetic	Using the body to express feelings, thoughts, and solve problems; using hands to handle objects skillfully.	Offers children a concrete, specific, and personal way to think about thought and represent their knowledge.	• Role play • Story re-enactments • Pantomime • Dramatic play • Dance and movement
Interpersonal	Distinguishing among the intentions, moods, and feelings of others by being sensitive to voice, gesture, and facial expressions; responding sensitively to others' feelings and moods.	Enables children to explore feelings, moods, and points of view of others and to respond sensitively to them.	• Improvisation • Pantomime • Role play • Pretend • Puppets
Intrapersonal	Detecting one's own moods, needs, desires; looking both inward and outward.	Helps children to test out and reflect on their own feelings and moods in socially acceptable ways and to think about their responses to others.	• Dramatic play • Pantomime • Improvisation • Readers' theater • Puppets
Verbal/Linguistic	Using words and language to express one's own thoughts and to understand others.	Allows children to create dialogue, solve problems, and express feelings, thoughts, and ideas.	• Dramatic play • Improvisation • Readers' theater • Puppets • Role play • Pretend • Story re-enactments

TEACHERS' REFLECTIONS ON THE DRAMATIC ARTS

Preservice Teachers

"I now know there is an important role for an audience when using drama in the classroom. The children will always have some special involvement."

"Since using drama in my student teaching, I have heard children talk who never spoke in class before."

Inservice Teachers

"When I use story drama with my fourth graders, I notice that the children are empowered by their retellings or re-creating versions of their own. They have a much clearer understanding of sequential story events and their retellings are growing increasingly more accurate."

"I learned to address the role of the child rather than the child when intervening in dramatic play. For instance, if John is playing the role of the wolf, I say, 'Wolf, what are you going to do now that . . .'"

Your Reflections

• What role do you think drama has in the curriculum?

• How would you integrate drama experiences in your curriculum?

• How might your knowledge and beliefs about drama enhance or inhibit children's creative thinking?

The Meaning of Enactment

Five-year-old Haley was captivated by the story of *Perfect the Pig* (Jeschke, 1985). In this story, a homeless, flying piglet is found, loved, and cared for by a young woman who names the pig Perfect. Perfect is stolen and abused by a man who operates a carnival sideshow, then is happily reunited with the woman when a judge awards her custody. After hearing this story, Haley pretends to be *Perfect*, experiencing the feelings and thoughts of the pig. She also decides which props ("I'll need wings") and behaviors ("This is how he oinks when he needs help") she needs to enact that role.

Enactment occurs when children adopt the actions, feelings, thoughts, and behaviors of people in particular situations. This ability emerges at about age 3 and signals a child's developing imagination. Enactment is potentially the most powerful kind of learning because children can:

• Assume roles, create dialogue, feel emotions, use their bodies, and make decisions.
• Use personal experiences to talk about and solve problems.
• Develop knowledge of appropriate roles, actions, and behaviors.
• See others' points of view.
• Try out new and emerging skills.
• Explore the forms and functions of language (Gelineau, 2004; McCaslin, 2006; Wilhelm & Edmiston, 1998).

Children learn about their world not only from their interactions with it, but also from the way their world interacts with them. These concrete, personal experiences provide the basis for their developing abstract thinking. Because drama is always concrete, specific, and personal, it helps children more easily understand how their physical and social worlds work and connect. In other words, the dramatic mode is a powerful way of knowing.

Infants and toddlers enact events that they have directly experienced, such as diapering and feeding; *preschool and kindergarten* children add to these incidents with more imaginative and make-believe situations, such as preparing meals for a family or taking care of a baby. *Elementary children* often imagine themselves in real-life problem-solving situations, such as controlling a space shuttle in outer space or enacting their own or others' narrative stories and historical events like the Revolutionary War or Greek mythology. Enactment helps all children stretch their imaginations, share experiences safely, and explore feelings, emotions, and

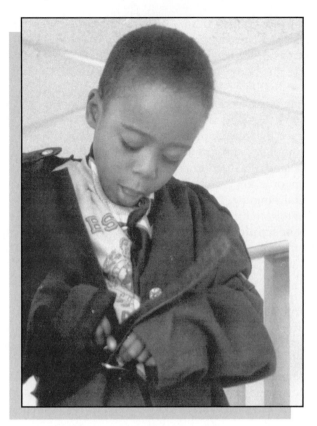

Enactment is a powerful kind of learning.

ideas in socially acceptable ways (Heathcote & Wagner, 1999; O'Neill, 1995; Roe, Smith, & Burns, 2005).

Forms of Enactment

Enactment occurs in three forms: (1) informal drama, (2) story or interpretive drama, and (3) formal or scripted drama. These drama forms can be differentiated by their degree of spontaneity versus formality (Tompkins, 2006). Following are the characteristics and an example of each form.

1. Informal drama is the most spontaneous type of enactment. It includes dramatic and sociodramatic play as well as improvisation, pantomime, and some movement activities. In informal drama, *young children* spontaneously take on a role or behavior of someone else (such as pretending to direct traffic as a police officer), use an object to stand for something else (such as sitting on a block and driving an "imaginary tractor" around fields), and use make-believe to act out familiar events (such as enacting a trip to a fast-food restaurant). There is no audience and the teacher acts as an observer or facilitator. *School-age children* engage in informal drama when they step into someone else's shoes and take their perspective and enact their own scripts based on familiar life situations (such as family celebrations of holidays), literature (such as a play based on the dramatic story of a little fruit bat, *Stellaluna* [Cannon, 1993]), or media experiences (such as the film *Jumanji*).

2. Story or interpretive drama involves interpreting someone else's ideas and words rather than creating new ideas and words. Children through Grade 4 often enact favorite stories they have heard and read or they create original stories. Take, for example, the book *Amazing Grace* (Hoffman, 1991). Grace is an African American child with a flair for drama. She pretends to be a nurse whose patients' lives are in her hands, imagines that she is the African trickster Anansi the Spider, and pretends to be a peg-legged pirate. When the class decides to enact Peter Pan, her peers tell Grace that she cannot play the lead role because she is female and black. With her mother's and grandmother's support, Grace pursues her dream. This story really lends itself to interpretation because Grace is practicing some form of enactment on every page. Story drama is particularly valuable in stimulating children's oral language and reading comprehension because they have to grasp the whole story to interpret it dramatically.

3. Formal or scripted drama, the most structured form of drama, involves a polished production of a prepared script before an audience (McCaslin, 2006). In scripted drama, the children memorize lines and someone directs. Because it is product-oriented, scripted drama focuses more on technique rather than self-expression (Bolton, 1985) and is most appropriate for children in Grade 4 or beyond. These children often write and perform, and may even direct, their own formal dramatic productions. Current thinking in the field of early childhood education is against the use of formal or scripted drama for young children through the primary grades unless, of course, children choose to create and produce their own plays (Tompkins, 2006). Table 6.2 arranges these types of enactment from least to most formal, compares the preparation time needed for each form, contrasts the role of the players and audience, analyzes materials needed, and examines implications for student learning.

Informal drama and story drama are the only forms of drama that belong in the early childhood curriculum. They offer purposeful ways to develop children's subject area knowledge as well as their imagination, thinking, nonverbal communication, and self-confidence. All three types are appropriate for children in Grade 4. In the next section we will see how drama supports all children's learning.

THE IMPORTANCE OF THE DRAMATIC ARTS IN THE CURRICULUM

For all children, the dramatic arts are a powerful vehicle for understanding difficult concepts by enacting ideas, communicating ideas based upon shared meaning, and identifying personal thoughts and feelings about oneself and others (Fennessey, 1995; Furman, 2000a; Gelineau, 2004; Podlozny, 2000; Wilhelm & Edmiston, 1998; Zemelman, Daniels, & Hyde, 2005). The dramatic arts contribute to learning in four main ways.

1. *Dramatic arts stimulate children's imagination and respect their individuality.* When children put themselves in another's life or situation, their interpretation of a role or situation is unique and has no right or wrong answers (McCaslin, 2006). One child might play the role of the wolf in "Little Red Riding Hood" as sly, another as mean, and still another as foolish. These possibilities involve children in a low risk group experience. A side benefit is that children's language and culture gain respect as they participate in drama activities both in their native language and in the majority language of the culture.

TABLE 6.2 Three Types of Enactment

Informal Drama/Dramatic Play	Story or Interpretive Drama	Formal/Scripted Drama
Least Formal ←		→ Most Formal
Characteristics		
Unrehearsed, spontaneous, invented enactment of roles and behaviors of familiar people or characters. Most characteristic of 3- to 8-year-olds.	Invented, improvised interpretation of ideas and stories using voices, gestures, and facial expressions; involves some rehearsal and is more formal.	Memorizing a written script; performing polished plays before an audience.
Preparation Time		
Minimal: children initiate roles, behaviors, actions, dialogue, and movements based on something familiar.	Moderate: children rehearse reading, interpret story, and enact roles.	Extensive: children memorize parts, dialogue, and gestures.
Roles of Players and Audience		
Active: children move freely from role of audience to that of player or director; not designed for an audience.	Active: children can be director, actor, critic, audience.	Passive: roles must be rehearsed to play; audience watches.
Materials		
Simple, familiar props; some realistic.	Simple or no props.	Elaborate costumes, props, scenery.
Implications for Student Learning		
Exerts powerful influence on ability to negotiate, concentrate, cooperate, and understand character traits; can be used with children's favorite or original stories.	Increases children's confidence in using scripted drama; allows for cooperative work with peers, reflection, revision, and increased concentration.	Should be used only at the children's suggestion and be child-directed.

2. *Dramatic arts require cooperation and teamwork.* A group of fourth graders, for example, asked their teacher if they could make up a skit. With only 40 minutes to prepare, they decided on the theme of ancient Rome, a topic they were study-ing, and wrote a script about a chariot race and a slave who wins his freedom by defeating a gladiator. The children collected props such as jump ropes, construc-tion paper, and rulers and invited their classmates to watch their skit and become improvised characters. In this snapshot, we see the children's cooperation, concen-tration, social acceptance, and give and take—all fundamental democratic princi-ples upon which our education is based.

3. *Dramatic arts provide opportunities to be actors and audiences.* Whether chil-dren are enacting or observing, they are simultaneously imagining the situations and problems of others. After learning about Kwanzaa in their first-grade class, some children shared their pantomimes and frozen pictures of celebrating the bounty of the earth. Some children were the *actors* for their peers and assumed the gestures and body movements related to their portrayals; others were *spectators* and assumed the role of critic and audience giving each child responsibility.

The dramatic arts explicitly contribute to each subject area. They are a subject in their own right whose skills must be taught in order to support learning in other

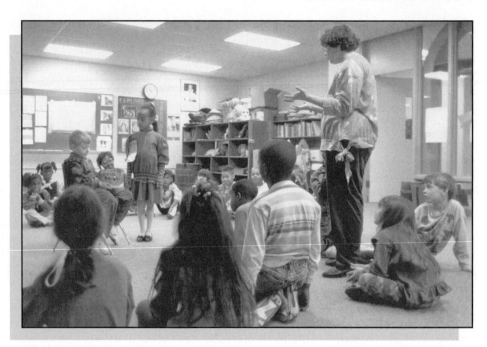

Some drama experiences provide opportunities for children to be both actors and audiences.

subject areas. In the following enactment of a restaurant theme, Kellie and Tammie, 4-year-old twins, and Brenda, a college student, are co-playing. Consider how this dramatic play episode contributes to the twins' developing imagination, ability to cooperate, effective language and literacy skills, perspective-taking ability, and appreciation of drama.

> **Kellie:**   Oh, here's your table. *(she gestures toward the table)*
> **Brenda:** Well, what should we eat, Tammie? What do you have here, Kellie?
> **Kellie:**   Well, we have pork chops, lima beans, and fish sticks.
> **Tammie:** That sounds good. We'll take it. *(Kellie exits and returns with a "tray"—two parts of a plastic sweater-drying rack)*

The girls continue their play, name their restaurant "King's," order drinks, and then ask for a check.

> **Tammie:** I want my check to be five dollars.
> **Kellie:**   Five dollars . . . and eighty-six cents.
> **Tammie:** Okay.
> **Brenda:** Do you have any money?
> **Tammie:** Oh, yeah. I have a lot of money. Oh. I forgot. I don't have a lot of money. *(starts rummaging through her purse and begins to giggle)*

In this restaurant scene, Kellie and Tammie were using drama to stimulate their imagination. Both girls' strong mental images of a restaurant helped them to create and enact the roles of customer and server as well as to embellish and ad-lib the scenario they created. When Kellie needed a tray to serve the food in the restaurant, she was problem-solving as she used two parts of a plastic sweater-drying rack for this prop. Through drama, children relive their experiences by creating their own worlds and experiment with solutions to real-life problems (McCaslin, 2006).

Drama also provides meaningful opportunities for children to practice literacy skills. It elicits more verbal play and richer language than in any other setting (Christie & Johnson, 1983; Furman, 2000b; Tompkins, 2006), develops narrative competence when children invent stories that contain essential story elements, displays children's knowledge of the functions of reading and writing (McMaster, 1998; Wiltz & Fein, 1996), and increases both children's confidence in their abilities to speak language and the value they place on communicating precisely (McMaster, 1998). Play episodes such as this one give children opportunities to use all of the various forms and functions of language (Halliday, 1975).

The dramatic arts also contribute to children's perspective-taking ability. When children actually become someone else, they learn the behaviors and feelings of that character or role, see how people affect others, and come to better understand an event or situations. By becoming slaves and gladiators in their skit, the students gained a deeper understanding of the masters' treatment of slaves and gladiators in ancient Rome and of their effect on them. Even very young children may glimpse insights that help in understanding people and, therefore, in living. In the restaurant episode, Kellie and Tammie practiced appropriate behaviors for eating in a restaurant. They also watched Brenda, the college student, model the customer role by asking, "Well, what should we eat, Tammie? What do you have here, Kellie?"

Early drama experiences build children's appreciation of drama as an art form. Today's children are tomorrow's audiences and players. School is an important context for them to gain an understanding of what drama is and how it comes into being. As so poignantly stated by Gavin Bolton (1985), a recognized expert in drama education, "Drama allows children to experience the complexities of today's world and to be prepared to live in the twenty-first century" (p. 156). Therefore, the dramatic arts are not a "frill"—they are a curricular basic.

 ## APPROPRIATE DRAMATIC ARTS ACTIVITIES

Appropriate drama experiences allow children to communicate and learn in meaningful ways through active, creative experiences in all subject areas. Some of the most appropriate drama experiences include dramatic and sociodramatic play, story play, pantomime, puppets, readers' theater, and story drama and are described below. Rich drama experiences help children do the following:

1. Develop improved skills in reading, listening, speaking, writing, comprehension, and acting.
2. Build skill in thinking analytically and acting decisively and responsibly.
3. Strengthen the ability to concentrate, follow directions, cooperate, and negotiate.
4. Deepen understanding of subject area content.
5. Show their knowledge in different forms (Crawford, 2004; Hennings, 2003; Tompkins, 2006; Wilhelm & Edmiston, 1998).

Dramatic and Sociodramatic Play

Four-year-old Michelle dons a surgeon's cap, hangs a stethoscope around her neck, and examines "Spotty," a large teddy bear. She uses a spoon to give her patient a shot, scribbles a prescription on a scrap of paper from the play area, and hands it to her playmate, Jacob.

A group of kindergartners are being air traffic controllers and helping planes land during a blizzard. They talk about how many controllers can fit into the control tower and which planes belong to which controller. These children are engaged in dramatic and sociodramatic play.

Why Use Dramatic and Sociodramatic Play?

In dramatic and sociodramatic play, children can be both actors and directors. As actors, children actually experience the feelings, thoughts, and behaviors of the roles they are playing. As directors, they imagine the thoughts, feelings, and behaviors associated with a role and coach the actors. Playing both roles in dramatic and sociodramatic play helps children:

- Construct an understanding of how the world works by stepping into the shoes of another person (Jalongo & Isenberg, 2008).
- Negotiate with players who have different needs and views (Furman, 2000a).
- Express their inner feelings (Mayesky, 2009).
- Practice language and literacy skills as they assume different roles (Roe et al., 2005; Tompkins, 2006).
- Use printed words in play that can later become sight words (Roe et al., 2005; Tompkins, 2006).
- Explore freely and imaginatively the more structured forms of drama (McCaslin, 2006).

Using Dramatic Play in the Classroom

Ms. Senack has set up a beach theme center that includes assorted related materials such as a large ocean poster, a child-sized beach chair, a small umbrella, a collection of shells, water toys, and cassette tapes for her 4-year-old class. Ari spreads his towel along the sand, then checks his bag for sunglasses and sand toys. Shayna locates her portable radio and skips over stations until she finds the appropriate music. "Hey, Ari!" Shayna asks, "do you like this song? Let's pretend we are teenagers!" Eventually, they use towels to bury themselves and call themselves "dancing sand people." At the sand table, they engage in the following dialogue:

Ari:	Put all the shells you want in your pile. Don't get them mixed up. These are mine! *(gets a magnifying glass from the science table)* Look, this one is really dirty!
Shayna:	Let me see! *(Ari hands her the magnifying glass, and Shayna examines the shell)* That's not dirt! That's the way the shell is. It comes like that! You just don't know 'cause only if you have a 'fying glass can you see what it looks like underneath.
Ari:	My mom sometimes uses shells for plates. She has really big shells and puts our food on them.
Shayna:	Here's some macaroni and cheese! *(hands Ari a shell with some sand on it)*

This beach theme play illustrates the use of two tools for enhancing role play—prop boxes, or dramatic play kits, and dramatic play centers.

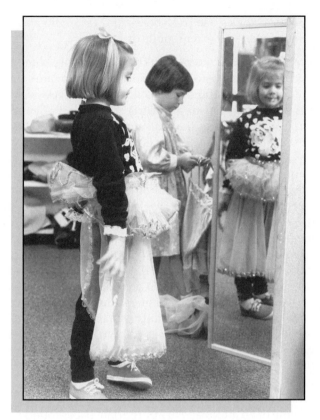

In dramatic play, children experience the actual
feelings, thoughts, and behaviors of the roles they enact.

Prop Boxes and Dramatic Play Kits

Prop boxes or dramatic play kits contain a collection of real items that are related in some way, such as a picnic basket, plastic food, a tablecloth, and plastic ants. Using real items can stimulate children's imaginative play with particular concepts, situations, and roles. Prop boxes do the following:

- Promote experiences with real materials and tools related to a theme (a toolbox).
- Sustain children's interest in their theme play (books, posters, records, and tapes related to the theme).
- Increase opportunities for family involvement by contributing materials and using literature-based prop boxes from school in the home setting.
- Provide opportunities to enact familiar roles (deposit slips and checks for a banker or boots, a net, and a fishing pole for a fisherman) (Barbour & Desjean-Perrotta, 2002; Edwards, 2006; Fikani, 2007; Myhre, 1993).

Well-planned prop boxes enhance dramatic and sociodramatic play. Younger children need adequate props, space, and time to pursue dramatic play even though their roles and themes shift frequently. Older children, whose play may be more sophisticated, can plan their play and often negotiate roles and responsibilities. At all ages, children use the props in many different ways. Be certain, however, that all of the items are safe to use and free of dangerous or loose parts.

The following strategies use prop boxes and dramatic play kits to support children's enactments that will extend units of study.

1. *Brainstorm themes that interest the children.* Choose some themes that are very familiar (such as a grocery store or a farm), others that are somewhat familiar (such as a gas station or a TV studio), and still others that are even less familiar to children (such as a travel agency or a construction project). Be certain to provide adequate background experiences that will support children's enactment.

2. *Collect storage containers.* Strong boxes with lids (such as those that contain photocopy paper) or clean, dry 5-quart ice cream tubs work well for this purpose. Label the outside of the container with the theme ("The Three Bears" or "Chinese New Year") and draw a picture or paste on a photo that will help children identify each container's contents. You might also invite the children to paint and decorate these boxes.

3. *Generate a list of possible items to include in the prop box.* Ask children, parents, colleagues, and local businesses to contribute items. Clothing, especially old uniforms and costumes, and recycled materials such as old toys and household articles are generally useful. Invite families to provide materials such as clothing, accessories, or props for a particular piece of literature to be studied in the classroom. Stories such as *The City Mouse and the Country Mouse* (Stevens, 1987), *Sylvester and the Magic Pebble* (Steig, 1969), and *Stone Soup* (Brown, 1975) lend themselves to family involvement.

4. *Identify your goals for the theme or unit.* What vocabulary could children use in their drama? How will you introduce the theme and related activities so that they build on what children know? You may want to include some books that correspond to the theme or an audiotape of appropriate background music or sounds. Record these ideas and tape them inside the cover of the prop box to serve as a guide for parents, substitute or student teachers, or administrators. These ideas will help keep the dramatic play well connected to the goals of the unit. Figure 6.1 shows one way to label a prop box. Figure 6.2 (p. 208) gives examples of what to include in a puppet prop box and a medical prop box.

Dramatic Play Centers

Dramatic play centers can contain general family living materials or materials focused on a topic familiar and interesting to a particular group of children. They encourage children's spontaneous play with a variety of roles (Howe, Moller, Chambers, & Petrakos, 1993; Woodward, 1985). Play centers make a topic, such as nutrition or careers, more real to children, and build interest in it. Use the following four strategies to encourage children's enactment in play centers.

1. *Provide a variety of background experiences.* Use pictures, stories, and discussion about the theme to build prior knowledge. Children need to be familiar with roles in order to enact them.

2. *Create an attractive physical setting.* Posters, books, and materials can transform an area of the classroom. The physical setting should invite children to enter the area and can stimulate their imaginations.

3. *Provide safe, simple, and durable props.* Select props that are well suited to children's ages, interests, and abilities. Simple props such as a cape or a magic mirror inspire children to enact roles and behaviors. You will want to check periodically that your props are in good repair and are being used properly.

4. *Involve children in planning.* Encourage children to suggest ideas for themes and to develop new theme corners periodically. Children can make and

Information to be taped *inside* the lid or cover of the prop box	Theme: _____ Goals for Center: _____ Vocabulary: _____ Introduction Procedure: _____ Field Trips and Resource People: _____
Information on the *outside* of the prop box	Theme: _____ Props (costumes, real things, objects): _____ Materials in Box: _____ Suggested Supplements: _____ Child-Made Materials: _____
Adult roles	Observer: Watch play. Collaborator: Add a new prop, ask a question, help children gain entry to the play. Model: If invited, join the play and model a role or action and then leave. Mediator: Help children find peaceful solutions to conflicts. Safety Monitor: Check for hazards, worn or damaged materials, clutter.

Figure 6.1   Prop Box Guide

collect the necessary props. When introducing a new theme corner, jointly establish limits such as the number of children who can be there at any one time. Figure
6.3 (p. 209) shows a dramatic play center for a fast-food restaurant that incorporates goals, materials, and related activities. Figure 6.4 (p. 210) lists other ideas for
dramatic play centers and shows a doctor's office.

Story Play

Story play, also called *story dictation,* is a form of guided drama that uses children's
own stories as the content for enactment (Paley, 1992, 2004). In story play, children
can be both writers and actors by dictating stories to an adult or by writing their
own stories that later become plays to dramatize. As authors, children choose
which of their friends might play certain roles as the teacher reads the original stories. Story play in the preschool and kindergarten years is a natural transition to
the journal writing and shared reading and writing typically encountered in the
primary grades (Vukelich, Christie, & Enz, 2002). In Grades 1–4, story drama provides a way for young writers to compose meaning on multiple levels and facilitates children's ownership of their imaginative work within the drama world,
which reappears in their writing (Crumpler and Schneider, 2002).

Figure 6.2 Materials
for Puppet and
Medical Prop Boxes

Puppet Prop Box:

Paper plates, paper bags, craft sticks, tongue depressors,
buttons, sequin pieces, wallpaper pieces, cotton balls,
construction paper, pipe cleaners, yarn, glue, scissors,
markers, tape, books about puppetry and puppet making.

Medical Prop Box:

Dolls, stuffed animals, doll-sized furniture, doctor
kit, stethoscope, tongue depressors, plastic digital
thermometer, plastic syringes, bandages, eye
chart, white shirts for uniforms, pad, pencil,
telephone, appointment book, shower cap, empty
pill containers, scale, patient folders, coupons for
medical supplies and products, magazines, books
and posters about doctors and nurses.

Why Use Story Play?

Vivian Paley (1992, 2004) reports that children who see their own stories enacted are motivated to write other stories for dramatization so that they can become story players. Many teachers use children's own stories to dramatize to
support children's language and literacy development and to build a strong
sense of community in the classroom. In this way, enactment provides all children an opportunity to be "story tellers," to express their ideas both verbally
and nonverbally, to increase their communicative competence, and to participate in a simple yet powerful dramatic experience. Story play is predicated on
the idea that children can learn to read and write more easily if they use their
own words because they have more meaning for them. Story play is one way to
include shy children, second-language learners, and children with special
needs into classroom drama.

Using Story Play in the Classroom

Story play begins by encouraging children to write their own stories or to dic-
tate stories to an adult who writes them down. Older children can write their
own stories for later enactment to a small group or to the whole class. One by
one, each child author chooses a role to play from his or her story and selects
classmates to play different roles. The child author may also serve as the director as the teacher reads the child's story aloud. Periodically, select an original
story to keep in each child's portfolio so that you can see his or her storytelling
abilities progress over time.

Goal	Vocabulary	Teacher-Provided Props
To increase children's ability to choose and enact roles	Restaurant	Uniforms
	Drive-through	Play money
	Cashier	Trash can, dishcloth, mop
	Cook	Stove
	Menu	Cups, straws, trays
	Food	Assorted containers
	Customer	Cooking utensils
	Trash can	Pencils
	Cash register	Cards for taking orders
	Tables and chairs	Wall posters of food & prices

Child-Provided Props	Introducing the Center	Related Activities
Hats	1. Discuss eating in a fast-food restaurant.	1. Take a field trip and eat in a fast-food restaurant.
Aprons		
Menus	2. Discuss roles of workers and customers.	2. Invite employees to talk with the children about their work.
Signs		
Decorated car made from box	3. Introduce imprinted items from different restaurants and have children sort and classify them.	3. Collect cups, napkins, hats, and other objects.
Price list		
Styrofoam containers		4. Cook and taste different kinds of potatoes.

Figure 6.3   Dramatic Play Center for a Fast-Food Restaurant
Note: Data from Isbell (1995).

The story play procedure validates children's attempts at writing and telling stories. The more ways children can elaborate their own ideas, the more complex their stories will become and the better insight they will have about narrative structure.

Pantomime

Pantomime, a type of informal drama, is a good starting point for the dramatic arts. In pantomime, children use gestures and movement to communicate ideas, feelings, and actions—all without words. As part of their unit on the circus, a group of second graders were pantomiming eating cotton candy. Some children held their hands in front of their faces and bit off chunks of the cotton candy; others pulled some candy off the cones with their hands and ate it; still others just licked their hands and fingers. The teacher encouraged responses from the onlookers by asking, "How did you know it was cotton candy?" or "What else might the mimers have done to show you it was cotton candy and not an ice cream cone?" In this way, the second graders and their teacher used pantomime to give form to their ideas.

Figure 6.4
Suggestions for
Dramatic Play
Centers

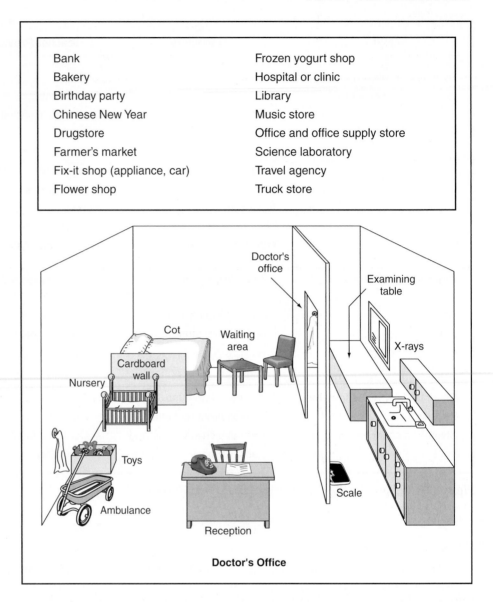

Bank	Frozen yogurt shop
Bakery	Hospital or clinic
Birthday party	Library
Chinese New Year	Music store
Drugstore	Office and office supply store
Farmer's market	Science laboratory
Fix-it shop (appliance, car)	Travel agency
Flower shop	Truck store

Doctor's Office

Why Use Pantomime?

Pantomime helps children feel comfortable with their bodies while interpreting ideas, feelings, and actions. Because it begins with physical experience, it makes concepts more concrete. Specifically, pantomime helps children:

1. Develop the confidence and tools needed for later story dramatization.
2. Communicate nonverbally.
3. Convey their understanding of characters and events through gesture and movement.
4. Develop skills in acting, concentrating, listening, language, and audience awareness (Edwards, 2006; Hennings, 2003; McCaslin, 2006).

Because mime uses no words or dialogue, it is particularly valuable for children who are English Language Learners, who have speech or hearing problems, or who are very shy. It helps them develop the confidence to express themselves through body language. In pantomime, all children can be successful because they do not have to use verbal communication.

Using Pantomime in the Classroom

It is a good idea to introduce pantomime first as a whole-group activity. Once children feel comfortable using their bodies to act out situations, they can begin to explore simple characterizations and role-play common experiences. Children express themselves more freely when many children and the adults participate. *Preschool and kindergarten* children need help getting started with pantomime. The less experienced children are, the more background and modeling they need to stimulate their imaginations before they can create their own interpretations. Children respond positively to teachers' suggestions, such as, "Show me with your body that it is cold outside" or "Let's pretend you are a stick floating down a quiet stream." Young children also like to interpret their actions and gestures to music or pantomime characters from a favorite story, such as "The Three Billy Goats Gruff."

School-age children enjoy miming parts of favorite stories as well as making up original and humorous skits for group pantomime. They also can be encouraged to pantomime individuals currently in the news, such as politicians or sports figures. In this way, they explore sophisticated variations of actions or feelings and respond favorably to teachers acting as choreographers in changing their actions (Hennings, 2003). The more children observe nonverbal behaviors, the more able they are to add body language and gestures to their own nonverbal repertoire. One third-grade teacher, for example, asked the children to pantomime the characters from *Mufaro's Beautiful Daughters* (Steptoe, 1987), a book they were reading. She invited the children to respond as a group to her calls: "The king is looking for a wife. You are Manyara, a selfish, mean, spoiled child and you are very jealous of your sister, Nyasha. Show me with your body what you would look like when you found out the king might ask Nyasha to be his wife. You are Nyasha, Manyara's kind, considerate, and beautiful sister; show me what you would look like when you found out that Manyara wanted to be the king's wife. Show me anger, jealousy, kindness, and beauty." As the context changes, the children interpret and invent the appropriate movements, such as body stiffness, facial and arm gestures, and sharpen their imaginations as they became one of Mufaro's daughters.

Because all children like to make and do things, miming interests them. Children can best mime actions that they have experienced and that they can easily imagine. Some appropriate mime activities for *young children* are:

1. Acting out familiar nursery rhymes such as "Jack and Jill" or "One, Two, Buckle My Shoe."
2. Showing what it is like to do your favorite after-school activity, such as riding a bike or working in the family garden.
3. Being a character or an animal in favorite songs. Short songs, such as "I'm a Little Teapot," are good introductions to mime and song.
4. Modeling familiar actions such as brushing teeth, washing hands, riding on a crowded bus, or eating in the school cafeteria. Children also like to mime throwing balls of different sizes, eating a dripping ice cream cone, or washing dishes.
5. Imagining they are other creatures, such as a tiger stalking through the jungle looking for food, a kitten lapping some milk, or a wriggling worm.

Elementary children who have little experience with mime also need practice and modeling before they can be comfortable with mime. Teaching mime in a group conveys the message that there are many ways to interpret characters and events.

Some appropriate mime activities for *elementary children* are as follows:

1. Showing the different stages in a life cycle such as a caterpillar or mealworm.
2. Imagining they are slaves traveling along the Underground Railroad.
3. Acting out historical events such as the Boston Tea Party, landing on the moon, or the "shot heard 'round the world" at Lexington, Massachusetts.

Puppets

Puppets make powerful teaching tools. They invite children to explore their imagination and share it with others. Puppets are the perfect props for all forms of drama!

Why Use Puppets?

Puppets add life to the classroom by naturally fostering creativity, imagination, and arts-based learning. In today's product-oriented world, they help children convey feelings, emotions, values, and ideas. They are particularly motivating for the listener because they carry a bit of mystery with them.

For children, creating and using puppets is what makes the learning valuable rather than focusing on the puppet as a finished product. Teachers can use puppets to enhance their own creativity, view children in different roles, nurture affective development, and as teaching tools for all of the subject areas.

A puppet can be a nonthreatening vehicle for the following:

- Self-expression, storytelling, improvisation, and enactment (Mayesky, 2009; Norton, 2007).
- Risk taking and building confidence in speaking abilities (Fikani, 2007; Hennings, 2003).
- Social negotiation (McCaslin, 2006).
- Releasing emotions, distinguishing between reality and fantasy, and practicing life experiences (Fikani, 2007; Hunt & Renfro, 1982).

Many puppets are simple, safe, and easy for children to create and use. A wooden spoon easily becomes a person when given a face; a mitten can be transformed into an animal by adding eyes and a nose. If puppets are to become real tools for unlocking children's creative potential, they must be easily accessible for children. Figure 6.5 lists ideas for making puppets.

Using Puppets in the Classroom

Here are some suggestions for class work with puppets.

1. *Provide opportunities for children to experiment with different puppets.* Before they create their own, have them hold the puppets in front of them or over their heads. Introduce a mirror so that they can explore the puppet's movements, voice, and gestures. Young children find it easiest to manipulate puppets with moving mouths so that they can use dialogue if they choose (Hunt & Renfro, 1982; Sawyer, 2008).

2. *Create a puppet center.* Keep a box of puppet-making materials such as scraps of fabric, paper tubing and plates, recycled buttons, yarn, and popsicle

Finger, Glove, and Mitten Puppets

Draw characters on fingers with washable markers.

Cut fingers from old work gloves or rubber gloves.

Cut a hole in old Ping-Pong balls and draw a face.

Bottle lids that are large and deep may be painted or decorated.

Use commercial finger puppets.

Decorate cardboard tubes (e.g., old bandage tube).

Box Puppets

Assorted small boxes (e.g., small candy carton, pudding, or cereal boxes for hand and finger puppet)

Assorted large boxes (e.g., cereal) for larger puppets

Assorted envelopes of all colors and sizes

Paper Bag Puppets

Assorted brown and white bags to be decorated with materials for face puppets

Assorted brown and white bags to be decorated for the body and use the fingers through the flattened bottom as the face.

Grocery bags become body puppets (called humanettes: half people, half bag)

Stick Puppets

Draw faces on assorted sticks (e.g., tongue depressors, Popsicle sticks).

Draw faces on wooden clothespins to make storytelling puppets.

Draw faces on lightweight cardboard.

Use a tongue depressor attached to a paper plate for a paper plate puppet.

Make pipe cleaner and wooden spoon puppets.

Ball Puppets

Use a Styrofoam ball for the head.

Decorate old tennis balls.

(Continued)

Figure 6.5 Ideas for Making Puppets

Cloth Puppets

Use a sock for a puppet's head and body.

Cut out and stitch a body, add a head.

Use a king-size pillowcase.

Masks

Eye masks from light cardboard

Tagboard face mask

Materials

Assorted fabric scraps of different textures; assorted sticks; assorted bags; assorted small boxes of different sizes and shapes; button eyes; colored paper; crayons; markers; egg cartons; envelopes; felt; glue; old panty hose and socks; pom-poms; rubber bands; sequins; scissors; stapler; Styrofoam balls and packing materials; tape; wire hangers; yarn.

Storage: Using common recyclable materials enhances play with puppets and makes storage attractive and accessible. Teachers have successfully used the following items: aprons with pockets; cardboard six-packs; egg cartons; expanding hanging baskets; hat or wine rack; photocopy paper boxes; multiple skirt hangers; plastic gallon containers or 2-liter plastic bottles; shoe box, bag, or rack.

Figure 6.5   *(Continued)*

sticks available. Locate the center away from the normal traffic pattern so children can gather and use their puppets in informal enactments. *Preschoolers and kindergartners* enjoy using paper plates or other recycled materials to invent puppets. *Primary-grade* children often use the puppet center to create silhouette stick puppets of favorite book characters to share informally with one another. Notice the confidence in first grader Brittany's comments while working with a friend in the puppet center:

Brittany: Oh, I love puppets. They are so cute. Hmmm . . . what can I make? I think I'll make a girl. Can I make two? Okay, then I'll make a girl and a boy. We can do a little play then. I'll be the girl and you can be the boy.

3. *Use puppets to help children express feelings with their voices.* Encourage children to use high- or low-pitched voices, or animal sounds such as squeaking, growling, or chirping. For example, a kindergarten teacher uses paper plate puppets with happy, sad, surprised, and frightened faces on them. She tells a short story, stops, and asks a child to respond using one of the puppets and an appropriate voice.

4. *Teach children some basic puppet actions.* Children can experiment with moving a puppet's head up and down to communicate "yes," moving the hands to indicate "come here" or "good bye," or moving the puppet to signal an action like running or jumping. If children are planning a puppet show and have difficulty manipulating puppets and saying the words at the same time, suggest mak-

Puppets are the perfect props for all forms of drama.

ing an audiotape. Making a recording in advance gives them the chance to focus on the puppet's actions (McCaslin, 2006; Sawyer, 2008).

5. *Create puppets that illustrate what children are learning.* A group of third graders created puppets dressed to represent the different social classes in ancient Rome. The children wrote their own scripts and performed puppet skits for younger children. A fourth-grade teacher invited her children to make African masks to illustrate important ceremonial events of that culture. Studying the symbolism and different uses of masks captures the interests of elementary children who are intrigued about learning about the people who created such masks (McCaslin, 2006). To see Samantha making a puppet using concepts she has learned in math and science, watch the video, "Samantha Makes an Octopus Puppet" online at MyEducationLab.

6. *Provide guidelines for safety and management.* To maximize the value of puppets in the classroom, involve children in establishing limits and responsibilities in using puppets. For example, puppets can be used for talking with one another, creating a puppet show, or retelling a story. Teachers should not allow puppets to be used as action figures in "hand-to-hand" combat.

Story Drama

Story drama, a type of interpretive drama, is based on the reenactment of familiar stories, poems, fables, or original stories. Sometimes called story retelling, story drama often consists of a teacher-led group with children creating scenes from familiar literature that use both dialogue and movement (Booth, 2005; Vukelich et al., 2002). Preschool and kindergarten children enjoy dramatizing cumulative tales such as *Henny Penny* (Galdone, 1968) or *Over in the Meadow* (Keats, 1971) or picture books such as *Look out, Suzy Goose* (Horacek, 2008). First and second graders enjoy dramatizing scenes from longer stories such as *Ramona the Brave* (Cleary, 1975), *Doctor De Soto* (Steig, 1982), or *Knots on a Counting Rope* (Martin & Archambault, 1987). Children in third and fourth grades enjoy enacting and debating character

MyEducationLab

Go to MyEducationLab and select the topic "Play." Under Activities and Applications, watch the video Samantha Makes an Octopus Puppet.

conflicts in longer stories such as *Number the Stars* (Lowry, 1989), *Shiloh* (Naylor, 1991), or *Holes* (Sachar, 1998).

Why Use Story Drama?

Story drama supports children's understanding of story structure, characterization, language usage, and perspective-taking. Research shows that enacting stories (1) improves reading comprehension by enabling readers to determine what is important and understand the main idea (Furman, 2000b; Jalongo, 2007; Kelner & Flynn, 2006); (2) promotes speaking, listening, critical, and creative reading skills by interpreting familiar material (Hennings, 2003); (3) heightens students' awareness of sequence of events, personalities, dialogue, and mood (Roe et al., 2005); (4) increases the ability to speak clearly and use appropriate vocabulary (Roe et al., 2005); and (5) enables children to experience the feelings and behaviors of others (McCaslin, 2006; Tompkins, 2006). In story drama, children control the length and interpretation of the particular retelling.

Using Story Drama in the Classroom

The following strategies will help you choose and adapt stories to dramatize:

    1. *Choose stories with immediate action, a simple plot, few characters, and appealing dialogue that children can easily put into their own words.* Children must be familiar with the story and characters if they are to re-create the plot and the conversation. Folk tales such as *How Many Spots Does a Leopard Have?* (Lester, 1990) or *Fables* (Lobel, 1980) fit this criterion.

    2. *Involve children actively in the selection of the story.* Choosing stories to enact builds interest in dramatization. Stories suitable for dramatization, such as *The Mixed-Up Chameleon* (Carle, 1984), *One Fine Day* (Hogrogrian, 1971), *The Doorbell*

Story drama supports children's understanding of story structure, characterization, language usage, and perspective-taking.

Rang (Hutchins, 1986), and *The Phantom Tollbooth* (Juster, 1988), should be readily available in the classroom library.

3. *Be a facilitator.* Prepare questions in advance to help children focus on both story and drama elements. For example, in reenacting the story of *Charlotte's Web* (White, 1952), you might ask, "I wonder how Wilbur felt being the new animal and the only pig on the farm. Show me with your body and your voice. If you were an animal on Mr. Zuckerman's farm, what would you do to help Wilbur? Show me with your body and your voice. Imagine you are Wilbur. What are you thinking about? Show me."

4. *Provide ample time and space for children to plan the dramatization, decide which parts to read or enact, and explore the nature of their characters.* Each child must determine how a character feels and thinks before trying to act like that character. In one first-grade reenactment of *Caps for Sale* (Slobodkina, 1947) children asked one another these questions to help them better understand the character of the peddler: Where do you live? Where did you get your caps? How will you shake your fingers, shake both hands, stamp your feet, and throw your caps on the ground? How will you act like a monkey in the trees?

5. *Reflect on the reenactment.* All children can evaluate their story dramas. Always begin with the strengths of the enactment. Ask questions that will help children focus on the drama elements of voice, action, diction, and movement of the characters. In their next reenactment, note the changes in children's voices, body movements, and imagination.

Readers' Theater

Readers' theater, another form of interpretive drama, is an oral reading of a story or script by a group of readers. In selecting literature for readers' theater, choose stories with a simple plot; a clear ending; characters that are understandable through their dialogue, and repetitive words or phrases, if available (Norton, 2007). In readers' theater, children assume a role, read aloud, and interpret the parts of the script that relate to their particular role. Props are not necessary. This form of drama focuses on children's use of the drama tools of facial and vocal expressions, gestures, and imagination to interpret a play or story in a nonstaged performance. Sometimes a narrator sets the tone, but this is not necessary. Children in third and fourth grades often develop their own scripts from familiar stories, which involve deciding on important dialogue and narration.

Because readers' theater incorporates practice before presentation, less proficient readers can often be successful in oral reading and interpretation (Forsythe, 1995; Hennings, 2003; Norton, 2007). Although readers' theater was designed for older children, it is easily adaptable to primary-grade children and nonreaders using a memorized big book on an easel or by telling the story using a felt board.

Why Use Readers' Theater?
In readers' theater, children focus only on the oral interpretation of the material, facial expressions, and simple gestures. Unlike formal, scripted drama, they are not pressured to memorize lines or use elaborate props. During readers' theater, the audience receives information and responds to the participants. Readers' theater is a particularly useful form of drama for incorporating multicultural stories, such as *Abiyoyo* (Seeger, 1986) or *Tar Beach* (Ringgold, 1991); deepening children's language proficiency by finding and enacting words through such books as *Chicka Chicka*

Boom Boom (Martin & Archambault, 1989) that begin with certain sounds, such as the *b* in *button;* practicing reading in a supportive environment, enabling less-able readers to experience fluency and comprehension in a low-anxiety setting; and providing a strategy for fostering language acquisition for second-language learners (Burke & O'Sullivan, 2002).

Using Readers' Theater in the Classroom

Teachers typically use the following procedure for readers' theater (Norton, 2007):

1. Select material that is action based, exciting, and capable of interpretation in a dramatic fashion and that can be read without help. Folktales such as "Chicken Little" and stories in verse such as *The Adventures of Taxi Dog* (Barracca & Barracca, 1990) meet these criteria.
2. Provide several group read alouds and then choose or assign parts.
3. Have readers sit on the floor or stand, with their books in front of them, while they read and act out parts as they follow along with the material.
4. Choose a narrator or director to read the title, announce the characters, describe the setting, and connect the parts to the whole. Practice reading and revising oral interpretations.

The scenarios[1] that follow illustrate appropriate uses of readers' theater with preschool/kindergarten, first–second grade, and third–fourth grade children.

READERS' THEATER FOR PRESCHOOL/KINDERGARTEN

Margy Scalia's preschoolers are focusing on the folktale "The Three Little Pigs." She encouraged the children to explore the folktale through dramatic play by adding pig and wolf puppets to the puppetry center and simple costume pieces to the dramatic-play area to support dramatic retellings of the tale and to make up their own versions. When the children were familiar with the tale, Ms. Scalia extended her literacy activities through an informal variation of readers' theater.

To do this, Ms. Scalia created prompt cards with pictures and printed text for a few of the simple words that were repeated throughout the story that she reviewed with the children, giving them an opportunity to touch them and look at the words and pictures before using them in a story. Some children were fascinated by the cards while others quickly moved on to different activities. Ms. Scalia was used to the children's different interests and did not force anyone's participation. After a few practice tries of holding up a card and having the children say the printed and illustrated word aloud, they told the story with Ms. Scalia serving as the narrator and the children joining in with the prompt card words and other familiar phrases. Afterwards, Ms. Scalia added the cards to the classroom's literacy center for the children's own story making. A few of the children had so enjoyed the activity that they often pulled out cards so that the entire class could tell the story of "The Three Little Pigs."

---

[1]Scenarios on pages 218–219 are courtesy of Kelli Jo Kerry Moran, Indiana University of Pennsylvania.

READERS' THEATER FOR FIRST AND SECOND GRADES

Ms. Lee invited her second graders to volunteer to play Anansi, a trickster from the Ashanti culture of West Africa, as told in the African tale *Anansi the Spider* (McDermott, 1972) in the upcoming readers' theater. She had selected a play that fit the interests and developmental level of her second graders and had read the story with the children before beginning the readers' theater activity; they were already familiar with the plot and characters.

Each child assumed a role, with most roles being shared by two or three children. One of Ms. Lee's greatest challenges in large-group activities was making the activity appropriate for all skill levels. This time she assigned each child's part at the appropriate reading level and used rebus scripts to support those children unable to read the entire text. After a week's worth of daily practice, Ms. Lee and the children felt ready to do an in-class, informal performance with a few teachers as a supportive audience. Ms. Lee noticed especially how Jarom and Elsie had practiced and reread the script so many times that by the end of the week they were confident and able to read their parts with ease and expression. Ms. Lee had never seen them try so hard.

READERS' THEATER FOR THIRD AND FOURTH GRADES

Josh Morales had just finished grading the readers' theater scripts his fourth-grade class had completed for the culminating activity of their civil rights unit. The quality of their work was impressive and Josh was finally glad that his cooperating teacher had insisted that he integrate language arts into his social studies unit. Readers' theater had been a good fit because it incorporated all the elements of language arts and helped Josh achieve an additional objective of helping the children develop a more empathetic understanding of the obstacles faced by civil rights leaders.

A few days later, Josh brought in a series of scripts about Martin Luther King, Jr., and taught the children some basic readers' theater conventions such as turning their back to the audience to indicate being "off stage." He modeled expressive reading and had the children brainstorm other ways to make readers' theater more effective. Then he created small groups of children, with each group given a different script. The groups negotiated their own roles and practiced those roles the next day. Not only were the subsequent performances great, but it was obvious that real social studies and language arts learning had taken place.

Appropriate drama experiences develop children's concentration, cooperation, imagination, use of body and voice, and expression of their ideas and understanding. They also build children's self-esteem, self-confidence, and understanding of the values, beliefs, and culture of others. These experiences can be integrated across the curriculum in all subject areas as described in Table 6.3, which shows how to integrate the tableau strategy for children of all ages.

TABLE 6.3 Integrating the Curriculum: Using Tableau

Integrating drama across the curriculum is one way to help children come to understand abstract ideas by enacting them concretely. Because integration means bringing all parts together to make a unified whole, you want to consider teaching the skills and concepts in drama as well as those in other subject areas such as language arts or science for connected learning.

There is considerable debate around integrating drama into the curriculum. Some believe that true integration teaches drama as a subject in its own right with specific goals and objects that are paired with the goals and objectives of other subject areas. Others believe that drama should be used as a specific teaching strategy or vehicle for teaching other subjects. As you move toward integrating drama as a discipline in its own right, you will want to keep in mind the objectives for both drama and the other subject(s) you are teaching (Bolton, 1985; Consortium of National Arts Education Associations 1994; Crawford, 2004; Gelineau, 2004; McCaslin, 2006; Wilhelm & Edmiston, 1998). While there are infinite ways to weave drama across the curriculum, we will illustrate how one such drama technique, *tableau,* can be integrated across the curriculum.

What is tableau?

Tableau is a drama technique in which actors do not speak or move. Sometimes tableau is called living picture, frozen picture, or living statue because characters literally "freeze" in expressive poses, gestures, and movements that represent a significant event, subject, scene, picture, or character to create a "human statue." Using their *bodies,* individuals, pairs, small or whole groups move like a character they pretend to be. Using their *imagination,* they see the character and the situation they are playing in their mind's eye and make them real. To be effective, children must also cooperate and concentrate as they take turns, create relationships, and maintain roles. A tableau should have a strong focal point and consist of a variety of levels, actions, and character intentions (Changing Education Through the Arts [CETA], 2005; Fay & Whaley, 2004; Kelner & Flynn, 2006; Tortello, 2004).

Why use tableau?

In the classroom, tableau gives children control over how to show their learning. This dramatic art offers a creative, controlled way for all children to focus on a specific moment, to practice visualization, and to use varying levels of space (e.g., stand, sit, bend, lie down) to express what they understand. It also challenges students to identify a character's objective or an object's purpose and/or relevance in a specific situation, serves as an introduction to acting, and provides a low risk experience with drama for teachers (CETA, 2005, Living Pictures Course).

Why is tableau suitable for children with special needs?

Tableau is particularly effective with English Language Learners because it is highly engaging, uses no language, and can be used with individuals or small and large groups. In tableau, all children can participate and express their knowledge through their bodies, which in turn helps language development (Fay & Whaley, 2004). For children who lack confidence or organizational skills, tableau offers a chance for them to improve those skills as well as to practice cooperation, concentration, and work in groups.

Tableau is a particularly powerful integration strategy because children can show what they know. In *language arts,* they can use tableau to interpret text and character traits, in *math* and *science,* they can explore the chronology of life cycles, while in *social studies and health,* they can focus on pivotal aspects of major events and concepts.

	COMMUNICATION Literacy, Language Arts and Technology	THE SCIENCES Mathematics/Science	SOCIAL STUDIES Social Studies/ Health and Safety
Preschool/ Kindergarten *Individuals*	Act out movements from an action picture chosen from a shoebox picture collection and then FREEZE to look like part of the picture, such as a child jumping, flying like an airplane, lapping milk from a dish like a kitten, galloping like a horse, or holding a baby.	Have children invent their own gestures and body movements for favorite animals or feelings and then freeze in those positions. Observers can talk about what they see. Children can also freeze their bodies into shapes—for objects like a bride, shapes that change such as an egg to a chicken, and shapes that move like a top.	Use gestures, facial expressions, and movement to show safe and unsafe ways to cross the street, or show concepts of time by sequencing events of the day, such as eating breakfast, riding the school bus, being in school, and getting ready for bed.

(Continued)

TABLE 6.3 Integrating the Curriculum: Using Tableau—continued

	COMMUNICATION Literacy, Language Arts and Technology	THE SCIENCES Mathematics/Science	SOCIAL STUDIES Social Studies/ Health and Safety
First/Second Grade *Pairs and Small Groups*	In pairs or small groups, children can revisit favorite book passages or characters and create frozen pictures that show characters' feelings or imagine a picture and communicate that idea to others. They may also freeze actions of special words in a story like glide, jiggle, or quake.	When studying life cycles of plants, a caterpillar, or a frog, invite children to choose a special part of the life cycle to make a frozen picture. Have some groups organize their frozen pictures for the beginning of the life cycle, others in the middle of the life cycle, and others at the end of the life cycle. Invite comments after the presentations.	Use gestures, facial expressions, and body movement to communicate basic social studies concepts as families. Compare similarities and differences between the home life of different families such as different ways of eating, sleeping, and greeting people after reading *The Boy of the Three-Year Nap* (Snyder, 1988).
Third/Fourth Grade *Whole Class Divided into Groups*	Using small groups, have each group create more complex tableaus based on poetry, folktales, and fairy tales, such as *The Princess and the Pea*. Children can bring a character to life from their frozen picture when the teacher "touches the shoulder" of a child in the frozen picture to hear the character's thoughts aloud.	In a study of earth and space science, have four groups create frozen pictures of the four parts of the water cycle, evaporation, condensation, precipitation, and collection. Use as an introductory or a concluding activity.	Use tableau as a culminating activity for a unit or an intermediate activity for a book they are reading. After reading the first three chapters of *Roll of Thunder, Hear My Cry* (Taylor, 2002), children can role-play and then FREEZE their solution to a racial conflict in the story for the character Little Man, who is outraged at being given a book that is cast off from a white school. OR After a unit on Martin Luther King, have children create different historic civil rights moments (e.g., civil rights marches, voting, segregated buses). In each of these moments tableau combines imagination with historic information to dramatize a powerful moment, integrating emotion into learning—greatly increasing remembering.

The class then reviews each group's work, reflecting on the criteria established and touching on areas such as:

- Interpretation
- Blocking
- Physical gesture
- Addressing the audience

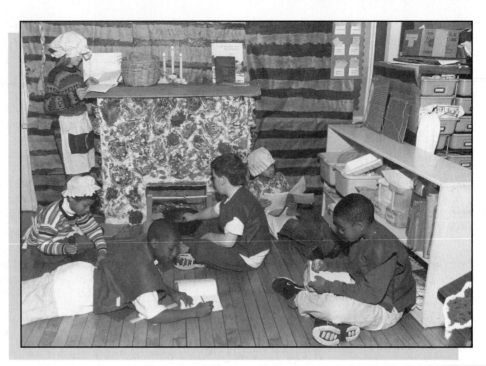

Appropriate drama experiences develop children's concentration, cooperation, imagination, use of body and voice, and self-expression.

 ## TEACHERS' ROLES AND RESPONSIBILITIES

Teachers exert a powerful influence over children's dramatic expression. As facilitators, teachers must both prepare and follow-up on children's dramatizations (McCaslin, 2006; Wilhelm & Edmiston, 1998). The following roles and responsibilities will strongly affect how you use drama in your classroom.

1. *Teach children both drama skills and content area skills.* Get comfortable with teaching the basic drama skills of *body, voice, imagination, concentration,* and *cooperation.* Children need to practice these skills so they can express what they are enacting. Help them to transform their *bodies* to move like a character by modeling and providing feedback on how the posture, poses, and gestures they use tell about a character or situation. You can also encourage them to transform their *voices* into whatever they are portraying to help them connect to characters. Children's *imagination* is an important tool as children step into a role or situation (scene), make it real and engage both the actors and the audience. Finally, children need to *cooperate* with one another and *concentrate* in order to remain focused on their body, voice, and imagination. Both the drama skills and the content skills need to be taught separately before you can expect children to be able to put them together to show what they know.

2. *Define the space to be used.* How space is arranged sends strong messages about how to use that space for drama. You will want to provide specific space for dramatic activity (such as a puppet stage), enough personal space so that children do not touch each other, and clear pathways to enter and exit those spaces.

3. *Model a behavior or attribute.* Modeling is one of the most effective drama strategies. Watch, however, for the appropriate moment to do this. In drama, teachers should not impose their ideas on children. Rather, they should encourage children to develop their own ideas, value their responses, support their improvisations, and encourage them to believe in themselves and their abilities. When Mr. Martinez's kindergartners wanted to enact a firefighting scene, they needed a prop to use as a fire hose. He invited them to problem-solve, asking, "What kind of object do you need?" Children suggested that it should be long, rounded, skinny, and sort of stretchy. They decided to use a plastic Slinky.

4. *Ask questions that provoke imagination and thinking.* Before any drama activity, find out what children know or want to know about the content and roles. For example, when Mr. Sanchez's first graders were planning to enact different kinds of camping vacations after reading *Bailey Goes Camping* (Henkes, 1985), *Three Days on a River in a Red Canoe* (Williams, 1981), and *Stringbean's Trip to the Shining Sea* (Williams, 1988) he asked the children to talk about what they knew about camping. He also asked them questions such as "Where will you all sleep?" "How will you prepare your food?" and "What will you do for fun on your trip?" By understanding his children's experiences, Mr. Sanchez challenged their thinking, which helped them enact more complex camping themes.

5. *Address the roles of the participants and audience.* For any drama experience to be successful and engaging, you will need to discuss the roles of the participants and audience prior to the activity. All children, whether taking a role as actor or audience member, must agree to work in a pretend situation, agree to the wishes of the group over the wishes of an individual, participate without monopolizing the scene, and commit to work without making fun or provoking laughter among classmates (Flynn, 2000; Kelner & Flynn, 2006). For particular situations, specific rules, such as keeping one's hands to oneself, may be needed.

6. *Allow adequate time.* Children need ample time to plan, carry out, and sustain their dramatic activity. Drama requires time to recruit players, locate materials and props, negotiate roles and plots, and carry out agreed-on ideas. To capitalize on this you will need to schedule ample blocks of time for dramatic arts (Johnson et al., 1999).

7. *Reflect with children.* Talking about specific roles and situations as well as the children's use of voice, body movements, concentration, and cooperation during and after the drama helps children develop the necessary drama skills to express their thoughts and feelings. Give children the opportunity to reflect on the drama skill, the content skill, and how they might revise each area. To illustrate, Ms. Wengel's second graders had created a shoe display as part of their Social Studies unit on clothing. It contained a variety of styles of *real shoes*, such as slippers, boots, running shoes, and ballet shoes. It also contained shoe catalogs and photos of *old-fashioned shoes* and *boots* as well as the children's own pictures of shoes of the future that the children used to sort, classify, measure, and make purchases. Ms. Wengel helped the children *reflect* on the different styles by asking them to think about how it would be to walk, put on, clean, lace and buckle, and make old-fashioned shoes and shoes of the future. How would those differ from the shoes and boots they were wearing today? By watching and listening to others' ideas and responses, they could then incorporate these *actions and movements* into future dramatizations of different shoes and how they reflected the time and culture. You can structure reflection through journaling, a reflection form with questions, having partners share a topic or questions you assign, and using small group and whole class discussions. Ask the other children to consider what they saw. What did they think was on the characters' minds? Is it worthwhile to invite several groups of students to dramatize the same scene and have the class discuss the aspects of the situation that each performance brings to light?

Talking with children about their drama, assuming different roles, and providing time, space, and resources are the building blocks of the dramatic arts. This foundation provides all children with the opportunities to explore appropriate dramatic arts experiences. In the next section, we introduce you to ways to make accommodations in drama for diverse learners.

CURRICULUM ACCOMMODATIONS FOR DIVERSE LEARNERS IN THE DRAMATIC ARTS

Dramatic experiences increase children's visual and auditory processing ability and their memory skills. Through drama, children are able to make abstract ideas concrete in ways they often cannot do through words alone (Gregoire & Lupinetti, 2005). Taking on the role of another helps children discover others' perspectives and try them out in a safe, nonthreatening environment.

Tips for Drama in an Inclusive Classroom
- Use props to make learning concrete. Many children do not know how to use "pretend" props.
- Begin with simple activities. Try an easy task such as acting like an animal or making faces and then add skills requiring oral language along with the dramatic presentation.
- Adopt a buddy system if children have difficulty moving, listening, or understanding a dramatic activity.
- Keep activity levels high and short so students remain engaged.
- Invite children to take leadership roles.
- Maintain a safe and supportive environment that encourages risk taking and reduces anxiety.
- Provide long-term projects, such as turning a story or historical event into a play for the class, to increase children's interest in the dramatic arts.

Specific Suggestions for Diverse Learners
The drama strategies that have been discussed throughout this chapter can be easily accommodated for the following learners:

Children with Learning Disabilities
Because progress in literacy acquisition is related to exposure to printed material, the more a child with a reading disability relates to and interacts with literature, the stronger reader he or she becomes (Lyon, 2003).

- When using story drama or readers' theater, make sure that scripts match the child's reading ability. Have children practice their part in small groups or with an adult.
- When using story play, encourage children to write as much as they can on their own; then type up the story so that it is readable. Have children practice what they have written and then take on the role of "director" of their own play.
- When introducing content vocabulary, begin by reading the words to children and encourage the children to act them out. Reinforce reading skills by providing vocabulary reading cards and practicing with partners.

English Language Learners

Drama activities such as body movement, choral speaking, tableau, and pantomime use children's concentration without the pressure of verbalization. Naturally immersing English Language Learners in oral language allows them to create and interpret familiar character roles, situations, and events (de Leon, 2002; Sawyer, 2008).

- Choose bilingual stories for dramatization and puppet play and encourage children to act out parts in their native language. If children are not comfortable enough to participate orally, invite them to have a role in designing and making scenery or props.

Children with Social/Emotional Challenges

Drama often is a way for children with social/emotional challenges to interact, to understand the perspective of others, and to play with voice tone and range, the skills they are unable to do on their own (Deasy, 2002). Sometimes, these children may be reluctant to join in an activity, which is okay.

- Invite children with social and emotional challenges to be a part of the audience and to make the choice when they are ready to join the activity.
- Use puppets, masks, or other props with children to take the attention away from them, allowing them to feel more open to express themselves (Pearson, 2000).

Children with Physical Exceptionalities

These children can participate in drama activities by taking the role of the narrator in a retelling, the puppeteer in a dramatization, or as a group member in choral speaking.

- Make sure that any puppets the children use or make are able to be manipulated based on their needs.
- During story reenactment, clear a large enough space to allow for easy movement. If using tableau, clearly show children how they can achieve different physical levels using their body parts in a frozen position.

    Above all, encourage children with exceptionalities to take risks in a safe environment; they will, no doubt, surprise you. In the next section, we look at how you can meet the Theater Arts Standards in all areas of your curriculum.

MEETING STANDARDS THROUGH APPROPRIATE DRAMA ACTIVITIES

Incorporating Theater Arts Standards in Your Curriculum

The Goals 2000: Educate America Act (1996), named the arts as a core academic subject. The act calls for education standards that define what America's schoolchildren should know and be able to do in the arts by the time they complete high school. The standards, developed by the Consortium of National Arts Education Associations, address four arts disciplines—dance, music, theater, and visual arts—and are categorized in grade-level clusters.

What follows is a list of the national theater standards by grade cluster K–4 followed by one idea of how you can appropriately teach both a theater and another subject area standard.

1. Improvisation

Standard #1 (K–4): Script writing by planning and recording improvisations based on personal experience and heritage, imagination, literature, and history

Standard #2 (K–4): Acting by assuming roles and interacting in improvisations

Preschool–kindergarten: Preschool children often study family life and role-play family members as part of their *social studies* curriculum. In the classroom's family living area, children decide who will be the parents and children. They gather props and assume different family roles, such as cooking breakfast, feeding the baby, getting ready for school, and going to work.

First grade–second grade: As part of a *social studies unit* on "Families around the World," children create their own passports and use them to visit families from different countries and cultures. Each family plans and pantomimes a short skit to illustrate who is in the family, what each member does, what life is like in their country, how they get around, and how the climate influences their life. Children record their observations in their passports as they visit each family around the world.

Third grade–fourth grade: To prepare for an upcoming dramatic enactment as part of their *social studies unit* on the Revolutionary War, the children create "The Boston Tea Party: Live on the Scene." They write 1-to-2-minute monologues of the character and role they are portraying, and practice their monologues while standing up, bending over, sitting down, lying on their backs, running in place, and doing jumping jacks. After discussing how the movements affect their abilities to project their voices and use good diction, all children have an opportunity to enact their monologue. The children in the audience may provide feedback on their voices by raising a green piece of paper to show that the monologue was loud enough, with clear diction, and not too fast, or a red piece of paper to show that the monologue needed improvement in one or more of these areas.

2. Designing and Directing

Standard #3 (K–4): Designing by visualizing and arranging environments for classroom dramatizations

Standard #4 (K–4): Directing by planning classroom dramatizations

Preschool–kindergarten: During a *science unit* on weather, preschool children learn how to dress appropriately for different environments. Seasonal clothing and toys in prop boxes give children the opportunity to enact dressing appropriately during different seasons. For example, when asked to enact playing in the summer, children might choose a shovel and pail and put on sunglasses, sandals, and a hat while pretending to play in the sand.

First grade–second grade: As part of a *social studies and science unit* on habitats and Native American environments, children participate in choral readings and discussions of Byrd Baylor's book *The Desert Is Theirs* (Baylor & Parnall, 1975). The culminating activity for the unit is an interactive museum, in which groups of children portray frozen picture scenes from the book. The children decide who will enact the people and animals in the desert habitat, how they might look, and what props and scenery they will need. Teachers and children view the exhibits "coming to life" with the children enacting their scene in the story.

Third grade–fourth grade: After discussing historical information about "the shot heard 'round the world" and the Boston Massacre, children design and enact a modern-day talk show of the historical event. The children decide who should be the show host, co-host, cue-card holder, and lighting and sound technicians, and which people to interview. The role of the talk show audience allows for open debates with the interviewees. The children work collaboratively and use their five senses to help visualize and create the appropriate scenery, lighting, and sound for the show's setting using similar skills and abilities they need from both social studies and language arts.

3. Researching, Comparing, and Analyzing Art Forms

Standard #5 (K–4): Researching by finding information to support classroom dramatizations

Standard #6 (K–4): Comparing and connecting art forms by describing theater, dramatic media (such as film, television, and electronic media), and other art forms

Preschool–kindergarten: After reading *The Cat in the Hat* (Seuss, 1957) and watching the animated video, children discuss the characteristics of both real and imaginary characters. With art supplies, they design imaginary puppets to act in an improvised puppet show. The teacher invites children to describe what they like to eat, wear, and do for fun, making a natural connection with *language arts* skills.

First grade–second grade: For a unit on continents, children work in groups to research, design, write, and perform in commercials for a fictitious travel agency. Each commercial features pertinent information about the continent and reasons one would want to visit and utilizes important *language arts* skills and abilities.

Third grade–fourth grade: As part of a *social studies unit* on the Civil War, children research, design, write, and perform in a courtroom drama debating slavery from the perspectives of the abolitionists and the southern planters (Fennessey, 2000). The children look at courtroom debates in movies to find ways to add visuals, music, and movement to make their arguments more compelling. In this example, children need to rely heavily on *oral language* skills.

4. Analyzing and Utilizing Forms of Media

Standard #7 (K–4): Analyzing and explaining personal preferences and constructing meanings from classroom dramatizations and from theater, film, television, and electronic media productions

Standard #8 (K–4): Understanding context by recognizing the role of theater, film, television, and electronic media in daily life

Preschool–kindergarten: As part of their *science unit* on the zoo, preschool children discuss how animals communicate. They use movement and sounds to show their feelings and to convey their needs. The children enact different scenarios such as "a hungry lion," "a sleepy bear," or "an angry gorilla." During each enactment, the teacher and students discuss what movements and sounds gave them clues as to how the animal was feeling or what the animal needed.

First grade–second grade: After reading *The Daring Escape of Ellen Craft* (Moore & Young, 2002), children work in groups to reenact scenes from the suspenseful story of two slaves determined to escape to freedom. Each group develops one of the following story parts: exposition, rising action, conflict, crisis and resolution. One group reenacts what they think is necessary background information for the characters and setting. At the end of their enactment, the teacher calls out "Freeze," and the next group of children (rising action) take their place and begin their reenactment. The groups continue to enact their parts of the story until the story is complete. At the conclusion, the children discuss how reenacting a story helps in comprehending the parts of a story. This example illustrates the meaningful integration of language arts, social studies, and drama standards.

Third grade–fourth grade: Children studying citizenship education and democratic values hold real or mock elections for classroom delegates to the school's student council. Each class selects a candidate to support and designs a political campaign for that candidate. The children collaborate to help their candidate with press conferences, debates, campaign commercials, and public service announcements. After the election, the children analyze and discuss the most and least effective strategies in each candidate's campaign. Here is another example of the meaningful connections between theater standards and social studies content.

 ## CHAPTER SUMMARY

1.   Drama contributes to every child's learning and is an essential part of a child-centered classroom. Enactment enhances the development of children's imaginative thinking, problem solving, language and literacy development, perspective-taking abilities, and appreciation of drama as an art form.
2.   Drama focuses on children's natural expression of thoughts, feelings, and ideas rather than on a polished theatrical performance.
3.   Drama activities occur in three forms. *Informal drama* uses children's natural, pretend behavior to enact roles, behaviors, and actions in such activities as role-play or pantomime. *Story or interpretive drama* involves some rehearsal, and participants use voice, gestures, and facial features to interpret someone else's ideas and words. *Scripted or formal* drama uses a memorized script performed for an audience.
4.   Teachers exert a powerful influence over children's dramatic expression. How teachers select and present drama experiences significantly influences how children will develop their creative potential.

Frequently Asked Questions About the Dramatic Arts

I am just a classroom teacher and do not have drama expertise. How can I use drama in my classroom?

Using the dramatic arts is about teaching in a way that naturally connects *what* you want to teach with *how* you teach it so that all children have powerful opportunities to learn (Crawford, 2004). You can slowly integrate drama into your curriculum as you learn along with your children. Consider making statements of possibility, such as I'm learning how to use my voice to express feelings; I'm learning how to use my body to show actions, or I'm learning how to use my imagination to put myself in someone else's shoes. Two very easy ways to get started are simple theater games (see Appendix C for many suggestions) and storytelling during which you use your voice, body, and imagination as you capture children's attention. Getting comfortable and adept at embracing classroom drama is a valuable tool for engaging children in expressing their understandings in a new form.

In this high stakes testing environment, how can I incorporate drama when I have worksheets, scripted lessons, and workbooks to do each day?

Studies show that imaginative expression through drama is an effective way to promote literacy outcomes (Wagner, 2003). According to Wagner (2003), drama produces maturity in student writing and with word-writing fluency; drama produces second- and third-grade writers whose writing shows better organization, ideas, and style than those children who have not experienced intentional attention to drama in the classroom; and dramatic role playing improves persuasive writing of fourth graders.

Wagner concludes that studies show "dramatic play in kindergartners correlates with word-writing fluency, and educational drama under a teacher's guidance is effective in improving subsequent writing in studies at second, third, and fourth grade levels. Other studies show the power of drama to improve reading and writing through choral reading of poetry, storytelling, and story drama." For example, experiences with drama promote a better understanding of narrative structure, build critical skills in vocabulary and sentence structure, and deepen comprehension in Language Arts (Crawford, 2004; Kelner & Flynn, 2006). In social studies, drama brings to life the past, present, and future of the people who inhabit the earth; deepens appreciation for other people's ways and points of view; and sharpens skills such as mapping.

How do I engage extremely shy children in drama activities?

Drama enables children to work together in groups or teams to create, direct, and interpret meaningful situations. However, for a shy student, drama activities can be very intimidating. Teachers need to resist the temptation to coax shy children into participation, because they often need additional time to observe others before participating in drama activities. Shy children may choose to watch their classmates or sit on the sidelines until they feel comfortable that their efforts will be accepted and encouraged before they actually participate. Teachers can use puppets, masks, or other props that children can either stand behind or use to take the attention away from them and feel more open to express themselves (Pearson, 2000). Additionally, teachers also need to practice the art of *side coaching,* a drama technique in which the leader gives suggestions or comments from the sidelines to heighten and advance as well as control the playing (Heinig, 1993; Kirk, Gallagher, & Anastasiow, 2007).

5.   Appropriate drama experiences for children include dramatic and sociodramatic play, story play, pantomime, puppets, readers' theater, and story drama. Each of these drama forms can be integrated into every subject area and can meet national standards.

 Discuss: Perspectives on the Dramatic Arts

1.   Many educators believe that the answer to our educational problems is a "back to basics" philosophy. What arguments would you put forth to convince other educators that drama is basic to an early childhood curriculum?

Web Sites and Resources for Dramatic Arts

http://aaronshep.com/rt/

Children's author Aaron Shepard provides many resources for readers' theater, including the acclaimed Reader's Theater Editions series of free
  scripts. Each script includes the length of the play, description of the genre,
  culture, theme, and number and ideal age of readers.

http://artsedge.kennedy-center.org/

ArtsEdge offers free, arts-integrated, standards-based teaching materials for
  classroom use. It also provides student materials and guidelines for arts-
  based instruction and assessment.

http://library.thinkquest.org/5291/

Children's Creative Theater, an Education World Reviewed Site, Graded A+,
  includes the history of theater, a glossary of theater terms, theater games,
  theater resources for all age levels, an original skit, and the opportunity to
  visit a children's theater online.

2. Teachers have an important role in integrating the dramatic arts across the
   curriculum. What teaching behaviors would you expect to see from a
   teacher who supports children's growth through drama?

3. Review the opening case study of first-grade children preparing to enact the
   story "The Little Red Hen." Why do you think Ms. Clark devoted one week
   to this activity? If a colleague criticized Ms. Clark for "wasting time," how
   might Ms. Clark respond without being overly defensive?

4. As a beginning teacher, how much experience with drama do you need to
   have? What are the minimum skills and values you will need to incorporate
   drama successfully into your curriculum?

5. Research describes the positive effects of dramatization on children's
   reading comprehension. Review some of the children's literature mentioned
   in this chapter. In what ways do these particular books encourage story
   drama in the classroom?

PART 3
CREATIVE TEACHING AND ASSESSMENT

Chapter 7

Designing Environments That Support Creativity and the Arts

The arts create an environment that is ripe for student learning and development. Teachers can bring non-arts school subjects into this space— to be taught and learned through integrated instruction.

From Lauren M. Stevenson and Richard J. Deasey (2005), *Third Space: When Learning Matters*, p. 51

 PERSPECTIVES ON THE CLASSROOM ENVIRONMENT

Preschool–Kindergarten

When Ms. Ring had surgery, she missed two weeks of school and a substitute taught her class. On the day Ms. Ring returns to her classroom, she is shocked by what she sees. There may be a place for everything, but nothing is in its place. Puzzle pieces are in the toy box, on the floor, and buried in the sand table. Dolls and stuffed toys are sticky with glue, raisins are squashed into the carpet, and crayons are mixed in with the woodworking tools. The substitute had brought in sieves, sifters, and soil so that the children could categorize and label the soil as rocks, gravel, or sand. Now those materials are everywhere. Before Ms. Ring took sick leave, she conferred with the substitute and felt confident in her creative classroom. Now Ms. Ring has doubts. Her classroom is no longer an environment that supports creativity. It is, in her words, a "disaster area"—unsupervised, unstructured, and unplanned.

First Grade–Second Grade

When you walk into Ms. Keier's second-grade classroom, you immediately notice that there are no desks, there is soft lighting around the room, including small lights that border the bulletin boards, and a few low, round tables that children work at. Two years ago, Ms. Keier decided to arrange her room in this way "to create a home away from home" for her and the children. When you visit Ms. Keier's second grade, you will notice that the children are working around a few low, round tables with flowers on them, on the floor, and in the centers. There are no desks. In the literacy area, you see a couch with soft pillows and a large stuffed bear, book bins labeled with the kinds of books they contain, and a large area rug.

Third Grade–Fourth Grade

Ms. Rapoza and Ms. Liu are deeply committed to using the arts to teach their third and fourth graders. On any given day, you might see these children working in small groups in interest centers; acting out concepts from social studies or from the literature they are reading; writing and illustrating stories and poetry in response to works of art they are studying; moving individually and together to show what they know about the cycles and patterns in science and math; and drawing their observations of natural objects in science. You will also see children's work carefully displayed with detailed descriptions of the lesson outcomes as well as teacher and student reflections. The children in these classes represent ten different countries of origin and over 20 different languages are spoken at home.

These scenarios highlight how classroom environments influence learning. Carefully designed classroom environments are "a planned arrangement of ideas, people, time, space, and resources" (McLean, 1995, p. 7) that is essential to successful teaching and learning. Environments that support children's creativity and the arts create a sense of belonging and ownership, build on children's natural curiosity and joy of learning, and allow personal initiative to flourish while developing respect and trust for others and for learning. Planning a creative environment is as important as planning for instruction. Each must harmonize with the goals of the program and/or curriculum.

In the following section, we provide the theoretical and research foundation for classroom environments that support creativity and arts-based learning.

THEORETICAL AND RESEARCH BASE: FEATURES OF CREATIVE CLASSROOM ENVIRONMENTS

Recall some of your own classrooms in which you were comfortable, felt valued, and looked forward to learning as compared to those in which you were uncomfortable, felt devalued, and felt like learning was a chore. In the first case, the quality of your classroom environment was positive; in the latter case, the quality was negative. Classroom environments that nurture creative work have three basic features: *climate, space,* and *time* (Bransford, Brown, & Cocking, 1999; Frost, Shinn, & Jacobs, 1998; Garreau & Kennedy, 1991; Jones, 1977; Kauchak & Eggen, 2007). Each is discussed next.

Climate

Climate refers to the emotional and academic feeling one gets from the environment and dictates to what extent children can be productive, engaged thinkers and learners. Classrooms that *promote* children's creative thought have the following:

- *Teachers* who care about children and their creative thought, have high expectations for all students' success, support children's efforts in both the art forms and the subject areas, and create aesthetically stimulating classrooms.
- *Children* who feel emotionally safe to take risks, are absorbed in learning, and have choices about work to be done.
- *Materials* that capture and sustain children's interest and imagination, are stored attractively and orderly, and have powerful images that spark ideas.
- *Design features* that evoke a warm, homelike quality, such as carpeted surfaces; soft, light colors; and comfortable furniture in a safe and orderly environment.

On the other hand, classrooms that *hinder* children's creativity are product-oriented and have the following:

- *Teachers* who criticize creative thinking, do not expect all students to be successful, and teach in unattractive rooms.
- *Children* who are passive learners, worry about being criticized, have few choices, and are unlikely to be risk takers.
- *Materials* that elicit one correct answer, suggest a "hands-off" approach to learning, and are stored on crowded shelves.
- *Design features* that evoke an institutional feeling, such as neutral colors, unmovable furniture, or an abundance of uncoordinated patterns.

Consider these features as you think about the feeling emanating from each of the classrooms described in the opening scenarios on classroom environments. In

Ms. Ring's classroom, the substitute allowed a disorderly environment for materials. How do you think the children in Ms. Ring's classroom felt when the substitute was there? In contrast, Ms. Rapoza's and Ms. Liu's classrooms were arranged in interest centers, displays of children's original work filled the room and the halls and provided evidence of children's learning and thinking, the classrooms were alive with activity, and the arts provided a meaningful way for children to demonstrate their knowledge. Clearly, the climate in each of these classrooms is different and dependent upon the philosophy and beliefs of its teachers. In what ways do these classrooms provide a place that is safe, orderly, conducive to creative thought, and challenging for all learners? You can also view the artifact "One-eyed Creature" online at MyEducationLab and think about ways in which you can provide a safe environment for creative expression in your classroom.

Classroom climate is greatly influenced by an environment's aesthetic appeal (Crawford, 2004; Edwards, Gandini, & Forman, 1999; New, 2004; Sanoff, 1995). The schools in the Reggio Emilia section of Italy have environments that are explicitly created to appeal to children's aesthetic senses. A visitor to such a school might see environments full of light, color, plants, and mirrors selected for their aesthetic characteristics. Great care is taken to create a beautiful environment—detail is given even to such seemingly inconsequential considerations as how bathrooms are decorated, how materials are stored, and how lunches and snacks are presented. The environment in Reggio Emilia schools is warm and beautiful, and is taken as seriously as is instruction (Edwards et al., 1999). To learn more about Reggio Emilia schools, watch the video "Reggio Emilia" online at MyEducationLab.

Published rating scales and accreditation procedures provide guidelines and items for the design of creative environments for children of all ages. These scales provide the salient items and criteria needed to design high-quality, classroom environments. Appendix B lists and describes seven such scales.

Space

Space includes the degree to which the classroom environment is organized to develop active, creative thinkers. At a minimum, you will need some open space where children can engage in dramatic retellings, express their understandings of what they are learning through movement, and enjoy each others' creative work. Young children need at least 25–30 square feet to play productively and to minimize disputes (Rettig, 1998; Smith & Connolly, 1980). Effective use of space involves flexible use of materials, defined places for quiet and noisy activities, private space, and accommodations for children with special needs.

- *Flexible use of materials.* Effective teachers use easels, movable cabinets, storage shelves, and tables to define areas so that children can work individually, in small groups, or in a whole group. The more flexible the materials and furnishings within a space, the more possible it is to maximize the potential of any room regardless of its size or shape. If, for example, children are in a school building that is undergoing renovations and want to reconstruct what they are seeing with blocks or other large materials, flexible furnishings allow for spaces to be increased and decreased in response to the children's current project needs.
- *Defined places for quiet and noisy activities.* Well-balanced classroom space separates quiet and boisterous activity and creates safe traffic patterns. It also provides small spaces necessary for young children to create

MyEducationLab

Go to MyEducationLab and select the topic "Visual Arts." Under Activities and Applications, view the artifact One-eyed Creature *and answer the questions provided.*

MyEducationLab

Go to MyEducationLab and select the topic "Curriculum." Under Activities and Applications, watch the video Reggio Emilia.

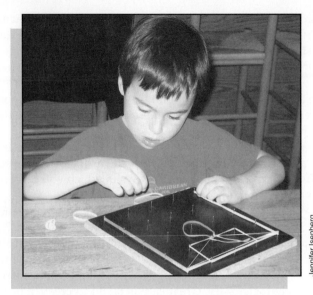

Jennifer Isenberg

Creative classrooms greatly influence children's capacity to think creatively, to engage in complex play, and to learn.

imaginative playworlds in which they can engage for long periods of time. These arrangements give both children and teachers more control and choice over their creative work and their play (Clayton, 2001; Crawford, 2004; Kritchevsky, Prescott, & Walling, 1977). Many teachers are quite inventive in using classroom space creatively.

- *Private space.* Teachers sometimes underestimate children's need for private space. Some children need a periodic rest from the activity of the classroom in a place to restore energy or to think quietly before resuming classroom work. Certain activities, such as listening to a story tape, may be enjoyed more fully in a secluded place. If classrooms lack such places, children often create their own, such as the first graders who found that the space underneath their teacher's seldom used desk was a favorite place to read. Figure 7.1 lists ways of creating small spaces in your setting to increase the quality of children's play and creative thought.
- *Accommodations for children with special needs.* Adapting space for children with special needs helps them feel part of the classroom community. A child in a wheelchair, for example, will need additional space to maneuver or sit at a table. Children who are impulsive often need two distinct spaces—one space to work alone and one space to be in a group. Children with communication disorders need environments that minimize noise and

Figure 7.1
Suggestions for Creating Small Spaces
Note: Data from Wellhousen (2002).

- *Lofts,* which use both upper and lower spaces at the same time.
- *Alcoves,* which often occur between shelves.
- *Closets,* with the door removed, which can become learning centers.
- *Screens,* which create a cozy space and enable teachers to monitor children.
- *Appliance boxes,* which become another center or an imaginary place.

promote language learning by having many opportunities to talk. How you arrange and use your space will impact how you will use your time to nurture children's creative work.

Time

Time clearly conveys the importance of an activity or experience. More than 200 years ago, Benjamin Franklin referred to time as "the stuff of life." The same could be said about time and teaching, for many teachers think there never is enough time to cover the material. Unfortunately, much classroom time is used inefficiently and inappropriately.

There is no doubt that the creative process takes time. All children need enough time to explore, develop, and complete their ideas. Time influences three dimensions of creative thought—self-expression and self-regulation, attention span, and complex thinking.

- *Time influences children's self-expression and self-regulation.* When children have enough time during the school day to engage in creative experiences, they become more self-directed learners. When children have long blocks of time, their thinking is more constructive, cooperative, and expressive than with short, interrupted time periods. In a full-day preschool or kindergarten, for example, 30 minutes per day of play is a minimum (Johnson, Christie, & Wardle, 2005). Teachers who are sensitive to time factors must be able to decide when to extend or stop an activity or when to capitalize on a "teachable moment." Classroom environments that have ample time tend to foster children's imaginative spirit and original thinking.
- *Time affects children's attention span.* Many teachers erroneously believe that because children have short attention spans, activities must be changed constantly. When children are engaged in meaningful learning, they can concentrate for comparatively long periods of time. In the schools of Reggio Emilia, for example, very young children remain with a topic for as long as they show an interest in it. Often these topics last for several months (Edwards et al., 1993; New, 2004). In elementary schools children remain with inventions and investigations for long periods of time because the projects are highly interactive and engaging.
- *Time affects the complexity of children's thought.* When children have ample time, they can tap into the kinds of creative processes used by inventors— curiosity, persistence, imagination, communication, and problem solving. Higher levels of play, such as sociodramatic play, require considerable amounts of time to plan and carry out an activity that is particularly engaging and meaningful to the child (Edwards et al., 1999; Garreau & Kennedy, 1991; Tegano, Moran, DeLong, Brickey, & Ramassini, 1996). Long blocks of time increase children's ability to move from exploration to more complex forms of investigative play with materials, people, and events. To illustrate, one primary-grade teacher helped her children observe and record changes of plant growth over time. The children classified that data by similarities and differences in types of plants, answered questions using scientific processes, and concluded their study with cooking, dramatizing, and illustrating the plant growth cycle. In this example, long blocks of time investigating a process (change in plant growth) helped children deepen their conceptual understanding (Wassermann, 2000).

The features of creative classroom environments—climate, space, and time—are critical foundations for children's creative processes. Classrooms that allow time for children to explore, inquire, and utilize its contents within safe and secure settings support children's creative processes as well as their changing needs, interests, and abilities. Classroom environments that are responsive to all children are a prerequisite to learning. Figure 7.2 contains key features of quality classroom environments that affect children's creative processes.

Softness	Hardness
Describes the feeling of the environment.	
Carpeted areas	Hard surfaces (wood or linoleum)
Soft, comfortable, and mobile furniture	Immobile furniture
Warm, soft vocal tones	Drab colors
Open	**Closed**
Describes how materials, storage patterns, and schedule enhance or restrict children's creative interactions with materials and with each other.	
Unlimited possibilities for use (e.g., collage and water)	Limited alternatives (e.g., puzzles and matching games)
Many possibilities (e.g., construction materials)	Materials to be used in one way
Visible and accessible storage	No visible or reachable storage
Simple	**Complex**
Describes the extent to which materials and equipment sustain children's interests. Simple materials do not hold children's attention very long; complex materials contribute to children's imagination.	
Single use not fostering manipulation (e.g., slides, puzzles, swings)	Combine two different materials (e.g., art, dramatic play); supercomplex materials: combine three or more materials (e.g., sand, tools, and water)
High Mobility	**Low Mobility**
Concerns the degree of children's physical activity.	
Gross motor, active physical activities (e.g., climbing, jumping)	Small motor, sedentary activities (e.g., drawing, writing)
Intrusion	**Seclusion**
Concerns boundaries and opportunities for privacy.	
Adds new people and materials to the environment; children free to move about; cross-age grouping and teachable moments	Defined private spaces for seclusion and minimal stimulation
Risk	**Safety**
Concerns opportunities for risk taking and environmental safety.	
Opportunities to experiment with new materials, ideas, and ways of playing in careful ways	Protects children from hazards
Large Group	**Individual**
Addresses the balance between large- and small-group learning opportunities throughout the day.	
Story time, musical experiences, group games, morning meeting	Lap reading, one-to-one reading, individual activities

Figure 7.2   Key Features of Creative Environments
Note: Data from Jones (1977) and Prescott (1984).

TEACHERS' REFLECTIONS ON CLASSROOM ENVIRONMENTS

Preservice Teachers

"As a student teacher, I noticed the children often started cleaning up at centers almost as soon as they initiated an activity because so little time was allotted there. When I had responsibility for full-time teaching, I extended the time blocks and saw its benefits on children's creative thinking."

"I used to think that classrooms should be serious, 'no nonsense' places to learn. I now believe that warm, safe, and homey environments are more beneficial to fostering creative thinking."

Inservice Teachers

"The idea of the environment as the 'third teacher' has prompted joyful wanderings in my own head of the possibilities associated with this notion. How to make this happen in my kindergarten class is daunting to me now, but I am convinced of the need for it and am pursuing it."

"As a school board member, I was asked to examine the playground space at one of our elementary schools and hesitated at first. Playground space just did not shout out creative thinking or priority to me in this time of high accountability and focus on test scores. Now, I realize how the playground can hold the key to hands-on extensions and expand children's view of their life, the world, and the future."

Your Reflections

- What do you think are the effects of the classroom environment on children's and teachers' thinking?

- How might your knowledge and beliefs about a creative environment influence children's self-expression and learning?

- Explain how you would go about designing your own classroom environment and provide a rationale for your decisions.

DESIGNING INDOOR ENVIRONMENTS FOR CREATIVITY AND ARTS-BASED LEARNING

In enriched classroom environments, children experience a balance of self-selected, self-directed, and teacher-selected activities. Picture these two third-grade classrooms. In Mr. Lee's class, the day begins with centers containing activities and projects selected by the children as part of their unit of study on the solar system. Some children are constructing models of planets; others are researching the distances between each planet and the sun; still others are investigating moon shapes and illustrating the different phases; and others are publishing original books, plays, and poetry about what they see in the night sky. Following centers, the children gather in a circle for their morning meeting. Mr. Lee likes the group circle arrangement for whole group because it minimizes distractions and creates a sense of belonging. Mr. Lee places traditional, whole-group activities (such as problem solving, planning events of the day, sharing, and academic or social skill development) after centers to capitalize on children's high interest in starting to learn early in the day. Next door in Ms. Gorman's classroom, the children spend the first hour and a half of each day in a language arts block. They remain seated at their desks as they begin their day with traditional openings, such as attendance, the calendar, the lunch count, and the weather. Ms. Gorman follows these opening activities with a group skill lesson and a lengthy period of teacher questions to individual children about the lesson. She constantly reminds the children to pay attention and often isolates several from the group by sending them to the "thinking chair" for becoming distracted.

Notice how the children in Mr. Lee's classroom are eager to learn, have choices of selected learning activities, and talk with their teachers and peers. Mr. Lee's classroom has a flexible schedule and organization, contains a variety of interest centers, and has well-managed transitions and routines that meet children's needs. Conversely, in Ms. Gorman's room, the arrangement is invariant, there are no interest centers, one activity blurs into another, and routines are established for teacher convenience, dictated by the schedule. In this case, Ms. Gorman's classroom environment does not provide rich opportunities for children's creative work, while Mr. Lee's arrangement supports children's creative work. The following section describes two important features of quality indoor environments that nurture creative work—*room arrangement* and *arts-based centers*.

Room Arrangement

Room arrangement refers to the way space is organized. It can be planned, such as the art center and the area around it, or unplanned, such as a cubbyhole between two shelving units that attracts children. The arrangement of your classroom has a big impact on the way children function with one another and with materials (Clayton, 2001; Hyson, 2008; McLean, 1995; Prescott, 1984).

When arranging the classroom for creative experiences, keep in mind the following principles:

1. *The environment communicates messages about appropriate behavior.* If you are invited to dinner, you would behave differently at a cookout with paper plates and plastic utensils than at a formal dinner party with china, silver, and crystal. Room arrangement works in the same way. It dictates how children may interact and use materials and affects their work pace. Well-organized space facilitates movement, creative expression, and arts-based learning. In contrast, poorly organized space invites interruptions, decreases children's attention spans, increases the likelihood of conflicts, and demands more teacher direction about rules and regulations (Jalongo & Isenberg, 2008; Johnson et al., 2005).

2. *Space must be easy to supervise.* Teachers need to be able to scan the room from all vantage points to observe and monitor children. In this way, teachers can facilitate behaviors that support learning goals and redirect those that do not. It is equally important to distinguish between the child's and the adult's environment. Teachers and children view their surroundings from different perspectives. Both usually attend to what is at their eye level (Bredekamp & Copple, 1997; Clayton, 2001).

3. *Materials must be accessible and easy to use.* Ms. Reich teaches a class of 2-year-olds and has arranged the manipulative toys such as large Tinkertoys and shape sorters along low, open shelves that face a carpeted area away from traffic flow. Because toddlers usually dump manipulatives on the floor to play with them, Ms. Reich provided the space for them to do so. From a developmental perspective, this teacher made her toys easy to use. Making materials accessible to children enhances children's sense of ownership of the classroom, encourages creative problem solving, and fosters exchanges of materials from one part of the classroom to another (Isbell & Exelby, 2001).

4. *Be alert to traffic patterns.* Well-arranged rooms provide clear pathways for a smooth and easy flow of traffic throughout the room. When centers are too close to one another and children cannot freely move among them, children interfere with each other. This usually causes conflict. To maintain freedom of movement that enables children to focus on their creative processes, paths should not be used for any other purpose. Unclear paths often distract children on their way to a space or disrupt activities by leading children to intrude in others' ongoing play or to accidentally knock over materials (Clayton, 2001). You can see how one preschool teacher creates spaces for easy traffic flow within the classroom by watching the video "Room Arrangement: Preschool" online at MyEducationLab.

Room arrangement is a powerful tool in an environment that aims to nurture children's creative work. Figure 7.3 shows room arrangements for three age groups: toddlers, preschoolers/kindergartners, and children in Grades 1–4.

Arts-Based Centers

Arts-based centers are places where individuals or small groups of children engage in activities that promote problem solving. A center-based learning environment focuses on the question, "What do the children need to learn and how will they learn it?" Arts-based centers help teachers nurture children's creative expression

MyEducationLab

Go to MyEducationLab and select the topic "Environments." Under Activities and Applications, watch the video Room Arrangement: Preschool and answer the questions provided.

Figure 7.3 Room Arrangements

For Toddlers

Figure 7.3
(*Continued*)

For Preschoolers/Kindergartners

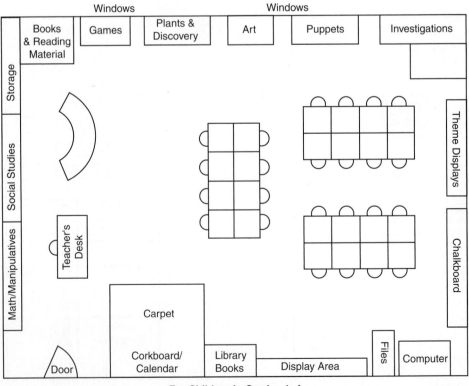

For Children in Grades 1–4

through a variety of activities. They offer a way to integrate the curriculum, develop multicultural awareness, teach to all of children's intelligences, and nurture children's spontaneity and originality (Christie et al., 2005; Isbell & Exelby, 2001; Mayesky, 2009; Sloane, 1999). Carefully designed arts-based centers contain a variety of easily accessible books, materials, resources, and supplies that:

- Promote active learning, planning, decision making, problem solving, originality, and interaction in all subject areas.
- Increase social and verbal interaction and various forms of play among peers.
- Require children to choose how to manage their time and when to move to another activity.
- Reflect children's interests and cultural backgrounds.

Arts-Based Centers for Different Age Levels

Arts-based centers are appropriate for children of all ages. While centers can and should take into account individual needs, interests, and levels of learning, some adaptations must be made for children at different ages.

Toddlers need centers that contain a variety of play materials with different levels of complexity, as well as time for exploration (Johnson et al., 2005; Mayesky, 2009; Rettig, 1998). They must have low, open shelves to display and help the children find materials that reflect familiar people and places matched to the children's developmental level. Toddlers also need materials that encourage exploration and large motor development with climbing and push-pull toys, provide a private space to watch others play or to rest with a soft toy, and offer sensory and creative experiences with music, science, pretense, construction, manipulatives, and sand and water to encourage different types of play.

Preschoolers and kindergartners need centers that meet all of the requirements for toddlers and contain a variety of interesting materials and supplies that can be used to role-play pretend games (such as hats and shoes) and to construct (such as wood, glue, and blocks). The materials must reflect the expanding world of their community, their culture, and their increasing interest in all subject areas; the activities must promote problem solving (Copple & Bredekamp, 2006).

First and second graders need centers that support their developing logical thinking skills, engage them in learning, support belonging to a peer group, integrate subjects meaningfully across the curriculum, and help them demonstrate competence in a particular area. Their learning experiences should capitalize on their need to be active learners and enable them to feel competent and successful.

Third and fourth graders tend to like resources that include literacy materials, challenge cards, hands-on learning, and ongoing projects (Hyson, 2008; Sloane, 1999). Chapter Eight details the variety of age-appropriate materials children can use in arts-based centers. Regardless of age, all children require centers to explore opportunities to connect their learning through art, drama, music, and play (Cornett, 2007).

Teachers who use arts-based centers need to consider the essential elements of space, special requirements, and safety and supervision (Crawford, 2004; Isbell & Exelby, 2001; Sloane, 1999). The following section provides suggestions for managing arts-based centers in your classroom.

Managing Arts-Based Centers in a Creative Classroom

Centers require management to capitalize on children's natural curiosity. In general, you will want to start slowly in introducing centers and be certain to teach children the basic skills needed to participate in a center activity. Arts-based centers should help children feel comfortable expressing themselves through an art form such as drawing, enacting, or writing, and contain all the materials needed to complete an activity, including instructions, checklists, progress sheets, and options for exploring the concepts and theme. The following techniques will help you manage a center-based environment (Crawford, 2004; Sloane, 1999; Wassermann, 2000):

1. *Create centers that are appropriate for a particular group of children.* Knowing the needs, interests, and background of your students is important for establishing a center that invites children's participation. You might ask, "What is appropriate for children to learn at this center?" "How will the children who use this center be able to express what they know?" Managing centers involves assessing what students know and can do, soliciting children's ideas about units of study and help in collecting items for that unit, and involving children in planning procedures for its use. Consider, for example, Mr. Kennedy's second-grade classroom. There are two large child-created displays related to their unit on insects. One display contains a variety of three-dimensional imaginative insects created by the children at the art center. Another presents children's illustrated stories about their creations. These centers contain interesting and accessible materials that invite children's participation, are attractively stored in color-coded plastic baskets and tubs, and are clearly labeled to help children keep them properly organized.

2. *Introduce the center with guidelines for its use.* Some teachers provide mini "field trips" before using a center. These excursions help children understand the center's boundaries, highlight the materials and equipment available for use, and give children a sense of how much time they have for sustained play, exploration, and investigation. They also help children know what learning goals are expected. In Mr. Kennedy's second grade, he organizes children's work as well as materials. Children use individual mailboxes made from recycled 2-liter or gallon jugs with the tops cut off, egg cartons as scissors holders, and a clothesline to display their art. Organizing children's work provides children with a sense of order that fosters their ability to gain a sense of control over their environment, as illustrated here.

3. *Use planning boards, procedure charts, and learning contracts.* These tools encourage children to recognize the beginning and end of an activity, develop planning and organizational skills related to their own activities, manage their time, work independently and with others, assume responsibility for their own activities, and reflect on their decisions (Nielsen, 2006; Sloane, 1999; Wassermann, 2000). Planning boards also help teachers limit the number of children in a center activity at any one time, evaluate and change centers as needed, and observe children's choices. Planning boards and procedure charts can be easily made from pegboard or tagboard, pictures or labels for centers, and name tags. Some teachers use a magnetic board with small magnets or magnetic tape strips on the board and paper clips glued on the back of cards. For children who are not yet readers, children's names and the names of the centers can be illustrated pictorially. Figure 7.4 illustrates a planning board used with preschoolers, kindergartners, and first graders; Figure 7.5 (p. 246) illustrates procedure charts used with primary-grade children.

Figure 7.4   A Planning Board

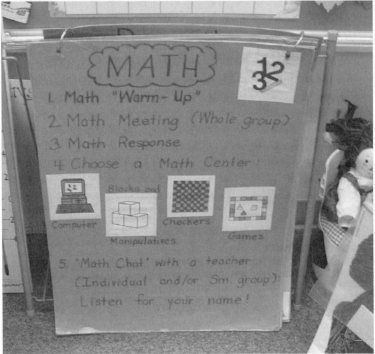

Figure 7.5   Procedure Charts
Note: Courtesy of Gail V. Ritchie, Center Ridge Elementary School, Fairfax, VA.

Learning contracts are an organizational tool to guide independent study and promote autonomy, facilitate instruction and monitor learning, and diversify learning for children (Tomlinson, 1999). Contracts allow children to choose what work to do, when to work, with whom to work, and where to work. For example, after studying different animals, some second graders contracted to extend their knowledge through art by making drawings or models of their favorite animal; others wrote original stories; still others created original scenarios, such as "Meet My Pet Boa Constrictor." Figure 7.6 illustrates learning contracts for preschoolers/kindergartners; Figure 7.7 (p. 248) illustrates learning contracts for first and second graders; and Figure 7.8 (p. 249) illustrates learning contracts for third and fourth graders.

4. *Assume specific teacher roles to facilitate learning.* Teachers can use centers to observe and assess children for social or skill use and document children's progress. Teachers can also meet with individual children to guide their center choices that are related to specific learning goals. Moreover, teachers can use center time to model behavior for children who are reluctant to participate in a center project, support children's ideas and projects through listening or participating as a co-player where needed, or pose questions that will keep children engaged in learning.

5. *Document children's progress and evaluate center use.* Documentation helps teachers identify what children are learning through center activity. Because children are engaged in a variety of experiences at the same time, it is important to

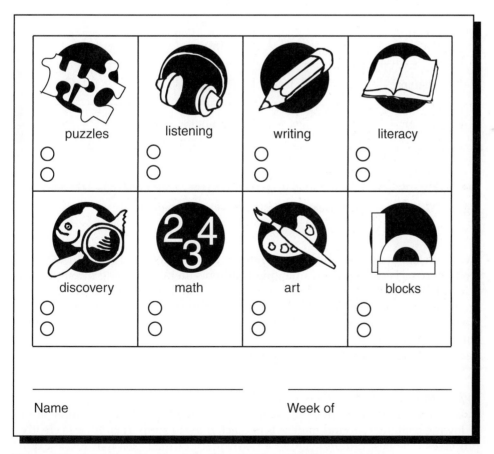

Figure 7.6   Learning Contract for Preschoolers/Kindergartners

Name _____   Week of _____

Language Arts		Math	
_____ ○		_____ ○	
_____ ○		_____ ○	
Social Studies		Science	
_____ ○		_____ ○	
_____ ○		_____ ○	

Skill Group

Lunch 🍎📖		Story 📖		Recess 🏀	
Blocks	○ ○		Literacy	○ ○	
Listening	○ ○		Puzzles	○ ○	
Projects	○ ○		Computer	○ ○	

Figure 7.7   Learning Contract for First and Second Graders

have a system in place to show what children can do. (Refer to Figure 2.1 in Chapter Two for a checklist for documenting children's literacy learning through play.) It is equally important for teachers continually to ask themselves whether children are engaged in meaningful activity and whether the centers provide ongoing opportunities and challenges. Moreover, a key part of the evaluation is to watch for children's waning interest. They may need additional props or materials or may need to start brainstorming ideas for a new theme.

Types and Uses of Arts-Based Centers

Indoor centers can be permanent, temporary, or rotating and include some of the following commonly found materials and activities to support children's creative processes. The best centers include a rich variety of materials that invite exploration, experimentation, problem solving, and connections to real life.

Biography of an Artist

1. Choose one of the following biographies to learn about an artist's life:

_____ *Sebastian: A Book about Bach* (Winter)

_____ *When Miriam Sang* (Ryan)

_____ *Michaelangelo* (Stanley)

_____ *Alvin Ailey* (Pinkney)

_____ *Duke Ellington: The Piano Prince and His Orchestra* (Pinkney)

2. Find out about your artist's life and talent as an artist, musician, or dancer. What dreams did he or she have and how did he or she fulfill them?

3. Share your findings in one of the following ways:

   a. Illustrate an interesting incident about your artist and write about why you illustrated what you did.

   b. Write a skit about your favorite part of the biography.

   c. Make a model of the artist you read about.

   d. Interview a classmate who has read this book or another book about your artist.

   e. Use computer art to represent a big idea about your artist.

   f. Other—specify: _____.

I plan to read _____, share by _____, and complete my work by _____.

Student _____

Teacher _____

Date _____

Figure 7.8   Learning Contract for Third and Fourth Graders

Art Center.   The art center enables children to investigate and create using a wide variety of materials. Some teachers display works from famous artists in or near the center to enhance aesthetic appreciation. The art center should be located near a water source. If not, use plastic sheeting to cover carpeted areas or tables when children are using messy materials.

Most art centers can be used to encourage active learning and to help children express their understanding of what they are learning. For example, in one preschool classroom, two children were designing a menu and a cover for their Mexican restaurant theme center. They used the art center to illustrate the menu and then used it to elaborate on their play. In a third-grade class, Horace used the art center to create a glove finger puppet as a prop for his story on dragons. Mrs. Ritchie's fourth graders created flyers advertising pets available for adoption to help the local animal shelter as a follow-up to reading *Shiloh* (Naylor, 1991). The students researched facts about the available pets and created an advertisement for one of them, which included a drawing of the animal, its age, and what it liked to eat and play with. In these classrooms, the centers provided a vehicle for integrating the curriculum and using the different art forms. Chapter Four contains a detailed list of appropriate uses of art materials.

Block and Construction Center.   Blocks and construction materials (such as Unifix cubes and Legos) help children develop essential classification and seriation skills and concepts, as well as increase their social and problem-solving skills. The block and construction center should be located away from busy traffic areas and in an area with ample space for construction. It should contain a wide assortment of blocks and accessories, such as human figures, road signs, and small-wheeled vehicles for young children and a variety of construction sets and materials for older children. Literacy materials and tools are also important so that children may sketch their "blueprints" on paper, label a building they've created, or write a story about their experience. Blocks should be accessible on open shelves marked with paper silhouettes of each block size and shape. Placing the center adjacent to the dramatic play center for younger children increases the interchange among centers (Hirsch, 1996; Vergeront, 1996). Chapter Eight contains more detailed information on blocks and construction materials.

Discovery and Science Center.   In this "hands-on" center, children actively explore materials and activities that help bring science to life through exciting opportunities to see, hear, smell, touch, and feel science as they develop scientific and conceptual understandings. Children gain firsthand experiences with concepts about animals, vegetation, and minerals, as well as the equipment used to study them such as scales, magnets, and simple measurement tools. Materials for study may include boxes of collected items, such as shells or rocks, for sorting, classify-

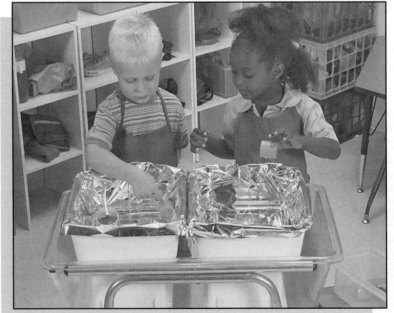

Children can develop scientific understandings through exploration with a variety of scientific materials.

ing, comparing and contrasting, and old appliances or radios with different tools to take apart the used items. Often children use these materials for ongoing projects in other centers. To illustrate, one kindergartner took the magnifying glass from the discovery center to examine sick animals she was tending in the dramatic-play area during a play theme on the veterinarian's office. A fourth grader added information about his plant's growth to the classroom graph. The discovery and science center also includes experiences with sand, rice, and water that offer many opportunities for teaching about safety issues with the materials being used.

Drama Center.   The drama center can extend children's exploration and expansion of roles, behaviors, social skills, and language. It also promotes career and cultural awareness as children explore various occupations and cultures. Drama centers are often transformed into thematic units of study, such as a bakery during a unit on economics, a shoe store during a unit on measurement, and an artist's studio during a unit on famous artists. Regardless of the theme, a drama center provides rich opportunities for building literacy skills and concepts. When pencils, pads, telephone books, literature books, and other print materials are added to this center, children's voluntary use of literacy is encouraged (Christie et al., 2003). Prop boxes, described in Chapter Six, are appropriate in this center and enhance children's creative work.

Library and Literacy Center.   This center invites children to read a variety of print materials and should be located in a quiet area of the classroom. It should be attractive, inviting, stocked with books that match children's interests and their topics of study, and comfortable for browsing and reading. Some teachers have used a rocking chair, a seat removed from a car, or an old bathtub filled with pillows in their literacy centers. An ample supply of familiar and interesting books in different formats

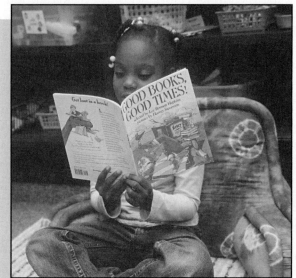

A literacy center should be attractive, inviting, stocked with books that match children's interests and their topics of study, and comfortable for browsing and reading.

such as story and information books, wordless and predictable books, riddles, rhymes, and child-made books should be easily accessible and displayed on bookshelves. The center should also contain printed signs and questions that invite children to explore the book selections. Some teachers include the Sunday comics, old catalogues, puppets and prop boxes for retelling stories, recycled copies of children's magazines, and mobiles of information about a featured author. Interesting writing materials, such as recycled colored paper from a print shop and unusual pens and pencils, should be available. For *younger children*, this center encourages early literacy play—an important precursor to learning to read and write (Christie et al., 2003; Morrow, 2009). For *older children*, this center provides ample opportunities for self-selected books that range from easy-to-read materials (such as magazines) to a variety of high-quality literature (such as fiction and poetry) to match students' ability and interest levels as well as opportunities to discuss and share literature.

Manipulative and Math Center.   Manipulative materials, such as colored blocks, buttons, counting frames, and cubes, encourage children's growing mathematical understanding of numbers, classification, ordering, comparing, measuring, estimating, and counting. The center needs to be located near low, open shelves that contain an organized system for storing manipulatives and math games such as dominoes. Writing materials, a chalkboard, and a flannel board should also be available for children to create their own math stories and explore and practice mathematical skills and concepts. Chapter Eight contains an extensive list of appropriate manipulative materials for different ages.

Media and Music Center.   This center uses electronic media (such as CDs, computers, audio tapes, and videotapes) as vehicles for play and playful expression as well as opportunities to invent music with different material (such as PVC pipes for listening to and creating sounds, child- and teacher-created musical instruments, and music for listening and movement). The media and music center needs to be located away from extreme heat, cold, and glare but near an electrical outlet. Many teachers find that laminated posters with rebus-type instructions on operating and caring for the equipment are useful. Computers should be placed on tabletops at eye level and should be arranged so that two or three children may work together at any one time (Swaminathan & Wright, 2003). The media and music center should be as open and accessible as other centers so that children can use the equipment for play and investigation. It should also contain a variety of music for children to listen to, simple musical instruments for children to create their own music, music and instruments from other cultures that children can explore, and opportunities for recording (Kemple, Batey, & Hartle, 2004).

Technology Center.   Technology can be used to expand a child's understanding about a topic or reinforce concepts already learned in the classroom. Age-appropriate software maximizes children's learning by enhancing their inventive thinking, self-expression, teamwork, and creation of high-quality products, all of which are essential skills for the twenty-first century (Haugland, 2001; NAEYC, 1996b). Selecting appropriate Web sites is also important. Whether it is an information site, which helps children gain new knowledge and answer questions; a communication site, which puts children in touch with others; or a publication site, which provides a place for children to post their work, all sites must be evaluated using stringent criteria and specific evaluation tools (Swaminathan & Wright, 2003).

Writing Center. In this center, often placed near the library center to prompt children to write about what they are reading, children experiment with writing and illustrating in many forms, from scribbling or drawing to composing poems and stories. Sometimes they come here from other centers to make signs or captions for their work. Arts-based writing centers contain chalkboards, a stapler, glue, pencils, markers and crayons, and an assortment of papers in various sizes, shapes, and colors for writing and illustrating. Magazines, newspapers, old catalogues, scissors, and glue are also available for children to illustrate stories or add to their creations. Some teachers have children keep a box of children's drawings for others to use to create stories (Christie et al., 2003). To see how one teacher has a defined space for each center and uses a common theme for center activities, watch the video "Using Centers to Foster Learning" online at MyEducationLab.

Centers offer children more than just good opportunities to engage in an activity; they offer children the chance to explore, investigate, and utilize their ideas in new and creative ways. It is unlikely that you will use all of these centers simultaneously. Most teachers use about six permanent centers that are aligned with their classroom, program, and school goals. Teachers periodically transform these centers to be aligned with ongoing themes and units the children are studying at a particular time. When using arts-based centers as a teaching strategy, be sensitive to children's pace of learning and help them move comfortably from one activity to another by paying attention to transitions and routines.

Transitions and Routines

Transitions are times during the day when children move from one activity to the next. In a classroom with centers and choices, each transition requires children to make a decision. *Routines* are regular and predictable activities that form the basis of the daily schedule; they help children sense the passage of time (for example, snack follows cleanup or math follows lunch) and anticipate events (such as by playing a musical selection at the end of each day).

Transitions and routines consume 20 to 35 percent of the preschooler's day and about 15 percent of an elementary child's day (Jalongo & Isenberg, 2008). Unless appropriately planned, they can be difficult and stressful periods for both children and teachers because children's sense of time differs with age and engagement. Failure to plan for transition times encourages inappropriate behaviors, boredom, and increased dependence on the teacher (Hemmeter, Ostrosky, Artman, & Kinder, 2008; Hyson, 2008). Following are characteristics of appropriate transitions and routines.

- *Establish a signal for listening and attending.* Use a simple rhythmic clap, or a prop like a tambourine or an oatmeal box as a class signal for preparing to transition to another activity. Be sure to keep this simple and practice it so that it stays effective all year long.
- *Cue students about how much time is left for an activity.* All children need to know how much time is left for an activity. You can announce, "In three minutes we will be meeting at the rug. Use this time to finish your activity and put away your materials."
- *Incorporate the arts for transitions.* Use familiar music to move *young children* to a new activity, such as singing the song "Riding in an Airplane," by Raffi, for preschool children who then can pretend to fly to the art tables equipped with paper, markers, and photographs of airplanes and make appropriate airplane noises along the way. This will connect their study of

MyEducationLab

Go to MyEducationLab and select the topic "Environments." Under Activities and Applications, watch the video Using Centers to Foster Learning.

transportation with music and art and assure a positive transition. For *elementary children*, use drama to create a morning class news show with children assuming different roles such as news reporter, weather reporter, and travel reporter who can report on characters from literature or events from social studies.

- *Plan for the transition from indoors to outdoors.* Some children may be engaged in an indoor activity and might be hesitant to leave; others may prefer indoor activities but need the opportunity to be outdoors. Giving a warning to prepare children for the next experience or location is essential. Planned transitions and routines that are developmentally appropriate are essential for children of all ages. They differ from other activities in purpose, length, and frequency and depend on the age of the children and the available physical facilities. Thoughtful planning provides a structured yet flexible environment that is predictable, minimizes chaos, and empowers children (Hemmeter et al., 2008; Kohn, 1993). Figure 7.9 provides tips for managing transitions and routines for children.

Routines are an integral part of learning and offer both children and teacher more control over their environment.

Arrival

- Prepare materials and activities before children arrive.
- Be available to greet children.
- Prepare engaging activities that attract children's attention and are easy to monitor.
- In extended-day settings, communicate any unusual behaviors or concerns to staff and teachers who follow you.
- Ask parents who want to talk to stay for a moment, if feasible, or call them later to arrange a time.
- Construct an attendance chart, center planning board, or procedure charts so that children can sign in and choose activities as they arrive.

Opening Group Time

- Begin this part of the day after children have had a chance to explore the environment.
- Introduce choices for the day and ask children to decide what they will do.
- Use this time to review or create any classroom rules related to using a particular center or piece of equipment. When children help set these limits, they are more likely to internalize them.
- Demonstrate the appropriate use of new materials.

Cleanup

- Give notice. Children need a 10-, a 5-, and then a 1-minute warning to begin cleanup.

(Continued)

Figure 7.9   Tips for Managing Routines and Transitions
Note: Data from Clayton (2001) and Hemmeter, Ostrosky, Artman, & Kinder (2008).

- Play tape-recorded music and have children listen for something special as they put away materials.
- Use a song to announce that cleanup time is approaching and sing while cleaning up.
- Organize a precleanup circle. Decide how to divide the tasks so that each child picks up a certain number of objects or a particular kind of object (such as everything that is smaller than a shopping bag or everything that has a metal part) or use a cleanup helpers' board.
- Model the behaviors you want to see from the children.
- Follow cleanup with an interesting activity that children can anticipate with enthusiasm.
- Create rhymes to familiar tunes that refer to putting away materials or helping ("This is the way we clean our room . . . ").

Departure
- Establish a departure ritual such as hearing a story, using a clapping pattern, creating a body pattern or enjoying a song together.
- Briefly preview 1 or 2 interesting things that will take place the next day or later that week.
- Use tote or paper bags for papers, newsletters, and other forms of communication.
- Be available to say good-bye.

Transitions from One Activity to Another
- Develop a repertoire of songs and finger plays to be used as children move from one place to another. Use a song or finger play (for example, "Two Little Blackbirds;" ask one child to name another by color of clothing, kinds of fasteners on shoes, or name card).
- Have books ready for children to read while others finish their activities and get ready to join the group.
- Use a mystery box, puppets, a riddle ("I see something red, white, and blue with stars on it"), finger plays, or quiet songs.

For Children in Grades 1–4:
- Review the day and talk about tomorrow.
- Plan ahead on how to move from one activity to another.
- Have materials ready for the next activity.
- Assign children responsibilities for transitions ("Katie, please gather the scissors").
- Have children move from one activity to another at their own pace, when possible.

Just as teachers regularly consider the design of the indoor environment, they also need to consider the design of the outdoor environment. An engaging outdoor environment stimulates innovative thinking, imagination, and other creative habits of mind. In the next section, we examine the outdoor environment.

DESIGNING OUTDOOR ENVIRONMENTS FOR CREATIVITY AND ARTS-BASED LEARNING

Many teachers view the outdoor environment as a place to release excess energy. This narrow view neglects the outdoors as an important setting for stimulating children's creative ways of thinking by providing the space and freedom they need to try things out (Rivkin, 1995; Sutterby & Frost, 2006; Sutterby & Thornton, 2005; Tovey, 2007).

Think about Ms. Ogur's concerns about her preschoolers' outdoor environment. On her playground there were three tricycles, two balls, and a combination swing set/climbing apparatus for 15 children to share. The children often squabbled over the materials. Ms. Ogur knew that these disputes were caused, in part, by not having a rich, challenging, place for children to explore, investigate, be curious, and wonder with materials, equipment, and peers.

After talking with other colleagues and reading professional literature on outdoor play for preschoolers, she discovered that some materials have different levels of complexity (Kritchevsky et al., 1977) and can be classified as follows:

- **Simple units** that have a single, obvious use, with no subparts for children to manipulate or create (such as swings and tricycles).
- **Complex units** that have subparts of two very different kinds of materials for children to manipulate (such as water and plastic containers, or sand and digging tools). This category also includes single play materials that have many diverse possibilities (for example, art materials such as dough and paint, a box of books, or a jump rope).
- **Supercomplex units** that have three or more subparts that children can combine and juxtapose (such as sand, digging tools, and water). Supercomplex units hold children's attention and interest the longest because children have many opportunities to manipulate and juxtapose the parts and integrate them into their play themes.

Ms. Ogur then decided to enrich the outdoor space environment by adding some complexity to it. She brought out a wagon; created an obstacle course from old, worn tires; and made some simple traffic signs out of scrap lumber and paint. She also brought out the police officer's hat from the dramatic-play center and markers and scrap paper from the literacy center. From these simple additions, the children created elaborate play about accidents, traffic, parking, and speeding. Some children even created and handed out parking tickets. On other occasions, the children used the wagon as an ambulance to transport an accident victim to the hospital, where another elaborate scenario was enacted. Ms. Ogur even used the traffic signs to reinforce bicycle safety practices.

Ms. Ogur illustrates what a resourceful teacher can do to make the outdoor environment more stimulating and challenging even with limited resources. She also demonstrates how well-planned outdoor environments have the potential to stimulate learning and be more inclusive. Teachers like Ms. Ogur, who view the outdoor environment as a support for children's creativity and imagination know that the more children can wonder, be curious, and make connections to possibilities, the more their creative thinking will develop (Sutterby & Frost, 2006; Tovey, 2007).

Types of Playgrounds

Basically, there are three types of playgrounds: traditional, adventure, and creative (Frost, 2004; Rivkin, 1995). Each differs in origin, types of equipment and materials, targeted age groups, and purpose. Each also differs in promoting or constraining the amount of children's physical activity and social interaction.

Traditional playgrounds originated in the early part of the twentieth century and were designed for physical exercise to emphasize gross motor play. They are often not well maintained or supervised, are built on dangerously hard surfaces, and are not consistent with what we know about children's learning and development, yet they are prevalent in elementary school playgrounds (Frost & Woods, 1998; Frost et al., 2008). Since the late 1970s, wooden superstructures with a variety of apparatuses have replaced some of this steel equipment and plastic has begun to replace wood. Traditional playgrounds:

- Contain large, steel, immovable equipment (such as climbing bars, slides, and swings)— mostly simple units—to be used for one single purpose: exercise.
- Lack variety and challenge that often results in boredom.
- Favor physically able children who can take advantage of the play opportunities available.
- May appeal to less physically able children who are reluctant to participate in these types of gross motor activities.

Adventure or "junk" playgrounds, originating in Denmark in the middle of the twentieth century and uniquely European, are designed to provide supervised, creative play opportunities for urban children. Adventure playgrounds:

- Contain unconnected tools and materials that enable children to build, create, and pretend using materials in a free and open atmosphere.
- Offer children options (such as building, gardening, using sand or water, and cooking).
- Have adults who function as play leaders, support children's ideas, act as facilitators, and support children's freedom to learn through discovery in an enriched environment. These types of playgrounds never were very popular in this country because of our concerns with safety, the unavailability of trained play leaders, and concerns that the adventure playground was not as aesthetically pleasing to adults' eyes.

Creative/contemporary playgrounds, adapted in the twentieth century from the adventure playground concept, are a way to integrate elements of adventure playgrounds into contemporary settings. They provide children with a more stimulating environment for play than that of a traditional playground. Creative playgrounds:

- Contain a superstructure with movable parts (such as boards, ramps, and wheels).
- Are action-oriented, provide safe underneath surfaces, and offer a variety of stimulating materials and equipment.
- Promote all forms of play (functional, constructive, dramatic, and games).
- Offer children numerous possibilities for social interaction (Barbour, 1999). Creative playgrounds are "developmentally pleasing and aesthetically rich" (Frost & Woods, 1998, p. 234).

Playgrounds that provide many possibilities for children are important creative environments. Their design has certain features that enhance all forms of children's play and creativity.

Features of Quality Outdoor Environments

Outdoor environments provide many benefits for all children and should be utilized year round (Frost, 2004; Rivkin, 1995; Sutterby & Thornton, 2005). High-quality outdoor environments should focus on four primary features: equipment and materials, safety, supervision, and storage. Figure 7.10 is a checklist of criteria to use for the outdoor environment.

Place an X under the appropriate response to see if your outdoor environment encourages opportunities for creative learning.

Adequate Space

Does the environment	Y	N
• Stimulate all four types of play—exercise, constructive, dramatic, and games with rules?	____	____
• Provide appropriate spaces for individuals and small groups of children according to their ages, physical sizes, interests, and abilities?	____	____
• Ensure that movement from one zone to another will be safe and manageable?	____	____
• Offer a visually pleasing area in which the natural elements and fabricated structures complement each other?	____	____
• Provide overall cohesiveness rather than discrete, unconnected objects or structures?	____	____
• Foster a sense of flow from one activity to another?	____	____
• Provide varied ground surfaces such as hardtop for games and vehicles, grass, water, soft mulch or sand, hilly and flat areas, construction areas, sunlight, and shade?	____	____
• Offer easy access to coats, toilets, and drinking fountains?	____	____
• Provide protected storage for equipment?	____	____
• Contain space for walking, running, and skipping?	____	____
• Include a shaded area with tables and benches for art activities, table games, or snacks?	____	____

Materials

Does the environment	Y	N
• Offer ample opportunities to use age-appropriate, complex materials?	____	____
• Promote independent and creative uses of flexible materials such as sand, water, dramatic play, and superstructures with room for many children?	____	____

(Continued)

Figure 7.10   Checklist for the Outdoor Environment

Note: Data from Frost (2004); National Association for the Education of Young Children (1996a); National Program for Playground Safety (1999); and Sutterby & Thornton (2005).

- Contain equipment and materials for active and quiet play and for solitary, parallel, and cooperative play? _____ _____
- Contain materials for dramatic play (e.g., car, boat)? _____ _____
- Provide materials for gross motor development (e.g., climbers, wide slides)? _____ _____
- Provide a sand area located away from people, with proper covering to protect it from inclement weather and animals? _____ _____
- Include a water area with a variety of materials for experimentation, problem solving, and exploration? _____ _____
- Contain a variety of balls? _____ _____
- Contain nonlocomotor materials for stretching, carrying, and swinging? _____ _____
- Contain manipulative materials for throwing, kicking and catching? _____ _____

Activities and Experiences

Does the environment   Y   N

- Provide for children's interactions with materials, peers, and adults through proper storage, defined spaces, and interest areas? _____ _____
- Offer a range of activities, experiences, and equipment with "loose parts" that children can adapt to their own play schemes? _____ _____
- Provide large equipment for gross motor development; loose parts and natural materials for constructive play; enclosed structures for dramatic play; linked platforms for social play; semiprivate spaces for hiding; and nature areas for gardening? _____ _____

Safety   Y   N

- Are adults actively supervising the play area? _____ _____
- Is the equipment in good repair, in working order, and free of sharp edges? _____ _____
- Are there fences at least 5 feet high with lockable gates that work well? _____ _____
- Are there 8–10 inches of sand, mulch, or pea gravel under climbing and moving equipment that cushion falls? _____ _____
- Is there some type of edging (e.g., railroad ties) to contain the cushioning materials? _____ _____
- Is the area free of litter (e.g., broken glass)? _____ _____

Equipment and Materials

Outdoor equipment and materials should hold children's interest over time and promote creative thought through all four forms of play (Frost, 2004; National Association for the Education of Young Children [NAEYC], 1996a). Equipment should be sturdy, safe, and age-appropriate. High-quality equipment and materials feature movable parts; a combination of simple, complex, and supercomplex materials; a wide variety of experiences and activities; and well-defined spaces.

Movable parts are pieces that children can manipulate and use to improvise. Lightweight objects of different sizes, shapes, and textures; boards or ramps; and organic materials such as sand and water can be moved from place to place within the play area as children choose. They also add complexity to the environment. Movable parts provide for flexibility, diversity, novelty, and challenge, which are all important ingredients for creative thought, socialization, and learning.

Complexity refers to the number of possibilities the material offers children. The more possibilities the material has, the more likely it is to hold children's interest and attention because children can do more with it (Kritchevsky et al., 1977). If too much of the equipment is designed to be used by one child at a time or to be used in just one way, it severely limits the outdoor environment's complexity. For example, a large tire swing that can hold two or more children offers more options than a swing on a swing set.

Diversity or variety refers to the number of ways materials can be used, regardless of their complexity. It influences how children get started in their activity (NAEYC, 1996a). A variety of materials offer children necessary choices to create their own forms of play. Many teachers use play crates to add variety to the outdoors. Figure 7.11 provides examples of props and play crates for use outdoors.

Well-defined spaces are those in which both the amount and the arrangement of space facilitate children's play patterns. Accreditation criteria of the National Association for the Education of Young Children (1996a) and the National Academy of Early Childhood Programs (2004) require a minimum of 75 square feet of play space outdoors per child. When the outdoor space is designed using these criteria, children retain ownership over their play, practice persistence, develop feelings of competence and engage in decision-making and problem-solving.

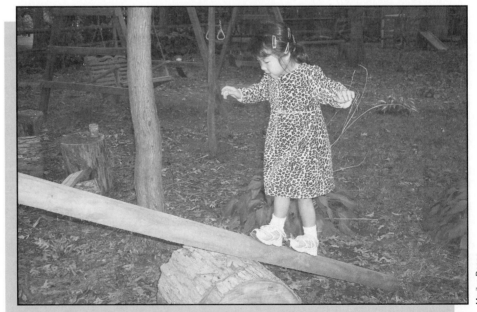

Marilyn Deppe

Outdoor environments provide many benefits for all children and should be utilized year-round.

> **Play crates** organize materials on the playground and extend children's interests from the classroom to the outdoors. Store materials in durable wood or plastic storage containers that are easily transportable from indoors to outdoors.

Automobile Repair		
Mat	Filters	Flashlight
Auto parts catalogue	Nuts and bolts	Wrench
Keys	Bicycle pump	Piece of hose

Fishing		
Plastic boat	Cane poles	Small stool (optional)
Fishnet	Rod and reel	Play fish
Plastic worms	Rubber snakes	Minnow bucket
Rubber lizards	Tackle box	Cricket box

Gardening		
Stakes	Seed packets	
Garden tools	Gardening catalogue	
Small rakes	Flowerpots	
Child-size garden gloves		

Beach		
Sunglasses	Ice chest	Swimming tube
Seashells	Beach towel	Diving mask
Pail and shovel	Air mattress	Paperback books

Camping		
Knapsack	Sleeping bag	Canteen
Flashlight	Plastic dishes	Tent
Sticks for fire	Mosquito repellent	

Figure 7.11   Props and Play Crates for the Outdoor Environment
Note: Data from Odoy & Foster (1997).

Well-planned outdoor environments meet all of children's needs, including physical and mental flexibility.

Safety

A safe outdoor environment is essential. Yet national survey data reveal that today's playgrounds are unsafe, causing a dramatic increase in childhood playground injuries over the past two decades (Frost, 2004; NAEYC, 1996a; National Program for Playground Safety [NPPS], 1999; Thomason & Thrash, 1999; Thompson, Hudson, & Mack, 2000). Safe playgrounds:

- Are well designed and adequately maintained.
- Have storage facilities, suitable surfacing materials, and accessibility.
- Provide features children prefer, such as dramatic-play materials and nature areas.

Barbara Schwartz/Merrill

Safety is an important issue in the design and construction of outdoor playground equipment.

- Focus on all developmental areas.
- Are developmentally appropriate.
- Are used with safety orientation for staff or children.

Supervision

It is estimated that about 40 percent of playground injuries are related to inadequate supervision. Thus, we suggest the following guidelines for better safety and supervision in outdoor settings:

1. Have the same ratio of adults in the outdoor environment as you do in the indoor environment. Make sure that the adults who monitor the outdoor environment have knowledge of injury prevention and first aid.

2. Circulate around the area rather than standing in a group and talking.

3. Set clear, reasonable limits about what children may do, such as sitting down on the slide.

4. Give special attention to swings or climbers where there is a lot of activity and potential for injury.

5. Place 8 to 10 inches of fall-absorbing material, such as pea gravel or bark mulch, under and around all moving equipment (such as swings and rotating devices), because falls are the number one cause of playground injuries to children (U.S. Consumer Product Safety Commission, 2002). Be sure to include a retaining border to hold the material and replenish it frequently.

Storage

Storage facilities house the materials that children use to develop and extend their play and creative thought. The location of the storage is critical. Accessible storage saves time in transporting materials and encourages responsibility in children. Think about storage that is:

- *child-scaled* to facilitate taking out and putting away equipment.
- *weathertight and vandalproof* to protect the equipment.
- *multipurpose,* contains space for teacher storage, and allows children to play on the structure.

These characteristics of high-quality outdoor environments apply to children of all ages. However, some adaptations need to be made for specific age groups.

Outdoor Environments for Children of Different Ages

Like indoor environments, outdoor environments must be designed with children's ages and developmental levels in mind. They support a range of learning and developmental goals, including a sense of competence, cooperation, and creativity through a variety of activities.

Infant and Toddler Years

Outdoor environments for *infants and toddlers* should meet their rapidly increasing motor and social development, their boundless energy and curiosity, and their clear need for autonomy. Infant and toddler playgrounds have *unique safety* issues (Frost et al., 2008; Frost & Woods, 1998; Stephenson, 2002). For this age group, give special attention to the following:

- *Ground cover* that cannot be ingested, such as pea gravel.
- *Hazardous material* that may have accumulated overnight, such as broken objects, sharp edges, or foreign objects.
- *Swing seats* that include a strap to prevent falling.
- *Safety barriers* that protect infants and toddlers from traffic, fall hazards, and pools of water.
- *Shade* for sun- and heat-sensitive infants (Frost et al., 2008).

Infants and toddlers also need opportunities for a wide range of sensory experimentation and exploration with a few simple, safe, age-appropriate choices. Adding materials of different textures, such as sticks, bugs, or tree bark, or clear pathways to walk on, touch, and explore, enhances their play. They need stimulating equipment close to the ground, such as tunnels or simple climbing structures; dramatic-play options; movable parts for stacking, gathering, and dumping; and natural experiences with living plants and animals (Frost et al., 2008; Rivkin, 1995; Stephenson, 2002).

Some interesting additions for *toddler outdoor environments* include the following:

- Hanging inflatable objects from a tree and having children try to "catch one" with a cardboard tube.
- Painting the pathways, equipment, or fence with small buckets of water and large brushes.
- Washing dishes and furniture with pans of warm, soapy water, sponges, and scrub brushes.

Preschool/Kindergarten Years

Outdoor environments for *preschoolers and kindergartners* should promote all four forms of play—functional, constructive, dramatic, and games with rules to support these children's need for vigorous gross motor play and increased interest in role playing and games. The environment should develop a wide range of skills and abilities. It should contain a convenient and accessible storage facility for portable materials, a grassy area for group games, a place for privacy to accommodate children's need for solitary and parallel play, and a variety of child-sized equipment for motor development (Debord, Hestenes, Moore, Cosco, & McGinnis, 2002; Frost et al., 2008). The best outdoor environments for preschool and kindergarten children include a complex superstructure with a combination of movable parts (for example, raw materials such as sand, water, and assorted lumber boards) and climbing structures with lots of moving parts, such as swings, bars, ladders, hanging ropes and structures with potential for dramatic-play activities.

Try some of these activities to add novelty and complexity to the outdoor environment:

- Turn wheeled vehicles into another vehicle by taping on a sign and adding appropriate props nearby to stimulate dramatic play.
- Use a large, empty carton and other appropriate props to create a service station area for wheeled vehicles, a bank drive-through, or a roadside produce stand.
- Use props and play crates designed for outdoor play that stimulate creativity and the imagination as shown in Figure 7.11.
- Use bubbles with an assortment of recycled materials, such as berry baskets and straws, for bubble wands.
- Encourage children to paint along the fence by clipping easel paper on it; leave the paintings up for an art show.
- Read *A Rose for Pinkerton* (Kellogg, 1981) and *Pet Show* (Keats, 1972) and then have a pet show with children's stuffed animals. Make judges' clipboards out of cardboard and clothespins, stands for the animals out of recycled ice-cream tubs, and prize ribbons out of used gift wrap.
- Create nature collages using shoebox lids and white glue to make collages of natural materials located on or near the outdoor environment.
- Create nature areas for children to focus on the aesthetic aspects of the outdoors.

First Grade–Fourth Grade

Environments for children in *Grades 1 through 4* should encourage natural investigation and challenge imagination. These children prefer structures with numerous physical challenges, such as climbers, equipment and spaces for social development, and safe places for group games. Following are some suggestions that challenge school-age children in outdoor areas.

- Plan and conduct a scavenger hunt. Use a variety of clues that incorporate riddles, listening, or writing. Tie the scavenger hunt into the unit of study where possible.
- Provide chalk so that children can make outdoor games, such as hopscotch or foursquare, or create shadow drawings.
- Tie-dye old T-shirts and dry them along a fence. Then use another color for more complex and symmetrical designs.
- Do a shadow play in the afternoon. Invite children to enact various roles and use cardboard silhouettes for props. Have the audience watch the show on the ground rather than the players themselves.

- Assign "fitness" homework, such as walking, hopping, jumping rope, counting steps, or stretching that improves fitness.
- Create a nature area, such as a butterfly garden, to connect with ongoing projects in the classroom.

Outdoor environments can foster all children's creative thought through a variety of planned uses of space, activities, experiences, and materials. You can see how one teacher uses the outdoor environment as a learning experience by watching the video "Science" online at MyEducationLab.

Teachers who believe in the power of the environment for learning must assume roles that guide children's creative processes.

MyEducationLab

Go to MyEducationLab and select the topic "Math, Science, and Technology." Under Activities and Applications, watch the video Science.

TEACHERS' ROLES AND RESPONSIBILITIES IN A CREATIVE ENVIRONMENT

What we as teachers believe about creativity and arts-based learning influences our classroom environment. We would be wise to keep in mind the words of Jeffrey Bloom (2006): ". . . creativity in any kind of endeavor . . . operates from passion. People who operate from a basis of passion tend to set very high standards for themselves, be persistent in reaching their goals, and be willing to take risks. Your work with children needs to encourage and support the development of these characteristics" (p.255).

The following suggestions will help you promote children's creative habits of mind and send messages that enable children to function comfortably, productively, and effectively together.

1. *View yourself as a creative teacher.* Ask yourself the following questions: In what ways do I support children's creativity and build an arts-based environment? Do I have original ideas? Do I provide opportunities for children who respond in unusual ways to engage in creative development? Could I identify the most creative children in my class? Creative teachers exhibit spontaneity, sensitivity, open-mindedness, and a high tolerance for ambiguity. Their classroom environments maximize student participation and engagement, support learner-centered teaching, encourage children to "live the question," reward imaginative ideas, and encourage children's self-evaluation (Edwards, 2007; Jalongo & Isenberg, 2008).

2. *Consider the environment a powerful learning tool.* When teachers are knowledgeable about space, time, and materials they can often anticipate how children will use them. Predicting behavior in this way promotes children's independence, active involvement, and sustained attention (McLean, 1995). The environment can also be used to manage tasks. A predictable schedule, for example, helps all children learn the rhythm of the day and feel able to participate. Carefully arranged and displayed materials invite children's participation in appropriate ways with a minimum of adult intervention. One preschool teacher uses children's photographs for taking attendance and rebus recipes for preparing snacks. Such tools reduce the amount of time teachers devote to routine administrative tasks, freeing them to focus on children's creativity and arts-based learning.

In the next section, we discuss possible adjustments to the indoor and outdoor environments to accommodate diverse learners.

ACCOMMODATIONS FOR DIVERSE LEARNERS

All children need environments that foster a sense of curiosity and wondering. With some simple adjustments, it is easy to create arts-based, creative environments that support diverse learners (Klein, Cook, & Richardson-Gibbs, 2001). We first make suggestions for modifying the indoor physical environment, then suggest ways to modify center activities, and finally suggest ways to modify the outdoor environment to meet the needs of diverse learners.

Tips for Modifying the Indoor Physical Environment to Support Diverse Learners

- Understand the child's exceptionality so that appropriate accommodations allow for full participation and a focus on the child's abilities.
- Provide a "buddy" who can help introduce and model classroom routines and activities.
- Modify the physical environment, such as space, furniture location, noise, and light.
- Modify centers with some simple adjustments in materials, equipment, and careful planning.

Classroom Accommodations for Children with Physical Disabilities
- Provide large spaces in which children can easily move and work.
- Maintain clear pathways in the classroom for easy movement.
- Position tables so that children in wheelchairs are at the same level as their peers.

Classroom Accommodations for Children with Hearing Impairments
- Have children sit away from noisy backgrounds, such as windows, doors, and heating/cooling systems.
- Encourage children to move freely around the classroom so they can hear better and see the faces of their peers.
- Use carpet and corkboard walls to reduce classroom noise.

Classroom Accommodations for Children with Visual Impairments
- Orient children to the location of materials, centers, pathways and exits using the child's desk as a focal point.
- Familiarize the child to the school environment once he or she is oriented to the classroom. When outdoors, explicitly show the child which play materials, equipment, activities, and playmates are available.
- Designate a peer "sight guide" for special activities, such as fire drills and assemblies.
- Use lighting that does not cast shadows or a glare on schoolwork and activities.

Tips for Modifying Centers to Support Diverse Learners

- When planning for centers, consider the skill level of all learners.
- Label all materials, question charts, and center instructions with both text and visual icons.
- Tape-record directions so that both readers and nonreaders know what to do.

Specific Suggestions for Modifying Centers for Diverse Learners

Literacy Center

Provide a variety of reading materials across age and ability levels such as:

- Picture books
- ABC books
- Easy readers
- Predictable pattern books
- Books and recordings from different cultures and countries
- Display books used during story time to elicit retelling and reading "practice."

Writing Center

Use a variety of materials for struggling authors such as:

- Pencil grips
- Felt-tip pens instead of pencils for children with limited motor abilities
- Pads of paper
- Large-lined paper: Lines may need to be of a different color or "raised" off the paper
- Handwriting posters
- Word walls to facilitate spelling
- Writers' dictionaries for older students who struggle with spelling
- Letter magnets, stamps, and stencils to encourage exploration of letters and their placement within words

Math/Science Center

- Provide a wide arrangement of differently sized manipulatives to accommodate students with fine motor or dexterity difficulties.
- Arrange activities that allow for other students to model or assist struggling peers in a group setting.
- Include a variety of measuring instruments such as rulers, tape measures, and yardsticks.

Technology Center

- Incorporate Web sites or software that can read directions or text on the screen.
- Choose software that has levels of difficulty ranging from easy to hard.
- Teach children to enable the computer to read back what they have written. Most word processing products have this capability built in.

Tips for Modifying the Outdoor Environment to Support Diverse Learners

- Understand that playing outdoors offers a change from the classroom environment and provides opportunities for children to develop gross motor, self-help, and social skills.
- Consider access (for example, all entryways should be as level as possible) and surfaces (for example, children with mobility challenges need a smooth, stable surface to walk on and something relatively soft to fall on).
- Provide challenges with differing degrees of difficulty, such as balance beams of different lengths, simple obstacle courses, or noncompetitive games.

Specific Suggestions for Modifying the Outdoor Environment to Support Diverse Learners

Accommodations for Children with Physical Challenges

- Adapt playground equipment by positioning it so that children can attain maximum range of reach, motion, muscle control, and visual contact.
- Place equipment lower or use a low table at wheelchair height that is sturdy enough to withstand leaning for a child in a wheelchair.

Accommodations for Children with Visual or Hearing Impairments

- Mark areas with audible and visual cues (such as wind chimes or bells) or have a playmate wear a brightly colored vest to provide a visual clue (Wellhousen, 2002).
- Attach Braille labels to materials to help children with low vision.

Accommodations for Children with Diverse Cognitive Needs

- Keep vocabulary simple, incorporate noncompetitive games, and shorten obstacle courses.
- Provide additional supervision for monitoring safety on equipment, limiting the number of materials available for choice, and communicating clear boundaries to those children who require it.

To capitalize on children's creative thought, teachers need to create environments that are responsive to the needs of all learners. Quality classrooms should be filled with numerous resources, such as books, videos, and databases, to encourage self-directed learning and provide learning experiences that offer multiple opportunities for children to work with a variety of peers in collaborative small-group contexts (Edmiston & Fitzgerald, 2000). All children need to learn in an environment they can trust. A carefully designed environment that supports creativity and the arts provides such an environment that reflects national standards.

MEETING STANDARDS THROUGH CREATIVE ENVIRONMENTS

Professional organizations for teachers all have a set of standards for establishing high-quality classroom environments. These standards indicate that the classroom environment should support children's honest expression and thinking, and help children feel ownership in their learning by having some choice and input into their work and its completion, assessment, and display. All teachers are expected to be able to design environments that contribute to the success of every learner.

Figure 7.12 provides quality indicators of classroom environments, guided by national standards. It includes examples that foster positive relationships, positive learning outcomes, a positive emotional climate, and a positive physical environment. Use Figure 7.12 to discuss other examples that contribute to these key indicators of environments that support creativity and arts-based learning.

While the following four standards come from different professional organizations, each addresses the same essential elements. Read the standards to identify

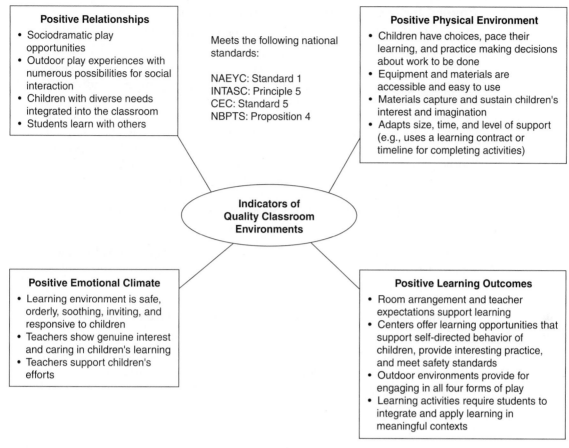

Figure 7.12   Indicators of Creative Environments

the common elements among them. What else would you add from this chapter? Then, choose an age level (infants/toddlers, preschool/kindergarten, first through fourth grade) for which you will create a "state of the art" environment. Now, write a scenario for one of the following that includes:

- all indicators for a particular age level
- some indicators for the same age level
- no indicators for the same age level

Compare and contrast your scenario with a peer and recommend three changes based on your conversation. Be willing to add other indicators and examples from the chapter that would provide evidence for your choices.

National Standards on Classroom Environments

National Association for the Education of Young Children (NAEYC)

Standard 1: Child Development and Learning

Teachers use their understanding of young children and their needs and of multiple interacting influences on child development and learning to create environments that are healthy, respectful, supportive, and challenging for all children.

Council for Exceptional Children (CEC)

Standard 5: Learning Environments and Social Interactions

Special educators actively create learning environments for individuals with exceptional learning needs (ELN) that foster cultural understanding, safety and emotional well-being, positive social interactions, and active engagement of individuals with ELN. In addition, special educators foster environments in which diversity is valued and individuals are taught to live harmoniously and productively. Special educators shape environments to encourage the independence, self-motivation, self-direction, personal empowerment, and self-advocacy of individuals with ELN. Special educators help their general-education colleagues integrate individuals with ELN in regular environments and engage them in meaningful learning activities and interactions.

Interstate New Teacher Assessment and Support Consortium (INTASC)

Principle 5

The teacher uses an understanding of individual and group motivators and behaviors to create a learning environment that encourages positive social interaction, active engagement in learning, and self-motivation.

National Board for Professional Teaching Standards (NBPTS)

Proposition 4

Teachers are responsible for managing and monitoring student learning. Accomplished teachers create, enrich, maintain, and alter instructional settings to capture and sustain the interest of their students. They make the most effective use of time in their instruction.

 ## CHAPTER SUMMARY

1. Designing the classroom environment is as important as planning for instruction.
2. Creative classroom environments have three basic features: climate, space, and time. *Climate* refers to the emotional and academic tone one gets from the environment and dictates to what extent children can be productive learners; *space* includes the degree to which the classroom environment contributes to active, creative thinkers; and *time* conveys the importance of an activity and affects children's expression, attention span, and complexity of thought.
3. Room arrangement refers to the way space is organized. When arranging a creative environment, consider what it communicates to children; how easily the space can be supervised; how accessible the materials are; and be alert to traffic patterns.
4. There are many types and uses of arts-based centers. Centers organize space and promote active learning, planning and decision making, problem solving, originality, and interaction. Centers can be managed through careful guidelines for their use, planning boards, procedure charts, and/or contracts.
5. Transitions are times when children move from one activity to another. Routines are activities that occur regularly and form the basis of the daily schedule. Planned transitions and routines ensure predictability and a sense of security for all children.

Frequently Asked Questions About Creative Environments

Can I have a creative classroom even if I am not particularly creative? How will children benefit from such a classroom?

In her book, *Why Our Schools Need the Arts*, Jessica Hoffman Davis (2008) talks about how every teacher, regardless of artistic ability, needs to teach about and through the arts. No early childhood educator can be an expert in all the subjects he or she is required to teach, including the arts. But every early childhood teacher can capitalize on young children's natural creativity with a variety of artistic media and pay close attention to what children are learning. According to Davis (2008), they "learn about learning—about what to do with mistakes, how to ask good questions that advance learning, and how to make sense of the world with the many skills acquired in school" (p. 37). In arts-friendly classrooms, you would want to feel comfortable inviting children into arts-based learning and to model appropriate attitudes toward the arts. As a teacher who values creativity, you will want to (1) show respect for all children's works of art as their way of interpreting their world; (2) ask inquiry-based questions about both the process and the product that focus on what they want to know and do; (3) promote children's imagination and expression through "what if"? questions and activities that give children the opportunity to express their own feelings and appreciate those of others; (4) value opportunities to develop ideas and products that are not "right or wrong," and (5) encourage children to reflect on their work and begin to think about how they are doing and what they want to do next. This kind of environment teaches children "about what it means to be human and enable them to experience their humanity in thought and action" (Davis, 2008, p. 78).

Is recess necessary in today's classroom?

Nationally, 64 percent of children do not participate in any daily unstructured physical activity (Jensen, 1998). A combination of long work hours for parents, scheduled after-school activities, and schools' increased focus on academics (National Association of Early Childhood Specialists in State Departments of Education [NAECSSDE], 2002) has jeopardized recess as an integral part of childhood. Recess is an essential component of the total educational experience for elementary-age children. It provides children with discretionary time and opportunities to engage in physical activity that helps to develop healthy bodies and minds (National Association for Sport and Physical Education, 2001). Unstructured physical play is a developmentally appropriate outlet for reducing stress in children's lives, improves children's attentiveness, and decreases restlessness (NAECSSDE, 2002). Eric Jensen (1998) makes a strong case for how physical activity stimulates brain development by increasing neural connections. Play is an active form of learning that unites the mind, body, and spirit of children. Up until age 9, children's learning occurs best when the whole self is involved (NAECSSDE, 2002).

How can I ease newcomers into my classroom routines when they know little or no English?

Only when students feel comfortable with your classroom's social and academic routines will optimal second-language acquisition and academic learning occur. Using Maslow's (1970) hierarchy of human needs as a foundation, you will want to assure safety, security, and a sense of belonging. To help second-language learners feel safer and more secure, you might assign a personal buddy, who speaks the child's language and follows the predictable routines in your classroom, to each newcomer. This plan creates a sense of security for all students but is especially important for students who are new to the language and culture of the school. In fact, your predictable routines may be the first stable feature some students have experienced in a long time. To help second-language learners achieve a sense of belonging, you might seat new students in the middle or front of the room, integrating them early in cooperative groups, and help them follow predictable routines.

All children need environments that foster creativity and arts-based learning in which they can plan for their own learning, identify resources and materials, and interact with one another.

6.   Outdoor environments need the same attention to space, materials, equipment, and safety as indoor environments. They need simple, complex, and supercomplex units to hold children's interest over time and challenge their imagination.

7.   There are three types of playgrounds—traditional, adventure, and creative. Action-oriented playgrounds contain a superstructure with movable apparatuses, loose parts, and safe underneath surfaces.

8. What teachers believe about creativity and arts-based learning influences their classroom environment. Teachers need to view themselves as creative and consider the environment as a learning tool.

9. With some simple adjustments to the indoor and outdoor environments, it is easy to adapt arts-based and creative environments to support the needs of diverse learners.

 Discuss: Perspectives on Classroom Environments

1. Think about your most pleasurable play environment as a child. How does this relate to what you know about the importance of environments to support creative growth?

2. Visualize your ideal classroom, both indoors and outdoors. In what ways do you think your beliefs about creativity influence your mind's-eye view of the indoor and outdoor environment?

3. Refer to the case study at the beginning of the chapter. What were Ms. Ring's reactions to the state of her classroom when she returned from leave? Were her reactions justified? On what basis? How will she go about re-creating a creative environment? If Ms. Ring's substitute asked you how she could improve her classroom, what would you suggest? Why?

4. Some teachers admit that they never think much about the outdoor environment and treat it just as a way to have children expend energy. What do you think of this practice? Why?

5. In your creative classroom environment, how would you respond to a parent or a colleague who said, "But they are just playing! When are they going to learn something?" What would you say and why?

Chapter 8

Using Creative Materials and Resources Effectively

When children have the chance to notice, collect, and sort materials, and when teachers respond to their ideas, the children become artists, designers, and engineers. When children are simply given materials to use without the chance to explore and understand them, the materials do not become part of their world.

Walter Drew and Baji Rankin, 2004, p. 42

CLASSROOM PERSPECTIVES ON MATERIALS AND RESOURCES

Preschool–Kindergarten

In the block area, five boys and girls are constructing a pirate ship from hollow wooden blocks. In the absence of pirate garb, the children make do with cowboy boots, vests, and construction worker hard hats. One child, sitting in front, steers the ship while the "lookout" paces about. A child dashes from the block area to the housekeeping area, snatches the "jewelry case," then darts back to her fellow pirates. Suddenly, the cry goes up, "Jewels! We've found the treasure! We're rich! Jewels, jewels, jewels!" With great noise and excitement, the pirates display their necklaces, bracelets, and rings. In the days that follow, the children extend this pirate theme by adding a treasure map to assist with their forays and decorating boxes to use as treasure chests.

First Grade–Second Grade

It is October in Ms. Thomas's first grade and the children are learning about plants. After some brainstorming, the first graders decide to make a class Big Book about pumpkins, and build a giant pumpkin patch. So Ms. Thomas reads different pumpkin books to them during the next few days and gathers a variety of different materials and resources for the children to investigate pumpkins. The children explore pumpkins by carving pumpkins of different sizes and shapes, counting pumpkin seeds, measuring different-sized pumpkins, estimating the number of objects that would fit inside the class plastic pumpkin, collecting and sorting pumpkins of different shades of orange, and determining whether pumpkins could sink and float. From their investigations, the children create a pumpkin patch made from giant paper pumpkins, illustrate stages of pumpkin growth on the computer and on paper, write books, enact the life cycle of the pumpkin, make pumpkin bread and muffins, and construct a model of the inside of the pumpkin.

Third Grade–Fourth Grade

In Ms. Wong's fourth-grade class, the children are studying about the California gold rush. To demonstrate their understanding, Ms. Wong invites the children to teach others about the gold rush. Some children create songs, raps, and poems; others create skits and games to express their knowledge. Their original products use materials that show people arriving from all over the world on horseback, by foot, on wagon trains, and by ship to look for gold. Each of the representations includes references to facts and concepts such as panning for gold, using sluice boxes, and constructing tent towns. The children also use props and language that illustrate the clothing the miners wore (such as denim jeans), the food they ate (such as sour-dough bread and pancakes), and the tools they used.

As these three episodes illustrate, the effective use of materials and resources supports children's creative thinking, their play, and their artistic expression. In these classroom scenarios, 4-year-olds used objects symbolically to initiate and carry out their pirate play theme; first graders used writing and illustrating, en-actment, and construction to demonstrate their understanding of pumpkins as a plant; and fourth graders used props, role play, and games to express their knowl-edge of the gold rush. The children's responses to materials revealed their origi-nal uses of common materials (using the jewels as a treasure), role playing (enacting the life cycle of a pumpkin), and games (showing people, tools, and food in the gold rush).

THEORETICAL AND RESEARCH BASE: THE IMPORTANCE OF MATERIALS AND RESOURCES

Materials are the concrete tools that children use to explore, experiment, investi-gate, and understand their world. All children have the same need for the effec-tive use of materials to do their work well because materials are the vehicles used in classrooms to study and learn the knowledge, skills, and attributes associated with each of the curriculum areas. For teachers, then, three concepts are impor-tant to understanding the effective use of creative materials and resources: (1) their historical development, (2) their convergent or divergent nature, and (3) their safety.

History of Toys and Playthings

Have you ever thought about how early toys and materials originated and what they were like? Children's toys and playthings have a long history in education. In fact, the materials we provide for children reflect social, political, and cultural is-sues. In colonial America, for example, boys played with simulated hunting and fishing materials, while girls played with corncob dolls. Near the turn of the cen-tury, construction toys were strictly for boys; homemaker toys were strictly for girls (Hewitt & Roomet, 1979; Mergen, 1982).

During the Industrial Revolution in the mid-1800s, toys specifically de-signed for children also became industrialized. When wheeled toys, board games, dolls, and doll furniture first appeared, they were mass-produced on the assembly line. At the turn of the century, during the child-study movement, childhood was recognized as a distinct period of development and children were no longer viewed as miniature adults. To reflect this movement, toy manufactur-ers began producing educational toys. During this time, Dr. Maria Montessori also introduced an array of sensory materials for children with mental retarda-tion. Lacing frames, knob puzzles, and graduated cylinders were just a few of Montessori's contributions to educational toys. She is also credited with originat-ing the concept of "self-correcting" toys—toys that can be used in a particular se-quence and a specified way. These materials slowly became part of some early childhood programs.

In the 1920s, toy manufacturers invited educators to help develop materials that would stimulate children's imagination and self-expression. Influenced by the ideas of child development specialists and educators such as John Dewey, early childhood educators provided firsthand experiences for children with concrete, imaginative materials such as blocks, clay, paint, and wood. Additionally, they encouraged children under age 6 to play with language and rhythms and to invent their own games (Monighan-Nourot, 1990). Today, the same child may play with an heirloom set of nesting dolls from her great-grandmother's era, a rag doll from her grandmother's day, a Barbie doll from her mother's era, and modern dolls for both boys and girls.

In today's world, technology has brought new dimensions to objects with which children can play. Children play with media-related figures that replicate television characters. These highly structured toys limit children's creativity and often increase the level of violence found in play (Levin, 1999). They also play with electronic figures that can communicate feelings and hold high appeal for young children. The advent of "digital objects" that exist only inside a computer, and objects that children can animate once they have created them, have the potential for changing the world of materials for children both at home and in the classroom. While some early childhood educators question the value of such materials, play with digital media and in virtual playgrounds can still have the features of make-believe, opportunities for self-expression, and relate to children's experiences. The following sections outline some basic considerations in using materials and resources to enhance children's creative thinking.

 # CONVERGENT AND DIVERGENT MATERIALS

The materials children use influence their growing knowledge, their play possibilities, and their expression of ideas. Some materials lead to single or prescribed uses and encourage convergent thinking. Windup toys, talking dolls, and coloring books are generally considered **convergent** materials. These materials lead children to think about a single or correct way to use them. There is little opportunity to use such materials in novel ways.

Other materials lead to multiple uses and are more open-ended. Blocks, sand, and water encourage thinking about possibilities and are considered divergent materials. Divergent materials invite a variety of children's responses through exploration, experimentation, and original thinking that stimulate their problem-solving ability.

Think about Amy and Tony, 4-year-olds who watched with great interest as their caregiver was preparing to recycle some materials. Among them was a baby carriage with wobbly wheels, prompting Amy to ask, "Could we have the wheels from the carriage to play with?" What appealed to them were the divergent properties of the wheels—the endless possibilities for creative play. In the weeks that ensued, the wheels became a steering wheel for a camper, a home for wooden animals, and a tray for food in the children's restaurant play.

Divergent or open-ended materials—blocks, carpentry tools, dress-up clothes, paints and markers, modeling dough, mud, sand, and water—are usually the most valuable (Bisgaier & Samaras, 2004; Drew & Rankin, 2004; Hendrick & Weissman, 2006; Johnson et al., 2005). These materials do the following:

1. *Enable children to use their imaginations in original and satisfying ways.* After 3-year-old Melissa had eye surgery, she used a spoon from the housekeeping area to operate on the eyes of a toy dog and wrapped the dog in bandages made from paper towels. She created a new use for the spoon while practicing what she knew about an eye operation.

2. *Deepen children's understandings through meaningful connections.* When first grader Jamal painted subway stops on a class mural about different types of transportation, he investigated the properties of art—color, line, and form. When Jamal added a ticket booth, an engineer, and shapes for subway seats, he demonstrated what he knew about subways as a means of transportation.

3. *Encourage children to work cooperatively.* In Ms. Anderson's second-grade unit on the community, the children used blocks to build a city; sand to sculpt the terrain; paper, pencils, rulers, and protractors to make scale models of the buildings; and earth-moving toys to create roads. They learned more from their experience than if they had completed dot-to-dot papers and worksheets on community helpers.

4. *Have no right or wrong uses, are failure-proof, and build self-esteem.* When 5-year-old Taso carefully dressed up as a cook and proudly stood before a long mirror, he exuded a sense of self-confidence and competence. The dress-up gear enabled him to view himself in a role he could not directly experience.

5. *Are process-oriented rather than product-oriented.* After hearing the rhyming verse of *Jamberry* (Degen, 1983), a story about a bear who rejoices in finding all kinds of berries, a group of kindergartners repeatedly chanted, "One berry, two berry, pick me a blueberry." Their sheer delight in the rhythm and rhyme from this captivating piece of literature produced giggles and laughter as they elaborated and created other silly *Jamberry* rhymes. Here, play with language illustrates the children's interest in process over product.

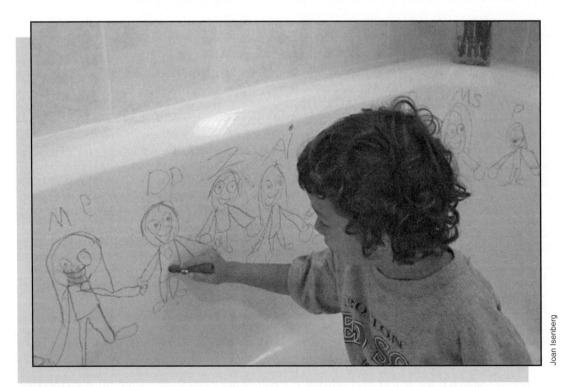

The materials children use influence their knowledge, their play possibilities, and their expression of ideas.

Divergent materials offer children unlimited possibilities. To capitalize on this potential, children must have opportunities to explore, manipulate, investigate, and use all types of materials.

Using Creative Materials Safely and Appropriately

The materials children use can either enhance or hinder their creative thinking and artistic expression (Charney, 2002). The best materials are relevant to children's development and the curriculum that fosters their imagination, and can be used for more than one topic or activity. What qualities should you look for in using safe, age-appropriate materials and equipment? Safe materials use appropriate dyes, are high-density, have no carcinogenic plastic parts, are flame retardant, and are in good condition. When using materials, remember it is the play, exploration, and experimentation itself that contributes to children's creativity, imagination, and learning. Table 8.1 provides guidelines for using materials safely and appropriately.

TABLE 8.1   Using Materials Safely and Appropriately

Guideline	Example
Use Materials That:	
• Hold children's interest and can be used in more than one way	Construction materials; modeling materials; generic toy figures
• Promote creativity and problem solving by enabling children to decide what to do	Building sets; board games; pretend materials
• Can be used with other materials for changing and more complex play	Blocks, housekeeping, and literacy materials
• Add new dimensions to children's play	People and animal props; natural materials, dress-up clothes, and housewares; balls; medical kits
• Are safe, are durable, and work for children with disabilities	Read labels for age and safety recommendations; check toys periodically for wear and damage; supervise for proper use of toys; store toys on shelves or safe boxes
Avoid Materials That:	
• Can be used in only one way	Programmed or mechanical toys that limit children's imaginations
• Promote violent and stereotypical play behaviors	Action figures and props connected to television programs and movies
• Appeal to a single age or developmental stage	Materials with very small pieces for very young children or games that require considerable academic skill; puzzles with too many pieces
• Are unsafe, are not durable, and do not work for children with disabilities	Outdoor toys that cannot withstand different kinds of weather; materials with toxic paint; dolls whose heads and eyes can be easily removed

Note: Data from Bronson (1995), Johnson, Christie, & Yawkey (1999), Levin (1999), and Moyer (1995).

TEACHERS' REFLECTIONS ON MATERIALS AND RESOURCES

Preservice Teachers

"After observing my preschoolers use blocks, I am amazed at what they can do. The children used geometric shapes for food, medicine, furniture, amusement parks, and counting. This helped me see the many possibilities in just one material."

"When I added board games such as Cootie and The Very Hungry Caterpillar to my second-grade centers, I watched the children practice social skills ('How many and who can play?'), problem-solve ('since only six can play, we'll play next time'), think strategically ('I only need two more turns before . . . '), and use school skills ('I rolled a six on the number cube . . . 1, 2, 3 . . . '). The children's responses to these games convinced me of their appropriateness."

Inservice Teachers

"My eyes are now open to a multitude of materials that promote convergent and divergent thinking. With a variety of found materials, I have created 'Imagination Boxes' that the children use to construct and invent objects."

"In my third-grade classroom, my students used Legos as a vehicle to create a three-dimensional representation of different habits they were studying. They brainstormed ways to construct these habits so they accurately represented what they wanted to show."

Your Reflections

- What do you think are age-appropriate materials, resources, and games?

- How do you think materials nurture children's creative thinking?

- How might you learn about the value of different types of toys, play materials, and imaginative resources?

As you integrate creativity and the arts into your curriculum, you will want to consider the types of materials that invite children's creative thought. In the next section, we describe the varying types of materials and their uses.

TYPES OF MATERIALS

Two-year-old Allysun clutches a fat red crayon and vigorously scribbles on a large piece of paper. She is absorbed with her markings and the gliding movement of the crayon across the paper's smooth surface.

Four-year-olds Lourdes and Maria, children of migrant workers in a Head Start classroom, pack, unpack, and repack boxes with dishes and food and talk about where they will next live.

Six-year-old twins Caroline and Diana are building tunnels and bridges with blocks as part of their unit on transportation.

Eight-year-olds Kim and Brady are engrossed in a game of checkers. They carefully contemplate their next strategic moves.

Ten-year-olds Jacob and Sara like to organize relay races during recess. They use balls, ropes, running, throwing, and jumping in different ways to vary the races that they organize and invent.

Each of these children is using a range of materials in age-appropriate ways. Materials can be categorized into six groups that serve as concrete learning tools. The following section describes these types of materials, which include skill/concept, gross motor, manipulative, construction, self-expressive, and natural, everyday materials (Isenberg & Quisenberry, 2002; Johnson et al., 2005; Moyer, 1995).

Skill/Concept Materials

Skill and concept materials are prescriptive and product-oriented. Children commonly practice skills such as eye-hand coordination, sorting, classifying, and counting with them. Typical materials in this category consist of board games such as Lotto, card games such as Fish, all types of books, attribute blocks, Cuisenaire rods, and perception materials such as lacing beads and puzzles. These materials have limited possibilities for creative and divergent thinking.

Gross Motor Materials

Gross motor materials stress large muscle activity and skill development. Children use them primarily to explore and practice motor abilities and to develop strength in large muscle coordination. Typical gross motor materials for *younger children* include balls, climbers, pull toys, riding toys, and ropes. *Older children* tend to like team sports, throwing, catching, relay races, and rope courses. As motor development increases due to activity, these materials have the potential to encourage divergent and inventive thinking when used in supportive environments.

Manipulative Materials

Manipulative materials (sometimes called fine motor materials) develop small muscles in children's fingers and hands, basic concepts, imaginative thinking, and eye-hand coordination. Children's use of manipulative materials provides important opportunities for literacy and numeracy development; offers concrete experiences with basic attributes of color, size, and shape; provides opportunities for cooperative problem solving; and increases awareness of cultural diversity. Typical fine motor materials for children through the *primary years* include beads, building sets, crayons, dough, geoboards, markers, jigsaw puzzles, lacing and sewing frames, pegs, pencils, pop-up boxes, and scissors. *Third and fourth graders* enjoy practice with a variety of tools, such as protractors, rulers, templates, and brushes, and tasks such as weaving, carving, drawing, and cartooning.

Construction Materials

Construction materials have separate pieces that can be combined in different ways and encourage children to create different ways to do so. These materials include blocks (units, pattern, parquetry), building sets (Lincoln Logs, Tinkertoys), two- and three-dimensional shapes (triangles, cubes, cylinders), and woodworking materials (hammer, nails, wood scraps, white glue). Construction materials offer endless possibilities and support coordination and inventive thinking. The number of pieces influences how children choose to combine pieces and determine when their product is finished.

Self-Expressive Materials

Self-expressive materials encourage children to experiment with different roles, feelings, and behaviors and express them through drama, music, and art. Materials in this category include dolls, dress-up clothes, computer music and art, housekeeping toys, markers, miniature life toys such as Weebles or bendable people, musical instruments, literature of all types, puppets, works of art, and children's own bodies. Children determine how the materials will be used, invent personalities and roles, and respond imaginatively. As a result, self-expressive materials promote a sense of pride and accomplishment in children.

Natural and Everyday Materials

Natural and everyday materials have specific, nonplay purposes. Children decide how to use them, employ imaginative and divergent thinking, and imitate and model adult roles with them. Everyday materials might include such household items as boxes, buttons, carpentry tools, and pots and pans. Natural materials include sticks, twigs, leaves, rocks, pinecones, sand, mud, and water. Use of natural and everyday materials brings life to the classroom and helps children make it their own, as in the program for preschoolers that used a majority of "found" materials such as palm branches, PVC pipes, and large cardboard tubes to provide children with challenging opportunities outside as well as inside (Yinger and Blaszka, 1995). Figure 8.1 suggests appropriate uses for recycled materials, and Table 8.2 describes the types of materials, their specific uses, lists the child's role, and the potential creative possibilities in each category.

To make the most of each material, teachers and children need to consider possibilities. This might involve altering the object in some way. For example, think of an empty detergent bottle. A toddler might fill and empty it; a preschooler might experiment with the number and location of holes punched in it and the rate of water flowing out; an elementary-school child might add plastic tubing and create a siphon. In this way, one recycled piece of plastic has become a challenging yet developmentally appropriate resource for each child. You can see an example of one use of recycled materials you might include in your classroom and how children might use them by viewing the artifact "Recycled Paper Picture" found online at MyEducationLab.

MyEducationLab

Go to MyEducationLab and select the topic "Visual Arts." Under Activities and Applications, view the artifact Recycled Paper Picture *and answer the questions provided.*

DEVELOPMENTALLY APPROPRIATE MATERIALS

Developmentally appropriate materials are concrete, real, and meaningful to children (Bredekamp & Copple, 1997). They support child-initiated learning and learner-centered teaching, stimulate the imagination, facilitate recall about meaningful experiences, and aid communication. Through extensive interactions with real materials and with others, children through fourth grade come to understand the people, events, and things in their world. Thus, developmentally appropriate materials should fill classrooms with things to do, things to

Goals
• To help children think creatively—"Let's see what we can make!" • To encourage children to work together—"Oh, no! We can't let it fall!" • To involve children in inventing patterns—"First red, then blue, then yellow, now red again." • To build children's problem-solving skills—"If I do this, I think it might . . . " • To allow children to explore ideas—"I wonder what would happen if . . . " • To support creating and inventing—"Teacher, look at what I made!"
Sources

• Ask *families* to collect decorating items (wallpaper, fabric, paint chips, framing materials); craft and hobby items (yarn, wood scraps, lace, buttons); kitchen items (plastic containers, egg cartons, paper towel tubes, plastic caps, detergent bottles); machines and machine parts (old telephones, alarm clocks, typewriters, computer parts).
• Gather materials from *businesses* too:
  • Restaurants (bags, straws, cups, bowls, trays, spoons, corks, boxes, ice cream cartons)
  • Building supply and home centers (lumber, sawdust, wood curls, nails, wire, wallpaper books, linoleum tiles, plastic pipe pieces, carpet samples, ceramic tile pieces)
  • Cleaners and tailors (buttons, hangers, large spools, fabric scraps)
  • Camera stores and frame shops (usable expired film, plastic film cylinders, matboard pieces, frame scraps)
  • Factories (plastic injection molders, die cutters)
  • Packaging companies (plastic scraps and punch-outs in a wide variety of colors and shapes, gaskets, washers, sponge-type foam, and Styrofoam)
  • Newspaper plant or printer (card stock, newsprint, fancy papers of many types)
  • Grocery, drug, and department stores (boxes, divided cartons, countertop or floor displays)

Storage Suggestions
1. Create a central storage "warehouse" for materials. 2. Label the storage bins and involve children in sorting materials. 3. Provide small plastic baskets for children to transport materials from the storage area to the work area. 4. Develop a collection schedule so that materials arrive at predetermined times. 5. Put labeled containers next to the door for collecting donated materials.

Figure 8.1   Appropriate Uses for Recycled Materials
Note: Based on Drew & Rankin (2004) and Jalongo & Stamp (1997b).
Note: Be sure to check for contamination hazards prior to use.

touch, and things to learn. These kinds of materials foster self-directed learning, of which creativity is a natural by-product. In the following sections, we describe developmental characteristics and age-appropriate play materials for infants/toddlers, preschoolers/kindergartners, and first through fourth grade children. We also suggest how you can use these materials appropriately with children of different ages.

TABLE 8.2 Materials for Divergent Thinking

	Types of Material					
	Skill/Concept	**Gross Motor**	**Manipulative**	**Construction**	**Self-Expressive**	**Natural and Everyday**
Illustrative Examples	Card and board games; lacing, sorting, and stacking materials	Balls, indoor/outdoor climbers, pull and riding toys	Puzzles, interlocking plastic and wooden sets, nuts and bolts, table blocks	Blocks, interlocking building sets, markers, paper, scissors	Dolls, dress-up clothes, housekeeping toys, markers, musical instruments, puppets	Buttons, natural materials, pots and pans, carpentry tools
Intended Use	Teach skills and concepts. Structured and outcome-oriented.	Emphasize large muscle development.	Emphasize small muscle development and eye-hand coordination.	Contain materials with separate parts to make things.	Relate to child's role or identity and creative expression in art.	Have clear nonplay uses in the adult world.
Child's Role	Responds to materials with senses, both physically and intellectually.	Responds, explores, and practices gross motor skills.	Responds, explores, and practices fine motor and perception skills.	Creates with multiple pieces. Determines beginning and end of project.	Decides how to use material. Invents situations, personalities, and roles. Responds imaginatively to materials.	Determines use and incorporates into activity.
Potential for Divergent Thinking	Limited number of uses. Structure imposed by material. Little opportunity for creative expression.	Some opportunity for creative and imaginative input in language, depending upon the environmental conditions and the role of the teacher.		Multiple combinations possible, depending upon number of pieces available.	Multiple possibilities to respond and invent scenes and express language and ideas.	Self-motivating and versatile materials encourage children to imitate and model adult roles and behavior.

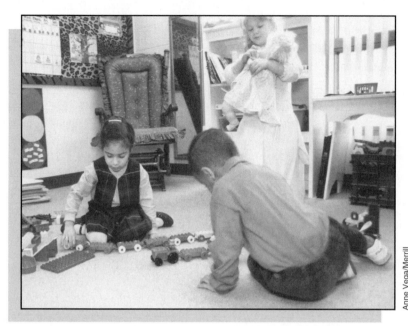

Developmentally appropriate materials are concrete, real, and meaningful to children.

Infants and Toddlers

Infants and toddlers learn by feedback from sensory exploration and social interaction. As infants roll, reach, grasp, and crawl they need a variety of textured objects to view and to reach. Because infants repeat interesting, pleasant experiences, they need toys and objects that make pleasant sounds (such as mobiles and musical toys); are soft and squeezable (such as soft fabric toys with different textures and soft fabric-covered balls); and are simple and realistic (such as cloth picture books and bath toys).

Toddlers actively struggle with issues of independence, show great interest in children their own age, and have a high energy level. They test out materials and are fascinated by finding new and different ways to use them. Both infants and toddlers need materials for looking, feeling, listening, grasping, and moving that are carefully matched to their abilities. Toddlers also prefer materials that:

- Make sounds or movements, such as musical toys.
- Fit together, pull apart, and stack, such as fill-and-dump toys, sorting boxes, and blocks.
- Stimulate pretend play, such as pots and pans, simple dress-up clothes, and empty containers.
- Can be read and examined, such as board books and photo albums.
- Pull and push, such as large cartons and wagons.

Although a variety of materials is necessary, infants and toddlers need only a few at one time. Tables 8.3 (p. 286) and 8.4 (p. 287) provide examples of developmentally appropriate materials for infants (birth to age 1) and toddlers (ages 1–3).

TABLE 8.3   Developmentally Appropriate Materials for Infants (Birth–Age 1)

Type of Material	Appropriate Materials	Examples
Skill/concept	Books/records and tapes	Soft cloth and thick cardboard books; lullabies, voices of familiar caretakers
	Games	Peek-a-Boo, So Big, Where Is the Baby? and other socially interactive games
Gross motor	Active play	Push/pull toys; large balls, infant bouncers
Manipulative	Fine motor	Simple rattles, teethers, sturdy cloth toys, squeeze and squeak toys, colorful mobiles, activity boxes for the crib; clutch and texture balls; stacking toys
Construction	Blocks	Soft rubber blocks
	Puzzles	Two-to-three-piece puzzles of familiar objects
Self-expressive	Dolls and soft toys	Soft baby dolls, plush animals
	Puppets	Soft hand puppets
	Dramatic play	Large, unbreakable mirrors attached to the crib or wall
	Sensory	Tactile toys; colorful visuals; auditory toys; suitable teethers
Natural and everyday	Household	Pots and pans; plastic containers

Note: For further information see Bronson (1995), Johnson, Christie, & Wardle (2005), and Moyer (1995).

Your Role

The following guidelines will help you nurture infants' and toddlers' self-expression with materials:

1. *Use only materials that meet safety standards.* Avoid materials that have sharp points or edges, as well as nails, wires, or pins that can be swallowed or have parts that can lodge in children's ears and throats. Be sure that materials are painted with nontoxic or lead-free paint, do not require electricity, can be easily cleaned, and cannot pinch fingers or catch hair.

2. *Provide a rich sensory environment with plenty of materials.* Infants and toddlers need to experience materials with all of their senses. Teachers who create a "crawling trail" made from scraps of distinctively different textures of fabrics, such as satin, lace, corduroy, and flannel, are providing a sensory environment that intrigues and involves infants and toddlers. Toddlers need plenty of materials and containers to collect, fill, dump, and stack objects. Simple, small, plastic containers of all sizes and shapes, cloth sacks, a variety of cardboard tubing, and empty wooden spools are necessary for water, sand, and manipulative play. Toddlers also enjoy attractive, everyday, safe objects and often use one object to represent another. Blocks, water, sand, and dress-up clothes appeal to toddlers' imaginations.

3. *Use appropriate social games.* Infants and toddlers respond positively to Peek-a-Boo, So Big, Trot, Trot to Boston and other familiar social routines. These highly repetitive games have simple rules through which infants and toddlers learn the beginning of turn taking, the rhythms of conversation, and the bonds of social relationships.

TABLE 8.4   Developmentally Appropriate Materials for Toddlers (Ages 1–3)

Type of Material	Appropriate Materials	Examples
Skill/concept	Books/records and tapes	Simple picture books and poems about familiar places and people; records and tapes of children's songs, folk songs, nursery rhymes, popular songs, songs from other cultures; movement and exercise music
	Games	Social interaction games with adults, such as Pop Goes the Weasel, Ring-a-Round-a-Rosy, and Round and Round the Garden
Gross motor	Active play	Toys to push and pull; toys with objects; ride-on toys
	Outdoor	Low slides and climbers, tunnels of oversized cardboard boxes for crawling, variety of balls, sand and water materials
Manipulative	Fine motor/perception	Colored paddles, dressing dolls, activity boxes, pop-up toys operated by pushing a button, nesting and stacking toys; toys to put together and take apart; large colored beads and spools, sewing and lacing cards, large shape sorters, pegboards, with a few large pegs, frames for zipping and snapping
	Puzzles and form boards	Simple two-to-three-piece puzzles and form boards with familiar shapes and objects; puzzles with books
Construction	Building sets	Small, lightweight sets of 15–25 pieces before 18 months; solid wooden unit blocks (20–40 pieces); wooden hollow blocks and accessories; interlocking building sets
	Carpentry	Assorted pounding toys with large wooden pegs or balls, plastic hammers, plastic pliers, thick
	Styrofoam boards	
Self-expressive	Dolls and soft toys	Soft-bodied or rubber dolls; simple caretaking accessories
	Dramatic play	Toy telephone, full-length mirror; miniature dishes, pots and pans; dress-up clothes; shopping cart
	Sensory	Soft, cuddly, easy-to-hold, safe toys; modeling dough; visual and auditory stimuli; sensory games and boxes
	Art/music	Rhythm instruments, bells, large crayons, markers, unlined paper
Natural and everyday	Sand and water	Sponges, small shovel, pail, cups, plastic containers for dumping and filling, baster, molds
		Pots and pans, plastic containers, cooking utensils; real objects that are familiar to children

Note: For further information, see Bronson (1995), Johnson, Christie, & Wardle (2005), and Moyer (1995).

Preschoolers and Kindergartners

Preschoolers and kindergartners show an increasing social ability, a fascination with adult roles, a growing mastery over their small and large muscles, and a deep passion for make-believe play that peaks at about age 5. Their simple, unstructured play includes family roles, such as Mommy, Daddy, Grandma, and Baby, and roles of familiar people outside the family, such as a supermarket checker or truck driver. These children use both realistic and nonrealistic props and accessories.

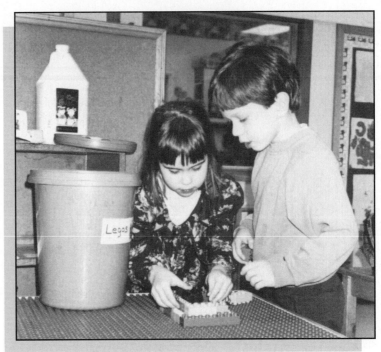

Joan Isenberg

Materials for preschoolers should support their developing social skills and imagination.

Materials for preschoolers and kindergartners should support their developing social skills, interest in adult roles, growing imaginations, increasing motor skills, and rapidly expanding vocabularies. They need the following:

- Dramatic-play props such as discarded adult clothes from familiar adult roles, and literacy tools to write.
- Realistic replicas or models of useful objects such as telephones and cars.
- Construction materials, such as simple building sets, to create products.
- Sensory materials, such as sand and water, to explore.
- Manipulative materials, such as simple puzzles, to test ideas concretely.
- Wheeled vehicles to demonstrate gross motor skills and to facilitate social interaction.
- Picture books about familiar themes such as transportation, families, and communities that represent people and objects from other cultures.
- Everyday objects such as boxes, cardboard tubing, and an assortment of plastic caps.

Table 8.5 provides examples of developmentally appropriate materials for preschool and kindergarten children.

Your Role

Teachers need to keep in mind the following guidelines when providing materials for preschoolers and kindergartners:

1. *Include adequate props and materials both indoors and outdoors.* Younger children and less-skilled players need more-realistic props, such as miniature cars,

TABLE 8.5 Developmentally Appropriate Materials for Preschool and Kindergarten Children (Ages 3–6)

Type of Material	Appropriate Materials	Examples
Skill/concept	Books/records	Picture books, simple and repetitive stories and rhymes, animal stories, pop-up books, simple information books, wide variety of musical recordings
	Games	Socially interactive games with adults, such as What If; matching and lotto games based on colors and pictures, such as picture bingo or dominoes; games of chance with a few pieces that require no reading, such as Chutes and Ladders; flannel board with pictures, letters, storybook characters
Gross motor	Active play	Push and pull toys; ride-on toys; balls of all kinds; indoor slide and climber; rocking boat
	Outdoor	Climbers, rope ladders, balls of all sizes, old tires, sand and water materials
Manipulative	Fine motor	Dressing frames; toys to put together and take apart; cookie cutters, stamp and printing materials, finger paint, modeling dough, small objects to sort and classify; bead stringing with long, thin string; pegs and small pegs; colored cubes, table blocks, magnetic board/letters/numbers and shapes; perception boards and mosaics

	Puzzles and form boards	Fit-in or framed puzzles
		    For 3-year-olds: from 4 to 20 pieces
		    For 4-year-olds: from 15 to 30 pieces
		    For 5-year-olds: from 15 to 50 pieces
		Large, simple jigsaws; number/letter/clock puzzles

	Investigative	Toys, globe flashlight, magnets, lock boxes, weather forecasting equipment, scales, balances, stethoscopes
Construction	Building sets	Small and large unit blocks; large hollow blocks; from age 4, interlocking plastic blocks with pieces of all sizes
	Carpentry	Workbench, hammer, preschool nails, saw, sandpaper, pounding benches, safety goggles
Self-expressive	Dolls and soft toys	Realistic dolls and accessories; play settings and play people (e.g., farm, hospital)
	Dramatic play	Dress-up clothes, realistic tools, toy camera, telephone, household furniture
	Sensory	Tactile boxes; auditory and musical materials such as smelling and sound boxes; cooking experiences
	Art/music	All rhythm instruments, music boxes; large crayons, paint, paste, glue, chalkboard and chalk, sewing kits, collage materials, markers, modeling dough, blunt scissors
Natural and everyday	Sand and water	Sandbox tools, bubbles, water toys
		Old clocks, radios, cameras, telephones; telephone books; mirrors; doctor kits; typewriter; magazines; fabric scraps; computer; cash register and receipts; measuring cups and muffin tins

Note: For further information see Bronson (1995), Johnson, Christie, & Wardle (2005), and Moyer (1995).

people, or tools, to support and sustain their play and engage their thinking. Older children and more advanced players need less-realistic materials for variety and flexibility of play themes, although they still enjoy realistic props. One preschool teacher noticed, for example, that a bridal veil, a bouquet of plastic flowers, and an old tuxedo jacket that she found at a secondhand store stimulated considerable excitement and elaborated play in the dress-up corner. Be certain to include natural and everyday objects that are likely to be meaningful for the child, such as a stuffed toy dog with a bowl, leash, brush, and bone.

2. *Model the use of open-ended materials when necessary.* As children use more highly developed imagination, encourage them to use less-realistic props. One kindergarten teacher brought a square block to the post office theme corner and suggested: "Let's pretend this is a package that just came in the mail." Be certain to leave the area once interactions are established.

3. *Develop your own imagination.* One of Mr. Phelps's kindergartners brought in a pith helmet and sombrero to add to the dress-up corner. Rather than simply leaving the gear on a hat rack, Mr. Phelps thought about the possibilities and invented a game that the children loved called Expedition. He put a piece of blue cloth on the floor and put the balance beam over it with a rubber crocodile below. He strategically positioned other animals around the room too. Soon, the children's activity took on many new dimensions—sinking in the quicksand, swinging from a pretend vine, and getting lost in the jungle. Each time Mr. Phelps introduced a new picture book such as *Junglewalk* (Tafuri, 1988), the children introduced new themes.

Now that you have read about materials for preschoolers and kindergartners, view the artifact "Frog and Toad Response" online at MyEducationLab and think about other materials that would be appropriate in your classroom for children ages 3 to 6 and where you would include them.

First Through Fourth Graders

First through fourth grade children are refining skills and talents that they prize, are relying more on support from their peer group, are becoming more logical thinkers, and are enjoying problem solving and inventing. Each of these qualities is clearly reflected in their expressive thinking. Materials for these children should reflect their need for realistic, rule-oriented, and peer activities. They need the following:

- Organized educational or physical games with rules, such as card, board, computer, and outdoor games that help them practice school skills, strategic thinking, decision making, and problem solving.
- Construction materials and puzzles, such as building sets, markers and stampers, and puzzles that have 50 to 500 pieces.
- Songs, chants, word games, and rituals, such as Scrabble, Boggle, or Word Yahtzee, as well as jokes, riddles, tongue twisters, and hyperbole. Mastery of games with rules also teaches a child how to follow instructions and preserve moral order. Table 8.6 lists a variety of developmentally appropriate materials for first through fourth grade children.

Your Role

Teachers must carefully consider how to use developmentally appropriate materials and resources to foster first through fourth graders' creative thought. The following guidelines will help you think broadly about such uses.

MyEducationLab

Go to MyEducationLab and select the topic "Early Literacy." Under Activities and Applications, view the artifact Frog and Toad Response *and answer the questions provided.*

TABLE 8.6   Developmentally Appropriate Materials for First Through Fourth Grade Children (Ages 6–10)

Type of Material	Appropriate Materials	Examples
Skill/concept	Books/records	Books on different cultures, recipe books, Caldecott and Newbery Award books and tapes, folktales, fables, historical fiction books in a series, biographies, jokes, riddles, tall tales; music of all types
	Games	Strategy and memory games; more-complex board and card games for problem solving and decision making; sports games
Gross motor	Active play	Organized group games
	Outdoor	Jump ropes, flying disks, bicycles, rope ladders, wagons, beanbags, assorted balls, sports sets
Manipulative	Fine motor	Gardening equipment, canister of buttons to sort and classify, weaving looms, sewing kits, combination locks, pickup sticks, Spirographs
	Puzzles	More complex puzzles with 50–100 pieces; puzzles of reproductions of paintings; form boards by famous artists
	Investigation	Science materials and kits; printing sets; terrariums and aquariums to create and observe
Construction	Building sets	Sets with realistic models, additional unit blocks, shapes, and accessories; props for roads and towns
	Carpentry	Add screwdrivers, vises, and accessories
Self-expressive	Dolls and soft toys	Dolls from other cultures; more detailed, smaller dolls; varied play settings and action figures
	Dramatic play	Storybook masks and costumes, walkie-talkies
	Sensory	Collecting toys in sets; clay and clay tools
	Art/music	Small crayons, chalk, watercolors, hole punchers, staplers, all musical instruments, basket-making materials, pottery wheel, stencil and craft kits
Natural and everyday	Sand and water	Add food coloring, funnels, pumps, hoses, plastic tubing, and assorted containers and utensils
		Simple cameras and film; computers, paper and pencils; items for "collections"

Note: For further information see Bronson (1995), Johnson, Christie, & Wardle (2005), and Moyer (1995).

1. *Use projects and investigative activities.* In their unit on ecosystems, a group of fourth graders created small habitats for their land snails. The children and their teacher collected gravel, moss, soil, rocks, bark, twigs, and plastic tanks and gallon jugs with air holes poked through the top. In pairs, the children observed, recorded, and researched their snail with magnifying glasses. They investigated their snail's reaction to a shining flashlight beam, a piece of wet lettuce, and some drops of water and compared their information with that of their classmates. They even compared the size of the snail to their own size and sought answers to their own questions about snails, such as what it means to be alive. To do this, they supplemented their observations with resources such as the Internet, information books, CD-ROMs, and interviews with friends who have pets. Some concluded their study with a group book about snails that contained illustrations from their own research; others created artistic displays of their work (Koch, 2005).

2. *Use materials that challenge children's thinking.* Developmentally appropriate materials take into account children's ages, needs, interests, abilities, and cultural backgrounds. Younger primary children take pride in demonstrating developing motor and intellectual skills and are fascinated with language play, number games, riddles, and jokes. They are intrigued by the sound ambiguity of knock-knock jokes, enjoy manipulating song lyrics like Raffi's "I like to oat, oat, oat oaples and banonos" and enjoy the ambiguous language of such books as *The King Who Rained* (Gwynne, 1970), while older children are intently interested in enacting and inventing humorous scripts.

3. *Arrange the classroom in interest centers.* As part of an integrated curriculum in one urban second-grade class, children used a sandbox as the centerpiece of the language arts center. Through their reading about knights and castles, they used the sand table to construct their own interpretation of elaborate sand castles. They also used materials in the art center to illustrate more detailed aspects of the medieval environments they were learning about (Barbour, Drosdeck, & Webster, 1987).

TECHNOLOGY MATERIALS, CREATIVE THINKING, AND THE ARTS

Technology is changing the availability of materials and resources for finding out answers to questions and how we communicate (Bers, 2008; Leu, Mallette, Karchmer, & Kara-Soteriou, 2005). It has given teachers and children access to works of art from all historical periods and across many cultures, opportunities to explore inventions, and information through searches and WebQuests. The Internet, in particular, has made whole museum collections widely available to students and teachers

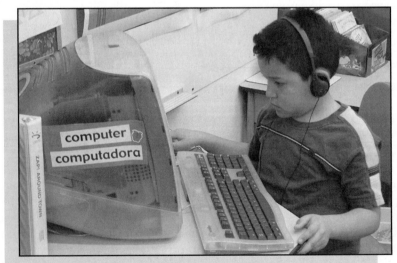

Hope Madden/Merrill

Computers are a part of daily life for children and can promote creative and imaginative experiences.

(Arts Education Partnership, 2004a). Teachers today use various technologies such as CD-ROM encyclopedias, computers and calculators, digital sound and visual image recording, and the Internet that can promote creative thought and arts-based learning across disciplines (Leu et al., 2005; March, 2004). Technological materials invite new ways of expressing ideas. They are tools that enable children to use many different ways to communicate, create, and control their own playful microworlds; they invite new creations by the imaginative child and enable children to play with real-world items, such as musical instruments, works of art, dolls, and story characters (Arts Education Partnership, 2004a; Swaminathan & Wright, 2003).

Technology materials that promote creative thought and arts-based learning are appropriate for all children. Research (Haugland, 2001) shows that creativity is significantly diminished in children who use drill-and-practice software for just 45 minutes per week. All adults who work with children and computers, an example of one kind of technology, need to know how to choose and use software that facilitates children's creative and artistic expression as well as their own roles in facilitating children's learning with computers.

Appropriate Software

Certain features of software promote children's creative thought and expression. Some of these include a simple design that has many possibilities, clear instructions so that children can use the program with little adult involvement, and easy access to and exit from the program (NAEYC, 1996b). Software that meets the needs and interests of children and enhances their creative thought and artistic expression enables them to do the following:

1. *Discover and invent with symbols.* When children use technology, they should have many opportunities to communicate their ideas through various symbols. Computer drawing programs such as Color Me, Crayola Make a Masterpiece, and Delta Draw encourage discovery as children experiment with the fill features, change and overlay colors and backgrounds, and invent stories about their creations. And virtual reality programs such as I Can Be a Dinosaur Finder, in which children become paleontologists, can provide rich symbolic experiences (Haugland, 2001).

2. *Foster inquiry, communication, and problem solving.* These computer materials provide children with possibilities for gathering information, making decisions, generating creative ideas and solutions, and testing their plans and solutions. Software that enables children to "build" their own stories by selecting particular backgrounds, icons, or characters capitalizes on children's divergent thinking and brings a story to life. With a simple click of the mouse, children can change a story's preset animals, characters, or objects to those of their own inventions. In Wiggins in Storyland, for example, *young children* can explore Wiggins the bookworm's living room, play tic-tac-toe on Wiggins's windows, hear classic stories read aloud, and make a snack for Wiggins to drink. Older children enjoy creating their own different story endings for Web stories by exploring software such as Create Your Own Adventure with Zeke (Swaminathan & Wright, 2003). In Oregon Trail, *older children* find themselves having to problem-solve survival issues by deciding how to equip their wagons with limited funds. Problem-solving software has limitless possibilities and fosters children's mental flexibility.

3. *Make connections to their units of study.* During dental health week, one second-grade teacher introduced the software program Color Me for the children to create bright illustrations for their original stories about healthy teeth. The second graders created scenic backgrounds and characters to illustrate their texts about toothbrushes as part of their study. Other programs like Cubby Magic: Folk Tales around the World use native adults to share stories, which can be read with and without rebus pictures. Children can also make their own illustrations or use rebus pictures to interpret multicultural ideas. The challenge for teachers is to choose software that enables children to explore possibilities within a technological world (Yelland, 1999).

4. *Apply a range of skills and encourage social interaction.* Some software requires children to use a very simple set of skills (such as matching and rhyming skills in Reader Rabbit) as opposed to the use of strategic thinking required in more open-ended programs such as paint programs or Kid Works 2. Programs like Millie and Bailey's Preschool use trial-and-error testing to match the right shoes to different-sized feet of customers while more open-ended software such as Thinkin' Things Collection 3 for older children, in which children draw a design on a two-dimensional rectangle that instantly appears in 3D as a spinning shape, focuses on the development of one of the new literacies, that of "visual thinking." The more time children have to explore possibilities with this program, the more intriguing the mental puzzles become to solve. Many software programs encourage children to work together. Other open-ended software for young children that fosters social interaction includes Millie's Math House, where children construct a mouse house together and take turns choosing shapes, and Facemaker, which enables children to create limitless kinds of faces.

The Internet

The Internet has already started to transform education through the emergence of e-learning. E-learning may help develop creativity and imagination, which are seen as essential skills for the twenty-first century (Pink, 2006; Thompson & Randall, 2001). One use of the Internet for elementary children is the use of WebQuests, an inquiry-oriented technology activity in which some or all of the information for learners comes from resources on the Internet. WebQuests, either short-term or long-term, should be designed to make the most of a learner's time and be real, relevant, and rich. The questions children seek to answer should be real, be meaningful, and lead to active learning (Swaminathan & Wright, 2003). For an extensive array of examples of WebQuests, go to http://webquest.sdsu.edu/materials.htm and click on "Find WebQuests."

To watch a teacher connecting a WebQuest to the children's study of dinosaurs, watch the video "A Dinosaur WebQuest" found online at MyEducationLab.

Go to MyEducationLab and select the topic "Math, Science, and Technology." Under Activities and Applications, view the video A Dinosaur WebQuest.

Your Role

Your primary responsibility with technology materials is to ensure that they are used as one of many learning tools for all children. You can do this in the following ways:

1. *Provide appropriate technology materials.* Software such as Bailey's Book House that enables very young children to create their own greeting cards and invitations; I Spy, which offers children the opportunity to select objects to search for in a microworld; or Storybook Weaver, which enables older children to create their own stories with a word processor and multicultural illustrations.

2. *Ensure equal access to technology for all children.* All children need opportunities to develop and refine subject-area skills and to have opportunities to develop interpersonal and intrapersonal skills through technological materials.

Whatever the software, girls and boys, children of color, and children with disabilities need equal access to this powerful technology.

   3. *Be an informed and critical user.*   You need to know what children can learn from the technology being used and celebrate all children's accomplishments by sharing tangible products of learning. For example, you might have children take digital photographs of objects that interest them and print and laminate them to create a personal sorting material. They can display and use their work and even bring it home to share. *Older children* can post their work on the class Web site or use software such as Thinkin' Things Collection 3 to create their own songs and games in a problem-solving environment and then share them with their peers or during an open house.

   4. *Promote artistic and creative thought*   that develops visual-spatial perception, such as Kid Pix 2 for very young children, who create stamped designs and artwork; or Crayola Make a Masterpiece for older children, who use animated traditional art tools (such as watercolor, oil, chalk, and markers), unusual art tools (such as popping corn), and magic effect tools for different styles (such as mosaics) to create computer art.

   In the next section, we describe other divergent materials that should be available in every classroom. These materials offer teachers many opportunities to take advantage of teachable moments or naturally occurring situations that enable you to teach on the spot.

 ## OTHER DIVERGENT MATERIALS AND RESOURCES

Certain divergent materials are basic for all children—blocks, modeling materials, sand, and water. These materials offer many possibilities for children to express their ideas and feelings, grow naturally with children, and can be used for more than one topic or activity.

Blocks

In his autobiography, Frank Lloyd Wright (1932) enthusiastically recalled his kindergarten experiences with blocks: "The smooth, shapely maple blocks with which to build, the sense of which never afterward left the fingers: so form became feeling" (p. 11). With blocks, children are free to design imaginative constructions, create structures and determine what to do with them, as can be seen in a glimpse of Ms. Mitsoff's first-grade classroom. Ms. Mitsoff rearranged her room to double the block-building space. Throughout the year, her first graders used the blocks as the focal point for their units of study. In their unit on the farm, for example, the children conceptualized, built, and played in a farm containing stalls for cows, a henhouse, a main farmhouse, and a barn. They also assumed different roles, including those of the farmer, milker, and egg collector. Ms. Mitsoff noticed her children practicing the following concepts:

- Science concepts as they observed, compared, and interpreted findings on ways to collect, store, and deliver milk.
- Math concepts as they estimated the distance between the farmhouse and the henhouse.

- Social studies concepts as they re-created the roles of the farm workers.
- Literacy concepts as they named and labeled their structures and considered books as references.
- Art concepts as they repeated patterns in their symmetrical buildings.

Types and Uses

There are many different types of blocks—hollow blocks, unit blocks, and table blocks. *Hollow blocks* are large wooden blocks that have an opening for carrying. Children often use these blocks to build large structures. *Unit blocks* should be made from hard wood, have smooth and rounded corners and edges, and be accurate so that children can build without frustration. To build structures, children need precisely measured unit blocks including units, double units, quadruple units, wedges, triangles, cylinders, and half-rounds. *Table blocks* are small, colored cubed blocks that children use alone or in pairs around a table. They often include unusual shapes that invite children's inventiveness. Figure 8.2 illustrates the various unit block shapes.

Children pass through the following seven stages in block building (Hirsch, 1996):

- Stage 1: Carrying—Very young children carry blocks around but do not use them to build.
- Stage 2: Building begins—Children make mostly rows, either horizontal (on the floor) or vertical (stacked). There is much repetition in this early building pattern.
- Stage 3: Bridging—Two blocks with a space between them, connected by a third block.

Figure 8.2
Illustrations of Block Shapes

Square

Unit

Double Unit

Quadruple Unit

Pillar and Half Pillar

Large and Small Triangle

Large and Small Cylinder

Ramp

Elliptical Curve

Quarter Circle

"Y" Switch

Gothic Door

Arch and Quarter Circle

Roof Board

- Stage 4: Enclosures—Blocks placed in such a way that they enclose a space.
- Stage 5: Decorative patterns—When facility with blocks is acquired, much block symmetry can be observed. Buildings, generally, are not yet named.
- Stage 6: Naming structures for enactment—Before reaching this stage, children may also have named their structures, but the names were not necessarily related to the function of the building.
- Stage 7: Resembling reality—Children's buildings often reproduce or symbolize actual structures they know, and there is a strong impulse toward enactment around the block structures.

To see a teacher facilitating block play among children in the block center, watch the video "Building Blocks: Small Group Activity" found online at MyEducationLab.

Your Role

Using blocks is central to children's learning in all areas. For example, blocks contribute to children's literacy development as they gain experience with symbolic representation, a basic abstract aspect of the reading and writing process; they promote visual and spatial literacy as children select particular blocks for their constructions; they help children develop the fine motor strength needed for writing; and they enable children to develop their oral language skills by communicating about their plans and needs for their structures. Use the following guidelines to maximize the potential learning through blocks for children of all ages.

- Store blocks on low, open shelves for easy access.
- Provide an adequate supply of blocks—200 blocks for a group of ten 3-year-olds. A complete set of more than 750 blocks is not too many for an older group of 20 children.
- Allocate enough floor space for building out of the traffic patterns and away from a quiet activity area.
- Provide enough time for building (45 to 60 minutes).
- Provide props and accessories such as cars and animals.
- Maintain a periodic physical presence in the area to attract children to the block center.
- Label shelves with the shape of the long side of the block in view so children can locate materials quickly, perceive the relationships of the blocks to one another, practice classification skills, and assist with cleanup.
- Use blocks in ways other than building, such as a matching or measuring game with blocks of a specific size.
- Develop a genuine appreciation for block playing (Hirsch, 1996).

Modeling Materials

Dough and clay are three-dimensional, sensory materials that offer children possibilities for expressing knowledge, thoughts, and feelings. *Younger children* enjoy pounding, squeezing, and rolling these materials. *Older children* do the same but also represent and/or create familiar objects or people. Where possible, consider letting the children mix the dough themselves. Figure 8.3 (p. 298) contains some simple recipes for modeling materials.

Modeling materials allow children to explore, manipulate, discover, create, and observe changes in physical properties. Children can learn the attributes of

MyEducationLab

Go to MyEducationLab and select the topic "Play." Under Activities and Applications, watch the video Building Blocks: Small Group Activity *and answer the questions provided.*

Figure 8.3 Recipes for Modeling Materials

Clay Substitute
1 cup flour
1/2 cup salt
1/3 cup water

Vegetable Dye
1 cup flour
1/2 cup salt
1 teaspoon powdered alum
1/2 cup water

Sawdust Dough
2 cups sawdust
3 cups flour
1 cup salt
Water as needed

Cornstarch Dough
1 cup cornstarch
2 cups baking soda
1/4 cup cold water
Food coloring

Play Dough
1 cup salt
1/2 cup cornstarch
1/2 cup boiling water

Peanut Butter Dough (edible)
1 cup honey
1 cup peanut butter
2 cups dried milk

Goop
1 cup cornstarch
1 cup water
Add food coloring and pour into plastic tub
(Messy but unique!)

Soapy Clay
2 cups detergent flakes
2 tablespoons water
Food coloring, if desired

modeling materials through the changes they make involving consistency (from wet to dry), color (from primary to secondary), identity (from a ball to a snake), space (from small to large), and weight (from light to heavy).

These "hands-on" experiences with transformations help children make connections between actions and events, a fundamental understanding for the development of logical thinking. Children need plenty of dough for modeling to be satisfying. Be certain to focus on the process of the material and avoid pushing children to create a product.

Sand and Water

Sand and water are readily available, inexpensive, satisfying resources that help children explore concepts and release tension. Children learn science concepts, such as the effects of objects dropped on water; math concepts such as volume, by guessing the number of cups of water needed to fill a larger container; and social interaction skills.

Sand and water are particularly absorbing and relaxing materials for children. Children can release tension as they pour water back and forth in containers or let sand gradually sift through their fingers. When children use sand and water, they are often quite calm and cooperative.

Using sand and water should take place both indoors and outdoors. Some teachers place the sand or water in large plastic tubs or in specially prepared tables. Other teachers substitute rice, shelled corn, or birdseed for indoor sandboxes when sand is unavailable. The inside of an old truck tire laid flat makes a serviceable outdoor sandbox. Be certain to cover the sandbox when the children are not using it so that a stray animal does not foul it. Check outdoor sandboxes frequently for insect infestations too.

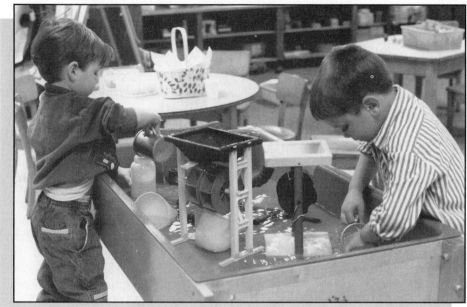

Anne Vega/Merrill

Water is a particularly rewarding and relaxing material for children of all ages.

Your Role

When using sand and water, consider the following:

- Use sand and water together so children can mold the mixture.
- Vary the equipment so that children are continually challenged to think of new uses. Some common materials for sand and water play include various-sized molds, sponges, plastic bottles and containers of assorted sizes, flexible plastic tubing, measuring cups and spoons, and small replicas of cars, buildings, and boats. Plastic aprons are also useful.
- Ask open-ended questions such as, "Why do you think the water is coming out so slowly?" or "I wonder what would happen if you added water to your sand mound?"
- Decide in advance on simple rules so that water and sand do not get tracked around the classroom. Have materials available so that children take responsibility for cleanup.

All materials need to be matched to children's abilities and interests. They are their tools for understanding their world. You have a key role in providing materials and resources that promote the release of children's creative and artistic expression. They provide a different experience from games.

ORGANIZED GAMES

In the following scenario, think about triplets playing games at different ages. Rosa, Dolly, and Norman are now fourth graders. When they were toddlers, they played social games, such as This Little Piggy and Hide the Keys. As preschoolers, they played running and chasing games and simple spinning games of chance, such as Hi-Ho Cherry-O. In these games, rules did not matter. Now Rosa plays on the school soccer team and practices soccer skills wherever she can. Dolly actively seeks friends to play strategy games such as Rummy and Clue. And Norman thrives on memory and word games such as Twenty Questions and Scrabble.

The games Rosa, Dolly, and Norman played are typical and served as a valuable resource for promoting their creative thought. In the next section, we describe the value of games, child-constructed games, and how to make games with children of all ages.

What Is a Game?

A **game** is a form of play in which children follow an agreed-upon set of rules, predetermine an outcome, assign players specific roles, and assign sanctions for violations (DeVries, 1998; Hughes, 1999; Kamii & DeVries, 1980). Dictionary definitions usually include the elements of rules, competition, and winning.

Most children's games involve physical skill, chance, strategy, or some combination of these elements to determine the outcome. In games of physical skill such as jump rope or stickball, motor skill is essential. Games of chance, such as the simple board game Winnie the Pooh, rely on dice or a spinner. Games of strategy, such as checkers or Boggle, require decision-making skills and compel players to take turns, follow complex directions, and employ complicated strategies. Organized sports are often considered strategy games because they require a player to plan strategies and imagine oneself in the opponent's role.

The Value of Games

Games are one material that contributes to children's creative-thinking, decision-making, social skills, and problem-solving skills. Games themselves are motivating for many children because the desire to play them comes from within. For many children, games provide a means to learn new skills and to practice known skills. Some educators believe that organized games for young children are developmentally inappropriate, thwart creativity, and encourage competition. Others believe that they can be appropriate if teachers positively confront the competitive element (DeVries, 1998; Kamii & DeVries, 1980; National Association for Sport and Physical Education [NASPE], 2002; Riley, San Juan, Klinker, & Ramminger, 2008).

Games for school-age children should capitalize on their increased coordination, desire to challenge themselves, interest in facts and how things work and why things happen, and genuine love of group games. When group games match children's developmental levels, children do the following:

- Develop *cooperative behaviors and strategic thinking* by experiencing others' thinking and relating it to their own. One third grader, for instance, talked about setting up a "double jump" in checkers, indicating her thinking in relation to her actions.
- Practice *autonomy* by choosing whether to play the game and to follow its rules. To illustrate, when Carmella's kindergarten friends wanted to play shadow tag, she chose another activity because she did not want to be "it."
- Engage in *problem solving* by deciding how to follow rules and play fairly. For example, a group of first graders was trying to start a game of Go Fish but could not begin their play until they solved the problem of who was to go first.

- Practice *critical thinking* by monitoring each other's actions. In a game of dominoes, it is common to hear one child tell another, "That domino doesn't have the same number of dots. You can't use that one" (Johnson et al., 2005; Van Hoorn et al., 2007).

Games suitable for *young children* have one or two simple rules, include all children who want to participate, encourage children to figure things out for themselves, and do not stress being first, winning, or losing. Young children like noncompetitive guessing games such as "I'm thinking of something in the room that is . . . ," simple sorting and matching games, simple board games (if they can change the rules), and basic running and chasing games.

Children in *first through fourth grades* need strategy games that develop problem-solving and decision-making abilities while encouraging them to think about others' thoughts and feelings. Board games and active outdoor group games are typical of this age for both boys and girls. With an emphasis on involvement, mutual enjoyment, and respect, group games can promote basic intellectual, social, and creative skills in children through fourth grade.

Competition Versus Cooperation

Games should be a positive experience for all children. All children should benefit from the physical challenge, exercise, problem solving, and strategic thinking while simultaneously enjoying a sense of belonging to the group, a commitment to goals, and enhanced cooperative skills, all of which contribute to academic success. If teachers make it clear that the goal of a game is doing as well as each child can, then games can enhance cooperation. To illustrate, Ms. Ake's second graders were involved in relay races. When she reminded them that the goal of these races was to do their very best, she noticed how they urged one another on in their three-legged races as they jointly figured out ways to get quickly to the other side of the room.

Cooperation means operating together. It involves negotiating to arrive at an agreement that is acceptable to all. As a result, some disputes and conflicts are inevitable. When children play games cooperatively, they construct rules for themselves as they begin to experience others' viewpoints. An emphasis on cooperative games encourages children to play together rather than against one another by focusing on group participation, sharing, giving each player an opportunity to play, and making rules that suit the players. Cooperative games help children develop a sense of teamwork, loyalty to the group, and knowledge of how to get along with others. Because Western culture is inherently competitive, it is a challenge for teachers to handle competition constructively in classrooms.

Your Role

Consider this group of elementary children playing Marble Run, a commercial game in which children combine small blocks with slides and intricate grooves into a course for the marble. As the children excitedly invent new courses, they exclaim, "Now, let's try this!" or "Look at it go!" Their teacher commented, "This is their favorite game because it has so many possibilities and combinations. When I say, 'It's game time,' I have to be sure to say 'Only four children can use Marble Run.' It is truly the favorite game in our classroom."

The teacher's role, in this case, was that of observer and manager as she freed the children to utilize the many available combinations. There was no correct way to play the game. The children constructed the rules in ways that made sense to them.

When using games in your classroom provide opportunities for children to modify rules and create their own games. In that way, games such as Marble Run, as they are being played, become a powerful vehicle for developing intellectual and social autonomy. You can help children modify game rules by doing the following:

1. *Supporting their initiatives in games.* The children playing Marble Run were encouraged to play the game in many different ways. Sometimes the game involved races; at other times it became a maze. Each group of players could initiate the way to play the game and then negotiate rules for it.

2. *Focusing on noncompetitive games.* Children who compete can and do also cooperate in games as well as other activities. All children function best when they actively participate in most or all of the game instead of being excluded or eliminated by focusing on winning or losing. Appendix C describes appropriate, noncompetitive ball games, quiet games, singing games, running games, and partner games that can be introduced into the curriculum to enhance cooperation.

3. *Allowing them to modify rules during the game.* Even though the children usually started one of the Marble Run games with a race of some kind, they often decided to change it in midstream to a different game. Their teacher supported their thinking about all of the variations they invented by using positive language that empowered them to think about the many possibilities inherent in the game.

Games are useful for active and quiet times, for transitions from one activity to another, and as a resource for fostering specific learning outcomes. Therefore, you will need to develop a repertoire of games that foster a cooperative spirit that will last children through their lives.

 ## CHILD-CONSTRUCTED GAMES

Child-constructed games promote children's understanding and acceptance of rules as well as their ability to cooperate, compete, and think flexibly. Unfortunately, children in today's world spend less time spontaneously inventing games and more time using prepared commercial games with predetermined instructions, rules, and outcomes or in organized team sports. This limits their opportunities to make, revise, and follow their own rules with their peers and to control their social interactions. In the next section, we describe the power of children's invented games on their divergent thinking, artistic expression, and overall development.

Invented Games

Inventing games makes rules meaningful and relevant for children (Castle, 1998). They help children do the following:

1. *Become autonomous learners.* Second grader Andy made a simple baseball game from oak tag, markers, and colored dots. When other children were excited about using it and helped him modify the game, Andy gained confidence in his ability as an independent yet collaborative learner.

2. *Practice basic skills.* Julia wanted to create her own version of hopscotch on the playground outdoors. She practiced her writing to label the asphalt with chalk and to write the game's rules; she used reading skills to read her rules to a friend; and she incorporated mathematics when figuring out the procedures and format of her hopscotch game.

3. *Develop organizational skills.* In invented games, children plan the game, construct it, play it with others, discover its problems, and make changes. Some of Ms. Spencer's fourth-grade girls invented a board game called Shopping. The object was to move along a path to purchase various department store items. While playing the game, they discovered that their rule of getting the exact number on the dice to move the number of spaces remaining on the game board left them sitting for many turns waiting to complete the game. So they agreed to change the rules.

Invented games encourage mutual self-interest in rules and rule making and differ greatly from teacher-imposed rules. They provide an appealing and satisfying vehicle for children to apply knowledge and skills, increase their understanding of rules, see others' ideas and points of view, and improve their social interaction skills. Older children can make board games based on the content they are studying, while younger children might invent games based on stories they are reading. Think about the following second graders in Mr. Green's classroom. Paolo, Kristin, and Sarah are struggling readers and have some difficulty with basic arithmetic operations. For one hour every Wednesday afternoon, Mr. Green expects all of his second graders to invent their own games, either alone or with a partner, using assorted available materials. Let's look at the games of Kristin, Sarah, and Paolo.

Kristin made the "Go Here and There Game" alone and then taught it to her friend. Her simple path game included starting and finishing points, some obstacles along the way, a few game cards, and an individual card for rules. During play her friend asked, "Where are the place cards?" Kristin said, "Oops, I forgot them" and went back to make them.

Sarah's game reflects the solar system unit her class is studying. It includes all the planets, Saturn's rings, a darkened background indicating night, and the sun and stars. She made cards for the number of spaces to move forward and back, as well as outer-space instructions like "Tack a peas [take a piece] of the moon rock and stay." She used existing dice to designate turns and dried beans for markers. Her simple rules read as follows: "RULES: Start from the moon go to the Erath and the first person to get there wens." When she tried to teach the game to a friend the next week, she quickly discovered that she had no labels on the dots telling players when to choose a card. As a result, the game could not begin. Sarah then made the necessary modifications.

Paolo's game, Colorland, is also a simple path game containing a clear beginning and end, periodic spots to pick cards, a place labeled "card," and many cards sending players to jail or helping them escape from jail. Two of his cards read "brach owt of jail [break out of jail]" and "Go 5 steps forwerd." Paolo has played his game several times with his classmates. His final version evolved from the many questions his friends asked while playing.

Notice that in all three cases, children were refining the format of their games, practicing skills in context, and collaborating with peers. Child-constructed games provide children with the opportunity to construct and use rules in relevant ways, to apply content they are studying, to see others' points of view, and to figure things out autonomously or cooperatively.

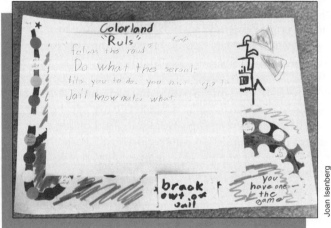

Three invented games.

Making Games with Children

The following guidelines will help you include game making in your classroom.

1. *Find information and collect facts.* Before making a game, the children need to determine what information they need. If children are studying environmental issues, for example, this is a good time to review the content learned during the unit and clarify what they still want to know. This is also the time for children to gather books and other informational resources to verify facts.

2. *Make a rough draft.* As in the writing process, making a rough draft of the game board, cards, content, and accessories helps children to plan. It provides an organizational framework for thinking and working together for a common outcome.

3. *Make the game.* Have a variety of free and inexpensive materials available, such as file folders, poster board of all sizes and colors, beans, markers, sticky dots, labels, plastic bread ties, old magazines, calendar numbers, and assorted plastic bottle caps. Expect children to decide the type of game to make (board, card, and motor) and invent it. Their games will usually look like games that are familiar to them, yet the content and the play of the game will vary.

4. *Play the game.* Playing the games helps children notice problems and pitfalls. Children "go back to the drawing board" willingly to produce a playable game.

5. *Revise the game to achieve more accuracy.* Revision means literally "to see again." As children revise their games, they re-see and re-think them until they achieve excellence in the finished product. The revision process provides multiple opportunities for creative expression, constructive conflict resolution, and practice in self-evaluation. By observing, recording, and comparing children's progress with invented games throughout the year, teachers have a powerful learning, teaching, and assessment tool that appeals to children of all ages (Castle, 1998; Surbeck & Glover, 1992).

As with all other areas of the curriculum, you will need to make accommodations with your materials and resources to meet the needs and interests of diverse learners. We discuss some possible accommodations in the next section.

CURRICULUM ACCOMMODATIONS FOR DIVERSE LEARNERS

Classroom materials can easily be modified to accommodate diverse learners. To appropriately accommodate materials, you will need to understand each child's physical, social, and cognitive level of functioning. By carefully observing children as they use different materials, you will know which materials and resources in your classroom may need modification.

Tips for Adapting Materials and Resources in the Classroom

- Build a library of curriculum materials spanning several grade levels to give you ideas and content for using materials and resources on all levels.
- Provide books on tape and a player for use during quiet reading times. Have older children listen to tapes of books that are being read aloud to the class.
- Include picture instructions in games so that nonreaders can understand the rules of play.

- Read books that reflect cultural and ethnic diversity such as, *Knots on a Counting Rope* (Martin & Archambault, 1987), *I Hate English* (Levine, 1990), *Speak English for Us, Marisol!* (English & Sanchez, 2000), and *My Name is Yoon* (Recorvits & Swiatkowska, 2003).
- Design centers to foster exploration of cultural traditions and backgrounds such as, Hanukah, Chinese New Year, and Kwanzaa.
- Challenge gifted and talented children with more complex tasks, such as inventing computer games, designing experiments, and creating riddles, jokes, and poems.

Specific Suggestions for Diverse Learners

Children Who Are English Language Learners (ELL)

English Language Learners (ELLs) need many ways to express their knowledge and to practice speaking skills. Games naturally immerse ELLs in a language-rich experience that can be easily adapted to meet their needs. Try the following modifications when using games with ELLs:

- Simplify the rules or content of a game; for example, sight word bingo may include pictures as well as words or fewer spaces to cover.
- Create games in which there is no clear winner to increase self-confidence.
- Introduce games that require little or no reading for students who are just beginning to learn English; for example, "Go Fish," "Candy Land," or "Chutes and Ladders."

Children with Sensory Integration Impairments

Children with hearing or vision loss and those who struggle with fine or large motor skills benefit from tactile, auditory, and visual materials that make sounds, vibrate, and have a texture or scent. For children with sensory integration impairments, try:

- Tactile maps for exploration
- Large-type print kits
- Braille materials, such as a menu in the housekeeping area
- Toys that emit light
- Bright, shiny, contrasting-colored materials
- Raised slant boards for reading and writing
- Rice table for exploration
- Allowing time to get and put away materials so they learn to become self-sufficient.
- Providing real-life materials whenever and wherever possible.

Other classroom materials can easily be modified so that children can be successful with them, such as:

- Providing large-knobbed puzzles for easier manipulation.
- Including oversized building set pieces, such as wooden blocks or Mega blocks, within Lego and block collections.
- Outlining finished puzzle pieces on a board template for easier placement.
- Raising edges on outer edge puzzle pieces using tape or glue for easier tactile discrimination.
- Providing materials with tactile differences to encourage exploration, such as stuffed animals, wooden blocks, and plastic cars.

Children with Physical Disabilities

Children with physical disabilities need materials that can easily be manipulated. Be sure that children with physical disabilities have enough space to engage with materials that does not restrict their movement. Place materials within easy reach so children have independent access. Other modifications for children with physical disabilities include the following:

- Use larger beads, looms, and needles for those who have trouble navigating fine motor skills.
- Keep materials within a child's reach by placing them in a box lid or cookie sheet.
- Place rubber pads, "Scoot guard," or Velcro under materials and toys to keep them from sliding out of reach.
- Lower basketball hoops.
- A child in a wheelchair can be the jump rope turner for others to jump rope.

As teachers, we are responsible for teaching so all children can learn and be successful in school. Each of us needs to take time to think about our children and curriculum, to reflect on what works and why, and what we need to do next for children. Sharing materials, resources, and ideas with your colleagues can help you attain the standards for which you are accountable. We look at those standards next.

MEETING STANDARDS THROUGH THE EFFECTIVE USE OF CREATIVE MATERIALS AND RESOURCES

Teachers often find that providing materials and resources for creative thinking and arts-based learning is challenging because they feel less prepared than in academic subjects. Materials and resources that promote creative thought and expression are connected to standards across disciplines and require both "hands on" and "minds on" learning (Beeghly & Prudhoe, 2002; Wassermann, 2000; Zemelman, Daniels, & Hyde, 2005). These materials invite children to tinker and experiment, visualize and model, brainstorm and role-play, inquire and problem-solve as well as to paint, draw, dramatize, act out, and dance their understanding. Using materials in this way parallels the types of play discussed in Chapter Two (functional play, dramatic play, sociodramatic play, and games with rules).

Many museums and arts organizations have fine Web sites that provide information, lesson plans, and activities for teachers to use materials and resources effectively. Still, teachers are responsible for selecting the most appropriate materials and resources; deciding when, where, and how to make them accessible; and answering the questions, "What classroom materials and resources promote standards-based teaching?" and "How do different teaching materials and resources affect learning?"

What follows are examples of ways you can incorporate creative materials and resources into your curriculum. These examples are followed by the appropriate national content, arts, and teacher-education standards.

Materials and Resources for English Language Arts

Example

Read the book *Dance with Me* (Esbensen, 1995), a collection of 15 poems about different kinds of dance steps illustrated in pastels. The poems portray everyday objects and events from the author's perspective, such as the tap-dance sounds of raindrops falling on the roof in a summer storm, a baby tapping a beat with her reflection in the mirror, and a woman dancing as she weeds her garden. Readers see ordinary subjects such as bubbles, waves, and dust and through different lenses.

Preschool/Kindergarten

Using the poem "Bubbles" from the book *Dance with Me* (Esbensen, 1995), invite children to become "bubbleologists" and study bubbles. With some bubble solution and a variety of wands, have them explore, investigate, and make bubbles. Encourage them to describe their bubbles—color, shape, size, number, length, and duration—and determine which wands work best.

Possible Activities

- Use pastel colors to write and/or illustrate poems inspired by "Bubbles."
- Use rhythm instruments to make sound effects for the reading of "Bubbles."
- Create rebus picture words for bubbles of different shapes.
- Brainstorm ways to float like bubbles.

First Grade–Fourth Grade

Possible Activities

- Redefine the ordinary: Create an interesting poem about something ordinary in your daily life (use movement, voice, action, person, place, and thing).
- Use the Internet to discover dance steps from around the world and apply them to ordinary objects.
- Construct a cardboard model of something ordinary and share your construction with a friend.

Connection to English/Language/Arts Standards

The Arts (Dance): Understanding choreographic principles, processes, and structures. Applying and demonstrating critical and creative thinking skills in dance.

Language Arts: Students apply a wide range of strategies to comprehend, evaluate, and appreciate texts. They draw upon their prior experiences, their interactions with other readers and writers, and their knowledge of word meaning and other texts.

Science (Physical Science): Students develop an understanding of the properties of objects and materials.

Teacher Education:

INTASC—Principle 1, Content Pedagogy

NAEYC—Standard 4, Teaching and Learning, and Substandard 4c, Understanding Content Knowledge in Early Education

Materials and Resources for Science

Materials and resources for science should promote sustained inquiry and understanding (Bloom, 2006; Worth & Grollman, 2003). Effective science teaching requires the availability and organization of a broad range of basic scientific materials, equipment, media, and technology as well as specific tools for particular topics and learning experiences. Teachers must balance safety, proper use, and availability with students' needs to participate actively in designing experiments, selecting tools, and constructing apparatus, all of which are critical to the development of an inquiry stance.

Science literacy also involves the use of materials and resources outside the school, such as science centers and museums. The school's indoor and outdoor physical environment can easily be used as a living laboratory for the study of natural phenomena and should be used as a resource for science study wherever the school may be located.

Example

Preschool/Kindergarten

Appropriate basic materials include aluminum foil and plastic wrap; basic rock, mineral, and shell collections; assortments of seeds, beans, and peas; egg cartons; food coloring; hand lenses; magnets of various sizes and shapes; measuring cups and spoons; rubber balls of various sizes; scales; shoe boxes; small plastic animals and trays; and trade books.

Possible Activities

- Investigate color changes with food coloring and eyedroppers.
- Mix modeling dough and observe changes.
- Construct a model out of dough.
- Use found or recycled materials to create collages to compare and contrast changes.

First Grade–Fourth Grade

In addition to the preceding materials, use balloons, barometers, batteries, beakers, calculators, charts of regional birds, rocks, minerals, compasses, graduated cylinders, plastic containers, tubing, straws, prisms, pulleys, and safety goggles.

Possible Activities

- Use an "invention sketchpad" to create an invented animal, food, game, or machine. Draw "ideas" on the sketchpad and then use some of the basic materials to create your invention.
- Write a story about your invention.
- Search the Internet to find out about your favorite inventor and what materials he or she used to create an invention.
- Take an invention walk around your school to identify all the things that have been invented.
- Make "junk bags" by filling lunch bags with items from your basic science materials and have the children invent something in teams.

Sources for Free and Inexpensive Materials

Environmental Protection Agency Public Information Center and Library
http://www.epa.gov

National Aeronautics and Space Administration (NASA) NASA Education Division NASA Headquarters 300 E Street SW Washington, DC 20546
http://www.nasa.gov

National Science Foundation Division of Pre-College Education 4201
    Wilson Blvd Arlington, VA 22230
www.nsf.gov

Outstanding Science Trade Books for Students K–12
    Recommended reading levels arranged by seven topical categories
http://www.nsta.org/ostbc

Connection to Science Standards

NSES Teaching Standard D: Teachers of science design and manage learning environments that provide students with the time, space, and resources needed for learning science. In doing this, teachers make available the science tools, materials, media, and technological resources accessible to students and identify and use resources outside the school.

Teacher Education:

INTASC—Principle 1, Content Pedagogy

NAEYC—Standard 4, Teaching and Learning, and Substandard 4c, Understanding Content Knowledge in Early Education

Materials and Resources for Social Studies

Example

In a study of author Gary Soto, children learn about the Hispanic culture through the author's works. For younger children, read *Chato's Kitchen* (1997), a story of five mice who move next door to a cat and who end up being friends and celebrating with an elaborate fiesta. For older children, read *Neighborhood Odes* (1992), a collection of 21 poems set in a Chicano neighborhood that portray common things such as the music of an ice cream vendor's truck, the top of a refrigerator where old bread lies in plastic, and dust released into the air when a boy strums a guitar, which is evoked by the form of the poems, which fall in long vertical columns with short lines. Woodcut illustrations capture the culture of the Chicano community. The odes celebrate fireworks, pets, grandparents, tortillas, and the library.

Preschool/Kindergarten
Possible Activities

- Design a book of your favorite poems.
- Make quesadillas.
- Draw a self-portrait of characters and create a portrait gallery.
- Investigate local neighborhoods and explore Mexican and Mexican American culture.
- Create a collage picturing your favorite things in your house (toys, food, furniture).
- Create puppets to represent historical figures.
- Explore museum sites for contributions of Hispanic figures.
- Learn folk songs and singing games of the culture.

First Grade–Fourth Grade
Possible Activities

- Create a new country with favorite food, sport, greeting, main form of transportation, flag, national anthem, name of country, and motto.

- Invent games (Memory, Concentration) that use the images in Soto's poems.
- Create an ode about a favorite person or object in your daily life.
- Play a game from one of the countries.
- Visit some key Web sites such as those of *National Geographic,* the Getty Museum, and Exploratorium to locate other links to the Hispanic culture and to explore Mexican American art.

Connection to Social Studies and Arts Standards

Social Studies (Culture): Students explore how cultures express themselves through the arts.

Frequently Asked Questions About Materials and Resources

I have so much English to teach to children who are English language learners. Why should I use games with them?

Children in schools today speak more than 400 different languages. For all children, engaging in simulations; drama games; story, word, and writing games; and outdoor games can improve their learning, offer a different way to express knowledge, and create an atmosphere of ease, original thinking, and imaginative thought. Games create experiences with language and ideas, and "experience is the glue that makes learning stick" (Peregoy & Boyle, 2005, p. 131). For English-language learners at all levels, games encourage students to work on motivating projects; provide scaffolds for oral language, where evident; and focus on easy use of oral language, exploding the myth that games are not appropriate for nonnative language learners (Kindler, 2002).

I have children from many different countries in my classroom. How do I know what kinds of materials to choose, because I cannot teach about all of these different cultures?

The materials that children use are powerful vehicles for multicultural education because they are visual representations of others' feelings, behaviors, artifacts, and traditions. Using materials "rooted in cultural traditions may help children identify more deeply with their cultures and share their cultures with others. When integrated into the teaching of other subjects, the arts provide a vehicle for students to introduce their life experiences into the classroom in purposeful ways for their recognition of their peers and teachers" (Arts Education Partnership, 2004b, p. 26). Students from diverse backgrounds can also use art materials to engage with each other and to build understanding of race, culture, and socioeconomic status. Materials, therefore, should reflect the individuality of children and adults in that setting (Isenberg & Quisenberry, 2002; Ramsey, 1998; Wootton, 2004).

In my student teaching classroom, some children are gifted and also second-language learners. What kinds of materials and resources do these children need?

Many myths surround children who are gifted second-language learners. These children need a language-rich environment that integrates critical and higher-order thinking as well as the use of multiple intelligences. It is not true that these children are less capable, are unable to articulate, or do not work as well in groups or independent research projects (Castellano, 2003). Because of their often exceptional verbal ability, high-achieving preschool children need to use more language play, such as riddles, jokes, and poems, and more logical, rules-oriented games. Children who are academically talented enjoy playing or inventing computer games that are intellectually demanding, solving advanced problems in mathematics, exploring ideas, testing hypotheses, and judging the quality of their solutions. Investigations, learning centers, and contracts offer children many possibilities to use their gifts.

In every classroom, children need a variety of creative materials and resources that hold their fascination, challenge their thinking, keep them engaged, and support meaningful play and creative thought. See Appendix E for sources for free and inexpensive classroom materials and resources.

Social Studies (Global Connections): Students explore how exposure to diversity found in cultural universals (dancing, cooking, and hospitality) may lead to global understandings or misunderstandings.

Social Studies (Culture): Students investigate how different cultures, groups, and societies are similar and different across common situations.

The Arts (Visual Arts): Understanding and applying media, techniques, and processes.

Understanding the visual arts in relation to history and cultures.

Teacher Education:

  INTASC—Principle 1, Content Pedagogy

  NAEYC—Standard 4, Teaching and Learning, and Substandard 4c, Understanding Content Knowledge in Early Education

 ## *Web Sites to Visit*

http://www.exploratorium.edu
Hands-on exhibits devoted to inquiry-based teaching and learning.

http://www.thegateway.org
Provides access to lesson plans, curriculum units, and other education resources.

http://www.puzzlemaker.com
Allows users to create puzzles and games for newsletters, flyers, handouts, or classroom assignments.

http://www.terra-quest.com
Includes information about ecology, travel, environments and wildlife, and history.

http://webquest.sdsu.edu
Provides an inquiry-oriented resource to those using the WebQuest model to teach with the Internet.

http://www.field-guides.com
Field trips for children of all ages in a variety of subject areas.

http://www.smithsonianeducation.org/
Smithsonian Institute Education Internet Resources
Provides lesson plans in all subject areas and field trip information for all grade levels.

http://whale.wheelock.edu/whalenet-stuff/curriculum.html
Provides lesson plans for teachers about whales.

 ## CHAPTER SUMMARY

1. Throughout history, children in all cultures have played with materials. The types of materials available are affected by economic, cultural, and political issues and strongly influence children's self-expression, inventiveness, and divergent thinking.

2. Materials that hold the most promise for creative thought and arts-based learning have multiple uses, encourage inventiveness and problem solving, and are process-oriented.

3. Children should experience a balance of materials, including skill/concept, manipulative, construction, self-expressive, and natural and everyday materials.

4. Developmentally appropriate materials, which are concrete, real, meaningful, and stimulating to the imagination, should be available to children of all ages. Younger children need sensory materials to explore and investigate in dramatic play, art, music, construction, and manipulative play. Older children also need realistic, rule-oriented, and peer-related activities.

5. Technology materials are one of many classroom learning tools. They enable children to control their symbolic world, apply new and familiar skills, enhance their social interactions, foster self-directed learning, solve problems, and connect information to what they know and are studying.

6. Organized games can be a significant aspect of the curriculum if presented and played appropriately. They encourage autonomy, decision making, cooperation, and use of rules.

7. Teachers should offer opportunities for children to invent, teach, and play their own games as part of the curriculum.

8. Using a variety of creative materials and resources is one of the best ways for teachers to adapt the curriculum to a wide range of children's abilities, interests, and cultural backgrounds.

 ## *Discuss: Perspectives on Creative Materials*

1. Select, investigate, and explore a child's creative material from your current setting. Think about the possible ways children could use it. If you can, observe different children using the same material. Keep a list of the children's uses. Compare your list with those who selected a similar material. How did infants/toddlers, preschoolers/kindergartners, and children in Grades 1 to 4 use the material?

2. Reread the chapter's opening quotation. Describe how your thinking has changed since reading this chapter.

3. Incorporating invented games into the curriculum provides many opportunities for learning. Discuss these opportunities and suggest ways to include them as part of a thematic unit.

4. Why should children use creative materials? List some of these materials and briefly state a rationale for including each in the curriculum.

5. Refer to the chapter-opening classroom scenarios. Why was it important for the children's teachers to provide these kinds of materials? What was their role? Defend your thinking.

6. Observe a child who is using a material for the first time. Refer to the discussion of the uses of materials in this chapter and describe his or her behaviors. How do the behaviors fit the progression?

Chapter 9

Assessing the Creative Processes and Products of Children

Mary Renck Jalongo
and Marilyn J. Narey

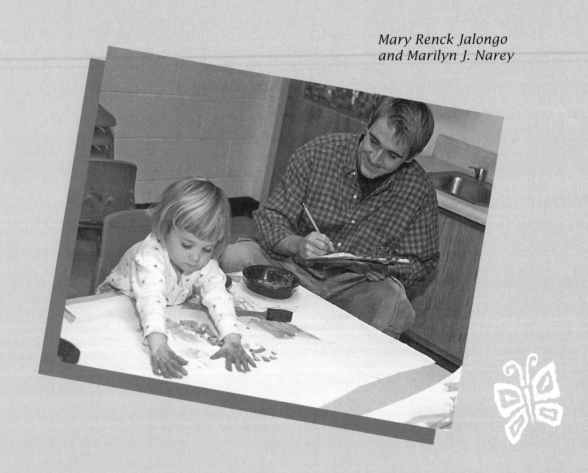

The creative work of students, if taken seriously, can and must be assessed and evaluated.

Lars Lindström, 2006, p. 64

CLASSROOM PERSPECTIVES ON ASSESSMENT OF CREATIVE WORK

Preschool—Kindergarten

In response to state academic standards, six kindergarten teachers in the district have planned an integrated unit on life cycles that incorporates the arts and creative expression. Experiences for the children include planting seeds to watch them grow and observing the metamorphosis of a chrysalis into a butterfly. Each day features a story such as *The Tiny Seed* (Carle, 2001), *One Little Seed* (Greenstein, 2004), *Big Yellow Sunflower* (Barry, 2008), and *Monarch and Milkweed* (Frost, 2008). The children maintain science journals, dramatize life cycles, create music to accompany their presentations of the life cycles, and work in groups to create picture books about the growth of other plants and animals. The students also participate in a sociodramatic play center representing a plant nursery complete with cash register, plastic pots and plants, and materials for making signs and writing receipts. To assess student understanding, the teachers use observational notes of play, a rubric to score the picture books, and recordings of the dramatizations and songs.

First Grade—Second Grade

Most teachers are familiar with pages from the sketchbooks of famous people, such as Leonardo da Vinci, that were used to record thinking, imaginings, plans, and inventions. The naturalist Charles Darwin produced dozens of sketchbooks to record scientific observations, and Queen Victoria created a watercolor memoir of her children. Following these traditions, the teachers of first graders have decided to introduce small, blank spiral-bound notebooks that their students will use as sketchbooks over the course of the school year. They begin by looking at examples in children's books such as Janet Stevens's (1996) *From Pictures to Words: A Book about Making a Book*. Then the teachers provide time each day for children to work in the sketchbooks in their preferred ways. Three students settle near a window, choosing to work near one another and initiate a dialogue; one is seated on the floor next to the aquarium to study the fish. The teachers do not write on the students' actual drawings because it might suggest to the children that words are more important than their visual expression (Anning, 1999). Periodically, the teachers meet with one student or groups of students to share their work. The children's weekly entries, collected over several months and combined with the teachers' observational notes, are shared with families at conference time.

Third Grade—Fourth Grade

The third-grade teachers have collaborated with the music teacher on a yearlong project that will enable all students to finish the year with a record of their musical explorations. The project begins when the teachers and the children bring in favorite tapes, CDs, or music videos. The teachers introduce the project by playing various musical selections over a period of a week or two. They explain to the students that they will experiment with music and sounds to produce a personal CD or a music video. Every day, time is set aside so that children can work with instruments (such as keyboards and recorders), construct and play handmade instruments, or compose melodies and/or lyrics and schedule recording sessions. An array of picture books about music and composers—such as the song picture book *The Train They Call the City of New Orleans* (Goodman & McCurdy, 2003) as well as books about people who craft musical instruments, such as *Made in Mexico* (Laufer, 2000) and *Pictures at an Exhibition* (Celenza, 2003)—are shared. The students also get inspiration from videotapes that focus on music and musicians such as *Duke Ellington: The Piano Prince and His Orchestra* (Weston Woods, 2000) and *This Land Is Your Land* (Weston Woods, 2000), a video about the songs of Woody Guthrie. Students attend concerts performed by the high school students, go on a field trip to see an orchestra play at a nearby university, and work with the musicians-in-residence program. Each third grader's recorded piece is stored in an envelope and labeled with the student's name. The final musical CDs are shared and discussed by the student with peers and teacher in terms of the student's goals. In each of these cases, teachers are assessing children's creative growth and artistic expression.

ASSESSMENT CHALLENGES IN CREATIVITY AND THE ARTS

Assessment "involves identification of goals and purposes, selection of procedures, methods, and measures, coordination of timing, analysis of data, interpretation of results, and formulation of responses to the results" (Dorn, Madeja, & Sabol, 2004, p. 22). One basic principle of assessment is that it must be linked with the written curriculum and the instruction that takes place in class (Goodlad, 2007; Popham, 2004).

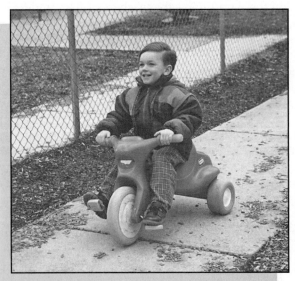

Anthony Magnacca/Merrill

Assessment needs to take the teacher's goals and the child's purposes into account.

Contemporary assessment of creative processes and products poses some unique assessment challenges (Sefton-Green & Sinker, 2000). In general, some of these challenges are:

> First, what is the nature of the arts learning experience, and if we can sufficiently understand it, how are we to capture or measure it? Second, are the learning disciplines of art, music, dance, and drama similar enough to each other to merit being grouped together as "arts education," or are we better off dissecting each discipline separately? And finally, what kinds of outcomes should we expect as a result of arts learning, or, to put it another way, how do the arts contribute to human development? (Horowitz & Webb-Dempsey, 2002, p. 98)

When such assessment issues surface in the classroom, teachers are the ones who are obligated to resolve them. A place to begin is to accept that *creative processes and products are multidimensional and complex.* Therefore, assessments of children's creative growth benefit from an interdisciplinary perspective, focusing on creative qualities demonstrated under a variety of circumstances and across subject areas. This also means that teachers seeking to document creative thinking and arts-based learning need to focus on what children know, understand, and can do (Wiggins & McTighe, 2005). Suppose that a teacher is presenting a unit on media literacy in which children are given the resources to invent a commercial (Burton, 2006). Assessment criteria might include such things as the quality of their investigative work, the inventiveness of the product, the ability to use models, and the child's capacity for self-assessment (Lindström, 2006).

Another idea that teachers need to understand is that *creative thought and art works are not adequately assessed by standardized tests.* Most standardized tests are paper-and-pencil, "one right answer" tasks that compare one child's performance to the performance of a group of peers—all things that can be at odds with creative processes (Sternberg, 2006). Even tests that are designed to assess creativity sometimes rely rather heavily on a single creative behavior (such as artistic ability) or tend to assess problem solving under very restrictive conditions (Chae, 2003; Kim, 2006; Urban, 2005). Suppose that a researcher is assessing creativity during block play and provides the child with a small set of wooden blocks, then observes the child's block play during a short time period. The researcher may conclude that the child exhibits little originality. But the child may be accustomed to incorporating other miniature toys in her block play, may work exceptionally well with other children in creating large unit block structures, or may be extraordinarily imaginative with construction toys at home. The restrictive format of the test simply could not tap into the child's capabilities.

A third assumption that teachers need to accept is that *creative thinking and artwork require real-life contexts to be valid.* A high score on a test of creativity does not provide an authentic, everyday indication of the child's creative thought and expression, such as the ability to construct an imaginative diorama based on a favorite story. The more removed from direct, hands-on, actual experience a task becomes, the less likely that it will be a good predictor of exceptional "real-world" performance. Figure 9.1 (p. 318) provides an overview of appropriate assessment tasks, tools, and outcomes by three different groups: (1) the teacher, (2) the child, and (3) parents, families, and the community at large.

Teachers—both the regular classroom teachers and specialist teachers in the arts—consider their knowledge of assessment methods to be insufficient (Dorn, Madeja, & Sabol, 2003). Yet if teachers leave creative products and the arts out of the assessment loop, these pursuits will be eclipsed by other areas of the curriculum

Appropriate Assessment Tasks

- Are opportunities for learning
- Enable every child to succeed at some level
- Are embedded in the curriculum
- Connect content, process, and work habits
- Acknowledge children's accomplishments
- Give children opportunities to demonstrate what they have learned
- Provide clear expectations and standards of excellence

Appropriate Assessment Tools

- Emphasize dialogue and self-reflection
- Are part of a comprehensive assessment plan
- Show the child's rate of progress
- Identify skills that still need to be developed
- Provide direction to teachers as they plan
- Suggest ways that parents and families might support play, creative expression, and the arts at home and in the community

Appropriate Assessment Outcomes

- Document not only what children are learning (content, skills) but also how they are learning it (processes)
- Engage educators, other professionals, families, and communities in rich and meaningful dialogue about the value of assessment in the arts, creativity, and play
- Convince parents, families, and communities of the contributions of creative expression, play, and the arts to children's lives

Figure 9.1   Appropriate Assessment Tasks, Tools, and Outcomes

Note: Data from Educators in Connecticut's Pomperaug Regional School District 15 (1996), and Isenberg & Farley (1990).

that are tied to standards and testing. A very common mistake in evaluating children's work is making snap judgments about whether a child's work is "advanced." Performing a task earlier does not necessarily mean it has been performed better. For example, a child who draws a stick person of a ballet dancer before most of his or her peers is producing a stereotype. Imitating stereotypes has nothing to do with creativity and the arts, even if it does appear ahead of most peers. On the other hand, a child who uses rudimentary lines yet captures the fluid motion of ballet deserves a positive evaluation even if the drawing does not "look like" a ballet dancer all that much. Teachers need to promote children's knowledge, skills, and understanding in making the arts, presenting the arts, and appraising their own work and that of others. "Children may have strengths in one particular area (a physically disabled child may be potentially a very talented choreographer) and may be more skilled in one aspect of a particular art form (for example, strong rhythmic ability, but difficulty in singing a melody)" (Peter, 1998, p. 169). Methods of assessment need to be relevant, appropriate, and capable of documenting effort and progress as well as attainment of specific goals and achievement.

Observational notes play an important role in assessment.

THEORETICAL AND RESEARCH BASE: IDENTIFICATION OF TALENT AND GIFTEDNESS

Talent refers to "general, pervasive, relatively natural abilities as well as learned skills that guide and facilitate human behavior in practical and career-related domains of human activity" (Feldhusen, 2001, p. 5). Many educators are puzzled about how to respond appropriately when a child with remarkable talents, gifts, or achievements arrives in their classrooms. There are several reasons for this reaction. The first has to do with the mismatch between the child and the planned curriculum. Teachers may fear that the child will be uninterested and may resent a child if the entire first-grade language arts curriculum is based on learning to read and the child arrives at school capable of reading the teacher's manual. Another explanation for educators' mixed emotions concerning extraordinarily talented children is that U.S. society has not come to terms with reconciling excellence and equity. In fact, a little more than half of the states have no systematic gifted education plan. This disregard is a reflection of U.S. society's streak of anti-intellectualism that tends to treat high cognitive functioning as weird or highbrow. It also reflects educators' reluctance to "single out" children as talented, fearing that it might hurt other children's feelings. A third influence on attitudes toward gifted students is the availability of resources. When resources are scarce, there is a tendency to concentrate on children with learning problems whose needs seem more pressing. These influences, singly or in combination, often lead people to the erroneous conclusion that gifted children will "do just fine on their own."

Yet, as Davidson and Davidson (2004) argue:

> True social justice means providing an education that challenges all students to the extent of their abilities—gifted children included. Blessed with brilliant minds and enormous skill, these highly intelligent students may not seem to warrant much help, but they have special needs, too. They deserve far more attention than America's education system currently offers them. The nation's future depends on their energies and talents, and wasting their childhoods because of inertia, ignorance, or ideology is as shortsighted as writing off children because of religion or race. (p. 23)

Nathan, a first grader, exemplifies some of the problems that occur when teachers do not recognize children's gifts and talents. His teacher is presenting a lesson on units of measure. She tells the children to look at several objects to be measured on a workbook page and asks, "What are some different ways that we could tell someone how long the line is without using a ruler?" Children make a variety of suggestions, such as using paper clips, erasers, or finger widths. Then the teacher calls on Nathan, who says, "You could ask an ant to walk across the line and tell you how many steps he took." Nathan's teacher assumed that he was being flippant, so she replied, "And I know a little boy who is going to be walking right down to the principal's office if he doesn't behave." His teacher could not see that, in Nathan's family, this response would have been regarded as original, spontaneous, and indicative of a good sense of humor. Nathan was mortified by his teacher's harsh criticism and virtually stopped participating in class. From that day forward, even when he was called on to speak, he responded by parroting back one-word or short answers that the teacher expected.

How can educators counteract this tendency to overlook talent in ways that diminish children as individuals, cause them to question why they don't "fit in," or force them to endure the frustration of having powers that they cannot put to use? Figure 9.2 offers suggestions for working with students who have particular gifts and talents.

As Nathan's bad experience illustrated, a major challenge to assessment of children's creative expression and arts-based learning often is the teacher's misguided notions. Even though teachers claim to support creativity in schools, "in actual classroom practice . . . high skill in memorization and accurate recall are often preferred to critical thinking or independent decision making" (Cropley, 2001, p. 137). Evidently, teachers throughout the world regard creativity as a disruptive force, based on research conducted in countries as diverse as Turkey, Australia, Nigeria, and the United States (Cropley, 2001; Scott, 1999).

Several studies have found that, when teachers are asked to name a child who is particularly creative or asked to recommend a student for a gifted and talented program, teachers tend to choose the well-mannered "briefcase" children and fail to recognize the abilities of (or even express dislike for) nonconformist, creative, "bohemian" children (Dawson, 1997; Hunsaker, 1994; Westby & Dawson, 1995). Even when everyone agrees that a child possesses gifts and talents, the response to that ability can be inappropriate. A common misconception is that talented children do not need to work that hard; however, as Piirto (2001) observes, "The world is full of talented people, but fully creative people do a lot of hard work" (p. 64). Talent alone is not enough because a high ability does not necessarily lead to high levels of performance. In addition, talented children may be overly praised and rewarded by adults just for possessing gifts, but students are not necessarily given special help in making the most of their gifts. Accurate, qualified feedback from role models and mentors is important in the development of talent, and the child should

- Treat learning as a joy, value intellectual discovery, and embrace excellence within the school culture.

- Adapt the curriculum to fit the gifted child with the same level of commitment that is made for children with learning disabilities and difficulties.

- Recognize the many different ways in which talents and gifts can appear, for example, in children with special needs (e.g., Autism spectrum disorders), in one domain only (e.g., bodily/kinesthetic), in multiple domains (e.g. ver-bal/linguistic and intrapersonal), in children who lack opportunities (e.g., a low-income child with musical talent but few family/community resources to pursue it), and in children with extensive out-of-school experience (e.g., extensive training in the martial arts).

- Teach children to accept, encourage, and admire remarkable achievements in other children rather than feel threatened by them .

- Do not force children to study material they have mastered already.

- Do not define gifted programs as "enrichment" or more work at the same level; give them the opportunity to "stretch" and pursue advanced work.

- Use a variety of strategies as appropriate to meet learning goals (such as distance learning, independent study, mentoring, subject-matter acceleration, and grade skipping).

- Use flexible grouping strategies that respect competency in each subject rather than the child's age.

- Do not make participation in gifted programs a hardship (as by pulling children out of class, forcing them to miss important material).

- Encourage collaboration among adults (parents, families, administrators, teachers, community members) to pursue the goal of helping to optimize every child's potential.

- Offer competitions and talent searches so students can get a sense of their capabilities in comparison with others; celebrate high achievers' accomplishments.

- Recognize the special needs of gifted students (such as career planning and counseling needs and opportunities to pursue favorite subjects in depth).

- Provide ongoing professional development for teachers so that they can nurture talent, including their own, and continue their own education to make sure they meet the needs of all special learners and know the gifted education policies of the nation and the state.

Figure 9.2 Teaching Practices That Support Students with Gifts and Talents

Note: Data from Davidson & Davidson (2004).

have access to people who have some expertise (Piirto, 2001). When such mentorship is provided, the results are impressive. Artist-in-residence programs in schools throughout the United States give children an opportunity to work alongside artists, musicians, and writers as well as gain keen insights into their work habits.

Another difficulty with defining and identifying talents and giftedness is that these concepts are defined by the culture. If we rely only on our own ideas and ignore the cultural context in which children grew up, we not only neglect other cultures but also diminish opportunities for children (Sternberg, 2007). To illustrate, most schools use a standardized test and preestablished cutoff score as the main way to identify children for gifted and talented programs yet "There is no one test that will adequately represent all of the diverse cultures of the world, any more than there is any one language that will represent these cultures" (Sternberg, 2007, p. 6).

For all of these reasons—teachers' failure to understand gifts and talents, misconceptions about children's creative and artistic behavior, school systems' apparent inability to provide the amount and kind of support necessary, and poor understanding of cultural differences—many of the most brilliant minds throughout history have been labeled as troublemakers and misfits during their school careers. Keep this in mind as you meet children who defy your expectations, challenge your authority, and prompt you to rethink the curriculum.

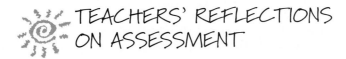

TEACHERS' REFLECTIONS ON ASSESSMENT

Preservice Teachers

"We had a terrific art program with real artists who visited the children and worked with them. The children's artwork was amazing! Now our art teacher is leaving to work with a museum program and I wonder what will happen. When I talked with him, he said that he enjoyed working with the children but did not feel that his efforts were valued all that much. The administration is so focused on test scores and meeting standards in reading and math that, every time the budget was cut, there was talk of eliminating his position."

Inservice Teachers

"According to our state's academic standards, all kindergarten students must be tested to determine their 'reading readiness.' As a result, the kindergarten curriculum has become like boot camp for first grade. Everything else, it seems, has been overshadowed by preparation for reading readiness tests. The test scores are used as much as a way to control teachers as they are to evaluate the children's achievement. Each school's average test score and district rankings are posted on the state's Department of Education web site and teachers' reputations rise or fall based on how well their kids did during a particular year. The entire district has gone test crazy because our funding is based on demonstrating continuous improvement in test scores."

Your Reflections

- How do these teachers think about assessment?

- What problems have they identified concerning support for creative expression and the arts?

- What issues have they raised about assessment?

ASSESSMENT: WHY, WHAT, AND HOW

The term *student assessment* may conjure up visions of tests, checklists, gold stars, report cards, and program evaluations. *Assessment* may include all of these things but it is much more. As a general concept in education, assessment is the process of discovering children's knowledge, abilities, and interests (Popham, 2001); it is the "continual process of observing and recording and otherwise documenting the work that children do and how they do it, as a basis for a variety of educational decisions that affect the child" (Bredekamp, 1991, p. 21). Assessment involves much more than testing for the purpose of providing grades. It is critical to understand the assessment's purpose (Why assess?), focus (What is assessed?), and methods (How will it be assessed?). Attention to the why, what, and how helps ensure that the assessment process will be appropriate and the results will be worthwhile. To view an artifact used for assessment, look at the worksheet designed to evaluate emotions online at MyEducationLab.

MyEducationLab

ALEX

Go to MyEducationLab and select the topic "Assessment/ Documentation." Under Activities and Applications, view the artifact Assessing Emotions Worksheet. *How might such a strategy support socioemotional growth?*

Why Assess: Identifying the Purpose

The National Association for the Education of Young Children (NAEYC) and the National Association of Early Childhood Specialists in State Departments of Education (NAECSSDE) call on teachers to thoughtfully consider the real purposes of assessment. Assessment of creative thinking and arts-based learning should help teachers to:

- *Identify and respond appropriately to the needs of individual children,* for example, gaining deeper insight into their creative thought processes, documenting their growth in the arts, and communicating this with parents/families.
- *Make instructional decisions that benefit the child,* for example, designing an individualized educational plan, making accommodations that enable them to participate in creative thinking and the arts, and providing opportunities to optimize children's gifts and talents.
- *Evaluate program effectiveness,* for example, evaluating the success of a new curriculum model, preparing an accreditation report, and collecting data from parents/families about arts opportunities in the home.

What to Assess: Finding a Focus

After identifying the purpose of the assessment, the teacher must clarify what will be assessed: Content knowledge? Children's understanding of processes and procedures? Evidence of effort and progress? Performance skills and techniques? The quality of the product? A starting point for meaningful assessment is the lesson objectives. If a first-grade lesson focuses on learning to mix paint colors to match the colors observed in fall leaves, then the child's ability to mix a variety of colors is what should be evaluated. Criteria such as neatness, creativity, attitude, or behavior have little place in this assessment. If the first-grade lesson objective is for children to represent themselves through drawing with theme "I am raking the fall leaves," a teacher might begin by asking children to draw this. Then the teacher would bring in a rake, ask children to observe how both hands are used to hold the rake, demonstrate the adjustments made if the rake is taller than the child, notice how arms have to bend, and visualize how big the pile of leaves might be in proportion to the child. Assessment would be based on evidence of these understandings and changes in the children's drawings from the first draft to the second try.

How to Assess: Selecting the Approach

One approach to assessment that is often overlooked is formative assessment. Formative assessment occurs "along the way" to adjust to learners' needs and it is particularly important for children with special needs because it recognizes effort and progress (Doran & Fleischman, 2005; McTighe & O'Connor, 2005; Stiggins, 2007). Examples of formative assessment are notes from a class discussion, small-group interactions, journal entries, skill inventories, homework assignments, or pretests (Tomlinson & McTighe, 2006).

During formative assessment teachers also recognize the need for changes in the physical environment (materials, equipment, room arrangement) as well as ped-agogical approaches (ways of giving instructions, demonstration of techniques, composition of groups, reorganization of content). Lyla, a 5-year-old, offers a good example of formative assessment. She tells her teacher that she wants to make a doll. When the teacher offers crayons, paints, and paper, Lyla responds, "No, I need things to make it squooshier"—in other words, this young child sought to make a doll out of fabric that would be stitched and stuffed. Through formative assessment, her teacher was able to offer the support Lyla needed to accomplish her goal—fab-ric, buttons, yarn, scissors, paper to make a pattern, and an adult with a sewing ma-chine to stitch the edges of the two pieces of the cloth together so that the kindergartner could stuff it with polyester fiberfill, like a pillow. At that point, Lyla was ready for summative assessment, the evaluation that occurs after a learning ex-perience has been completed. Other examples of summative assessments are musi-cal performances, displays of children's artwork, presentations by a child to a panel of experts, and, of course, tests. Teachers may allow the students to demonstrate learning in a variety of modes such as posters, brochures, skits, and so on but, all too often, these products are not graded or are weighted less when grading and this sends the message that these products don't count for much. Figure 9.3 summarizes assessment methods used by teachers, children, and families and communities.

Prepared by the Teacher

General Guidelines: Observing young children's play, creative expression, and artworks is intended to provide a more holistic view of what children know and can do with their creative thinking processes. Teachers need to invent a system for gathering observations regularly. All observations should be dated, keyed to program goals, and filed systematically in student work portfolios to facilitate charting children's progress over time.

- **Anecdotal records** highlight student attitudes, preferences, judgments, and participation. The teacher can make notes for younger students; older students can write their own. These notes should be dated and collected over time to demonstrate patterns of growth.
- **Checklists, developmental profiles, or logs** compare one child's progress with that of the typically developing child.
- **Conference notes** from discussions with individual children or groups of children about the content and process of their creative work demonstrate what was accomplished during major projects.
- **Interviews** with children demonstrate their emerging understanding of creativity and the arts.
- **Documentation panels** provide evidence of the learning that was achieved through the course of a major project. These large displays that chronicle the life cycle of a project are commercial-artist-quality documentation of children's accomplishments (Carter & Curtis, 1995; Chard, 1998; Jalongo & Stamp, 1997b).

(Continued)

Figure 9.3   Overview of Assessment Methods Used by the Teacher, the Child, and Families/Communities

---

Produced and Assessed by the Child

General Guidelines: In order to teach children the skills of self-evaluation, they should bear responsibility for identifying their best work and providing a rationale for its inclusion in their portfolios.

- **Self-selected work samples** may include one-dimensional works (e.g., paintings, drawings, writing) as well as photographs, sketches, and videotapes or audiotapes of works or displays.
- **Rating scales or checklists** encourage children to bring their artistic decision making to a conscious level as they are working on a project, evaluate their group's performance, or assess the overall quality of a culminating activity.
- **Child-led conferences** enable the child to present his or her work to parents and families.

Assessed by the Family/Community

General Guidelines: Parents, families, and community members need to be involved in assessing children's growth.

- **Conferences with parents and families** provide them with the opportunity to review the child's work over time.
- **Review of live or taped individual or group performances** enable parents, families, and community members to see the child's/children's conceptualization, presentation, quality, personalization, and cooperation.
- **Responses to portfolios of children's work** give families an opportunity to provide written feedback on the child's work.

TEACHERS' ROLES AND RESPONSIBILITIES

Where assessment is concerned, "Teachers have an obligation to promote pupils' knowledge, skills and understanding in *making* the arts (developing their skills), in *presenting* the arts (realizing a work of art, choreographing a dance, composing a piece of music, scripting a play) and in *appraising* their own work and that of others discriminately and constructively. Children may have strengths in one particular area (a physically disabled child may be potentially a very talented choreographer) and may be more skilled in one aspect of a particular art form (for example, strong rhythmic ability, but difficulty in singing a melody). Teachers need to work to pupils' strengths" (Peter, 1998, p. 169). Working to children's strengths requires teachers to be observers, interactors, and evaluators.

The Role of Observer

"One of the most valuable yet rarely acknowledged assessment tools in educational practice is the sustained, thoughtful day-to-day observation of student behavior by a competent, professional teacher" (Wassermann, 1989, p. 368). In the role of observer, teachers pay attention to what children do while remaining on the sidelines. Appropriate observations of children do the following:

- Use direct observational data and avoid high-inference, value-laden terminology.
- Accurately record the observable behavior of the child, both verbal and nonverbal.

Sharing assessment information with parents and families is an essential way of supporting creative thinking and the arts.

- Describe the context in which the behavior occurred—the time, setting, circumstances, and behaviors of other children or adults related to the episode.
- Become the basis for planning a high-quality program.

How does observation support children's learning? A third-grade teacher has involved his gifted and talented students in a unit on inventions. He shares some examples from *Toys! Amazing Stories Behind Some Great Inventions* (Wulffson, 2000), *Accidents May Happen* (Jones & O'Brien, 1997), *The Kid Who Invented the Popsicle* (Wulffson, 1999), *The Kids' Invention Book* (Erbach, 1997), *Brainstorm: The Stories of Twenty American Kid Inventors* (Tucker, 1995), and *Girls Think of Everything: Stories of Ingenious Inventions by Women* (Thimmesh, 2000) with the students. The third graders' first assignment is to apply their emerging research skills in locating authoritative print and electronic sources that describe inventions and inventors of an item found in their household or classroom. As the children work at the library, their teacher places a baseball cap backward on his head as a signal to the students that he is writing down what he sees and should not be disturbed unless it is an emergency (Strachota, 1996). Over the next 15 minutes, he records episodes of student behavior on his laptop along with the date, the activity, and the child's initials. At the end of the month, he will sort the notes using the child's initials and generate a report to place in each child's file. These data will be useful in discussing the child's work habits with parents and families at conference time. What can a teacher learn from observation? During the library session the teacher noticed that some of the children were unfocused at first and decided that his instructions were not sufficiently clear. A few were seeking information about inventions they had heard about previously (such as the telephone and the steam engine) instead of focusing on the stipulation that the invention had to be an item they could demonstrate during their presentation. As this brief description illustrates, there are three main purposes for anecdotal records: (1) to document individual student growth, (2) to demonstrate students'

Student: C. J.   Observer: M. T.
Date: 9/24/10   Time: 2:45
Location: School library   Activity: Researching inventors

Ch. are deciding on an inventor. C. J.: "I'm going to do the Wright Bros. and airplanes." J. J.: "I think we have to be able to show the thing they invented when we talk about it. How are you going to show a plane?" C. J. comes over and asks, "Is it okay if my report is on the Wright Brothers? J. J. said we have to show whatever it is when we talk about it." I remind him of the instructions and criteria for evaluation and he says, "What about this book about kids who invented things? I can bring a Popsicle to school."

Figure 9.4   Example of an Anecdotal Record

progress toward program goals, and (3) to assess the value of the learning activity. To see a video of a teacher conducting an observation, go to MyEducationLab online and watch "Observing Children in Authentic Contexts." Figure 9.4 is a sample anecdotal record from the third graders' project on modern inventors and inventions.

Three additional observational tools are checklists, rating scales, and rubrics. *Checklists* are used to indicate the presence or absence of a behavior (Does your child play a musical instrument? Yes/No). *Rating scales* are used when it is important to know to what degree something occurs (In a typical week, how many times do you and your child read and discuss a children's book? 0, 1–2, 3–5, 6–7, 8 or more). There are many commercially available checklists and rating scales that teachers and caregivers can use as is or adapt to suit their needs (Seely, 1994). A *rubric* is a particular type of rating scale that specifies the level of performance and links it to a grade. During the invention theme, the culminating activity was for each child to create and videotape a short, evening news–type story about the invention that he or she had selected. Figure 9.5 (p. 328) is an example of the scoring rubric that the teacher developed to assess the quality of the third graders' presentations. For more on rubrics, see Mason and Steedly, 2006.

Audio and video recording are mechanical means of observing that become the teacher's eyes and ears while he or she continues to engage in classroom activities. Video recording can also be an excellent means of involving the child in self-evaluation. Movement, dance, and drama experiences viewed by both teacher and child often provoke spontaneous self-critique by the child: "Oh, you can't see my puppet's face!" or "I like the way I made my streamers move like the wind during the weather dance." Students learn to become more thoughtful observers of their own work when teachers emphasize important aspects of the process and product. Children's early experiences with self-evaluation build a foundation for self-critique and assessment that is valuable throughout life.

The Role of Interactor

Interaction includes the teacher's daily face-to-face exchanges with students as well as more structured and planned types of interaction, such as conducting a conference or interview with a child and recording the results. In contrast to observation, where the teacher remains out of the action, the role of interactor gets teachers involved in dialogue with the child about his or her creative/artistic processes and products. A kindergarten teacher, for example, meets with each of her students

MyEducationLab

Go to MyEducationLab and select the topic "Assessment/ Documentation." Under Activities and Applications, watch the video Observing Children in Authentic Contexts *and complete the activity.*

Accuracy of Information

3	2	1
Information is accurate and well-documented	Most information is accurate and well-documented	Information contains errors of fact and is not supported by sources

Content of Assignment

3	2	1
Invention and inventor are contemporary	Invention and inventor are modern	Invention and inventor are from a historical era

Sources Used

3	2	1
Multiple authoritative sources were consulted	At least one authoritative source was consulted	Few or none of the sources consulted were authoritative

Use of Example

3	2	1
Student provides a actual example of an everyday item	Student provides an image of the item	Student does not provide an example or image

Structure of Presentation

3	2	1
Very clear and well organized	Moderately clear and well-organized	Not clear and/or well organized

News Story Format

3	2	1
Is concise and in the format of a news story	Is reasonably concise and in the format of a news story	Is not concise and/or in the format of a news story

Effectiveness of Presentational Style

3	2	1
Very effective use of voice and gesture during presentation	Moderately effective use of voice and gesture during presentation	Ineffective use of voice and/or gesture presentation

Figure 9.5   Scoring Rubric for a News Story About an Invention

about their writing for 10 minutes, once a week. Usually these meetings begin with a brief review of the child's writing portfolio and discussion aimed at getting a sense of the child's goals and progress toward those goals. In preparation for conferences, the teacher also interviews each child on the topic of writing. When she asks Caleb the first question on the interview, "Tell me about your writing," he responds with the writing sample and explanation found in Figure 9.6.

Audio and video recording methods represent significant advantages where interaction is concerned. It often is not possible for a teacher to interact with a child and make notes at the same time, so mechanical means offer an

Caleb: This says "cat" and "dog" and that's a big "G" and one hundred and one. That's just my name and . . . yeah, my name, Caleb. And one hundred and ten and . . . uh . . . nine and six. And this is a five and a four and a fancy four and a thirteen. See? I made this pretend word and then I can find words in it. I have to underline the letters so I don't forget . . . Watch this! D-o-d—that spells dad! And m-o-m spells mom. Wait. Oh, wait. D-a-d spells dad! Here's a "u" and an "o." Wait, here's a fancy "u" and this is a fancy "o." Watch! This is a little "t" and this here is a littler "t" and now they're connected together!

Figure 9.6 Caleb's Writing

opportunity to analyze the quality of the interactions. Ms. Maloney, a student teacher, set up a pet store in conjunction with a unit on economics. Through the use of video, Ms. Maloney is able to "step back" from her teaching and analyze the interaction between her and Lori, the second-grade girl who invited her into the role of customer.

Lori:	This is my pet store. May I help you today, miss? Are you looking for anything in particular?
Teacher:	Yes, I would like to buy my nephew an unusual gift. He is going to be 10 years old on Monday.
Lori:	Well, isn't that just special! I hope that he is a nice boy. What kinds of animals does he like?
Teacher:	He likes dinosaurs and wild animals.
Lori:	Well, we are out of dinosaurs. I just sold the last one yesterday and I did not order any more. The animals are just too large for my store. We do have some parakeets and fish.
Teacher:	Do you have any parrots? They are a wild animal.
Lori:	Yes, I just happen to have one, beautiful colors on it.
Teacher:	I'll take it. He is just beautiful. Can he be taught to talk? I heard that some of them can learn to talk, is that true?
Lori:	First of all, before you get too confused, this is a she. This particular type of bird can be taught to talk, but it takes a lot of time.
Teacher:	What else do I need?
Lori:	You'll need a cage, food, and some items for the bird to play with.
Teacher:	Well, how much do I owe you for the bird, cage, food, and two toys?
Lori:	The total price is $225.33.
Teacher:	Do you take MasterCard?
Lori:	Yes.

This teacher's behavior illustrates the types of environment, materials, and climates that foster creativity that are summarized in Figure 9.7.

By recording and analyzing this interaction, Ms. Maloney has a clearer sense of Lori's ability to take on a role, to "think on her feet," to understand basic concepts about economics as well as pet care (the topic of a previous unit), and ability to communicate. It also offers a more holistic evaluation of Lori's emerging understanding of economic principles, business ethics, and customer relations.

Part of becoming effective in the role of interactor is intervening to "nudge" children's growth. If a preschool teacher notices that a particular child has never ventured into the block area, she could invite him into the area. If children's interest in the block center wanes, the teacher might supply additional items, such as small wooden people, animals, vehicles, and road signs to rekindle enthusiasm. Asking good questions, such as those in Figure 9.8 (p. 332) is another tool for fulfilling the role of interactor.

The Role of Evaluator

In this role, the teacher collects samples of students' work at various stages, arranges them to highlight growth, and analyzes them to make instructional decisions. Evaluation of processes and products may be incidental or planned, use teacher-developed materials or commercially available materials, and use different methods of recording (written, oral, or mechanically recorded). Evaluating what children have learned

Classroom Environment, Materials, and Climate

Creative teachers:

- Create organizational and structural conditions that allow open and flexible distribution of roles, themes, problems, and activities.
- Provide challenging and stimulating learning materials.
- Offer opportunities to work with varied materials under different conditions.
- Establish a classroom climate that permits alternative solutions.

Professional Attitudes and Values

Creative teachers:

- Provide support and positive feedback for problem finding, not just problem solving.
- Serve as a model of creative thought.
- Tolerate ambiguity and accept alternative solutions.
- Expect and accept humor and playfulness from children.

Social Support for Creativity

Creative teachers:

- Have a cooperative, socially integrative style of teaching.
- Make it possible for children to participate in joint projects with self-selected partners.
- Surprise students with recognition for creative processes and products.
- Extend mastery of factual knowledge through collaboration.

Recognition and Respect for Children's Creativity

Creative teachers:

- Enable self-directed work that allows for a high degree of initiative, spontaneity, and experimentation.
- Encourage and accept constructive nonconformist behavior.
- Take children's questions seriously and tolerate "sensible," bold errors.
- Help students learn to cope with frustration and failure.
- Reward courage as much as being right.
- Actively teach creative strategies.
- Foster intense concentration and task commitment through high motivation and interest in self-selected topics.
- Increase autonomy in learning by recognition and self-evaluation of progress.

Figure 9.7   What Do Creativity-Fostering Teachers Do?
Note: Data from Clark (1996), Cropley (2001), and Urban (1996, 2005).

is linked with curriculum and instruction from the very start. Assessment is not an "afterthought," but rather an integral component of the original plan.

Where creative thinking and arts-based learning are concerned, evaluation often relies on *performance assessment*. Some of the defining characteristics of performance assessment are:

- The tasks performed by children are relevant and interesting.
- Both the products and the processes used to achieve them are evaluated.

For the Teacher: A Guide to Asking Better Questions

Some simple changes in our ways of posing questions can encourage children to think more critically. As children hear cognitive terms in everyday use and practice the thinking skills that accompany these labels, they will begin to internalize these words and incorporate them into their own vocabularies.

Instead of saying . . .
"Let's look at these two pictures."

Say:
"Let's *compare* these two pictures."

Instead of asking . . .
"What do you think will happen when . . ."

Ask:
"What do you *predict* will happen when . . . ?"

Instead of asking . . .
"What did you think of the story?"

Ask:
"What *conclusions* can you draw about this story?"

Instead of asking . . .
"How do you know that's true?"

Ask:
"What *evidence* do you have to support . . . ?"

A Framework for the Child's Self-Questions about Problem Solving

---

Circle the strategy or strategies that you used to solve the problem.

?   I guessed.

   I looked for a pattern.

   I made a list.

   I drew a picture.

   I made a web or diagram.

   I solved a simpler problem.

   I worked backward.

   I made a table.

✓   I experimented with several different strategies.

   I asked somebody for clues.

   I collaborated with a group.

Figure 9.8   Questions That Encourage Creative Problem Solving
Note: Data from British Ministry of Education and Costa (1993).

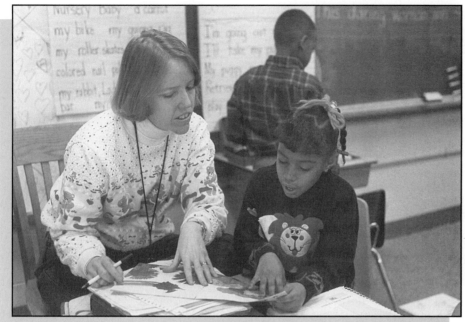

Skillful questioning by teachers supports children's creative thinking.

- Students develop skills in self-evaluation as they take greater responsibility for selecting their best work.
- Students' attitudes and feelings are considered as well as knowledge and skills.
- Results of the assessment are used to optimize children's learning.
- Assessment data are used to improve classroom practice and make informed instructional decisions.
- Results of the assessment produce a holistic picture of student performance.

Take, for example, the performance assessment of skills in music. A young child might demonstrate understanding of tempo (fast/slow) by tapping rhythm sticks rapidly in response to a lively tune and slowly in response to a lullaby; or a group of children might demonstrate the concept of dynamics (loud/soft) by playing the game Radio, in which they make their voices softer or louder in response to an oversized cardboard dial that represents the volume control on a radio; or to demonstrate the concept of rhythm ("with the beat") by responding to cue cards (of clapping hands, snapping fingers, or stomping feet) that depict ways of moving their bodies "in time" with different musical selections. Likewise, older children might demonstrate their understanding of pitch and melody by doing the following:

- Singing at a prescribed pitch.
- Gesturing with hands to illustrate whether the pitch of notes is going up or down on the scale.
- Playing a pattern on a melody instrument, such as a xylophone.
- Standing up each time they recognize a pattern of musical notes.

All of these examples illustrate performance assessment because they allow the child to demonstrate understanding. Performance assessment can also be summative—that is, conducted at the conclusion of a learning process. One of the most commonly used types of summative performance assessment in creativity and the arts is the portfolio (Boughton, 2005). To see a video about student portfolios, watch "Portfolio Exhibitions" online at MyEducationLab. Figure 9.9 offers general guidelines for portfolios and Figure 9.10 (p. 336) provides an example of a child's portfolio. Advances in technology and digital imaging make it possible to store and retrieve permanent records of the students' work as visual images rather than retain the child's original work (Dorn, Madeja, & Sabol, 2003). Other types of summative performance assessment include creative-writing journals, musical performances, debates or panel discussions in social studies, an exhibit of scale models constructed by the children, demonstrations of a craft that the child has mastered, videos of a play, and technology-based presentations that combine images, music, and dance.

Teachers might also consider more unusual formats such as student-designed board games, illustrated books and comic books, and musical scores and lyrics. A third-grade teacher has shared the picture books *Talking Walls* (Knight & O'Brien, 1995), *Murals: Walls that Sing* (Ancona, 2003), and *Talking Walls: The Stories Continue* (Knight & O'Brien, 1997) with her students as part of an integrated unit on social studies and art. The culminating activity is for small groups of children to produce murals that will be displayed in a glass case in the lobby of the school. Each group has to agree upon a style and purpose for the mural. The evaluation rubric for this project was shared with the students prior to beginning the murals and is used by the teacher, the individual children, and the class to evaluate the various murals on completion. Additionally, visitors to the building are asked to sign a guest book and comment on the children's work. After each group's mural is completed and on display, the small group explains the style that they selected and their purpose for the particular mural. One group, for example, chose to produce a mural with the characteristics of cave paintings discovered in France. They worked together to meet the challenge of simulating the rough-hewn texture of a cave wall and decided to wrinkle tan craft paper and staple it over some crumpled recycled paper. They also deliberated on ways to produce muted colors that might have been produced using natural sources. Their stated purpose for the mural was to use the style of cave art to depict a story. Discussion with their peers highlighted creative processes ("How did you get it to look old?") and products ("Which walls did you use to get the ideas for the animals?").

Note that the evaluation of this project was not approached as a contest. That is because an overreliance on competitions linked with tangible rewards can undermine creativity (Fawson & Moore, 1999). This is thought to occur in two major ways: partly by constraining the response (as when the child chooses a less innovative response to avoid rejection and please the teacher) and partly by diverting attention from the intrinsic rewards of the task (as when the child becomes preoccupied with hurrying to win instead of a slow and careful process) (Joussement & Koestner, 1999). Tangible rewards sometime decrease the pleasure children associate with learning as they focus on the prize (Levin & Greenwald, 2001). External rewards have their place, however. When a reward is linked to clearly defined and specified creative behaviors it may encourage higher levels of performance (Eisenberger & Armeli, 1997). Contests and tangible rewards, while commonplace, need to be used judiciously.

It is also necessary to build children's skills in self-evaluation with comments and questions such as:

- Tell me about how you worked with your group today. What did you contribute?
- Describe some of the things you liked about your work.
- Did this project give you any problems? What did you do about it?

What Is a Portfolio?

A portfolio is a carefully selected collection of student work samples that highlight individual effort, progress, and learning. Just as professional artists' portfolios are used in interviews to highlight what they can do, children's portfolios are a way of documenting learning.

Why Use Portfolios to Assess Creative Thought and Expression?

- Portfolios reveal and document children's learning in many different modes, on real-world tasks, over a period of time.
- Portfolios encourage self-evaluation in students.
- Portfolios help teachers make instructional decisions.
- Portfolios document student growth and progress in a way that parents/families can understand.

How Are Portfolios Used?

Armstrong (1994) recommends "the 5 Cs of portfolio development":

1. *Celebration.* Use portfolios to acknowledge and validate children's products and accomplishments during the year.
2. *Cognition.* Use portfolios to encourage students to reflect on their own work.
3. *Communication.* Use portfolios to inform families, administrators, and colleagues about children's growth and progress.
4. *Cooperation.* Use portfolios as a way for groups of children to collectively produce and evaluate their own work.
5. *Competency.* Use portfolios to establish a set of standards by which one child's work can be compared with other children's performance or with a benchmark established by the teacher.

What Is Included in a Portfolio?

Children's portfolios should not be cartons filled with every imaginable item ever produced by the child during the course of the year. Rather, they should be focused and organized by learning goals. If a teacher has the language arts goal that children read and respond to a variety of picture books, for instance, the file might contain a log of the books read by the child and stories or artwork inspired by children's books. If exploring different media is a curriculum goal in art, one of the folders might contain a sample of paintings, chalk drawings, batik, and a photograph of sculptures the child constructed out of clay, wood, and paper. To demonstrate the child's attainment of another art program goal, the refinement of a form, a folder might contain sketches of the work at successive stages and the finished product.

How Should Portfolios Be Stored and Maintained?

An expandable file with accordion-folded sides is a good portfolio. Individual folders that are keyed or color-coded to program goals can be placed inside the expandable file to organize the child's work. Include a table of contents so that teachers, administrators, parents, and children can use it.

Figure 9.9   Using Portfolios to Assess Creative Thinking and Arts-Based Learning

The child was sitting on his mom's lap at the kitchen table as she was writing out some bills. The child was imitating actions made by Mom: moving the pen over the paper.

1. Daniel's first marks—12 months: random scribbling

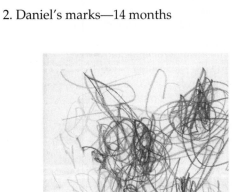

At this stage of development it is not appropriate to ask the child to "tell you about" his or her drawing. Instead, provide feedback such as "I like the lines that you made," or if you have observed the child working quickly, say, "those lines look really fast," or if the child has seemed to be interested in trying out various colors of crayons or markers, say, "I see all of those colors you drew."

2. Daniel's marks—14 months

3a and b. Daniel's marks—19 months: circular scribble

Figure 9.10   Portfolio of a Childs Grow th Over Time

After the child created the scribbled lines, it reminded him of a pirate ship he had recently watched on a television cartoon show, and he made the major developmental step in his visual language development by naming his scribble.

4. Daniel's marks become a visual representation—24 months: naming the scribble

The child drew this with some prompting. Talking about grandma coming for a visit: "You can make a picture of Gram while we are waiting. Draw Grandma's head. Where are Grandma's eyes? Her mouth? Do you think she went to the beauty shop to get her hair fixed this morning? Does she have long arms to hug you when she comes? What kind of shoes will she wear?"

5. Daniel's first drawing of a human figure—26 months: beginning of preschematic stage

6a and b. Daniel's drawings of Mommy and Daddy—27 months: preschematic stage

(Continued)

7a–b. Daniel's self-portraits—ages 2 years, 3 months to 2 years, 10 months

Daniel drew this portrait of Dad, perhaps concentrating on body "divisions" of neck, waist, etc. When the drawing was complete, he observed, "Daddy looks like a zebra." In this preschematic drawing the child is moving back and forth between drawing with intent (the symbol for his father) and interpreting his marks (the lines look like stripes on a zebra).

8. "Daddy looks like a zebra"—2 years, 8 months

Drawing need not be a formal process. Materials can be made available for any time a child wants to use them. This drawing was done at the pool during a break from swimming.

9. "At the Pool"—2 years, 9 months

Figure 9.10 *(Continued)*

10. "I Am Cutting My Birthday Cake"—age 4 years

At age 4, Daniel is moving from the preschematic stage to the schematic stage as he demonstrates great control in his ability to draw a descriptive schema for himself, the four candles on the birthday cake and the letters spelling out "Happy Birthday." Note how he has drawn the table in a fold-over fashion: he "knows" that each table leg is connected to a corner. His visual representation is an attempt to explain this knowledge.

11. "He-Man"—age 5 years

This drawing on his fifth birthday party invitation shows further development in his schema for a person as Daniel represents his favorite action hero, He-Man. Note the similarities and differences in this example and in example 10.

12. "Knights in Armor"—age 5 years

Daniel continues to develop his schema for people, which are often characters from adventure shows or books. During this time he is also creating props, costumes, and sets for make-believe play with his action figure characters. Note that the legs are now drawn as shapes, rather than lines.

(Continued)

Daniel drew his table partner in kindergarten after his teacher instructed the class to carefully observe what the other child was wearing, what color of eyes and hair they had, etc. Although clothing is not usually included in the schema, the teacher's prompt to carefully observe what their partner was wearing resulted in a detailed drawing of the other child's sailor-type outfit with an anchor and other nautical symbols.

13. "A Picture of the Person Sitting Across from Me, Charbel"—age 5 years

Following the teacher's prompt, Daniel drew this picture of himself and Dad playing ball. Note the detail of five fingers and the stripes on his new shirt. He illustrates how the ball is thrown and then hit with the bat by making multiple images of the ball. This time relationship is common at this stage as the child attempts to communicate meaning. The intent is not to say that there are multiple balls, but to explain that the ball is moving through time and space.

14. Detail from "Things I Did Over the Warm Spring Weekend"—age 5

Daniel drew this during the last week of kindergarten. At the end of the school year the kindergarten class was finally allowed to use the gym, since the older grades were having Phys. Ed. classes outdoors. The large space with its shiny wooden floor was the setting for a favorite game, "Duck, Duck, Goose." The uniqueness of the experience made Daniel choose it in response to his teacher's request to draw their favorite day in kindergarten. He carefully drew to explain the game: classmates sitting in a circle on the wooden floor with one walking around the circle.

15. "My Favorite Day in Kindergarten"—age 5 and 3/4 years

Figure 9.10 *(Continued)*

16. "Tree"—Age 5 and 3/4 years

At the schematic stage, children usually draw a baseline and a skyline, which indicates a means of ordering their spatial relationships and a means of connecting themselves to their environment. Usually there is no three-dimensional quality in their spatial concept. Daniel's frequent drawing and thoughtful observation, however, probably inspired the overlapping in this drawing. The sky, although not drawn all the way down to the ground, is seen through the branches of the tree, a use of three-dimensionality not typical for this age.

17. "If I Were President"—age 7 years

Here Daniel's drawing shows characteristics of what Lowenfeld termed the stage of dawning realism. Use of overlapping, the profile view, and the attention to detail, such as the shoe laces, are signs that Daniel is moving out of the schematic stage.

18. Anniversary card (an attempt at perspective)—age 9 years

Here Daniel uses a classic comic strip character (copying comic strip characters is common during this stage) to create an anniversary card for his parents. He attempts and almost accurately achieves perspective on the door wall, but still draws the floor tiles under Dagwood from an overhead view. At this stage, and not before, the child may formally be taught perspective and figure drawing techniques. For most children, this will occur by around age 11, although some, like Daniel, will show ability earlier and others, who have not had much opportunity to draw, will not be ready for this conceptual understanding until much later.

(Continued)

19. "A   Friend"—age 11 years

Daniel is clearly interested in portraying subject matter in a realistic manner. Here he uses shading to achieve a more three-dimensional quality, and his proportion when drawing people is more lifelike, based upon what his eyes see, rather than what his brain knows.

20. "Woodpecker"—age 11 and 1/2

Daniel continues to attempt to portray visual reality in painting as well as drawing.

Figure 9.10   *(Continued)*

- What are some things you could do for yourself? What did you need help with?
- What did you do to help others?
- When you had some trouble, explain how you solved the problem.
- What were some of the new ideas that you had?
- What did you do the best of all?
- Were there things that you didn't try? How did you feel about that?
- Is there a particular piece of work that you feel proud of? Tell me about it.
- Tell me what you did when . . . (data from Wassermann, 2000).

MyEducationLab

Go to MyEducationLab and select the topic "Assessment/ Documentation." Under Activities and Applications, view the artifact Self-Monitoring Worksheet. How does a tool like this support children's self-evaluation?

To view an artifact that assists the child in self-evaluation, look at the "Self-Monitoring Worksheet" online at MyEducationLab.

Communication with families, the community, and your colleagues about assessment is crucial. If you fail to help others understand why you approach teaching as you do, you are likely to be met with resistance if you depart from the more traditional approaches. When you begin a unit of study, be certain to let others know what you are doing, and why. Letters from teachers to families are a simple yet effective way of communicating. Figure 9.11 is a sample letter to families that introduces a new teaching theme. Note that it has several key features. First, it keeps educational

Dear Parents and Families of Kindergartners:

Understanding patterns is an important skill for young children.

Recognizing patterns is essential for learning to read and write, to create works of art, to appreciate music, to participate in dance, and to listen to stories. Next week, we will begin our study of patterns. Children will be learning that:

Patterns are repetitions. Printed fabric is a pictorial pattern, a picket fence is an architectural pattern, a jump-rope rhyme is a pattern of sound, words are patterns of letters, and so forth.

Patterns can be found everywhere. There are social patterns, such as please and thank you; there are visual patterns, such as wallpaper; there are auditory patterns, such as clapping to the beat of music, and so forth.

Patterns occur in nature. The change of seasons is a pattern, a spider's web is a pattern, tracks in the snow are patterns.

Children can make patterns. A child can draw a border around a picture, invent motions to go with a song, or use the computer to generate patterns.

Patterns are found in different cultures. African Kente cloth is a pattern, Chinese characters form patterns, Navajo pottery is decorated with patterns, and company logos are patterns.

You will see your child bringing home geometric patterns that were produced on the computer, word search pages where the child highlights patterns of words, and patterns produced with a stamp pad and various stamps. Please display your child's work and invite him or her to talk with you about patterns.

Around your home and in the community, consider playing a "Pattern Hunt" game. For instance, while setting the table, you might say, "See if you can make a pattern of bowl, spoon, glass for everyone in the family." Stopped at a traffic light, you might say, "I spy a pattern—red, yellow, green. Do you see the pattern?"

Thank you for helping your child to understand patterns.

Sincerely,

Figure 9.11 Sample Letter to Parents and Families

jargon to a minimum and is written in clear, simple language that is supported with concrete examples. Second, it explains what children are learning and how parents and families can help. Third, it has a positive tone so that families get a sense of your enthusiasm for teaching and efforts to motivate their child to learn. You may want to try writing a similar letter to accompany a thematic unit that you are planning.

Published Scales

Over the years, many experts have attempted to quantify creativity and predict potential in the arts. There are various formal scales for assessing creative products, see Cropley (2001). Nevertheless, measurement tools frequently fall short when we try to reduce complex processes to numerical ratings. Even if we do succeed in assigning a numerical value to creative processes or products, we are left with the task of interpreting those numbers. As Wassermann (1989) points out, numbers themselves do not have meaning. It takes human intelligence to make sense out of them. The results of published scales should always be viewed as one indicator in a comprehensive form of assessment rather than the "final word" on a child's play, creativity, or gifts and talents.

✺ RETHINKING ASSESSMENT IN CREATIVITY AND THE ARTS

Teachers frequently are perplexed when it comes to evaluating children's creative growth and artwork and are often at a loss about how to assess these things (Johnson, 2003). As a result, teachers may take the easy way out and not evaluate it at all. When they decide to do this, everyone—child, family, administrators, community—assumes that the arts don't count. Under these circumstances, teachers tend to err at one of two extremes (Bresler, 1993). At one end of the spectrum is the little-intervention approach (Gilbert, 1996), characterized by little evaluation or, for that matter, instruction ("Go ahead and make anything you want"). Teachers defend the little-intervention approach by arguing that any hint of structure or challenge will inhibit the child's creativity. They may mistakenly conclude that assessment will damage the child's self-esteem. Yet teachers actually do make judgments about children's creative processes and art products all the time. They may mentally separate the day's works into the "good" ones; they single out certain students as the class artists, giving them the special assignments of creating room decorations for the holidays; or they select students for various roles in a dramatic performance. These evaluations are intuitive and usually not publicly acknowledged. Often, they are based upon the teacher's preconceived notions of how child art should look or what characteristics are desirable for a child performance. Thus, in many not-so-subtle ways, the actions of teachers who argue for the little-intervention approach often contradict their own philosophical stance, and the absence of thoughtful teacher monitoring or evaluation results in programs of little substance.

At the opposite end of the spectrum is the production-oriented approach, in which cookie-cutter-type products are the norm. In the production-oriented approach, evaluation is not based on originality; rather, it is based on how closely the end product resembles the model provided by the teacher for children to copy. The problem here is that the resulting products fail to stimulate children's intellects or to engage them effectively in the arts.

A third way of abdicating responsibility for creativity and arts-based learning is by "leaving all that to the specialists," those teachers who have specialized training in art and music. There are several problems here. The first and most obvious is that not every school has a music or art teacher and, even if they do, many of these teachers are without their own classroom space and are expected to teach hundreds of children of various ages for short periods of time (often just 20 or 30 minutes) one time per week (Olson, 2002). To further complicate matters, many arts specialists have had little preservice instruction in assessment methods (Colwell, 1998). Therefore, even if these teachers can meet the challenge of the conditions under which they teach, they must educate themselves or rely on their own educational experiences as a student, which usually based assessment on criteria such as attendance, attitude, and cooperation rather than attainment of any arts objectives (Colwell, 1998).

The solution lies between the two extremes of laissez-faire and complete teacher control. We recommend that teachers find a balance point that allows room for improvisation, choice, and spontaneity yet encourages children to do their best through evaluation and feedback. Use art vocabulary, provide genuine art materials and experiences, demonstrate proper techniques, extend the child's learning what is commonly known, done, or widely available. The next section discusses how national standards can be used to support these efforts.

MEETING STANDARDS

Assessment of Creative Works

In today's schools student work that is not linked to standards and assessed in some systematic way is treated as less important and less vital to educational purposes. If work is not assessed, it can be expected to be on the endangered list when resources are in short supply. Fortunately, several national organizations have generated standards and guidelines that can provide a framework for assessment in the arts, such as the National Advisory Committee on Creative and Cultural Education (1999) in the United Kingdom and the publication of the Consortium of National Arts Education Associations (1994), *National Standards for Arts Education: What Every Young American Should Know and Be Able to Do in the Arts*. Guidelines for assessment of creative work are in Figure 9.12 (p. 346).

The next section describes several classroom projects that meet these standards.

Assessment in Music and Movement

Preschool

What: Child's movement/dance performance

Why: Assessment of child's understanding of movement in personal space and large muscle motor skills

How: Following explorations of walking, hopping, and other simple movements (in place) in personal space and as locomotor movements across a large defined space, children will demonstrate their ability to understand the difference among the various ways of moving their bodies.

Primary

What: Student's movement performance

Why: Assessment of student's understanding of the aesthetic quality of "texture" in visual art, music, and movement

How: Following explorations of the quality of "texture" in a variety of media, students will demonstrate understanding of texture by responding with appropriate movement to visual and musical prompts (e.g., a march versus a waltz).

Assessment of Creative Growth

Preschool

What: Child's attitudes, actions (verbal, visual, and kinesthetic), responses, communicated observations regarding encounters with his or her environment, and interactions with people, animals, and objects.

Why: Documentation of child's creative growth

How: At this level, assessment can be the responsibility of the teacher through a portfolio collection of narratives of teacher observations of the child along with photographs and artifacts of creative responses, including

Appropriate assessment of creative work:

- Is founded on expanded definitions of intelligence and creativity.
- Is fair (gives all students an equal opportunity to participate) and adapted to special needs of individual students.
- Is oriented toward students but planned and monitored by teachers who can clearly state the purpose of the assessment, identify the domain to be assessed, understand the assessment strategy or task, prepare the actual task or exercise, devise a scoring plan, and report the results.
- Integrates assessment of creative thought and the arts with the curriculum.
- Evaluates creative work at multiple levels and from multiple perspectives.
- Provides ongoing (formative) feedback as well as feedback on the finished work (summative).
- Focuses on "real-world" tasks and considers the particulars of the context in which creative works are generated.
- Includes both informal and formal assessment strategies.
- Considers not only the products but also the processes.
- Provides opportunities for students to revisit the work, refine, and revise.
- Is responsive to knowledge of disciplinary content, skills, and processes of a discipline, requisite motor skills in a discipline, appropriate procedures in particular contexts, self-appraisal of strengths and weaknesses in a discipline, and insight into the dispositions and values associated with achievement in a domain.
- Is concerned with determining students' preconceptions and changing their misconceptions.
- Is linked to standards and referenced to criteria.
- Is supportive of collaborative and cooperative learning.

Figure 9.12   Appropriate Assessment of Creative Work
Note: Data from Beattie (1997).

but not limited to those appropriately classified as art. The teacher should date entries and periodically review each child's development for the purposes of developing instruction, creating appropriate environments and opportunities, and sharing with parents and other caregivers.

Primary

What: Student's individual creative investigations, solutions, and responses

Why: Documentation of student's creative growth

How: Student's personal creativity journal. At the beginning of the school year, engage students in discussion of creative people, soliciting their perceptions and prior knowledge. Read stories of diverse creative lives and involve students in locating stories about others. Implement the long-term project of keeping a personal creativity journal. Suggest that the journal include reflections about attributes of creative people that students admire from their reading and from personal acquaintance, their personal assessments of their own areas of creativity, documentations of their creative responses and endeavors, and investigations that they wish to pursue. Periodically schedule the sharing of the journals in class or small-group discussion, asking questions about development in individual perceptions of what creativity is, how the student demonstrated creativity, and how the student has demonstrated growth as evidenced by thought processes, responses, products, and so on.

Performance-Based Assessment of Integrated Learning Experience

Preschool

What: Child's ability to visually represent and dramatically communicate the ideas from a character in a picture book or the media.

Why: Assessment of child's reading comprehension

How: Model making/dramatic play. An important aspect of literacy instruction is comprehension. In order to assess children's understanding of a story, the teacher can encourage them to create visual representations in the form of models to communicate ideas. Models can provide children who are not so articulate in the classroom an opportunity to express their understandings (Pahl, 1999). It is probably not necessary to provide instruction for model making, only materials and opportunity. Many children engage in this form of creative production quite naturally by inventing elaborate props to include in their play. A kindergarten boy, for example, designed a small three-dimensional paper picnic basket and paper food for Iron Man and The Incredible Hulk superheroes to take on their road trip; he also devised a shoebox elevator to take them to the top floor (via an attached string pulled through the stair railing) of an office building.

Primary

What: The student's ability to create and communicate an accurate representation of a selected mathematical concept through movement/dance performance

Why: Children need to understand the underlying concepts in mathematics before computation makes sense to them.

How: In lieu of a traditional end-of-unit or semester assessment of the students' understanding of various mathematical concepts (e.g., subtraction, division, multiplication), the teacher could incorporate the medium of dance. Dance is a physical language that speaks the integrated response from the mind and the body, so assessments should evaluate expressiveness and meaning-making (Johnson, 2003; Ross, 1994). By using the medium of movement/dance as a means of communicating understanding, teachers not only address those often-neglected students with kinesthetic intelligence but also encourage all students to think in a new way by "translating" what they know into a different set of symbols. The teacher should begin by modeling ways that movement/dance can explain a concept. Take, for instance, the math concept of one-to-one correspondence. The teacher can "choreograph" and provide directions to students to demonstrate this idea. Following this demonstration, students can work in small groups to create a movement/dance piece that effectively explains a mathematical concept. Formative assessment might consist of critically analyzing video or live performances to examine how dancers portray size and space relationships, power, subtleties of movement, and so on. The final assessment will be of each student's effective communication through the movement/dance piece his or her understanding of the math concept.

 ## CONCLUSION

In an interview, E. Paul Torrance (quoted in Cramond, 2001), one of the pioneers in creativity research, talked about his 30-year study of "beyonders," individuals from various countries and walks of life whose creative achievement was remarkable in their chosen domain (Torrance, 2004). The characteristics that these individuals shared were a delight in deep thinking, a tolerance of mistakes, a passion for their work, a clear sense of purpose and mission, an acceptance of being different, a level of comfort with being a minority of one, and a relative lack of concern about being "well rounded." Based on this research, Torrance and his colleagues advised children to pursue their interests with intensity, work to their strengths, learn to self-evaluate, seek out mentors and teachers, ignore admonitions about being well-rounded, and learn to be interdependent (Henderson, Presbury, & Torrance, 1983). Such advice, based on studies of those who excelled in their chosen fields and functioned at very high levels of creativity, are suggestive of the type of changes that need to be made in schools and programs.

As you think about assessment of creative growth and in the arts, keep in mind that effective assessment enables teachers "to diagnose student strengths and weak-

Frequently Asked Questions About Assessment

It seems that there really isn't much time for creative activities. Don't creative pursuits take time away from serious learning?

Creative and artistic pursuits *are* serious learning because they deal with complex thought processes as children are asked to compare, classify, deduce, investigate, inquire, invent, analyze errors, construct support, deal with abstractions, appreciate multiple perspectives, make decisions, solve problems, and evaluate products (Beattie, 1997; Marzano, Pickering, & McTighe, 1993).

What determines the value of a creative product?

Creative products are not inherently good for society; they also can be put to destructive ends. Therefore, it makes sense to guide children in examining the underlying values of creative work. In fact, many of the activities that are used

to teach media literacy take this approach (Semali & Watts Pailliotet, 1999). An advertiser might spend hundreds of thousands of dollars on a creative idea for promoting a product. But whose interests are being served? Who is most likely to be taken in by the appealing advertisement? What are the consequences for society at large if questionable claims and business practices are allowed to proliferate? Society is inundated with unstructured problems like this one, not the neat, predictable, and orderly kinds of questions too often presented in school. If we seek to prepare children for the future, we must think beyond what is customary and conventional and devote attention to the thoughtful critique of creative products in society.

How reliable is assessment by a panel of judges?

Increasingly, there is an emphasis on the contribution of the creative product or response as judged by an appropriate group of observers; in other words, a consensual process is used to assess creativity (Amabile, 2001; Priest, 2001). The strength of a team of assessors is that it can help to reduce bias. It is critical that creative processes and products be part of the overall assessment plan in the curriculum.

nesses early on and on a regular basis, to monitor student progress, to improve and adapt instructional methods in response to assessment data, and to use information about students individually and as a group to manage the classroom more effectively" (Beattie, 1997, p. 2). Teachers must examine their understandings of the role of creativity in their own lives, in their classroom, and in society. How is it exhibited, how is it valued and what end does it serve? They must teach children to critically examine creativity in their work, school, and society. Perhaps the most important role of the teacher in child-centered assessment is to view children as informants about their own growth and as partners in the assessment process.

 ## CHAPTER SUMMARY

1. Assessment of creative thinking and arts-based learning is a highly controversial issue; many inappropriate practices are commonplace. Teachers are urged to rely on the standards of major professional organizations, use a wide range of formative and summative assessment methods, integrate creative thinking and the arts with other subject areas, and convey the results to children and their families.
2. Meaningful assessment of creative thought is linked to the lesson objectives, state standards, and national standards. Comprehensive assessment includes data on the learner's attitudes, processes, efforts, and finished products.
3. In general, the purposes for assessing creativity are to gain insight about creativity, evaluate progress, identify talents, provide enrichment, and optimize each child's growth in creative thinking and arts-based learning.
4. Tools for assessment of creativity and the arts include such things as observations, checklists, rating scales, interviews, conferencing, portfolios, rubrics, and tests—all collected over time.
5. It is essential for teachers to make assessment accommodations for children with special needs and to design adaptations that enable children with gifts and talents so that all children's creative thinking and arts-based learning can reach its full potential.

 ### Discuss: Assessment Issues in Creative Expression and Art

1. The principal visits your classroom and comments, "Why are the children drawing during reading class?" How would you respond?
2. Recall some occasions when you were asked to evaluate your own performance. How did that make you feel? Was your self-assessment accurate? Useful? How did your self-evaluation compare with other people's assessments of your performance?
3. When a large city school district announced that it would identify elementary schools for the study of music, dance, and languages, urban parents got in line the night before and literally camped out to get their children enrolled in a particular school. What does this behavior tell you about families' interest in traditionally "nonacademic" subjects? What will you do to change practices that often exclude children, particularly poor and minority children, from participating?

Chapter 10

Children's Creative Work in Diverse Families and Communities

Before we can begin to establish meaningful relationships with families we must make sure to establish an inviting classroom climate that implicitly and explicitly communicates that this is a place where families are valued. . . This culture of collaboration is effectively communicated to parents through the implicit messages sent by teachers through the visual representations throughout the physical space, the tone of all communication to families (formal and informal), and perhaps most importantly, the frequency and consistency of active and positive communication between home and school.

Leigh M. O'Brien and Sham'ah Md-Yunus, 2007, p. 236

CLASSROOM PERSPECTIVES ON CULTURE, FAMILY, AND THE ARTS

Preschool—Kindergarten

Ms. Ochoa teaches kindergarten in an economically depressed rural area where some of the children live in trailer courts. She overhears two children who are building a house with blocks as they discuss their concept of a home:

Bradley: No, you can't live in a trailer; you've got to live in a house.
Carol Ann: But I do live in a trailer.
Bradley: A trailer is for camping. You've gotta live in a house, or maybe an apartment.

In response to this disagreement, Ms. Ochoa initiates a "Where do they live?" bulletin board/collage. Her pictures come from local real estate advertising booklets as well as copies of magazines such as *National Geographic* and *Old House Journal*. She also finds UNICEF cards and calendars that contain photographs and children's drawings of homes from around the world. The children use these materials as resources to create their own impressive display of different homes for human beings. To extend the project even further, Ms. Ochoa invites a Habitat for Humanity volunteer to speak with the children about her work and to share photos of the homes that she has helped to renovate, including her own. As a result of Ms. Ochoa's efforts, every child's concept of what a home can be or become is expanded.

First Grade—Second Grade

The state academic standards for language arts require students to understand different points of view in a story and to produce compositions that demonstrate that ability. In a class for gifted and talented second graders, their teacher decides to use "fractured fairy tales" as a way of developing the students' perspective-taking abilities (Holder & Pearle, 2005). She plans a four-day unit using the following concepts, books, and activities.

Monday

Question: How can a change in setting affect point of view in a story?

Children's Literature: The Cowboy and the Black-Eyed Pea (Johnston, 1996)—a Texas version of the fairy tale "The Princess and the Pea"; two regional variants of "The Three Little Pigs": *The Three Little Javelinas* (Lowell, 1992) and *The Three Little Pigs and the Fox: An Appalachian Tale* (Hooks, 1997).

Activity: Have students work in small groups to select a new setting for a familiar folk or fairy tale, retell it, then complete a chart that compares/contrasts the two.

Tuesday

Question: How does telling a tale from a different character's point of view change the plot?

Children's Literature: The True Story of the Three Little Pigs! (Scieszka, 1989); *The Wolf Who Cried Boy* (Hartman, 2004).

Activity: Use the book *Mufaro's Beautiful Daughters* (Steptoe, 1987) with the group to invent a script in which the story is told from the mean sister's point of view. Then distribute copies of familiar fairy tales, such as "Rapunzel," "Sleeping Beauty," and "Rumplestiltskin," and have children work with a partner to create a script for a scene depicting a different character's perspective.

Wednesday

Question: How might characters with different points of view communicate with one another through writing?

Children's Literature: The Jolly Postman, or, Other People's Letters (Ahlberg & Ahlberg, 1986); *Three Days on a River in a Red Canoe* (Williams, 1981); *Stringbean's Trip to the Shining Sea* (Williams, 1988); *Mailing May* (Tunnell, 2000); *Nettie's Trip South* (Turner, 1987).

Activity: Create a letter, postcard, greeting card, or e-mail message from one story character to another.

Thursday

Question: What can a prequel reveal about a character's reasons or motives for interpreting events in a particular way?

Children's Literature: Discuss books and movies in a series such as *Star Wars, Lord of the Rings,* and *Harry Potter.* Provide examples of storyboarding (a sequential set of drawings that depict the action in a film). Use Janet Stevens's *Tops and Bottoms* (1995), which alludes to Aesop's fable "The Tortoise and the Hare" and attributes Hare's financial problems to a bet he made (and lost) with Tortoise.

Activity: Work in small groups to create a storyboard of the fable "The Tortoise and the Hare," which predates the story of *Tops and Bottoms.* Encourage the students to emphasize the characters' motives and then discuss how these events might have influenced Hare's behavior.

Third Grade—Fourth Grade

The national literacy standards for 9- and 10-year-old children in many countries throughout the world include teaching them to locate, interpret, and apply factual information effectively. In the refutational approach, students are supplied with a written document that includes some deliberate errors of fact (Lynch & Harris, 2000). The students then work individually, in pairs, or in small groups and use their reference skills and tools, including the Internet, to locate authoritative infor-mation that can support or refute key statements made in the text. Ms. Peterson's fourth graders, for example, are studying Australian animals and she has distributed a brief text that includes both accurate and inaccurate information. It states that a platypus has a poisonous stinger and that koalas are outgoing and kept as pets. (The first statement is true—a platypus does have a stinger to protect itself—and the second is false; koalas are wild animals that are not kept as pets.) She leads students in investigating various topics and invites them to create maps, diagrams, and a field guide that address common misconceptions. At the conclusion of the project, each student writes a paragraph summarizing the gaps that were filled in and the errors that were corrected.

 ## DEFINING CULTURAL PERSPECTIVES ON CREATIVITY AND THE ARTS

"The common language of creativity transcends race, country, culture, and economic level" (Meador, 1999, p. 324). Consider the following descriptions of how four different countries conceptualize creative thinking in their populations:

- After Canada was ranked 15th internationally in research and development, the government issued a report in 2003 that challenged the citizenry to foster a "culture of creativity," to make sweeping changes in the educational system, and to move into the top five. Canadians are being urged to become more inventive, entrepreneurial, and technologically advanced. Now the pressure is on Canadian citizens, particularly teachers, to "think outside the box" and to address a national sense of inferiority in creative thought and participation in the arts.

- Ideas about intelligence extend well beyond memorization of facts in two African countries. In rural Kenya, it was found that there are four distinct terms used to describe intelligence—rieko (knowledge and skills), luoro (respect), winjo (comprehension of how to handle real-life problems), and

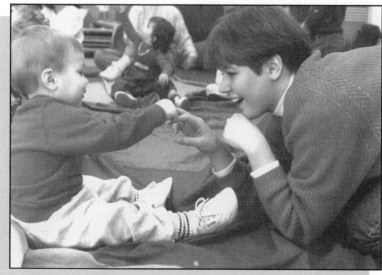

How do diverse families encourage children's creativity?

paro (initiative) (Sternberg, 2007, p. 3). In Zimbabwe, the word for intelligence, *ngware*, actually means to be prudent and cautious, particularly in social relationships (Sternberg, 2007, p. 2).

- During the early 2000s, the U.K. government was anxious to raise standards and set targets in literacy, an approach that tended to overshadow the arts. The government legislated that all language arts programs for young children would include "The Literacy Hour" (a program similar to what U.S. teachers would refer to as balanced reading, with time for reading aloud, writing, discussion, and so forth). An emphasis on literacy (and numeracy) overshadowed the arts and, in response, "expected outcomes" were specified for art as well, yet, as Barnes (2002) points out, art galleries throughout the world are filled with unexpected outcomes, not legislated ones!

- In China, over 178 million children attend elementary and secondary school, the official purpose of art in "the national curriculum is to foster patriotism, morality, and socialism." Although traditional art instruction in China emphasizes direct instruction in technique and imitation of the masters, teachers recognize their responsibility to enlarge the children's vision and allow them to create according to their imaginations (Perry, 1998; Rong & Shi, 2001). The importance of a combination of characteristics that transcend the cognitive is far from new. The Chinese have a concept they refer to as *zuoren*, which refers to the process of becoming a human being in the fullest sense. Li (2004) lists seven categories of meanings of *zuoren* as: (1) pursuing fulfillment of life, (2) self-strengthening without ever stopping, (3) developing high moral character, (4) seeking knowledge, (5) maintaining harmonious social relations, (6) striving for a successful career, and (7) contributing to society.

As these snapshots of four diverse countries have illustrated, "Creativity is one of the most precious qualities human beings possess, and so is intelligence. These two qualities are needed by society to help us deal with the enormously complicated problems we constantly face" (Cohen & Gainer, 1995, p. 195). There is little doubt that the international community needs resourceful, imaginative, inventive, and ethical problem solvers who will make a significant contribution to society. Of course, the way that nations envision their futures exerts a powerful influence on ideas about creativity and intelligence. Wealthy nations often view innovation as the way to maintain their privileged status while

> In technologically less developed countries where both physical survival and survival of the national identity are more important than world dominance, creativity is often seen as the key to rapid economic and social development, especially modernization and its hoped-for benefits of improved education, nutrition, and health care, tolerance of minorities, democracy and political stability. (Cropley, 2001, p. 5)

According to many experts and leaders in the field, contemporary society needs the following:

1. Students who possess "resilience and flexibility, a creative and integrative way of thinking, and a certain psychological sturdiness in the way they face new circumstances in the company of other people" (Minuchin, 1987, p. 254).

2. A school curriculum that encourages "experimentation, risk-taking, flexibility, autonomy" and children who have acquired "a mode of learning that places responsibility on them and that allows them the freedom to try, to test, to innovate, and to be creative" (Tetenbaum & Mulkeen, 1986, p. 99).

3. A workforce that is responsible and self-disciplined and can move from one challenge to another, adapt quickly to change, produce innovative solutions to problems, and acquire expertise in more than one area (Research and Policy Committee, 1985; Tetenbaum & Mulkeen, 1986). Tomorrow's workers must be able to "figure out what they need to know, where to get it, and how to make meaning of it" (Task Force on Teaching as a Profession, 1986, p. 20).

4. A citizenry capable of reading, writing, and computing at high levels; analyzing and interpreting data, drawing conclusions, and making decisions; and functioning as part of a community (Boyer, 1995; Etzioni, 1993).

To learn more about cultural diversity and creativity watch "Incorporating the Home Experiences of Culturally Diverse Students in the Classroom, Parts 1–4" online at MyEducationLab.

The Influence of Parents and Families on Talent

Jonathan Kozol (1997) points out that:

> Children are not simply "embryonic workers." They have value in themselves for who they are already. Children are not just "preparatory grown-ups." They are alive right now and must be valued, blessed, and treasured for the multitude of gifts they bring to us as a society, not for the added value they may bring to IBM. . . . Business needs team players who are not resistant or iconoclastic and do not waste precious time with metaphors or ethics. But society needs prophets, poets, troublemakers, saints and rebels, beautiful dreamers, glorious eccentrics. (p. 6)

Many parents/families would be uncomfortable with what Kozol is advocating yet they exercise a powerful influence on children's creative growth and artistic expression. Families can place very different values on creativity and the arts; for example, when the ability to meet basic needs is in jeopardy, there is an understandable tendency to favor jobs and careers that are practical and dependable sources of income. On the other hand, when resources are plentiful, families may be more willing

Go to MyEducationLab and select the topic "Diversity." Under Activities and Applications, watch the video Incorporating the Home Experiences of Culturally Diverse Students in the Classroom, Parts 1–4 *and complete the activity.*

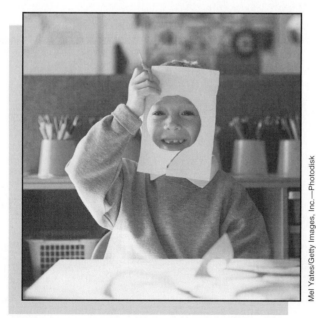

Mel Yates/Getty Images, Inc.—Photodisk

Creative thought contributes to the individual, the cultural group, and society at large.

to allow a child to pursue nontraditional careers because they are in a better position to give their children financial support to acquire skills that take a long time to develop (e.g., learning to play the piano). Even when finances are not the main consideration, families may be more interested in seeing their child "fit in" or may urge their child to follow in a parent's footsteps. Conversely, other parents and families may insist that their child depart from much of what their family represents and dream of the day when a child's stunning talent or advanced education enables him or her to accomplish this. The aspirations of parents for a child can range all of the way from wishing for complete conformity to dreaming of trailblazing—and everywhere in between. Hopes and dreams that parents have for children with disabilities are even more complex and are, all too often, undermined by the low expectations of others (Baum & Reis, 2004; Newman & Sternberg, 2004; Rogers, 2007).

A child's gifts and talents also affect parents'/families' view of creativity and the arts because "When the child's abilities are truly prodigious, parental and social investments need to be prodigious as well" (Csikszentmihalyi, Rathunde, & Whalent, 1993, p. 26). Even when children do not appear to have remarkable talents and gifts in a particular skill, such as singing, parents and families continue to play a crucial role. Studies show that most families make music part of their child's daily experience from infancy; however, there is a sharp decline in parental singing and playing music for children commencing in toddlerhood as parents/families may begin to emphasize literacy with print activities, often to the detriment of singing and playing music (Custodero, 2006). Figure 10.1 describes what parents and families can do to support children's talent, growth, and development in creativity and the arts.

Another reason that parents and families are so influential is that many creative endeavors and arts-based learning activities occur outside the school setting, often at home or in other out-of-school contexts. It is customary for children to practice musical instruments, dances, and produce works of visual art at home. Nearly 80 percent of elementary students reported engaging in art-making at home (Dorn, Madeja, & Sabol, 2003). Their top three reasons for doing so were to have

Much of the young child's creative thinking and arts-related activity occurs in out-of-school settings.

Tolerance. Accept that a child's creative ideas do not always work out to adults' satisfaction or even to the child's personal satisfaction. Children should not be punished and humiliated when ideas fail. In fact, one of the defining characteristics of geniuses is the ability to generate many different ideas and to know which ones are worth pursuing.

Space. Provide children with a private, relatively undisturbed, space in which their creative work can be done. Lois Ehlert, the well-known children's book author and illustrator who is famous for her collages, attributes her growth as an artist to the fact that her parents allowed her to have a large, old table of her own in the basement where she could collect bits and scraps and objects and use them to invent. She was not required to clean it up or put it away and it was always available for her use.

Materials. Children need at least some tools that will support and inspire creative exploration—scissors, crayons, paste, simple musical instruments, picture books. The chief architect of the arts and crafts movement, Frank Lloyd Wright, attributed his interest in architecture to a set of wooden blocks he received as a child.

Support. Children need adults who recognize and support their efforts. A passion for creative problem solving and the arts begins with enjoyment as children enter into these pursuits with curiosity and interest. When hockey great Mario Lemieux was a child, his parents created an indoor place for him and his brother to practice skating by putting water in the foyer and allowing it to freeze.

Role Models. Children need to see adults enjoying and participating in the arts and creative thinking. Something as simple as thinking out loud to demonstrate how you arrive at a creative solution can reap surprising benefits. The parent who repairs a household item and shares the problem-solving strategy with the child is teaching him or her to imagine different possibilities and persist until a satisfactory solution is found. It is also important for parents and families to make children aware of the true stories behind the great contributors of their era and previous eras so children can see that the path is not clear and easy.

Parents/families can shape children's talent in several significant ways, including:

- modeling perseverance and industriousness,
- offering advice or giving explicit instruction
- instilling a desire or expectation in children to participate in an activity
- setting high standards and encouraging self-evaluation
- offering moral support and keeping children motivated
- proposing new challenges
- reorganizing their lives to permit their children's abilities to flourish

Figure 10.1   How Parents and Families Can Nurture Creativity in Children
Note: Based on Baldwin (2001), Greenspan, Soloman, & Gardner (2004), and Piirto (1998)

fun (82 percent), to relax (60 percent) or to express their ideas (56 percent), and their evaluation criteria for artwork made at home were (1) use of the artistic elements, (2) skill with art materials, (3) details in their work, (4) neatness of the product, and (5) personal satisfaction with the outcomes of their efforts (Dorn, Madeja, & Sabol, 2003). Neighborhood children often collaborate to perform a puppet play, start a club, or master a craft. Whether it is ballet, woodworking, or creative writing, much of the training, practice, support, and performance occurs at home and therefore depends on parents and families.

The Influence of Peer Culture on Talent

In a society characterized by rapid change, children may find it difficult to relate to adults whose cultural experiences have differed so dramatically from their own. Under these circumstances, children tend to form a strong peer culture and tend to rely

---

What kind of adult do you hope children will become? Read through the list and put a star next to the characteristics that teachers ought to encourage the most. Then go back through the list and circle the traits that you think your parents and family would have valued the most in a child. Compare/contrast the two lists. Then compare your lists with those of classmates.

_____ Adventurous	_____ Intuitive
_____ Accepts challenges	_____ Likes school
_____ Affectionate	_____ Likes to work alone
_____ Altruistic	_____ Never bored
_____ Appreciative	_____ Obedient
_____ Athletic	_____ Persistent
_____ Becomes preoccupied with tasks	_____ Physically attractive
_____ Careful	_____ Physically strong
_____ Cautious	_____ Playful
_____ Competitive	_____ Popular
_____ Compassionate	_____ Polite
_____ Completes work on time	_____ Proud
_____ Confident	_____ Quiet
_____ Conforming	_____ Rebellious
_____ Considerate of others	_____ Receptive to ideas of others
_____ Cooperative	_____ Refined
_____ Courageous	_____ Remembers well
_____ Creative	_____ Respectful of adults
_____ Curious	_____ Self-sufficient
_____ Desires to excel	_____ Sense of beauty
_____ Determined	_____ Sense of humor
_____ Emotional	_____ Sensitive
_____ Energetic	_____ Sincere
_____ Fearful	_____ Socially well adjusted
_____ Fits in with peers	_____ Spirited in disagreement
_____ Friendly	_____ Supportive
_____ Gets good grades	_____ Talkative
_____ Healthy	_____ Thorough
_____ Humanitarian	_____ Unwilling to accept things on others say-so
_____ Independent in judgment	_____ Versatile
_____ Industrious	_____ Visionary
_____ Intelligent	_____ Willing to take risks
_____ Inquisitive	

Figure 10.2   What Traits Do You Hope to Foster in Children?

on advice from other children. There is little question that peers exert a powerful influence on children's talents and the development of expertise and, contrary to the
commonly held view that extraordinarily talented children are rejected by peers,
Greenspan, Solomon, and Gardner (2004) found that "Children developed strong relationships with their domain-related peers and provided moral and technical support to one another. Peers who did not participate in children's activities played an
equally important role by sympathizing with the lengthy hours children were required to devote to their activities and by demonstrating enthusiasm for their involvement . . . the children in our study successfully navigated and utilized both
groups of friends in the development of their talent" (p. 132).

In consideration of peer and parent/family influences, it is essential for educators to shore up any deficiencies that might exist so that every child will have an
opportunity to experience the satisfactions of creative thought processes and products. As a starting point, reflect on one fundamental question concerning the role
of creative thinking and the arts in children's futures: What kind of human beings
do we hope that children will become? Figure 10.2 (on the previous page) presents
a list of human characteristics that adults might consider to be important for children to develop. Look through the list and reflect on the top five traits that you
hope to nurture in your students. How does your list of five compare with the lists
that classmates produce? More often than not, a group of early childhood and elementary teachers will arrive at some consensus on the essential characteristics. As
you review your college class's top five, consider this question: Which of these
traits, based on what you have read in this book, could be enhanced and extended
through creative thinking and the arts? Usually, the answer is "All of them."

As the next section describes, the social context exerts a major influence on
the development of talent.

THEORETICAL AND RESEARCH BASE: MULTIPLE INTELLIGENCES

Over the past decade, our view of human intelligence has expanded and enlarged.
In the past, there was a tendency to think of intelligence as a singular trait—the
general capacity of the human being for storing, retrieving, and processing information. In contrast to this simplistic view, Howard Gardner (1993a) defines intelligence as "the ability to solve problems, or to fashion products that are of
consequence in a particular cultural setting or community" (p. 15). He has proposed that there are nine—and possibly more—types of intelligence. He argues
that each way of thinking is sufficiently distinctive to warrant a special category.
The nine types of intelligence are as follows:

1. *Verbal/linguistic* intelligence with words and language, such as the skill
   possessed by a writer or a person who can speak several languages fluently.
2. *Logical/mathematical* intelligence with sequential thinking and numerical
   reasoning ability, such as the abilities possessed by a mathematician or
   scientist.
3. *Bodily/kinesthetic* wisdom about one's own body and its movements, such as
   the intelligence possessed by a figure skater or a wide receiver in football.
4. *Visual/spatial* intelligence in using "the mind's eye" to work with images
   and see their interrelationships, such as the intelligence needed by an
   architect.

5. *Musical/rhythmic* intelligence having to do with sound patterns, mastery of musical notation, and musical talent, such as the skills of a composer or performer.

6. *Interpersonal* intelligence in dealing with human interaction and perceptivity about how to resolve social problems, such as the abilities of a skilled counselor or therapist.

7. *Intrapersonal* wisdom about the self that leads to self-knowledge and personal growth, such as the intelligence of a person who fully understands how he or she learns.

8. *Environmental/naturalist* intelligence having to do with adapting to and learning about the physical environment, both natural and human-made. Examples of careers for naturalists are marine biologist, city planner, and forest ranger.

9. *Philosophical/moral* Although research on this type of intelligence is not as well developed as it is for the previous eight, those who possess philosophical/moral intelligence are capable of seeing the big picture and getting to the heart of the matter. These individuals raise questions of significance and grapple with ethical considerations effectively. Examples of professions that would rely on this form of intelligence are judges and clergy.

To find out more, watch the "Addressing Multiple Intelligences in a Project" video online at MyEducationLab.

Furthermore, Gardner argued that only the first two forms of intelligence—verbal/linguistic and logical/mathematical—were routinely emphasized in American schools and that, as a result, much human potential was being wasted. Many other educators agree that we need to plan programs that respect these different ways of knowing (Hatch, 1997). Examples of teaching themes for preschool, first grade, and third grade that emphasize each of the nine intelligences are in Table 10.1.

Go to MyEducationLab and select the topic "Curriculum." Under Activities and Applications, watch the video Addressing Multiple Intelligences in a Project *and complete the activity.*

Ideally all schools would (a) cultivate skills that are valued in community and society, (b) approach new concepts and subjects in a variety of ways, and (c) personalize instruction as much as possible (Latham, 1997). One reason for this is that creativity is, to some extent, specific to particular domains (Simonton, 2003). Different roles such as music video director, crime scene investigator, or vocalist on a nationally televised talent show obviously require different forms of creative thought and expression.

TEACHERS' REFLECTIONS ON CREATIVITY, FAMILIES, AND COMMUNITIES

Preservice Teachers

"I completed two field experiences in teaching. One of the schools was in a low-income rural area and the parents and families were really in support of technology; they also turned out in large numbers for any musical performances by the children. At the other school, most kids had better computers at home than at school and the parents and families were already thinking about how their kids would get into a good college. Still, these parents seemed to associate the arts with being cultured rather than as a career path for their children."

TABLE 10.1 Teaching Themes Based on Multiple Intelligences

The Nine Intelligences	Preschool MI Theme on Colors	First-Grade MI Theme on Patterns	Third-Grade MI Theme on Pets
Verbal/Linguistic	Read concept books about colors (e.g., *Who Said Red?* [Serfozo, 1992]), produce class books about various colors (e.g., *What Is Green? Our Favorite Colors*), learn to recognize the names of the primary colors, conduct a simple survey to discover favorite colors of classmates and family members, invent a class version of a book that features colors, such as *Brown Bear, Brown Bear, What Do You See?* (Martin, 1967), learn color names in a different language, read *Naming Colors* (Dewey, 1995), learn the chant *My Crayons Talk* (Hubbard, 1996).	Define the concept of patterns by finding examples of patterns in the classroom, explore word patterns (e.g., chants, rhymes, and raps), write couplets, listen for patterns in story language (e.g., "but it was too small," "but it was too large," "and it was just right"), recite a poem with a refrain in unison, search for patterns in groups of words that rhyme (e.g., *mall, hall, fall, wall*), read and perform a story in rhyme such as *Chicka Chicka Boom Boom* (Martin & Archambault, 1989).	Identify animal sounds, discuss chapter books about pets, maintain a detailed observational log about a classroom pet, create group booklets with practical information about the care and feeding of pets, tape-record reports about a particular type of pet, read the classified section of the newspaper to see what pets are for sale, visit pet rescue Web sites to see what pets are available (e.g., mustangs, greyhounds), make a vocabulary book of words for groups of animals (e.g., *flock, herd*).
Logical/Mathematical	Use paint samples to arrange hues from light to dark and produce color "families," develop a color chart after experimenting with food coloring (e.g., blue and red make ____), play sorting games with attribute blocks—flat, plastic blocks in three colors (red, yellow, and blue), three shapes (circle, triangle, square), and three sizes (small, medium, large), play a matching game with the color word on one side of a puzzle piece and a picture of a crayon that color on the matching piece.	Examine patterns in mathematical equations (e.g., adding 1 to a number), recognize the fact that subtraction problems can be checked by adding the two bottom numbers, produce pictorial patterns on the computer using various types of software, use a number line on the floor to count by ones, twos, and so forth, watch the video *How the Leopard Got Its Spots* and note the patterns in animals' fur (e.g., zebra stripes, giraffe spots), as well as the patterns in the soundtrack of African choir music.	Count the number of pets owned by everyone in the class, create a simple bar graph of the favorite pets owned by the class, list the common features of domesticated animals, rank-order pets from most to least popular, identify the most unusual pet owned by anyone in the group, match various pets to their preferred food choices, analyze the consequences of neglecting pets' care, figure out how much it would cost to raise a cat or dog for a year using a pet supply catalog.

(Continued)

TABLE 10.1 Teaching Themes Based on Multiple Intelligences (continued)

The Nine Intelligences	Preschool MI Theme on Colors	First-Grade MI Theme on Patterns	Third-Grade MI Theme on Pets
Bodily/Kinesthetic	Make finger and hand prints of different colors, use a simplified computer keyboard with keys in different colors, play a simple teacher-made color game on a plastic shower curtain or tablecloth on the floor, group children according to the color of their clothing for an activity, decorate plain cloth dolls for each child so that the doll's features can be made to match the child's hair color, eye color, etc., use hard candy to match colors to flavors (e.g., red for cherry, yellow for lemon), take a color walk after reading *Colors Everywhere* (Hoban, 1997).	Create a product using a pattern (e.g., in and out for weaving), make pattern cards for others to follow using large wooden beads and string, give children a chance to arrange their bodies into letter patterns (e.g., a task card that asks three children to make their bodies into a capital letter A), make patterns using an ink pad and stamps made from styrofoam, use wallpaper book samples to search for repeated patterns and sort them into groups on the floor, make rubbings of patterns (e.g., bottom of shoe).	Compare the relative sizes of pets to one another and oneself, invent a dance that characterizes a particular animal's style of moving, give a demonstration of how to groom a pet (e.g., a 4-H student showing how to care for a cow's feet), research and analyze how pets move (e.g., how a horse gallops, a snake slithers).
Visual/Spatial	Use word configuration (the outline or shape of the word) to match color words to the correct shape; use swatches of fabric to match colors, sort individual boxes of crayons into plastic containers of all the same color of crayon, identify the colors that typically go with various foods (e.g., apples as yellow, red, green or combinations of these), sort plastic fruits and vegetables by colors, discover the magic of mixing colors in *White Rabbit's Color Book* (Baker, 1995).	Create designs using parquetry blocks, design patterned borders for original picture books, make and follow cue cards to show the gestures that accompany an action song (e.g., "Little Cabin in the Woods"), print out common signs in various colors from the computer and make into a color-sorting game, look at a piece of landscaping software to see how patterns are used, use architectural blocks to build a structure and make a diagram of the structure.	Make sculptures of various pets, examine a pet closely and create life-size silhouettes, identify animal tracks and match them to the animals that made them, design a poster to encourage responsible pet ownership, create diagrams of pets labeled with the proper terminology (e.g., *mane*, *withers*, and *fetlock* for a horse), take a video visit to a veterinarian's office or animal shelter.
Musical/Rhythmic	Sing color songs (e.g., "Jenny Jenkins" or "Mary Wore Her Red Dress"), learn a color song in another language (e.g., "De Colores"), use a toy xylophone with colored keys and a color-coded piece of music for a simple nursery tune and learn to play a song.	Participate in simple dances and musical games (e.g., square dance steps), move "in time" with music (e.g., swaying), lead a rhythm band, watch a captioned musical video for children; recite a cumulative rhyme (e.g., "The House That Jack Built"), sing a song with a chorus or a refrain.	Find or invent an instrumental selection that captures the feelings associated with various pets, sing songs about animals, choose a rhythm that matches the characteristic movement of a pet, compose a song about a pet using music software.

Intelligence			
Interpersonal	Work with a partner or a small group to develop a poster collage of colors, read a story about different skin tones, make a big poster-sized book on colors and share it with another class, use color paddles (wooden frames with tinted plastic inside) to look at things with a partner and discuss how a change in color changes the object.	Infer the steps in a process by observing others (e.g., how to operate a videotape, learn a jump rope game, play hopscotch), work with a partner to learn a rhyme with a clapping pattern ("Miss Lucy"), solve a simple secret code such as numbering the letters of the alphabet, examine fabrics of different cultures such as batik or Kente Colors (Chocolate, 1996).	Participate in a class project designed to safeguard the welfare of pets in the community, interview a pet shop owner, arrange a classroom visit with an expert on animal care, correspond by e-mail with volunteers at the local animal shelter.
Intrapersonal	Think about the feelings associated with various colors (e.g., red as fiery, yellow as sunshine), choose dress-up clothes based on favorite colors, use the paint feature of a piece of art software to try out several colors for an object or a picture before deciding which one to save or print out.	Look for daily routines that are patterns of behavior (e.g., getting ready for school), identify patterns of sound that are pleasant (e.g., ticking of a clock), experiment with a piece of software to make patterns until a satisfying combination is produced.	Maintain a journal of activities enjoyed with a pet, describe reasons for choosing a particular pet as a favorite, prepare a statement of beliefs about animal rights, write a persuasive argument for choosing a dog or cat rather than a kitten or puppy and homeless animal rather than a pedigreed pet.
Naturalist/ Environmental	Take a color walk, sort fallen leaves by color, search for animals who are hidden by their protective coloration in pictures, look at how different book illustrators use color and compare/contrast (e.g., Tomie de Paola and Ed Young), document how colors in nature change (e.g., watching an amaryllis bulb grow).	Look for repeated patterns in the environment (e.g., sunrise/sunset, a picket fence), listen for patterns of sound in nature (e.g., ocean waves) and patterns of sound from objects invented by people (e.g., train), make a collection of advertising logos and analyze them for patterns.	Investigate the requirements of various animals, learn more about animals whose habitats are threatened by humans, investigate the Web site of the Humane Society of the United States (HSUS).
Philosophical/Moral	Why do people connect colors to the weather and also to feelings (e.g., yellow sunshine, a gray day, blue skies, white clouds, etc.)?	How might repeated patterns become boring and cause us to lose interest? What do storytellers, musicians, and artists do to keep us interested and surprise us?	Investigate the illegal sale of exotic or endangered species as pets. What does the law require if these animals are found? What is the punishment? Does the punishment fit the crime?

Note: Based on Gardner (1993b) and Armstrong (1987).

Inservice Teachers

"After reading an article about the educational uses of virtual reality (Cyranek, 2002), I have begun to think about it as a tool for learning rather than just an arcade game. It has possibilities as a more visual and interactive way of developing understanding and motivating students to apply what they have learned."

Your Reflections

- How are perspectives about creative thought and artistic expression affected by the individual child and family?

- Why is it important for teachers to evaluate their personal beliefs, classroom practices, and potential biases about creative expression and the arts?

- How can teachers persuade others that creative thought and the expressive arts make essential contributions to society?

Brain Research and Creative Thinking

Historically speaking, many deeply rooted dichotomies have dominated Western philosophy. Most people still believe, for example, that the following pairs of words are opposites: reason/imagination, science/art, and cognition/emotion. Even contemporary thinking contributes its own potential set of dichotomies by oversimplifying the results of brain research and treating the left side of the brain as analytical and practical and the right side as intuitive and holistic. This sort of either/or thinking is not supported by the experts (Bruer, 1997; Lindsey, 1998/1999; Shore, 1997). As a society, we need to put these fragments back together again and recognize that the same brain that thinks also feels, and that the same brain that stores factual information also imagines what is not yet possible.

Complete this sentence: "The brain is like _____." If you are like most of your contemporaries, you said "a computer." In the 1950s, most people would have responded with "a machine." Examining the symbols or metaphors that we use to describe the human brain provides a glimpse into society's depth of understanding about the brain and its functioning. Now that we have increasingly sophisticated research about the brain, neither of these comparisons is adequate; a machine is too simple and a computer too linear. In fact, the dividing line between human capacity and the capacity of computers in many people's minds is creative thought. Donna Jo Napoli's (2003) discussion of whether computers ever can be expected to carry on a conversation just like a human being illustrates this point. True, some computer programs can respond to any question or statement with a preprogrammed statement or question from a database; they may even "learn" from the human and modify the program. Either way, these sophisticated pieces of equipment still are not fluent conversational partners because they cannot respond to nuance and "fill in the blanks." To illustrate, Napoli (2001) offers the following question: "Why won't you go into that room?" and asks the reader to reflect on what a computer would do with the following answers: "Spiders." "Superstition." "No shoes." "No windows." "No reason." "I won't tell you." "Guess." (p. 107). Such nonlinear problem solving is required in daily interactions as well as in works of genius.

The human mind is capable of running multiple chains of thought simultaneously. Consider an ordinary task such as signing your name. Exactly what did you do when producing your signature? Analyze every detail of what is involved—the knowledge and skills that you needed, the experiences you had previously, every step involved in the task. If you brainstorm a list of everything involved, such as holding the pen, positioning the paper, forming each letter of the alphabet, making your signature distinctive, and knowing where to sign, you could probably come up with dozens of facts, subskills, actions, beliefs, values, and attitudes. Yet you probably did not think about any of those abilities in isolation or consciously analyze what you were doing (Neve, Hart, & Thomas, 1986). Your brain handled all of the necessary steps for you (Kline, 1995). While you were signing, your brain was helping you think about other things as well, such as the fact that you need to do some laundry, that it's raining outside, and that your chair is uncomfortable—in other words, your brain is not only running multiple chains of thought at the same time (Neve, Hart, & Thomas, 1986), but is also combining, editing, recombining, and readjusting them along the way. In fact, your brain could assemble a new pattern instantly if you were called on to sign 10 cover letters for job applications, versus signing a thank-you note to a friend, versus signing your name on a marriage license. From this point of view, (1) the brain's primary drive is to relate things to the real world, (2) the human brain is exceptionally effective at perceiving and processing patterns, and (3) learning is actually the acquisition of useful patterns of thought (Carnine, 1990; Kline, 1995).

Therefore, teaching in a way that is consistent with how the human brain works is compatible with everything that you have learned from this book thus far about creative expression and play. Figure 10.3 (p. 366) is an overview of the environmental, mental, emotional, and developmental conditions that foster creativity and respect the brain's natural way of functioning.

How Basic Is Creative Thinking?

A teacher held up a piece of purple construction paper and said, "What color is this?" Cris, a 5-year-old, thought for a moment and then answered, "graple." The teacher who is thinking inflexibly moves on, saying, "Can somebody help Cris?" But the teacher who really listens and respects children thinks about Cris's answer. It makes perfect sense. Cris has noticed—perhaps through direct experiences with lollipops or beverages—that grape is the flavor associated with the color purple and has invented a word to make sense out of this observation. A good teacher might marvel out loud, saying with a tone of pleasure and surprise in her voice, "Grape-flavored things are usually purple, aren't they?" Cris's response falls somewhere between the historical dichotomies: between reason and feeling, between logic and imagination, between "left brain" and "right brain." That largely uncharted territory between what are incorrectly regarded as bipolar opposites is where genius lies. Every child—not just the compliant, the economically advantaged, or the gifted and talented—has creative potential just waiting to be set free by a great teacher. Figure 10.4 (p. 367) identifies the 12 qualities of genius that teachers must recognize and promote in all children.

Educators overlook the genius of childhood if they allow rationality and logic to overshadow the child's natural affinity for nonliteral thinking (Egan, 2006; Egan, Stout, & Takaya, 2007). Rollo May (1975) poses a question that every educator should take to heart: "In our day of dedication to facts and hardheaded objectivity, we have disparaged imagination. . . . What if imagination and art are not frosting at all, but the fountainhead of human experience?" (pp. 149–150). Perhaps we have had it backward. Skills mastery is not the price of admission to creativity, as often is reflected in teachers' behavior. Students who are experiencing difficulties in mathematics or reading, for instance, may be assigned only low-level drill on the computer while classmates who are mastering these subjects are given opportunities to use the computer to design original materials, such as simulations. Children

- Researchers report that approximately half of the child's critical brain development occurs before kindergarten (Simmons & Sheehan, 1997).
- According to a study conducted by the National Goals Panel, the major risk factors for children under age 3 are inadequate prenatal care, isolated parents, substandard child care, poverty, and insufficient attention (Carnegie Corporation, 1994).
- A child is born with 100 billion neurons, which make over 50 trillion connections, called synapses. During the first 3 years of life, many more neural connections are made, literally trillions more than the brain can possibly use. Over time, those that are rarely or never used are eliminated, a process called "pruning" (Begley, 1997; Nash, 1997).
- The way in which the child is raised affects how the child's brain is wired; in other words, the early years are "when we create the promise of a child's future" (Simmons & Sheehan, 1997).
- A young child's brain development suffers if the child is not permitted to live in a healthy, safe, and stimulating environment (Jenson, 2006). Researchers at Baylor College of Medicine found that children who don't play much or who are rarely touched develop brains 20 to 30 percent smaller than normal for their age (Nash, 1997).
- Research on the human brain suggests that three things contribute significantly to a child's well-being: (1) good prenatal care, (2) warm and loving attachments between young children and adults, and (3) positive, age-appropriate stimulation from the time of birth (Newberger, 1997).
- The connection between early experience and later experience is so strong that it led researchers to conclude that "early social and emotional experiences are the seeds of human intelligence" (Hancock & Wingert, 1997, p. 36).
- Neuroscientists have identified "windows of opportunity," particular time periods when the brain's circuitry matures. Different regions of the brain actively develop and mature according to certain timetables. During these periods, there is heightened sensitivity to environmental influences (Puckett, Marshall, & Davis, 1999).
- The child-centered, "whole child" practices of early childhood education are consistent with what neuroscience has identified as ways of enriching the brain (Jalongo, 2008).

Figure 10.3   Facts and Figures About Brain Research

who are in the gifted program may have mentors out in the community while others do not. Clearly, all children can benefit from using technology in creative ways and from good mentors. Yet schools often penalize children with an "eat your vegetables first" mentality about creative and artistic development. Often it is the opportunity for joyful creative expression that inspires learners to refine their skills.

Consider, for example, two children from different families who are learning to play the piano. Svetlana is an 8-year-old whose family immigrated to the United States from Russia. She has been taking lessons since she was 5, and has several talented musicians in her ancestry. Nevertheless, she says in complete candor to a visitor: "Please, just don't ask me to play the piano. I hate it." Zhu, the second child, first became interested in the piano as a toddler because she liked to sit on her grandfather's lap and experiment with the sounds made by the different keys. Sometimes they would sing songs together. Svetlana's parents believe that early, intensive drill on the technical skills will enable their child to realize her potential

1. **Curiosity:** A full-scale, active exploration of the world and ideas driven by the urge to make meaning and gain understanding.

Children have active imaginations and natural curiosity.

2. **Playfulness:** Experimenting with things and ideas in a spontaneous, intrinsically motivated way that is not bound by others' rules.

Children, even in the desperate circumstances of a war-torn country or natural disaster, manage to make playthings from the rubble.

3. **Creativity:** The ability to look at things differently, make surprising connections, and generate useful products.

Children are particularly adept at connecting the seemingly unconnected and creating interesting juxtapositions.

4. **Wonder:** Being awestruck by the world and astonished by what others might take for granted.

Children experience the world afresh and are amazed by what they encounter even when it seems commonplace to adults.

5. **Imagination:** Producing rich and varied images, even of things that do not exist.

Children's eidetic imagery—the richness of their mental images—is so strong that a frightening picture comes alive and nightmares seem real.

6. **Wisdom:** Delving beneath the surface to get to the heart of the matter.

Children have a fresh way of looking at things that often escapes their elders, who rely on years of experience.

7. **Inventiveness:** Producing surprising results from "hands-on" creativity.

Children are discoverers. They put the simplest materials to funny and sometimes bizarre uses. They play with the wrappings while the expensive gift sits idly by.

8. **Vitality:** Being awake to sensory input, responding to it fully, and actively engaged in experiences.

Children are noted for their energy levels and the passion with which they pursue their interests.

9. **Sensitivity:** Responding vividly to stimuli, thereby enriching what is experienced.

Children have a deep, yet naïve response to music, literature, and art.

10. **Flexibility:** Capitalizing on the plasticity of the mind.

Children move easily between fantasy and reality, between the inner world and outer world.

11. **Humor:** Breaking out of routine and leaving behind seriousness.

The child's sense of humor is at first slapstick, then incongruity, then word play.

12. **Joy:** Something that emanates from within when new connections, insights, feats, or skills are made.

The child finds delight in simple accomplishments.

Figure 10.4   Twelve Qualities of Genius in Every Child: Implications for Early Education
Note: Based on Armstrong (1998).

and surpass even the impressive achievements of her family members. There is little question that both children can play the piano at an advanced level; however, Svetlana's motivation and interest have been compromised by incessant drill and pressure. Which child is more likely to use music to enrich life? And who is more likely to develop the individual, interpretive style that is the hallmark of a great pianist? Teachers and parents must remember that although mastery of techniques is important, it should not be developed at the expense of creativity (Hope, 1990). Part of working effectively with diverse families is helping them to recognize this.

TEACHERS' ROLES AND RESPONSIBILITIES

Educators have been criticized for decades for failing to foster creative thinking and artistic expression in their students. In 1950, J. P. Guilford, who was noted for his research into the structure of the intellect, became the president of the American Psychological Association. In his address, he asked "Why is there so little apparent correlation between education and creative productiveness?" (Fasko, 2001). In 1970, Charles Silberman noted that it was impossible to spend any prolonged period visiting public school classrooms without being appalled by the destruction of spontaneity, the joy of learning, the pleasure of creating, and self-esteem. What has been done to change this situation during the last three decades? Some would argue that very little progress has been made because the conditions that support creativity still have not been met (see Figure 10.5).

In order to work effectively with diverse families, first, *recognize the family and cultural influences that shaped your self-image as a creative thinker*. What makes some teachers confident that they are creative thinkers? Why does the performance of some teachers improve with experience while the performance of others declines over the years? Figure 10.6 (p. 369) highlights the major influences on teachers' creativity.

It is interesting to reflect on the characteristics that are associated with creative teaching and how to develop them in yourself, something that Figure 10.7 (p. 370) guides you to do.

Second, *identify what gets in the way of creative thinking and engagement in the arts*. Imagine that you are assigned to write a lesson plan and urged to "be creative." Think about all of the influences that might inhibit you from doing your best. Your insecurity might come from:

- *Fear of taking a risk.* Often, college students do not feel sufficiently safe and secure to "break out" and take the risks associated with being different. External pressures such as grades, peer ridicule, or the censure of the instructor might make us overly fearful of making a mistake. Internal feelings, such as not wanting to appear foolish or not wanting to be noticed, also inhibit creativity.
- *Premature criticism.* Teachers sometimes reject ideas almost immediately. A student teacher might write a lesson plan and keep deleting what was

Environmental	Room arrangement that facilitates hands-on learning Independent access to materials Variety of media and resource materials
Mental	Flexible and stimulating environment Challenging (but not overwhelming) tasks Activities adapted to children's special needs
Emotional	Respect for children's contributions Support to take risks with new ideas and activities Honest, individualized praise
Developmental	Children's rates and styles of growth expected to vary Individual differences prized; cultural differences celebrated

Figure 10.5   Conditions That Support Creative Thought
Note: Data from Shallcross (1981).

➜ Education

Teachers without specific training in creativity are not well equipped to serve as models of creativity for their students.

Conversely, teachers who are well informed about creative thinking processes can exert a powerful influence on their students' work.

➜ Expectations

When teachers feel pressured to teach only the material that is tested, used to rank schools, or used to decide who is a "good" teacher, this inhibits their willingness to try new things.

Conversely, when teachers work in settings that expect and support new and interesting things from them, they are more likely to attempt new things and approach challenges positively.

➜ Resources

When materials are in very scarce supply, it can interfere with planning for instruction and providing opportunities to be creative.

Conversely, when inviting materials are readily available, teachers are more likely to put them to use in their classrooms.

➜ Recognition

When teachers' efforts to do more than follow the book and cover the material are disregarded, they sometimes give up and fall into the well-traveled ruts of marginal or "burned-out" teachers.

Conversely, when teachers gain the respect of their peers and leaders for daring to be different, they are more likely to continue to grow and develop as creative practitioners.

➜ Hope

When teachers feel oppressed by lack of freedom, they feel disrespected and become apathetic and disaffected.

Conversely, when teachers are given choices, challenges, and support, they are more likely to rise to the occasion.

➜ Opportunities

When teachers are deprived of opportunities for professional development in the area of creativity, they tend to teach the same things in the same ways, year after year.

Conversely, when teachers have opportunities to learn about and try out creative teaching strategies, they are more likely to expand their teaching repertoires beyond the ordinary.

➜ Rewards

When teachers struggle to do more than what is minimally required and do not receive intrinsic or extrinsic rewards, their motivation to teach creatively is diminished.

Conversely, when teachers enjoy the satisfaction of a job well done and the admiration of others, they feel validated, encouraged, and energized to continue teaching creatively.

Figure 10.6   Influences on Teachers' Creativity

Note: Based on Csikszentmihalyi (1996), Piirto (1998), and Rodd (1999).

written, struggling to make the plan perfect from the very start rather than playing with ideas. Only after many possibilities are generated should teachers begin to exercise their more judgmental side.

- *Need for control.* If educators follow the safe, predictable path, they feel more in control of the situation. Writing a plan that is dry and ordinary, yet meets the minimal requirements, is a way of exercising control over uncertainty. Similar concerns affect parents' and families' behavior. They may encourage

Nonconformist—Do I tend to behave, act, and think in unique ways? Am I capable of departing from routines, rules, and conventions? Am I committed to supporting children's creativity in spite of difficulties or other people's lack of support?

Inventor—When confronted with a daunting task, do I have the ability to generate a positive outcome through my resourcefulness and nonstereotypic thinking?

Self-Starter—Am I curious? Do I pursue my interests? Am I interested in knowing all that I can about something? Do I continue striving for a certain goal, not quitting until it is reached? Do I get involved in many different projects simultaneously?

Energizer—Am I willing to invest energy above and beyond what is required? Can I persuade others to join in?

Player—Do I create, understand, and take part in unexpected ideas and take pleasure in humor? Do I use humor effectively to deal with embarrassing or difficult situations?

Observer—Do I notice and remember details? Do I learn as much as possilbe by observing others?

Spontaneous—Do I have the capacity to respond quickly and appropriately to unfamiliar situations?

Figure 10.7   Will You Become a Creative Teacher? A Self-Assessment
Note: Based on Csikszentmihalyi (1996) and Dinca (1999).

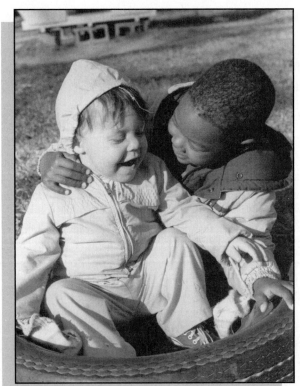

When adults embrace diversity, children emulate this behavior.

Leadership Through Advocacy

- Learn to articulate your beliefs about the value of creative expression and play, even to those who are skeptical or nonsupportive.
- Take action to defend children's right to safe and healthy opportunities for play by engaging in activities such as cleaning up a playground and painting the equipment.
- Band together with respected colleagues to propose programs and policies that support children's creativity and play.

Administrative Leadership

- Join a task force, committee, or service organization that focuses on children's creative expression and play.
- Revamp the curriculum to infuse more opportunities for children to express themselves creatively and have time to play.
- Lead a group of colleagues in taking action to make your center or school an environment more conducive to children's and teachers' creativity.

Community Leadership

- Work with the community to develop an attractive display of children's work at the mall, in the local bank, or at a festival or fair.
- Join a discussion group on the Internet and share what you have learned about children's creative expression and play with parents and families.
- Seek sources of funding support for arts projects, including business sponsorship, grants, and other means of financial backing for the arts.

Conceptual Leadership

- Write a position paper on some area of children's creative expression, have it reviewed carefully by experts, then post it on the Web.
- Develop an informative bulletin board, newsletter, flyer, or other means of communication that can be shared with the general public.
- Join a group of classmates and a faculty member in making a professional conference presentation on children's creative expression and play.

Leadership Through Career Development

- Join a professional organization that supports children's creative expression and play, such as the National Association for the Education of Young Children, the Association for Childhood Education International, or the Reggio Emilia network.
- Scan the professional journals, such as *Early Childhood Education Journal, Childhood Education,* and *Young Children,* and surf the Net regularly for new information from organizations such as the Council for Exceptional Children, Americans for the Arts, and Music Educators National Conference.
- Further your education by volunteering to offer arts experiences for children, participating in conference sessions on creativity and play, and pursuing an advanced degree.

Figure 10.8 Leadership Activities to Support Children's Creativity and the Arts
Note: Based on Kagan & Bowman (1997).

children to take the predictable route, jump to the right answer, or fear that support for creativity will spiral out of control and cause disobedience.

Third, we need to *embrace responsibility for promoting children's growth in creativity and the arts* by:

1. Keeping the interests of children and families uppermost in our minds when making decisions.
2. Respecting each child's culture, ethnicity, language, religion, age, disability, and gender.
3. Communicating, assessing, and intervening in fair, unbiased, and appropriate ways that combine caring about children with educating them.
4. Interacting with children and their families with compassion, wisdom, and competence.
5. Preparing children for a productive, meaningful place in society (Mortimer, 2004; Noddings, 2005).

Fourth, we must learn to *function as leaders in promoting creativity and the arts.* Teachers also bear responsibility for functioning as advocates, and Figure 10.8 (p. 371) provides guidelines for demonstrating your leadership in supporting creativity and the arts.

MEETING STANDARDS THROUGH MULTICULTURAL EDUCATION AND THE ARTS

As Charles Silberman (1970) stated nearly 40 years ago, "Education should prepare people not just to earn a living but to live a life—a creative, humane, and sensitive life" (p. 114). Take, for example, concerns about violence in schools and society.

Barbara Schwartz/Merrill

Changing demographics will increase diversity in classrooms.

From	To
Fear and Chaos ➜	**Joy and Control**

Example: A child may resist using finger paints because they are "messy" and the child has been told to stay neat, yet with protective clothing, encouragement, and experimentation, that same child can relish the opportunity to make a finger painting.

Boredom and Routine ➜	**Engagement and Surprise**

Example: Children are immersed in cartoon-style art at discount stores, as holiday decorations, at fast-food restaurants, and in the media, yet when they are given real works of art to examine closely and discuss, they break away from the ordinary and develop an aesthetic response to what is extraordinary and highly valued in society.

Frustration and Low Self-Esteem ➜	**Mastery and Pride in Attainment**

Example: When first learning a simple folk dance, children may find it confusing or awkward, yet when they have supportive guidance and opportunities to practice, they experience the joy of mastering the dance and performing it gracefully.

Other Directedness and External Evaluation ➜	**Self-Directedness and Self-Evaluation**

Example: Many of the questions and tasks that children encounter in school have one correct answer. Opportunities for creative expression give children greater responsibility for selecting tasks, pursuing them at their own pace, and evaluating both processes and products in terms of their personal satisfaction and sense of completeness.

Isolation and Exclusion ➜	**Belonging and Community**

Example: Many creative children are cast in the role of outsiders in a society that values conformity and compliance, yet with opportunities to creatively address problems, to pursue a passion in the arts, or to participate in dramatic play, the strengths and talents of students who do not fit someone else's mold can be revealed and appreciated.

Figure 10.9   The Humanizing Influence of Opportunities for Creative Expression

How might opportunities for creative expression support violence prevention efforts? The word *violence* originates in a word meaning "life force"; it has the same root word as *vital.* Originally, the word *violence* did not have the host of negative meanings that we attribute to it today. If we begin to think about violence as an outburst of life, we begin to see connections between creativity, or the life force put to positive use, and the contemporary understanding of violence, or the life force put to destructive purposes. The goal of education never should be to cause children to become emotionally "flat." Rather, it should channel their interests, passions, and curiosities into socially acceptable and productive outlets. As Charles Fowler (quoted in O'Neil, 1994) contends, "We are creatures of feeling as well as thought, and schools that recognize that basic fact and address it are better schools. . . . Our spirit needs as much nurturing as any other part of our mind. Schools that ignore it are cold and desolate places. Remember: If we fail to touch the humanity of students, we have not really touched them at all" (p. 4). Figure 10.9 illustrates the humanizing influence that creative expression and the arts can have on children.

Work with diverse families requires teachers who know them, care about them, and act accordingly (Banks, 1996). You can view the artifact "Family and Home Picture," which illustrates diversity, online at MyEducationLab. Culturally speaking, the purpose of the arts is "to destabilize fixed ideas and existing identities;

MyEducationLab

Go to MyEducationLab and select the topic "Family/Parent Involvement." Under Activities and Applications, view the artifact Family and Home Picture. *As you look at the artifact, think about how families influence children's creative development.*

TABLE 10.2 Levels of Multicultural Education and Implications for Creativity and the Arts

Levels	Definition	Connections with Creativity and the Arts
Level 1: Contributions	Some contributions to creativity and the arts are acknowledged and mentioned, but the curriculum does not change significantly.	Provide students with many examples of art forms from different cultures (see Artcyclopedia.com); introduce them to less well-known inventors and artists who may have been overlooked; and show respect for different art forms, for example, avoid referring to art as "primitive" or "naïve."
Level 2: Additive	Something more significant is added to the curriculum without altering the total program. As a result, these projects are not an "official" part of the curriculum and may be abandoned when personnel changes occur.	Consider schoolwide projects that focus on creative individuals and artists who were marginalized, such as African American inventors.
Level 3: Transformation	Multicultural perspectives are infused throughout the program and have resulted in major, enduring curricular changes.	Contributions become a centerpiece of the curriculum rather than an "add on"—for example, a community might make storytelling a strand that runs throughout the curriculum and across the grade levels or an ongoing school art gallery in a location where parents will see and respond to it (Moore, 2003).
Level 4: Decision Making and Social Activism	This level includes the previous three levels and extends beyond them by focusing on positive changes to society. It encourages students to make decisions and act upon the concepts, issues, or problems they have identified.	Children are encouraged to challenge the status quo in the arts. For example, a group of students in rural Appalachia might select expanding social recognition of folk art as their goal. At Levels 1 and 2, they might view examples of folk art and represent themselves using a traditional folk art form, such as a carving, a toy, a doll, or a quilt with the support of their community. Local artists could mentor the students in their chosen art form and students could work to gain media and community recognition for the artists at a folk art festival.

Note: Levels based on Banks, (1996).

to help us find a new way of seeing, of hearing, of thinking, of feeling . . . And to find from those experiences new ways of experiencing our communities, our neighbors, our society" (Nolan, quoted in Jones et al., 1996, p. 48). Table 10.2 above, summarizes four levels of multicultural education identified by Banks (1996) and ways to support them via creative thinking and arts-based learning.

To summarize, the visual arts support multicultural education by helping children understand (1) the relevance and significance of art in human experience, (2) the

Frequently Asked Questions About Creativity, Diverse Families, and Communities

Do creative children usually become creative adults?

Based on extensive study of the early life of geniuses, Howe (2004) concluded that their patterns of development as children did not differ drastically from those who matured into unexceptional adults. Predictions about which children will become highly creative and productive as adults are notoriously inaccurate because creative gifts and contributions develop over time and are influenced by purpose, play, and chance (Gruber & Davis, 1988). Creative capacities can be underdeveloped, diminished, and ruined. Creativity is a complex developmental system that is shaped by at least seven influences: (1) cognitive processes; (2) social and emotional processes; (3) family aspects, both while growing up and current; (4) education and preparation, both informal and formal; (5) characteristics of the domain and field; (6) sociocultural contextual aspects; and (7) historical forces, events, and trends (Feldman, 1999, pp. 171–172).

What is a genius?

Defining genius is difficult because although it is used to label a person, it actually refers to the person's major creative achievements; "it is an accolade rather than a description" (Howe, 2004, p. 106). "Geniuses are, to say the least, an extremely diverse group. Some think predominantly in words, others contemplate images; some geniuses are highly intuitive, others are sharply analytical in their reasoning. But where character and temperament are concerned, shared attributes are more common . . . terms such as *curious, determined* and *diligent* apply to almost all highly creative achievers whose early lives I have explored . . . it is hard to think of any geniuses who have not relished hard work, or who have not been dogged in pursuit of their aims" (Howe, 2004, pp. 105, 110).

It seems that creativity is mainly innate, that some people are creative while others simply are not. Do you agree?

Creativity is a potential. Other traits such as interest, motivation, planning, attention, persistence, leadership, self-confidence, and self-esteem affect creativity (Amabile, 2001; Naglieri, 2001; Robinson & Clinkenbeard, 1998; Ryan & Deci, 2000). Stunning creative thought does not simply appear. Rather, it is the product of years of learning, thought, and preparation (Weisberg, 1993), and it is common to refer to the "3/10 rule"—at least 3 hours of practice per day for 10 years in order to become an expert in a field (Sternberg, 2004). Creative thought is domain specific and affected by the particulars of the situation (Han & Marvin, 2002). A person who is highly creative in one domain and environment, for example, has "street smarts" may not shine in another situation, such as the corporate boardroom. Therefore, children need to experience a wide range of interesting activities in order to discover their creative potential in different contexts.

What can we learn from geniuses?

Perhaps the most important lesson is that being smart is not enough. "The lives and experiences of geniuses provide numerous demonstrations of the necessity for human qualities that go beyond the narrowly cognitive . . . little of enormous significance is achieved in the absence of diligence and the capacity for sustained hard work" (Howe, 2004, p. 117). Evidently, it is not a single, stunning talent that explains the lives of world-class geniuses, prodigies, and innovators; rather, it is a repertoire of strengths and a confluence of cultural circumstances that allow expression of remarkable achievements (Howe, 2004). We must abandon the myth of the lone genius and regard genius as multifaceted and socially constructed (Shavinina & Ferrari, 2004). For practical suggestions on how to increase creativity by emulating geniuses, see the work of Michael Gelb and Tony Buzan.

Are there ways to make yourself more creative?

Few people possess "Big C Creativity," or the eminent creativity of celebrated geniuses, while many possess "little c creativity," or problem-solving ability that is more widely distributed among people (Craft, 2000; Nakamura & Csikszentmihalyi, 2001; Ripple, 1989; Runco, 1996). Yet the contributions of everyday problem solving are so widespread and numerous that they may be just as valuable as the single, brilliant breakthrough. In Runco's (2004) review of the research, he identifies three general tactics that enable people to think more creatively: (1) change of perspective (taking time away from a task, incubating, traveling, or working backward); (2) use of analogies (developing productive mental models that lead to new insights, such as Eli Whitney inventing the cotton gin after watching a cat trying to catch a chicken through a fence); and (3) approaches that recombine (borrowing ideas from another field, such as Jean Piaget drawing from his studies of biology to arrive at cognitive developmental theory).

MyEducationLab

*Go to MyEducationLab
and select the topic
"Diversity." Under
Activities and
Applications, view the
artifact* Tina's Self-
Portrait. *As you look at
the artifact, think about
the genius of childhood.*

perspectives posed by people of various backgrounds, (3) the commonality and diversity of humankind, and (4) the child's personal power as a creator of and responder to art, as well as the responsibilities that come with that power (Delacruz, 1995b). Use the artifact "Tina's Self-Portrait" online at MyEducationLab to reflect on children's creativity.

 ## CONCLUSION

Richards (2001) contends that society needs a general shift toward greater creative openness and growth, not only because it is an important form of adaptation in a complex, chaotic society but also because it offers advantages for physical and psychological health to the individual. Thus, learning to think creatively and express oneself artistically are life skills; they are important ways to prepare children for whatever lies ahead. In the past, in the present, and in the future, our most enlightened educational visions will be connected by the common thread of imagination, creative thought, and enhanced opportunities for artistic expression. As we look ahead, it will no doubt be possible to trace society's greatest innovations and achievements back to an abiding respect for creative thought processes during childhood. For when we value creative thinking and creative expression in society, it becomes part of our social consciousness and social capital. Society then protects its reserves of creativity by fashioning networks of support that are capable of instilling confidence, promoting resilience, and multiplying ways of being intelligent in every person that commence in childhood and continue throughout life.

Effective and ethical educators in a culturally pluralistic and democratic society have a responsibility to make a commitment to all children and to respect all the cultural groups and communities that those children represent. Without that commitment and respect, educators are incapable of addressing the needs of the diverse groups of students entrusted to their care. As educators, we need to bear in mind that, as Albert Einstein observed, "All the valuable things, material, spiritual, and moral, which we receive from society can be traced back through countless generations to certain creative individuals" (quoted in Gelb, 2002, p. 17).

 ## CHAPTER SUMMARY

1. Creative expression and the arts are influenced by the social contexts in which they occur. The culture not only defines but also determines what "counts" as high ability, achievement, creativity, and art.

2. Parents, families, peers, instructors, and other significant others exert a powerful influence on the child's creative growth and artistic development. Much of the experimentation, practice, and participation in creative thinking and arts activities occurs in out-of-school settings.

3. Talent is important, but it is not enough. Even the most gifted individuals need systems of social support in order to realize their potential. Intelligence as it is commonly defined is not sufficient to result in high achievement either. Many "extracognitive" variables—those that rely on talents and gifts beyond knowledge—contribute to achievement and genius.

4. There is a need to teach children in ways consistent with what we know about the functioning of the human brain. Research suggests that young

children learn in a natural and integrative manner. Play, social interaction, and psychological safety and freedom all contribute to children's learning and creative expression.

5.   Promoting creative thinking and arts-based learning is a major way of supporting the goals of multicultural education.

Discuss: Contributions of Creativity and the Arts to Society

1.   "It has become increasingly clear that millions of contemporary adults . . . have grown up with little or no grounding in the arts, and do not even consider participating in an artistic discipline or attending an arts event when choosing among their leisure and entertainment options" (McDaniel & Thorn, 1997, p. 6). Would you classify yourself among these adults? Why or why not? What might the implications of rejecting the arts be for your values and attitudes as a teacher?

2.   President Franklin Delano Roosevelt once said, "Inequality may linger in the world of material things, but great music, great literature, great art, and the wonders of science are, and should be, open to all." Describe some practical ways that you could use your influence to promote equity in the arts and make families aware of opportunities within the community.

3.   At what point does parental challenge and support cross the line and become an instance of a parent "living through" a child? What is the difference between the "stage mom or dad" and a supportive parent? What goals need to be balanced to prevent children from being exploited? What would you do or say to help a child if it was obvious that the child's parent or family had become obsessed with making their child a star, to the detriment of the child?

Appendix A

Cross-Referenced Standards Guide

This guide identifies which creative arts topics correlate to specific national content area standards.

	Social Studies	Mathematics	Science/ Technology	Literacy	Language Arts
Creative Thought	pp. 93–97	pp. 93–97	pp. 26, 93–97	pp. 26–27, 93–97, 250–251	pp. 26–27, 93–97, 250–251
Drama	pp. 226–228	pp. 93, 226–228	pp. 226–228	pp. 226–228, 250	pp. 226–228, 250
Games	pp. 66–67, Appendix C	pp. 66–67, Appendix C	pp. 66–67, Appendix C	pp. 26–27, Appendix C	pp. 26–27, 66–67, Appendix C
Inventions/ Discovery/ Investigation	pp. 27–28, 97, 243–245, 269	pp. 27–28, 93, 252, 269	pp. 27–28, 93, 250, 269	pp. 27–28, 97, 269	pp. 27–28, 97, 269
Multiple Art Forms	pp. 93–97, 250, 308–312, 361–363	pp. 93–97, 250, 308–312, 361–363	pp. 93–97, 252, 308–312, 361–363	pp. 93–97, 252, 253, 308–312, 362–363	pp. 93–97, 250, 252, 253, 308–312, 361–363
Music/Dance/ Movement	pp. 93, 185–191	pp. 185–191	pp. 185–191	pp. 185–191	pp. 185–191
Play	pp. 66–67, 269	pp. 66–67, 250	pp. 66–67	pp. 66–67, 250	pp. 66–67
Puppetry	pp. 212–215	pp. 212–215	pp. 67, 212–215	pp. 67, 212–215	pp. 212–215
Tableau	pp. 220–221	pp. 220–221	pp. 220–221	pp. 220–221	pp. 220–221
Visual Arts	pp. 142–145, 249	pp. 142–145	pp. 142–145	pp. 94, 142–145	pp. 94, 142–145

Appendix B

Published Rating Scales to Evaluate Preschool Settings

Frost, J. L. (1986). Playground rating system: Ages 3–8. In J. S. McKee (Ed.), *Play: Working partner of growth* (pp. 66–67). Wheaton, MD: Association for Childhood Education International.

The rating system contains 39 items to evaluate three different areas of playground quality. It evaluates what the playground should contain, the condition and safety of the equipment, and the degree and quality of challenge and learning opportunities for children. Each item is rated on a scale from 0 ("Does Not Exist") to 5 ("Excellent; All Elements"). A score may be obtained for each individual area, as well as a total playground rating score.

Harms, T., & Clifford, R. M. (1989). *Family day care rating scale.* New York: Teachers College Press. 39 pages.

This scale defines family day care comprehensively and can be used for evaluating family day care settings. It provides ratings for space, materials, and learning activities among the six categories addressed to ensure that the environment is developmentally appropriate for young children. Each item is described in four levels of quality ranging from "Inadequate" (does not meet custodial needs) to "Excellent" (high-quality care).

Harms, T., & Clifford, R. M. (1995). *School-age care environment rating scale.* New York: Teachers College Press.

The SACERS provides a resource for identifying high-quality environments offered by schools and other organizations. The scale contains 49 items; organized within seven categories that include Space and Furnishings, Health and Safety, Activities, Interactions, Program Structure, and Staff Development.

Harms, T., Clifford, R. M., & Cryer, D. (1998). *Early childhood environment rating scale* (Rev. ed.). New York: Teachers College Press. 44 pages.

This rating scale provides guidelines for assessing the quality of the physical and social environments for young children in seven areas. Detailed guidelines are provided for room arrangement, furnishings, and displays, as well as for creative activities.

Harms, T., Cryer, D., & Clifford, R. M. (1990). *Infant/toddler environment rating scale.* New York: Teachers College Press. 48 pages.

This rating scale contains assessment criteria for children in group care up to 30 months of age. Criteria for furnishings and displays for children, space, learning activities, and program structure are among the seven categories rated from "Inadequate" (not meeting custodial care needs) to "Excellent" (describing high-quality care).

Jones, E. (1977). *Dimensions of teaching-learning environments.* Pasadena, CA: Pacific Oaks.

This rating scale describes the physical setting and the teacher's behavior along four dimensions: soft/hard, simple/complex, intrusion/seclusion, and high mobility/low mobility. It views these dimensions along a continuum and explores the possibilities of arranging environments within them.

National Association for the Education of Young Children. (1998). *Accreditation criteria and procedures of the National Association for the Education of Young Children.* Washington, DC: Author.

Contains standards for early childhood programs set by the profession. A portion of these standards describes nine aspects of the physical environment. The scale focuses on the arrangement of the environment, selection of materials, and interactions between adults and children.

Appendix C

Noncompetitive Games for Children

BALL GAMES

Preschoolers/Kindergartners

Call Ball
Form a circle with one child in the center who tosses the ball while calling another child's name. This child tries to catch the ball after the first bounce. The child continues with other children.

Basket Ball
Children stand before a plastic basket and toss the ball into the basket. The game may be played individually, in pairs, or in groups. Emphasis is on trying to hit the mark rather than keeping score, so move the basket closer or farther away to adjust the challenge level.

School-Age Children

Letter or Number Ball
As players pass a small ball around a circle, have them say a letter or a number. Players may count or say the alphabet in unison if they go in order.

Tennis
Make "rackets" out of a nylon stocking stretched over a coat hanger. Children can bat a ping-pong ball back and forth using the racket.

Lap Ball
Players form a circle and sit close to one another, with shoulders touching. They try to pass a ball around the circle from lap to lap without using their hands.

Sound Ball
Stand in a circle and hold an *imaginary ball*. Make eye contact with a child across the circle and toss the imaginary ball to that child while making an accompanying

sound, such as tossing a very heavy ball and making a groaning sound with it. The child who catches the imaginary ball passes it to another child and makes a new sound. Focus on weight, size, and texture.

QUIET GAMES
Preschoolers/Kindergartners
Nursery Rhymes
Say the rhyme and follow up with action. For example: "Jack and Jill went up (children reach up high) the hill. Jack falls down (children touch the ground)." Other favorite nursery rhymes include "Humpty Dumpty," "Mary Had a Little Lamb," and "Baa Baa Black Sheep."

Toyshop
Have children pretend they are toys. When called on, each child imitates the sound and action of the toy and continues until someone guesses the name of the toy.

Clap and Tap Names
In this game, say a child's name and have the group repeat it several times, establishing a rhythm for the name. Then have the children clap the rhythm of the name while they say it. Ask them to use their feet while saying the name and, last, to move forward on that rhythm.

School-Age Children
On My Way to School . . .
Form a circle with one child in the center who says, "On my way to school this morning, I saw . . . " and then imitates what he or she saw. Others guess the imitation. The one guessing correctly goes into the center, and the game begins again.

Buzz
Players take turns counting one number at a time. Whenever they have to say a number with seven in it, they say buzz instead. If a player accidentally says *seven* (or *seventeen,* or *twenty-seven*), then the game begins again at number one.

Guess My Numbers
Have pairs of children trying to guess each other's birthdays, number of siblings, birthday month and day, number of letters in their last name, the digits in their telephone number, and any other number-related fact that children can think of. They can give hints such as higher or lower to help lead their partner to the correct answer.

SINGING GAMES
Preschoolers/Kindergartners
Charlie over the Water
Players join hands in a circle. One player, Charlie, is in the center. The circle moves to the left while chanting:

> *Charlie over the water,*
> *Charlie over the sea,*

Charlie caught a blackbird
But he can't catch me.

On the word *me* the players quickly squat. Charlie tries to tag a player before he or she gets into the squat position. The tagged child then becomes "Charlie."

Round and Round Went the Gallant Ship

In this game, children dance around in a circle with clasped hands, reciting the following verse and "bobbing" down quickly as the ship goes to the bottom of the sea:

Three times round went our gallant ship,
And three times round went she;
Three times round went our gallant ship,
Then she sank to the bottom of the sea.

A tumble as the ship goes down adds much to the spirit of the play.

Did You Ever See a Lassie?

One child is in the middle of a circle. Other children grasp hands and circle around the child in the center while singing the first two lines. During lines three and four, the children drop hands and imitate the child in the middle, who thinks up some special way to hop.

Did you ever see a lassie (laddie), a lassie, a lassie,
Did you ever see a lassie, do this way and that?
Do this way and that way, and this way and that way,
Did you ever see a lassie do this way and that?

School-Age Children

Riggety Jig

The children form a standing circle. One child begins to skip inside the circle to the following tune:

As I was going down the street
Down the street, down the street
As I was going down the street
Hi Ho, Hi Ho, Hi Ho.

A handsome fellow (pretty girl) I chanced to meet
Chanced to meet, chanced to meet
A handsome fellow (pretty girl) I chanced to meet
Hi Ho, Hi Ho, Hi Ho.

With the chosen partner, both children skip around the circle to the following tune:

Riggety jig, jig, and away we go
Away we go, away we go
Riggety jig, jig, and away we go
Hi Ho, Hi Ho, Hi Ho.

Others clap the tune.

Singing Syllables

After one player leaves the room, the rest of the group decides on a word to sing. If the word is *November*, for example, some players will sing "No No No," some will sing "vem vem vem," and the rest will sing "ber ber ber," all at the same time.

Now the player who left the room returns and tries to figure out what the word is. Everyone gets a turn to be the guesser, with, of course, a new word sung each time.

RUNNING GAMES
Preschoolers/Kindergartners
Squirrel and Nut
The children sit in a circle with heads down and hands open. One child, the squirrel, drops the "nut" (a piece of chalk or crayon) into the hands of any other child. That child immediately gets up and tries to catch the squirrel, who is safe by reaching the place of the second child. If not caught, the other child becomes the squirrel.

Cat and Mice
The cat hides behind something. Four or five "mice" creep up to the cat's hiding place and start scratching on the floor. Their scratching is the signal for the cat to start chasing them, and they are safe only on reaching their holes (places). Any mouse who is tapped becomes the cat. Other mice are then chosen, and the game begins again.

Drop the Handkerchief
One child runs around the circle and drops a handkerchief behind another player. That player picks up the handkerchief and runs around the circle in the direction opposite to that of the first player. The one who reaches the vacant place left in the circle becomes "it." Then the game is repeated.

Musical Chairs
One version of musical chairs is to play music and have children find a chair *or* a lap when the music stops. A chair is removed each time, but everyone finds a seat (by sitting on a lap).

School-Age Children
Numbers Change
Players stand in a large circle and are numbered consecutively. One player, in the center, calls two numbers (not his or her own). The center player tries to secure one of their places. The one who is left without a place now becomes the center player.

In the classroom, the number caller (who also has a number) stands in front of the room and calls two numbers. While players change places, the caller tries to take a seat vacated by one of the runners whose number was called.

Kitty in the Corner
The children form a circle on the floor. Four chairs are placed in four corners of a square. A fifth child is in the middle. When the teacher calls "Kitty in the corner," the children in the chairs change places while the child in the center seeks to get into one of the chairs. The displaced child then chooses someone to take his or her place until all have had a turn.

Squirrels in Trees
The group is divided and numbered in threes. Numbers 1 and 2 join hands to represent the tree. Number 3 is the squirrel and stands in the circle formed by the other two. There should be one or more odd squirrels without trees. The groups of threes are scattered over the play space. At a signal from a leader or the teacher, the squirrels attempt to get into trees. Only one squirrel is allowed in one tree at the same time. Someone is always left without a tree. As soon as all trees are full, the game is repeated.

PARTNER GAMES
Preschoolers/Kindergartners
Repeat
One player says a word that the other player repeats. Continue repeating the same word until one player wants to stop, which is the tricky part.

Finish My Action
One player begins an imaginary action, such as brushing teeth or raking leaves. When that player stops, the partner finishes the action. Then the partners switch roles.

Parachute Ball
Have several children hold up the handles on a colorful parachute and have adults nearby the parachute. Place a ball in the center of the parachute so everyone has to work together to launch the ball in the air. Talk about what to do to get the ball higher in the air.

School-Age Children
Copycat
With a partner, decide who will be the mirror and who will be the copycat. Players must face each other as they stay together mirroring actions.

Puppeteers
One player is the puppet on the ground, unable to move. Along comes the puppeteer, who brings the puppet to life with pretend strings. The puppeteer pulls the strings, and the puppet responds to every tug. Allow everyone a chance to be the puppeteer as well as to be the puppet.

Ali Baba and the Forty Thieves
Two players stand facing each other a few feet apart. One of the players sings the words "Ali Baba and the forty thieves" to any made-up tune, at the same time doing a hand movement, such as clapping. When the singer is finished, the second player repeats the song and the motions exactly; at the same time, the first player sings the phrase again and does something different with his or her hands—hitting one arm with the opposite hand, for example.

For the next round, the second player must copy this second set of movements, along with continuing to sing, and so on, with both players singing "Ali Baba and the forty thieves" over and over, each doing a different hand movement. The activity continues until one of the players forgets the line.

What Are You Doing?
A child pantomimes an action, such as eating ice cream. The person next to him asks, "What are you doing?" and that person answers by naming a different activity, such as planting seeds. The child who asks the question then mimes planting seeds and the game continues around the circle with different actions mimed.

Machines and More
Each player as part of a small group works together to create a collaborative pantomime that represents different machines, such as a dishwasher, car, bicycle, or computer. The groups work for a few minutes to agree on roles and what to do; the others guess the machine being pantomimed.

REFERENCES

Crawford, L. (2004). *Lively learning: Using the arts to teach the K–8 curriculum.* Greenfield, MA: Northeast Foundation for Children.

Gregson, B. (1984). *The outrageous outdoor games book.* Carthage, IL: Fearon.

Kamii, C., & DeVries, R. (1980). *Group games in early education: Implications for Piaget's theory.* Washington, DC: National Association for the Education of Young Children.

Orlick, T. (1978, 1982). *The cooperative sports and games book* and *The second cooperative sports and games book.* New York: Pantheon.

Riley, D., San Juan, R., Klonker, J., & Ramminger, A. (2008). *Social & emotional development: Connecting science and practice in early childhood settings.* St. Paul, MN: Redleaf Press.

Rowe, S., & Humphries, S. (1994). *Playing around: Activities and excursions for social and cooperative learning.* London: Forbes.

Sobel, J. (1983). *Everybody wins: Non-competitive games for young children.* New York: Walker.

Appendix D

Case Study: Dittos and Elegant Costumes

Case methodology is a form of problem-based instruction for adults. Cases help learners experience situations that they are *likely to experience* in their professional settings. Use this case to help you analyze problems of communicating about play to parents and colleagues, to set goals about play for your own professional setting, and to share your ideas about appropriate ways to respond to parental concerns about too much play in the classroom.

DITTOS AND ELEGANT COSTUMES

"What do you think of this, Clara?" asked her principal, setting a three-page single-spaced letter from a parent in front of Clara just a few minutes before school began one morning. Clara, her assistant, and her student teacher were busy preparing the room for the students' arrival, and the contents of the letter came as a complete surprise to her. As she read she felt her anger rise and a flush move from her neck up to her cheek then to her forehead as she tried to hold on to some sense of composure.

"We want Lauren moved from Miss Sparks' kindergarten class immediately," the letter began. "There is no comparison between the two classes. All Lauren does is play, play, play. She is not learning a thing. The class never does anything. The children in Mrs. Wolfe's class put on a play just last week with elegant costumes. Each child had memorized long parts and lots of songs. Our neighbor's child is in Mrs. Wolfe's class, and his pictures come home looking like they are supposed to. And the ditto sheets that they do are really helping him learn."

There was more, but Clara looked up at the principal with hurt in her eyes. "Lauren's parents just don't understand. They don't want to understand that there are other ways of teaching young children besides elaborate productions and ditto sheets—perhaps even better ways. What shall we do?"

"I don't know, Clara. I need to think about it for awhile. But I know that I will need to talk with Lauren's parents soon."

"I have talked with them so many times myself," said Clara, "but somehow it just doesn't do any good. I hate it, being put on the defensive this way."

The principal left, leaving Clara to try to salvage what remained of her morning. Soon the children arrived, and she became swept up in the momentum of the day's activities. She had no time to reflect on her own teaching philosophy and style until much later, during free choice activity time. She looked out over her class busily engaged in learning activities of their own choosing: on the floor, at tables, standing up, sitting down, moving around, quiet and chatty.

Her eyes caught Jenny. Jenny was up to her elbows in soapsuds, her face intent, her eyes sparkling. There was a daub of white at the end of her nose. "A, B, C, D, E," Jenny sang to herself as she wrote letters in the soap on the table's surface.

Clara walked over to Tommy. His eyebrows were puckered, and his whole countenance concentrated on his task. Tommy was hammering a nail at the woodworking table.

"Look, Miss Sparks! With one nail, the pieces wiggle. Two nails hold it steady," he exclaimed.

Sally and Louise then approached Clara, their heads covered with scarves, each carrying a basket.

"We're on our way to Grandma's house, Miss Sparks," said Louise. "Would you like a cookie?"

"Only if you'll be careful never to talk with strangers," replied Clara.

"Oh, we won't. We never do," the girls answered, moving on again around the room, the path invisible to all but their own eyes.

Clara continued to watch the children, jotting down a note here and there for her anecdotal records, involving herself where necessary to keep the flow of learning strong and creative. As she worked, she felt her confidence return, and at the end of the free choice time she continued her day with renewed vigor. She liked what she was doing. She was convinced that her child-centered approach to teaching was right for children.

On the way home that afternoon Clara gathered her anecdotal records about Lauren. She needed to touch base with the principal before leaving the building to clarify her own role in the matter and to find out what the principal planned to do next.

She walked out past the other kindergarten room with its displays of children's work on the walls, each one a carbon copy of the next.

"Good night," Clara called to her colleague, Mrs. Wolfe, still in her classroom.

"Oh, Clara, could we talk a minute?" Mrs. Wolfe answered. Clara stopped and went in.

"I don't know how to say this, Clara, so I'll just say it," Mrs. Wolfe began. "Lauren's mother stopped in to see me today and told me that she asked to have Lauren moved to my room. She said that many of her neighbors feel the same way about you, and that the discussions about kindergarten in the neighborhood are angry ones. They're out to get you, Clara, and I thought you'd want to know."

Clara looked at her colleague, stunned. . . .

Study Questions

Think about the above case and write down your thoughts about these questions. Be prepared to use your responses to share with your group at another class meeting.

1. What is the problem here? Why? Explain what you mean.
2. What are the issues in this case? Explain. Give an example from the case to illustrate each one.
3. How powerful is the neighborhood gossip mill? What are some appropriate ways to deal with it?

4. To what and to whom is Clara responsible? Explain.
5. What is the role of the principal? Why?
6. If you were Clara, what would you do and why?

Source: Courtesy of George Mason University Case Writing Team.

Appendix E

Resources for Creative Materials

SELECTING AND USING SAFE PLAY MATERIALS

Bronson, M. (1995). *The right stuff for children birth to age 8.* Washington, DC: National Association for the Education of Young Children.
Provides a detailed list of age-appropriate materials that are organized by different types of play.

Moyer, J. (Ed.). (1995). *Selecting educational equipment and materials for school and home.* Wheaton, MD: Association for Childhood Education International.
Contains lists of materials and equipment for classrooms for children ages birth through age 10 as well as a listing of developmentally appropriate materials that promote each type of play.

U.S. Consumer Product Safety Commission. (1993, 1994). *Which toy for which child? A consumer's guide for selecting suitable toys: Ages birth through five* and *Which toy for which child? A consumer's guide for selecting suitable toys: Ages six through twelve.*
List basic safety guidelines and age-appropriate toys and materials. For additional information, write to: U.S. Consumer Product Safety Commission, Washington, DC 20207.

FREE CLASSROOM MATERIALS

For 120 decks of cards and 100 sets of dice to use as number cards for math and that are free of charge, write a letter stating you are a teacher and would like to have the cards and dice for use in your classroom. Include your name and address and send to:

Sands Hotel-Casino
136 S. Kentucky Ave.
Atlantic City, NJ 08401 (Allow 4 months for processing your request.)

FOLKLIFE AND CULTURAL ARTIFACTS

For advisory information on folklife resources and cultural artifacts, contact the following national, regional, or local agencies.

National Agencies

American Folklife Center
Library of Congress
101 Independence Ave. S.E.
Washington, DC 20540-4610
(202) 707-5510

New York Center for Urban Folk Culture
72 E. 1st St.
New York, NY 10003
(212) 529-1955

Regional Agencies

Southern Arts Federation
1401 Peachtree St. N.E., Suite 460
Atlanta, GA 30309
(404) 874-7244

Western Folklife Center
P.O. Box 1570
Elko, NV 89803
(775) 738-7508

State and Community-Based Agencies

Most states and local communities support a Council on the Arts that should be able to assist you with materials and other useful resources for classroom applications. Be sure you tell the contact person you are an early childhood educator.

Local Community Resources for Free, Recyclable, and Usable Materials

Use these materials for projects and other activities. Be sure to tell your source what you are looking for and why you need it. Most community businesses are eager to help. Try the following resources:

Carpet and Flooring Stores for carpet scraps and samples, linoleum, tiles, and wallpaper books

Drugstores for plastic containers, pill bottles, vials, and display boards

Ice Cream Stores for cardboard containers and plastic spoons

Office Supply Stores for assorted envelopes, supplies, surplus paper and forms, damaged but safe good, outdated boxes, Styrofoam pieces

Remember, too, that the families are the best resources for home recyclables such as plastic lids and containers, egg cartons, meat trays, assorted containers, and plastic cartons.

Glossary

Note to the student: A glossary should be used to help you remember terms with which you are familiar. For a deeper understanding of any of these terms, we encourage you to reread the chapter sections in which those terms appear. The chapter reference is in parentheses.

active learning Concrete experiences that are "hands-on," challenging, and relevant to the learner. (Chapter 2)

adventure or "junk" playgrounds Collections of tools and materials that allow children to build, create, and pretend using these items outdoors. (Chapter 7)

aesthetic Having to do with feelings, ideas, and perceptions about beauty. (Chapter 5)

affective Describes feelings or emotional responses. (Chapter 5)

autocratic Demanding obedience, following specific rules, and imposing inflexible standards on behavior. (Chapter 3)

behaviorism The view that a person's environment is the most important variable in shaping his or her development. (Chapter 3)

brainstorming Generating as many ideas as possible without evaluating them in order to enhance creativity. (Chapter 6)

center-based classroom A classroom arranged into various areas each containing interesting and accessible materials that offer children choices and support their independence. (Chapter 7)

child-centered Describes activities and programs that base decisions and policies on the needs of the children and place concerns about the learners first. (Chapter 7)

classical theories Theories about play that sought to explain the causes and purposes of play from the nineteenth century through World War I. (Chapter 2)

climate The feeling created by a learning environment. (Chapter 7)

cognitive Having to do with knowledge, understanding, and intellectual growth. (Chapter 5)

cognitive-development theory Jean Piaget's view of how children's intellectual abilities develop and progress through a series of stages. (Chapter 2)

complex units Units with subparts made of two totally different elements for children to manipulate or invent. (Chapter 7)

conflict resolution A problem-solving process enabling children to understand and resolve their disputes or disagreements peacefully. (Chapter 3)

construction materials Varied materials that children can combine and recombine to build something. (Chapter 8)

constructive play Creating or engaging in problem-solving behavior according to a preconceived plan. (Chapter 2)

constructivism The belief that children are more than passive recipients of information and actively build their own understandings. Based on Piaget's cognitive-developmental theory. (Chapter 3)

controlled scribbles Scribbles with a definite shape that are produced when the child has better control over the writing implement. (Chapter 4)

convergent Describes materials or experiences that lead children to think about a single answer or one right way of arriving at a solution. (Chapter 8)

cooperative learning Working collaboratively in a group to achieve a common goal. (Chapter 3)

creative/contemporary playgrounds Superstructures with movable parts that are action-oriented, provide safe underneath surfaces, and promote all forms of play. (Chapter 7)

creative teachers Educators who are committed to supporting children's play and facilitating children's creative expression. (Chapter 3)

creativity A thinking and responding process that involves connecting with our previous experience, responding to stimuli, and generating at least one unique combination. (Chapter 1)

democratic Having high expectations, understanding child development, showing and expecting respect, allowing decision making, and setting reasonable limits for behavior and practices. (Chapter 3)

developmentally appropriate materials Materials, experiences, and activities that are carefully matched to the children's developmental levels. (Chapter 8)

divergent Describes materials and experiences designed to elicit many different student responses that promote exploration, experimentation, and problem-solving. (Chapter 8)

dramatic play The child's use of props, plot, and roles to symbolize real or imaginary experiences. Also referred to as pretend, fantasy, make-believe, or symbolic play. Dramatic play is typical of 2- to 7-year-olds. (Chapter 2)

enactive stage The developmental stage during which physical activity and music are intertwined. (Chapter 5)

enactment Adopting actions, feelings, thoughts, and behaviors of people in particular situations. This ability typically begins at age 3. (Chapter 6)

formal or scripted drama   The most structured dramatic form, which includes a prepared script used in a practiced production and is viewed by an audience. (Chapter 6)

functional play   Simple, pleasurable, repeated movements with objects, people, and language to learn new skills or to gain mastery of a physical or mental skill. Also referred to as sensorimotor, practice, or exercise play and typical of infants and toddlers. (Chapter 2)

game   A form of play in which children follow a set of predetermined rules and procedures and assign players specific roles. (Chapter 8)

gross motor materials   Materials designed to foster large muscle activity and coordination. (Chapter 8)

hands-on materials   Manipulatives that children can use to enhance their understanding and learning; promote learning by doing. (Chapter 6)

hollow blocks   Large wooden blocks with an opening for carrying. (Chapter 8)

humanism   The belief that people are capable of controlling their lives through choice, creativity, and self-realization. (Chapter 3)

iconic stage   The developmental stage during which children use pictures and real objects to represent ideas and experiences. (Chapter 5)

imagination   The ability to form rich and varied mental images or concepts of people, places, things, and situations that are not present. (Chapter 1)

indirect guidance   Child-centered strategies that teachers use to plan, arrange, and manage people and classroom space, materials, and schedules. (Chapter 3)

informal drama   Spontaneous enactments that include dramatic and sociodramatic play, pantomime, and movement activities. (Chapter 6)

investigative play   Actively exploring and experimenting during play. (Chapter 3)

learner-centered art   Allowing children to direct their own work, valuing the process as much as the product, and fostering originality rather than conformity. (Chapter 4)

manipulative materials   Concrete materials that aid small muscle activity in the fingers and hands, basic concepts, and eye-hand coordination. (Chapter 7)

medium   The means or channel through which the artist conveys a message. (Chapter 4)

modern theories   Theories of play, prominent after World War I, that emphasize the consequences of play for children. (Chapter 2)

multicultural education   Learning that respects and celebrates children's diversity (ethnic, racial, religious). (Chapter 6)

naming of scribbling   Children's verbal labeling of a scribble they have produced. (Chapter 4)

natural and everyday materials   Materials with specific nonplay purposes—such as rocks, leaves, sand, buttons, and pots and pans—that children can use to employ imaginative and divergent thinking and to imitate and model adult roles. (Chapter 8)

nonrepresentational drawing   A stage in children's drawing in which drawings do not resemble the items being represented. (Chapter 4)

one-way communication   A focus on messages from the school to the family. (Chapter 3)

permissive   Having a disinterested attitude that results in an inconsistent environment and fails to promote children's self-control. (Chapter 3)

play-debrief-replay   Wassermann's three-step model for organizing instruction and challenging primary-grade children's divergent thinking. (Chapter 3)

practice theory   A theory that proposes that play prepares children for the future roles and responsibilities needed to survive in their culture. (Chapter 2)

preschematic   Describes children's drawings that are just beginning to represent the object being depicted, yet are difficult for adults to interpret without the child's explanation. (Chapter 4)

process   An emphasis on the way something (such as a piece of artwork) is produced, including the problem-solving strategies used and the originality or inventiveness exhibited. (Chapter 4)

project   An in-depth study that is usually initiated, planned, and evaluated by the children. (Chapter 3)

prop boxes or dramatic play kits   Collections of real items or props that have a relation to one another. For example, a chef's hat, apron, cookware, and plastic food could be in a prop box for a restaurant center. (Chapter 6)

psychoanalytic theory   A theory that perceives play as an important outlet for emotional release and for developing self-esteem as children learn to control their thoughts, bodies, objects, and social behaviors. (Chapter 2)

random scribbling   Random marks that are produced by toddlers when the writing implement happens to make contact with the writing surface. (Chapter 4)

readers' theater   A form of interpretive drama during which readers assume a role, read, and orally interpret the parts of the story that relate to their role. (Chapter 6)

recapitulation theory   A theory that proposes that play enables children to revisit activities of their ancestors and shed any negative behaviors in order to prepare them for living in today's world. (Chapter 2)

recreation/relaxation theory   A theory that suggests that play replenishes or "re-creates" energy used in work. (Chapter 2)

referent   An object or symbol that stands for something else. (Chapter 4)

repeated shapes   A stage in children's drawing where scribbling is well controlled and small geometric shapes are repeated, almost like designs. (Chapter 4)

representational art A stage in children's drawing in which the drawings begin to resemble the items being depicted. (Chapter 4)

representational use Children's intentionally planning and acting on ideas and ways familiar to their world. (Chapter 8)

room arrangement The way space is organized for children's learning and movement. (Chapter 7)

schematic A category of children's drawings in which the child's work clearly resembles the objects drawn. (Chapter 4)

self-expressive materials Resources that encourage children to experiment with various roles, feelings, and behaviors and express them through drama, music, and art. (Chapter 8)

simple units Play materials that have no apparent use with no subparts for children to manipulate or create. (Chapter 7)

skill and concept materials Materials that are prescriptive and product-oriented. (Chapter 8)

sociocultural theory A view that learning occurs in a social context and is fundamentally social in nature. The major vehicle for learning is interaction with an emulation of role models. (Chapter 2)

sociodramatic play Symbolic play that involves two or more children who communicate verbally about the play episode and enact social roles. (Chapter 2)

space The degree to which the physical environment is arranged to develop active, creative thinkers. (Chapter 7)

story or interpretive drama Interpretive drama creating a rendition or reenactment of someone else's ideas and words, often based on children's literature. (Chapter 6)

story play or story dictation Guided drama using children's original stories as the content for enactment. (Chapter 6)

supercomplex units Play materials having three or more subparts that children can juxtapose. (Chapter 6)

surplus-energy theory A view that human beings have certain amounts of energy to be used for survival, and the excess energy not spent forms a surplus that is expended through play. (Chapter 2)

symbolic play The child's use of props, plot, and roles to symbolize real or imaginary experiences. Also referred to as pretend, dramatic or sociodramatic, fantasy, or make-believe play. Symbolic play is typical of 2- to 7-year-olds. (Chapter 2)

symbolic stage The developmental stage during which a child uses abstract symbols, especially language, to represent ideas and experiences. (Chapter 5)

table blocks A variety of small, colored cubed blocks used alone or in pairs on a table or hard surface. (Chapter 8)

three-way communication Collaborating among the home, school, and community to support children's creative expression. (Chapter 3)

time A feature of creative environments that conveys a clear message about the importance of an activity or experience. (Chapter 7)

toys Materials specifically designed for children's play and learning. Toys and playthings reflect their society, politics, and cultural issues. (Chapter 8)

traditional playgrounds Playgrounds containing large, steel, immovable equipment designed for physical exercise outdoors. (Chapter 7)

two-way communication A dialogue between schools and families that encourages and respects families' contributions to the interaction. (Chapter 3)

unit blocks A set of large, smooth hardwood blocks in a wide array of shapes used for constructive play and large building projects on the floor. (Chapter 8)

water table A raised frame that holds a large container of water so that several children can stand next to it and engage in water play with toys, various types of plastic containers, or tubing. (Chapter 8)

References

Alberto, P., & Fredrick, L. (2000). Teaching picture reading as an enabling skill. *Teaching Exceptional Children, 33*(1), 60.

Allison, J. (2004). Ask the expert: Jeannette Allison on the project approach. In M. Jalongo & J. Isenberg (Eds.), *Exploring your role: A practitioner's introduction to early childhood education* (2nd ed.). Upper Saddle River, NJ: Merrill/Prentice Hall.

Alper, C. D. (1999). Early childhood music education. In C. Seefeldt (Ed.), *The early childhood curriculum* (pp. 237–263). New York: Teachers College Press.

Althouse, R., Johnson, M. H., & Mitchell, S. T. (2003). *The colors of learning: Integrating the visual arts into the early childhood curriculum.* New York: Teachers College Press and Washington, DC: National Association for the Education of Young Children.

Amabile, T. M. (1983). *The social psychology of creativity.* New York: Springer-Verlag.

Amabile, T. M. (1986). The personality of creativity. *Creative Living, 15*(3), 12–16.

Amabile, T. M. (1989). *Growing up creative.* New York: Crown.

Amabile, T. M. (2001). Beyond talent: John Irving and the passionate craft of creativity. *American Psychologist, 56,* 333–336.

Amann, J. (1993). *Theme teaching with great visual resources: How to involve and educate students using large, high-quality, low-cost art reproductions.* Rosemont, NJ: Modern Learning Press.

Anderson, W., & Lawrence, J. E. (2006). *Integrating music into the elementary classroom (media edition with CD).* Belmont, CA: Wadsworth.

Andress, B. (1998). *Music for young children.* Fort Worth, TX: Harcourt Brace College.

Andrews, L. J., & Sink, P. E. (2002). *Integrating music and reading instruction: Teaching strategies for upper-elementary grades.* Reston, VA: The National Association for Music Educators (MENC).

Annarella, L. A. (1999). *Using creative drama in the writing process.* (ERIC Document Reproduction Service No. ED434379)

Anning, A. (1999). Learning to draw and drawing to learn. *International Journal of Art & Design Education, 18*(2), 163–172.

Anning, A., & Ring, K. (2004). *Making sense of children's drawings.* Berkshire: Open University Press.

Armistead, M. E. (2007). Kaleidoscope: How a creative arts enrichment program prepares children for kindergarten. *Young Children, 62*(6) 86–93.

Armstrong, T. (1987). *In their own way.* New York: St. Martin's Press.

Armstrong, T. (1994). *Multiple intelligences in the classroom.* Alexandria, VA: Association for Supervision and Curriculum Development.

Armstrong, T. (1998). *Awakening genius in the classroom.* Alexandria, VA: Association for Supervision and Curriculum Development.

Arts Education Partnership. (2004a). *The arts and group learning.* Retrieved July 25, 2004, from *http://www.aep-arts.org/PDF%20Files/OpportunitiesResearch.pdf*

Arts Education Partnership. (2004b). *The arts and special student populations.* Retrieved July 25, 2004, from *http://www.aep-arts.org/PDF%20Files/OpportunitiesResearch.pdf*

Art Ideas for Special Artists, 2008 *http://www.edbydesign.com/specneedsres/specialart/index.html*

ArtExpress. (2002). Adapting materials for children with disabilities. Retrieved April 20, 2008, from *http://www.wiu.edu/users/mfkls1/artexpress/adaptat.html*

Bae, J. (2004). Learning to teach the visual arts in an early childhood classroom: The teacher's role as guide. *Early Childhood Education Journal, 31*(4), 247–253.

Baer, J. (1994). Why you still should not trust creativity tests. *Educational Leadership, 52*(2), 71–73.

Bafumo, M. E. (2005). The arts in your classroom. *Teaching PreK–8, 35*(6), 8.

Baldwin, A. Y. (2001). Understanding the challenge of creativity among African Americans. *Journal of Secondary Gifted Education, 12*(3), 121–125.

Bamford, A. (2006). *The wow factor: Global research compendium on the impact of the arts in education.* Münster, Germany: Waxmann Münster.

Banks, J. (Ed.). (1996). *Education, transformative knowledge, and action: Historical and contemporary perspectives.* New York: Teachers College Press.

Banks, J. A. (2001). *Cultural diversity and education: Foundations, curriculum, and teaching.* Boston: Allyn & Bacon.

Barab, S. A., & Landa, A. (1997). Designing effective interdisciplinary anchors. *Educational Leadership, 54*(6), 52–55.

Barasch, D. S. (1997, November). Creativity. *Family Life,* 54–59.

Barbour, A. C. (1999). The impact of playground design on the play behaviors of children with differing levels of physical competence. *Early Childhood Research Quarterly, 14*(1), 75–98.

Barbour, A., & Desjean-Perrotta, B. (2002). *Prop box play: 50 themes to inspire dramatic play.* Beltsville, MD: Gryphon House.

Barbour, N., Drosdeck, S., & Webster, T. (1987). Sand: A resource for the language arts. *Young Children, 42*(2), 20–25.

Barnes, R. (2002). *Teaching art to young children, 4–9* (2nd ed.). London: Routledge Falmer.

Barnhart, C. L., & Barnhart, R. K. (1983). *The world book dictionary.* Chicago: Thorndike-Barnhart.

Barrett, M. (2006). Inventing songs, inventing worlds: The 'genesis' of creative thought and activity in young *children's* lives. *International Journal of Early Years Education, 14*(3), 201–220.

Barrett, T. (1997). *Talking about student art.* Worcester, MA: Davis.

Barrett, T. (2004). Improving student dialogue about art. *Teaching Artist Journal, 2*(2), 87–94.

Barry, F. (2008). Big yellow sunflower. Somerville, MA: Candlewick Press.

Basinger, L., & Killian, J. N. (2004). Classroom instrument preferences among 4- to 9-year-olds in a free-play setting.

UPDATE: Applications of Research in Music Education, 23(1), 1–6.

Baum, S., & Reis, S. M. (Eds.). (2004). *Twice-exceptional and special populations of gifted students,* Vol. 7 (Essential Readings in Gifted Education). Thousand Oaks, CA: Sage Publications.

Baumrind, D. (1967). Child care practices anteceding three patterns of preschool behavior. *Genetic Psychology Monographs, 75,* 43–88.

Baumrind, D. (1993). The average expectable environment is not good enough: A response to Scarr. *Child Development, 64*(5), 1299–1317.

Baxendell, B. W. (2003). Consistent, coherent, creative: The 3C's of graphic organizers. *Teaching Exceptional Children, 35*(3), 46–53.

Bayless, K. M., & Ramsey, M. E. (1990). *Music: A way of life for the young child.* Upper Saddle River, NJ: Merrill/Prentice Hall.

Beattie, D. K. (1997). *Assessment in art education.* Worcester, MA: Davis.

Beattie, D. K. (2000). Creativity in art: The feasibility of assessing current conceptions in the school context. *Assessment in Education: Principles, Policy & Practice, 2*(7), 175–202.

Beaty, J. (2009). *Preschool appropriate practices* (3rd ed.). Clifton Park, NY: Delmar Cengage Learning.

Beeghly, D. G., & Prudhoe, C. M. (2002). *Litlinks: Activities for connected learning in elementary classrooms.* Boston: McGraw-Hill.

Begley, S. (1997, Spring-Summer). How to build a baby's brain. [Special issue]. *Newsweek, 129,* 28–32.

Bennett, N., Wood, L., & Rogers, S. (1997). *Teaching through play: Teachers' thinking and classroom practice.* Buckingham, England: Open University Press.

Bergen, D. (2002). Finding humor in children's play. In J. L. Roopnarine (Ed.), *Conceptual, social-cognitive, and contextual issues in the fields of play* (Vol. 4, pp. 209–220). Westport, CT: Ablex.

Bergen, D., & Coscia, J. (2000). *Brain research and childhood education.* Olney, MD: Association for Childhood Education International.

Berk, L. (2005). *Infants, children, and adolescents* (5th ed.). Boston: Allyn & Bacon.

Berk, L., Mann, T., & Ogan, A. (2006). Make-believe play: Wellspring for development of self regulation. In D. Singer, R. Golinkoff, & K. Hirsch-Pasek (Eds.), *Play = learning: How Play Motivates and Enhances Children's Cognitive and Social-Emotional Growth* (pp. 74–100). New York: Oxford University Press.

Bernstein, P. (1990). On breaking 100 in music. In F. Wilson & F. Roehmann (Eds.), *Music and child development: Proceedings of the 1987 Denver Conference* (pp. 400–419). St. Louis, MO: Mosby.

Bers, M. B. (2008). *Blocks to robots: Learning with technology in the early childhood classroom.* New York: Teachers College Press.

Besemer, S. P., & O'Quin, K. (1999). Confirming the three-factor creative product analysis matrix model in an American sample. *Creativity Research Journal, 12,* 287–296.

Bisgaier, C. S., & Samaras, T., with Russo, M. (2004). Using wood, glue, and words to enhance learning. *Young Children, 59*(4), 22–29.

Blizzard, J. (1999). Quoted in L. Mann, Dance education: The ultimate sport. *ASCD Education Update, 41*(5), 1, 3, 8.

Bloom, B. (1964). *Stability and change in human characteristics.* New York: Wiley.

Bloom, J. W. (2006). *Creating a classroom community of young scientists* (2nd ed.). New York: Routledge.

Bloom, A., & Hanny, J. (2006). Integrating art from around the world into the classroom. *Phi Delta Kappan, 87*(8), 641.

Bodrova E., & Leong D. J. (2007). Tools of the Mind: The Vygotskian Approach to Early Childhood Education. Upper Saddle River, NJ: Merrill/Prentice Hall.

Bolton, G. (1985). Changes in thinking about drama in the classroom. *Theory into Practice, 24*(3), 151–157.

Booth, D. (2005). *Story drama: Creating stories through role playing, improvising, and reading aloud* (2nd ed.). Portland, ME: Stenhouse Publishers.

Boughton, D. (2005). From fine *art* to visual culture: *Assessment* and the changing role of *art* education. *International Journal of Education through Art, 1*(3), 211–223.

Boyd, A. E. (1989, July–August). *Music in early childhood.* Paper presented at the 21st International Conference on Early Education and Development, Hong Kong. (ERIC Document Reproduction Service No. ED310863)

Boyer, E. L. (1995). *The basic school: A community for learning.* Princeton, NJ: Carnegie Foundation for the Advancement of Teaching.

Bransford, J., Brown, A., & Cocking, R. (Eds.). (1999). How people learn. Washington, DC: National Academy Press.

Bredekamp, S. (Ed.). (1991). Guidelines for appropriate curriculum content and assessment in programs serving children 3 through 8. *Young Children, 46*(3), 21–38.

Bredekamp, S., & Copple, C. (Eds.). (1997). *Developmentally appropriate practice in early childhood programs* (Rev. ed.). Washington, DC: National Association for the Education of Young Children.

Brenneman, K., & Louro, I. F. (2008). Science journals in the preschool classroom. *Early Childhood Education Journal, 36*(2), pp. 113–119.

Bresler, L. (1993). Three orientations to arts in the primary grades: Implications for curriculum reform. *Arts Education Policy Review, 94*(6), 29–35.

Brickman, N. A. (1999). *Creative representation: High/Scope preschool key experiences.* Ypsilanti, MI: High/Scope Educational Research Foundation.

Bromley, K. (1998). *Language arts: Exploring connections* (3rd ed.). Boston: Allyn & Bacon.

Bronson, M. (1995). *The right stuff for children birth to 8: Selecting play materials to support development.* Washington, DC: National Association for the Education of Young Children.

Bronson, M. B. (2006) Developing social and emotional competence. In D. F. Grillo (Ed.), *K today: Teaching and learning in the kindergarten year* (pp. 47–56). Washington, DC: National Association for the Education of Young Children.

Browne, A. (2003) The shape game. New York: Farrar, Straus and Giroux.

Bruer, J. (1997). Education and the brain: A bridge too far. *Educational Researcher, 26*(8), 4–16.

Bruner, J. (1968). *Toward a theory of instruction.* New York: Norton.

Bruner, J. S. (1966). What we have learned about early learning. *European Early Education Research Journal, 4*(1), 5–16.

Burke, A. F., & O'Sullivan, J. C. (2002). *A handbook for using drama in the second language classroom.* Portsmouth, NH: Heinemann.

Burnaford, G., Brown, S., Doherty, J., & McLaughlin, H. J. (2007). *Arts integration frameworks, research, and practice: A literature review.* Washington, DC: Arts Education Partnership.

Burns, M. T. (2002). Musical creativity. *Teaching Music, 9*(2), 40–45.

Burton, J. M. (2001). Lowenfeld: An(other) look. *Art Education, 54*(6), 33–42.

Burton, L. (2006). Getting started! Media education in the early years. *Screen Education, 44,* 90–96.

Cabrera, J. (2006). *Ten in the bed.* New York: Holiday House.

Caine, G., & Caine, R. N. (1997). *Education at the edge of possibility.* Alexandria, VA: Association for Supervision and Curriculum Development.

Caine, R. N., & Caine, G. (1991). *Teaching and the human brain.* Alexandria, VA: Association for Supervision and Curriculum Development.

Carnegie Corporation. (1994). *Starting points: Meeting the needs of our youngest children.* Retrieved January 28, 2005, from *http://www.carnegie.org/starting-points/startpt1.html*

Carnine, D. (1990). New research on the brain: Implications for instruction. *Phi Delta Kappan, 71*(5), 372–377.

Carpenter, B., & Shevlin, M. (2004). Creating an inclusive curriculum. In N. Walsh & H. Gash (Eds.), *Lives and times: Practice, policy and people with disabilities* (pp. 81–92). Canada: Rathdown Press.

Carter, M., & Curtis, D. (1995). *Training teachers: A harvest of theory and practice.* St. Paul, MN: Redleaf Press.

Casey, T. (2005). *Inclusive play: Practical strategies for working with children aged 3 to 8.* Thousand Oaks, CA: Sage Publications.

Casey, T. (2007). *Environments for outdoor play.* Thousand Oaks, CA: Sage Publications Inc.

Casler, K., & Keleman, D. (2007). Reasoning about artifacts at 24 months: The developing teleo-functional stance. *Cognition, 103,* 120–130.

Cassell, J. (2004). Towards a model of technology and literacy development: Story listening systems. *Journal of Applied Developmental Psychology, 25*(1), 75–105.

Castellano, J. A. (2003). *Special populations in gifted education: Working with diverse gifted learners.* Boston: Allyn & Bacon.

Castle, K. (1998). Children's rule knowledge in invented games. *Journal of Research in Childhood Education, 12*(2), 197–209.

Caulfield, R. (1999). Mozart effect: Sound beginnings? *Early Childhood Education Journal, 27*(2), 119–122.

Cecil, N. L., & Lauritzen, P. (1994). *Literacy and the arts for the integrated classroom: Alternative ways of knowing.* New York: Longman.

Chae, S. (2003). Adaptation of a picture-type creativity test for pre-school children. *Language Testing, 20,* 179–188.

Changing Education Through the Arts. (2005). The John F. Kennedy Center for the Performing Arts: Living Pictures Course. Washington, DC: Author.

Chard, S. (1998). *The project approach: Managing successful projects (Book 2).* New York: Scholastic.

Charney, R. S. (2002). *Teaching children to care: Classroom management for ethical and academic growth, K–8.* Greenfield, MA: Northeast Foundation for Children.

Checkley, K. (1997). The first seven . . . and the eighth. *Educational Leadership, 55*(1), 8–15.

Chenfeld, M. B. (2002). *Creative experiences for young children* (3rd ed.). Portsmouth, NH: Heinemann.

Christie, J. (2001). Play as a learning medium—revisited. In S. Reifel (Ed.), *Theory in context and out* (Vol. 3, pp. 357–366). Westport, CT: Ablex.

Christie, J. F., Enz, B., & Vukelich, C. (2007). *Teaching language and literacy: Preschool through the elementary grades* (3rd ed.). Boston: Allyn & Bacon.

Christie, J. F., & Johnson, E. P. (1983). The role of play in social-intellectual development. *Review of Educational Research, 53*(1), 93–115.

Clark, B. (1988). *Growing up gifted* (3rd ed.). Upper Saddle River, NJ: Merrill/Prentice Hall.

Clark, C. (1996). Working with able learners in regular classrooms. *Gifted and Talented International, 11,* 34–38.

Clasen, D., Middleton, J., & Connell, T. (1994). Assessing artistic and problem-solving performance in minority and nonminority students using a nontraditional multidimensional approach. *Gifted Child Quarterly, 38,* 27–32.

Clawson, M. (2002). Play of language–minority children in an early childhood setting. In J. L. Roopnarine (Ed.), *Conceptual, social-cognitive, and contextual issues in the fields of play* (Vol. 4, pp. 99–116). Westport, CT: Ablex.

Clayton, M. K. (2001). *Classroom spaces that work.* Greenfield, MA: Northeast Foundation for Children.

Clemens, S. G. (1991). Art in the classroom: Making every day special. *Young Children, 46*(2), 4–11.

Click, P. M., & Parker, J. (2009). *Caring for school-age children* (5th ed.). Clifton Park, NY: Delmar/Cengage Learning.

Coates, E., & Coates, A. (2006). Young children talking and drawing. *International Journal of Early Years Education, 14*(3), 221–241

Cobb, E. (1977). *The ecology of imagination in childhood.* New York: Columbia University Press.

Cobb, S., Mallett, A., Pridmore, T., & Benford, S. (2007). Interactive flashlights in special needs education. *Digital Creativity, 18*(2), 69–78.

Cohen, E. P., & Gainer, R. S. (1995). *Art: Another language for learning* (3rd ed.). Portsmouth, NH: Heinemann.

Collins, R. (1998). *The sociology of philosophies: A global theory of intellectual change.* Cambridge, MA: Harvard University Press.

Colwell, R. (1998). Preparing student teachers in assessment. *Arts Education Policy Review, 99*(4), 29–36.

Consortium of National Arts Education Associations. (1994). *National standards for arts education: Dance, music, theater, and visual arts: What every young American should know and be able to do in the arts.* Reston, VA: Music Educators National Conference.

Consortium of National Arts Education Associations. (2002). *Authentic connections.* Reston, VA: Author.

Copple, C., & Bredekamp, S. (2006). *Basics of developmentally appropriate practice: An introduction for teachers of children 3 to 6.* Washington, DC: National Association for the Education of Young Children.

Corbey-Scullen, L., & Howell, J. (1997). Out of the housekeeping corner and onto the stage: Extending dramatic play. *Young Children, 52*(6), 82–88.

Cornett, C. E. (2007). *Creating meaning through literature and the arts: An integration resource for classroom teachers.* Upper Saddle River, NJ: Pearson Merrill/Prentice Hall.

Coufal, K. L., & Coufal, D. C. (2002). Colorful wishes: The fusion of drawings, narratives, and social studies. *Communication Disorders Quarterly, 23*(2), 109–121.

Cox, M. V., & Ralph, M. L. (1996). Young children's ability to adapt their drawings of the human figure. *Educational Psychology, 16*(3), 245–256.

Craft, A. (1999). *Teaching creativity: Philosophy and practice.* London: Routledge.

Craft, A. (2000). *Creativity across the primary curriculum: Framing and developing practice.* London: Routledge.

Cramond, B. (2001). Interview with Paul E. Torrance on creativity in the last and next millennia. *Journal of Secondary Gifted Education, 12*(3), 116–120.

Crawford, L. (2004). *Lively learning: Using the arts to teach the K–8 curriculum.* Greenfield, MA: Northeast Foundation for Children.

Creasey, G., Jarvis, P., & Berk, L. (1998). Play and social competence. In O. Saracho and B. Spodek (Eds.), *Multiple perspectives on play in early childhood education* (pp. 116–143). Albany: State University of New York Press.

Cropley, A. (1997). Fostering creativity in the classroom. In M. Runco (Ed.), *The creativity research handbook* (pp. 83–113). Cresskill, NJ: Hampton Press.

Cropley, A. (1999). Definitions of creativity. In M. Runco & S. Pritzker (Eds.), *Encyclopedia of creativity* (Vol. 11, pp. 511–524). San Diego: Academic Press.

Cropley, A. J. (2001). *Creativity in education and learning: A guide for teachers and educators.* London: Kogan Page.

Crumpler, T., & Schneider, J. (2002). Writing with their whole being: A cross study analysis of children's writing from five classrooms using process drama. *Research in Drama Education, 7*(1), 75–78.

Crumpecker, C. (2004). They came two by two. *Arts and Activities, 135*(5), 30–31.

Csikszentmihalyi, M. (1996). The creative personality. *Psychology Today, 29*(4), 36–40.

Csikszentmihalyi, M., Rathunde, K., & Whalent, S. (1993). *Talented teenagers.* New York: Cambridge University Press.

Cummings, P. (1992). *Talking with artists.* New York: Bradbury.

Cummings, P. (1993). *Talking with artists II.* New York: Bradbury.

Custodero, L. A., & Johnson-Green, E. A. (2003). Passing the cultural torch: Musical experience and musical parenting of infants. *Journal of Research in Music Education, 51*(2), 102–114.

Custodero, L. (2006). Singing practices in 10 families with young children. *Journal of Research in Music Education, 54*(1), 37–56.

Custodero, L., & Johnson-Green, E. A. (2007). Caregiving in counterpoint: Reciprocal influences in the musical parenting of younger and older infants. *Early Child Development and Care, 178*(1), 15–39.

Cyranek, G. (2002). Social implications of virtual worlds. *Digital Creativity, 13*(1), 1–2.

D'Amboise, J. (1991). Quoted in Music Educators National Conference, *Growing up complete: The imperative for music education* (p. 5). Reston, VA: Author.

Dacey, J. S. (1989). *Fundamentals of creative thinking.* Lexington, MA: Heath.

Dacey, J. S., & Lennon, K. H. (1998). *Understanding creativity: The interplay of biological, psychological, and social factors.* San Francisco: Jossey-Bass.

Danko-McGhee, K., & Slutsky, R. (2003). Preparing early childhood teachers to use art in the classroom. *Art Education, 56*(4), 12–18.

Dansky, J. L. (1980). Make-believe: A mediator of the relationship between play and associative fluency. *Child Development, 51,* 576–579.

Dansky, J. L., & Silverman, I. W. (1973). Effects of play on associative fluency in preschool children. *Developmental Psychology, 9,* 38–43.

Darrow, A. A. (1985). Music for the deaf. *Music Educators Journal, 71*(6), 33–35.

Darrow, A., & Loomis, D. M. (1999). Music and deaf culture: Images from the media and their interpretation by deaf and hearing students. *Journal of Music Therapy, 26*(2), 88–107.

Davidson, J., & Davidson, B. (2004). *Genius denied: How to stop wasting our brightest young minds.* New York: Simon & Schuster.

Davila, D. E., & Koenig, S. M. (1998). Bringing the Reggio concept to American educators. *Art Education, 51*(4), 18–24.

Davis, G., & Rimm, S. (1994). *Education of the gifted and talented* (3rd ed.). Needham Heights, MA: Allyn & Bacon.

Davis, J., & Gardner, H. (1992). The cognitive revolution: Consequences for the understanding and education of the child as artist. In B. Reimer & R. A. Smith (Eds.), *The arts, education, and aesthetic knowing* (pp. 92–123). Chicago: University of Chicago Press.

Davis, J. H. (2008). *Why our schools need the arts.* New York: Teachers College Press.

Dawson, V. L. (1997). In search of the wild Bohemian: Challenges in the identification of the creatively gifted. *Roeper Review, 19*(3), 148–152.

de Bono, E. (1971). *New think.* New York: Avon.

de Bono, E. (1992). *Teach your child how to think.* New York: Viking.

de León, A. G. (2002, Fall). Moving beyond storybooks: Teaching our children to read and learn. *Carnegie Reporter,* 3–11.

Debord, K., Hestenes, L. L., Moore, R. C., Cosco, N., & McGinnis, J. R. (2002). Paying attention to the outdoor environment is as important as preparing the indoor environment. *Young Children, 57*(3), 32–35.

Deiner, P. L. (2005). *Resources for educating children with diverse abilities* (4th ed.). Albany, NY: Thomson Delmar Learning.

DeVries, P. (2008). Parental perceptions of music in storytelling sessions at a public library. *Early Childhood Education Journal, 35*(5), 473–478.

DeVries, R. (1998). Games with rules. In D. P. Fromberg & D. M. Bergen (Eds.), *Play from birth to twelve and beyond: Contexts, perspectives, and meanings* (pp. 409–415). New York: Garland.

Dewey, J. (1916). *Democracy and education.* New York: Macmillan.

Dewey, J. (1938). *Experience and education.* New York: Macmillan.

Diamond, B. J., & Moore, M. A. (1995). *Multicultural literacy: Mirroring the reality of the classroom.* White Plains, NY: Longman.

Diamond, A., Barnett, S., Thomas, J., & Munro, S. (2007). Preschool Program Improves Cognitive Control Science 30(318), pp. 1387–1388.

Diamond, M., & Hopson, J. (1999). *Magic trees of the mind: How to nurture your child's intelligence, creativity, and healthy emotions from birth through adolescence.* New York: Penguin.

Dinca, M. (1999). Creative children in Romanian society. *Childhood Education, 75*(6), 355–358.

Doctoroff, S. (2001). Adapting the physical environment to meet the needs of all young children for play. *Early Childhood Education Journal, 29*, 105–109.

Dodge, D. T., Colker, L. J., & Heroman, C. (2002). *The creative curriculum for preschool* (4th ed.). Washington DC: Teaching Strategies.

Doran, H., & Fleischman, S. (2005, November). Research matters/challenges of value-added assessment. *Educational Leadership, 63*(3), 85–87.

Dorn, C. M., Madeja, S. S., & Sabol, F. R. (2004). *Assessing expressive learning.* Mahwah, NJ: Lawrence Erlbaum.

Drew, W. F., & Rankin, B. (2004). Promoting creativity for life using open-ended materials. *Young Children, 59*(4), 38–45.

DuCharme, C. C. (1991, April). *The role of drawing in the writing processes of primary grade children.* Paper presented at the Association for Childhood Education International Study Conference, San Diego, CA.

Duffy, B. (1998). *Supporting creativity and imagination in the early years.* Buckingham, England: Open University Press.

Duncum, P. (2002). Clarifying visual culture art education. *Art Education, 55*(3), 6–11.

Dunkin, A. (2006). *Dancing in your school: A guide for preschool and elementary school teachers.* Hightstown, NJ: Princeton Book Company.

DuPont, S. (1992). The effectiveness of creative drama as an instructional strategy to enhance the reading comprehension skills of fifth-grade remedial readers. *Reading Research and Instruction, 31*(3), 41–52.

Dyson, A. H. (1993). *Social worlds of children learning how to write.* New York: Teachers College Press.

Ebbeck, M. (1996). Children constructing their own knowledge. *International Journal of Early Years Education, 4*(2), 5–27.

Eckhoff, A. (2008). The importance of art viewing experiences in early childhood visual arts: The exploration of a master art teacher's strategies for meaningful early arts experiences. *Early Childhood Education Journal.*

Eckhoff, A., & Urbach, J. (2008). Understanding imaginative thinking during childhood: Sociocultural conceptions of creativity and imaginative thought. *Early Childhood Education Journal.* 36(2), pp. 179–186.

Edmiston, B. (2000). Drama as ethical education. Research in Drama Education, 5(1), 63-84.

Educators in Connecticut's Pomperaug Regional School District 15. (1996). *A teacher's guide to performance-based learning and assessment.* Alexandria, VA: Association for Supervision and Curriculum Development.

Edwards, C., Gandini, L., & Forman, G. (Eds.). (1993). *The hundred languages of children: The Reggio Emilia approach to early childhood education.* Norwood, NJ: Ablex. (ERIC Document Reproduction Service No. ED355034)

Edwards, C. P., Gandini, L., & Forman, G. E. (Eds.). (1999). *The hundred languages of children: The Reggio Emilia approach to early childhood education—advanced reflections.* Greenwich, CT: Ablex.

Edwards, Gandini, Hill, Cadwell, & Schwall (2005).

Edwards, L. C. (2007). *The creative arts: A process approach for teachers and children* (4th ed.). Upper Saddle River, NJ: Merrill/Prentice Hall.

Efland, A. D. (2004). The entwined nature of the aesthetic: A discourse on visual culture. *Studies in Art Education, 45*(3), 234–251.

Egan, K. (1988). The origins of imagination. In K. Egan and D. Nadaner (Eds.), *Imagination and education* (pp. 91–127). New York: Teachers College Press.

Egan, K. (2006). *Teaching literacy: Engaging the imagination of new readers and writers.* Thousand Oaks, CA: Corwin Press.

Egan, K., & Nadaner, D. (Eds.). (1988). *Imagination and education.* New York: Teachers College Press.

Egan, K., Stout, M., & Takaya, K. (Eds.). (2007). *Teaching and learning outside the box: Inspiring imagination across the curriculum* (pp. 101–166). New York: Teachers College Press.

Eisenberger, R., & Armeli, S. (1997). Can salient reward increase creative performance without reducing intrinsic creative interest? *Journal of Personality and Social Psychology, 72*, 652–663.

Eisner, E. (1976). *The arts, human development and education.* Berkeley, CA: McCuthen.

Eisner, E. (1990). Who decides what schools teach? *Phi Delta Kappan, 71*, 523–525.

Eisner, E. (1999). The uses and limits of performance assessment. *Phi Delta Kappan, 80*(9), 658–660.

Eisner, E. W. (1994). *Cognition and curriculum reconsidered* (2nd ed.). New York: Teachers College Press.

Eisner, E. W. (1998). *The kind of schools we need: Personal essays.* Portsmouth, NH: Heinemann.

Eisner, E. W. (2003). Preparing for today and tomorrow. *Educational Leadership, 61*(4), 6–10.

Elgas, P. M., Prendeville, J., Moomaw, S., & Kretchmer, R. R. (2002). Early childhood classroom setup. *Child Care Information Exchange, 143*, 17–20.

Elias, C. L., & Berk, L. E. (2002). Self-regulation in young children: Is there a role for sociodramatic play? *Early Childhood Research Quarterly, 17*(2), 216–238.

Ellis, M. J. (1973). *Why people play.* Upper Saddle River, NJ: Merrill/Prentice Hall.

Epstein, A. S. (2001). Thinking about art: Encouraging art appreciation in early childhood settings. *Young Children, 56*(3), 38–43.

Epstein, A. S., & Trimis, E. (2002). *Supporting young artists. The development of the visual arts in young children.* Ypsilanti, MI: High/Scope Educational Research Foundation.

Ericsson, K. A., & Charness, N. (1994). Expert performance: Its structure and acquisition. *American Psychologist, 49*(8), 725–747.

Erikson, E. (1950). *Childhood and society.* New York: Norton.

Erikson, E. H. (1963). *Childhood and society.* New York: Norton.

Erwin, E., & Schreiber, R. (1999). Creating supports for young children with disabilities in natural environments. *Early Childhood Education Journal, 26*(3), 167–171.

Etzioni, A. (1993). *The spirit of community: Rights, responsibilities, and the communitarian agenda.* New York: Crown.

Fasko, D. (2001). Education and creativity. *Creativity Research Journal, 13*(3/4), 317–327.

Faulkner, D., Coates, E., Craft, A., & Duffy, B. (2006). Creativity and cultural innovation in early childhood education. *International Journal of Early Years Education, 14*(3), 191–199.

Fawson, P. C., & Moore, S. A. (1999). Reading incentive programs: Beliefs and practices. *Reading Psychology, 20*, 325–340.

Fay, K., & Wholey, S. (2004). *Becoming one community: Reading and writing with English language readers.* Portland, ME: Stenhouse.

Feeney, S., Christensen, D., & Moravcik, E. (Eds.). (1991). *Who am I in the lives of children?* Upper Saddle River, NJ: Merrill/Prentice Hall.

Feldhusen, J. F. (1995). Creativity: Knowledge base, metacognitive skills, and personality factors. *Journal of Creative Behavior, 29*(4), 255–268.

Feldhusen, J. F. (2001). Multiple options as a model for teaching the creatively gifted child. In M. D. Lynch & C. R. Harris, (Eds.), *Fostering creativity in children, K–8* (pp. 3–13). Needham Heights, MA: Allyn & Bacon.

Feldhusen, J. F., & Goh, B. E. (1995). Assessing and accessing creativity: An integrative review of theory, research, and development. *Creativity Research Journal, 8*(3), 231–247.

Feldman, D. H. (1999). The development of creativity. In R. J. Sternberg (Ed.), *Handbook of creativity* (pp. 169–186). New York: Cambridge University Press.

Fello, S., Paquette, K. R., & Jalongo, M. R. (2006/2007). Talking drawings: Improving intermediate students' comprehension of expository science text. *Childhood Education, 83*(2), 80–86.

Felton, H., & Stoessiger, R. (1987, September). Quality learning: The role of process in art and mathematics. *National Association for Drama in Education,* 14–21.

Fennessey, S. (1995). Living history through drama and literature. *The Reading Teacher, 49*(3), 16–19.

Fennessey, S. (2000). *History in the spotlight: Creative drama and theatre practices for the social studies classroom.* Portsmouth, NH: Heinemann.

Ferrari, M. (2004). Educating selves to be creative and wise. In L. V. Shavinina & M. Ferrari (Eds.), *Beyond knowledge: Extracognitive aspects of high ability* (pp. 136–168). Mahwah, NJ: Erlbaum.

Fields, M., Groth, L., & Spangler, K. (2007). *Let's begin reading right* (6th ed.). Upper Saddle River, NJ: Merrill/Prentice Hall.

Fikari, C. (2007). Play, props, and puppets: The role of dramatic play in the development of academic language for intermediate–level ELL students. *Focus on Elementary, 20*(2), 1–5. Olney, MD: ACEI.

Fisher, D., & McDonald, N. (2004). Stormy weather: Leading purposeful curriculum integration with and through the arts. *Teaching Artist Journal, 2*(4), 240–248.

Fishkin, A. S., Crammond, B., & Olszewski-Kubilius, P. (1999). Issues in studying creativity in youth. In A. S. Fishkin, B. Crammond, & P. Olszewski-Kubilius (Eds.), *Investigating creativity in youth: Research and methods.* Cresskill, NJ: Hampton Press.

Fleith, D. (2000). Teacher and student perceptions of creativity in the classroom environment. Roeper Review, 22(3), 148.

Flohr, J. W., Miller, D. C., & Debeus, R. (2000). EEG studies with young children. *Music Educators Journal, 87*(2), 28–33.

Flynn, L. L., & Kieff, J. (2002). Including everyone in outdoor play. *Young Children, 57*(3), 20–26.

Flynn, R. M. (2000). *From story to stage: Dramatizing literature using creative problem solving* [Pamphlet]. Washington, DC: John F. Kennedy Center for the Performing Arts.

Forman, G. (1998). Constructive play. In D. P. Fromberg & D. M. Bergen (Eds.), *Play from birth to twelve and beyond: Contexts, perspectives, and meanings* (pp. 392–400). New York: Garland.

Forsythe, S. J. (1995). It worked! Readers theater in second grade. *The Reading Teacher, 49*(3), 264–265.

Fox, D. B. (1989). MusicTIME and music times two: The Eastman infant-toddler music program. In B. Andress (Ed.), *Promising practices in prekindergarten music* (pp. 13–24). Reston, VA: Music Educators National Conference.

Fox, D. B. (1991). Music, development, and the young child. *Music Educators Journal, 77*(5), 42–46.

Freire, P. (1973). *Pedagogy of the oppressed.* New York: Seabury.

Freud, S. (1958). *On creativity and the unconscious* (I. F. Grant Doff, Trans.). New York: Harper & Row. (Original work published 1928)

Fritz, A. (2002). Keynote address for IDATER '98—Creativity: From philosophy to practice. Retrieved January 28, 2005, from *http://www.21learn.org/arch/articles/fritz.html*

Fromberg, D. P. (1998). Play issues in early childhood education. In C. Seefeldt & A. Galper (Eds.), *Continuing issues in early childhood education* (2nd ed.; pp. 190–212). New York: Teachers College Press.

Fromberg, D. P. (1999). A review of research on play. In C. Seefeldt (Ed.), *The early childhood curriculum: Current findings in theory and practice* (3rd ed., pp. 27–53). New York: Teachers College Press.

Fromberg, D. P. (2002). *Play and meaning in early childhood education.* Boston: Allyn & Bacon.

Fromberg, D. P., & Bergen, D. M. (Eds.). (2006). *Play from birth to twelve and beyond: Contexts, perspectives, and meanings* (2nd ed.). New York: Taylor & Francis, Inc.

Frost, J. L. (2004). Common issues and concerns about outdoor play environments. In M. Jalongo & J. Isenberg (Eds.), *Exploring your role: A practitioner's introduction to early childhood education* (p. 175). Upper Saddle River, NJ: Merrill/Prentice Hall.

Frost, J. L., Shinn, D., & Jacobs, P. (1998). Physical environments and children's play. In O. Saracho & B. Spodek (Eds.), *Multiple perspectives on play in early childhood education* (pp. 255–294). Albany, NY: State University of New York Press.

Frost, J. L., & Woods, I. C. (1998). Perspectives on play in playgrounds. In D. P. Fromberg & D. M. Bergen (Eds.), *Play from birth to twelve and beyond: Context, perspectives, and meanings* (pp. 232–240). New York: Garland.

Frost, J. L., Wortham, S. C., & Reifel, S. (2008). *Play and child development* (3rd ed.). Upper Saddle River, NJ: Pearson Education.

Furman, L. (2000a). In support of drama in early childhood education, again. *Early Childhood Education Journal, 27*(30), 173–178.

Furman, L. (2000b). Using drama and theater to provide literacy development: Some basic classroom applications. *Research in Drama Education, 7*(1), 61–69.

Gainer, B. (1997). Marketing arts education: Parental attitudes toward arts education for children. *Journal of Arts Management, Law & Society, 26*(4), 253–268.

Gaitskell, C. D., Hurwitz, A., & Day, M. (1982). *Children and their art: Methods for the elementary school* (4th ed.). Dubuque, IA: Brown.

Gajdamaschko, N. (2005). Vygotsky on imagination: Why an understanding of the imagination is an important issue for schoolteachers. *Teaching Education, 16*(1), 13–22.

Gallas, K. (2003). *Imagination and literacy: A teacher's search for the heart of meaning.* New York: Teachers College Press.

Gallenstein, N. (2005). Never too young for a concept map. *Science and Children, 43*(1), 44–47.

Gandini, L., Hill, L., & Cadwell, L. (Eds.) (2005*). In the spirit of the studio: Learning from the atelier of Reggio Emilia.* New York: Teachers College Press.

Garcia, C., Garcia, L., Floyd, J., & Lawson, J. (2002). Improving public health through early childhood movement programs. *Journal of Physical Education, Recreation, and Dance, 73*(1), 27–32.

Gardner, H. (1993a). *Frames of mind: The theory of multiple intelligences* (10th anniversary ed.). New York: Basic Books.

Gardner, H. (1993b). *Multiple intelligences: The theory in practice.* New York: Basic Books.

Gardner, H. (2000). *Intelligence reframed: Multiple intelligences for the 21st century.* New York: Basic Books.

Gardner, H. (2007). *Five minds for the future.* Boston, MA: Harvard Business School Publishing.

Garreau, M., & Kennedy, C. (1991). Structure time and space to promote pursuit of learning in the primary grades. *Young Children, 46*(4), 46–51.

Gelb, M. J. (2002). *Discover your genius: How to think like history's ten most revolutionary minds.* New York: Quill/HarperCollins.

Gelineau, R. P. (2004). *Integrating the arts across the elementary school curriculum.* Belmont, CA: Thomson-Wadsworth.

Gershon, J., & Gershon, D. *Judy and Dave's Online Songbook.* Retrieved January 27, 2008, from All Together Now Entertainment at *http://judyanddavid.com/index2.html*

Geyer, B., & Geyer, F. (2005). *Teaching Early Concepts with Photos of Kids.* New York: Scholastic, Inc.

Gilbert, J. (1996). Developing an assessment stance in primary art education in England. *Assessment in Education: Principles, Policy & Practice, 3*(1), 55–74.

Glover, J. (1980). *Becoming a more creative person.* Upper Saddle River, NJ: Merrill/Prentice Hall.

Gluschankof, C. (2002). The local musical style of kindergarten children: A description and analysis of its natural variables. *Music Education Research, 4,* 37–49.

Gold, R., & Cuming, G. J. (1999). Age-appropriate dance. *Dance Magazine, 78.*

Goleman, D., & Kaufman, P. (1992). The art of creativity. *Psychology Today, 25*(2), 40–47.

Golomb, C. (2004). *The child's creation of a pictorial world.* Mahwah, NJ: Erlbaum.

Goodenough, F. (1975). Measurement of intelligence by drawings. New York: Ayer. (orig. pub. 1954).

Goodlad, J. (2007). Kudzu, rabbits, and school reform. In A. C. Ornstein, E. F. Pajak, & S. B. Ornstein (Eds.), *Contemporary issues in curriculum* (4th ed., pp. 51–58). Boston, MA: Allyn & Bacon.

Gordon , A. M., & Browne, K. W. (2007). *Beginning essentials in early childhood education.* Clifton Park, NY: Delmar/Cengage Learning.

Gould, P., & Sullivan, J. (2004). *The inclusive early childhood classroom: Easy ways to adapt learning.* Beltsville, MD: Gryphon House.

Green, J. (2001). Socially constructed bodies in American dance classrooms. *Research in Dance Education, 2*(2), 155–173.

Greenberg, M. (1979). *Your children need music.* Upper Saddle River, NJ: Merrill/Prentice Hall.

Greenspan, D. A., Solomon, B., & Gardner, H. (2004). The development of talent in different domains. In L. V. Shavinina & M. Ferrari (Eds.), *Beyond knowledge: Extracognitive aspects of high ability* (pp. 119–135). Mahwah, NJ: Erlbaum.

Gregoire, M., & Lupinetti, J. (2005). Supporting diversity through the arts. *Kappa Delta Pi Record, 41*(4), 159–163.

Griffiths, N. (2001). Storysacks, reading: Reading and language information center. *The University of Reading.* www.storysacks.com

Gromko, J. E., & Poorman, A. S. (1998). The effect of music training on preschoolers' spatial-temporal task performance. *Journal of Research in Music Education, 46*(2), 173–181.

Gronlund, G. (2001). Academics in the preschool and kindergarten years—Let me tell you how. *Young Children, 56*(2), 42–43.

Gruber, H. E., & Davis, S. N. (1988). Inching our way up Mount Olympus: The evolving-systems approach to creative thinking. In R. J. Sternberg (Ed.), *The nature of creativity* (pp. 243–270). New York: Cambridge University Press.

Gruber, H. E., & Wallace, D. B. (1999). The case study method and evolving systems approach for understanding creative people at work. In R. J. Sternberg (Ed.), *The handbook of creativity* (pp. 93–115). New York: Cambridge University Press.

Guilford, J. P. (1984). Varieties of divergent production. *Journal of Creative Behavior, 18,* 1–10.

Guralnick, M., & Hammond, M. (1984). Peer-related social interactions of developmentally delayed young children: Development and characteristics. *Developmental Psychology, 20,* 815–827.

Guralnick, M., & Hammond, M. (1999). Sequential analysis of the social play of young children with mild developmental delays. *Journal of Early Intervention, 22,* 243–256.

Hall, M. A. (1989). Music for children. In B. Andress (Ed.), *Promising practices in prekindergarten music* (pp. 47–57). Reston, VA: Music Educators National Conference.

Hallahan, D. P., & Kauffman, J. M. (2002). *Exceptional learners: Introduction to special education* (9th ed.). Needham Heights, MA: Allyn & Bacon.

Halliday, M. A. K. (1975). *Explorations in the functions of language.* London: Edward Arnold.

Han, K., & Marvin, C. (2002). Multiple creativities? Investigating domain-specificity of creativity in young children. *Gifted Child Quarterly, 46,* 98–109.

Han, M., Benavides, A., & Christie, J. (2001). Bilingual children's language usage. In S. Reifel (Ed.), *Theory in context* (Vol. 3). Westport, CT: Ablex.

Hancock, L., & Wingert, P. (1997, Spring-Summer). The new preschool. [Special Issue]. *Newsweek, 129,* 36–37.

Harding, S. (2005). Outdoor play and the pedagogic garden. In J. Moyles (Ed.), *The excellence of play* (2nd ed., pp. 138–153). London: Open University Press.

Hargreaves, D. J., Galton, M. J., & Robinson, S. (1996). Teachers' assessments of primary children's classroom work in the creative arts. *Educational Research, 38*(2), 199–211.

Harris, J. R. (1998). *The nurture assumption: Why children turn out as they do.* New York: Free Press.

Harrison, A. (1984). Creativity, class and boredom: Cognitive models for intelligent activities. *Journal of Education, 166*(2), 150–169.

Harrison, C. (1999). Visual representation of the young gifted child. *Roeper Review, 21*(3), 189–195.

Hartman, J. A., & Eckerty, C. (1995). Projects in the early years. *Childhood Education, 71*(3), 141–148.

Hatch, T. (1997). Getting specific about multiple intelligences. *Educational Leadership, 54*(6), 26–29.

Haugland, S. (2001). What role should technology play in young children's learning? Part 2. Early childhood classrooms in the 21st century: Using computers to maximize learning. *Young Children, 55*(1), 12–18.

Haugland, S., & Wright, J. (1997). *Young children and technology: A world of discovery.* Boston: Allyn & Bacon.

Healey, D., & Rucklidge, J. J. (2005). An exploration into the creative abilities of children with ADHD. *Journal of Attention Disorders, 8,* 88–95.

Healy, J. (1996). How to uncover the natural creative abilities in your child. *Brown University Child and Adolescent Behavior Letter, 12*(4), 5–6.

Hearron, P., & Hildebrand, V. (2009). *Guiding young children* (8th ed.). Upper Saddle River, NJ: Merrill/Prentice Hall.

Heath, S. B., & Wolf, S. (2005). Focus in creative learning: Drawing on art for language development. *Literacy, 39*(1), 38–45.

Heathcote, D., & Wagner, B. J. (1999). *Drama as a learning medium.* Portsmouth, NH: Heinemann.

Heberholz, B. (1974). *Early childhood art.* Dubuque, IA: Brown.

Heinig, R. B. (1993). *Creative drama for the classroom teacher* (4th ed.). Upper Saddle River, NJ: Merrill/Prentice Hall.

Heller, P. G. (1996). Many ways of knowing: Using drama, oral interaction, and the visual arts to enhance reading comprehension. *The Reading Teacher, 45*(8), 580–584.

Helm, J. H., & Beneke, S. (Eds.). (2003). *The power of projects: Meeting contemporary challenges in early childhood classrooms.* New York: Teachers College Press and Washington, DC: National Association for the Education of Young Children.

Hemmeter, M. L., Ostrosky, M. M., Artman, K. M., & Kinder, K. A. (2008). Planning transitons to prevent challenging behavior. *Young Children, 63*(3), 18–25.

Henderson, M., Presbury, J., & Torrance, E. P. (1983). *Manifesto for children.* Staunton, VA: Full Circle Counseling.

Hendrick, J. (2001). *The whole child* (7th ed.). Upper Saddle River, NJ: Merrill/Prentice Hall.

Hendrick, J., & Weissman, P. (2006). *The whole child* (8th ed.). Clifton Park, NY: Delmar Cengage Learning.

Henkes, R. (1989). The child's artistic expression. *Early Child Development and Care, 47,* 165–176.

Hennebery, S., Soto, G., & Yu, B. (2007). Supporting the development of narrative skills of an eight-year old child who uses an augmentative and alternative communication device. *Child Language Teaching and Therapy, 23*(1), 27–45.

Hennessey, B. A. (1994). The consensual assessment technique: An examination for the relationships between ratings of process and product creativity. *Creativity Research Journal, 7,* 193–208.

Hennings, D. G. (2003). *Communication in action: Teaching literature-based language arts* (8th ed.). Boston: Houghton Mifflin.

Hestenes, L., & Carroll, D. (2000). The play interactions of young children with and without disabilities: Individual and environmental influences. *Early Childhood Research Quarterly, 15,* 229–246.

Hewitt, K., & Roomet, L. (1979). *Educational toys in America: 1800 to the present.* Burlington, VT: Robert Hall Fleming Museum/University of Vermont.

Hicks, J. (2001). How do you cure a sick horse? *Art Education, 54*(2), 6–10.

Hildebrandt, C. (1992). Creativity in music and early childhood. *Young Children, 53*(6), 68–74.

Hileman, K. (2008). *Welcome to our Classroom Museum.* Retrieved January 27, 2008, from Teaching Pre K–8 at *http://www.teachingk8.com/archives/articles/welcome_to_our_classroom_museum_by_keil_hileman.html*

Hill, P. S. (1923). *A conduct curriculum for the kindergarten and first grade.* New York: Scribner's.

Hirsch, E. S. (1996). *The block book* (3rd ed.). Washington, DC: National Association for the Education of Young Children.

Hirsch-Pasek, K., Fyer, D., & Golinkoff, R. M. (2003). *Einstein never used flash cards: How our children really learn and why they need to play more and memorize less.* Emmaus, PA: Rodale Books.

Holden, C. (1987, April). Creativity and the troubled mind. *Psychology Today, 21*(4), 9–10.

Holder, C., & Pearle, L. (2005). Fracturing fairy tales: The stories of two teacher-learners. *Knowledge Quest, 33*(4), 19–20.

Hollander, S., & Richwine, P., (2004). Picture this: Museums and collections of picture-book art. *Book Links, 13*(6), 30–33.

Holmes, R., & Geiger, C. (2002). The relationship between creativity and cognitive ability in preschoolers. In J. L. Rooparine (Ed.), *Conceptual, social-cognitive, and contextual issues in the fields of play* (Vol. 4, pp. 127–148). Westport, CT: Ablex.

Hope, S. (1990). Technique and arts education. *Design for Arts in Education, 91*(6), 2–14.

Hope, S. (1991). Policy making in the arts and school change. In Council of Arts Accrediting Associations, *Briefing Paper* (pp. 1–5). Reston, VA: Author.

Horibe, F. (2001). *Creating the innovation culture: Leveraging visionaries, dissenters and other useful troublemakers in your organization.* New York: Wiley.

Horowitz, J., & Webb-Dempsey, J. (Spring, 2002). Future directions for multi-arts research. In The Arts Education Partnership (Eds.)., The compendium of arts research. Washington, DC: The Council of Chief State School Officers.

Howe, H. (1993). *Thinking about our kids: An agenda for American action.* New York: Free Press.

Howe, M. J. A. (2004). Some insights of geniuses into the causes of exceptional achievements. In L. V. Shavinina & M. Ferrari (Eds.), *Beyond knowledge: Extracognitive aspects of high ability* (pp. 105–117). Mahwah, NJ: Erlbaum.

Howe, N., Moller, L., Chambers, B., & Petrakos, H. (1993). The ecology of dramatic play centers and children's social and cognitive play. *Early Childhood Research Quarterly, 8*(2), 235–252.

Hughes, F. P. (1999). *Children, play and development* (3rd ed.). Boston: Allyn & Bacon.

Hull, K., Goldhaber, J., & Capone., A. (2002). *Opening doors: An introduction to inclusive early childhood education.* New York: Houghton Mifflin.

Humpal, M. E., & Wolf, J. (2003). Music in the inclusive environment. *Young Children, 58*(2), 103–107.

Hunsacker, S. L. (1994). Creativity as a characteristic of giftedness: Teachers see it, then they don't. *Roeper Review, 17*(1), 11–15.

Hunt, J. M. (1961). *Intelligence and experience.* New York: Ronald Press.

Hunt, T., & Renfro, N. (1982). *Puppetry in early childhood education.* Austin, TX: Nancy Renfro Studios.

Hutinger, P. L. (1997). *The Expressive Arts Project: A final report.* Macomb, IL. (ERIC Document Reproduction Service No. ED415646)

Hyson, M. (2008). *Enthusiastic and engaged learners: Approaches to learning in the early childhood classroom.* New York: Teachers College Press and Washington, DC: NAEYC.

Hyson, M. C., & Christiansen, S. L. (1997). Developmentally appropriate guidance and the integrated curriculum. In C. Hart, D. Burts, & R. Charlesworth (Eds.), *Integrated curriculum and developmentally appropriate practice* (pp. 257–284). Albany: State University of New York Press.

IbcTech. (2007). *Fun and fantastic fingerplays.* Retrieved January 27, 2008, from *http://www.thebestkidsbooksite.com/fingerplays-for-kids.cfm*

Isaacs, S. (1933). *Social development in young children.* London: Routledge & Kegan Paul.

Isaksen, S. G. (1992). *Nurturing creative talents: Lessons from industry about needed work-life skills.* Buffalo, NY: Creative Solving Group.

Isbell, R. (1995). *The complete learning center book.* Beltsville, MD: Gryphon House.

Isbell, R. T., & Exelby, B. (2001). *Early learning environments that work.* Beltsville, MD: Gryphon House.

Isbell, R., Sobel, J., Lindauer, L., & Lowrance, A. (2004). The effects of storytelling and story reading on the oral language complexity and story comprehension of young children. *Early Childhood Education Journal, 32*(3), 157–163.

Isbell, R. T., & Raines, S. C. (2006). *Creativity and the arts with young children.* Clifton Park, NY: Delmar/Cengage.

Isen, A. M., Daubman, K. A., & Nowicki, G. P. (1987). Positive affect facilitates problem solving. *Journal of Personality and Social Psychology, 52,* 1121–1131.

Isenberg, J., & Farley, M. (1990). *Reading assessment program review committee.* Richmond: Virginia Department of Education.

Isenberg, J., & Quisenberry, N. (2002). Play: Essential for all children. *Childhood Education, 79*(1), 33–39.

Isenberg, J. P., & Raines, S. C. (1992). Peer conflict and conflict resolution among preschool children. In J. Gittler & L. Bowen (Eds.), *Annual review of conflict knowledge and conflict resolution* (Vol. 3, pp. 21–40). New York: Garland.

Jackson, P. W., & Messick, S. (1965). The person, the product, and the response: Conceptual problems in the assessment of creativity. *Journal of Personality, 33,* 309–329.

Jalongo, M. R. (1991). Children's play: A resource for multicultural education. In E. B. Vold (Ed.), *Multicultural education in the early childhood classroom* (pp. 52–56). Washington, DC: National Education Association.

Jalongo, M. R. (2002). *Early childhood language arts* (3rd ed.). Boston: Allyn & Bacon.

Jalongo, M. R. (2003). The child's right to creative thought and expression (International Position Paper of the Association for Childhood Education International). *Childhood Education, 79*(4), 218–228.

Jalongo, M. R. (2004). *Young children and picture books* (2nd ed.). Washington, DC: National Association for the Education of Young Children.

Jalongo, M. R., & Collins, M. (1985). Singing with young children! Folk music for nonmusicians. *Young Children, 40,* 17–22.

Jalongo, M. R., & Isenberg, J. P. (2008). *Exploring your role: An introduction to early childhood education* (3rd ed.). Upper Saddle River, NJ: Merrill/Prentice Hall.

Jalongo, M. R., & Ribblett, D. (1997). Using song picture books to support emergent literacy. *Childhood Education, 74*(1), 15–22.

Jalongo, M. R., & Stamp, L. N. (1997). Appendix D: Picture book versions of songs, chants, fingerplays, and action rhymes. In M. R. Jalongo & L. N. Stamp, *The arts in children's lives: Aesthetic education in early childhood* (pp. 157–256). Boston: Allyn & Bacon.

Jefferson, B. (1963). *Teaching art to children: The values of creative expression.* Boston: Allyn & Bacon.

Jensen, E. (1998, Spring). Quoted in K. Rasmussen, Arts education: A cornerstone of basic education. *ASCD Curriculum Update, 2.*

Jensen, E. (2000). Moving with the brain in mind. *Education Leadership, 58*(1), 34–37.

Jensen, E. (2006). *Enriching the brain: How to maximize every learner's potential.* San Francisco, CA: Jossey-Bass.

Johnson, A. (1998). How to use creative dramatics in the classroom. *Childhood Education, 75*(1), 2.

Johnson, D. (2003). Activity theory, mediated action and literacy: Assessing how children make meaning in multiple modes. *Assessment in Education, 10*(1), 103–129.

Johnson, D., Johnson, R., & Holubec, E. (1998). *Cooperation in the classroom.* Boston: Allyn and Bacon.

Johnson, J., Christie, J., & Wardle, F. (2005). *Play, development and early education.* Boston: Pearson Education, Inc.

Johnson, J. E., Christie, J. F., & Yawkey, T. D. (1999). *Play and early childhood development* (2nd ed.). New York: Longman.

Johnson, M. (2008). Developing verbal and visual literacy through experiences in the visual arts. *Young Children, 63*(1), 74–79.

Jones, D., McConnell, B., & Normie, G. (Eds.). (1996). *One world, many cultures.* Papers from the 4th International Conference on Adult Education and the Arts, Caredenden, Scotland: Fife Regional Council. (ERIC Document Reproduction Service No. ED414470)

Jones, E. (1977). *Dimensions of teaching-learning environments.* Pasadena, CA: Pacific Oaks.

Jones, E., & Cooper, R. (2006). *Playing to get smart.* New York: T.C. Press.

Jones, M., & Ross, B. (2005). Picturing a story. *Teaching PreK–8, 35*(6), 50–51.

Jones, T. (2005). Incorporate diversity into your classroom. *Intervention in School and Clinic, 41*(1), 9–12.

Joussement, M., & Koestner, R. (1999). Effect of expected rewards on children's creativity. *Creativity Research Journal, 12*(4), 231–239.

Justice, L. M., Pence, K. L., & Beckham, A. R. (2005). *Scaffolding with storybooks: A guide for enhancing young children's language and literacy achievement.* Newark, DE: International Reading Association.

Kagan, S. L., & Bowman, B. T. (Eds.). (1997). *Leadership in early care and education.* Washington, DC: National Association for the Education of Young Children.

Kagan, S., & Lowenstien, A. (2004). School readiness and children's play: Contemporary oxymoron or compatible option? In E. Zigler, D. G. Singer, & S. Bishop-Josef (Eds.), *Children's play: The roots of reading* (pp. 59–76). Washington, DC: Zero to Three Press.

Kamii, C., & DeVries, R. (1980). *Group games in early education: Implications of Piaget's theory.* Washington, DC: National Association for the Education of Young Children.

Kantrowitz, B. (1997, Spring-Summer). Off to a good start. [Special Issue]. *Newsweek, 129,* 6–9.

Kasten, W. C., Kristo, J., McClure, A., & Garthwait, W. (2004). *Living literature: Using children's literature to support reading and language arts.* Upper Saddle River, NJ: Merrill/Prentice Hall.

Katz, L. G. (1988). *Early childhood education: What research tells us.* Bloomington, IN: Phi Delta Kappa.

Katz, L. G., & Chard, S. C. (2000). *Engaging children's minds: The project approach* (2nd ed.). Norwood, NJ: Ablex.

Kauchak, D. P., & Eggen, P. D. (2007). *Learning and teaching: Research-based methods.* New York: Allyn & Bacon.

Kay, S. I., & Subotnik, R. F. (1994). Talent beyond words: Unveiling spatial, expressive, kinesthetic and musical talent in young children. *Gifted Child Quarterly, 38*(2), 70–74.

Kelley, L., & Sutton-Smith, B. (1987). A study of infant musical productivity. In J. C. Peery, I. W. Peery, & T. Draper (Eds.), *Music and child development* (pp. 35–53). New York: Springer-Verlag.

Kelner, L. B., & Flynn, R. (2006). *A dramatic approach to reading comprehension.* Portsmouth, NH: Heinemann.

Kellogg, R. (1979). *Children's drawings/children's minds.* New York: Avon.

Kemple, K. M., Batey, J. J., & Hartle, L. C. (2004). Music play: Creativity centers for music play and exploration. *Young Children 59*(4), 30–37.

Kemple, K. M., & Nissenberg, S. A. (2000). Nurturing creativity in early childhood education: Families are part of it. *Early Childhood Education Journal, 28*(1), 67–71.

Kendrick, M., & McKay, R. (2004). Drawings as an alternative way of understanding young children's constructions of literacy. *Journal of Early Childhood Literacy, 4*(1), 109–128.

Kerka, S. (2002). *Adult learning in and through the arts.* Columbus, OH: ERIC Clearinghouse on Adult, Career, and Vocational Education. ERIC Digest Number 236. (EDO-CE-02-236)

Kerlavage, M. S. (1995). A bunch of naked ladies and a tiger: Children's responses to adult works of art. In C. M. Thompson (Ed.), *The visual arts in early childhood learning* (pp. 56–62). Reston, VA: National Art Education Association.

Kerr, B. A., & Cohn, S. J. (2001). *Smart boys: Talent, manhood, and the search for meaning.* Scottsdale, AZ: Great Potential Press.

Kim, A., Vaughn, S., Wanzek, J. & Wei, S. (2004). Graphic organizers and their effects on the reading comprehension of students with LD: A synthesis of research. *Journal of Learning Disabilities, 37*(2), 105–118.

Kim, K. H. (2006). Can we trust creativity tests? A review of the Torrance Tests of Creative Thinking. *Creativity Research Journal, 18,* 3–14.

Kinkade, T. (2002). The child's heart in art. *American Artist, 66*(716), 12.

Kindler, A. L. (2002). *Survey of the states' limited English proficient students and available educational programs and services: 1999–2000 report.* Washington, DC: George Washington University and National Clearinghouse for English Language Acquisition and Language Instruction Educational Programs.

Kindler, A. M. (1996). Myths, habits, research, and policy: The four pillars of early childhood education. *Arts Education Policy Review, 97*(4), 24–30.

Kindler, A. M. (Ed.). (1997). *Child development in art.* Reston, VA: National Art Education Association.

Kirk, S., Gallagher, J., & Anastasiow, N. (2003). *Educating exceptional children* (10th ed.). New York: Houghton Mifflin.

Klein, M. D., Cook, R. E., & Richardson-Gibbs, A. M. (2001). *Strategies for including children with special needs in early childhood settings.* Albany, NY: Thomson Delmar Learning.

Kline, L. W. (1995). A baker's dozen: Effective instructional strategies. In R. W. Cole (Ed.), *Educating everybody's children: Diverse teaching strategies for diverse learners* (pp. 21–41). Alexandria, VA: Association for Supervision and Curriculum Development.

Koch, J. (2005). *Science stories* (3rd ed.). Boston: Houghton Mifflin.

Kohn, A. (1987, September). Art for art's sake. *Psychology Today, 21*(9), 52–57.

Kohn, A. (1993). Choices for children: Why and how to let students decide. *Phi Delta Kappan, 75*(1), 8–21.

Kohn, A. (1996). *Beyond discipline: From compliance to community.* Alexandria, VA: Association for Supervision and Curriculum Development.

Korn-Bursztyn, C. (2002). Scenes from a studio: Working with the arts in an early childhood classroom. *Early Childhood Education Journal, 30*(1), 39–46.

Kozol, J. (1997). Students' needs or corporate greed? *Education Digest, 63*(1), 3–6.

Kress, G. (1997). *Before writing: Rethinking the paths to literacy.* New York: Routledge.

Kritchevsky, S., Prescott, E., & Walling, L. (1977). *Planning environments for young children: Physical space* (Rev. ed.). Washington, DC: National Association for the Education of Young Children.

Landreth, G., & Homeyer, L. (1998). Play as the language of children's feelings. In D. P. Fromberg & D. M. Bergen (Eds.), *Play from birth to twelve and beyond: Contexts, perspectives, and meanings* (pp. 193–198). New York: Garland.

Lang, S. S. (1999). Music: Good not only for the soul, but the brain. *Human Ecology Forum, 27*(2), 24.

Latham, A. S. (1997). Research link: Quantifying MI's gains. *Educational Leadership, 55*(1), 84–85.

Lee, E. A., & Seo, H. (2006). Understanding of creativity by Korean elementary teachers in gifted education. *Creativity Research Journal, 18*(2), 237–242.

Leu, D. J., Mallette, M. H., Karchmer, R. A., & Kara-Soteriou, J. (2005). Contextualizing the nerw literacies of infromation and communication technologies in theory, research, and practice. In R. A. Karchmer, M. H. Mallette, J. Kara-Soteriou, & D. J. Leu (Eds.), *Innovative approaches to literacy education: Using the Internet to support new literacies* (pp. 1–10). Newark, DE: International Reading Association.

Levin, D. (1999, November). Rethinking children's play: Changing times, changing needs, changing responses. *National PTA Magazine,* 8–11.

Levin, J., & Greenwald, N. L. (2001). Swimming against the tide: The creative child as a late bloomer. In M. D. Lynch &

C. R. Harris, (Eds.), *Fostering creativity in children, K–8* (pp. 71–77). Needham Heights, MA: Allyn & Bacon.

Lewis, A. G. (1983). *Listen, look, and sing (Grades 1, 2, and 3).* Morristown, NJ: Silver Burdett.

Li, J. (2004). High abilities and excellence: A cultural perspective. In L. V. Shavinina & M. Ferrari (Eds.), *Beyond knowledge: Extracognitive aspects of high ability* (pp. 187–208). Mahwah, NJ: Erlbaum.

Li, R. (1996). *A theory of conceptual intelligence: Thinking, learning, creativity, and giftedness.* Westport, CT: Praeger.

Lindsey, G. (1998/99). Brain research and implications for early childhood education. *Childhood Education, 75*(2), 97–100.

Lindstrom, L. (1997). Integration, creativity, or communication? Paradigm shifts and continuity in Swedish art education. *Arts Education Policy Review, 99*(1), 17–24.

Littleton, D. (1989). Children's play: Pathways to music learning. In B. Andress (Ed.), *Promising practices: Pre-kindergarten music education* (pp. ix–xiii). Reston, VA: Music Educators National Conference.

Lowenfeld, V., & Brittain, W. L. (1982). *Creative and mental growth* (7th ed.). New York: Macmillan.

Lyon, R, (2003). Reading disabilities: Why do some children have difficulty learning to read? What can be done about it? *Perspectives, 29*(2). Retrieved December 15, 2007, from *http://nhida.org/docs/ReadingDisabilities.pdf*

MacKinnon, D. W. (1978). *In search of human effectiveness.* Buffalo, NY: Creative Education Foundation.

Majure, J. (1995). It's playtime. *Arthritis Today, 9*(1), 46–51.

Mang, E. (2005). The referent of children's early songs. *Music Education Research, 7*(1), 3–20.

Mantione, R. D., & Smead, S. (2003). *Weaving through words: Using the arts to teach reading comprehension strategies.* Newark, DE: International Reading Association.

Manzo, K. K. (2002). Arts programs enhance some skills, study says. *Education Week, 21*(36), 5.

March, T. (2004). Webquests: The fulcrum for systemic curriculum improvement. Retrieved January 28, 2005, from http://center.uoregon.edu/ISTE/NECC2004/handout_files_live/KEY_160238/webquest_fulcrum_necc.pdf

Marion, M. (2007). *Guidance of young children* (7th ed.). Upper Saddle River, NJ: Merrill/Prentice Hall.

Martindale, C. (2001). Oscillations and analogies: Thomas Young, MD, FRS, genius. *American Psychologist, 56,* 342–345.

Marzano, R. J., Pickering, D., & McTighe, J. (1993). *Assessing student outcomes: Using the Dimensions of Learning Model.* Alexandria, VA: Association for Supervision and Curriculum Development.

Maslow, A. (1970). *Motivation and personality* (2nd ed.). New York: Harper Row.

Mason, C. Y., & Steedly, K. M. (2006). Rubrics and an arts integration community of practice. *Teaching Exceptional Children, 39*(1), 36–43.

Maxim, G. (1989). *The very young: Guiding children from infancy through the early years* (3rd ed.). Upper Saddle River, NJ: Merrill/Prentice Hall.

May, R. (1975). *The courage to create.* New York: Norton.

Mayesky, M. (2009). *Creative activities for young children* (9th ed.). Clifton Park, NY: Delamar/Cengage Learning.

Mazur, K. (2004). An introduction to inclusion in the music classroom. *General Music Today, 18*(1), 6.

McAlpine, D. (1996). Characteristics of gifted children. In D. McAlpine & R. Moltzen (Eds.), *Gifted and talented: New Zealand perspectives* (pp. 43–62). Palmerston North, NZ: Massey University ERDC Press.

McCaslin, N. (2006). *Creative drama in the classroom and beyond* (8th ed.). Boston: Allyn & Bacon.

McCune, L. N., & Zanes, M. (2001). Learning, attention, and play. In S. Golbeck (Ed.), *Psychological perspectives on early childhood education* (pp. 92–106). Mahwah, NJ: Erlbaum.

McDaniel, N., & Thorn, G. (1997). *Learning audiences: Adult arts participation and the learning consciousness.* Washington, DC: John F. Kennedy Center for the Performing Arts/Association of Performing Arts Presenters.

McGinnis, J. R. (2002). Enriching the outdoor environment. *Young Children, 57*(3), 28–30.

McIntyre, K. L. (2005). *Cultural dances and stories from around the world: A discovery of world cultures through dance and drama curriculum designed for grades K–5.* Irvine, CA: Center for Learning through the Arts. Available at *http://repositories.cdlib.org/clta/artsbridge/20050701KM*

McKean, B. (2000). Arts everyday: Classroom teachers' orientation toward arts education. *Arts and Learning Research, 16*(1), 177–194.

McLaughlin, N. (2001). Optimal marginality: Innovation and orthodoxy in Fromm's revision of psychoanalysis. *Sociological Quarterly, 42*(2), 271–287.

McLean, S. V. (1995). Creating the learning environment: Context for living and learning. In J. Moyer (Ed.), *Selecting educational equipment and materials* (pp. 5–13). Wheaton, MD: Association for Childhood Education International.

McLeod, L. (1997). Children's metacognition: Do we know what they know? And if so, what do we do about it? *Australian Journal of Early Childhood, 22*(2), 6–11.

McMaster, J. C. (1998). "Doing" literature: Using drama to build literacy. *The Reading Teacher, 51*(7), 574–675.

McTighe, J., & O'Connor, K. (2005, November). Seven practices for effective learning. *Educational Leadership, 63*(3), 10–17.

Meador, K. (1999). Creativity around the globe. [Special issue]. *Childhood Education, 75,* 324–325.

Meier, D. R. (2004). *Young child's memory for words: Developing first and second language and literacy.* New York: Teachers College Press.

Mergen, B. (1982). *Play and playthings: A reference guide.* Westport, CT: Greenwood Press.

Merrill, J. D. (2004). Rhythmic and vocal creativity builds music skills. *General Music Today, 17*(3), 14–20.

Merriman, W.E. & Marazita, J.M. (2004). Young children's awareness of their own lexical ig-norance: Relations to word mapping, memory processes, and beliefs about change. In D.T. Levin (Ed.), Thinking and seeing: Visual Metacognition in adults and children (pp. 57-74). Cambridge, MA: MIT Press.

Mindes, G. (1998). Can I play too? Reflections on the issues for children with disabilities. In D. P. Fromberg & D. M. Bergen (Eds.), *Play from birth to twelve and beyond: Contexts, perspectives, and meanings* (pp. 208–214). New York: Garland.

Minuchin, P. (1987). Schools, families and the development of young children. *Early Childhood Research Quarterly, 2,* 245–254.

Mitchell, L. C. (2004). Making the most of creativity in activities for young children with disabilities. *Young Children, 59*(4), 46–49.

Monighan-Nourot, P. (1990). The legacy of play in American early childhood education. In E. Klugman & S. Smilansky (Eds.), *Children's play and learning: Perspectives and policy implications* (pp. 59–85). New York: Teachers College Press.

Montgomery, J., & Martinson, A. (2006). Partnering with music therapists: A model for addressing students' musical and extramusical goals. *Music Educators Journal, 92*(4), 34–39.

Moore, K. B. (2003). How to create a school art show. *Early Childhood Today, 17*(7), 1–3.

Moore, T. (2002). If you teach children, you can sing. *Young Children, 57*(4), 84–85.

Morado, C., Koenig, R., & Wilson, A. (1999). Miniperformances, many stars! Playing with stories. *The Reading Teacher, 53*(2), 116–123.

Morin, F. (2001). Composing dances with children. *JOPERD: The Journal of Physical Education, Recreation & Dance, 72*(6), 43–50.

Morrow, L. (2009). *Literacy development in the early years: Helping children read and write* (4th ed.). Boston: Allyn & Bacon.

Mortimer, H. (2004). Hearing children's voices in the early years. *Special Education Needs Support for Learning, 19*(4), 169–174.

Mosco, M. (2005). Getting the information graphically. *Arts & Activities, 138*(1), 44.

Moyer, J. (Ed.). (1995). *Selecting educational equipment and materials for school and home.* Wheaton, MD: Association for Childhood Education International.

Murray, C. G. (2007). *Simple signing with young children: A guide for infant, toddler, and preschool teachers.* Beltsville, MD: Gryphon House.

Myhre, S. M. (1993). Enhancing your dramatic play area through the use of prop boxes. *Young Children, 48*(5), 6–11.

Naglieri, J. A. (2001). Understanding intelligence, giftedness and creativity using the PASS Theory. *Roeper Review, 23*(3), 151–156.

Nakamura, J., & Csikszentmihalyi, M. (2001). Catalytic creativity: The case of Linus Pauling. *American Psychologist, 56,* 337–341.

Napoli, D. J. (2003). *Language matters: A guide to everyday questions about language.* New York: Oxford University Press.

Narey, M. J. (Ed.). (2009). Making meaning: Constructing multimodal perspectives of language, literacy, and learning through arts-based early childhood education. Dordrecht, The Netherlands: Springer.

Narey, M. J. (2009, in press).

Nash, J. M. (1997, February 3). Fertile minds. *Time, 149*(5), 48–56.

National Academy of Early Childhood Programs. (2004). Accreditation criteria and procedures of the NAEYC. Washington, DC: National Association for the Education of Young Children.

National Advisory Committee on Creative and Cultural Education. (1999). *All our futures: Creativity, culture, and education.* London: DfEE.

National Art Education Association. (1999). *Purposes, principles, and standards for school art programs.* Reston, VA: Author.

National Association of Early Childhood Specialists in State Departments of Education. (2002). *Recess and the importance of play.* A position statement on young children and recess. Retrieved January 28, 2005, from *http://naecs.crc.uiuc.edu/position/recessplay.html*

National Association for the Education of Young Children. (1996a). *Playgrounds: Keeping outdoor learning safe.* Release #5. Washington, DC: Author.

National Association for the Education of Young Children. (1996b). Position statement: Technology and young children—ages three through eight. *Young Children, 5*(6), 11–16.

National Association for Sport and Physical Education. (2001). *Recess in elementary schools* (Position paper). Reston, VA: Author.

National Association for Sport and Physical Education (NASPE). (2002). *Early childhood physical activity guidelines.* Reston, VA: Author.

National Center on Education and the Economy (2007). *Tough choices, tough times, the report of the new commission on the skills of the American workforce.* Washington, DC: Author

National Institute of Arts and Disabilities. *http://www.niadart.org/*

National Institute of Mental Health. (2008). *Autism spectrum disorders (Pervasive developmental disorders).* Retrieved February 21, 2008 from *http://www.nimh.nih.gov/health/publications/autism/complete-publication.shtml*

National Program for Playground Safety. (1999). *Our children. National PTA Magazine, 25*(2), 17.

Neelly, L. P. (2002). Practical ways to improve singing in early childhood classrooms. *Young Children, 57*(4), 80–83.

Neeley, P., Neeley, R., Justen, J., & Tipton-Sumner, C. (2001). Scripted play as a language intervention strategy for preschoolers with development disabilities. *Early childhood Education Journal, 28,* 243–246.

Nespeca, S. M. (2005). Join in! Picture books that invite participation. *Book Links, 14*(5), 48–51.

Neve, C. D., Hart, L. A., & Thomas, E. C. (1986). Huge learning jumps show potency of brain-based instruction. *Phi Delta Kappan, 68*(2), 143–148.

New, R. (2004). *The Reggio Emilia approach: Provocations and partnerships with U.S. early childhood educators.* In J. Rooparnine and J. Johnson (Eds.), *Approaches to early childhood education.* Columbus, OH: Merrill/Prentice-Hall.

Newberger, J. J. (1997). New brain development research: A wonderful window of opportunity to build public support for early childhood education! *Young Children, 52*(4), 4–9.

Newman, J. (Ed.). (1990). *Finding our own way.* Portsmouth, NH: Heinemann.

Nicholson, M. W., & Moran, J. D. (1986). Teachers' judgments of preschoolers' creativity. *Perceptual and Motor Skills, 63,* 1211–1216.

Nielsen, D. M. (2006). *Teaching young children: A guide to planning your curriculum, teaching through learning centers, and just about everything else.* (2nd ed.). Thousand Oaks, CA: Corwin Press.

Noddings, N. (2005). What does it mean to educate the whole child? *Educational Leadership, 63,* 8–13.

Norton, D. E. (2007). *Literacy for life*: Boston: Allyn & Bacon.

O'Brien, L. M. (2003). The rewards and restrictions of recess: Reflections on being a playground volunteer. *Childhood Education, 79,* 161–168.

O'Neill, S. (2002). *Young people and music participation project: Practitioner report and summary of findings.* University of Keele (*http://www.keele.ac.uk/depts/ps/ESRC*).

Ockelford, A., Welch, G., & Zimmermann, S. (2002). Music education for pupils with severe or profound and multiple difficulties—current provision and future need. *British Journal of Special Education, 29*(4), 178–182.

Odoy, H., & Foster, S. (1997). Creating play crates for the outdoor classroom. *Young Children, 52*(6), 12–16.

Olson, J. L. (2002). Children at the center of art education. *Art Education, 56*(4), 33–42.

Olson, K. (2006, November 8). The wounds of schooling. *Education Week, 26*(11), 28–29.

O'Neill, C. (1995). *Drama worlds: A framework for process drama.* Portsmouth, NH : Heinmann.

O'Neil, J. (1994, January). Looking at the art through new eyes: Visual arts programs pushed to reach new goals, new students. *ASCD Curriculum Update*, 1–8.

Osborn, A. (1972). *Your creative power: How to use imagination.* New York: Scribner's. (Original work published 1948)

Osborne, J. (2003). Art and the child with autism: Therapy or education? *Early Child Development and Care, 173*(4), 411–423.

Owocki, G. (1999). *Literacy through play.* Portsmouth, NH: Heinemann.

Pahl, K. (1999). Making models as a communicative practice: Observing meaning making in a nursery. *Reading,* 114–119.

Pakulsky, L. A., & Kaderavek, J. N. (2004). Facilitating literacy using experience books: A case study of two children with hearing loss. *Communication Disorders Quarterly, 25*(4), 179–188.

Paley, V. (1992). *You can't say you can't play.* Cambridge, MA: Harvard University Press.

Paley, V. G. (2004). *A child's work: The importance of fantasy play.* Chicago: University of Chicago Press.

Palmer, M., & Sims, W. L. (Eds.). (1993). *Music in prekindergarten: Planning and teaching.* Reston, VA: Music Educators National Conference.

Papalia, D. E., Olds, S. W., & Feldman, R. D. (2007). *A child's world: Infancy through adolescence* (10th ed.). New York: McGraw-Hill.

Papert, S. (1993). *The children's machine: Rethinking school in the age of the computer.* New York: Basic Books.

Pappalardo, R. G. (1990). Curricular issues: The visual arts and students with disabilities. In A. L. Nyman & A. J. Jenkins (Eds.), *Issues and approaches for art students with special needs* (pp. 42–54). Reston, VA: National Art Education Association.

Parker, W. C. (2009). *Social studies in elementary education* (13th ed.). Boston: Allyn & Bacon/Merrill.

Parten, M. (1932). Social participation among preschool children. *Journal of Abnormal and Social Psychology, 27*(2), 243–269.

Pearson, M. (2000). All the classroom's a stage! *Education World.* Retrieved March 18, 2004, from *http://www.education-world.com/a curr/curr226.shtml*

Pellegrine, A. & Holmes, R. M. (2006). *The role of recess in primary school.* In Singer, D., Golinkoff, M., & Hirsch-Pasek, K. (Eds.), *Play = learning: How play motivates and enhances children's cognitive and social-emotional growth.* (pp. 36–53). New York: Oxford University Press.

Pepler, D., & Ross, H. S. (1981). The effects of play on convergent and divergent problem-solving. *Child Development, 52*, 1202–1210.

Peregoy, S. F., & Boyle, O. F. (2005). *Reading, writing, and learning in English as a Second Language classroom: A classroom resource for K–12 teachers* (4th ed.). Boston: Allyn & Bacon.

Perkins, D. (1984). Creativity by design. *Educational Leadership, 42*, 18–25.

Perry, P. (1998). Art in a million schools: Art education in China. *Journal of Art and Design Education, 17*(3), 311–314.

Persellin, D. (1998). Quoted in M. P. Pautz, Teaching prekindergarten music. *Teaching Music, 5*(5), 40–43.

Peter, M. (1998). 'Good for them, or what?' The arts and pupils with SEN. *British Journal of Special Education, 25*(4), 168–172.

Peter, M. (2003). Drama, narrative and early learning. *British Journal of Special Education, 30*(1), 21–27.

Peterson, M. (1979). *Stay in tune* [record/cassette]. Summit, NJ: Meg Peterson Enterprises.

Peterson, R. E. (2001/2002). Establishing the creative environment in technology education. *Technology Teacher, 61*(4), 7–11.

Petrakos, H., & Howe, N. (1996). The influence of the physical design of the dramatic play center on children's play. *Early Childhood Research Quarterly, 11*(1), 63–67.

Piaget, J. (1952). *The origins of intellect.* New York: International University Press.

Piaget, J. (1962). *Play, dreams and imitation in childhood* (C. Gategno & F. M. Hodgson, Trans.). New York: Norton.

Piirto, J. (1992). *Understanding those who create.* Dayton: Ohio Psychology Press.

Piirto, J. (2001). How parents and teachers can enhance creativity in children. In M. D. Lynch & C. R. Harris (Eds.), *Fostering creativity in children, K–8* (pp. 49–67). Needham Heights, MA: Allyn & Bacon.

Pink, D. H. (2006). *A whole new mind: Why right-brainers will rule the future.* New York: Riverbend Books.

Pintrich, P. R., & Schunk, D. (2002). *Motivation in education: Theory, research, and applications* (2nd ed.). Upper Saddle River, NJ: Merrill/Prentice Hall.

Pitri, E. (2001). The role of artistic play in problem solving. *Art Education, 54*(3), 40–51.

Plucker, J. A., & Beghetto, R. A. (2004). Why creativity is domain general, why it looks domain specific, and why the distinction does not matter. In R. J. Steinberg, E. L. Grigorenko, & J. L. Singer (Eds.), *Creativity: From potential to realization* (pp. 153–167). Washington, DC: American Psychological Association.

Popham, W. J. (2001). *The truth about testing: An educator's call to action.* Alexandria, VA: Association for Supervision and Curriculum Development.

Popham, W. (2004). Curriculum, instruction, and assessment: Amiable allies or phony friends? *Teachers College Record, 106*(3), 417–428.

Potter, F. (1985). "Good job!" How we evaluate children's work. *Childhood Education, 61*(3), 203–206.

Prescott, E. (1984). The physical setting in day care. In J. Greenman & R. Fuqua (Eds.), *Making day care better: Training, evaluation, and the process of change* (pp. 44–65). New York: Teachers College Press.

Podlozny, A. (2000). Strengthening verbal skills through the use of classroom drama: A clear link. *Journal of Aesthetic Education, 34*(3–4), 239–276.

Papalia, D. E., Olds, S. W., & Feldman, R. D., (2007). *Human development* (10th ed.). Boston: McGraw-Hill.

Priest, T. (2001). Using creativity assessment to nurture and predict compositional creativity. *Journal of Research in Music Education, 49*(3), 245–257.

Prudhoe, C. M. (2003). Picture books and the art of collage. *Childhood Education, 80*(1), 6–11.

Puckett, M., Marshall, C. S., & Davis, R. (1999). Examining the emergence of brain development research: The promises and the perils. *Childhood Education, 76*(1), 8–12.

Qualley, C. (1986). *Safety in the art room.* Worcester, MA: Davis.

Rabkin, N., & Redmond, R. (2006). The arts make a difference. *Educational Leadership, 63*(5), pp. 60–64.

Ramsey, P. (1998). Diversity and play: Influences of race, culture, class, and gender. In D. P. Fromberg & D. M. Bergen (Eds.), *Play from birth to twelve and beyond: Contexts, perspectives, and meanings* (pp. 23–34). New York: Garland.

Rankin, B. (1995, February). Displaying children's work. *Scholastic Early Childhood Today,* 34–35.

Rappaport, L., & Schulz, L. (1999). *Creative play activities for children with disabilities: A resource book for teachers and parents.* Champaign, IL: Human Kinetics.

Rasmussen, K. (1998, Spring). Arts education: A cornerstone of basic education. *ASCD Curriculum Update,* 1–3, 6–7.

Ratey, J. J. (2001). *A user's guide to the brain: Perception, attention, and the four theaters of the brain.* New York: Pantheon.

Raths, L. E., Wassermann, S., Jonas, A., & Rothstein, A. (1986). *Teaching for thinking: Theory, strategies and activities for the classroom.* New York: Teachers College Press.

Ray, J. J. (1997). For the love of children: Using the power of music in "English as a Second Language" programs. (Doctoral dissertation, University of California, Los Angeles, 1997). *Dissertation Abstracts International, 58,* 07A.

Raywid, M. A. (1995). A teacher's awesome power. In W. Ayers (Ed.), *To become a teacher: Making a difference in children's lives* (pp. 78–85). New York: Teachers College Press.

Rea, D. (2001). Maximizing the motivated mind for emergent giftedness. *Roeper Review, 23*(3), 157–164.

Read, Write, Think. (2007). *Classroom activity: Printing inventory.* Retrieved January 27, 2008, from *http://www.readwritethink. org/calendar/calendar_day.asp?id=276*

Reifel, S. (2001). (Ed.). *Theory in context and out* (Vol. 3). Westport, CT: Ablex.

Reiff, J. C. (1997). Multiple intelligences, culture, and equitable learning. *Childhood Education, 73*(5), 301–304.

Research and Policy Committee. (1985). *Investing in children.* Washington, DC: Committee for Economic Development.

Rettig, M. (1998). Environmental influences on the play of young children with disabilities. *Education and Training in Mental Retardation and Developmental Disabilities, 33*(2), 189–194.

Richards, R. (2001). Millennium as opportunity: Chaos, creativity, and Guilford's structure of intellect model. *Creativity Research Journal, 13*(3/4), 249–265.

Riley, D., San Juan, R. R., Klinker, J., & Ramminger, A. (2008). *Social and emotional development: Connecting science practice in early childhood settings.* St. Paul, MN: Redleaf Press.

Ripple, R. E. (1989). Ordinary creativity. *Contemporary Educational Psychology, 14,* 189–202.

Rivkin, M. S. (1995). *The great outdoors: Restoring children's right to play outside.* Washington, DC: National Association for the Education of Young Children.

Roberts, B. C. (2004). Jazzy Miz Mozetta. New York: Farrar, Straus and Giroux

Robinson, A., & Clinkenbeard, P. R. (1998). Giftedness: An exceptionality examined. *Annual Review of Psychology, 49,* 117–139.

Robinson, K. (2001). Mind the gap: The creative conundrum. *Critical Quarterly, 43*(1), 41–45.

Rodd, J. (1999). Encouraging young children's critical and creative thinking skills: An approach in one English elementary school. *Childhood Education, 75*(6), 350–354.

Roe, B. D., Smith, S. H., & Burns, P. C. (2005). *Teaching reading in today's elementary schools* (9th ed.). New York: Houghton Mifflin.

Roebuck, E. (1999). Stravinsky's *Firebird* and young children. *Music Educators Journal, 86*(1), 34–37.

Roeper, B., & Davis, D. (2000). Howard Gardner: Knowledge, learning and development in drama and arts education. *Research in Drama Education, 5*(2), 217–233.

Rogers, C. (1961). *On becoming a person.* Boston: Houghton Mifflin.

Rogers, C. (1991). Toward a theory of creativity. In A. Rothenberg & C. Hausman (Eds.), *The creativity question* (pp. 296–305). Durham, NC: Duke University Press. (Original work published 1954)

Rogers, C. (2007). Experiencing an inclusive education: Parents and their children with special educational needs. *British Journal of Sociology Education, 28*(10), 55–68.

Rong, X. L., & Shi, T. (2001). Inequality in Chinese education. *Journal of Contemporary China, 10*(26), 107–124.

Ross, J. (1994). The right moves: Challenges of dance assessment. *Arts Education Policy Review, 96*(1), 11–17.

Rotigel, J. (2003). Understanding the young gifted child: Guidelines for parents, families, and educators. *Early Childhood Education Journal, 30*(4), 209–214.

Rouleau, S., & Buchberg, W. *Eric Carle author study.* Retrieved January 27, 2008, from Scholastic Inc. *http://content.scholastic.com/browse/article.jsp?id=3234*

Roush, B. E. (2005). Drama rhymes: An instructional strategy. *The Reading Teacher, 58*(6), 584–587.

Rowe, G. (1987). *Guiding young artists: Curriculum ideas for teachers.* Portsmouth, NH: Heinemann.

Rubin, K. H., Fein, G. S., & Vandenberg, B. (1983). Play. In E. M. Hetherington and P. H. Mussen (Eds.), *Handbook of child psychology: Vol. 4. Socialization, personality and development* (pp. 698–774). New York: Wiley.

Rule, A. C. (2007). Helping children improve their reasoning. *Early Childhood Education Journal 35*(1), 13–18.

Runco, M. (1997). *Handbook of creativity* (Vol. 1). Cresskill, NJ: Hampton Press.

Runco, M. A. (1986). Predicting children's creative performance. *Psychological Reports, 59,* 1247–1252.

Runco, M. A. (1996). *Eminent creativity: Everyday creativity and health.* Norwood, NJ: Ablex.

Runco, M. A. (2004). Creativity as an extracognitive phenomenon. In L. V. Shavinina & M. Ferrari (Eds.), *Beyond knowledge: Extracognitive aspects of high ability* (pp. 17–37). Mahwah, NJ: Erlbaum.

Runco, M. A. (Ed.). (1994). *Problem finding, problem solving, and creativity.* Norwood, NJ: Ablex.

Runco, M. A., & Pritzker, S. (1999). *Encyclopedia of creativity.* San Diego, CA: Academic Press.

Ryan, P. M. (2002). When Marian sang. New York: Scholastic.

Ryan, R. L., & Deci, E. L. (2000). Self-determination theory and the facilitation of intrinsic motivation, social development, and well-being. *American Psychologist, 55,* 68–78.

Rybczynski, M., & Troy, A. (1995). Literacy-enriched play centers: Trying them out in "the real world." *Childhood Education, 72*(1), 7–12.

Sanoff, H. (1995). *Creating environments for young children.* Mansfield, OH: BookMasters.

Santrock, J. W. (2005). *Child development* (11th ed.). Boston: McGraw-Hill.

Sapon-Shevin, M., Dobbelgere, A., Carrigan, C., Goodman, K., & Mastin, M. (1998). Everyone here can play. *Educational Leadership, 56*(1), 42–45.

Savva, A., & Trimis, E. (2005). Young children's responses to contemporary exhibits: The role of artistic experiences. *International Journal of Education and the Arts, 6*(13), unpaged.

Sawyer, K. R. (2003). Introduction. In K. R. Sawyer, V. John-Steiner, S. Moran, R. J. Sternberg, D. H. Feldman, J. Nakamura, & M. Csikszentmihalyi (Eds.), *Creativity and development* (pp. 3–11). Oxford: Oxford University Press.

Sawyer, W. (2008). *Growing up with literature* (5th ed.). Clifton Park, NY: Delmar Cengage Learning.

Scarlett, W. G., & New, R. S. (2007). Play. In R. New & M. Cochran (Eds.), *Early childhood education: An international encyclopedia* (Vol. 3, pp. 626–633). Westport, CT: Praeger.

Scarlett, W. G., Naudeau, S., Salonius-Pasternak, D., & Ponte, J. (2004). *Children's play*. Thousand Oaks, CA: Sage.

Schickendanz, J. A. (2008). *Increasing the power of instruction: Integration of language, literacy, and math across the preschool day*. Washington, DC: National Association for the Education of Young Children.

Schiller, M. (1995). Reggio Emilia: A focus on emergent curriculum and art. *Art Education, 48*(3), 45–50.

Schiller, P., & Willis, C. (2006). Bugs, Bugs, Bugs: 20 Songs and over 250 Activities for Young Children. Beltsville, MD: Gryphon House.

Schiller, P., & Willis, C. (2006). School Days: 28 Songs and Over 250 Activities for Young Children. Beltsville, MD: Gryphon House. p. 179 Serafin, 1994

Schirrmacher, R. (1988). *Art and creative development for young children*. Albany, NY: Delmar.

Scott, C. L. (1999). Teachers' biases toward creative children. *Creativity Research Journal, 12*, 321–328.

Seely, A. E. (1994). *Professional's guide: Portfolio assessment*. Westminster, CA: Teacher Created Materials.

Sefton-Green, J., & Sinker, R. (Eds.). (2000). *Evaluating creativity: Making and learning by young people*. London: Routledge.

Semali, L. M., & Watts Pailliotet, A. (Eds.). (1999). *Intermediality: The teachers' handbook of critical media literacy*. Boulder, CO: Westview Press.

Shaftel, F. R., & Shaftel, G. (1982). *Role playing in the curriculum* (2nd ed.). Upper Saddle River, NJ: Merrill/Prentice Hall.

Shallcross, D. (1981). *Teaching creative behavior*. Upper Saddle River, NJ: Merrill/Prentice Hall.

Sharp, C. (2004). Developing young children's creativity: What can we learn from research. *Topic, 32*, 5–12.

Shavinina, L. V., & Ferrari, M. (2004). Extracognitive facets of developing high ability: Introduction to some important issues. In L. V. Shavinina & M. Ferrari (Eds.), *Beyond knowledge: Extracognitive aspects of high ability* (pp. 3–13). Mahwah, NJ: Erlbaum.

Sheets, R. H. (2006). *What is diversity pedagogy theory?* Retrieved from May 10, 2008 *http://www6.tltc.ttu.edu/rsheets/web/What%20is%20diversity%20Pedagogy.pdf*

Sheldon, K. M. (1995). Creativity and self-determination in personality. *Creativity Research Journal, 8*(1), 25–36.

Shore, R. (1997). *Rethinking the brain: New insights into early development*. New York: Families and Work Institute.

Silberman, C. E. (1970). *Crisis in the classroom: The remaking of American education*. New York: Random House.

Simeonova, D. I., Chang, K. D., Strong, C., & Ketter, T. A. (2005). Creativity in familial bipolar disorder. *Journal of Psychiatric Research, 39*, 623–631.

Simonton, D. K. (1996). *Selected papers in genius and creativity*. Norwood, NJ: Ablex.

Simonton, D. K. (1997). Historiometric studies of creative genius. In M. A. Runco (Ed.), *The creativity research handbook* (Vol. 1, pp. 3–28). Cresskill, NJ: Hampton Press.

Sims, W. L., & Cecconi-Roberts, L. (2003). *Availability and use of recorded music in selected prekindergarten classrooms*. Paper presented at the 15th International Symposium for Research in Music Behavior. Chicago, Illinois.

Singer, D., & Singer, S. L. (2005). *Imagination and play in the electronic age*. Cambridge, MA: Harvard University Press.

Singer, D. G., Golinkoff, R. M., & Hirsch-Pasek, K. (Eds.). (2006). *Play = learning: How play motivates and enhances children's cognitive and social-emotional growth*. New York: Oxford University Press.

Singer, D. G., & Singer, J. L. (1998). Fantasy and imagination. In D. P. Fromberg & D. M. Bergen (Eds.), *Play from birth to twelve and beyond: Contexts, perspectives, and meanings* (pp. 313–318). New York: Garland.

Singer, J. L. (1973). *The child's world of make-believe*. New York: Wiley.

Singer, J. L. (2006). *Epilogue: Learning to play and learning through play*. In D. Singer, R. Golinkoff, & K. Hirsch-Pasek (Eds.), *Play = learning: How Play Motivates and Enhances Children's Cognitive and Social-Emotional Growth*, (pp. 251–262). New York: Oxford University Press.

Singer, J. L., & Singer, D. G. (1985). *Make believe: Games and activities to foster imaginative play in young children*. Glenview, IL: Scott Foresman.

Sloane, M. (1999). Learning resource centers: Engaging primary students. *Childhood Education, 75*(2), 76–82.

Smilansky, S. (1968). *The effects of sociodramatic play on disadvantaged preschool children*. New York: Wiley.

Smilansky, S., & Shefatya, L. (1990). *Facilitating play: A medium for promoting cognitive, socio-emotional and academic development in young children*. Gaithersburg, MD: Psychosocial and Educational Publications.

Smith, F. (1992). Learning to read: The great debate. *Phi Delta Kappan, 73*(6), 423–435, 438–441.

Smith, N., & The Drawing Study Group. (1998). *Observation drawing with children*. New York: Teachers College Press.

Smith, N. R. (1982). The visual arts in early childhood education: Development and the creation of meaning. In B. Spodek (Ed.), *Handbook of research in early childhood education* (pp. 87–106). New York: Free Press.

Smith, P. K., & Connolly, K. J. (1980). *The ecology of preschool behavior*. Cambridge, England: Cambridge University Press.

Snyder, S. (1995). *Share the music, K–6*. New York: Macmillan/McGraw-Hill.

Spodek, B., & Saracho, O. N. (Eds.). (1998). *Multiple perspectives on play in early childhood education*. Albany: State University of New York Press.

Stankiewicz, M. A. (2000). Discipline and the future of art education. *Studies in Art Education, 41*(4), 301–313.

Starko, A. J. (2001). *Creativity in the classroom: Schools of curious delight.* Mahwah, NJ: Erlbaum.

State of Florida Department of State. (1990). *Children and the arts: A sourcebook of experiences for Florida's pre-kindergarten early intervention program.* Gainesville, FL: Author. (ERIC Document Reproduction Service No. ED330454)

Stephenson, A. (2002). What George taught me about toddlers and water. *Young Children,* 10–14.

Sternberg, R. J. (1998). Principles of teaching for successful intelligence. *Educational Psychologist, 33*(2/3), 65–72.

Sternberg, R. J. (2004). Wisdom and giftedness. In L. V. Shavinina & M. Ferrari (Eds.), *Beyond knowledge: Extracognitive aspects of high ability* (pp. 169–186). Mahwah, NJ: Erlbaum.

Sternberg, R. J., & Lubart, T. I. (1996). Investing in creativity. *American Psychologist, 51*(7), 677–688.

Sternberg, R. J. (2006, February 22). Creativity is a habit. *Education Week, 25*(24), 64–47.

Sternberg, R. J. (2007). *Cultural dimensions of giftedness and talent. Roeper Review, 29*(3), 160–165.

Stevenson, L. (2004). *The arts and school change.* Washington, DC: Arts Education Partnership.

Stevenson, L. M., & Deasy, R. J. (2005). *Third space: When learning matters.* Arts Education Partnership, 2005, Washington, DC.

Stiggins, R. (2007). Assessment through the student's eyes. *Educational Leadership, 64*(8), 22–26.

Stinson, S. W. (1990). Dance for education in early childhood. *Design for Arts in Education, 91,* 34–41.

Stooke, R. (1998). Teaching through play. *Research in Drama Education, 3*(2), 272–277.

Strachota, B. (1996). *On their side: Helping children take charge of their learning.* Greenfield, MA: Northeast Foundation for Children.

Stremmel, A. (1997). Diversity and the multicultural perspective. In C. H. Hart, D. C. Burts, & R. C. Charlesworth (Eds.), *Integrated curriculum and developmentally appropriate practices: Birth to age eight* (pp. 363–388). Albany: State University of New York Press.

Strom, R. D., & Strom, P. S. (2002). Changing the rules: Education for creative thinking. *Journal of Creative Behavior, 36*(3), 183–200.

Surbeck, E., & Glover, M. (1992). Seal revenge: Ecology games invented by children. *Childhood Education, 69*(3), 275–280.

Sutterby, J. A., & Frost, J. L. (2006). Making playgrounds fit for children and children fit for playgrounds. *Young Children, 57*(3), 36–42.

Sutterby, J., & Thornton, C. (2005, May). *The developmental benefits of outdoor play. Young Children.* 60(3), 26–33

Sutton-Smith, B. (1986). The spirit of play. In G. Fein & M. Rivkin (Eds.), *The young child at play: Reviews of research* (Vol. 4, pp. 3–16). Washington, DC: National Association for the Education of Young Children.

Swaminathan, S., & Wright, J. (2003). Educational technology in the early childhood and primary years. In J. P. Isenberg & M. R. Jalongo (Eds.), *Major trends and issues in early childhood education: Challenges, controversies, and insights* (pp. 136–149). New York: Teachers College Press.

Szekely, G. (1996). Preparation for a new art world. *Art Education, 49*(4), 6–13.

Szyba, C. M. (1999). Why do some teachers resist offering appropriate, open-ended art activities for young children? *Young Children, 54*(1), 14–20.

Taggart, C. C. (2000). Developing musicianship through musical play. In National Association for Music Education [MENC], *Spotlight on early childhood music education* (pp. 23–36). Reston, VA: MENC.

Tarnowski, S. (1999). Musical play and young children. *Music Educators Journal, 86*(1), 26–29.

Task Force on Teaching as a Profession. (1986). *A nation prepared: Teachers for the 21st century.* Washington, DC: Carnegie Forum on Education and the Economy.

Taylor, B. (1999). *A child goes forth: A curriculum guide for preschool children.* Upper Saddle River, NJ: Merrill/Prentice Hall.

Taylor, I. A. (1975). An emerging view of creative actions. In I. A. Taylor and J. W. Getzels (Eds.), *Perspectives in creativity* (pp. 297–325). Chicago: Aldine.

Tegano, D. W., Moran, J. D., III, DeLong, A. J., Brickey, J., & Ramassini, K. K. (1996). Designing classroom spaces: Making the most of time. *Early Childhood Education Journal, 23*(3), 135–141.

Tegano, D. W., Sawyers, J. K., & Moran, J. D. (1989). Problem-finding and solving in play: The teacher's role. *Childhood Education, 66*(2), 92–97.

Temmerman, N. (2000). An investigation of the music activity preferences of pre-school children. *British Journal of Music Education, 17,* 51–60.

Tennent, L., & Berthelsen, D. (1997). Creativity: What does it mean in the family context? *Journal of Australian Research in Early Childhood Education, 1,* 91–103.

Tetenbaum, T. J., & Mulkeen, T. A. (1986). Computers as an agent for educational change. *Computers in the Schools, 2*(4), 91–103.

Thomason, C., & Thrash, D. (1999). Play it safe: A pre-installation checklist that could mean an injury and liability free playground. *Children and Families, 8*(1), 40–46.

Thompson, C. M. (1997). Teaching art in elementary schools: Shared responsibilities and distinctive roles. *Arts Education Policy Review, 99*(2), 15–22.

Thompson, D., Hudson, S., & Mack, M. (2000, March/April). The "ins and outs" of designing play areas for early childhood settings. *Early Childhood News,* 6–13.

Thompson, P., & Randall, R. (2001). Can e-learning spur creativity, innovation, and entrepreneurship? *Educational Media International, 38*(4), 289–293.

Tiedt, P., & Tiedt, I. (2000). *Multicultural teaching: A handbook of activities, information, and resources* (6th ed.). Boston: Allyn & Bacon.

Tieso, C. L. (2007). Patterns of overexcitabilities in identified gifted students and their parents. *Gifted Child Quarterly, 51(1),* 11–22.

Tolbert, M. (2005). Using active group games to develop basic life skills. *Young Children, 60*(4), 72–78.

Tomlinson, C. (1999). *The differentiated classroom: Responding to the needs of all learners.* Alexandria, VA: Association for Supervision and Curriculum Development.

Tomlinson, C. A., & McTighe, J. (2006). *Integrating differentiated instruction and understanding by design.* Alexandria, VA: Association for Supervision and Development.

Tompkins, G. E. (2002). *Literacy for the 21st century* (3rd ed.). Upper Saddle River, NJ: Merrill/Prentice Hall.

Tompkins, G. (2006). *Language arts essentials.* Upper Saddle River, NJ: Merrill/Prentice Hall.

Torbert, M. (2005). *Using active group games to develop basic life skills. Young Children, 60*(4), 72–78.

Torff, B. (2000). Encouraging the creative voice of the child. *NAMTA Journal, 25*(1), 195–214.

Tortello, R. (2004). Tableaux visuals in the literacy classroom. *The Reading Teacher, 58*(2), 206–208.

Torrance, E. P. (1993). The beyonders in a thirty-year study of creative achievement. *Roeper Review, 15,* 131–134.

Torrance, E. P. (1995). *Why fly? A philosophy of creativity.* Norwood, NJ: Ablex.

Tovey, H. (2007). *Playing outdoors: Spaces and places, risk and challenge.* New York: McGraw-Hill.

Trawick-Smith, J. (1998). Why play training works: An integrated model for play intervention. *Journal of Research in Childhood Education, 12*(2), 117–129.

Tudge, J., & Caruso, D. (1988). Cooperative problem-solving in the classroom: Enhancing young children's cognitive development. *Young Children, 44*(1), 46–57.

Turner, M. E. (1999). Child-centered learning and music programs. *Music Educators Journal, 86*(1), 30–35.

Ulbricht, J. (1998). Interdisciplinary art education reconsidered. *Art Education, 51*(4), 13–17.

Upitis, R. (1990). *This too is music.* Portsmouth, NH: Heinemann.

Urban, K. K. (1996). Encouraging and nurturing creativity in school and workplace. In U. Munander & C. Semiawan (Eds.), *Human resource development* (pp. 78–97). Jakarta: University of Indonesia Press.

Urban, K. K. (2005). Assessing creativity: The Test for Creative Thinking-Drawing Production (TCT-DP). *International Education Journal, 6,* 272–280.

U.S. Consumer Product Safety Commission. (2002). *A handbook for public safety.* Washington, DC: U.S. Government Printing Office.

U.S. Department of Education, Office of Educational Research and Improvement (1993). *National excellence: A case for developing America's talent.* Washington, DC: U.S. Government Printing Office.

Valentine, V. (2008). The best kind of play for kids: NPR. Retrieved February 27, 2008 from *http://www.npr.org. templates/story/story.php?storyID573598288*

Van Hoorn, J. J., Monighan-Nourot, P., Scales, B., & Alward, K. (2007). *Play at the center of the curriculum* (3rd ed.). Upper Saddle River, NJ: Merrill/Prentice Hall.

Varnon, D. (1997). Enriching remedial programs with the arts. *Reading and Writing Quarterly, 13*(4), 325–332.

Vergeront, J. (1996). *Places and spaces for preschool and primary (indoors).* Washington, DC: National Association for the Education of Young Children.

Verriour, P. (1994). *In role: Teaching and learning dramatically.* Markham, Canada: Pippin.

Vize, A. (2005). Making art activities work for students with special needs. *Arts & Activities.* Retrieved February 15, 2008, from *http://findarticles.com/p/articles/mi_m0HTZ/is_4_138/ai_n15922950*

Vukelich, C., Christie, J., & Enz, B. (2002). *Helping young children learn language and literacy.* Boston: Allyn & Bacon.

Vygotsky, L. (1925). *The psychology of art.* Cambridge, MA: MIT Press.

Vygotsky, L. (1986). *Thought and language.* Cambridge, MA: MIT Press.

Vygotsky, L. S. (1933). The role of play in development. In M. Cole, V. John-Steiner, S. Scribner, & E. Souberman

(Eds.), *Mind in society* (pp. 92–104). Cambridge, MA: Harvard University Press.

Vygotsky, L. S. (1967). Play and its role in the mental development of the child. *Soviet Psychology, 12,* 62–76.

Vygotsky, L. S. (1978). *Mind in society: The development of higher psychological processes.* Boston: Harvard University Press.

Wagner, B. J. (2003) Imaginative expression. In J. Flood, D. Lapp, J. Squire, & J. Jensen (Eds.), *Handbook of research on teaching the English language arts* (2nd ed., pp. 1008–1025). Mohawk, NJ: Lawrence Erlbaum.

Walker, B. (2004). *Diagnostic teaching of reading: Techniques for instruction and assessment* (2nd ed.). Upper Saddle River, NJ: Merrill/Prentice Hall.

Wallas, G. (1926). *The art of thought.* New York: Harcourt Brace.

Walling, D. R. (2001). Rethinking visual arts education: A convergence of influences. *Phi Delta Kappan, 82*(7), 626–631.

Walsh, D. J. (1993). Art as socially constructed narrative: Implications for early childhood education. *Arts Education Policy Review, 94*(6), 18–24.

Warnock, M. (1977). *Schools of thought.* London: Faber & Faber.

Wassermann, S. (1989). Reflections on measuring thinking, while listening to Mozart's *Jupiter Symphony. Phi Delta Kappan, 70*(5), 365–370.

Wassermann, S. (1990). *Serious players in the classroom: Empowering children through active learning experiences.* New York: Teachers College Press.

Wassermann, S. (2000). *Serious players in the primary classroom* (2nd ed.). New York: Teachers College Press.

Webster, A., Campbell, C., & Jane, B. (2006). Enhancing the creative process for learning in primary technology education. *International Journal of Technology and Design Education, 16*(3), 221–235.

Webster, P. R. (1990). Creativity as creative thinking. *Music Educators Journal, 76*(9), 22–28.

Weinberger, N. M. (1998). The music in our minds. *Educational Leadership, 56*(3), 36–40.

Weininger, O. (1988). "What if" and "as if": Imagination and pretend play in early childhood. In K. Egan & D. Nadaner (Eds.), *Imagination and education* (pp. 141–149). New York: Teachers College Press.

Weinstein, R. (1995). Quoted in R. W. Cole (Ed.), *Educating everybody's children: Diverse teaching strategies for diverse learners* (p. 18). Alexandria, VA: Association for Supervision and Curriculum Development.

Weisberg, R. W. (1993). *Creativity: Beyond the myth of genius.* New York: Freeman.

Wellhousen, K. (2002). *Outdoor play everyday: Innovative play concepts for early childhood.* Albany, NY: Delmar.

Werner, P., Timms, S., & Almond, L. (1996). Health stops: Practical ideas for health-related exercise in preschool and primary classrooms. *Young Children, 51*(6), 48–55.

Westby, E. L., & Dawson, V. L. (1995). Creativity: Asset or burden in the classroom? *Creativity Research Journal, 8*(1), 1–10.

Wheeler, E. J. (2004). *Conflict resolution in early childhood.* Upper Saddle River, NJ: Merrill/Prentice Hall.

White, M. M. Moore, E., DeRegniers, B. S., & CArr, J. (Eds.). (1998). *Sing a song of popcorn: Every child's book of poems.* New York: Scholastic.

Whitehurst, T., & Howells, A. (2006). 'When something is different people fear it': Children's perceptions of an arts-based inclusion project. *Support for Learning, 21*(1), 40–44.

Wiggins, G., & McTighe, J. (2005). *Understanding by design—Expanded 2nd edition*. Alexandria, VA: Association for Supervision and Curriculum Development.

Wilcox, E. (1994). Unlock the joy of music. *Teaching Music, 2,* 34–35, 46.

Wilcox, E. (2000). Music, brain research, and better behavior. *Education Digest, 65*(6), 10–15.

Wilhelm, J. D., & Edmiston, B. (Eds.). (1998). *Imagining to learn: Inquiry, ethics, and integration through drama*. Portsmouth, NH: Heinemann.

Willems, M. (2005). Leonardo, the terrible monster. New York: Hyperion.

Williams, V. (1988). *Stringbean's trip to the shining sea*. New York: HarperCollins.

Williams, W. M., Brigockas, M. G., & Sternberg, R. J. (1997). *Creative intelligence for school*. New York: Harper-Collins.

Wilson, F., & Roehmann, F. (Eds.). (1990). *Music and child development: Proceedings of the 1987 Denver Conference*. St. Louis, MO: MM3 Music.

Wilt, J., & Watson, T. (1977). *Listen!* Waco, TX: Creative Resources.

Wiltz, N. W., & Fein, G. (1996). Evolution of a narrative curriculum: The contributions of Vivian Gussey Paley. *Young Children, 51*(3), 61–68.

Wing, L. (1995). Play is not the work of the child: Young children's perceptions of work and play. *Early Childhood Research Quarterly, 10*(2), 223–247.

Wohlschlaeger, A., & Wohlschlaeger, A. (1998). Mental and manual rotation. *Journal of Experimental Psychology: Human Perception and Performance, 24*(2), 387–412.

Wolf, D. P., & Pistone, N. (1995). *Taking full measure: Rethinking assessment through the arts*. New York: College Entrance Examination Board.

Wood, C. (2001). *Yardsticks: Children in the classroom ages 4–14*. Greenfield, MA: Northeast Foundation for Children.

Woodward, C. (1985). Guidelines for facilitating sociodramatic play. In J. Frost & S. Sunderlin (Eds.), *When children play* (pp. 291–295). Wheaton, MD: Association for Childhood Education International.

Woolfolk, A. (2007). *Educational psychology*. Boston: Allyn & Bacon.

Wootton, K. (2004). Community this and community that. In L. Smyth & L. Stevenson, *You want to be part of everything: The arts, community, and learning*. Washington, DC: Arts Education Partnership.

Worth, K., & Grollman, S. (2003). *Worms, shadows and whirlpools: Science in the early childhood classroom*. Jointly published by Heinemann, Education Development Center, and NAEYC, Portsmouth, NH: Newton, MA: Washington, DC.

Wright, F. L. (1932). *An autobiography*. New York: Longman.

Wright, S. (1997). Learning how to learn: The arts as core in an emergent curriculum. *Childhood Education, 73*(6), 361–365.

Yelland, N. (1999). Technology as play. *Early Childhood Education Journal, 26*(4), 217–220.

Yenawine, P. (1998). Visual art and student-centered discussions. *Theory into Practice, 37*(4), 314–322.

Yinger, J., & Blaszka, S. (1995). A year of journaling—A year of building with young children. *Young Children, 51*(1), 15–20.

Young, R. (2006). Super-size stringing beads. *Scholastic Parent & Child, 14*(4), 63–64.

Young, S. (2002). Young children's spontaneous vocalizations in free-play: Observations of two-to three-year-olds in a day-care setting. *Bulletin of the Council for Research in Music Education, 54*(1), 37–56.

Young, S. (2003a). *Music with the under fours*. New York: Taylor & Francis, Inc.

Youngquist, J., & Pataray-Ching, J. (2004). Revisiting "play": Analyzing and articulating acts of inquiry. *Early Childhood Education Journal, 31*(3), 171–178.

Zeece, P. D. (2008). When is a frog a book or a book a frog? *Early Childhood Education Journal*

Zemelman, S., Daniels, H., & Hyde, A. (2005) *Best practice: Today's standards for teaching and learning in America's schools* (3rd ed.). Portsmouth, NH: Heinemann.

Zigler, E., & Bishop-Josef, S. (2006). The cognitive child versus the whole child: Lessons from 40 years of Head Start. In D. Singer, R. Golinkoff, & K. Hirsch-Pasek (Eds.), *Play = learning: How play motivates and enhances children's cognitive and social-emotional growth* (pp. 15–35). New York: Oxford University Press.

Zimmerman, E., & Zimmerman, L. (2000). Art education and early childhood education: The young child as creator and meaning maker within a community context. *Young Children, 55*(6), 87–92.

Zur, S. S., & Johnson-Green, E. (2008). Time to transition: The connection between free play and school readiness. *Childhood Education, 84*(5), 295–300.

Zwirn, S. G., & Graham, M. (2005). Crossing borders: The arts engage academics and inspire children. *Childhood Education, 81*(5), 267–276.

Children's Books, Recordings, and Software

Books and Recordings

Aardema, V. (1981). *Bringing the rain to Kapiti Plain*. New York: Scholastic.

Ackerman, D. (1988). *Song and dance man*. New York: Knopf.

Ahlberg, J., & Ahlberg, J. (1986). *The jolly postman, or, Other people's letters*. New York: Little, Brown.

Aimera, M., & Ivanko, J. D. (2004). *To be an artist*. Watertown, MA: Charlesbridge Publishing.

Aliki. (2002). *Ah, music!* New York: HarperCollins.

Ancona, G. (2003). *Murals: Walls that sing*. S. Tarrytown, NY: Cavendish Children's Books.

Andersen, H. C., & Locker, T. (1987). *The ugly duckling*. New York: Macmillan.

Anderson, M. T. (2002). *Handel, who knew what he liked*. Cambridge, MA: Candlewick Press.

Anderson, M. T. (2003). *Strange Mr. Satie*. New York: Viking.

Andreae, G. (2001). *Giraffes can't dance*. New York: Orchard/Scholastic.

Baker, A. (1995). *White rabbit's color book*. New York: Kingfisher.

Barracca, D., & Barracca, S. (1990). *The adventures of Taxi Dog*. New York: Trumpet.

Barry F. (2008). *Big yellow sunflower*. Somerville, MA: Candlewick Press.

Barton, B. (1981). *Building a house*. New York: Greenwillow.

Bayes, L. (1983). Bear hunt. On *Circle around* [audio recording]. Seattle, WA: Tickle Tune Typhoon.

Baylor, B., & Parnall, P. (1975). *The desert is theirs*. New York: Simon & Schuster.

Beaumont, K. (2004). *Baby danced the polka*. New York: Dial.

Belton, S. (1993). *From Miss Ida's porch*. New York: Simon & Schuster.

Bradman, T. (2008). *Daddy's lullaby*. New York: Simon & Schuster.

Brenner, B. (2003). *The boy who loved to draw: Benjamin West*. Boston: Houghton Mifflin.

Briggs, R. (1978). *The snowman*. New York: Random House.

Brown, L. K., & Brown, M. (1990). *Visiting the art museum*. New York: Puffin.

Brown, M. (1975). *Stone soup*. New York: Scribner's.

Brown, M. (1985). *Hand rhymes*. New York: Dutton.

Brown, A. (2003). *The Shape Game*. New York: Farrar, Straus and Giroux.

Buchanan, K. (1994). *It rained on the desert today*. Flagstaff, AZ: Northland.

Bunting, E. (1990). *How many days to America: A Thanksgiving story*. Boston: Houghton Mifflin.

Bunting, E. (2002). *Sing a song of piglets: A calendar in verse*. Boston: Clarion.

Cameron, P. (1961). *"I can't," said the ant*. New York: Coward.

Cannon, J. (1993). *Stellaluna*. San Diego, CA: Harcourt Brace Jovanovich.

Carle, E. (1969). *The very hungry caterpillar*. New York: HarperCollins/World.

Carle, E. (1984). *The mixed-up chameleon*. New York: HarperCollins.

Carle, E. (1993). *Today is Monday*. New York: Putnam.

Carle, E. (2001). *The tiny seed* (Reprinted). New York: Aladdin.

Carter, D. A. (2001). *If you're happy and you know it, clap your hands*. New York: Cartwheel/Scholastic.

Carter, D. A. (2001). *Old MacDonald had a farm*. New York: Cartwheel/Scholastic.

Castañeda, O. (1996). *Abuela's weave*. New York: Lee & Low.

Catalanotto, P. (2001). *Emily's art*. New York: Simon & Schuster.

Celenza, A. H. (2003). *Pictures at an exhibition*. Watertown, MA: Charlesbridge.

Chin, C. (1997). *China's bravest girl*. Emeryville, CA: Children's Book Press.

Chocolate, D. (1996). *Kente colors*. New York: Walker.

Christelow, E. (2006). *Five little monkeys jumping on the bed*. New York: Clarion (big book version).

Cleary, B. (1975). *Ramona the brave*. New York: Morrow.

Cocca-Leffler, M. (2001). *Edgar Degas: Paintings that dance*. New York: Putnam.

Cockburn, V., & Steinbergh, J. (1991). *Where I come from! Poems and songs from many cultures*. Chestnut Hill, MA: Talking Stone Press.

Coleman, E. (2000). *To be a drum*. Morton, IL: Albert Whitman.

Cooper, E. (2001). *Dance!* New York: Greenwillow.

Creech, S. (1995). *Walk two moons*. New York: HarperCollins.

Cuyler, M. (2008). *Monster mess*. Margaret McElderry.

Crews, D. (1978). *Freight train*. New York: Greenwillow.

Degen, B. (1983). *Jamberry*. New York: Harper & Row.

Delibes, L. (1986). Coppelia. In M. Greaves, *Petrushka (A little box of ballet stories)*. New York: Dial.

Dewey, A. (1995). *Naming colors*. New York: HarperCollins.

Dillon, L., & Dillon, D. (1983). *Why mosquitoes buzz in people's ears: A West African tale*. New York: Puffin.

Dillon, L., & Dillon, D. (2002). *Here's Bojangles: Think of that!* New York: Scholastic.

Dorros, A. (1991). *Abuela*. New York: Dutton.

English, K., & Sanchez, E. O. (2000). *Speak English for us, Marisol!* Illinois: Albert Whitman & Co.

Erbach, A. (1997). *The kids' invention book*. Minneapolis, MN: Lerner.

Esbensen, B. (1995). *Dance with me*. New York: HarperCollins.

Flack, M. (1932). *Ask Mr. Bear*. New York: Macmillan.

Flournoy, V. (1985). *The patchwork quilt*. New York: Dial.

Fogelin, A. (2000). *Crossing Jordan*. Atlanta, GA: Peachtree.

Frost, H. (2008). *Monarch and Milkweed*. New York: Athensum.

Gackenbach, D. (1977). *Harry and the terrible whatzit*. New York: Seabury.

Galdone, P. (1968). *Henny Penny*. New York: Seabury.

Garza, C. (1990). *Family pictures/Cuadros de familia*. San Francisco: Children's Book Press.

Gauch, P. L. (1999). *Presenting Tanya, the ugly duckling*. New York: Putnam/Philomel.

Gelsanliter, W., & Christian, F. (1993). *Dancin' in the kitchen*. New York: Putnam.

Gerstein, M. (2002). *What Charlie heard*. New York: Frances Foster.

Gibbons, G. (1982). *Tool book*. New York: Holiday House.

Glazer, T. (1982). *On top of spaghetti*. New York: Doubleday.

Gollub, M. (2000). *The jazz fly*. Summerland Key, FL: Tortuga Press.

Goodman, S., & McCurdy, M. (2003). *The train they call the City of New Orleans*. New York: Putnam.

Gray, L. M. (1996). *My mama had a dancing heart*. New York: Orchard.

Gray, N. (1988). *A country far away*. New York: Orchard.

Greenberg, J., & Jordan, S. (2002). *Action Jackson*. Brookfield, CT: Roaring Brook Press.

Greenstein, E. (2004). *One little seed*. New York: Viking.

Greigo, M. (1980). *Tortillitas para mama*. New York: Holt, Rinehart & Winston.

Grifalconi, A. (1986). *The village of round and square houses*. New York: Little, Brown.

Grifalconi, A. (1987). *Darkness and the butterfly*. New York: Little, Brown.

Grimes, N. (1994). *Meet Danitra Brown*. New York: Lothrop, Lee & Shepard.

Gulbis, S. (2001). *I know an old lady who swallowed a fly*. New York: Cartwheel/Scholastic.

Gwynne, F. (1970). *The king who rained*. New York: Simon & Schuster.

Haley, G. E. (1988). *A story, a story*. New York: Simon & Schuster.

Hall, D., & Cooney, B. (1984). *Ox-cart man*. New York: Live Oak Media.

Hartman, B. (2004). *The wolf who cried boy*. New York: Puffin.

Hawkins, C., & Hawkins, J. (1984). *Boo! Who?* New York: Holt.

Hayes, A., & Thompson, K. (1995). *Meet the orchestra*. Stillwater, MN: Voyager Books.

Hendershot, J. (1987). *In coal country*. New York: Knopf.

Henderson, K. (1999). *The baby dances*. Boston: Candlewick Press.

Henkes, K. (1985). *Bailey goes camping*. New York: Greenwillow.

Highwater, J. (1981). *Moonsong lullaby*. New York: Lothrop, Lee & Shepard.

Hines, A. G. (2001). *Whose shoes?* New York: Harcourt Brace.

Hoban, T. (1985). *A children's zoo*. New York: Greenwillow.

Hoban, T. (1997). *Colors everywhere*. New York: Greenwillow.

Hoberman, M. A. (2001). *Miss Mary Mack*. Boston, MA: Little, Brown & Company.

Hoffman, M. (1991). *Amazing Grace.* New York: Dial.

Hogrogrian, N. (1971). *One fine day.* New York: Macmillan.

Hooks, W. G. (1997). *The three little pigs and the fox: An Appalachian tale.* New York: Aladdin.

Horacek, P. (2008). *Look out, Suzy Goose.* Somerville, MA: Candlewick Press.

Hubbard, P. (1996). *My crayons talk.* New York: Holt.

Hutchins, P. (1985). *The very worst monster.* New York: Greenwillow.

Hutchins, P. (1987). *Rosie's Walk.* New York: Scholastic.

Hutchins, P. (1986). *The doorbell rang.* New York: Greenwillow.

Jave, J. (2002). *Horace and Morris join the chorus (But what about Dolores?)* New York: Atheneum/Simon & Schuster.

Jeschke, S. (1985). *Perfect the pig.* New York: Holt.

Johnson, A., & Huliska-Beith, L. (2004). *Violet's music.* New York: Dial.

Johnston, R. (1996). *The cowboy and the black-eyed pea.* New York: Putnam.

Johnston, T. (1984). *The quilt story.* New York: Putnam.

Jonas, A. (1989a). *Color dance.* New York: Greenwillow.

Jonas, A. (1989b). *The quilt.* New York: Greenwillow.

Jones, C. F., & O'Brien, J. (1997). *Accidents may happen.* New York: Delacorte.

Juster, N. (1988). *The phantom tollbooth.* New York: Random House.

Keats, E. J. (1962). *The snowy day.* New York: Viking.

Keats, E. J. (1971). *Over in the meadow.* New York: Four Winds Press.

Keats, E. J. (1972). *Pet show.* New York: Macmillan.

Kellogg, S. (1981). *A rose for Pinkerton.* New York: Dial.

Kelley, T. (2001). *Claude Monet: Sunshine and water lilies.* New York: Putnam.

Kennedy, J. (1983). *Teddy bear's picnic.* La Jolla, CA: Green Tiger Press.

Kimmelman, L. (2000). *Dance, sing, remember: A celebration of Jewish holidays.* New York: HarperCollins.

Kleven, E. (2002). *Ernst.* New York: Tricycle Press.

Knight, M. B., & O'Brien, A. S. (1995). *Talking walls.* Gardiner, ME: Tilbury House.

Knight, M. B., & O'Brien, A. S. (1997). *Talking walls: The stories continue.* Gardiner, ME: Tilbury House.

Koscielniak, B. (2000). *The story of the incredible orchestra: An introduction to musical instruments and the symphony orchestra.* Boston: Houghton Mifflin.

Krull, K. (1993). *Lives of the musicians: Good times, bad times (and what the neighbors thought).* San Diego, CA: Harcourt Children's Books.

Kuskin, K. (1982). *The Philharmonic gets dressed.* New York: HarperCollins.

Ladysmith Black Mambazo. (1994). There come our mothers. On *Gift of the tortoise* [CD]. Redway, CA: Music for Little People.

Laufer, P. (2000). *Made in Mexico.* Washington, DC: National Geographic Society.

Lester, J. (1990). *How many spots does a leopard have?* New York: Scholastic.

Leuck, L., & Buehner, M. (2002). *My monster mama loves me so.* New York: Harper/Trophy.

Levine, E. (1990). *I hate English!* New York: Scholastic.

Liao, J. (2006). *The sound of colors: A journey of the imagination.* Boston: Little, Brown & Company.

Lithgow, J. (2003). *I'm a Manatee* [book and CD]. New York: Simon & Schuster Children's Publishing.

Lobel, A. (1970). *Frog and Toad are friends.* New York: Harper & Row.

Lobel, A. (1980). *Fables.* New York: Harper & Row.

London, J. (1996). *Hip Cat.* San Francisco: Chronicle Books.

Lowell, S. (1992). *The three little javelinas.* Hong Kong: Northland.

Lowry, L. (1989). *Number the stars.* New York: Yearling.

Mahy, M., & MacCarthy, P. (1993). *Seventeen kings and forty-two elephants.* New York: Dutton.

Manning, M. J. (2003). *The ants go marching.* Honesdale, PA: Boyds Mills Press.

Marcus, L. S. (2001). *Side by side: Five favorite picture-book teams go to work.* New York: Walker.

Martin, B. (1995). *Brown bear, brown bear, what do you see?* New York: Holt.

Martin, B., & Archambault, J. (1987). *Knots on a counting rope.* New York: Holt.

Martin, B., & Archambault, J. (1989). *Chicka chicka boom boom.* New York: Simon & Schuster.

Mayer, M. (1968). *There's a nightmare in my closet.* New York: Dial.

Mayer, M. (1977). *Frog goes to dinner.* New York: Dial.

McDermott, G. (1972). *Anansi the Spider.* New York: Holt, Rinehart, and Winston.

McPhail, D. (1999). *Mole music.* New York: Holt.

McPhail, D. (2000). *Drawing lessons from a bear.* New York: Little, Brown.

Medina-Serafin, M. (1998). Fiesta musical. On *A child's celebration of the world* [CD]. Redway, CA: Music for Little People.

Mendez, P. (1989). *The black snowman.* New York: Scholastic.

Merz, J. J. (2004). *That dancin' dolly.* New York: Viking.

Meyrick, K. (1990). *The musical life of Gustav Mole.* New York: Child's Play.

Mills, L. (1991). *The rag coat.* Boston: Little, Brown.

Mitchell, B. (1992). *Raggin': A story about Scott Joplin.* Minneapolis, MN: Carolrhoda.

Mitton, T. (2002). *Down by the cool of the pool.* New York: Scholastic.

Moore, C., & Young, M. (2002). *The daring escape of Ellen Craft.* Minneapolis, MN: Lerner.

Moss, L. (2001). *Our marching band.* New York: Putnam.

Moss, L., & Petit-Roulet, P. (2003). *Music is.* New York: Putnam.

Moss, L., & Priceman, M. (1995). *Zin! Zin! Zin!: A violin.* New York: Simon & Schuster.

Naylor, P. R. (1991). *Shiloh.* New York: Pearson Scott Foresman.

Newman, T. M., & Sternberg, R. J. (Eds.). (2004). *Students with both gifts and learning disabilities: Identification, assessment, and outcomes* (Neuropsychology and Cognition, Vol. 25). New York: Kluwer Academic.

Oneyefulu, I. (1997). *A is for Africa.* New York: Puffin.

Oppenheim, J., & Reid, B. (1988). *Have you seen birds?* New York: Scholastic.

Orgill, R. (1997). *If only I had a horn: Young Louis Armstrong.* Boston: Houghton Mifflin.

Orozco, J. (2004). *Fiestas: A year of Latin American songs of celebration.* New York: Puffin.

Paul, A. W. (2000). *The seasons sewn: A year in patchwork.* San Diego, CA: Voyager.

Peck, J. (1998). *The giant carrot.* East Rutherford, NJ: Penguin-Putnam.

Pilkey, D. (1993). *Dogzilla.* San Diego, CA: Harcourt Brace Jovanovich.

Pinkney, A. D. (1998). *Duke Ellington: The Piano Prince and his orchestra.* New York: Jump Sun.

Pinkney, A. D. (2002). *Ella Fitzgerald: The tale of a vocal virtuosa.* New York: Jump Sun.

Pinkney, B. (1994). *Max found two sticks.* New York: Simon & Schuster.

Pinkney, J. (2003). *God bless the child.* New York: HarperCollins.

Polacco, P. (1988a). *Rechenka's eggs.* New York: Philomel.

Polacco, P. (1988b). *The keeping quilt.* New York: Simon & Schuster.

Polacco, P. (1990). *Chicken Sunday.* New York: Simon & Schuster.

Raffi. (1984). *A young children's concert with Raffi* [video recording]. Hollywood, CA: Shoreline/Troubadour.

Raffi. (2008). *Songs of our world.* [CD].

Raschka, C. (1997). *Charlie Parker played be bop.* New York: Orchard.

Raschka, C. (2002). *John Coltrane's giant steps.* New York: Atheneum/Simon & Schuster.

Ray, D. K. (2001). *Hokusai: The man who painted a mountain.* New York: Farrar, Straus & Giroux.

Recorvits, H., & Swiatkowska, G. (2003). *My name is Yoon.* New York: Farrar, Straus & Giroux.

Reid, B. (1993). *Two by two.* New York: Scholastic.

Renshaw, A. (2007). *The art book for children: Book Two.* New York: Phaidon Press.

Renshaw, A., & Ruggi, G. W. (2005). *The art book for children: Book One.* New York: Phaidon Press.

Reynolds, P. H. (2003). *The dot.* Cambridge, MA: Candlewick Press.

Ringgold, F. (1991). *Tar beach.* New York: Scholastic.

Roth, S. L. (2003). *Hanukkah, oh Hanukkah.* New York: Dial.

Rylant, C. (1995). *Dog heaven.* New York: Blue Sky Press.

Sachar, L. (1998). *Holes.* New York: Random House.

Say, A. (1993). *Grandfather's journey.* Boston: Houghton Mifflin.

Say, A. (2003a). *Emma's rug.* Boston: Houghton Mifflin.

Say, A. (2003b). *Snow music.* New York: Greenwillow.

Say, A. (2004). *Music for Alice.* Boston: Houghton Mifflin.

Schotter, R., & Sewall, M. (1988). *Captain Snap and the children of Vinegar Lane.* New York: Orchard.

Schroeder, A. (1989). *Ragtime tumpie.* Boston: Little, Brown.

Scieszka, J. (1989). *The true story of the three little pigs!* New York: Penguin.

Seeger, P. (1986). *Abiyoyo.* New York: Macmillan.

Sendak, M. (1963). *Where the wild things are.* New York: Harper.

Serfozo, M. (1992). *Who said red?* New York: Aladdin.

Seuss, Dr. (1949). *Bartholomew and the oobleck.* New York: Random House.

Seuss, Dr. (1957). *The cat in the hat.* New York: Random House.

Shafer, A. C. (2003). *The fantastic journey of Pieter Bruegel.* New York: Dutton.

Shahan, S. (2009). *Spicy hot color: Colores picantes.* Atlanta, GA: August House.

Shannon, D. (2004). *Alice the fairy.* New York: Scholastic.

Showers, P. (1993). *The listening walk.* New York: Harper/Trophy.

Shulevitz, U. (1988). *Dawn.* New York: Farrar, Straus & Giroux.

Shulman, S. (2004). *Old MacDonald had a woodshop.* New York: Puffin.

Slobodkina, E. (1947). *Caps for sale.* New York: Scott.

Smith, S. F. (2004). *My country 'tis of thee.* New York: Cartwheel/Scholastic.

Snape, J., & Snape, C. (1991). *Frog odyssey.* New York: MacRae.

Snyder, S. (1988). *The boy of the three-year nap.* New York: Scholastic.

Soto, G. (1992). *Neighborhood odes.* New York: Harcourt Brace.

Soto, G. (1997). *Chato's kitchen.* East Rutherford, NJ: Putnam.

Sounds of Blackness (1991). *The evolution of gospel* [audio recording]. New York: Polygram Records.

Spier, P. (1961). *The fox went out on a chilly night.* New York: Doubleday.

Spier, P. (1997). *Peter Spier's rain.* New York: Doubleday Books for Young Readers.

Stanley, D. (1996). *Leonardo da Vinci.* New York: HarperCollins.

Steig, W. (1969). *Sylvester and the magic pebble.* New York: Prentice Hall.

Steig, W. (1982). *Doctor De Soto.* New York: Farrar, Straus & Giroux.

Steptoe, J. (1987). *Mufaro's beautiful daughters.* New York: Lothrop, Lee & Shepard.

Stevens, J. (1987). *The city mouse and the country mouse.* New York: Holiday House.

Stevens, J. (1995). *Tops and bottoms.* San Diego, CA: Harcourt Brace Jovanovich.

Stevens, J. (1996). *From pictures to words: A book about making a book.* New York: Holiday House.

Sweet Honey in the Rock (1989). *All for freedom* [audio recording]. Redmond, CA: Music for Little People.

Taback, S. (1997). *There was an old lady who swallowed a fly.* New York: Penguin Books.

Tafuri, N. (1988). *Junglewalk.* New York: Greenwillow.

Taylor, E. (2008). *My friend the monster.* New York: Bloomsbury Children.

Taylor, M. (2002). *Roll of thunder, hear my cry.* New York: Puffin.

Thimmesh, C. (2000). *Girls think of everything: Stories of ingenious inventions by women.* Boston: Houghton Mifflin.

Tucker, T. (1995). *Brainstorm: The stories of twenty American kid inventors.* New York: Farrar, Straus & Giroux.

Tunnell, M. O. (2000). *Mailing May.* New York: HarperCollins.

Turner, A. (1987). *Nettie's trip south.* New York: Simon & Schuster.

Udry, J. (2002). *The moon jumpers.* New York: HarperCollins.

Van Allsburg, C. (1988). *Two bad ants.* Boston: Houghton Mifflin.

Venezia, M. (1995). *Aaron Copland (Getting to know the world's most famous composers).* San Francisco: Children's Press.

Venezia, M. (1999). *John Philip Sousa.* San Francisco: Children's Press.

Walker, A. (2006). *There is a flower at the tip of my nose smelling me.* New York: Harper/Collins.

Walker, R. D. (2005). *Once upon a cloud.* New York: Scholastic.

Walter, M. P. (1987). *Ty's one-man band.* New York: Simon & Schuster.

Warhola, J. (2003). *Uncle Andy's: A faabbbulous visit with Andy Warhol.* New York: Putnam.

Waters, K., & Slovenz-Low, M. (1990). *Lion Dancer: Ernie Wan's Chinese New Year.* New York: Scholastic.

Weeks, S. (2008). *If I were a lion.* New York: Scholastic.

Weiss, N. (1987). *If you're happy and you know it.* New York: Greenwillow.

Weitzman, J. P., & Glasser, R. P. (2002). *You can't take a balloon into the Museum of Fine Arts.* New York: Dial.

Wellington, M. (2002). *Squeaking of art.* New York: Dutton.

Wescott, N. B. (1987). *Peanut butter and jelly.* New York: Dutton.

Weston Woods. (2000a). *Duke Ellington: The Piano Prince and his orchestra* [video cassette]. New York: Top Dog Media.

Weston Woods. (2000b). *This Land Is Your Land* [video cassette]. New York: Top Dog Media.

White, E. B. (1952). *Charlotte's web.* New York: Harper & Row.

Williams, K. L. (1990). *Galimoto.* New York: Lothrop, Lee & Shepard.

Williams, K. L. (1994). *When Africa was home.* New York: Orchard.

Williams, S. (1992). *I went walking.* San Diego, CA: Harcourt Brace Jovanovich.

Williams, V. (1988). *Stringbean's trip to the shining sea.* New York: HarperCollins.

Williams, V. B. (1981). *Three days on a river in a red canoe.* New York: Greenwillow.

Williams, V. B. (1986). *Cherries and cherry pits.* New York: Greenwillow.

Williams, V. (1988). Stringbeans trip to the shining sea. New York: HarperCollins.

Winter, J. (1988). *Follow the drinking gourd.* New York: Knopf.

Wolff, A. (1984). *A year of birds.* New York: Dodd.

Wulffson, D. (2000). *Toys! Amazing stories behind some great inventions.* New York: Holt.

Wulffson, D. L. (1999). *The kid who invented the popsicle.* New York: Puffin.

Young, E. (1992). *Seven blind mice.* New York: Putnam.

Zelinsky, P. (1990). *The wheels on the bus.* New York: Dutton.

Zelinsky, P. O. (1986). *Rumpelstiltskin.* New York: Dutton.

Zelinsky, P. O. (1992). *Knick-knack paddy whack!* New York: Dutton.

Software

Bailey's Book House. (1993). Redmond, WA: Edmark.

Blue's Clues 1 2 3 Time Activities. (1999). Woodinville, WA: Humongous Entertainment.

Color Me. (1988). Northbrook, IL: Mindscape.

Crayola Make a Masterpiece. (2002). San Francisco: Selectsoft Publishing, 1999, Wisconsin Rapids, WI.

Cubby Magic: Folktales Around the World. (1999). Wisconsin Rapids, WI: Humanities Software.

Delta Draw. (1988). Cambridge, MA: Spinnaker.

Facemaker. (1986). Cambridge, MA: Spinnaker.

Fantastic Animals: Mix-Up Puzzler. (1990). New York: Bantam 500.

I Can Be a Dinosaur Finder. (1999). Carson, CA: Educational Insights.

I Spy. (1997). New York: Scholastic New Media.

Kid Desk! Internet Safe. (1999). Redmond, WA: Edmark.

Kid Pix 2. (1994). Novato: CA: Broderbund.

Kid Works 2. (1992). Torrance, CA: Davidson & Associates.

Millie and Bailey Preschool. (1997). Redmond, WA: Edmark.

Millie's Math House. (1993). Redmond, WA: Edmark.

Reader Rabbit. (1989). Fremont, CA: The Learning Company.

Richard Scarry's How Things Work in Busytown. (1990). Menlo Park, CA: Paramount.

SimCity 2000. (1994). Walnut Creek, CA: Maxis.

Storybook Weaver. (1992). Minneapolis, MN: MECC.

Thinkin' Things. (1993). Redmond, WA: Edmark.

Wiggins in Storyland. (1994). Fremont, CA: Media Vision.

Index

Note: Page numbers followed by letters *f* and *t* indicate figures and tables, respectively.